DATE DUE

BRODART   Cat. No. 23-221

Fixed Income Markets
Instruments, Applications, Mathematics

Fixed Income Markets
Instruments, Applications, Mathematics

Moorad Choudhry

John Wiley & Sons (Asia) Pte Ltd

Other Wiley Editorial Offices

John Wiley & Sons, Inc., 605 Third Avenue, New York, NY 10158-0012, USA
John Wiley & Sons Ltd, Baffins Lane, Chichester, West Sussex PO19 1UD, England
John Wiley & Sons (Canada) Ltd, 22 Worcester Road, Rexdale, Ontario M9W 1L1, Canada
John Wiley & Sons Australia Ltd, 33 Park Road (PO Box 1226), Milton, Queensland 4064, Australia
Wiley-VCH, Pappelallee 3, 69469 Weinheim, Germany

Library of Congress Cataloging-in-Publication Data
0-470-82136-1

Typeset in 10.5/13 points, Times by Paul Lim
Printed in Singapore by Saik Wah Press Pte Ltd
10 9 8 7 6 5 4 3 2 1

For Paula, *my exotic Kiwi –*
You're the best thing that ever happened to me...

Contents

Foreword

As one proceeds through this text, one cannot help but wonder whether one is exploring the world of fixed income or applied mathematics. Such subtlety should not be surprising given that the study of finance, like most sciences, has its foundation in mathematics. In many ways, much of the theoretical and practical advances in finance over the last 20 years are attributable to the increased utility of mathematical frameworks to better disaggregate and quantify financial risks (Black and Scholes' famous option pricing framework, for instance, has some basis on previous work in the area of fluid dynamics). It should not go unnoticed either that the increasing reliance on analytical models is in part accelerated, if not at least made feasible, by the availability of computers. The following chapters will give evidence as to just how scientific the discipline of finance has truly become.

Irrespective of the drivers or facilitators, the fact remains that the need for tools to better "define, value, … optimise" the complex products and risks transacted between financial counterparties and intermediaries is growing exponentially. Motivated by more than simple intellectual curiosity, the need for new technologies is congruent with, if not manifested by, the exponential growth of derivatives instruments. Broadly defined, these include all financial products that by design parse and transfer some or all of the component risks (credit, duration, … liquidity) inherent in one core market (bond, commercial paper, … equity) to "another". For our purposes, "another", refers to the new or "derivative" market created to specifically price and trade the newly isolated and transferable risk. Derivatives markets (interest rate swaps, credit derivatives, equity derivatives, convertibles, … and the "catch all" structured products) can only start and grow once the analytical tools to value and trade these 2nd order instruments are identified, developed and accepted.

As potential or seasoned practitioners of fixed income, one might ask why this is relevant. In simple terms, the leading opportunities going forward in fixed income are rooted in analytically identifying and mastering the next generation of derivatives instruments and markets. The derivatives markets are the ultimate expression of opportunity given that they embody the creation of a new market by definition. These markets evolve out of the growing necessity by financial risk managers (corporate treasurers, investment managers, … governments) for new instruments that offer them greater ability to identify, value and freely transfer the unique risks embedded in their financial portfolios. To the enlightened, the frontiers of the fixed income markets are being fuelled by the financial products designed to address and intermediate these risk management needs. Like any new market, however, the highest rewards are afforded to those participants who recognize the life cycle trends in financial products and capitalize on them while information is still fragmented and pricing transparency is yet to be established. The future leading intermediaries of fixed income will principally compete on their ability to identify risk management needs as well as how quickly and accurately they develop the instruments and valuation frameworks that price, and hence "define", the derivatives markets that grow around them.

By pioneering the market acceptance of a particular valuation framework for any new risk transfer product, one is positioning oneself to command and profit from the new market as it invariably moves through the typical product life cycle: *product creation* (response to a particular risk management need), *transparency* (development and acceptance of pricing frameworks), and ultimately *standardisation* (bid-offer or margin compression through increased volumes). Equally, it is also important that one recognises that financial product life cycles are increasingly shorter these days as technology permits faster information dissemination; as new product concepts filter through the market, they undergo a "Darwin-like" optimization as alternative valuation methods are deployed and assessed until there is convergence on an industry accepted approach. At this point, an accepted valuation technology is no longer a source of competitive advantage but rather a necessary faculty in order for a market participant to trade risks effectively (that is, on the same information basis as others). There is a growing awareness of the disadvantages that accrue to market participants who fall behind in the "valuation technology arms race"; it is one of the reasons why the concepts of "risk management" and "risk management tools" have become fundamental to any education in fixed income, and for that matter, future career potential. Again, the accelerated means by which new, and increasingly interconnected, markets achieve pricing standardisation today is attributable to the transparency that applied mathematics and computer processing have fostered.

Given the aforementioned trends, it is easy to see that the forward opportunities in fixed income revolve around financial engineering. It should go accepted that the frameworks for measuring the basic elements of fixed income instruments are highly developed and precise in terms of equilibrium models. The approach one uses for valuing a corporate bond any point in time, for instance, is broadly understood and agreed. One should use the teaching in this book to accumulate a sound grounding in the basic equilibrium pricing models already accepted. Going forward, however, the resources of fixed income science will be directed at the development of the next generation derivative markets that provide for the pricing and trading of the 3rd, 4th, ... N^{th} order relationships across markets (including existing derivate markets themselves).

Offering perspective on the future, the "next order" derivatives markets will travel along two paths: a Macro-economic and Micro-economic one. Given that most of the historical developments in financial engineering have been Micro-economic orientated, we will begin there. In terms of the Micro-economic evolution of derivatives markets, much of the work will continue around increased segmentation and valuation of the component risks embedded in single instruments; as mentioned, this theme is not new and has been at the core of 1st order derivatives market development. Returning back to our corporate bond example, inherent in this basic financial instrument are various risks such as duration, credit, ... currency risk. For these component risks, efficient derivatives markets have evolved allowing financial risk managers considerable flexibility to either enhance or decrease their exposure to these risks. What is interesting, however, is that with each risk segmentation in itself comes new questions and opportunities for further, "next order" tradable risks. For instance, the advent of credit derivatives has provided corporate bondholders with a tool to isolate and transfer pure credit risk only (perhaps all the end risk the bondholder is looking for is the residual risks left in the core instrument after credit risk immunisation: duration and currency).

Once a risk is parsed and captured in a tradable instrument, market participants begin to dissect, price and trade the behavioural characteristics of the new specific risk (i.e. the 1st, 2nd, ... order characteristics of the credit derivatives markets itself, already once removed from the bundled risks of the underlying corporate bond). Being at the forefront of single asset risk dissection, slice by slice, is the Micro-economic opportunity. Using our credit derivatives case as an example of next generation dissection, new products and markets are already being developed further by offering optionality on credit derivatives (that is, puts and calls on credit risk spreads specifically). This should not be surprising given that this evolution is following a similar dissection path as the first true derivative market: interest rate swaps (one has been able to purchase puts and calls on future interest rates for many years; the markets for interest rate risk have moved considerably down the 2nd, 3rd, ... generation product life cycle).

In terms of Macro-economic derivatives market expansion, the principle of dissection has a similar meaning although focused on core cross-marked opportunities (debt versus equity markets, for instance). The Macro-economic development path is still relatively new, but offers a significant alternative for derivatives market growth. It should be particularly interesting for new students of finance in that it represents the general shift towards making all markets more connected from a valuation and trading perspective. The best evidence of the trends towards a "unified" market framework (which as a concept we will come back to) is seen with an example: one can look to the newly forming market for "equity default swaps" as a case study.

Specifically, equity default swaps are derivative instruments now being offered to financial managers that have features drawn from both the fixed income and equity markets. In simple terms, these contracts have a fixed payout similar to a debt instrument but are triggered on equity rather than credit related events. In other words, the synthetic debt instrument that this contract represents pays a premium (that is, coupon) to the owner until the corresponding equity instrument's price falls below a pre-agreed threshold (30% of the stock's price at the time of entering the contract, for instance). At the time of triggering, the owner would generally be obligated to pay the amount that would have been lost (that is, defaulted) if this had been invested in the debt instrument directly. Conceptually, the contract has allowed a fixed income investor to replace bond default risk on a company with stock price depreciation risk on the same company.

These types of cross-market derivatives contracts are very important to the development of the financial markets broadly. In our example, an equity default swap contract starts to bridge the debt and equity markets in an analytical and observable way, allowing for risk pricing and tradability; it should not be a surprise that the value of a company's stock has some predictive bearing on the creditworthiness of the debt it issues as well. As this instrument evolves it will increase the understanding of the interrelationship that exists between debt and equity markets, providing benefits to both. It is fair to say that it is only a matter of time before the "equity default swap" market evolves and it too becomes subject to the 2nd, 3rd, ... N^{th} order dissection of itself (that is, a Micro-economic derivatives market path).

In summary, the use of mathematical frameworks (powered by computing technology) has helped bring increased transparency and efficiency to the markets, broadening our general understanding of financial risks significantly. The greater understanding has lead to the creation of new markets that either dissect further the component risks in any particular financial asset as well as capture the inter-relationships that exist across asset classes. Directionally, these are the trends that are feeding the growth of fixed income and the career opportunities within it.

For the students and future leaders of fixed income, the challenge I put forward is no different than that being pursed by physicists today. Instigated by Einstein, of course, these "scientists of the universe" are competing for the honour of solving the framework that captures the relationship of the "big to the small": The Unified Theory of the Universe. Although there are analytical frameworks that depict well the interactive behaviour of particles at the sub-atomic level as well as the stars and planets at the galactic level, there is yet to be one unified theory that can link these sciences (despite the fact that our intuition suggests that they are some how intertwined).

In many ways, the financial markets are moving in a similar trajectory: towards a deeper understanding of the relationships that govern both *component risks* (the "particle" risks that define an individual asset) and *cross-market risks* (the "gravitational" effects inter-linking individual markets). Is there a "unified theory of financial markets" out there somewhere? A holistic framework of analytical building blocks that together captures the interrelationships of all risks traded in the financial markets? I suspect there is; keep these points in mind as you explore the fixed income world page by page in this fine book.

Oldrich Masek
MD, Credit and Rate Markets
JPMorgan Chase Bank

Preface

This is a revised and updated version of the author's previous works in the field of bond markets, fixed-income securities and derivatives. It combines a discussion of the markets and the main instruments used (both cash and derivatives), together with applications across markets and some trading and hedging considerations.

The market in bond-market securities, also known as the fixed-income market, is large and diverse, and one that plays an important part in global economic development. The vast majority of securities in the world today are debt instruments, with outstanding volume estimated at over US$13 trillion. In this book, we provide a concise and accessible description of the main elements of the markets, concentrating on the instruments used and their applications. As it has been designed to be both succinct and concise, the major issues are introduced and described and, where appropriate, certain applications are also analysed. However, a detailed discussion of specific markets and conventions is left out.

The book is divided into four parts, covering introduction to bonds, selected market instruments and derivatives and trading strategy. The highlights include:

- detailed treatment of bond mathematics, including pricing and yield analytics. This includes modified duration and convexity;
- the concept of spot (zero-coupon) and forward rates, and the rates implied by market bond prices and yields;
- a description of yield-curve fitting techniques, and an account of spline fitting, using regression techniques;
- an introductory discussion of term-structure models;
- description of different types of bonds;
- coverage of money-market instruments and analysis;
- analysis of instruments such as callable bonds that feature embedded options;
- a discussion of mortgage-backed securities;
- a discussion of collateralised debt obligations;
- techniques used in the analysis of index-linked bonds;
- the use and applications of credit derivatives by participants in the fixed-income markets;
- a chapter on market risk;

- a chapter on trading techniques based on the author's personal experience.

This book contains much additional and new material added to what was first published in 2001. This material reflects developments in the market since that time. New and updated chapters include:

- a revised chapter on credit derivatives;
- an updated chapter on swaps including overnight-index swaps and a description of the latest Bloomberg screens;
- accessible analysis of the forward rate;
- a description of Covered bonds in the chapter on MBS;
- a section on index-linked derivatives added to the chapter on index-linked bonds;
- a section on warrants;
- a description of the latest developments in synthetic securitisation, including Total Return Swap-backed asset-backed commercial paper conduits;
- an updated chapter on collateralised debt obligations (CDOs) and Repack vehicles.

We have also endeavoured to update as far as possible the statistical data used in market illustrations.

Comments on the text are most welcome and should be sent to the author care of the publishers.

Website and further market research

For the latest market research from Moorad Choudhry, visit www.YieldCurve.com which also contains conference presentations and teaching aids written by the author and other YieldCurve.com associates.

A word on the mathematics

Financial subjects such as the debt-capital markets are essentially quantitative disciplines, and thus it is not possible to describe them, let alone analyse them, without recourse to a certain amount of numerical input. However, to maintain this book's accessibility, we have limited the level of mathematics used; as a result, many topics could not be reviewed in full detail. This is not, despite its sub-title (!), a maths book; there are very few derivations, for example, and fewer proofs. This has not, we feel, impaired the analysis, as the reader is still left with an understanding of the techniques required in the context of market instruments.

At the other end of the scale, we have sought to make the book as succinct and concise as possible, so a certain amount of general familiarity with the financial markets is assumed. In addition, there is no coverage of specific market conventions. Complete beginners may wish to review an introductory text — for example, the course companion for the SFA Registered Representatives exam or the securities part of Level I of the CFA qualification — before tackling this book. But generally, the writing style is designed to make the content accessible to a very wide readership. Finally, a certain amount of economic analysis is fairly relevant to a complete understanding of the debt markets, and it would do no harm for market participants to have an elementary grounding in this subject. There is a vast literature on this subject, and readers may wish to familiarise themselves with some of this as part of their learning before tackling this book.

Acknowledgments

Thanks to Oldrich Masek for the fantastic foreword – it is always a pleasure to work with you.

Thanks to Warren McCormick at HSBC, I'm still hoping to write a ticket with you after over 10 years (!), thanks to Bill Foley at ABN, Paul Bellinger at HSBC, Dave Thomas at Sumitomo and Derek Stevens at RBOS for helping to make my return to the market such a pleasure.

Thanks to Tom, Dan, Michelle and Gavin at KBC Bank London, and Francis, Jean-Pierre, Hans, Catherine and Bart at KBC Bank Brussels, as well as Jonathan Gold, Matthew White and Glenn Handley at Dresdner Kleinwort Wasserstein for making my return to dealing so welcome.

Finally, thanks to Simon Haigh at Computer Doctor for saving my PC – the one this book was written on! You're the hardest working chap I know!

Moorad Choudhry
June 2004

About the Author

Moorad Choudhry is Head of Treasury at KBC Financial Products in London. He was educated at Claremont Fan Court school, the University of Westminster and the University of Reading, before joining the London Stock Exchange in 1989. From there he joined Hoare Govett Securities Limited (later ABN Amro Hoare Govett Limited), where he was a gilt-edged market-maker and Treasury trader. Subsequently he was a sterling bond proprietary trader at Hambros Bank Limited. He later worked in structured finance services for JP Morgan Chase Bank in London.

Moorad is a Fellow of the Securities Institute and a Visiting Professor at the Department of Economics, London Metropolitan University. He obtained his Doctorate in Financial Economics from Birkbeck, University of London, and his MBA from Henley Management College.

Moorad was born in Bangladesh and lives in Surrey, England.

If ever you're ready,
To come on back to me,
Well just call me, and immediately,
I'll drop what I'm doing...

–   Edwyn Collins, *If Ever You're Ready*
(Demon Records) 1989

PART

I

Introduction to Bonds

In Part I, we describe the key concepts in fixed-income market analysis, which cover the basics of the bond instrument. The building blocks described here are generic and are applicable in any market. The analysis is simplest when restricted to plain vanilla *default-free* bonds; as the instruments become more complex we are required to introduce additional techniques and assumptions. Part I comprises five chapters. We begin with bond pricing and yield, followed by traditional interest-rate risk measures such as modified duration and convexity. This is followed by a look at spot and forward rates, the derivation of such rates from market yields, and the concept of the yield curve. Yield-curve analysis and the modelling of the term structure of interest rates is one of the most heavily researched areas of financial economics. The treatment here is kept as concise as possible, which sacrifices some detail, but bibliographies at the end of each chapter will direct interested readers on to what the author feels are the most accessible and readable references in this area.

While we do not describe specifics of particular markets, it is important to remember that the general concepts discussed here are pertinent to debt markets in any jurisdiction.

1

The Bond Instrument

Bonds are debt-capital market instruments that represent a cash flow payable during a specified time period heading into the future. This cash flow represents the interest payable on the loan and the loan redemption. So, essentially, a bond is a loan, albeit one that is tradeable in a secondary market. This differentiates bond-market securities from commercial bank loans.

In the analysis that follows, bonds are assumed to be default-free, which means that there is no possibility that the interest payments and principal repayment will not be made. Such an assumption is accurate when one is referring to government bonds such as US Treasuries, UK gilts, Japanese JGBs, and so on. However, it is unreasonable when applied to bonds issued by corporates or lower-rated sovereign borrowers. Nevertheless, it is still relevant to understand the valuation and analysis of bonds that are default-free, as the pricing of bonds that carry default risk is based on the price of risk-free government securities. Essentially, the price investors charge borrowers that are not of risk-free credit standing is the price of government securities plus some credit risk premium.

Bond-market basics

All bonds are described in terms of their issuer, maturity date and coupon. For a default-free conventional, or "plain-vanilla", bond, this will be the essential information required. Non-vanilla bonds are defined by further characteristics such as their interest basis, flexibilities in their maturity date, credit risk and so on. Different types of bonds are described in Part II of this book.

Figure 1.1 shows screen DES from the Bloomberg system. This page describes the key characteristics of a bond. From Figure 1.1, we see a description of a bond issued by the Singapore government, the 4.625% of 2010. This tells us the following bond characteristics:

Issue date	July 2000
Coupon	4.625%
Maturity date	1 July 2010
Issue currency	Singapore dollars
Issue size	SGD 3.4 million
Credit rating	AAA/Aaa

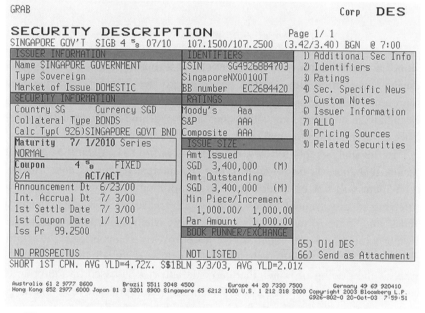

Figure 1.1 Bloomberg screen DES showing details of $4^5/_8$% 2010 issued by Republic of Singapore as at 20 October 2003
©Bloomberg L.P. Used with permission.

Calling up screen DES for any bond, provided it is supported by the Bloomberg, will provide us with its key details. Later on, we will see how non-vanilla bonds include special features that investors take into consideration in their analysis.

We will consider the essential characteristics of bonds later in this chapter. First, we review the capital market, and an essential principle of finance, the time value of money.

Capital market participants

The debt capital markets exist because of the financing requirements of governments and corporates. The source of capital is varied, but the total supply of funds in a market is made up of personal or household savings, business savings and increases in the overall money supply. Growth in the money supply is a function of the overall state of the economy, and interested readers may wish to consult the reference at the end of this chapter which includes several standard economic texts. Individuals save out of their current income for future consumption, while business savings represent retained earnings. The entire savings stock represents the capital available in a market. As we saw in the preface however the requirements of savers and borrowers differs significantly, in that savers have a short-term investment horizon while borrowers prefer to take a longer term view. The "constitutional weakness" of what would otherwise be *unintermediated* financial markets led, from an early stage, to the development of financial intermediaries.

Financial Intermediaries

In its simplest form a financial intermediary is a *broker* or *agent*. Today we would classify the broker as someone who acts on behalf of the borrower or lender, buying or selling a bond as instructed. However intermediaries originally acted between borrowers and lenders in placing funds as required. A broker would not simply on-lend funds that have been placed with it, but would accept deposits and make loans as required by its customers. This resulted in the first banks. A *retail bank* deals mainly with the personal financial sector and small businesses, and in addition to loans and deposits also provides cash transmission services. A retail bank is required to maintain a minimum cash reserve, to meet potential withdrawals, but the remainder of its deposit base can be used to make loans. This does not mean that the total size of its loan book is restricted to what it has taken in deposits: loans can also be funded in the wholesale market. An *investment bank* will deal with governments, corporates and institutional investors. Investment banks perform an agency role for their customers, and are the primary vehicle through which a corporate will borrow funds in the bond markets. This is part of the bank's corporate finance function; it will also act as wholesaler in the bond markets, a function known as *market making*. The bond issuing function of an investment bank, by which the bank will issue bonds on behalf of a customer and pass the funds raised to this customer, is known as *origination*. Investment banks will also carry out a range of other functions for institutional customers, including export finance, corporate advisory and fund management.

Other financial intermediaries will trade not on behalf of clients but for their own *book*. These include *arbitrageurs* and speculators. Usually such market participants form part of investment banks.

Investors

There is a large variety of players in the bond markets, each trading some or all of the different instruments available to suit their own purposes. We can group the main types of investors according to the time horizon of their investment activity.

Short-term institutional investors. These include banks and building societies, money market fund managers, central banks and the treasury desks of some types of corporates. Such bodies are driven by short-term investment views, often subject to close guidelines, and will be driven by the total return available on their investments. Banks will have an additional requirement to maintain *liquidity*, often in fulfilment of regulatory authority rules, by holding a proportion of their assets in the form of easily tradeable short-term instruments.

Long-term institutional investors. Typically these types of investors include pension funds and life assurance companies. Their investment horizon is long-term, reflecting the nature of their liabilities; often they will seek to match these liabilities by holding long-dated bonds.

Mixed horizon institutional investors. This is possibly the largest category of investors and will include general insurance companies and most corporate bodies. Like banks and financial sector companies, they are also very active in the primary market, issuing bonds to finance their operations.

Market professionals. This category includes the banks and specialist financial intermediaries mentioned above, firms that one would not automatically classify as "investors" although they will also have an investment objective. Their time horizon will range from one day to the very long term. They include the proprietary trading desks of investment banks, as well as bond market makers in securities houses and banks who are providing a service to their customers. Proprietary traders will actively position themselves in the market in order to gain trading profit, for example in response to their view on where they think interest rate levels are headed.

These participants will trade direct with other market professionals and investors, or via brokers. Market makers or *traders* (also called *dealers* in the United States) are wholesalers in the bond markets; they make two-way prices in selected bonds. Firms will not necessarily be active market makers in all types of bonds, smaller firms often specialise in certain sectors. In a two-way quote the *bid price* is the price at which the market maker will buuy stock, so it is the price the investor will receive when selling stock. The *offer price* or *ask price* is the price at which investors can buy stock from the market maker. As one might expect the bid price is always higher than the offer price, and it is this *spread* that represents the theoretical profit to the market maker. The bid-offer spread set by the market maker is determined by several factors, including supply and demand and liquidity considerations for that particular stock, the trader's view on market direction and *volatility* as well as that of the stock itself and the presence of any market intelligence. A large bid-offer spread reflects low liquidity in the stock, as well as low demand.

As mentioned above *brokers* are firms that act as intermediaries between buyers and sellers and between market makers and buuyers/sellers. Floor-based stock exchanges such as the New York Stock Exchange (NYSE) also feature a *specialist*, members of the exchange who are responsible for maintaining an orderly market in one or more securities. These are known as *locals* on the London International Financial Futures and Options Exchange (LIFFE). Locals trade securities for their own account to counteract a temporary imbalance in supply and demand in a particular security; they are an important source of *liquidity* in the market. Locals earn income from brokerage fees and also from pure trading, when they sell securities at a higher price than the original purchase price.

Markets

Markets are that part of the financial system where capital market transactions, including the buying and selling of securities, takes place. A market can describe a traditional stock exchange, a physical trading floor where securities trading occurs. Many financial instruments are traded over the telephone or electronically over computer links; these markets are known as *over-the-counter* (OTC) markets. A distinction is made between financial instruments of up to one year's maturity and instruments of over one year's maturity. Short-term instruments make up the *money market* while all other instruments are deemed to be part of the *capital market*. There is also a distinction made between the *primary market* and the *secondary market*. A new issue of bonds made by an investment bank on behalf of its client is made in the primary market. Such an issue can be a *public* offer, in which anyone can apply to buy the bonds, or a *private* offer where the customers of the investment bank are offered the stock. The secondary market is the market in which existing bonds and shares are subsequently traded.

World Bond Markets

The origin of the spectacular increase in the size of global financial markets was the rise in oil prices in the early 1970's. Higher oil prices stimulated the development of a sophisticated international banking system, as they resulted in large capital inflows to developed country banks from the oil-producing countries. A significant proportion of these capital flows were placed in *Eurodollar* deposits in major banks. The growing trade deficit and level of public borrowing in the United States also contributed. The last twenty years has seen tremendous growth in capital markets volumes and trading. As capital controls were eased and exchange rates moved from fixed to floating, domestic capital markets became internationalised. Growth was assisted by the rapid advance in information technology and the widespread use of financial engineering techniques. Today we would think nothing of dealing in virtually any liquid currency bond in financial centres around the world, often at the touch of a button. Global bond issues, underwritten by the subsidiaries of the same banks, are commonplace. The ease with which transactions can be undertaken has also contributed to a very competitive market in liquid currency assets.

The world bond market has increased in size more than fifteen times in the last thirty years. As at the end of 2003 outstanding volume stood at over $23 trillion.

The market in US Treasury securities is the largest bond market in the world. Like the government bond markets in the UK, Germany, France and other developed economies it also very liquid and transparent. Of the major government bond markets in the world, the US market makes up nearly half of the total. The Japanese market is second in size, followed by the German market. A large part of the government bond market is concentrated therefore in just a few countries. Government bonds are traded on major exchanges as well as *over-the-counter* (OTC). Generally OTC refers to trades that are not carried out on an exchange but directly between the counterparties. Bonds are also listed on exchanges, for example the NYSE had over 600 government issues listed on it at the end of 2003, with a total par value of $4.1 billion.

The corporate bond market varies in liquidity, depending on the currency and type of issuer of any particular bond. Outstanding volume as at the end of 1998 was over \$5.5 trillion. The global distribution of corporate bonds is shown at Figure 1.5, broken down by currency. The introduction of the euro across eleven member countries of the European Union in January 1999 now means that corporate bonds denominated in that currency form the second highest group.

Companies finance their operations in a number of ways, from equity to short term debt such as bank overdrafts. It is often advantageous for companies to fix longer term finance, which is why bonds are so popular. Bonds are also attractive as a means of raising finance because the interest payable on them to investors is tax deductible for the company. Dividends on equity are not tax deductible. A corporate needs to get a reasonable mix of debt versus equity in its funding however, as a high level of interest payments will be difficult to service in times of recession or general market downturn. For this reason the market views unfavourably companies that have a high level of debt. Corporate bonds are also traded on exchanges and OTC. One of the most liquid corporate bond types is the *Eurobond*, which is an international bond issued and traded across national boundaries. Sovereign governments have also issued Eurobonds.

Overview of the main bond markets

So far we have established that bonds are debt capital market instruments, which means that they represent loans taken out by governments and corporations. The duration of any particular loan will vary from two years to thirty years or longer. In this chapter we introduce just a small proportion of the different bond instruments that trade in the market, together with a few words on different country markets. This will set the scene for later chapters, where we look at instruments and markets in greater detail.

Domestic and international bonds

In any market there is a primary distinction between *domestic* bonds and other bonds. Domestic bonds are issued by borrowers domiciled in the country of issue, and in the currency of the country of issue. Generally they trade only in their original market. A *Eurobond* is issued across national boundaries and can be in any currency, which is why they are also sometimes called *international* bonds. It is now more common for Eurobonds to be referred to as international bonds, to avoid confusion with "euro bonds", which are bonds denominated in *euros*, the currency of twelve countries of the European Union (EU). As an issue of Eurobonds is not restricted in terms of currency or country, the borrower is not restricted as to its nationality either. There are also *foreign* bonds, which are domestic bonds issued by foreign borrowers. An example of a foreign bond is a *Bulldog*, which is a sterling bond issued for trading in the United Kingdom (UK) market by a foreign borrower. The equivalent foreign bonds in other countries include *Yankee* bonds (United States), *Samurai* bonds (Japan), *Alpine* bonds (Switzerland) and *Matador* bonds (Spain).

There are detail differences between these bonds, for example in the frequency of interest payments that each one makes and the way the interest payment is calculated. Some bonds such as domestic bonds pay their interest *net*, which means net of a withholding tax such as income tax. Other bonds including Eurobonds make *gross* interest payments.

Government bonds

As their name suggests government bonds are issued by a government or *sovereign*. Government bonds in any country form the foundation for the entire domestic debt market. This is because the government market will be the largest in relation to the market as a whole. Government bonds also represent the best *credit risk* in any market as people do not expect the government to go bankrupt. As we see in a later chapter, professional institutions that analyse borrowers in terms of their credit risk always rate the government in any market as the highest credit available. While this may sometimes not be the case, it is usually a good rule of thumb.[1] The government bond market is usually also the most *liquid* in the domestic market due to its size and will form the benchmark against which other borrowers are rated. Generally, but not always, the yield offered on government debt will be the lowest in that market.

United States

Government bonds in the US are known as *Treasuries*. Bonds issued with an original maturity of between two and ten years are known as *notes* (as in "Treasury note") while those issued with an original maturity of over ten years are known as *bonds*. In practice there is no real difference between notes and bonds and they trade the same way in the market. Treasuries pay

---

[1] Occasionally one may come across a corporate entity that one may view as better rated in terms of credit risk compared to the government of the country in which the company is domiciled. However the main rating agencies will not rate a corporate enitity at a level higher than its country of domicile.

semi-annual coupons. The US Treasury market is the largest single bond market anywhere and trades on a 24-hour basis all around the world. A large proportion of Treasuries are held by foreign governments and corporations. It is a very liquid and *transparent* market.

United Kingdom

The UK government issues bonds known as *gilt-edged securities* or *gilts.*[2] The gilt market is another very liquid and transparent market, with prices being very competitive. Many of the more esoteric features of gilts such as "tick" pricing (where prices are quoted in 32nds and not decimals) and *special ex-dividend* trading have recently been removed in order to harmonise the market with euro government bonds. Gilts still pay coupon on a semi-annual basis though, unlike euro paper. The UK government also issues bonds known as *index-linked* gilts whose interest and redemption payments are linked to the rate of inflation. There are also older gilts with peculiar features such as no redemption date and quarterly-paid coupons.

Germany

Government bonds in Germany are known as *bunds*, BOBLs or *Schatze*. These terms refer to the original maturity of the paper and has little effect on trading patterns. Bunds pay coupon on an annual basis and are of course, now denominated in euros.

Non-conventional bonds

The definition of bonds given earlier in this chapter referred to conventional or *plain vanilla* bonds. There are many variations on vanilla bonds and we can introduce a few of them here.

Floating Rate Notes. The bond marked is often referred to as the *fixed income* market, or the *fixed interest* market in the UK. Floating rate notes (FRNs) do not have a fixed coupon at all but instead link their interest payments to an external reference, such as the three-month bank lending rate. Bank interest rates will fluctuate constantly during the life of the bond and so an FRNs cash flows are not known with certainty. Usually FRNs pay a fixed margin or *spread* over the specified reference rate; occasionally the spread is not fixed and such a bond is known as a *variable rate note*.

---

[2] This is because early gilt issues are said to have been represented by certificates that were edged with gold leaf, hence the term gilt-edged. In fact the story is almost certainly apocryphal and it is unlikely that gilt certificates were ever edged with gold!

	Credit rating	Maturity range	Dealing mechanism	Benchmark bonds	Issuance	Coupon and day-count basis
Australia	AAA	2-15 years	OTC Dealer network	5, 10 years	Auction	Semi-annual, act/act
Canada	AAA	2-30 years	OTC Dealer network	3, 5, 10 years	Auction, subscription	Semi-annual, act/act
France	AAA	BTAN: 1-7 years OAT: 10-30 years	OTC Dealer network. Bonds listed on Paris Stock Exchange	BTAN: 2 & 5 year OAT: 10 & 30 years	Dutch auction	BTAN: Semi-annual, act/act OAT: Annual, act/act
Germany	AAA	OBL: 2, 5 years BUND: 10, 30 years	OTC Dealer network. Listed on Stock Exchange	The most recent issue	Combination of Dutch auction and proportion of each issue allocated on fixed basis to institutions	Annual, act/act
South Africa	A	2-30 years	OTC Dealer network. Listed on Johannesburg SE	2, 7, 10 and 20 years	Auction	Semi-annual, act/365
Singapore	AAA	2-15 years	OTC Dealer network	1, 5, 10 and 15 years	Auction	Semi-annual, act/act
Taiwan	AA-	2-30 years	OTC Dealer network	2, 5, 10, 20 and 30 years	Auction	Annual, act/act
United Kingdom	AAA	2-35 years	OTC Dealer network	5, 10, 30 years	Auction, subsequent issue by "tap" subscription	Semi-annual, act/act
United States	AAA	2-20 years	OTC Dealer network	2, 5, 10 years	Auction	Semi-annual, act/act

Table 1.1 Selected Government bond market characteristics

Term (years)	Australia	Canada	France	Germany	South Africa	Singapore	Taiwan	United Kingdom	United States
1	5.2154	2.749	2.3291	2.3747	4.71	0.937		4.9599	
2	5.2259	3.394	2.8375	2.7184	9.351	1.157	1.449	5.1033	2.7034
3	5.3451	2.6339	3.1998	3.0609				5.1633	3.1129
4	5.482	3.937	3.4966	3.3998	10.025			5.1685	
5	5.5761	4.2684	3.7222	3.6425		2.3085	2.3243	4.6946	3.9406
7	5.735	4.0704	4.014	4.0465		2.9583		5.2042	
10	5.8888	4.9984	4.395	4.3708	10.468	3.3355	3.0608	5.1863	4.8135
15	5.941		4.709			3.8989	3.1635	5.1504	
20		5.2426	4.776	4.8365	9.605		3.3507	4.9885	
30		5.4447	4.98	4.9481			3.5571	4.8596	5.3878

Table 1.2 Selected government bond markets, yield curves as at 21 June 2004

Source: Bloomberg L.P.

Because FRNs pay coupons based on the three-month or six-month bank rate they are essentially money market instruments and are treated by bank dealing desks as such.

Index-linked bonds. An index-linked bond as its coupon and redemption payment, or possibly just either one of these, linked to a specified index. When governments issue Index-linked bonds the cash flows are linked to a price index such as consumer or commodity prices. Corporates have issued index-linked bonds that are connected to inflation or a stock market index.

Zero-coupon bonds. Certain bonds do not make any coupon payments at all and these are known as *zero-coupon bonds*. A zero-coupon bond or *strip* has only cash flow, the redemption payment on maturity. If we assume that the maturity payment is say, $100 per cent or *par* the issue price will be at a discount to par. Such bonds are also known therefore as *discounted* bonds. The difference between the price paid on issue and the redemption payment is the interest realised by the bondholder. As we will discover when we look at strips this has certain advantages for investors, the main one being that there are no coupon payments to be invested during the bond's life. Both governments and corporates issue zero-coupon bonds. Conventional coupon-bearing bonds can be *stripped* into a series of individual cash flows, which would then trade as separate zero-coupon bonds. This is a common practice in government bond markets such as Treasuries or gilts where the borrowing authority does not actually issue strips, and they have to be created via the stripping process.

Amortised bonds. A conventional bond will repay on maturity the entire nominal sum initially borrowed on issue. This is known as a *bullet* repayment (which is why vanilla bonds are sometimes known as bullet bonds). A bond that repays portions of the borrowing in stages during the its life is known as an *amortised* bond.

Bonds with embedded options. Some bonds include a provision in their offer particulars that gives either the bondholder and/or the issuer an option to enforce early redemption of the bond. The most common type of option embedded in a bond is a *call feature*. A call provision grants the issuer the right to redeem all or part of the debt before the specified maturity date. An issuing company may wish to include such a feature as it allows it to replace an old bond issue with a lower coupon rate issue if interest rates in the market have declined. As a call feature allows the issuer to change the maturity date of a bond it is considered harmful to the bondholder's interests; therefore the market price of the bond at any time will reflect this. A call option is included in all asset-backed securities based on mortgages, for obvious reasons (asset-backed bonds are considered in a later chapter). A bond issue may also include a provision that allows the investor to change the maturity of the bond. This is known as a *put feature* and gives the bondholder the right to sell the bond back to the issuer at par on specified dates. The advantage to the bondholder is that if interest rates rise after the issue date, thus depressing the bond's value, the investor can realise par value by *putting* the bond back to the issuer. A *convertible* bond is an issue giving the bondholder the right to exchange the bond for a specified amount of shares (equity) in the issuing company. This feature allows the investor to take advantage of favourable movements in the price of the issuer's shares. The presence of embedded options in a bond makes valuation more complex compared to plain vanilla bonds, and will be considered separately.

Bond warrants. A bond may be issued with a *warrant* attached to it, which entitles the bond holder to buy more of the bond (or a different bond issued by the same borrower) under specified terms and conditions at a later date. An issuer may include a warrant in order to make the bond more attractive to investors. Warrants are often detached from their host bond and traded separately.

Finally there is a large class of bonds known as *asset-backed securities.* These are bonds formed from pooling together a set of loans such as mortgages or car loans and issuing bonds against them. The interest payments on the original loans serve to back the interest payable on the asset-backed bond. We will look at these instruments in some detail in a later chapter.

Time value of money

The principles of pricing in the bond market are exactly the same as those in other financial markets, which state that the price of any financial instrument is equal to the present (today's) value of all the future cash flows from the instrument. Bond prices are expressed as per 100 nominal of the bond, or "per cent". So for example, if the price of a US dollar-denominated bond is quoted as "98.00", this means that for every $100 nominal of the bond a buyer would pay $98.[3] The interest rate or discount rate used as part of the present value (price) calculation is key, as it reflects where the bond is trading in the market and how it is perceived by the market. All the determining factors that identify the bond, including the nature of the issuer, the maturity, the coupon and the currency, influence the interest rate at which a bond's cash flows are discounted, which will be similar to the rate used for comparable bonds. First, we consider the traditional approach to bond pricing for a plain-vanilla instrument, making certain assumptions to keep the analysis simple, and then we present the more formal analysis commonly encountered in academic texts.

Introduction

Bonds or *fixed-income*[4] instruments are debt-capital market securities and therefore have maturities longer than one year. This differentiates them from money-market securities. Bonds have more intricate cash-flow patterns than money-market securities, which usually have just one cash flow at maturity. This makes bonds more involved to price than money-market instruments, and their prices more responsive to changes in the general level of interest rates. There is a large variety of bonds. The most common type is the plain vanilla (or *straight, conventional* or *bullet)* bond. This is a bond paying a regular (annual or semi–annual) fixed interest payment or coupon over a fixed period to maturity or redemption, with the return of principal (the par or nominal value of the bond) on the maturity date. All other bonds are variations on this.

The key identifying feature of a bond is its Issuer, the entity that is borrowing funds by issuing the bond into the market. Issuers are generally categorized as one of four types: governments (and their agencies), local governments (or municipal authorities), supranational bodies such as the World Bank, and corporates. Within the municipal and corporate markets there is a wide range of issuers, each assessed as having differing abilities to maintain the interest payments on their debt and repay the full loan on maturity. This ability is identified by a *credit rating* for each issuer. The *term to maturity* of a bond is the number of years over which the issuer has promised to meet the conditions of the debt obligation. The maturity of a bond refers to the date that the debt will cease to exist, at which time the

---

[3] The convention in certain markets is to quote a price per 1000 nominal, but this is rare.

[4] The term "fixed income" originated at a time when bonds were essentially plain-vanilla instruments paying a fixed coupon per year. In the United Kingom, the term "fixed interest" was used. These days, many bonds do not necessarily pay a fixed coupon each year, for instance, asset-backed bond issues were invariably issued in an number of tranches, with each tranche paying a different fixed or floating coupon. The market is still commonly referred to as the fixed-income market, however.

issuer will redeem the bond by paying the principal. The practice in the bond market is to refer to the "term to maturity" of a bond as simply its "maturity" or "term". Some bonds contain provisions that allow either the issuer or the bondholder to alter a bond's term. The term to maturity of a bond is its other key feature. First it indicates the time period over which the bondholder can expect to receive coupon payments and the number of years before the principal is paid back. Secondly, it influences the yield of a bond. Finally, the price of a bond will fluctuate over its life as yields in the market change. The volatility of a bond's price is dependent on its maturity. All else being equal, the longer the maturity of a bond, the greater its price volatility resulting from a change in market interest rates.

The principal of a bond is the amount that the Issuer agrees to repay the bondholder on maturity. This amount is also referred to as the *redemption value, maturity value, par value* or *face value*. The coupon rate, or nominal rate, is the interest rate that the issuer agrees to pay each year during the life of the bond. The annual amount of interest payment made to bondholders is the coupon. The cash amount of the coupon is the coupon rate multiplied by the principal of the bond. For example, a bond with a coupon rate of 8% and a principal of $1000 will pay annual interest of $80. In the United States, the usual practice is for the issuer to pay the coupon in two semi-annual installments. All bonds make periodic coupon payments, except for one type that makes none. These bonds are known as zero-coupon bonds. Such bonds are issued at a discount and redeemed at par. The holder of a zero-coupon bond realises interest by buying the bond at this discounted value, below its principal value. Interest is therefore paid on maturity, with the exact amount being the difference between the principal value and the discounted value paid on purchase.

There are also floating-rate bonds (FRNs). With these bonds, coupon rates are reset periodically according to a pre-determined benchmark, such as three–month or six-month LIBOR. For this reason, FRNs typically trade more as money-market instruments than as conventional bonds.

A bond issue may include a provision that gives either the bondholder and/or the issuer an option to take some action against the other party. The most common type of option embedded in a bond is a *call feature*. This grants the issuer the right to call the debt, fully or partially, before the maturity date. A put provision gives bondholders the right to sell the issue back to the issuer at par on designated dates. A *convertible* bond is an issue giving the bondholder the right to exchange the bond for a specified number of shares (equity) in the issuing company. The presence of embedded options makes the valuation of such bonds more complex than plain-vanilla bonds.

Present value and discounting

As fixed-income instruments are essentially a collection of cash flows, we begin by reviewing the key concept in cash-flow analysis, that of discounting and *present value*. It is essential to have a firm understanding of the main principles of this before moving on to other areas. When reviewing the concept of the time value of money, assume that the interest rates used are the market-determined rates of interest.

Financial arithmetic has long been used to illustrate that £1 received today is not the same as £1 received at a point in the future. Faced with a choice between receiving £1 today or £1 in one year's time, we would not be indifferent given a rate of interest of, say, 10% that was equal to our required nominal rate of interest. Our choice would be between £1 today or £1 plus 10p – the interest on £1 for one year at 10% per annum. The notion that money has a time value is a basic concept in the analysis of financial instruments. Money has time value because of the opportunity to invest it at a rate of interest. A loan that has one interest payment on maturity is accruing simple interest. On short-term instruments, there is usually only the one interest payment on maturity, hence simple interest is received when the instrument expires. The terminal value of an investment with simple interest is given by 1.1 below.

$$F = P \left(1 + r \right) \tag{1.1}$$

where

F is the terminal value or future value
P is the initial investment or present value
r is the interest rate.

The market convention is to quote interest rates as annualised interest rates, which is the interest that is earned if the investment term is one year. Consider a three-month deposit of $100 in a bank, placed at a rate of interest of 6%. In such an example, the bank deposit will earn 6% interest for a period of 90 days. As the annual interest gain would be $6, the investor will expect to receive a proportion of this, which is calculated as follows:

$$\$6.00 \times 90 / 360$$

Therefore, the investor will receive $1.50 interest at the end of the term. The total proceeds after the three months is therefore $100 plus $1.50. Note, we use 90/360 as that is the convention in the US markets. For a small number of currencies, including Hong Kong dollars and Sterling, a 365-day denominator is used. If we wish to calculate the terminal value of a short-term investment that is accruing simple interest, we use the following expression:

$$F = P \left(1 + r \times \text{days} / \text{year}\right) \tag{1.2}$$

The fraction days/year refers to the numerator, which is the number of days the investment runs, divided by the denominator which is the number of days in the year. The convention in most markets (including the dollar and euro markets) is to have a 360-day year. In the sterling markets, the number of days in the year is taken to be 365. For this reason, we simply quote the expression as "days" divided by "year" to allow for either convention.

Let us now consider an investment of $100 made for three years, again at a rate of 6%, but this time fixed for three years. At the end of the first year, the investor will be credited with interest of $6. Therefore for the second year the interest rate of 6% will be accruing on a principal sum of $106, which means that at the end of year two the interest credited will be $6.36. This illustrates how compounding works, which is the principle of earning interest on interest. The outcome of the process of compounding is the future value of the initial amount. The expression is given in 1.3.

$$FV = PV \left(1 + r\right)^{n} \tag{1.3}$$

where

FV is the future value
PV is initial outlay or *present value*
r is the periodic rate of interest (expressed as a decimal)
n is the number of periods for which the sum is invested.

When we compound interest, we have to assume that the reinvestment of interest payments during the investment term is at the same rate as the first year's interest. That is why we stated that the 6% rate in our example was fixed for three years. We can see, however, that compounding increases our returns compared to investments that accrue only on a simple-interest basis.

Now let us consider a deposit of $100 for one year, at a rate of 6% but with quarterly interest payments. Such a deposit would accrue interest of $6 in the normal way but $1.50 would be credited to the account every quarter, and this would then benefit from compounding. Again assuming that we can reinvest at the same rate of 6%, the total return at the end of the year will be :

$$100 \times [(1 + 0.015) \times (1 + 0.015) \times (1 + 0.015) \times (1 + 0.015)]$$
$$= 100 \times [(1 + 0.015)^4]$$

which gives us 100×1.06136, a terminal value of $106.136. This is some 13 cents more than the terminal value using annual compounded interest.

In general, if compounding takes place m times per year, then at the end of n years mn interest payments will have been made and the future value of the principal is given by 1.4 below.

$$FV = PV(1 + r/m)^{mn} \qquad (1.4)$$

As we showed in our example, the effect of more frequent compounding is to increase the value of the total return when compared to annual compounding. The effect of more frequent compounding is shown below, where we consider the annualised interest-rate factors, for an annualised rate of 6%.

$$\text{Interest-rate factor} = (1 + r/m)^m$$

Compounding frequency		Interest-rate factor
Annual	$(1 + r)$	$= 1.060000$
Semi-annual	$(1 + r/2)^2$	$= 1.060900$
Quarterly	$(1 + r/4)^4$	$= 1.061364$
Monthly	$(1 + r/12)^{12}$	$= 1.061678$
Daily	$(1 + r/365)^{365}$	$= 1.061831$

This shows us that the more frequent the compounding, the higher the interest-rate factor. The last case also illustrates how a limit occurs when interest is compounded continuously. Equation 1.4 can be re-written as follows

$$FV = PV \left[\left(1 + \frac{r}{m} \right)^{m/r} \right]^{rn}$$

$$= PV \left[\left(1 + \frac{1}{m/r} \right)^{m/r} \right]^{rn}$$

$$= PV \left[\left(1 + \frac{1}{n} \right)^{n} \right]^{rn} \quad (1.5)$$

where $n = m/r$. As compounding becomes continuous and m and hence n approach infinity, the expression in the square brackets in (1.5) approaches a value known as e, which is shown below.

$$e = \lim_{n \to \infty}(1 + \frac{1}{n})^{n} = 2.718281\ldots$$

If we substitute this into 1.5 this gives us:

$$FV = PVe^{rn} \quad (1.6)$$

where we have continuous compounding. In (1.6), e^{rn} is known as the exponential function of rn and it tells us the continuously compounded interest rate factor. If $r = 6\%$ and $n = 1$ year then:

$$e^{r} = (2.718281)^{0.06} = 1.061837$$

This is the limit reached with continuous compounding.

The convention in both wholesale and personal (retail) markets is to quote an annual interest rate. A lender who wishes to earn the interest at the rate quoted has to place her funds on deposit for one year. Annual rates are quoted irrespective of the maturity of a deposit, from overnight to 10 years or longer. For example if one opens a bank account that pays interest at a rate of 3.5% but then closes it after six months, the actual interest earned will be equal to 1.75% of the sum deposited. The actual return on a three-year building society bond (fixed deposit) that pays 6.75% fixed for three years is 21.65% after three years. The quoted rate is the annual one-year equivalent. An overnight deposit in the wholesale or interbank market is still quoted as an annual rate, even though interest is earned for only one day.

The convention of quoting annualised rates is to allow deposits and loans of different maturities and different instruments to be compared on the basis of the interest rate applicable. We must be careful when comparing interest rates for products that have different payment frequencies. As we have seen from the foregoing paragraphs, the actual interest earned will be greater for a deposit earning 6% on a semi-annual basis than one earning 6% on an annual basis. The convention in the money markets is to quote the equivalent interest rate applicable when taking into account an instrument's payment frequency.

We saw how a future value could be calculated given a known present value and rate of interest. For example, $100 invested today for one year at an interest rate of 6% will generate $100 \times (1 + 0.06) = \$106$ at the end of the year. The future value of $100 in this case is $106. We can also say that $100 is the present value of $106 in this case.

In equation 1.3 we established the following future-value relationship:

$$FV = PV\,(1 + r)^{n}.$$

By reversing this expression we arrive at the present-value calculation given in 1.7.

$$PV = \frac{FV}{(1 + r)^{n}} \tag{1.7}$$

where the symbols represent the same terms as before. Equation 1.7 applies in the case of annual interest payments and enables us to calculate the present value of a known future sum.

To calculate the present value for a short-term investment of less than one year, we will need to adjust what would have been the interest earned for a whole year by the proportion of days of the investment period. Re-arranging the basic equation, we can say that the present value of a known future value is:

$$PV = \frac{FV}{\left(1 + r \times \frac{\text{days}}{\text{year}}\right)} \tag{1.8}$$

Given a present value and a future value at the end of an investment period, what then is the interest rate earned? We can re-arrange the basic equation again to solve for the *yield*.

When interest is compounded more than once a year, the formula for calculating present value is modified, as shown at (1.9).

$$PV = \frac{FV}{\left(1 + \dfrac{r}{n}\right)^{n}} \tag{1.9}$$

where, as before, FV is the cash flow at the end of year n, m is the number of times a year interest is compounded, and r is the rate of interest or discount rate. Illustrating this, therefore, the present value of $100 that is received at the end of five years at a rate of interest rate of 5%, with quarterly compounding is:

$$PV = \frac{100}{\left(1 + \frac{0.05}{4}\right)^{(4)(5)}}$$

$$= \$78.00$$

Interest rates in the money markets are always quoted for standard maturities – for example, overnight, tom next (the overnight interest rate starting tomorrow, or "tomorrow to the next"), spot next (the overnight rate starting two days forward), one week, one month, two months and so on, up to one year. If a bank or corporate customer wishes to deal for non-standard periods, an interbank desk will calculate the rate chargeable for such an "odd date" by interpolating between two standard-period interest rates. If we assume that the rate for all dates in between two periods increases at the same steady state, we can calculate the required rate using the formula for straight-line interpolation, shown at (1.10).

$$r = r_1 + (r_2 - r_1) \times \frac{n - n_1}{n_2 - n_1} \tag{1.10}$$

where

r is the required odd-date rate for n days
r_1 is the quoted rate for n_1 days
r_2 is the quoted rate for n_2 days.

Let us imagine that the one-month (30-day) offered interest rate is 5.25% and that the two-month (60-date) offered rate is 5.75%. If a customer wishes to borrow money for a 40-day period, what rate should the bank charge? We can calculate the required 40-day rate using the straight-line interpolation process. The increase in interest rates from 30 to 40 days is assumed to be 10/30 of the total increase in rates from 30 to 60 days. The 40-day offered rate would therefore be:

$$5.25\% + (5.75\% - 5.25\%) \times 10/30 = 5.4167\%.$$

What about the case of an interest rate for a period that lies just before or just after two known rates and not roughly in between them? When this happens we extrapolate between the two known rates, again assuming a straight-line relationship between the two rates and for a period after (or before) the two rates. So if the one-month offered rate is 5.25% while the two-month rate is 5.75%, the 64-day rate is:

$$5.25 + (5.75 - 5.25) \times 34/30 = 5.8167\%.$$

Discount factors

An n-period discount factor is the present value of one unit of currency (£1 or $1) that is payable at the end of period n. Essentially it is the present-value relationship expressed in terms of $1. If $d(n)$ is the n-year discount factor, then the five-year discount factor at a discount rate of 6% is given by

$$d(5) = \frac{1}{(1 + 0.06)^5} = 0.747258.$$

The set of discount factors for every time period from one day to 30 years or longer is termed the *discount function*. Discount factors may be used to price any financial instrument that is made up of a future cash flow. For example, what would be the value of $103.50 receivable at the end of six months if the six-month discount factor is 0.98756? The answer is given by:

$$0.98756 \times 103.50 = 102.212.$$

In addition, discount factors may be used to calculate the future value of any present investment. From the example above, $0.98756 would be worth $1 in six months' time, so by the same principle a present sum of $1 would be worth

$$1/d(0.5) = 1/0.98756 = 1.0126$$

at the end of six months.

It is possible to obtain discount factors from current bond prices. Assume a hypothetical set of bonds and bond prices as given in Table 1.3 below, and assume further that the first bond in the table matures in precisely six months' time (these are semi-annual coupon bonds).

Coupon	Maturity date	Price
7%	7-Jun-01	101.65
8%	7-Dec-01	101.89
6%	7-Jun-02	100.75
6.50%	7-Dec-02	100.37

Table 1.3 Hypothetical set of bonds and bond prices

Taking the first bond, this matures in precisely six months' time, and its final cash flow will be 103.50, comprising the $3.50 final coupon payment and the $100 redemption payment. The price or present value of this bond is 101.65, which allows us to calculate the six-month discount factor as:

$$d(0.5) \times 103.50 = 101.65$$

which gives $d(0.5)$ equal to 0.98213.

From this first step we can calculate the discount factors for the following six-month periods. The second bond in Table 1.3, the 8% 2001, has the following cash flows:

- $4 in six month s' time
- $104 in one year's time.

The price of this bond is 101.89, which again is the bond's present value, and this comprises the sum of the present values of the bond's total cash flows. So we are able to set the following:

$$101.89 = 4 \times d(0.5) + 104 \times d(1)$$

However, we already know $d(0.5)$ to be 0.98213, which leaves only one unknown in the above expression. Therefore we may solve for $d(1)$ and this is shown to be 0.94194.

If we carry on with this procedure for the remaining two bonds, using successive discount factors, we obtain the complete set of discount factors as shown in Table 1. 4. The continuous function for the two-year period from today is known as the discount function, shown at Figure 1.2.

Coupon	Maturity date	Term (years)	Price	d(n)
7%	7-Jun-01	0.5	101.65	0.98213
8%	7-Dec-01	1.0	101.89	0.94194
6%	7-Jun-02	1.5	100.75	0.92211
6.50%	7-Dec-02	2.0	100.37	0.88252

Table 1.4 Discount factors calculated using bootstrapping technique

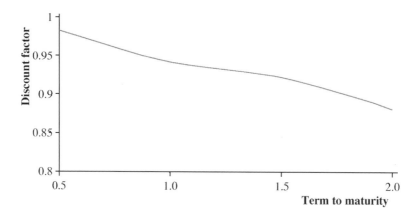

Figure 1.2 Hypothetical discount function

This technique, which is known as *bootstrapping*, is conceptually neat but presents problems when we do not have a set of bonds that mature at precise six-month intervals. In addition, liquidity issues connected with specific individual bonds can also cause complications. However, it is still worth being familiar with this approach.

Note from Figure 1.2 how discount factors decrease with increasing maturity: this is intuitively obvious, since the present value of something to be received in the future diminishes the further into the future we go.

Bond pricing and yield: The traditional approach

Bond pricing

The interest rate that is used to discount a bond's cash flows (and therefore called the discount rate) is the rate required by the bondholder. This is therefore known as the bond's yield. The yield on the bond will be determined by the market and is the price demanded by investors for buying it, which is why it is sometimes called the bond's return. The required yield for any bond will depend on a number of political and economic factors, including what yield is being earned by other bonds of the same class. Yield is always quoted as an annualised interest rate, so that for a bond paying semi-annually exactly half of the annual rate is used to discount the cash flows.

The fair price of a bond is the present value of all its cash flows. Therefore, when pricing a bond, we need to calculate the present value of all the coupon interest payments and the present value of the redemption payment, and sum these. The price of a conventional bond that pays annual coupons can therefore be given by (1.11).

$$P = \frac{C}{(1 + r)} + \frac{C}{(1 + r)^2} + \frac{C}{(1 + r)^3} + \cdots\cdots \frac{C}{(1 + r)^N} + \frac{M}{(1 + r)^N}$$

$$= \sum_{n=1}^{N} \frac{C}{(1 + r)^N} + \frac{M}{(1 + r)^N} \tag{1.11}$$

where

P is the price
C is the annual coupon payment
r is the discount rate (therefore, the required yield)
N is the number of years to maturity (therefore, the number of interest periods in an annually paying bond; for a semi-annual bond the number of interest periods is $N \yen 2$).
M is the maturity payment or par value (usually 100 per cent of currency).

For long-hand calculation purposes, the first half of (1.11) is usually simplified and is sometimes encountered in one of the two ways shown in (1.12).

$$P = C \left[\frac{1 - \left[\frac{1}{(1 + r)^N} \right]}{r} \right] \tag{1.12}$$

or

$$P = \frac{C}{r} \left[1 - \frac{1}{(1 + r)^N} \right]$$

The price of a bond that pays semi-annual coupons is given by the expression at (1.13), which is our earlier expression modified to allow for the twice-yearly discounting:

$$P = \frac{C/2}{(1 + \frac{1}{2}r)} + \frac{C/2}{(1 + \frac{1}{2}r)^2} + \frac{C/2}{(1 + \frac{1}{2}r)^3} + \cdots\cdots \frac{C/2}{(1 + \frac{1}{2}r)^{2N}} + \frac{M}{(1 + \frac{1}{2}r)^{2N}}$$

$$= \sum_{t=1}^{2T} \frac{C/2}{(1 + \frac{1}{2}r)^N} + \frac{M}{(1 + \frac{1}{2}r)^{2N}} \tag{1.13}$$

$$= \frac{C}{r}\left[1 - \frac{1}{(1 + \frac{1}{2}r)^{2N}}\right] + \frac{M}{(1 + \frac{1}{2}r)^{2N}}$$

Note how we set $2N$ as the power to which to raise the discount factor, as there are two interest payments every year for a bond that pays semi-annually. Therefore, a more convenient function to use might be the number of interest periods in the life of the bond, as opposed to the number of years to maturity, which we could set as n, allowing us to alter the equation for a semi-annually paying bond as:

$$P = \frac{C}{r}\left[1 - \frac{1}{(1 + \frac{1}{2}r)^{2N}}\right] + \frac{M}{(1 + \frac{1}{2}r)^{2N+1}} \tag{1.14}$$

The formula at (1.14) calculates the fair price on a coupon-payment date, so that there is no accrued interest incorporated into the price. It also assumes that there is an even number of coupon-payment dates remaining before maturity. The concept of accrued interest is an accounting convention, and treats coupon interest as accruing every day that the bond is held; this amount is added to the discounted present value of the bond (the *clean* price) to obtain the market value of the bond, known as the *dirty* price.

The date used as the point for calculation is the settlement date for the bond, the date on which a bond will change hands after it is traded. For a new issue of bonds, the settlement date is the day when the stock is delivered to investors and payment is received by the bond issuer. The settlement date for a bond traded in the secondary market is the day that the buyer transfers payment to the seller of the bond and when the seller transfers the bond to the buyer. Different markets will have different settlement conventions. For example, Australian government bonds normally settle 2 business days after the trade date (the notation used in bond markets is "T + 2") whereas Eurobonds settle on T + 3. The term *value date* is sometimes used in place of settlement date. However, the two terms are not strictly synonymous. A settlement date can only fall on a business date, so that an Australian government bond traded on a Friday will settle on a Tuesday. However, a value date can sometimes fall on a non-business day; for example, when accrued interest is being calculated.

If there is an odd number of coupon-payment dates before maturity, the formula at (1.14) is modified as shown in (1.15).

$$P = \frac{C}{r}\left[1 - \frac{1}{(1 + \frac{1}{2}r)^{2N+1}}\right] + \frac{M}{(1 + \frac{1}{2}r)^{2N+I}} \quad (1.15)$$

The standard formula also assumes that the bond is traded for a settlement on a day that is precisely one interest period before the next coupon payment. The price formula is adjusted if dealing takes place in between coupon dates. If we take the value date for any transaction, we then need to calculate the number of calendar days from this day to the next coupon date. We then use the following ratio i when adjusting the exponent for the discount factor:

$$i = \frac{\text{Days from value date to next coupon date}}{\text{Days in the interest period}}$$

The number of days in the interest period is the number of calendar days between the last coupon date and the next one, and it will depend on the day-count basis used for that specific bond. The price formula is then modified as shown at (1.16).

$$P = \frac{C}{(1 + r)^i} + \frac{C}{(1 + r)^{1+i}} + \frac{C}{(1 + r)^{2+i}} + \cdots\cdots \frac{C}{(1 + r)^{n-1+i}} + \frac{M}{(1 + r)^{n-1+i}}$$

$$(1.16)$$

where the variables C, M, n and r are as before. Note that (1.16) assumes r for an annually paying bond and is adjusted to $r/2$ for a semi-annually paying bond.

EXAMPLE 1.1

In these examples we illustrate the long-hand price calculation, using both expressions for the calculation of the present value of the annuity stream of a bond's cash flows.

1.1 (a)
Calculate the fair pricing of a US Treasury, the 4% of February 2014, which pays semi-annual coupons, with the following terms:
   $C = \$4.00$ per $100 nominal
   $M = \$100$
   $N = 10$ years (that is, the calculation is for value the 17th February 2004)
   $r = 4.048\%$

$$P = \frac{\$4.00}{0.04048} \left\{ 1 - \frac{1}{[1 + \frac{1}{2}(0.04048)]^{20}} \right\} + \frac{\$100}{[1 + \frac{1}{2}(0.04048)]^{20}}$$

$$= \$32.628 + \$66.981$$

$$= \$99.609 \text{ or } 99\text{-}19\text{+}$$

The fair price of the Treasury is $99-19+, which is composed of the present value of the stream of coupon payments ($32.628) and the present value of the return of the principal ($66.981).

This yield calculation is shown at Figure 1.3, the Bloomberg YA page for this security. We show the price shown as 99-19+ for settlement on 17 Feb 2004, the date it was issued.

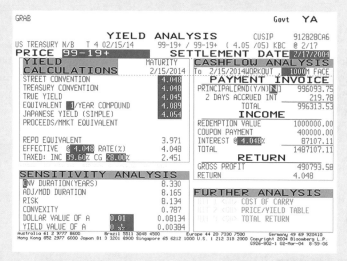

Figure 1.3 Bloomberg YA page for yield analysis

1.1(b)

What is the price of a 5% coupon sterling bond with precisely five years to maturity, with semi-annual coupon payments, if the yield required is 5.40%?

As the cash flows for this bond are 10 semi-annual coupons of £2.50 and a redemption payment of £100 in 10 six-month periods from now, the price of the bond can be obtained by solving the following expression, where we substitute $C = 2.5$, $n = 10$ and $r = 0.027$ into the price equation (the values for C and r reflect the adjustments necessary for a semi-annual paying bond).

$$P = 2.5 \left[\frac{1 - \left[\frac{1}{(1.027)^{10}}\right]}{0.027} \right] + \frac{100}{(1.027)^{10}}$$

$$= 21.65574 + 76.61178$$
$$= \$98.26752$$

The price of the bond is $98.2675 per $100 nominal.

1.1(c)

What is the price of a 5% coupon euro bond with five years to maturity paying annual coupons, again with a required yield of 5.4%?

In this case there are five periods of interest, so we may set $C = 5$, $n = 5$, with $r = 0.05$.

$$P = 5 \left[\frac{1 - \left[\frac{1}{(1.054)^{5}}\right]}{0.054} \right] + \frac{100}{(1.054)^{5}}$$

$$= 21.410121 + 76.877092$$
$$= £98.287213$$

Note how the annual-paying bond has a slightly higher price for the same required annualised yield. This is because the semi-annual paying sterling bond has a higher effective yield than the euro bond, resulting in a lower price.

1.1(d)

Consider our 5% sterling bond again, but this time the required yield has risen and is now 6%. This makes $C = 2.5$, $n = 10$ and $r = 0.03$.

$$P = 2.5 \left[\frac{1 - \left[\frac{1}{(1.03)^{10}}\right]}{0.03} \right] + \frac{100}{(1.03)^{10}}$$

$$= 21.325507 + 74.409391$$
$$= £95.7349$$

As the required yield has risen, the discount rate used in the price calculation is now higher, and the result of the higher discount is a lower present value (price).

1.1(e)

Calculate the price of our sterling bond, still with five years to maturity but offering a yield of 5.1%.

$$P = 2.5 \left[\frac{1 - \left[\frac{1}{(1.0255)^5} \right]}{0.0255} \right] + \frac{100}{(1.0255)^5}$$

$$= 21.823737 + 77.739788$$

$$= £99.563523$$

To satisfy the lower required yield of 5.1%, the price of the bond has fallen to £99.56 per £100.

1.1(f)

Calculate the price of the 5% sterling bond one year later, with precisely four years left to maturity and with the required yield still at the original 5.40%. This sets the terms in 1.1(b) unchanged, except now $n = 8$.

$$P = 2.5 \left[\frac{1 - \left[\frac{1}{(1.027)^8} \right]}{0.027} \right] + \frac{100}{(1.027)^8}$$

$$= 17.773458 + 80.804668$$

$$= £98.578126$$

The price of the bond is £98.58. Compared to 1.1(b) this illustrates how, other things being equal, the price of a bond will approach par (£100 per cent) as it approaches maturity.

There also exist *perpetual* or *irredeemable* bonds which have no redemption date, so that interest on them is paid indefinitely. They are also known as undated bonds. An example of an undated bond is the $3\frac{1}{2}$% War Loan, a UK gilt originally issued in 1916 to help pay for the 1914-1918 war effort. Most undated bonds date from a long time in the past and it is unusual to see them issued today. In structure, the cash flow from an undated bond can be viewed as a continuous annuity. The fair price of such a bond is given from (1.11) by setting $N = \infty$, such that :

$$P = \frac{C}{r} \qquad (1.17)$$

In most markets, bond prices are quoted in decimals, in minimum increments of 1/100^{ths}. This is the case with Eurobonds, euro-denominated bonds and gilts, for example. Certain markets – including the US Treasury market and South African and Indian government bonds, for example – quote prices in ticks, where the minimum increment is 1/32nd. One tick is therefore equal to 0.03125. A US Treasury might be priced at "98-05" which means "98 and five ticks". This is equal to 98 and 5/32^{nds} which is 98.15625.

EXAMPLE 1.2

What is the total consideration for £5 million nominal of a gilt, where the price is 114.50?

The price of the gilt is £114.50 per £100, so the consideration is:

1.145 × 5,000,000 = £5,725,000

What consideration is payable for $5 million nominal of a US Treasury, quoted at an all-in price of 99-16?

The US Treasury price is 99-16, which is equal to 99 and 16/32, or 99.50 per $100. The consideration is therefore:

0.9950 × 5,000,000 = $4,975,000.

If the price of a bond is below par, the total consideration is below the nominal amount; whereas if it is priced above par, the consideration will be above the nominal amount.

Bonds that do not pay a coupon during their life are known as zero-coupon bonds or strips, and the price for these bonds is determined by modifying (1.11) to allow for the fact that $C = 0$. We know that the only cash flow is the maturity payment, so we may set the price as:

$$P = \frac{M}{(1 + r)^N} \qquad (1.18)$$

where M and r are as before and N is the number of years to maturity. The important factor is to allow for the same number of interest periods as coupon bonds of the same currency. That is, even though there are no actual coupons, we calculate prices and yields on the basis of a quasi-coupon period. For a US dollar or a sterling zero-coupon bond, a five-year zero-coupon bond would be assumed to cover ten quasi-coupon periods, which would set the price equation as:

$$P = \frac{M}{(1 + \frac{1}{2}r)^n} \qquad (1.19)$$

We have to note carefully the quasi-coupon periods in order to maintain consistency with conventional bond pricing.

EXAMPLE 1.3

1.3(a)
Calculate the price of a gilt strip with a maturity of precisely five years, where the required yield is 5.40%.

These terms allow us to set $N = 5$ so that $n = 10$, $r = 0.054$ (so that $r/2 = 0.027$), with $M = 100$ as usual.

$$P = \frac{100}{(1.027)^{10}}$$

$$= £76.611782$$

1.3(b)
Calculate the price of a French government zero-coupon bond with precisely five years to maturity, with the same required yield of 5.40%.

$$P = \frac{100}{(1.054)^5}$$

$$= £76.877092$$

An examination of the bond price formula tells us that the yield and price for a bond are closely related. A key aspect of this relationship is that the price changes in the opposite direction to the yield. This is because the price of the bond is the net present value of its cash flows; if the discount rate used in the present value calculation increases, the present values of the cash flows will decrease. This occurs whenever the yield level required by bondholders increases. In the same way, if the required yield decreases, the price of the bond will rise. This property was observed in example 1.2. As the required yield decreased, the price of the bond increased, and we observed the same relationship when the required yield was raised.

The relationship between any bond's price and yield at any required yield level is illustrated in Figure 1.4, which is obtained if we plot the yield against the corresponding price; this shows a convex curve. In practice the curve is not quite as perfectly convex as illustrated in Figure 1.4, but the diagram is representative.

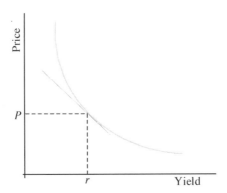

Fig 1.4 The price/yield relationship

SUMMARY OF THE PRICE/YIELD RELATIONSHIP

At issue, if a bond is priced at par, its coupon will equal the yield that the market requires from the bond.

If the required yield rises above the coupon rate, the bond price will decrease.

If the required yield goes below the coupon rate, the bond price will increase.

Bond yield

We have observed how to calculate the price of a bond using an appropriate discount rate known as the bond's yield. We can reverse this procedure to find the yield of a bond where the price is known, which would be equivalent to calculating the bond's internal rate of return (IRR). The IRR calculation is taken to be a bond's yield to maturity or redemption yield and is one of various yield measures used in the markets to estimate the return generated from holding a bond. In most markets, bonds are generally traded on the basis of their prices but because of the complicated patterns of cash flows that different bonds can have, they are generally compared in terms of their yields. This means that a market-maker will usually quote a two-way price at which she will buy or sell a particular bond, but it is the yield at which the bond is trading that is important to the market-maker's customer. This is because a bond's price does not actually tell us anything useful about what we are getting. Remember, that in any market there will be a number of bonds with different issuers, coupons and terms to maturity. Even in a homogenous market such as the Treasury market, different bonds and notes will trade according to their own specific characteristics. To compare bonds in the market, therefore, we need the yield on any bond and it is yields that we compare, not prices.

The yield on any investment is the interest rate that will make the present value of the cash flows from the investment equal to the initial cost (price) of the investment. Mathematically, the yield on any investment, represented by r, is the interest rate that satisfies equation (1.20) below, which is simply the bond price equation we've already reviewed.

$$P = \sum_{n=1}^{N} \frac{C_n}{(1 + r)^n} \qquad (1.20)$$

But as we have noted there are other types of yield measure used in the market for different purposes. The simplest measure of the yield on a bond is the current yield, also know as the flat yield, interest yield or running yield. The running yield is given by (1.21).

$$rc = \frac{C}{P} \times 100 \qquad (1.21)$$

where

rc is the current yield.

In (1.21) C is not expressed as a decimal. Current yield ignores any capital gain or loss that might arise from holding and trading a bond and does not consider the time value of money. It essentially calculates the bond coupon income as a proportion of the price paid for the bond, and to be accurate would have to assume that the bond was more like an annuity rather than a fixed-term instrument.

The current yield is useful as a "rough-and-ready" interest-rate calculation; it is often used to estimate the cost of or profit from a short-term holding of a bond. For example, if other short-term interest rates such as the one-week or three-month rates are higher than the current yield, holding the bond is said to involve a running cost. This is also known as *negative carry* or *negative funding*. The term is used by bond traders and market makers and leveraged investors. The carry on a bond is a useful measure for all market practitioners as it illustrates the cost of holding or funding a bond. The funding rate is the bondholder's short-term cost of funds. A private investor could also apply this to a short-term holding of bonds.

The yield to maturity or gross redemption yield is the most frequently used measure of return from holding a bond.[5] Yield to maturity (YTM) takes into account the pattern of coupon payments, the bond's term to maturity and the capital gain (or loss) arising over the remaining life of the bond. We saw from our bond price formula in the previous section that these elements were all related and were important components determining a bond's price. If we set the IRR for a set of cash flows to be the rate that applies from a start-date to an end-date we can assume the IRR to be the YTM for those cash flows. The YTM therefore is equivalent to the internal rate of return on the bond, the rate that equates the value of the discounted cash flows on the bond to its current price. The calculation assumes that the bond is held until maturity and therefore it is the cash flows to maturity that are discounted in the calculation. It also employs the concept of the time value of money.

As we would expect, the formula for YTM is essentially that for calculating the price of a bond. For a bond paying annual coupons, the YTM is calculated by solving equation (1.11). Note that the expression at (1.11) has two variable parameters, the price P and yield r. It cannot be re-arranged to solve for yield r explicitly and, in fact, the only way to solve for the yield is to use the process of numerical iteration. The process involves estimating a value for r and calculating the price associated with the estimated yield. If the calculated price is higher than the price of the bond at the time, the yield estimate is lower than the actual yield, and so it must be adjusted until it converges to the level that corresponds with the bond price.[6] For the YTM of a semi-annual coupon bond, we have to adjust the formula to allow for the semi-annual payments, shown at (1.13).

To differentiate redemption yield from other yield and interest-rate measures described in this book, we henceforth refer to it as *rm*.

---

[5] In this book the terms "yield to maturity" and "gross redemption yield" are used synonymously. The latter term is encountered in sterling markets.

[6] Bloomberg also uses the term "yield-to-workout", where "workout" refers to the maturity date for the bond.

EXAMPLE 1.4 Yield to maturity for semi-annual coupon bond

A semi-annual paying bond has a dirty price of \$98.50, an annual coupon of 6% and there is exactly one year before maturity. The bond therefore has three remaining cash flows, comprising two coupon payments of \$3 each and a redemption payment of \$100. Equation 1.12 can be used with the following inputs:

$$98.50 = \frac{3.00}{(1 + \frac{1}{2}rm)} + \frac{103.00}{(1 + \frac{1}{2}rm)^2}$$

Note that we use half of the YTM value rm because this is a semi-annual paying bond. The expression above is a quadratic equation, which is solved using the standard solution for quadratic equations, which is noted below.

$$ax^2 + bx + c = 0$$

$$x = \frac{-b \pm \sqrt{b^2 - 4ac}}{2a}$$

In our expression, if we let $x = (1 + rm/2)$, we can re-arrange the expression as follows:

$$98.50x^2 - 3.0x - 103.00 = 0$$

We then solve for a standard quadratic equation, and there will be two solutions, only one of which gives a positive redemption yield. The positive solution is $rm/2 = 0.037929$ so that $rm = 7.5859\%$.

As an example of the iterative solution method, suppose that we start with a trial value for rm of $r_1 = 7\%$ per cent and plug this into the right-hand side of equation 1.12. This gives a value for the right-hand side of:

$$RHS_1 = 99.050$$

which is higher than the left-hand side (LHS = 98.50); the trial value for rm was therefore too low. Suppose then that we try next $r_2 = 8\%$ and use this as the right-hand side of the equation. This gives:

$$RHS_2 = 98.114$$

$$rm = r_1 + (r_2 - r_1) \frac{RHS_1 - LHS}{RHS_1 - RHS_2}$$

our linear approximation for the redemption yield is $rm = 7.587\%$, which is near the exact solution.

Note that the redemption yield, as discussed earlier in this section, is the gross redemption yield, the yield that results from payment of coupons without deduction of any withholding tax. The net redemption yield is obtained by multiplying the coupon rate C by (1 − marginal tax rate). The net yield is what will be received if the bond is traded in a market where bonds pay coupon net, which means net of a withholding tax. The net redemption yield is always lower than the gross redemption yield.

We have already alluded to the key assumption behind the YTM calculation, namely that the rate rm remains stable for the entire period of the life of the bond. By assuming the same yield, we can say that all coupons are reinvested at the same yield rm. For the bond in example 1.4, this means that if all the cash flows are discounted at 7.59% they will have a total net present value of 98.50. This is patently unrealistic since we can predict with virtual certainty that interest rates for instruments of similar maturity to the bond at each coupon date will not remain at this rate for the life of the bond. In practice, however, investors require a rate of return that is equivalent to the price that they are paying for a bond and the redemption yield is, to put it simply, as good a measurement as any. A more accurate measurement might be to calculate present values of future cash flows using the discount rate that is equal to the market's view on where interest rates will be at that point, known as the forward interest rate. However, forward rates are implied interest rates, and a YTM measurement calculated using forward rates can be as speculative as one calculated using the conventional formula. This is because the actual market interest rate at any time is invariably different from the rate implied earlier in the forward markets. So a YTM calculation made using forward rates would not be realised in practice either.[7] We shall see later how the zero-coupon interest rate is the true interest rate for any term to maturity. However, despite the limitations presented by its assumptions, the YTM is the main measure of return used in the markets.

---

[7] Such an approach is used to price interest-rate swaps, however.

We have noted the difference between calculating redemption yield on the basis of both annual and semi-annual coupon bonds. Analysis of bonds that pay semi-annual coupons incorporates semi-annual discounting of semi-annual coupon payments. This is appropriate for most UK and US bonds. However, government bonds in most of continental Europe and most Eurobonds pay annual coupon payments, and the appropriate method of calculating the redemption yield is to use annual discounting. The two yields measures are not therefore directly comparable. We could make a Eurobond directly comparable with a UK gilt by using semi-annual discounting of the eurobond's annual coupon payments. Alternatively we could make the gilt comparable with the eurobond by using annual discounting of its semi-annual coupon payments. The price/yield formulae for different discounting possibilities we encounter in the markets are listed below (as usual we assume that the calculation takes place on a coupon payment date so that accrued interest is zero).

Semi-annual discounting of annual payments:

$$P_d = \frac{C}{(1 + \frac{1}{2}rm)^2} + \frac{C}{(1 + \frac{1}{2}rm)^4} + \frac{C}{(1 + \frac{1}{2}rm)^6} + \cdots \frac{C}{(1 + \frac{1}{2}rm)^{2N}} + \frac{M}{(1 + rm)^{2N}}$$

(1.22)

Annual discounting of semi-annual payments:

$$P_d = \frac{C/2}{(1 + \frac{1}{2}rm)^{\frac{1}{2}}} + \frac{C/2}{(1 + rm)} + \frac{C/2}{(1 + \frac{1}{2}rm)^{\frac{3}{2}}} + \cdots \frac{C/2}{(1 + rm)^N} + \frac{M}{(1 + rm)^N}$$

(1.23)

Consider a bond with a dirty price of 97.89, a coupon of 6% and a five years to maturity. This bond would have the following gross redemption yields under the different yield-calculation conventions:

Discounting	Payments	Yield to Maturity (%)
Semi-annual	Semi-annual	6.500
Annual	Annual	6.508
Semi-annual	Annual	6.428
Annual	Semi-annual	6.605

This proves what we have already observed; namely, that the coupon and discounting frequency will affect the redemption yield calculation for a bond. We can see that increasing the frequency of discounting will lower the yield, while increasing the frequency of payments will raise the yield. When comparing yields for bonds that trade in markets with different conventions, it is important to convert all the yields to the same calculation basis. Intuitively we might think that doubling a semi-annual yield figure will give us the annualised equivalent; in fact, this will result in an inaccurate figure due to the multiplicative effects of discounting and one that is an underestimate of the true annualised yield. The correct procedure for producing an annualised yields from semi-annual and quarterly yields is given by the expressions below.

The general conversion expression is given by (1.24):

$$rm_a = (1 + \text{interest rate})^m - 1 \tag{1.24}$$

where m is the number of coupon payments per year.

Specifically we can convert between yields using the expressions given at (1.25) and (1.26).

$$rm_a = [(1 + \tfrac{1}{2}rm_s)^2 - 1]$$
$$rm_s = [(1 + rm_a)^{\frac{1}{2}} - 1] \times 2 \tag{1.25}$$

$$rm_a = [(1 + \tfrac{1}{4}rm_q)^4 - 1]$$
$$rm_q = [(1 + rm_a)^{\frac{1}{4}} - 1] \times 4 \tag{1.26}$$

where rm_q, rm_s and rm_a are, respectively, the quarterly, semi-annually and annually compounded yields to maturity.

EXAMPLE 1.5

A UK gilt paying semi-annual coupons and a maturity of 10 years has a quoted yield of 4.89%. A European government bond of similar maturity is quoted at a yield of 4.96%. Which bond has the higher effective yield?

The effective annual yield of the gilt is:
$rm = (1 + \tfrac{1}{2} \bullet 0.0489)^2 - 1 = 4.9498\%$
Therefore, the gilt does indeed have the lower yield.

The market convention is sometimes simply to double the semi-annual yield to obtain the annualised yields, despite the fact that this produces an inaccurate result. It is only acceptable to do this for rough calculations. An annualised yield obtained by multiplying the semi-annual yield by two is known as a bond equivalent yield.

While YTM is the most commonly used measure of yield, it has one major disadvantage. The disadvantage is that implicit in the calculation of the YTM is the assumption that each coupon payment as it becomes due is re-invested at the rate *rm*. This is clearly unlikely, due to the fluctuations in interest rates over time and as the bond approaches maturity. In practice, the measure itself will not equal the actual return from holding the bond, even if it is held to maturity. That said, the market standard is to quote bond returns as yields to maturity, bearing the key assumptions behind the calculation in mind.

Another disadvantage of this measure of return arises where investors do not hold bonds to maturity. The redemption yield measure will not be of great value where the bond is not being held to redemption. Investors might then be interested in other measures of return, which we can look at later.

To reiterate then, the redemption yield measure assumes that:

- the bond is held to maturity
- all coupons during the bond's life are reinvested at the same (redemption yield) rate.

Therefore the YTM can be viewed as an it to maturity. Even then the actual realised yield on maturity would be different from expected or anticipated yield and is closest to reality perhaps where an investor buys a bond on first issue and holds the YTM figure because of the inapplicability of the second condition above.

In addition, as coupons are discounted at the yield specific for each bond, it actually becomes inaccurate to compare bonds using this yield measure. For instance, the coupon cash flows that occur in two years time from both a two-year and five-year bond will be discounted at different rates (assuming we do not have a flat yield curve). This would occur because the YTM for a five-year bond is invariably different from the YTM for a two-year bond. However, it would clearly not be correct to discount a two-year cash flow at different rates, because we can see that the present value calculated today of a cash flow in two years' time should be the same whether it is sourced from a short- or long-dated bond. Even if the first condition noted above for the YTM calculation is satisfied, it is clearly unlikely for any but the shortest maturity bond that all coupons will be reinvested at the same rate. Market interest rates are in a state of constant flux and would thus affect money reinvestment rates. Therefore, although yield to maturity is the main market measure of bond levels, it is not a true interest rate. This is an important result and we shall explore the concept of a true interest rate in Chapter 2.

Market yield measures

At Figure 1.3 we saw the Bloomberg page YA, used for yield analysis of fixed income instruments. Readers will notice from this figure that there are a number of different measures of yield shown on the page, all related to the standard yield-to-maturity calculation. This is because different markets and instruments use slightly different conventions when calculating yield-to-maturity.

All market yield measures define a bond's maturity date as the date when the final principal amount becomes due. This is almost invariably the stated maturity date of the bond, but in certain cases this date may fall on a non-business day, so the following working date is used instead.

Otherwise there are subtle differences in the way the different measures are calculated, although they may still give the same result. Here we explain these differences:

- **Street convention:** the standard yield-to-maturity calculation
- **True yield:** this is the standard yield-to-maturity calculated with coupon dates moved whenever they fall on a non-business day, to the next valid business day. Moving this date is pertinent to the yield measure because it affects the number of days in an interest period;
- **Treasury convention:** the yield calculated using simple interest for the first coupon period, and compounded interest for subsequent interest periods. Assume an actual/actual accrued interest basis (this term is explained in the next section);
- **Consortium yield:** this is used for bonds that use an actual/365 day-count basis, it assume 182.5 days in each (semi-annual) interest period;
- **DMO yield:** a yield associated with United Kingdom gilts, the street convention equivalent as defined by the UK Debt Management Office;
- **Equivalent/year compound:** this is the street convention method adjusted for actual cash flow and compounding frequency; it uses the actual date of cash flows as they would be received;

- **Japanese yield:** This is a simple yield calculation using the annualised cash flow, expressed as a percentage of the original clean price used at purchase;
- **Money market equivalent:** this is the yield of the bond but adjusted to make it equate to money market yield convention. It would only be used for a bond that had less than 365 days left to maturity. This calculation compounds the remaining coupon payments to the maturity date, and this total amount is used to calculate a yield, based on simple interest, quoted using the present value of the total cash flows. Assumes an actual/360 day count basis;
- **Repo equivalent:** this is the yield calculated with interest accumulated on an overnight basis, with bond priced fixed, and assuming actual/360 day basis;
- **Effective rate:** the bond yield realised by investing coupon income at a specified reinvestment rate from now until maturity.

Investors will use the yield measure appropriate to the market and instrument they are analysing.

Accrued interest, clean and dirty bond prices

Our discussion of bond pricing up to now has ignored coupon interest. All bonds (except zero-coupon bonds) accrue interest on a daily basis, and this is then paid out on the coupon date. The calculation of bond prices using present-value analysis does not account for coupon interest or *accrued interest*. In all major bond markets, the convention is to quote price as a *clean price*. This is the price of the bond as given by the net present value of its cash flows, but excluding coupon interest that has accrued on the bond since the last dividend payment. As all bonds accrue interest on a daily basis, even if a bond is held for only one day, interest will have been earned by the bondholder. However, we have referred already to a bond's *all-in* price, which is the price that is actually paid for the bond in the market. This is also known as the *dirty price* (or *gross price*), which is the clean price of a bond plus accrued interest. In other words, the accrued interest must be added to the quoted price to get the total consideration for the bond.

Accruing interest compensates the seller of the bond for giving up all of the next coupon payment even though she will have held the bond for part of the period since the last coupon payment. The clean price for a bond will move with changes in market interest rates; assuming that this is constant in a coupon period, the clean price will be constant for this period. However, the dirty price for the same bond will increase steadily from one interest payment date until the next. On the coupon date, the clean and dirty prices are the same and the accrued interest is zero. Between the coupon payment date and the next ex-dividend date the bond is traded cum dividend, so that the buyer gets the next coupon payment. The seller is compensated for not receiving the next coupon payment by receiving accrued interest instead. This is positive and increases up to the next ex-dividend date, at which point the dirty price falls by the present value of the amount of the coupon payment. The dirty price at this point is below the clean price, reflecting the fact that accrued interest is now negative. This is because after the ex-dividend date the bond is traded "ex-dividend"; the seller not the buyer receives the next coupon and the buyer has to be compensated for not receiving the next coupon by means of a lower price for holding the bond.

The net interest accrued since the last ex-dividend date is determined as follows :

$$AI = C \times \left[\frac{N_{xt} - N_{xc}}{DayBase}\right] \qquad (1.27)$$

where

AI	is the next accrued interest
C	is the bond coupon
N_{xc}	is the number of days between the ex-dividend date and the coupon payment date (seven business days for UK gilts)
N_{xt}	is the number of days between the ex-dividend date and the date for the calculation
$Day\ Base$	is the day-count base (365 or 360)

Certain bonds do not have an ex-dividend period (for example, Eurobonds) and accrue interest right up to the coupon date.

Interest accrues on a bond from and including the last coupon date up to and excluding what is called the value date. The value date is almost always the settlement date for the bond, or the date when a bond is passed to the buyer and the seller receives payment. Interest does not accrue on bonds whose issuer has subsequently gone into default. Bonds that trade without accrued interest are said to be trading flat or clean. By definition therefore,

clean price of a bond = dirty price − accrued interest.

For bonds that are trading ex-dividend, the accrued coupon is negative and would be subtracted from the clean price. The calculation is given by (1.28) below.

$$AI = -C \times \frac{\text{days to } next \text{ coupon}}{DayBase} \qquad (1.28)$$

As we noted, certain classes of bonds – for example, US Treasuries and Eurobonds – do not have an ex-dividend period and therefore trade cum dividend right up to the coupon date.

The accrued-interest calculation for a bond is dependent on the day-count basis specified for the bond in question. When bonds are traded in the market, the actual consideration that changes hands is made up of the clean price of the bond together with the accrued that has accumulated on the bond since the last coupon payment; these two components make up the dirty price of the bond. When calculating the accrued interest, the market will use the appropriate day-count convention for that bond. A particular market will apply one of five different methods to calculate accrued interest:

actual/365 Accrued = Coupon × days/365
actual/360 Accrued = Coupon × days/360
actual/actual Accrued = Coupon × days/actual number of days in the interest period
30/360 See below
30E/360 See below

When determining the number of days in between two dates, include the first date but not the second; thus, under the actual/365 convention, there are 37 days between 4th August and 10th September. The last two conventions assume 30 days in each month; so, for example, there are "30 days" between 10th February and 10th March. Under the 30/360 convention, if the first date falls on the 31st, it is changed to the 30th of the month, and if the second date falls on the 31st *and* the first date is on the 30th or 31st, the second date is changed to the 30th. The difference under the 30E/360 method is that if the second date falls on the 31st of the month, it is automatically changed to the 30th.

The accrued interest day-count basis for selected country bond markets is given at Table 1.3.

Market	Coupon Frequency	Day Count Basis	Ex-dividend period
Australia	Semi-annual	actual / actual	Yes
Austria	Annual	actual / actual	No
Belgium	Annual	actual / actual	No
Canada	Semi-annual	actual / actual	No
Denmark	Annual	30E/360	Yes
Eurobonds	Annual	30/360	No
France	Annual	actual / actual	No
Germany	Annual	actual / actual	No
Eire	Annual	actual / actual	No
Italy	Annual	actual / actual	No
New Zealand	Semi-annual	actual / actual	Yes
Norway	Annual	actual / 365	Yes
Spain	Annual	actual / actual	No
Sweden	Annual	30E/360	Yes
Switzerland	Annual	30E/360	No
United Kingdom	Semi-annual	actual / actual	Yes
United States	Semi-annual	actual / actual	No

Table 1.3 Selected country market accrued interest day-count basis

Van Deventer (1997) presents an effective critique of the accrued interest concept, believing essentially that it is an arbitrary construct that has little basis in economic reality. He states:

"The amount of accrued interest bears no relationship
to the current level of interest rates."

(Van Deventer, 1997 p.11)

This is quite true, the accrued interest on a bond that it is traded in the secondary market at any time is not related to the current level of interest rates, and is the same irrespective of where current rates are. As Example 1.6 makes clear, the accrued interest on a bond is a function of its coupon, which reflects the level of interest rates at the time the bond was issued. Accrued interest is therefore an accounting concept only, but at least it serves to recompense the holder for interest earned during the period the bond was held. It is conceivable that the calculation could be adjusted for present value but, at the moment, accrued interest is the convention that is followed in the market.

EXAMPLE 1.6

1.6(a): Accrual calculation for 7% Treasury 2002

This gilt has coupon dates of 7th June and 7th December each year. £100 nominal of the bond is traded for value 27th August 1998. What is accrued interest on the value date?

On the value date, 81 days have passed since the last coupon date. Under the old system for gilts, act/365, the calculation was:

$$7 \times 81/365 = 1.55342$$

Under the current system of act/act, which came into effect for gilts in November 1998, the accrued calculation uses the actual number of days between the two coupon dates, giving us:

$$7 \times 81/183 \times 0.5 = 1.54918$$

1.6(b)

Mansur buys £25,000 nominal of the 7% 2002 gilt for value on 27th August 1998, at a price of 102.4375. How much does he actually pay for the bond?

The clean price of the bond is 102.4375. The dirty price of the bond is: $102.4375 + 1.55342 = 103.99092$

The total consideration is therefore
$$1.0399092 \times 25,000 = £25,997.73$$

Example 1.6(c)

A Norwegian government bond with a coupon of 8% is purchased for settlement on 30th July 1999 at a price of 99.50. Assume that this is seven days before the coupon date and therefore the bond trades ex-dividend. What is the all-in price?

The accrued interest $= -8 \times 7/365 = -0.153424$

The all-in price is therefore $99.50 - 0.1534 = 99.3466$

Example 1.6(d)

A bond has coupon payments on 1st June and 1st December each year. What is the day-base count if the bond is traded for value date on 30th October, 31st October and 1st November 1999, respectively? There are 183 days in the interest period.

	30th October	31st October	1st November
Act/365	151	152	153
Act/360	151	152	153
Act/Act	151	152	153
30/360	149	150	151
30E/360	149	150	150

Selected Bibliography and References

The following readings are recommended; Sundaresan (1997) presents a high-quality overview of the debt markets as a whole, and there is much practical application as well as theoretical treatment. Higson (1995) is a very accessible treatment that places fixed-income instruments in the context of the capital markets as a whole, and is also very good for an introduction to financial arithmetic. All the Fabozzi references are excellent, as is Martellini *et al.*

Allen, S.L. and Kleinstein, A.D., *Valuing Fixed Income Investments and Derivative Securities*, New York Institute of Finance, 1991

Fabozzi, F., *Bond Markets, Analysis and Strategies*, Prentice Hall, 1989, chapter 2.

Fabozzi, F., *Bond Markets, Analysis and Strategies*, 2nd edition, Prentice Hall, 1993.

Fabozzi, F., *Fixed Income Mathematics*, 3rd edition, McGraw-Hill, 1997, p.190-192.

Fabozzi, F., (editor), *The Handbook of Fixed Income Securities*, 5th edition, McGraw-Hill, 1997.

Fabozzi, F., *Valuation of Fixed Income Securities and Derivatives*, 3rd edition, FJF Associates, 1998.

Fabozzi, F., *Treasury Securities and Derivatives*, FJF Associates, 1998.

Higson,C., *Business Finance*, Butterworth, 1995.

Martellini L., Priaulet, D., and Priaulet, S., *Fixed Income Securities*, John Wiley and Sons 2004

Questa, G., *Fixed Income Analysis for the Global Financial Market*, John Wiley & Sons, 1999.

Stigum, M. and Robinson, F., *Money Market and Bond Calculations*, Irwin, 1996.

Sundaresan, S., *Fixed Income Markets and their Derivatives*, South-Western, 1997.

Van Deventer, D. and Imai, K., *Financial Risk Analytics*, Irwin, 1997, p.9-11

Weston, J.F. and Copeland, T.E., *Managerial Finance*, Dryden, 1986.

2

Bond Instruments and Interest-rate Risk

In the introductory chapter we described the basic concepts in bond pricing. This chapter is really a continuity of the first and we discuss here the sensitivity of bond prices to changes in market interest rates, the key concepts of duration and convexity.

Duration, modified duration and convexity

Bonds pay a part of their total return during their lifetime, in the form of coupon interest, so that the term to maturity does not reflect the true period over which the bond's return is earned. Additionally, if we wish to gain an idea of the trading characteristics of a bond, and compare this to other bonds of, say, similar maturity, term to maturity is insufficient and so we need a more accurate measure. A plain-vanilla coupon bond pays out a proportion of its return during the course of its life, in the form of coupon interest. If we were to analyse the properties of a bond, we should conclude quite quickly that its maturity gives us little indication of how much of its return is paid out during its life, nor any idea of the timing or size of its cash flows, and hence its sensitivity to moves in market interest rates. For example, if comparing two bonds with the same maturity date but different coupons, the higher-coupon bond provides a larger proportion of its return in the form of coupon income than does the lower-coupon bond. The higher-coupon bond provides its return at a faster rate; its value is theoretically therefore less subject to subsequent fluctuations in interest rates.

We may wish to calculate an average of the time to receipt of a bond's cash flows, and use this measure as a more realistic indication of maturity. However, cash flows during the life of a bond are not all equal in value, so a more accurate measure would be to take the average time to receipt of a bond's cash flows, but weighted in the form of the cash flows' present value. This is, in effect, duration. We can measure the speed of payment of a bond, and hence its price risk relative to other bonds of the same maturity, by measuring the average maturity of the bond's cash-flow stream. Bond analysts use duration to measure this property (it is sometimes known as Macaulay's duration, after its inventor, who first introduced it in 1938).[1] Duration is the weighted average time until the receipt of cash flows from a bond, where the weights are the present values of the cash flows, measured in years. When he introduced the concept, Macaulay used the duration measure as an alternative for the length of time that a bond investment had remaining to maturity.

Duration

Recall that the price/yield formula for a plain-vanilla bond is as given at Equation (2.1) below, assuming complete years to maturity paying annual coupons, and with no accrued interest at the calculation date. The yield to maturity reverts to the symbol r in this section.

$$P = \frac{C}{(1 + r)} + \frac{C}{(1 + r)^2} + \frac{C}{(1 + r)^3} + \cdots\cdots \frac{C}{(1 + r)^N} + \frac{M}{(1 + r)^N} \tag{2.1}$$

If we take the first derivative of this expression we obtain (2.2)

$$\frac{dP}{dr} = \frac{(-1)C}{(1 + r)^2} + \frac{(-2)C}{(1 + r)^3} + \cdots\cdots + \frac{(-n)C}{(1 + r)^{n+1}} + \frac{(-n)M}{(1 + r)^{n+1}} \tag{2.2}$$

If we re-arrange (2.2), we will obtain the expression at (2.3), which is our equation to calculate the approximate change in price for a small change in yield.

$$\frac{dP}{dr} = \frac{1}{(1 + r)} \left[\frac{1C}{(1 + r)} + \frac{2C}{(1 + r)^2} + \cdots + \frac{nC}{(1 + r)^n} + \frac{nM}{(1 + r)^n} \right] \frac{1}{P} \tag{2.3}$$

---

[1] Macaulay, F., *Some theoretical problems suggested by the movements of interest rates, bond yields and stock prices in the United States since 1865,* National Bureau of Economic Research, NY, 1938. Although it is frequently quoted, it's rare to meet someone who has actually read this work. However, it remains a fascinating treatise and is well worth reading; it is available from Risk Classics publishing, under the title *Interest Rates, bond yields and stock prices in the United States since 1856.*

Readers may feel a sense of familiarity regarding the expression in brackets in equation (2.3) as this is the weighted average time to maturity of the cash flows from a bond, where the weights are, as in our example above, the present values of each cash flow. The expression at (2. 3) gives us the approximate measure of the change in price for a small change in yield. If we divide both sides of (2. 3) by P we obtain the expression for the approximate percentage price change, given at (2. 4).

$$\frac{dP}{dr}\frac{1}{P} = -\frac{1}{(1+r)}\left[\frac{1C}{(1+r)} + \frac{2C}{(1+r)^2} + \ldots + \frac{nC}{(1+r)^n} + \frac{nM}{(1+r)^n}\right]\frac{1}{P}$$

(2.4)

If we divide the bracketed expression in (2.4) by the current price of the bond P, we obtain the definition of Macaulay duration, given at (2.5).

$$D = \frac{\frac{1C}{(1+r)} + \frac{2C}{(1+r)^2} + \ldots + \frac{nC}{(1+r)^n} + \frac{nM}{(1+r)^n}}{P}$$

(2.5)

Equation (2.5) is simplified using Σ as shown by (2.6).

$$D = \frac{\sum_{n=1}^{N}\frac{nC_n}{(1+r)^n}}{P}$$

(2.6)

where C represents the bond cash flow at time n.

Example 2.1 calculates the Macaulay duration for an hypothetical bond, the 8% 2009 annual coupon bond.

EXAMPLE 2.1

Calculating the Macaulay duration for the 8% 2009 annual coupon bond

Issued	30th September 1999
Maturity	30th September 2009
Price	102.497
Yield	7.634%

Period (n)	Cash flow	PV at current yield*	n × PV
1	8	7.43260	7.4326
2	8	6.90543	13.81086
3	8	6.41566	19.24698
4	8	5.96063	23.84252
5	8	5.53787	27.68935
6	8	5.14509	30.87054
7	8	4.78017	33.46119
8	8	4.44114	35.529096
9	8	4.12615	37.13535
10	108	51.75222	517.5222
Total		102.49696	746.540686

* Calculated as $C/(1+r)n$

Macaulay Duration = 746.540686 / 102.497
                     = 7.283539998 years

Modified Duration = 7.28354 / 1.07634
                     = 6.76695

Table 2.1 Duration calculation for the 8% 2009 bond

The Macaulay duration value given by (2.6) is measured in years. An interesting observation by Galen Burghardt in *The Treasury Bond Basis* is that, "measured in years, Macaulay's duration is of no particular use to anyone" (Burghardt (1994), p.90). This is essentially correct. However, as a risk measure and hedge calculation measure, duration transformed into modified duration was the primary measure of interest-rate risk used in the markets, and is still widely used despite the advent of the value-at-risk measure for market risk.

If we substitute the expression for Macaulay duration (2.5) into equation 2.4 for the approximate percentage change in price we obtain (2.7) below.

$$\frac{dP}{dr}\frac{1}{P} = -\frac{1}{(1+r)}D \qquad (2.7)$$

This is the definition of modified duration, given as (2.8).

$$MD = \frac{D}{(1+r)} \qquad (2.8)$$

Modified duration is clearly related to duration, then. In fact we can use it to indicate that, for small changes in yield, a given change in yield results in an inverse change in bond price. We can illustrate this by substituting (2.8) into (2.7), giving us (2.9).

$$\frac{dP}{dr}\frac{1}{P} = -MD \qquad (2.9)$$

If we are determining duration long-hand, there is another arrangement we can use to shorten the procedure. Instead of equation (2.1), we use (2.10) as the bond price formula, which calculates price based on a bond being comprised of an annuity stream and a redemption payment, and summing the present values of these two elements. Again we assume an annual coupon bond priced on a date that leaves a complete number of years to maturity and with no interest accrued.

$$P = C \left[\frac{1 - \frac{1}{(1 + r)^n}}{r} \right] + \frac{M}{(1 + r)^n} \qquad (2.10)$$

This expression calculates the price of a bond as the present value of the stream of coupon payments and the present value of the redemption payment. If we take the first derivative of (2.10) and then divide this by the current price of the bond P, the result is another expression for the modified duration formula, given at (2.11).

$$MD = \frac{\frac{C}{r^2}\left[1 - \frac{1}{(1 + r)^n}\right] + \frac{n(M - \frac{C}{r})}{(1 + r)^{n+1}}}{P} \qquad (2.11)$$

We have already shown that modified duration and duration are related; to obtain the expression for Macaulay duration from (2.11) we multiply it by $(1 + r)$. This short-hand formula is demonstrated below in Example 2.2 for the same hypothetical bond, the annual coupon 8% 2009.

EXAMPLE 2.2

The 8% 2009 bond: using equation (2.11) for the modified duration calculation.

Coupon	8%, annual basis
Yield	7.634%
n	10
Price	102.497

Substituting the above terms into the equation we obtain:

$$MD = \frac{\frac{8}{(0.07634^2)}\left[1 - \frac{1}{(1.07634)^{10}}\right] + \frac{10(100 - \frac{8}{0.07634})}{(1.07634)^{11}}}{102.497}$$

$$MD = 6.76695$$

To obtain the Macaulay duration we multiply the modified duration by $(1 = r)$, in this case 1.07634, which gives us a value of 7.28354 years.

For an irredeemable bond duration is given by :

$$D = \frac{1}{rc} \qquad (2.12)$$

where $rc = (C/P_d)$ is the *running yield* (or *current yield*) of the bond. This follows from equation (2.6) as $N \rightarrow \infty$, recognizing that for an irredeemable bond $r = rc$. Equation (2.12) provides the limiting value to duration. For bonds trading at or above par, duration increases with maturity and approaches this limit from below. For bonds trading at a discount to par, duration increases to a maximum at around 20 years and then declines towards the limit given by (2.12). So, in general, duration increases with maturity, with an upper bound given by (2.12).

Properties of Macaulay duration

A bond's duration is always less than its maturity. This is because some weight is given to the cash flows in the early years of the bond's life, which brings forward the average time at which cash flows are received. In the case of a zero-coupon bond, there is no present value weighting of the cash flows, for the simple reason that there are no cash flows, and duration for a zero-coupon bond is equal to its term to maturity. Duration varies with coupon, yield and maturity. The following three factors imply higher duration for a bond:

- the lower the coupon
- the lower the yield
- broadly, the longer the maturity.

Duration increases as coupon and yield decrease. As the coupon falls, more of the relative weight of the cash flows is transferred to the maturity date and this causes duration to rise. Because the coupon on index-linked bonds is generally much lower than on vanilla bonds, this means that the duration of index-linked bonds will be much higher than for vanilla bonds of the same maturity. As yield increases, the present values of all future cash flows fall, but the present values of the more distant cash flows fall relatively more than those of the nearer cash flows. This has the effect of increasing the relative weight given to nearer cash flows and hence of reducing duration.

The effect of the coupon frequency. As we have already stated, certain bonds such as most Eurobonds pay coupon annually compared to, say, gilts, which pay semi-annual coupons. Again thinking of our duration fulcrum, if we imagine that every coupon is divided into two parts, with one part paid a half-period earlier than the other, this will represent a shift in weight to the left, as part of the coupon is paid earlier. Thus, increasing the coupon frequency shortens duration and, of course, decreasing coupon frequency has the effect of lengthening duration.

Duration as maturity approaches. Using our definition of duration we can see that initially it will decline slowly, and then at a more rapid pace as a bond approaches maturity.

Duration of a portfolio. Portfolio duration is a weighted average of the duration of the individual bonds. The weights are the present values of the bonds divided by the full price of the entire portfolio, and the resulting duration calculation is often referred to as a "market-weighted" duration. This approach is, in effect, similar to the duration calculation for a single bond. Portfolio duration has the same application as duration for a individual bond, and can be used to structure an immunized portfolio.

Modified duration

Although it is common for newcomers to the market to think intuitively of duration, much as Macaulay originally did, as a proxy measure for the time to maturity of a bond, such an interpretation is to miss the main point of duration, which is a measure of price volatility or interest-rate risk.

Using the first term of a Taylor's expansion of the bond price function,[2] we can show the following relationship between price volatility and the duration measure, which is expressed as (2.13) below.

$$\Delta P = -\left[\frac{1}{(1 + r)}\right] \times \text{Macaulay duration} \times \text{Change in yield} \qquad (2.13)$$

where r is the yield to maturity for an annual-paying bond (for a semi-annual coupon bond, we use $r/2$). If we combine the first two components of the right-hand side, we obtain the definition of modified duration. Equation (2.13) expresses the approximate percentage change in price as being equal to the modified duration multiplied by the change in yield. We saw in the previous section how the formula for Macaulay duration could be modified to obtain the modified duration for a bond. There is a clear relationship between the two measures. From the Macaulay duration of a bond can be derived its modified duration, which gives a measure of the sensitivity of a bond's price to small changes in yield. As we have seen, the relationship between modified duration and duration is given by (2.14).

$$MD = \frac{D}{1 + r} \qquad (2.14)$$

where MD is the modified duration in years. However it also measures the approximate change in bond price for a 1% change in bond yield. For a bond that pays semi-annual coupons, the equation becomes:

$$MD = \frac{D}{1 + \frac{1}{2}r} \qquad (2.15)$$

This means that the following relationship holds between modified duration and bond prices :

$$\Delta P = -MD \times \Delta r \times P \qquad (2.16)$$

---

[2] For an accessible explanation of the Taylor expansion, see Butler, C., *Mastering Value-at-Risk*, FT Prentice Hall, 1998, p.112–114.

In the UK markets, the term *volatility* is sometimes used to refer to modified duration but this is becoming increasingly uncommon to avoid confusion with option markets' use of the same term, which there often refers to implied volatility and is something different.

EXAMPLE 2.3 **Using modified duration**

An 8% annual coupon bond is trading at par with a duration of 2.74 years. If yields rise from 8% to 8.50%, then the price of the bond will fall by :

$$\Delta P = -D \times \frac{\Delta(r)}{1 + r} \times P$$

$$= -(2.74) \times \left(\frac{0.005}{1.080} \right) \times 100$$

$$= -£1.2685$$

That is, the price of the bond will now be £98.7315.

The modified duration of a bond with a duration of 2.74 years and yield of 8% is obviously:

$$MD = \frac{2.74}{1.08}$$

which gives us *MD* equal to 2.537 years.

In the earlier example of the five-year bond with a duration of 4.31 years, the modified duration can be calculated to be 3.99. This tells us that for a 1% move in the yield to maturity, the price of the bond will move (in the opposite direction) by 3.99%.

We can use modified duration to approximate bond prices for a given yield change. This is illustrated with the following expression:

$$\Delta P = -MD \times (\Delta r) \times P \tag{2.17}$$

For a bond with a modified duration of 3.99, priced at par, an increase in yield of 1 basis point (100 basis = 1%) leads to a fall in the bond's price of:

$$\Delta P = (-3.24/100) \times (+0.01) \times 100.00$$
$$\Delta P = \$0.0399, \text{ or } 3.99 \text{ cents}$$

In this case, 3.99 cents is the basis-point value of the bond, which is the change in the bond price given a 1 basis point change in the bond's yield. The basis-point value of a bond can be calculated using (2.18).

$$BPV = \frac{MD}{100} \cdot \frac{P}{100} \tag{2.18}$$

Basis-point values are used in hedging bond positions. To hedge a bond position requires an opposite position to be taken in the hedging instrument. So, if we are long a 10-year bond, we may wish to sell short a similar 10-year bond as a hedge against it. Similarly a short position in a bond will be hedged through a purchase of an equivalent amount of the hedging instrument. In fact, there are a variety of hedging instruments available, both on- and off-balance sheet. Once the hedge is put on, any loss in the primary position should, in theory, be offset by a gain in the hedge position, and vice-versa. The objective of a hedge is to ensure that the price change in the primary instrument is equal to the price change in the hedging instrument. If we are hedging a position with another bond, we use the BPVs of each bond to calculate the amount of the hedging instrument required. This is important because each bond will have different BPVs, so that to hedge a long position in, say, £1 million nominal of a 30-year bond does not mean we simply sell £1 million of another 30-year bond. This is because the BPVs of the two bonds will almost certainly be different. Also, there may not be another 30-year bond in that particular bond. What if we have to hedge with a 10-year bond? How much nominal of this bond would be required?

We need to know the ratio given at (2.19) to calculate the nominal hedge position.

$$\frac{BPV_p}{BPV_h} \tag{2.19}$$

where

BPV_p is the basis-point value of the primary bond (the position to be hedged)

BPV_h is the basis-point value of the hedging instrument.

The *hedge ratio* is used to calculate the size of the hedge position and is given at (2.20).

$$\frac{BPV_p}{BPV_h} \times \frac{\text{Change in yield for primary bond position}}{\text{Change in yield for hedge instrument}} \tag{2.20}$$

The second ratio in (2.20) is known as the *yield beta*.

Example 2.4 illustrates use of the hedge ratio.

Example 2.4 Calculating hedge size using basis-point value

A trader holds a long position of £1 million of the 8% 2019 bond. The modified duration of the bond is 11.14692 and its price is 129.87596. The basis-point value of this bond is therefore 0.14477. The trader decides, to protect against a rise in interest rates, to hedge the position using the 0% 2009 bond, which has a BPV of 0.05549. If we assume that the yield beta is 1, what nominal value of the zero-coupon bond must be sold in order to hedge the position?

The hedge ratio is:

$(0.14477/0.05549) \times 1 = 2.60894.$

Therefore, to hedge £1 million of the 20-year bond the trader shorts £2,608,940 of the zero-coupon bond. If we use the respective BPVs to see the net effect of a 1 basis point rise in yield, the loss on the long position is approximately equal to the gain in the hedge position.

Example 2.5 The nature of the modified duration approximation

Bond	8% 2009
Maturity (years)	10
Modified Duration	6.76695
Price duration of basis point	0.06936
Yield: 6.00%	114.72017
6.50%	110.78325
7.00%	107.02358
7.50%	103.43204
7.99%	100.0671311
8.00%	100.00000
8.01%	99.932929
8.50%	96.71933
9.00%	93.58234
10.00%	87.71087

Yield change	Price change	Estimate using price duration
down 1 bp	0.06713	0.06936
up 1 bp	0.06707	0.06936

Table 2.2 Nature of the modified duration approximation

Table 2.2 shows the change in price for one of our hypothetical bonds, the 8% 2009, for a selection of yields. We see that for a 1 basis point change in yield, the change in price given by the dollar duration figure, while not completely accurate, is a reasonable estimation of the actual change in price. For a large move, however, say 200 basis points, the approximation is significantly in error and analysts would not use it. Notice also for our hypothetical bond how the dollar duration value, calculated from the modified-duration measurement, underestimates the change in price resulting from a fall in yields but overestimates the price change for a rise in yields. This is a reflection of the price/yield relationship for this bond. Some bonds will have a more pronounced convex relationship between price and yield and the modified-duration calculation will underestimate the price change resulting from both a fall or a rise in yields.

Convexity

Duration can be regarded as a first-order measure of interest-rate risk: it measures the slope of the present value/yield profile. It is, however, only an approximation of the actual change in bond price given a small change in yield to maturity. Similarly for modified duration, which describes the price sensitivity of a bond to small changes in yield. However as Figure 2.1 illustrates, the approximation is an underestimate of the actual price at the new yield. This is the weakness of the duration measure.

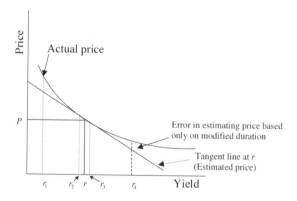

Fig 2.1 Approximation of the bond price change using modified duration

Reproduced with permission from Fabozzi, F., *Fixed Income Mathematics*, McGraw-Hill, 1997.

Convexity is a second-order measure of interest-rate risk; it measures the curvature of the present value/yield profile. Convexity can be regarded as an indication of the error we make when using duration and modified duration, as it measures the degree to which the curvature of a bond's price/yield relationship diverges from the straight-line estimation. The convexity of a bond is positively related to the dispersion of its cash flows; thus, other things being equal, if one bond's cash flows are more spread out in time than another's, then it will have a higher dispersion and hence a higher convexity. Convexity is also positively related to duration.

The second-order differential of the bond price equation with respect to the redemption yield r is:

$$\frac{\Delta P}{P} = \frac{1}{P}\frac{\Delta P}{P}(\Delta r) + \frac{1}{2P}\frac{\Delta^2 P}{\Delta r^2}(\Delta r)^2 \qquad (2.21)$$

$$= -MD(\Delta r) + \frac{CV}{2}(\Delta r)^2$$

where CV is the convexity.

From equation (2.21), convexity is the rate at which price variation to yield changes with respect to yield. That is, it describes a bond's modified duration changes with respect to changes in yield. It can be approximated by expression (2.22).

$$CV = 10^8\left(\frac{\Delta P'}{P} + \frac{\Delta P''}{P}\right) \qquad (2.22)$$

where

$\Delta P'$ is the change in bond price if yield increases by 1 basis point (0.01)
$\Delta P''$ is the change in bond price if yield decreases by 1 basis point (0.01)

Appendix 2.2 provides the mathematical derivation of the formula.

EXAMPLE 2.6

A 5% annual coupon is trading at par with three years to maturity. If the yield increases from 5.00 to 5.01%, the price of the bond will fall (using the bond price equation) to :

$$P'_d = \frac{5}{(0.0501)}\left[1 - \frac{1}{(1.0501)^3}\right] + \frac{100}{(1.0501)^3}$$

$$= 99.97277262$$

or by $\Delta P'_d = -0.02722737$. If the yield falls to 4.99 per cent, the price of the bond will rise to :

$$P''_d = \frac{5}{(0.0499)} \left[1 - \frac{1}{(1.0499)^3}\right] + \frac{100}{(1.0499)^3}$$

$$= 100.0272376$$

or by $P''_d = 0.027237584$. Therefore

$$CV = 5^8 \left(\frac{-0.0272284}{100} + \frac{0.0281623}{100}\right)$$

$$= 10.206$$

The unit of measurement for convexity using (2.22) is the number of interest periods. For annual coupon bonds this is equal to the number of years; for bonds paying coupon on a different frequency we use (2.23) to convert the convexity measure to years.

$$CV_{years} = \frac{CV}{C^2} \tag{2.23}$$

The convexity measure for a zero-coupon bond is given by (2.24).

$$CV = \frac{n(n + 1)}{(1 + r)^2} \tag{2.24}$$

Convexity is a second-order approximation of the change in price resulting from a change in yield. This is given by:

$$\Delta P = \tfrac{1}{2} \times CV \times (\Delta r)^2 \tag{2.25}$$

The reason we multiply the convexity by half to obtain the convexity adjustment is because the second term in the Taylor expansion contains the coefficient $\tfrac{1}{2}$. The convexity approximation is obtained from a Taylor expansion of the bond price formula. An illustration of Taylor expansion of the bond price/yield equation is given at Appendix 2.3

The formula is the same for a semi-annual coupon bond.

Note that the value for convexity given by the expressions above will always be positive; that is, the approximate price change due to convexity is positive for both yield increases and decreases.

EXAMPLE 2.7

2.7(a): Second-order interest-rate risk
A 5% annual coupon bond is trading at par with a modified duration of 2.639 and convexity of 9.57. If we assume a significant market correction and yields rise from 5% to 7%, the price of the bond will fall by:

$$\Delta P_d = -MD \times (\Delta r) \times P_d + \frac{CV}{2} \times (\Delta r)^2 \times P_d$$

$$= -(2.639) \times (0.02) \times 100 + \frac{9.57}{2} \times (0.02)^2 \times 100$$

$$= -5.278 + 0.1914$$

$$= -\$5.0866$$

to \$94.9134. The first-order approximation, using the modified-duration value of 2.639, is −\$5.278, which is an overestimation of the fall in price by \$0.1914.

2.7(b)
The 5% 2009 bond is trading at a price of £96.23119 (a yield of 5.50%) and has precisely 10 years to maturity. If the yield rises to 7.50%, a change of 200 basis points, the percentage price change due to the convexity effect is given by:

$$(0.5) \times 96.23119 \times (0.02)^2 \times 100 = 1.92462\%$$

If we use an HP calculator to find the price of the bond at the new yield of 7.50% we see that it is £82.83980, a change in price of 13.92%. The convexity measure of 1.92462% is an approximation of the error we would make when using the modified-duration value to estimate the price of the bond following the 200 basis-point rise in yield.

If the yield of the bond were to fall by 200 basis points, the convexity effect would be the same, as given by the expression at (2.25).

In example (2.7b) we saw that the price change estimated using modified duration will be quite inaccurate, and that the convexity measure is the approximation of the size of the inaccuracy. The magnitude of the price change as estimated by both duration and convexity is obtained by summing the two values. However, it only makes any significant difference if the change in yield is very large. If we take our hypothetical bond again, the 5% 2009 bond, its modified duration is 7.64498. If the yield rises by 200 basis points, the approximation of the price change given by modified duration and convexity is:

Modified duration = 7.64498 × 2 = −15.28996
Convexity = 1.92462

Note that the modified duration is given as a negative value, because a rise in yields results in a fall in price. This gives us a net percentage price change of 13.36534. As we saw in example (2.7b), the actual percentage price change is 13.92%. So, in fact, using the convexity adjustment has given us a noticeably more accurate estimation. Let us examine the percentage price change resulting from a fall in yields of 1.50% from the same starting yield of 5.50%. This is a decrease in yield of 150 basis points, so our convexity measurement needs to be re-calculated. The convexity value is:

$$(0.5) \times 96.23119 \times (0.0150)^2 \times 100 = 1.0826\%.$$

So the price change is based on:

Modified duration = 7.64498 × 1.5 = 11.46747
Convexity = 1.0826

This gives us a percentage price change of 12.55007. The actual price change was 10.98843%, so here the modified duration estimate is actually closer! This illustrates that the convexity measure is effective for larger yield changes only. Example (2.8) shows us that for very large changes, a closer approximation for bond price volatility is given by combining the modified duration and convexity measures.

EXAMPLE 2.8

The hypothetical bond is the 5% 2009, again trading at a yield of 5.50% and priced at 96.23119. If the yield rises to 8.50%, a change of 300 basis points, the percentage price change due to the convexity effect is given by:

$$(0.5) \times 96.23119 \times (0.03)^2 \times 100 = 4.3304\%$$

Meanwhile, as before, the modified duration of the bond at the initial yield is 7.64498. At the new yield of 8.50% the price of the bond is 77.03528 (check using an HP calculator).

The price change can be approximated using:
Modified duration = 7.64498 × 3.0 = −22.93494
Convexity = 4.3304

This gives a percentage price change of 18.60454%. The actual percentage price change was 19.9477%, but our estimate is still closer than that obtained using only the modified-duration measure. The continuing error reflects the fact that convexity is also a dynamic measure and changes with yield changes; the effect of a large yield movement compounds the inaccuracy given by convexity.

EXAMPLE 2.9 Using Microsoft Excel®

The Excel® spreadsheet package has two duration functions, *Duration* and *Mduration*, which can be used for the two main measures. Not all installations of the software may include these functions, which have to be installed using the "Analysis ToolPak" add-in macro. The syntax required for using these functions is the same in both cases, and for Macaulay duration is:
Duration (settlement, maturity, coupon, yield, frequency, basis).
The dates that are used in the syntax for Excel® version 5 are serial dates, so the user may need to use the separate function available to convert conventional date formats to the serial date for Excel®. All later versions of Excel recognise conventional date formats. The other parameters are:

- settlement: the settlement date
- maturity: the maturity date
- coupon: the coupon level
- yield: the yield to maturity
- frequency: annual or semi-annual
- basis: the day-count basis.

Once the parameters have been set up, Excel® will calculate the duration and modified duration for you.

Convexity is an attractive property for a bond to have. What level of premium will be attached to a bond's higher convexity? This is a function of the current yield levels in the market as well as market volatility. Remember that modified duration and convexity are functions of yield level, and that the effect of both is magnified at lower yield levels. As well as the relative level, investors will value convexity higher if the current market conditions are volatile. Remember that the cash effect of convexity is noticeable only for large moves in yield. If an investor expects market yields to move only by relatively small amounts, she will attach a lower value to convexity; and vice-versa for large movements in yield. Therefore the yield premium attached to a bond with higher convexity will vary according to market expectations of the future size of interest-rate changes.

The convexity measure increases with the square of maturity, and it decreases with both coupon and yield. As the measure is a function of modified duration, index-linked bonds have greater convexity than conventional bonds. We discussed how the price/yield profile will be more convex for a bond of higher convexity, and that such a bond will outperform a bond of lower convexity whatever happens to market interest rates. High convexity is therefore a desirable property for bonds to have. In principle, a more convex bond should fall in price less than a less convex one when yields rise, and rise in price more when yields fall. That is, convexity can be equated with the potential to outperform. Thus, other things being equal, the higher the convexity of a bond the more desirable it should in principle be to investors. In some cases investors may be prepared to accept a bond with a lower yield in order to gain convexity. We noted also that convexity is in principle of more value if uncertainty, and hence expected market volatility, is high, because the convexity effect of a bond is amplified for large changes in yield. The value of convexity is therefore greater in volatile market conditions

For a conventional vanilla bond, convexity is almost always positive. Negative convexity resulting from a bond with a concave price/yield profile would not be an attractive property for a bondholder. The most common occurrence of negative convexity in the cash markets is with callable bonds. We illustrated that for most bonds, and certainly when the convexity measure is high, the modified-duration measurement for interest-rate risk becomes more inaccurate for large changes in yield. In such situations it becomes necessary to use the approximation given by our convexity equation, to measure the error we have made in estimating the price change based on modified duration only. The expression was given earlier in this chapter.

The following points highlight the main convexity properties for conventional vanilla bonds.

A fall in yields leads to an increase in convexity. A decrease in bond yield leads to an increase in the bond's convexity; this is a property of positive convexity. Equally a rise in yields leads to a fall in convexity.

For a given term to maturity, higher coupon results in lower convexity. For any given redemption yield and term to maturity, the higher a bond's coupon, the lower its convexity. Therefore, among bonds of the same maturity, zero-coupon bonds have the highest convexity.

For a given modified duration, higher coupon results in higher convexity. For any given redemption yield and modified duration, a higher coupon results in a higher convexity. Contrast this with the earlier property; in this case, for bonds of the same modified duration, zero-coupon bonds have the lowest convexity.

Appendices

APPENDIX 2.1 Formal derivation of modified-duration measure

Given that duration is defined as:

$$D = \frac{\sum_{n=1}^{N} \dfrac{nC_n}{(1+r)^n}}{P} \, ,$$

(A2.1.1)

if we differentiate P with respect to r we obtain:

$$\frac{dP}{dr} = -\sum_{n=1}^{N} nC_n (1+r)^{-n-1}$$

(A2.1.2)

Multiplying A2.1.2 by $(1 + r)$ we obtain:

$$(1+r)\frac{dP}{dr} = -\sum_{n=1}^{N} nC_n (1+r)^{-n}$$

(A2.1.3)

We then divide the expression by P giving us:

$$\frac{dP}{dr}\frac{1+r}{P} = -\sum_{n=1}^{N} \frac{nC_n}{(1+r)^n P} = -D$$

(A2.1.4)

If we then define modified duration as $D/(1 + r)$ then:

$$-\frac{dP}{dr}\frac{1}{P} = MD$$

(A2.1.5)

Thus, modified duration measures the proportionate impact on the price of a bond resulting from a change in its yield. The sign in (A2.1.5) is negative because of the inverse relationship between bond prices and yields (that is, rising yields result in falling prices). So if a bond has a modified duration of 6.767, then a rise in yield of 1% means that the price of the bond will fall by 6.767%. As we discuss in the main text, however, this is an approximation only and is progressively more inaccurate for greater changes in yield.

APPENDIX 2.2 Measuring convexity

The modified duration of a plain-vanilla bond is:

$$MD = \frac{D}{(1+r)} \, .$$

(A2.2.1)

We know that:

$$\frac{dP}{dr}\frac{1}{P} = -MD. \tag{A2.2.2}$$

This shows that for a percentage change in the yield, we have an inverse change in the price by the amount of the modified-duration value.
If we multiply both sides of (A2.2.2) by any particular change in the bond yield, given by dr, we obtain expression (A2.2.3)

$$\frac{dP}{P} = -MD \times dr \tag{A2.2.3}$$

Using the first two terms of a Taylor expansion, we obtain an approximation of the bond price change, given by (A2.2.4).

$$dP = \frac{dP}{dr}dr + \frac{1}{2}\frac{d^2P}{dr^2}(dr)^2 + \text{approximation error} \tag{A2.2.4}$$

If we divide both sides of (A2.2.4) by P to obtain the percentage price change, the result is the expression at (A2.2.5).

$$\frac{dP}{P} = \frac{dP}{dr}\frac{1}{2}dr + \frac{1}{2}\frac{d^2P}{dr^2}(dr)^2 + \frac{\text{approximation error}}{P} \tag{A2.2.5}$$

The first component of the right-hand side of (A2.2.4) is the expression at (A2.2.3), which is the cash price change given by the duration value. Therefore, equation (A2.2.4) is the approximation of the price change. Equation (A2.2.5) is the approximation of the price change as given by the modified-duration value. The second component in both expressions is the second derivative of the bond price equation. This second derivative captures the convexity value of the price/yield relationship and is the cash value given by convexity. As such, it is referred to as dollar convexity in the US markets. The dollar convexity is stated as (A2.2.6).

$$CV_{dollar} = \frac{d^2P}{dr^2} \tag{A2.2.6}$$

If we multiply the dollar convexity value by the square of a bond's yield change, we obtain the approximate cash value change in price resulting from the convexity effect. This is shown by (A2.2.7).

$$dP = (CV_{dollar})(dr)^2 \tag{A2.2.7}$$

If we then divide the second derivative of the price equation by the bond price, we obtain a measure of the percentage change in bond price as a result of the convexity effect. This is the measure known as convexity and is the convention used in virtually all bond markets. This is given by the expression at (A2.2.8).

$$CV = \frac{d^2P}{dr^2}\frac{1}{2} \qquad (A2.2.8)$$

To measure the amount of the percentage change in bond price as a result of the convex nature of the price/yield relationship we can use (A2.2.9).

$$\frac{dP}{P} = \frac{1}{2}CV(dr)^2 \qquad (A2.2.9)$$

For long-hand calculations, note that the second derivative of the bond al assumptions apply to the expressions, that the bond pays aprice equation is A2.2.10, which can be simplified to (A2.2.11) and (A2.2.12). The usunnual coupons and has a precise number of interest periods to maturity. If the bond is a semi-annual paying one, the yield value r is replaced by $r/2$.

$$\frac{d^2P}{dr^2} = \sum_{n=1}^{N}\frac{n(n+1)C}{(1+r)^{n+2}} + \frac{n(n+1)}{(1+r)^{n+2}}M \qquad (A2.2.10)$$

Alternatively, we differentiate to the second order the bond price equation as given by (A2.2.11), giving us the alternative expression (A2.2.12).

$$P = \frac{C}{r}\left[1 - \frac{1}{(1+r)^n}\right] + \frac{100}{(1+r)^n} \qquad (A2.2.11)$$

$$\frac{d^2P}{dr^2} = \frac{2C}{r^3}\left[1 - \frac{1}{(1+r)^n}\right] - \frac{2C}{r^2(1+r)^{n+1}} + \frac{n(n+1)(100 - \frac{C}{r})}{(1+r)^{n+2}}$$

$$(A2.2.12)$$

APPENDIX 2.3 Taylor expansion of the price/yield function

Let us summarise the bond price formula as (A2.3.1), where C represents all the cash flows from the bond, including the redemption payment.

$$P = \sum_{n=1}^{N}\frac{C_n}{(1+r)^n} \qquad (A2.3.1)$$

We therefore derive the following:

$$\frac{dP}{dr} = -\sum_{n=1}^{N} \frac{C_n \cdot n}{(1 + r)^{n+1}} \qquad (A2.3.2)$$

$$\frac{d^2P}{dr^2} = \sum_{n=1}^{N} \frac{C_n \cdot n(n + 1)}{(1 + r)^{n+2}} \qquad (A2.3.3).$$

This then gives us:

$$\Delta P = \left[\frac{dP}{dr}\Delta r\right] + \left[\frac{1}{2!}\frac{d^2P}{dr^2}(\Delta r)^2\right] + \left[\frac{1}{3!}\frac{d^3P}{dr^3}(\Delta r)^3\right] + \ldots\ldots \qquad (A2.3.4)$$

The first expression in (A2.3.4) is the modified duration measure, while the second expression measures convexity. The more powerful the changes in yield, the more expansion is required to approximate the change to greater accuracy. Expression (A2.3.4) therefore gives us the equations for modified duration and convexity, shown by (A2.3.5) and (A2.3.6), respectively.

$$MD = -\frac{dP / dr}{P} \qquad (A2.3.5)$$

$$CV = -\frac{d^2P / dr^2}{P} \qquad (A2.3.6)$$

We can therefore state the following:

$$\frac{\Delta P}{P} = \left[-(MD)\Delta r\right] + \left[\frac{1}{2}(CV)(\Delta r)^2\right] + \text{residual error} \qquad (A2.3.7)$$

$$\Delta P = -\left[P(MD)\Delta r\right] + \left[\frac{P}{2}(CV)(\Delta r)^2\right] + \text{residual error} \qquad (A2.3.8)$$

EXAMPLE A2.3.1

Consider a three-year bond with (annual) coupon of 5% and yield of 5%. At a price of par we have:

$$\frac{dP}{dr} = -\left[\frac{5}{(1.05)^2} + \frac{5(2)}{(1.05)^3} + \frac{105(3)}{(1.05)^4}\right] = 263.9048$$

$$D = \frac{dP}{dr}\left[\frac{1 + r}{P}\right] = 263.9048\left[\frac{1.05}{100}\right] = 2.771$$

$$MD = \frac{2.771}{1.05} = 2.639$$

$$\frac{d^2P}{dr^2} = \left[\frac{5(1)(2)}{(1.05)^3} + \frac{5(2)(3)}{(1.05)^4} + \frac{105(3)(4)}{(1.05)^5}\right] = 957.3179$$

$$CV = \frac{d^2P \, / \, dr^2}{P} = \frac{957.3179}{100} = 9.573$$

Selected Bibliography and References

The references given in Chapter 1 are also very useful for duration, modified duration and convexity. Readers nevertheless may wish to have a look at the following texts. Burghardt's book, although a specialised subject not at all concentrating on interest-rate risk, nevertheless contains many useful insights and will help assist the reader to develop a deeper understanding of bond instruments. It is an excellent text. The same can be applied to Garbade (1996), another very high-quality work that contains many valuable insights on (among other things) duration, convexity and the practicalities of risk and hedging from a trader's perspective. It is well worth purchasing.

Bierwag, G.O., "Immunization, Duration and the term structure of interest rates", *Journal of Financial and Quantitative Analysis*, December 1977, p.725-741.

Bierwag, G.O., "Measures of duration", *Economic Inquiry 16*, October 1978, p.497-507.

Burghardt, G., *The Treasury Bond Basis*, McGraw-Hill, 1994.

Garbade, K., *Fixed Income Analytics*, MIT Press, 1996, chapters 3,4 and 12.

Macaulay, F., *The Movements of Interest Rates, Bond Yields and Stock Prices in the United States Since 1856*, RISK Classics Library, 1999.

3

Bond Pricing, Spot and Forward Rates

In this chapter, we present a brief overview of fixed-income analysis as it appears in the current literature. First, we illustrate basic concepts and then follow this with a discussion of yield-curve analysis and the term structure of interest rates.

Basic concepts

We are now familiar with two types of fixed-income security, zero-coupon bonds, also known as discount bonds or strips, and coupon bonds. A zero-coupon bond makes a single payment on its maturity date, while a coupon bond makes regular interest payments at regular dates up to and including its maturity date. A coupon bond may be regarded as a set of strips, with each coupon payment and the redemption payment on maturity being equivalent to a zero-coupon bond maturing on that date. This is not a purely academic concept – witness events before the advent of the formal market in US Treasury strips, when a number of investment banks had traded the cash flows of Treasury securities as separate zero-coupon securities.[1] The literature we review in this section is set in a market of default-free bonds,

---

[1] These banks included Merrill Lynch, Lehman Brothers and Salomon Brothers, among others (Fabozzi 1993). The term "strips" comes from Separate Trading of Registered Interest and Principal of Securities, the name given when the official market was introduced by the Treasury. The banks would purchase Treasuries which would then be deposited in a safe-custody account. Receipts were issued against each cash flow from each Treasury, and these receipts traded as individual zero-coupon securities. The market-making banks earned profit arising from the arbitrage difference in the price of the original coupon bond and the price at which the individual strips were sold. The US Treasury formalised trading in strips after 1985, after legislation had been introduced that altered the tax treatment of such instruments. The market in UK gilt strips trading began in December 1997. Strips are also traded in France, Germany, the Netherlands and New Zealand among other countries.

whether they are zero-coupon bonds or coupon bonds. The market is assumed to be liquid so that bonds may be freely bought and sold. Prices of bonds are determined by the economy-wide supply and demand for the bonds at any time, so they are macroeconomic and not set by individual bond issuers or traders.

Zero-coupon bonds

A zero-coupon bond is the simplest fixed-income security. It is an issue of debt, the issuer promising to pay the face value of the debt to the bondholder on the date the bond matures. There are no coupon payments during the life of the bond, so it is a discount instrument, issued at a price that is below the face or principal amount. We denote as $P(t, T)$ the price of a discount bond at time t that matures at time T, with $T \geq t$. The term to maturity of the bond is denoted with n, where $n = T - t$. The price increases over time until the maturity date when it reaches the maturity or par value. If the par value of the bond is £1, then the yield to maturity of the bond at time t is denoted by $r(t,T)$, where r is actually "one plus the percentage yield" that is earned by holding the bond from t to T. We have

$$P(t,T) = \frac{1}{[r(t,T)]^n} \tag{3.1}$$

The yield may be obtained from the bond price and is given by

$$r(t,T) = \left[\frac{1}{P(t,T)}\right]^{1/n} \tag{3.2}$$

which is sometimes written as

$$r(t,T) = P(t,T)^{-(1/n)} . \tag{3.3}$$

Analysts and researchers frequently work in terms of logarithms of yields and prices, or continuously compounded rates. One advantage is that it of this converts the non-linear relationship in (3.2) into a linear relationship.[2]

---

[2] A linear relationship in X would be a function $Y = f(X)$ in which the X values change via a power or index of 1 only and are not multiplied or divided by another variable or variables. So, for example, terms such as X^2, $\div X$ and other similar functions are not linear in X, nor are terms such as XZ or X/Z where Z is another variable. In econometric analysis, if the value of Y is solely dependent on the value of X, then its rate of change with respect to X, or the derivative of Y with respect to X, denoted dY/dX, is independent of X. Therefore, if $Y = 5X$, then $dY/dX = 5$, which is independent of the value of X. However, if $Y = 5X^2$, then $dY/dX = 10X$, which is not independent of the value of X. Hence this function is not linear in X. The classic regression function $E(Y \mid X_i)$ $= a + bX_i$ is a linear function with slope b and the regression "curve" is represented geometrically by a straight line.

The bond price at time t_2 where $t \leq t_2 \leq T$ is given by

$$P(t_2,T) = P(t,T)e^{(t_2-t)r(t,T)} \tag{3.4a}$$

which is natural given that the bond price equation in continuous time is

$$P(t,T) = e^{-r(t,T)(T-t)} \tag{3.4b}$$

so that the yield is given by

$$r(t,T) = -\log\left[\frac{P(t,T)}{n}\right] \tag{3.5}$$

which is sometimes written as

$$\log r(t,T) = -\left[\frac{1}{n}\right] \log P(t,T). \tag{3.6}$$

The expression in (3.4) includes the exponential function, hence the use of the term continuously compounded.

The term structure of interest rates is the set of zero-coupon yields at time t for all bonds ranging in maturity from $(t, t + 1)$ to $(t, t + m)$ where the bonds have maturities of $\{0,1,2,...m\}$. A good definition of the term structure of interest rates is given by Sundaresan, who states that it "...refers to the relationship between the yield to maturity of default-free zero coupon securities and their maturities." (Sundaresan 1997, p.176)

The yield curve is a plot of the set of yields for $r(t, t + 1)$ to $r(t, t + m)$ against m at time t. For example, Figures 3.1–3.3 show the zero-coupon yield curve for US Treasury strips and United Kingdom gilt strips, and the redemption yield curve for Chinese government bonds, on 20th October 2003.[3] Each of the curves exhibits peculiarities in its shape, although the most common type of curve is gently upward-sloping, as is the UK curve. The US and UK curves are compared to their yield-to-maturity curve as well. We explore further the shape of the yield curve later in this chapter.

---

[3] Note that the Chinese government bond yield curve relates to US$-denominated issues.

Fixed Income Markets

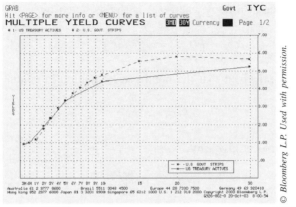

Figure 3.1 US Treasury zero-coupon yield curve, October 2003

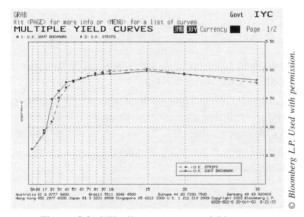

Figure 3.2 UK gilt zero-coupon yield curve

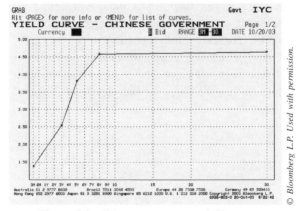

Figure 3.3 Chinese government yield curve

Coupon bonds

The majority of bonds in the market make periodic interest or coupon payments during their life, and are known as coupon bonds. We have already noted that such bonds may be viewed as a package of individual zero-coupon bonds. The coupons have a nominal value that is a percentage of the nominal value of the bond itself, with steadily longer maturity dates, while the final redemption payment has the nominal value of the bond itself and is redeemed on the maturity date. We denote a bond issued at time i and maturing at time T as having an w-element vector of payment dates $(t_1, t_2, \ldots, t_{w-1}, T)$ and matching date payments $C_1, C_2, \ldots, C_{w-1}, C_w$. In the academic literature these coupon payments are assumed to be made in continuous time, so that the stream of coupon payments is given by a positive function of time $C(t)$, $i < t < T$. An investor that purchases a bond; that is, the rate that discounts the bond's cash-flow stream C_w to its price $P(t, T)$. This is given by

$$P(t,T) = \sum_{t_i > t} C_i e^{-(t_i - t)r(t,T)} \qquad (3.7)$$

at time t that matures at time T pays $P(t, T)$ and will receive the coupon payments as long as she continues to hold the bond.[4]

The yield to maturity at time t of a bond that matures at T is the interest rate that relates the price of the bond to the future returns on the bond which says that the bond price is given by the present value of the cash-flow stream of the bond, discounted at the rate $r(t, T)$. For a zero-coupon (3.7) reduces to (3.5). In the academic literature, where coupon payments are assumed to be made in continuous time, the $\sum$ summation in (3.7) is replaced by the $\int$ integral. We will look at this in a moment.

In some texts, the plot of the yield to maturity at time t for the term of the bonds m is described as the term structure of interest rates but it is generally accepted that the term structure is the plot of zero-coupon rates only. Plotting yields to maturity is generally described as graphically depicting the yield curve, rather than the term structure. Of course, given the law of one price, there is a relationship between the yield-to-maturity yield curve and the zero-coupon term structure, and given the first one can derive the second.

---

[4] In theoretical treatment, this is the discounted clean price of the bond. For coupon bonds in practice, unless the bond is purchased for value on a coupon date, it will be traded with interest accrued. The interest that has accrued on a pro-rata basis from the last coupon date is added to the clean price of the bond, to give the market "dirty" price that is actually paid by the purchaser.

The expression at (3.7) obtains the continuously compounded yield to maturity $r(t, T)$. It is the use of the exponential function that enables us to describe the yield as continuously compounded.

The market frequently uses the measure known as current yield which is

$$rc = \frac{C}{Pd} \times 100 \tag{3.8}$$

where P_d is the dirty price of the bond. The measure is also known as the running yield or flat yield. Current yield is not used to indicate the interest rate or discount rate and therefore should not be mistaken for the yield to maturity.

Bond price in continuous time[5]

Fundamental concepts

In this section we present an introduction to the bond price equation in continuous time. The necessary background on price processes is introduced in the next chapter; readers will see the logic in this as we introduce term structure modelling there.

Consider a trading environment where bond prices evolve in a w-dimensional process

$$X(t) = [X_1(t), X_2(t), X_3(t), \ldots\ldots X_w(t)], t > 0 \tag{3.9}$$

where the random variables are termed state variables that reflect the state of the economy at any point in time. The markets assume that the state variables evolve through a process described as geometric Brownian motion or a Weiner process. It is therefore possible to model the evolution of these variables, in the form of a stochastic differential equation.

The market assumes that the cash-flow stream of assets such as bonds and (for equities) dividends is a function of the state variables. A bond is characterised by its coupon process

---

[5] See also Avellaneda (2000), Baxter and Rennie (1996), Neftci (2000), Cambell et al (1997), Ross (1999), and Shiller (1990). These are all excellent texts, and strongly recommended. For an accessible and highly readable introduction, Ross's book is worth buying for Chapter 4 alone, as is Avellaneda's for his Chapter 12. For a general introduction to the main pricing concepts, see Campbell et al (1997), Chapter 10. Chapter 3 in Jarrow (1996) is an accessible introduction for discrete-time bond pricing. Sundaresan (1997) is an excellent overview text on the fixed-income market as a whole, and is highly recommended. Further recommended references are given in the bibliography at the end of the chapter.

$$C(t) = C[X_1(t), X_2(t), X_3(t), \ldots\ldots X_w(t), t] \, . \qquad (3.10)$$

The coupon process represents the cash flow that the investor receives during the time that she holds the bond. Over a small incremental increase in time of dt from the time t the investor can purchase $1 + C(t)dt$ units of the bond at the end of the period $t + dt$. Assume that there is a very short-term discount security such as a Treasury bill that matures at $t + dt$, and during this period the investor receives a return of $r(t)$. This rate is the annualised short-term interest rate or short rate, which in the mathematical analysis is defined as the rate of interest charged on a loan that is taken out at time t and which matures almost immediately. For this reason, the rate is also known as the instantaneous rate. The short rate is given by

$$r(t) = r(t,t) \qquad (3.11)$$

and

$$r(t) = -\frac{\partial}{\partial T} \log P(t,t) \, . \qquad (3.12)$$

If we continuously reinvest the short-term security such as the T-bill at this short rate, we obtain a cumulative amount that is the original investment multiplied by (3.13).[6]

$$M(t) = \exp\left[\int_0^t r(s)ds\right] \qquad (3.13)$$

where M is a money-market account that offers a return of the short rate $r(t)$.

If we say that the short rate is constant, making $r(t) = r$, then the price of a risk-free bond that pays £1 on maturity at time T is given by

$$P(t,T) = e^{-r(T-t)} \qquad (3.13a)$$

What (3.13a) states is that the bond price is simply a function of the continuously compounded interest rate, with the right-hand side of (3.13a) being the discount factor at time t. At $t = T$ the discount factor will be 1, which is the redemption value of the bond and hence the price of the bond at this time.

---

[6] This expression uses the integral operator. The integral is the tool used in mathematics to calculate sums of an infinite number of objects, that is where the objects are uncountable. This is different to the Σ operator which is used for a countable number of objects. For a readable and accessible review of the integral and its use in quantitative finance, see Neftci (2000), p.59–66, a summary of which is given at Appendix 3.1.

Consider the following scenario. A market participant may undertake the following:

- it can invest $e^{-r(T-t)}$ units cash in a money-market account today, which will have grown to a sum of £1 at time T;
- it can purchase the risk-free zero-coupon bond today, which has a maturity value of £1 at time T.

The market participant can invest in either instrument, both of which we know beforehand to be risk-free, and both of which have identical payouts at time T and have no cash flow between now and time T. As interest rates are constant, a bond that paid out £1 at T must have the same value as the initial investment in the money-market account, which is $e_t^{-r(T-t)}$. Therefore equation (3.13a) must apply. This is a restriction placed on the zero-coupon bond price by the requirement for markets to be arbitrage-free.

If the bond was not priced at this level, arbitrage opportunities would present themselves. Consider if the bond was priced higher than $e_t^{-r(T-t)}$. In this case, an investor could sell short the bond and invest the sale proceeds in the money-market account. On maturity at time T, the short position will have a value of −£1 (negative, because the investor is short the bond) while the money market will have accumulated £1, which the investor can use to pay the proceeds on the zero-coupon bond. However, the investor will have surplus funds because at time t

$$P(t,T) - e^{-r(T-t)} > 0$$

and so will have profited from the transaction at no risk to himself.

The same applies if the bond is priced below $e_t^{-r(T-t)}$. In this case, the investor borrows $e_t^{-r(T-t)}$ and buys the bond at its price $P(t, T)$. On maturity the bond pays £1, which is used to repay the loan amount. However, the investor will gain because

$$e_t^{-r(T-t)} - P(t,T) > 0$$

Therefore the only price at which no arbitrage profit can be made is if

$$P(t,T) = e^{-r(T-t)} . \tag{3.13b}$$

In the academic literature the price of a zero-coupon bond is given in terms of the evolution of the short-term interest rate, in what is termed the risk-neutral measure.[7] The short rate $r(t)$ is the interest rate earned on a money-market account or short-dated risk-free security such as the T-Bill suggested above, and it is assumed to be continuously compounded. This makes the mathematical treatment simpler. With a zero-coupon bond we assume a payment on maturity of 1 (say $1 or £1), a one-off cash flow payable on maturity at time T. The value of the zero-coupon bond at time t is therefore given by

$$P(t,T) = \exp\left[-\int_t^T r(s)ds\right] \qquad (3.14)$$

which is the redemption value of 1 divided by the value of the money-market account, given by (3.13).

The bond price for a coupon bond is given in terms of its yield as

$$P(t,T) = \exp\left[-(T-t)r(T-t)\right] \qquad (3.15)$$

Expression (3.14) is very commonly encountered in the academic literature. Its derivation does not occur so frequently, however. We present it in Appendix 3.2, which is a summary of the description given in Ross (1999). This reference is highly recommended reading. It is also worth referring to Neftci (2000), Chapter 18.

The expression (3.14) represents the zero-coupon bond pricing formula when the spot rate is continuous or stochastic, rather than constant. The rate $r(s)$ is the risk-free return earned during the very short or infinitesimal time interval $(t, t + dt)$. The rate is used in the expressions for the value of a money-market account (3.13) and the price of a risk-free zero-coupon bond (3.15).

Stochastic rates in continuous time

In the academic literature the bond price given by (3.15) evolves as a martingale process under the risk-neutral probability measure $\tilde{P}$. This is an advanced branch of fixed-income mathematics, and is outside the scope of this book. However, it will be introduced in introductory fashion in the next chapter.[8] However, under this analysis the bond price is given as

---

[7] This is part of the arbitrage pricing theory. For detail on this, see Cox et al (1985), while Duffie (1992) is a fuller treatment for those with a strong grounding in mathematics.

[8] Interested readers should consult Nefcti (2000), Chapters 2, 17and 18. Another accessible text is Baxter and Rennie (1996), while Duffie (1992) is a leading-edge reference for those with a strong background in mathematics.

$$P(t,T) = E_t^{\tilde{p}}\left[e^{-\int_t^T r(s)ds}\right] \tag{3.16}$$

where the right-hand side of (3.16) is viewed as the randomly evolved discount factor used to obtain the present value of the £1 maturity amount. Expression (3.16) also states that bond prices are dependent on the entire spectrum of short-term interest rates $r(s)$ in the future during the period $t < s < T$. This also implies that the term structure at time t contains all the information available on short rates in the future.[9]

From (3.16) we say that the function {symbol} is the discount curve (or discount function) at time t. Avellaneda (2000) notes that the markets usually replace the term $(T - t)$ with a term meaning time to maturity, so the function becomes

$\tau \rightarrow P_t^{t+\tau}$, $\tau > 0$ where $\tau = (T - t)$.

Under a constant spot rate, the zero-coupon bond price is given by

$$P(t,T) = e^{-r(t,T)(T-t)} \tag{3.17}$$

From (3.16) and (3.17) we can derive a relationship between the yield $r(t, T)$ of the zero-coupon bond and the short rate $r(t)$, if we equate the two right-hand sides, namely

$$e^{-r(t,T)(T-t)} = E_t^{\tilde{p}}\left[e^{-\int_t^T r(s)ds}\right] \tag{3.18}$$

Taking the logarithm of both sides we obtain

$$r(t,T) = \frac{-\log E_t^{\tilde{p}}\left[e^{-\int_t^T r(s)ds}\right]}{T - t} \tag{3.19}$$

This describes the yield on a bond as the average of the spot rates that apply during the life of the bond, and under a constant spot rate the yield is equal to the spot rate.

With a zero-coupon bond and assuming that interest rates are positive, $P(t, T)$ is less than or equal to 1. The yield of the bond is, as we have noted, the continuously compounded interest rate that equates the bond price to the discounted present value of the bond at time t. This is given by

---

[9] This is related to the view of the short rate evolving as a martingale process. For a derivation of (3.16), see Neftci (2000), p.417.

$$r(t,T) = -\frac{\log(P(t,T))}{T - t} \qquad (3.20)$$

so we obtain

$$P(t,T) = e^{-(T-t)r(T-t)} \qquad (3.21)$$

In practice, this means that an investor will earn $r(t, T)$ if she purchases the bond at t and holds it to maturity.

Coupon bonds

Using the same principles as in the previous section, we can derive an expression for the price of a coupon bond in the same terms of a risk-neutral probability measure of the evolution of interest rates. Under this analysis, the bond price is given by

$$P_c = 100.E_t^{\tilde{P}}\left[e^{-\int_t^T r(s)ds}\right] + \sum_{n:t_n>t}^{N}\frac{C}{w}E_t^{\tilde{P}}\left[e^{-\int_t^{T_n} r(s)ds}\right] \qquad (3.22)$$

where

P_c is the price of a coupon bond
C is the bond coupon
t_n is the coupon date, with $n \leq N$, and $t = 0$ at the time of valuation
w is the coupon frequency[10]
and where 100 is used as the convention for principal or bond nominal value (that is, prices are quoted per cent, or per 100 nominal).

Expression (3.22) is written in some texts as

$$P_c = 100e^{-rN} + \int_n^N Ce^{-rn}dt \qquad (3.23)$$

We can simplify (3.22) by substituting Df to denote the discount factor part of the expression and assuming an annual coupon, which gives us

$$P = 100.Df_N + \sum_{n:t_n\geq t}^{N} C.Df_n, \qquad (3.24)$$

---

[10] Conventional or plain-vanilla bonds pay coupon on an annual or semi-annual basis. Other bonds, notably certain floating-rate notes and mortgage- and other asset-backed securities also pay coupon on a monthly basis, depending on the structuring of the transaction.

which states that the market value of a risk-free bond on any date is determined by the discount function on that date.

We know from Chapter 2 that the actual price paid in the market for a bond includes accrued interest from the last coupon date, so that price given by (3.24) is known as the clean price, and the traded price, which includes accrued interest, is known as the dirty price.

Forward rates

An investor can combine positions in bonds of differing maturities to guarantee a rate of return that begins at a point in the future. That is, the trade ticket would be written at time t but would cover the period T to $T + 1$ where $t < T$ (sometimes written as beginning at T_1 and ending at T_2, with $t < T_1 < T_2$). The interest rate earned during this period is known as the forward rate.[11] The mechanism by which this forward rate can be guaranteed is described in the box, following Jarrow (1996) and Campbell *et al* (1997).

The forward rate

An investor buys 1 unit of a zero-coupon bond maturing at time T, priced at $P(t, T)$ and simultaneously sells $P(t, T)/P(t, T + 1)$ bonds that mature at $T + 1$. From Table 3.1 we see that the net result of these transactions is a zero cash flow. At time T there is a cash inflow of 1, and then at time $T + 1$ there is a cash outflow of $P(t, T)/P(t, T + 1)$. These cash flows are identical to a loan of funds made during the period T to $T + 1$, contracted at time t. The interest rate on this loan is given by $P(t, T)/P(t, T + 1)$, which is therefore the forward rate. That is,

$$f(t,T) = \frac{P(t,T)}{P(t,T + 1)} \tag{3.25}$$

Together with our earlier relationships on bond price and yield, from (3.25) [we can define the forward rate in terms of yield, with the return earned during the period $(T, T + 1)$ being

$$f(t,T,T + 1) = \frac{1}{(P(t,T + 1)/P(t,T))} = \frac{(r(t,T + 1))^{(T+1)}}{r(t,T)^T} \tag{3.26}$$

---

[11] See the footnote on p.639 of Shiller (1990) for a fascinating insight on the origin of the term "forward rate", which Mr Shiller ascribes to John Hicks in his book *Value and Capital* (2nd edition, Oxford University Press, 1946).

	Time		
Transactions	t	T	$T+1$
Buy 1 unit of T-period bond	$-P(t,T)$	$+1$	
Sell $P(t,T)/P(t,T+1)T+1$ period bonds	$+[(P(t,T)/P(t,T+1)]P(t,T+1)$		$-P(t,T)/P(t,T+1)$
Net cash flows	0	$+1$	$-P(t,T)/P(t, T+1)$

Table 3.1

From (3.25) we can obtain a bond price equation in terms of the forward rates that hold from t to T,

$$P(t,T) = \frac{1}{\prod_{k=t}^{T-1} f(t,k)} \qquad (3.27)$$

A derivation of this expression can be found in Jarrow (1996), Chapter 3. Equation (3.27) states that the price of a zero-coupon bond is equal to the nominal value, here assumed to be 1, receivable at time T after it has been discounted at the set of forward rates that apply from t to T.[12]

When calculating a forward rate, it is as if we a writing an interest rate today that is applicable at the forward start date; in other words, we trade a forward contract. The law of one price, or no-arbitrage, is used to calculate the rate. For a loan that begins at T and matures at $T + 1$, similar to the way we described in the box above, consider a purchase of a $T + 1$ period bond and a sale of p amount of the T-period bond. The cash net cash position at t must be zero, so p is given by

$$P = \frac{P(t,T + 1)}{P(t,T)}$$

and to avoid arbitrage the value of p must be the price of the $T + 1$-period bond at time T. Therefore, the forward yield is given by

$$f(t,T + 1) = -\frac{\log P(t,T + 1) - \log P(t,T)}{(T + 1) - T} \qquad (3.28)$$

---

[12] The symbol Π means "take the product of", and is defined as $\prod_{i=1}^{n} x_i = x_1 \cdot x_2 \cdot \ldots \cdot x_n$, so that $\prod_{k=t}^{T-1} f(t,k) = f(t,t) \cdot f(t,t+1) \cdot \ldots \cdot f(t,T-1)n$, which is the result of multiplying the rates that obtain when the index k runs from t to $T - 1$.

If the period between T and the maturity of the later-dated bond is reduced, so we now have bonds that mature at T and T_2, and $T_2 = T + \Delta t$, then as the incremental change in time Δt becomes progressively smaller until we obtain an instantaneous forward rate, which is given by

$$f(t,T) = -\frac{\partial}{\partial T} \log P(t,T) \qquad (3.29)$$

This rate is defined as the forward rate and is the price today of forward borrowing at time T. The forward rate for borrowing today where $T = t$ is equal to the instantaneous short rate $r(t)$. At time t, the spot and forward rates for the period (t, t) will be identical; at other maturity terms they will differ. For all points other than at (t, t) the forward-rate yield curve will lie above the spot-rate curve if the spot curve is positively sloping. The opposite applies if the spot-rate curve is downward sloping. Campbell et al (1997, p.400-401) observe that this property is a standard one for marginal and average cost curves. That is, when the cost of a marginal unit (say, of production) is above that of an average unit, then the average cost will increase with the addition of a marginal unit. This results in the average cost rising when the marginal cost is above the average cost. Equally the average cost per unit will decrease when the marginal cost lies below the average cost.

EXAMPLE 3.1 The spot and forward yield curves

From the discussion in this section we see that it is possible to calculate bond prices, spot and forward rates provided that one has a set of only one of these parameters. Therefore, given the following set of zero-coupon rates, observed in the market, given in Table 3.2, we calculate the corresponding forward rates and zero-coupon bond prices as shown. The initial term structure is upward sloping. The two curves are illustrated in Figure 3.4.

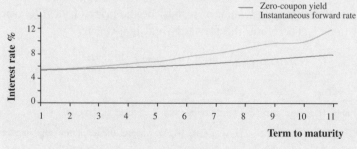

Figure 3.4 Hypothetical zero-coupon and forward yield curves

Term to maturity $(0, T)$	Spot rate $r(0, T)*$	Forward rate $f(0, T)*$	Bond price $P(0, T)$
0			1
1	1.054	1.054	0.94877
2	1.055	1.056	0.89845
3	1.0563	1.059	0.8484
4	1.0582	1.064	0.79737
5	1.0602	1.068	0.7466
6	1.0628	1.076	0.69386
7	1.06553	1.082	0.64128
8	1.06856	1.0901	0.58833
9	1.07168	1.0972	0.53631
10	1.07526	1.1001	0.48403
11	1.07929	1.1205	0.43198

Interest rates are given as $(1 + r)$

Table 3.2 Hypothetical zero-coupon yield and forward rates

There are technical reasons why the theoretical forward rate has a severe kink at the later maturity, but we shall not go into an explanation of this as it is outside the scope of this book.

Essentially, the relationship between the spot- and forward-rate curves is as stated by Campbell *et al* (ibid). The forward-rate curve will lie above the spot-rate curve if the latter is increasing, and will lie below it if the spot-rate curve is decreasing. This relationship can be shown mathematically; the forward rate or marginal rate of return is equal to the spot rate or average rate of return plus the rate of increase of the spot rate, multiplied by the sum of the increases between t and T. If the spot rate is constant (a flat curve), the forward-rate curve will be equal to it.

However, an increasing spot-rate curve does not always result in an increasing forward curve; only one that lies above it will produce this result. It is possible for the forward curve to be increasing or decreasing while the spot rate is increasing. If the spot rate reaches a maximum level and then stays constant, or falls below this high point, the forward curve will begin to decrease at a maturity point *earlier* than the spot-curve high point. In the example in Figure 3.4, the rate of increase in the spot rate in the last period is magnified when converted to the equivalent forward rate; if the last spot rate had been below the previous-period rate, the forward-rate curve would look like that in Figure 3.4(b).

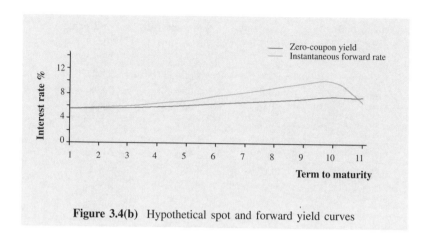

Figure 3.4(b) Hypothetical spot and forward yield curves

Calculating spot rates in practice

Researchers have applied econometric techniques to the problem of extracting a zero-coupon term structure from coupon bond prices. The most well-known approaches are described in McCulloch (1971, 1975), Schaefer (1981), Nelson and Siegel (1987), Deacon and Derry (1994), Adams and Van Deventer (1994) and Waggoner (1997), to name but a few. The most accessible article is probably the one by Deacon and Derry.[13] In addition, a good overview of all the main approaches is contained in James and Webber (2000), and Chapters 15–18 of their book provide an excellent summary of the research highlights to date.

We have noted that a coupon bond may be regarded as a portfolio of zero-coupon bonds. By treating a set of coupon bonds as a larger set of zero-coupon bonds, we can extract an (implied) zero-coupon interest-rate structure from the yields on the coupon bonds.

If the actual term structure is observable, so that we know the prices of zero-coupon bonds of £1 nominal value $P_1, P_2, ..., P_N$, then the price P_C of a coupon bond of nominal value £1 and coupon C is given by

$$P_c = P_1C + P_2C + ... + P_n(1 + C) \qquad (3.30)$$

Conversely if we can observe the coupon bond yield curve, so that we know the prices $P_{C1}, P_{C2},....., P_{CN}$, then we may use (3.30) to extract the

---

[13] This is in the author's opinion. Those with a good grounding in econometrics will find all these references both readable and accessible. Further recommended references are given in the bibliography.

implied zero-coupon term structure. We begin with the one-period coupon bond, for which the price is

$$P_{c1} = P_1(1 + C)$$

so that

$$P1 = \frac{P_{c1}}{(1 + C)} . \tag{3.31}$$

This process is repeated. Once we have the set of zero-coupon bond prices P_1, P_2,.....,P_{N-1} we obtain P_N using

$$P_N = \frac{P_{CN} - P_{N-1}C - \ldots\ldots - P_1C}{1 + C} . \tag{3.32}$$

At this point, we apply a regression technique known as ordinary least squares (OLS) to fit the term structure. The next chapter discusses this area in greater detail (we have segregated this so that readers who do not require an extensive familiarity with this subject may skip the next chapter). Interested readers should also consult the references at the end of Chapter 4.

Expression (3.30) restricts the prices of coupon bonds to be precise functions of the other coupon bond prices. In fact, this is unlikely in practice because specific bonds will be treated differently according to liquidity, tax effects and so on. For this reason we add an error term to (3.30) and estimate the value using cross-sectional regression against all the other bonds in the market. If we say that these bonds are numbered $i = 1,2,......,I$ then the regression is given by

$$P_{C_iN_i} = P_1C_i + P_2C_i + \ldots\ldots + P_{N_i}(1 + C_i) + u_i \tag{3.33}$$

for $i = 1,2,......,I$ and where C_i is the coupon on the ith bond and N_i is the maturity of the ith bond. In (3.33), the regressor parameters are the coupon payments at each interest period date, and the coefficients are the prices of the zero-coupon bonds P_1 to P_N where $j = 1, 2,....,N$. The values are obtained using OLS, as long as we have a complete term structure and that $I \geq N$.

In practice, we will not have complete term structure of coupon bonds and so we are not able to identify the coefficients in (3.33). McCulloch (1971, 1975) described a spline estimation method, which assumes that zero-coupon bond prices vary smoothly with term to maturity. In this approach, we define P_N, a function of maturity $P(N)$, as a discount function given by

$$P(N) = 1 + \sum_{j=1}^{J} a_j f_j(N) \tag{3.34}$$

The function $f_j(N)$ is a known function of maturity N, and the coefficients a_j must be estimated. We arrive at a regression equation by substituting (3.34) into (3.33) to give us (3.35), which can be estimated using OLS.

$$\prod_i = \sum_{j=1}^{J} a_j X_j + u_i , \quad i = 1, 2, \ldots, I \tag{3.35}$$

where

$$\prod_i \equiv P_{C_i N_i} - 1 - C_i N_i$$

$$X_{ij} \equiv f_j(N_i) + C_i \sum_{l=1}^{N_i} f_j(l) .$$

The function $f_j(N)$ is usually specified by setting the discount function as a polynomial. In certain texts, including McCulloch, this is carried out by applying what is known as a spline function. Considerable academic research has gone into the use of spline functions as a yield curve fitting technique; however, we are not able to go into the required level of detail here, which is left to the next chapter. Please refer to the bibliography for further information. For a specific discussion on using regression techniques for spline curve fitting methods, see Suits et al (1978).

Term structure hypotheses

As befits a subject that has been the target of extensive research, a number of hypotheses have been forward that seek to explain the term structure of interest rates. These hypotheses describe why yield curves assume certain shapes, and relate maturity terms with spot and forward rates. In this section, we briefly review these hypotheses.

The expectations hypothesis

Simply put, the expectations hypothesis states that the slope of the yield curve reflects the market's expectations about future interest rates. There are, in fact, four main versions of the hypothesis, each distinct from and not compatible with the others. The expectations hypothesis has a long history, first being described in 1896 by Fisher and later developed by Hicks (1946) among others.[14] As Shiller (1990) describes, the thinking behind it probably

---

[14] See the footnote on p.644 of Shiller (1990) for a fascinating historical note on the origins of the expectations hypothesis. An excellent overview of the hypothesis itself is contained in Ingersoll (1987), p.389–392.

stems from the way market participants discuss their view on future interest rates when assessing whether to purchase long-dated or short-dated bonds. For instance, if interest rates are expected to fall, investors will purchase long-dated bonds in order to "lock in" the current high long-dated yield. If all investors act in the same way, the yield on long-dated bonds will, of course, decline as prices rise in response to demand, and this yield will remain low as long as short-dated rates are expected to fall, and will revert to a higher level only once the demand for long-term rates is reduced. Therefore, downward-sloping yield curves are an indication that interest rates are expected to fall, while an upward-sloping curve reflects market expectations of a rise in short-term interest rates.

Let us briefly consider the main elements of the discussion. The unbiased expectations hypothesis states that current forward rates are unbiased predictors of future spot rates. Let $f_t(T,T + 1)$ be the forward rate at time t for the period from T to $T + 1$. If the one-period spot rate at time T is r_T then according to the unbiased expectations hypothesis

$$f_t(T,T + 1) = E_t[r_T] \qquad (3.36)$$

which states that the forward rate $f_t(T,T + 1)$ is the expected value of the future one-period spot rate given by r_T at time T.

The return-to-maturity expectations hypothesis states that the return generated from an investment of term t to T by holding a $(T - t)$-period bond will be equal to the expected return generated by a holding a series of one-period bonds and continually rolling them over on maturity. More formally we write

$$\frac{1}{P(t,T)} = E_t[(1 + r_t)(1 + r_{t+1})\ldots\ldots(1 + r_{T-1})] \, . \qquad (3.37)$$

The left-hand side of (3.37) represents the return received by an investor holding a zero-coupon bond to maturity, which is equal to the expected return associated with rolling over £1 from time t to time T by continually re-investing one-period maturity bonds, each of which has a yield of the future spot rate r_t. A good argument for this hypothesis is contained in Jarrow (1996, p.52), which states that essentially in an environment of economic equilibrium the returns on zero-coupon bonds of similar maturity cannot be significantly different, otherwise investors would not hold the bonds with the lower return. A similar argument can be put forward with relation to coupon bonds of differing maturities. Any difference in yield would not therefore disappear as equilibrium was re-established. However, there are a number of reasons why investors will hold shorter-dated bonds, irrespective of the yield available on them, so it is possible for the return-to-maturity version of the hypothesis not to apply. In essence, this version represents an equilibrium condition in which expected holding-period returns are equal, although it does not state that this return is the same from different bond-holding strategies.

From (3.36) and (3.37) we can determine that the unbiased expectations hypothesis and the return-to-maturity hypothesis are not compatible with each other, unless there is no correlation between future interest rates. As Ingersoll (1987) notes, although it would be both possible and interesting to model such an economic environment, it is not related to reality, as interest rates are highly correlated. Given positive correlation between rates over a period of time, bonds with maturity terms longer than two periods will have a higher price under the unbiased expectations hypothesis than under the return-to-maturity version. Bonds of exactly two-period maturity will have the same price.

The yield-to-maturity expectations hypothesis is described in terms of yields. It is given by

$$\left[\frac{1}{P(t,T)}\right]^{\frac{1}{T-t}} = E_t\left[\{(1 + r_t)(1 + r_{t+1})......(1 + r_{T-1})\}^{\frac{1}{T-t}}\right] \qquad (3.38)$$

where the left-hand side specifies the yield to maturity of the zero-coupon bond at time t. In this version, the expected holding period yield on continually rolling over a series of one-period bonds will be equal to the yield that is guaranteed by holding a long-dated bond until maturity.

The local expectations hypothesis states that all bonds will generate the same expected rate of return if held over a small term. It is given by

$$\frac{E_t[P(t + 1,T)]}{P(t,T)} = 1 + r_t \qquad (3.39)$$

This version of the hypothesis is the only one that is consistent with no-arbitrage, because the expected rates of return on all bonds are equal to the risk-free interest rate. For this reason, the local expectations hypothesis is sometimes referred to as the risk-neutral expectations hypothesis.

Liquidity premium hypothesis

The liquidity premium hypothesis arises from the natural desire for borrowers to borrow long while lenders prefer to lend short. It states that current forward rates differ from future spot rates by an amount that is known as the liquidity premium. It is expressed as

$$f_t(T,T + 1) = E_t[r_T] + \pi_t(T,T + 1) \ . \tag{3.40}$$

Expression (3.40) states that the forward rate {symbol} is the expected value of the future one-period spot rate given by r_T at time T plus the liquidity premium, which is a function of the maturity of the bond (or term of loan). This premium reflects the conflicting requirements of borrowing and lenders, while traders and speculators will borrow short and lend long, in an effort to earn the premium. The liquidity premium hypothesis has been described in Hicks (1946).

Segmented-markets hypothesis

The segmented-markets hypothesis seeks to explain the shape of the yield curve by stating that different types of market participants invest in different sectors of the term structure, according to their requirements. So, for instance, the banking sector has a requirement for short-dated bonds, while pension funds will invest in the long end of the market. This was first described in Culbertson (1957). There may also be regulatory reasons why different investors have preferences for particular maturity investments. A *preferred-habitat* theory was described in Modigliani and Sutch (1967), which states not only that investors have a preferred maturity but also that they may move outside this sector if they receive a premium for so doing. This would explain "humped" shapes in yield curves. The preferred-habitat theory may be viewed as a version of the liquidity-preference hypothesis, where the preferred habitat is the short-end of the yield curve, so that longer-dated bonds must offer a premium in order to entice investors to hold them. This is described in Cox, Ingersoll and Ross (1981).

Evidence on the Expectations Hypothesis

The actions of market investors would seem to suggest that the expectations hypothesis does not apply in practice. This is not surprising, because the increased risk associated with longer-dated securities, both interest-rate risk and credit risk, suggest that returns should increase monotonically along the term structure. This is not a new idea. Hicks (1946) first proposed the idea of a liquidity premium embedded in the term structure. Fama (1986) and Longstaff (1990) showed that short-term returns reflected a liquidity premium.

More recently, Dhillon and Lasser (1998) presented evidence of a monotonically increasing term premium for US Treasury strips. This is of course inconsistent with the expectations hypothesis. Nevertheless the result is not surprising, and reflects investor beliefs on the market. The existence of a liquidity premium, and an increasing relationship between liquidity premium and the maturity structure, reflects market belief on how the risk-return profile should behave.

Appendices

APPENDIX 3.1 The Integral

The approach used to define integrals begins with an approximation involving a countable number of objects, which is then gradually transformed into an uncountable number of objects. A common form of integral is the Riemann integral.

Given a calculable or deterministic function that has been graphed for a period of time, let us say we require the area represented by this graph. The function is $f(t)$ and it graphed over the period $[0, T]$. The area of the graph is given by the integral

$$\int_0^T f(s)ds \qquad \text{(A3.1.1)}$$

which is the area represented by the graph. This can be calculated using the Riemann integral, for which the area represented is shown at Figure A3.1.

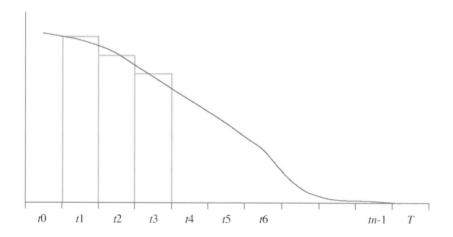

Figure A3.1 Calculating area using the integral

The general definition

To make the calculation, the time interval is separated into a n of intervals, given by $t_0 = 0 < t_1 < t_2 < \ldots\ldots < t_{n-1} < t_n < T$.

The approximate area under the graph is given by the sum of the area of each of the rectangles, for which we assume each segment outside the graph is compensated by the area under the line that is not captured by any of the rectangles. Therefore, we can say that an approximating measure is described by

$$\sum_{i=0}^{n} f\left[\frac{t_i + t_{i-1}}{2}\right](t_i - t_{i-1}) \qquad (A3.1.2)$$

This states that the area under the graph can be approximated by taking the sum of the n rectangles, which are created from the base x-axis which begins from t_0 through to T_n and the y-axis as height, described as

$$f((t_i + t_{i-1})/2) \ .$$

This approximation only works if a sufficiently small base has been used for each interval, and if the function $f(t)$ is a smooth function; that is, it does not experience sudden swings or kinks.

The definition of the Riemann integral is, given that

$$\max_{i} | t_i - t_{i-1} | \to 0 \ ,$$

defined by the limit

$$\sum_{i=0}^{n} f\left[\frac{t_i + t_{i-1}}{2}\right](t_i - t_{i-1}) \to \int_{0}^{T} f(s)ds \qquad (A3.1.3)$$

If the approximation is not sufficiently accurate, we can adjust it by making the intervals smaller still, which will make the approximation closer. This approach cannot be used if the function is not smooth; in mathematics this requirement is stated by saying that the function must be integrable or Riemann integrable.

Other integral forms are also used. A good introduction to these is given in Neftci (2000), Chapter 4.

Appendix 3.2 The derivation of the bond price equation in continuous time

This section is adapted from the approach described in Ross (1999), on p.54-56. This is an excellent reference, very readable and accessible, and is highly recommended. We replace Ross's use of investment at time 0 for maturity at time t with the terms t and T respectively, which is consistent with the price equations given in the main text. We also use the symbol M for the maturity value of the money-market account, again to maintain consistency with the expressions used in Chapters 2-4 of this book.

Assume a continuously compounded interest rate $r(s)$ that is payable on a money market account at time s. This is the instantaneous interest rate at time s. Assume further that an investor places x in this account at time s; after a very short time period of time h, the account would contain

$$x_h \approx x(1 + r(s)h) \qquad \text{A3.2.1)}$$

Say that $M(T)$ is the amount that will be in the account at time T if an investor deposits £1 at time t. To calculate $M(T)$ in terms of the spot rate $r(s)$, where{symbol}, for an incremental change in time of h, we have

$$M(s + h) \approx M(s)(1 + r(s)h) \qquad \text{(A3.2.2)}$$

which leads us to

$$M(s + h) - M(s) \approx M(s)r(s)h \qquad \text{(A3.2.3)}$$

and

$$\frac{M(s + h) - M(s)}{h} \approx M(s)r(s) \ . \qquad \text{(A3.2.4)}$$

The approximation given by (A3.2.4) turns into an equality as the time represented by h becomes progressively smaller. At the limit given as h approaches zero, we say

$$M'(s) = M(s)r(s) \qquad \text{(A3.2.5)}$$

which can be re-arranged to give

$$\frac{M'(s)}{M(s)} = r(s) \qquad \text{(A3.2.6)}$$

From expression (A3.2.6) we imply that in a continuous time process

$$\int_t^T \frac{M'(s)}{M(s)} ds = \int_t^T r(s) ds \qquad \text{(A3.2.7)}$$

and that

$$\log(M(T)) - \log(M(r)) = \int_t^T r(s) ds \qquad \text{(A3.2.8)}$$

However, we deposited £1 at time t, that is $M(t) = 1$, so from (A3.2.8)] we obtain the value of the money market account at T to be

$$M(T) = \exp\left[\int_t^T r(s) ds\right] \qquad \text{(A3.2.9)}$$

which was our basic equation shown as (A3.2.1).

Let us now introduce a risk-free zero-coupon bond that has a maturity value of £1 when it is redeemed at time T. If the spot rate is constant, then the price at time t of this bond is given by

$$P(t,T) = e^{-r(T-t)} \qquad \text{(A3.2.10)}$$

where r is the continuously compounded instantaneous interest rate. The right-hand side of (A3.2.10) is the expression for the present value of £1, payable at time T, discounted at time t at the continuously compounded, constant interest rate r.

So we say that $P(t, T)$ is the present value at time t of £1 to be received at time T. Since a deposit of $1/M(T)$ at time t will have a value of 1 at time T, we are able to say that

$$P(t,T) = \frac{1}{M(T)} = \exp\left[-\int_t^T r(s) ds\right] \qquad \text{(A3.2.11)}$$

which is our bond price equation in continuous time.

If we say that the *average* of the spot interest rates from t to T is denoted by $rf(T)$, so we have $rf(T) = \frac{1}{T}\int_t^T r(s) ds$, then the function $rf(T)$ is the term structure of interest rates.

Selected Bibliography and References

Adams, K. and Van Deventer, D., "Fitting Yield Curves and Forward Rate Curves with Maximum Smoothness", *Journal of Fixed Income* 4, 1994, p.52-62.

Avellaneda, M. and Laurence, P., *Quantitative Modelling of Derivative Securities*, Chapman & Hall/CRC, 2000, Chapters 10-12.

Baxter, M. and Rennie, A., *Financial Calculus*, Cambridge University Press, 1996, Chapter 5.

Cambell, J., Lo, A. and MacKinlay, A., *The Econometrics of Financial Markets*, Princeton University Press, 1997, Chapters 10-11

Cox, J., Ingersoll, J. and Ross, S., "An Inter-Temporal General Equilibrium Model of Asset Prices", *Econometrica* 53, 1985.

Deacon, M. and Derry, A., "Estimating the Term Structure of Interest Rates", *Bank of England Working Paper Series* No 24, July 1994.

Dhillon, V., and Lasser, D., "Term Premium Estimates from Zero-Coupon Bonds: New Evidence on the Expectations Hypothesis", *Journal of Fixed Income*, June 1998 pp. 52-58.

Duffie, D., *Dynamic Asset Pricing Theory*, Princeton University Press, 1992.

Fabozzi, F., *Bond Markets, Analysis and Strategies*, 2nd edition, Prentice Hall, 1993, Chapter 5.

Fabozzi, F., *Fixed Income Mathematics*, McGraw-Hill, 1997.

Fama, E., "Term Premiums and Default Premiums in Money Markets", *Journal of Financial Economics* 17, 1986, pp. 175-196

Gujarati, D., *Basic Econometrics*, 3rd edition, McGraw-Hill, 1995.

Hicks, J., *Value and Capital*, 2nd edition, Oxford University Press, 1946.

Ingersoll, J. Jr., *Theory of Financial Decision Making*, Rowman & Littlefied, 1987, Chapter 18.

James, J. and Webber, N., *Interest Rate Modelling*, Wiley, 2000.

Jarrow, R., *Modelling Fixed Income Securities and Interest Rate Options*, McGraw-Hill, 1996, Chapter 3.

Kitter, G., *Investment Mathematics for Finance and Treasury Professionals*, Wiley, 1999, Chapters 3 and 5.

Longstaff, F., "Time-varying Term Premiums and Traditional Hypotheses about the Term-Structure", *Journal of Finance* 45, 1990 pp.1307-1314

McCulloch, J., "Measuring the Term Structure of Interest Rates", *Journal of Business* 44, 1971, p.19-31

McCulloch, J., "The Tax-Adjusted Yield Curve", *Journal of Finance* 30, 1975, p.811-830.

Neftci, S., *An Introduction to the Mathematics of Financial Derivatives*, 2nd edition, Academic Press, 2000, Chapter 18.

Nelson, C. and Siegel, A., "Parsimonious Modelling of Yield Curves", *Journal of Business* 60(4), 1987, p.473-489.

Ross, Sheldon M., *An Introduction to Mathematical Finance*, Cambridge University Press, 1999.

Schaefer, S., "Measuring a Tax-Specific Term Structure of Interest Rates in the Market for British Government Securities", *Economic Journal* 91, 1981, p.415-438.

Shiller, R., "The Term Structure of Interest Rates", in Friedman, B. and Hanh, F., (eds), *Handbook of Monetary Economics*, Volume 1, North Holland, 1990, Chapter 13.

Suits, D., Mason, A. and Chan, L., "Spline Functions Fitted by Standard Regression Methods", *Review of Economics and Statistics* 60, 1978, p.132-139.

Sundaresan, S., *Fixed Income Markets and Their Derivatives*, South-Western, 1997.

Van Deventer, D. and Imai, K., *Financial Risk Analytics*, Irwin, 1997.

Van Horne, J., *Financial Management and Policy*, 10th edition, Prentice Hall, 1995.

Waggoner, D., "Spline Methods for Extracting Interest Rate Curves from Coupon Bond Prices", Working Paper, Federal Reserve Bank of Atlanta, 97-10, 1997.

In addition, interested readers may wish to consult the following recommended references on term structure analysis.

Constantinides, G., "A Theory of the Nominal Term Structure of Interest Rates", *The Review of Financial Studies* 5 (4), 1992, p.531-552.

Cox, J., Ingersoll, J. and Ross, S., "A Re-examination of Traditional Hypotheses about the Term Structure of Interest Rates", *Journal of Finance* 36, pp.769-799, 1981.

Cox, J., Ingersoll, J. and Ross, S., " A Theory of the Term Structure of Interest Rates", *Econometrica* 53, p.385-407, 1985.

Culbertson, J., "The Term Structure of Interest Rates", *Quarterly Journal of Economics* LXXI, p.489-504, 1957.

McCulloch, J.H., "A Reexamination of Traditional Hypotheses about the Term Structure: A Comment", *Journal of Finance* 63 (2), 1993, p.779-789.

Stambaugh, R., "The Information in Forward Rates: Implications for Models of the Term Structure", *Journal of Financial Economics* 21, 1988, p.41-70.

Shiller, R., Cambell, J. and Schoenholtz, K., "Forward Rates and Future Policy: Interpreting the Term Structure of Interest Rates", Brookings Papers on Economic Activity 1, 1983, p.173-223.

CHAPTER

4

Interest-rate Modelling

In the previous chapter, we introduced the basic concepts of bond pricing and analysis. We build on these concepts in this and the next chapter, which are a review of the initial and subsequent work conducted in this field. Term-structure modelling has been extensively researched in the financial economics literature; it is possibly the most heavily covered subject in that field. It is not possible to deliver a comprehensive summary in just two chapters, but we aim to cover the main topics to an in-depth level. As ever, interested readers are directed to the bibliography listing, which contains the more accessible titles in this area.

In this chapter, we review a number of interest-rate models, generally the more well-known ones. In the next chapter, we discuss some of the techniques used to fit a smooth yield curve to market-observed bond yields.

Introduction

Term structure modelling is based on theory describing the behavior of interest rates. A model would seek to identify the elements or factors that are believed to explain the dynamics of interest rates. These factors are random or *stochastic* in nature, so that we cannot predict with certainty the future level of any particular factor.[1] An interest-rate model must therefore specify a statistical process that describes the stochastic property of these factors, in order to arrive at a reasonably accurate representation of the behavior of interest rates.

---

[1] The word "stochastic" is derived from a term in ancient Greek, the word *stokhos* which means "a bull's eye". The connection? Throwing darts at a board and aiming for the bull's eye is a stochastic process, as it will contain a number of misses.

The first term-structure models covered in the academic literature described the interest-rate process as one where the short rate[2] follows a statistical process and where all other interest rates are a function of the short rate. So the dynamics of the short rate drive all other term interest rates. These models are known as one-factor models. A one-factor model assumes that all term rates follow on from when the short rate is specified; that is, they are not randomly determined. Two-factor interest-rate models have also been described. For instance, the model described by Brennan and Schwartz (1979) specified the factors as the short rate and a long-term rate, while a model described by Fong and Vasicek (1991) specified the factors as the short rate and short-rate volatility.

Basic concepts

The original class of interest-rate models described the dynamics of the short rate; the later class of models known as "HJM" models described the dynamics of the forward rate, and we will introduce these later. The foundation of interest-rate models is grounded in probability theory, so readers may wish to familiarise themselves with this subject. An excellent introduction to this is given in Ross (1999), which we referred to in the earlier chapter, while a fuller treatment is given in the same author's better known book, *Probability Models* (2000).

In a one-factor model of interest rates, the short rate is assumed to be a random or stochastic variable, with the dynamics of its behavior being uncertain and acting in an unpredictable manner. A random variable such as the short rate is defined as a variable whose future outcome can assume more than one possible value. Random variables are either discrete or continuous. A discrete variable moves in identifiable breaks or jumps. So, for example, while time is continuous, the trading hours of an exchange-traded future are not continuous, as the exchange will be shut outside business hours. Interest rates are treated in academic literature as being continuous, whereas, in fact, rates such as central-bank base rates move in discrete steps. A continuous variable moves in a manner that has no breaks or jumps. So, if an interest rate can move in a range from 5% to 10%, if it is continuous it can assume any value between this range; for instance, a value of 5.671291%. Although this does not reflect market reality, assuming that interest rates and the processes they follow are continuous allows us to use calculus to derive useful results in our analysis.

---

[2] We came across this expression in the previous chapter.

The short rate is said to follow a stochastic process, so although the rate itself cannot be predicted with certainty, as it can assume a range of possible values in the future, the process by which it changes from value to value can be assumed, and hence modeled. The dynamics of the short rate, therefore, are a stochastic process or probability distribution. A one-factor model of the interest rate actually specifies the stochastic process that describes the movement of the short rate.

The analysis of stochastic processes employs mathematical techniques originally used in physics. An instantaneous change in value of a random variable x is written as dx. The changes in the random variable are assumed to be normally distributed. The shock to this random variable that generates it to change value, also referred to as *noise*, follows a randomly generated process known as a Weiner process or geometric Brownian motion. This is described in Appendix 4 A variable following a Weiner process is a random variable, termed x or z, whose value alters instantaneously, but whose patterns of change follow a normal distribution with mean 0 and standard deviation 1. If we assume that the yield r of a zero-coupon bond follows a continuous Weiner process with mean 0 and standard deviation 1, this would be written $dr = dz$.

Changes or "jumps" in the yield that follow a Weiner process are scaled by the volatility of the stochastic process that drives interest rate, which is given by σ. So the stochastic process for the change in yields is given by $dr = \sigma dz$.

The value of this volatility parameter is user-specified; that is, it is set at a value that the user feels most accurately describes the current interest-rate environment. Users often use the volatility implied by the market price of interest-rate derivatives such as caps and floors.

So far we've said that the zero-coupon bond yield is a stochastic process following a geometric Brownian motion that drifts with no discernible trend. However, under this scenario, over time the yield would continuously rise to a level of infinity or fall to infinity, which is not an accurate representation of reality. We need to add to the model a term that describes the observed trend of interest rates moving up and down in a cycle. This expected direction of the change in the short rate is the second parameter in an interest-rate model, which in some texts is referred to by a letter such as a or b and in other texts is referred to as μ.

The short-rate process can therefore be described in the functional form given by (4.1)

$$dr = a\,dt + \sigma dz \qquad (4.1)$$

where

dr is the change in the short rate

a is the expected direction of change of the short rate or *drift*

dt is the incremental change in time

σ is the standard deviation of changes in the short rate

dz is the random process.

Equation (4.1) is sometimes seen with dW or dx in place of dz. It assumes that, on average, the instantaneous change in interest rates is given by the function adt, with random shocks specified by σdz. It is similar to a number of models, such as those first described by Vasicek (1977), Ho and Lee (1986), Hull and White (1991) and others.

To reiterate then, (4.1) states that the change in the short rate r over an infinitesimal period of time dt, termed dr, is a function of:

- the drift rate or expected direction of change in the short rate a
- a random process dz.

The two significant properties of the geometric Brownian motion are:

- the drift rate is equal to the expected value of the change in the short rate. Under a zero drift rate, the expected value of the change is also zero and the expected value of the short rate is given by its current value.
- the variance of the change in the short rate over a period of time T is equal to T, while its standard deviation is given by $\div T$.

The model given by (4.1) describes a stochastic short-rate process, modified with a drift rate to influence the direction of change. However, a more realistic specification would also build in a term that describes the long-run behavior of interest rates to drift back to a long-run level. This process is known as mean reversion, and is perhaps is best known by the Hull-White model. A general specification of mean reversion would be a modification given by (4.2)

$$dr = a(b - r)dt + \sigma dz \qquad (4.2)$$

where

b is the long-run mean level of interest rates

and where a now describes the speed of mean reversion. Equation (4.2) is known as an Ornstein-Uhlenbeck process. When r is greater than b, it will be pulled back towards b, although random shocks generated by dz will delay this process. When r is below b the short rate will be pulled up towards b.

Ito's lemma

Having specified a term-structure model, for market practitioners it becomes necessary to determine how security prices related to interest rates fluctuate. The main instance of this is where we wish to determine how the price P of a bond moves over time and as the short rate r varies. The formula used for this is known as Ito's lemma. For the background on the application of Ito's lemma, see Hull (1997) or Baxter and Rennie (1996). Ito's lemma transforms the dynamics of the bond price P into a stochastic process in the following form:

$$dP = P_r dr + \tfrac{1}{2} P_n (dr)^2 + P_t . \qquad (4.3)$$

The subscripts indicate partial derivatives.[3] The terms dr and $(dr)^2$ are dependent on the stochastic process that is selected for the short rate r. If this process is the Ornstein-Uhlenbeck process that was described in (4.2), then the dynamics of P can be specified as (4.4).

$$dP = P_r[a(b - r)dt + \sigma dz] + \tfrac{1}{2} P_n \sigma^2 dt + P_t \, dt \qquad (4.4)$$
$$= [P_r a(b - r) + \tfrac{1}{2} P_n \sigma^2 + P_t] \, dt + P_r \sigma dz$$
$$= a(r,t)dt + \sigma(r,t)dz$$

What we have done is to transform the dynamics of the bond price in terms of the drift and volatility of the short rate. Equation (4.4) states that the bond price depends on the drift of the short rate, and the volatility.

Ito's lemma is used as part of the process of building a term-structure model. The generic process this follows involves the following:

- specifying the random or stochastic process followed by the short rate, for which we must make certain assumptions about the short rate itself
- using Ito's lemma to transform the dynamics of the zero-coupon bond price in terms of the short rate
- imposing no-arbitrage conditions, based on the principle of hedging a position in one bond with one in another bond of a different

---

[3] This is the great value of Ito's lemma, a mechanism by which we can transform a partial differential equation.

maturity (for a one-factor model), in order to derive the partial differential equation of the zero-coupon bond price. We note that this is for a one-factor model: for a two-factor model we would require two bonds as hedging instruments

- solve the partial differential equation for the bond price, which is subject to the condition that the price of a zero-coupon bond on maturity is 1.

In the next section we review some of the models that are used in this process.

One-factor term-structure models

In this section, we discuss briefly a number of popular term-structure models and attempt to summarise the advantages and disadvantages of each which render them useful or otherwise under certain conditions and user requirements.

The Vasicek Model

The Vasicek model (1977) was the first term-structure model described in the academic literature, and is a yield-based one-factor equilibrium model. It assumes that the short-rate process follows a normal distribution. The model incorporates mean reversion and is popular with certain practitioners as well as academics because it is analytically tractable.[4] Although it has a constant volatility element, the mean reversion feature means that the model removes the certainty of a negative interest rate over the long term. However other practitioners do not favor the model because it is not necessarily arbitrage-free with respect to the prices of actual bonds in the market.

So the instantaneous short rate is described in the Vasicek model as

$$dr = a(b - r)dt + \sigma dz \qquad (4.5)$$

where a is the speed of the mean reversion and b is the mean reversion level or the long-run value of r.

z is the standard Weiner process or Brownian motion with a 0 mean and 1 standard deviation. In Vasicek's model, the price at time t of a zero-coupon bond that matures at time T is given by

---

[4] Tractability is much prized in a yield-curve model, and refers to the ease with which a model can be implemented; that is, with which yield curves can be computed.

$$P(t,T) = A(t,T)e^{-B(t,T)r(t)} \tag{4.6}$$

where $r(t)$ is the short rate at time t and

$$B(t,T) = \frac{1 - e^{-a(t,T)}}{a}$$

and

$$A(t,T) = \exp\left[\frac{(B(t,T) - T + 1)(a^2 b - \sigma^2/2)}{a^2} - \frac{\sigma^2 B(t,T)^2}{4a}\right]$$

The derivation of (4.6) is given in a number of texts (not least the original article!). We recommend section 5.3 in Van Deventer and Imai (1997) for its accessibility.

Note that in certain texts the model is written as

$$dr = \kappa(\theta - r)dt + \sigma dz$$

or

$$dr = \alpha(\mu - r)dt + \sigma dZ$$

but it just depends on which symbol the particular text is using. We use the form shown at (4.5) because it is consistent with our introductory discussion in the previous section.

In Vasicek's model, the short rate r is normally distributed so it can therefore be negative with positive probability. The occurrence of negative rates is dependent on the initial interest-rate level and the parameters chosen for the model, and is an extreme possibility. For instance, a very low initial rate, such as that observed in the Japanese economy for some time now, and volatility levels set with the market, have led to negative rates when using the Vasicek model. This possibility, which also applies to a number of other interest-rate models, is inconsistent with a no-arbitrage market because investors will hold cash rather than opt to invest at a negative interest rate.[5] However, for most applications the model is robust and its tractability makes it popular with practitioners.

The Ho and Lee model

The Ho and Lee model (1986) was an early arbitrage-free yield-based model. It is often called the "extended Merton model" as it is an extension

---

[5] This is stated in Black (1995).

of an earlier model described by Merton (1970).[6] It is called an arbitrage model as is it used to fit a given initial yield curve. The model assumes a normally distributed short rate, and the drift of the short rate is dependent on time, which makes the model arbitrage-free with respect to observed prices in the market, as these are the inputs to the model.

The model is given at (4.7).

$$dr = a(t)dt + \sigma dz \qquad (4.7)$$

The bond price equation is given as

$$P(t,T) = A(t,T)e^{-r(t)(T-t)} \qquad (4.8)$$

where $r(t)$ is the rate at time t and

$$\ln A(t,T) = \ln\left[\frac{P(0,T)}{P(0,t)}\right] - (T-t)\frac{\partial \ln P(0,t)}{\partial t} - \frac{1}{2}\sigma^2(T-t)^2 \ .$$

There is no mean reversion feature incorporated so that interest rates can fall to negative levels, which is a cause for concern for market practitioners.

The Hull and White model

The model described by Hull and White (1993) is another well-known model that fits the theoretical yield curve that one would obtain using Vasicek's model extracted from the actual observed market yield curve. As such, it is sometimes referred to as the "extended Vasicek model", with time-dependent drift.[7] The model is popular with practitioners precisely because it enables them to calculate a theoretical yield curve that is identical to yields observed in the market, which can then be used to price bonds and bond derivatives and also to calculate hedges.

The model is given at (4.9).

$$dr = a\left[\frac{b(t)}{a} - r\right]dt + \sigma dz \qquad (4.9)$$

where a is the rate of mean reversion and $\frac{b(t)}{a}$ is a time-dependent mean reversion.

---

[6] The reference in the bibliography is a later publication that is a collection of Merton's earlier papers.

[7] Haug (1998) also states that the Hull-White model is essentially the Ho and Lee model with mean reversion.

The price at time t of a zero-coupon bond with maturity T is

$$P(t,T) = A(t,T)e^{-B(t,T)r(t)}$$

where $r(t)$ is the short rate at time t and

$$B(t,T) = \frac{1 - e^{-a(t,T)}}{a}$$

$$\ln A(t,T) = \ln\left[\frac{P(0,T)}{P(0,t)}\right] - B(t,T)\frac{\partial P(0,t)}{\partial t} - \frac{v(t,T)^2}{2}$$

and

$$v(t,T) = \frac{1}{2a^3}\sigma^2(e-^{aT} - e^{at})^2(e^{2at} - 1) .$$

The Hall-White model is commonly used by derivatives traders.

Further one-factor term-structure models

The academic literature and market application have thrown up a large number of term-structure models as alternatives to the Vasicek model and models based on it such as the Hull-White model. As with these two models, each possesses a number of advantages and disadvantages. As we noted in the previous section, the main advantage of Vasicek-type models is their analytic tractability, with the assumption of the dynamics of the interest-rate allowing the analytical solution of bonds and bond instruments. The main weakness of these models is that they permit the possibility of negative interest rates. While negative interest rates are not a market impossibility,[8] the thinking would appear to be that they are a function of more than one factor, and that therefore modelling them using Vasicek-type models is not tenable. This aspect of the models does not necessarily preclude their use in practice, and will depend on the state of the economy at the time. To consider an example, during 1997–2000 Japanese money-market interest rates were frequently below $\frac{1}{2}$ of 1%, and at this level even low levels of volatility below 5% will imply negative interest rates with high probability if using Vasicek's model. In this environment, practitioners may wish to use models that do not admit the possibility of negative interest rates; perhaps those that model more than the short rate alone, so-called two-factor and

---

[8] Negative interest rates manifest themselves most obviously in the market for specific bonds in repo which have gone excessively special. However, academic researchers often prefer to work with interest-rate environments that do not consider negative rates a possibility (for example, see Black (1995)).

multi-factor models. We look briefly at these in the next section. First we consider, again briefly, a number of other one-factor models. As usual, readers are encouraged to review the bibliography articles for the necessary background and further detail on application.

The Cox, Ingersoll and Ross model

Although published officially in 1985, the Cox-Ingersoll-Ross model was apparently described in academic circles in 1977 or perhaps earlier, which would make it the first interest-rate model. Like the Vasicek model, it is a one-factor model that defines interest-rate movements in terms of the dynamics of the short rate. However, its incorporates an additional feature whereby the variance of the short rate is related to the level of interest rates, and this feature has the effect of not allowing negative interest rates. It also reflects a higher interest-rate volatility in periods of relatively high interest rates, and correspondingly lower volatility when interest rates are lower.

The model is given at (4.10).

$$dr = k(b - r)dt + \sigma\sqrt{r}dz \qquad (4.10)$$

The derivation of the zero-coupon bond price equation given at (4.11) is contained in Ingersoll (1987), Chapter 18. The symbol τ represents the term to maturity of the bond or $(T - t)$.

$$P(r,\tau) = A(\tau)e^{-B(\tau)r} \qquad (4.11)$$

where

$$A(\tau) = \left[\frac{2\gamma e^{(\gamma+\lambda+k)\frac{\tau}{2}}}{g(\tau)}\right]^{\frac{2kb}{\sigma^2}}$$

$$B(\tau) = \frac{-2(1 - e^{-\gamma\tau})}{g(\tau)}$$

$$g(\tau) = 2\gamma \mid (k + \lambda + \gamma)(e^{\gamma\tau} - 1)$$

$$\gamma = \sqrt{(k + \lambda)^2 + 2\sigma^2}$$

Some researchers[9] have stated that the difficulties in determining parameters for the CIR model have limited its use among market practitioners.

---

[9] For instance, see Van Deventer and Imai (1997) citing Fleseker (1993) on p.336, although the authors go on to state that the CIR model is deserving of further empirical analysis and remains worthwhile for practical application.

The Black, Derman and Toy model

The Black-Derman-Toy model (1990) also removes the possibility of negative interest rates and is commonly encountered in the markets. The parameters specified in the model are time-dependent, and the dynamics of the short-rate process incorporate changes in the level of the rate. The model is given at (4.12).

$$d[\ln(r)] = [\vartheta(t) - \phi(t)\ln(r)]dt + \sigma(t)dz \qquad (4.12)$$

The popularity of the model among market practitioners reflects the following:
- it fits the market-observed yield curve, similar to the Hull-White model
- it makes no allowance for negative interest rates
- it models the volatility levels of interest rates in the market.

Against this, the model is not considered particularly tractable or capable of being programmed for rapid calculation. Nevertheless, it is important in the market, particularly for interest-rate derivative market-makers. An excellent and accessible description of the BDT model is contained in Sundaresan (1997) on p. 240-244; Tuckman (1996) p.102-106 is also recommended.

Two-factor interest-rate models

As their name suggests, two-factor interest-rate models specify the yield curve in terms of two factors, one of which is usually the short rate. There are a number of possible factors that could be modeled when describing the dynamics of interest rates. For example, if defining the corporate-bond term structure, an additional factor might be the spread of identically rated bonds over the equivalent-maturity Treasury bond, known as the credit spread. The additional factors that could be modeled are listed below; note that models also exist that specify more than two factors, which are known as multi-factor models. Possible factors include:
- the short-term or instantaneous interest rate
- the long-term (say 10-year) interest rate
- short- and long-term real rates of interest
- the spread between the short-term and long-term interest rates, either the current level or the expected long-term level

- the corporate credit spread, either the current level or the long-term expected level
- the current rate of inflation
- the long-term average expected rate of inflation.

The choice of factors is dependent on the uses to which the model is being put; for example, whether for the pricing or hedging of derivative instruments or arbitrage trading. Other considerations will also apply; for instance, the ease and readiness with which model parameters can be determined. A particular issue in the use of two-factor and multi-factor models is the choice of factor. In this section we very briefly introduce a number of two-factor models, with references for readers who wish to learn about their derivation and application.

Brennan and Schwartz model

The Brennan-Schwartz model (1979) is a two-factor model that specifies the term structure in terms of the short rate and the long-term interest rate. The long-term rate is defined as the market yield observed on an irredeemable or perpetual bond, also known as an undated or consol bond. Both interest rates are assumed to follow what is known as a Gaussian-Markov process.[10] In the model, the dynamics of the logarithm of the short rate is defined as:

$$d[\ln(r)] = a[\ln(t) - \ln(r)]dt + \sigma_1 dz_1 \tag{4.13}$$

where p is a parameter that describes the relationship between the short rate and the long-term rate. The short rate r is related to the long-term rate and changes in response to moves in the level of the long-term rate l, which has the stochastic process of the following form:

$$dl = l[l - r + \sigma_2^2 + \lambda_2\sigma_2]dt + \lambda\sigma_2 dz_2 \tag{4.14}$$

where λ is the premium placed by the market on the risk associated with the long-term interest rate. In a later study by Longstaff and Schwartz (1992), the Brennan-Schwartz model was fitted with accurate results to market bond yields.

---

[10] A Markov process is one whose future behavior is independent of its past behavior, and is conditional on present behavior only. A Gaussian process is one whose marginal distribution, where marginals are random variables, is normal in behavior.

The extended Cox, Ingersoll and Ross (CIR) model

In further academic research,[11] the CIR model has been transformed into a two-factor model which specifies the interest rate as the function of two uncorrelated variables, both of which are assumed to follow a stochastic process. The model states:

$$dy_i = k_i(\theta_i - y_i)dt + \sigma_i\sqrt{y_i}dz_i \qquad (4.15)$$

where y_i are the independent variables. Under this model the authors derive the formula for the price of a zero-coupon bond as:

$$P(y1,y2,t,T) = A_1A_2e^{-B_1y_1-B_2y_2} \qquad (4.16)$$

where A and B are defined as before. In the 1992 article by Chen and Scott, this two-factor CIR model is shown to possess a number of advantages with a number of useful applications.

The Heath, Jarrow and Morton model

We have devoted a separate section to the approach described by Heath, Jarrow and Morton (1992) because it is a radical departure from the earlier family of interest-rate models. As usual, a fuller exposition can be found in the references listed in the bibliography.

The Heath-Jarrow-Morton (HJM) approach to the specification of stochastic state variables is different from that used in earlier models. The previous models describe interest-rate dynamics in terms of the short rate as the single or (in two- and multi-factor models) key state variable. With multi-factor models, the specification of the state variables is the fundamental issue in practical application of the models themselves. In the HJM model, the entire term structure, and not just the short rate, is taken to be the state variable. In Chapter 3, it was shown how the term structure can be defined in terms of default-free zero-coupon bond prices, yields, spot rates or forward rates. The HJM approach uses forward rates. So, in the single-factor HJM model the change in forward rates at current time t, with a maturity at time u, is captured by:

- a volatility function
- a drift function
- a geometric Brownian or Weiner process which describes the shocks or noise experienced by the term structure.

---

[11] See Chen and Scott (1992).

We present here a brief introduction to the HJM model. A recommended fuller treatment is presented in Chapter 8 of James and Webber (2000) and Chapter 5 of Baxter and Rennie (1996). The author suggests reading James and Webber first; both accounts, while presented as an "introduction", nevertheless require a good grounding in financial calculus.

The single-factor HJM model

To establish the HJM framework, we present our familiar simple interest-rate model. If we have a forward-rate term structure $f(0, T)$ that is T-integrable, the dynamics of the forward term structure may be described by:

$$df(t,T) = a(t,T)dt + \sigma dz \qquad (4.17)$$

where a is the drift rate and {symbol}the constant volatility level. The expression dz represents the geometric Brownian motion or Weiner process and is written as dW in some texts, or dW_t to represent the expression as applicable to the current time t. This is the stochastic differential equation for the forward rate. To transform this expression into the equation for the price of an asset we would apply Ito calculus, but this is something that we shall leave to specialised texts on financial mathematics. The forward rate expressed as an integral equivalent of (4.17) is

$$f(t,T) = f(0,T) + \int_0^t \sigma(s,T)ds + \sigma dz \qquad (4.18)$$

which assumes that the forward rate is normally distributed. Crucially, the different forward rates of maturity $f(0,1), f(0,2)....f(0, T)$ are assumed to be perfectly correlated. The random element is the Brownian motion dz, and the impact of this process is felt over time, rather than over different maturities.

As we noted, the term structure can be defined in terms of bond prices, yields, spot rates and forward rates. The HJM model is based on the instantaneous forward rate $f(t, T)$, and the single-factor version states that, given an initial forward-rate term structure $f(0, T)$ at time t, the forward rate for each maturity T is given by

$$df(t,T) = a(t,T)dt + \sigma(t,T)dz \qquad (4.19)$$

in the differential form, but which is usually seen in integral form:

$$f(t,T) = f(0,T) + \int_0^t a(s,T)ds + \int_0^t \sigma(s,T)dz_{(s)} \qquad (4.20)$$

where s is an incremental move forward in time (so that $0 \leq t \leq T$ and $t \leq s \leq T$). Note that the expressions at (4.19) and (4.20) are simplified versions of the formal model.

Under (4.19) and (4.20), the forward rate for any maturity period T will develop as described by the drift and volatility parameters $a(t, T)$ and $\sigma(t,T)$. In the single-factor HJM model, the random character of the forward-rate process is captured by the Brownian motion dz.[12] Under HJM, the primary assumption is that for each T, the drift and volatility processes are dependent only on the history of the Brownian-motion process up to the current time t, and on the forward rates themselves up to time t.

The multi-factor HJM model

Under the single-factor HJM model, the movement in forward rates of all maturities is perfectly correlated. This can be too much of a restriction for market application; for example, when pricing an interest-rate instrument that is dependent on the yield spread between two points on the yield curve. In the multi-factor model, each of the state variables is described by its own Brownian-motion process.[13] So, for example, in an m-factor model there would be m Brownian motions in the model, $dz_1, dz_2, \ldots\ldots, dz_m$. This allows each T-maturity forward rate to be described by its own volatility level $\sigma_i(t,T)$ and Brownian-motion process dz_i. Under this approach, the different forward rates given by the different maturity bonds that describe the current term structure evolve under more appropriate random processes, and different correlations between forward rates of differing maturities can be accommodated.

The multi-factor HJM model is given at (4.21).

$$f(t,T) = f(0,T) + \int_0^t a(s,T)ds + \sum_{i=1}^{m}\int_0^t \sigma(s,T)dz_i(s) \qquad (4.21)$$

Equation (4.21) states that the dynamics of the forward-rate process, beginning with the initial rate $f(0, T)$, are specified by the set of Brownian-motion processes and the drift parameter.

For practical application, the evolution of the forward-rate term structure is usually carried out as a binomial-type path-dependent process. However path-independent processes have also been used. The HJM approach has become popular in the market, both for yield-curve modelling and for pricing derivative instruments, due to the realistic effect of matching

---

[12] Note that certain texts use α for the drift term and W_t for the random term.
[13] For a good introduction, see Chapter 6 in Baxter and Rennie (1996).

yield-curve maturities to different volatility levels, and it is reasonably tractable when applied using the binomial-tree approach. Simulation modelling based on Monte Carlo techniques are also used. For further detail on the former approach, see Jarrow (1996).

Choosing a term-structure model

Selection of an appropriate term-structure model is more of an art than a science. The different types of model available, and the different applications and user requirements, mean that it is not necessarily clear-cut which approach should be selected. For example, a practitioner's requirements will determine whether a single-factor model or a two- or multi-factor model is more appropriate. The Ho-Lee and BDT models, for example, are *arbitrage* models, which means that they are designed to match the current term structure. With arbitrage (or arbitrage-free) models, assuming that the specification of the evolution of the short rate is correct, the law of no-arbitrage can be used to determine the price of interest-rate derivatives. There is also a class of interest-rate models known as *equilibrium* models, which make an assumption of the dynamics of the short rate in the same way as arbitrage models do, but are not designed to match the current term structure. With equilibrium models, therefore, the price of zero-coupon bonds given by the model-derived term structure is not required to (and does not) match prices seen in the market. This means that the prices of bonds and interest-rate derivatives are not given purely by the short-rate process. Overall then, arbitrage models take the current yield curve as described by the market prices of default-free bonds as given, whereas equilibrium models do not.

What considerations must be taken into account when deciding which term-structure model to use? Some of the key factors include:

Ease of application. The key input to arbitrage models is the current spot rate term structure, which is straightforward to determine using the market price of bonds currently trading in the market. This is an advantage over equilibrium models, whose inputs are more difficult to obtain.

Capturing market imperfections. The term structure generated by an arbitrage model will reflect the current market term structure, which may include pricing irregularities due to liquidity and other considerations. If this is not desired, it is a weakness of the arbitrage approach. Equilibrium models would not reflect pricing imperfections.

Pricing bonds and interest-rate derivatives. Traditional seat-of-the-pants market-making often employs a combination of the trader's nous, the range of prices observed in the market (often from inter-dealer broker screens) and gut feeling to price bonds. For a more scientific approach or for relative value trading,[14] a yield-curve model may well be desirable. In this case, an equilibrium model is clearly the preferred model, as the trader will want to compare the theoretical price given by the model compared to the actual price observed in the market. An arbitrage model would not be appropriate because it would taken the observed yield curve, and hence the market bond price, as given, and so would assume that the market bond prices were correct. Put another way, using an arbitrage model for relative-value trading would suggest to the trader that there was no gain to be made from entering into, say, a yield-curve spread trade. Pricing derivative instruments, such as interest-rate options or swaptions, require a different emphasis. This is because the primary consideration of the derivative market-maker is the technique and price of hedging the derivative. That is, upon writing a derivative contract the market-maker will simultaneously hedge the exposure using either the underlying asset or a combination of this and other derivatives such as exchange-traded futures. The derivative market-maker generates profit through extracting premium and from the difference in price over time between the price of the derivative and the underlying hedge position. For this reason, only an arbitrage model is appropriate, as it would price the derivative relative to the market, which is important for a market-maker. An equilibrium model would price the derivative relative to the theoretical market, which would not be appropriate since it is a market instrument that is being used as the hedge.

Use of models over time. At initial use the parameters used in an interest-rate model, most notably the drift, volatility and (if applicable) mean reversion rate reflect the state of the economy up to that point. This state is not constant, and so consequently, over time, any model must be continually re-calibrated to reflect the current state of the market. That is, the drift rate used today when calculating the term structure may well be a different value tomorrow. This puts arbitrage models at a disadvantage, as their parameters will be changed continuously in this way. Put another way, use of arbitrage models is not consistent over time. Equilibrium-model parameters are

---

[14] For example, yield-curve trades where bonds of different maturities are spread against each other, with the trader betting on the change in spread as opposed to the direction of interest rates, are a form of relative-value trade.

calculated from historic data or from intuitive logic, and so may not be changed as frequently. However, their accuracy over time may suffer. It is up to users to decide whether they prefer the continual tweaking of the arbitrage model over the more consistent use of the equilibrium model.

This is just the beginning; there are a range of issues which must be considered by users when selecting an interest-rate model. For example, in practice it has been observed that models incorporating mean reversion work more accurately than those that do not feature this. Another factor is the computer processing power available to the user, and it is often the case that single-factor models are preferred precisely because processing is more straightforward. A good account of the different factors to be considered when assessing which model to use is given in Chapter 15 of James and Webber (2000).

Appendix

APPENDIX 4.1 Geometric Brownian motion

Brownian motion was described in 1827 by the English scientist Robert Brown, and defined mathematically by the American mathematician Norbert Weiner in 1918. As applied to the price of a security, consider the change in price of a security as it alters over time. The time now is denoted as 0, with $P(t)$ as the price of the security at time t from now. The collection of prices $P(t)$, $0 \leq t \leq \infty$ is said to follow a Brownian motion with *drift* parameter μ and variance parameter σ^2 if for all non-negative values of t and T the random variable

$$P(t + T) - P(t)$$

is independent of all the prices P that have been recorded up to time t. That is, the historic prices do not influence the value of the random variable. Also the random variable is normally distributed with a mean uT and variance $\sigma_2 T$.

Standard Brownian motion has two drawbacks when applied to model security prices. The first and most significant is that, as the security price is a normally distributed random variable, it can assume negative values with non-negative probability, a property of the normal distribution. This cannot happen with equity prices and only very rarely, under very special conditions, with interest rates. The second drawback of standard Brownian motion is that the difference between prices over an interval is assumed to follow a normal distribution irrespective of the price of the security at the start of the interval. This is not realistic, as the probabilities are affected by the initial price of the security.

For this reason the geometric Brownian motion model is used in quantitative finance. Let us consider this now. Again, the time now is 0 and the security price at time t from now is given by $P(t)$. The collection of prices $P(t)$, $0 \leq t \leq \infty$ follows a geometric Brownian motion with drift μ and standard deviation or volatility σ if for non-negative values of t and T the random variable $P(t + T) / P(t)$ is independent of all prices up to time t. In addition, the value

$$\log\left[\frac{P(t + T)}{P(t)}\right]$$

is a normally distributed random variable with mean uT and variance $\sigma^2 T$.

What is the significance of this? It is this: once the parameters μ and σ have been ascertained, the present price of the security, and the present price only, determines the probabilities of future prices. The history of past prices has no impact. Also the probabilities of the ratio of the price at future time T to the price now are not dependent on the present price. The practical impact of this is that the probability that the price of a security doubles at some specified point in the future is identical whether the price now is 5 or 50.

For our purposes, we need only be aware that at an initial price of $P(0)$, the expected price at time t is a function of the two parameters of geometric Brownian motion. The expected price, given an initial price $P(0)$, is given by

$$E[P(t)] = P_0 e^{t(\mu + \sigma^2 / 2)} \tag{A4.1}$$

(A4.1) states that under geometric Brownian motion the expected price of a security is the present price increasing at the rate of $\mu + \sigma^2/2$.

The evolution of a price process, including an interest rate, under varying parameters is shown at Figure A4.1, with an initial price level at 100.

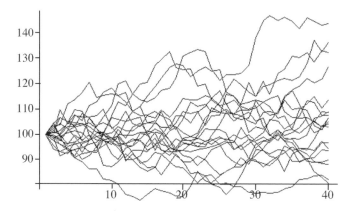

Figure A4.1 Evolution of Brownian or Weiner process

Selected Bibliography and References

Readers are first directed to the specific references cited in the text. If your interest is a general treatment of term-structure models, we suggest James and Webber (2000), while Baxter and Rennie (1996) is an excellent treatment of the mathematics involved. For a general exposition of the theory of the yield curve, Chapter 18 of Ingersoll (1987) is strongly recommended. Rebonato (1996) looks at the practical issues involved in implementing interest-rate models, and is a highly technical treatment. Finally, Van Deventer and Imai (1997) is an excellent, accessible account of, among other things, term-structure modelling and yield-curve smoothing techniques.

Baxter, M. and Rennie, A., *Financial Calculus*, Cambridge University Press, 1996, p.57-62.

Black, F., "Interest Rates as Options", *Journal of Finance*, December 1995, p.1371-1376.

Black, F., Derman, E. and Toy, W., "A One-Factor Model of Interest Rates and its Application to Treasury Bond Options", *Financial Analysts Journal*, Spring 1990, p.33-39.

Brennan, M. and Schwartz, E., "A Continuous Time Approach to the Pricing of Bonds", *Journal of Banking and Finance*, July 1979, p.135—155.

Campbell, J., "A Defence of Traditional Hypotheses about the Term Structure of Interest Rates", *Journal of Finance* 41 (1986), p.183-193.

Chen, R-R and Scott, L., "Pricing Interest Rate Options in a Two-Factor Cox-Ingersoll-Ross Model of the Term Structure", *Review of Financial Studies*, Winter 1992, p.613-636.

Cox, J., Ingersoll, J. and Ross, S., "A Theory of the Term Structure of Interest Rates", *Econometrica* 53, March 1985, p.385-407.

Fong, H.G. and Vasicek, O., "Fixed Income Volatility Management", *Journal of Portfolio Management*, Summer 1991, p.41-46.

Gibbons, M. and Ramaswamy, K., "The Term Structure of Interest Rates: Empirical Evidence", *Review of Financial Studies*, 1994.

Haug, E., *The Complete Guide to Option Pricing Formulas*, McGraw-Hill, 1998, Chapter 4.

Heath, D., Jarrow, R. and Morton, A., "Bond Pricing and the Term Structure of Interest Rates: A New Methodology for Contingent Claims Valuation", *Econometrica* 60, January 1992, p.77-105.

Ho, T. and Lee, S-b., "Term Structure Movements and Pricing Interest Rate Contingent Claims", *Journal of Finance*, December 1986, p.1011-1029.

Hull, J., *Options, Futures and other Derivatives*, 3rd edition, Prentice Hall, 1997, p.220-222.

Hull, J. and White, A., "Pricing Interest Rate Derivative Securities", *Review of Financial Studies*, 1990, p.573-592.

Ingersoll, J., Jr., *Theory of Financial Decision Making*, Rowman & Littlefield, 1987.

James, J. and Webber, N., *Interest Rate Modelling*, Wiley, 2000, Chapters 5-15.

Jarrow, R., *Modelling Fixed Income Securities and Interest Rate Options*, McGraw-Hill, 1996.

Merton, R., *Continuous Time Finance*, Blackwell. 1993, Chapter 11.

Rebonato, R., *Interest Rate Option Models*, Wiley, 1996.

Rebonato, R. and Cooper, I., "The Limitations of Simple Two-Factor Interest Rate Models", *Journal of Financial Engineering*, March 1996.

Sundaresan, S., *Fixed Income Markets and their Derivatives*, South Western Publishing, 1997.

Tuckman, B., *Fixed Income Securities*, Wiley, 1996.

Van Deventer, D. and Imai, K., *Financial Risk Analytics*, Irwin, 1997, Chapter 5.

Vasicek, O., "An Equilibrium Characterisation of the Term Structure", *Journal of Financial Economics*, 5, 1977, p.177-188.

Fitting the Yield Curve

In this chapter we consider some of the techniques used to actually fit the term structure. In theory, we could use the bootstrapping approach described earlier. For a number of reasons, however, this does not produce accurate results, and so other methods are used instead. The term-structure models described in the previous chapter defined the interest-rate process under various assumptions about the nature of the stochastic process that drives these rates. However, the zero-coupon curve derived by models such as those described by Vasicek (1977), Brennan and Schwartz (1979) and Cox, Ingersoll and Ross (1985) do not fit the observed market rates or spot rates implied by market yields, and generally market yield curves are found to contain more variable shapes than those derived using term-structure models. Hence, the interest-rate models described in Chapter 4 are required to be calibrated to the market and, in practice, they are calibrated to the market yield curve. This is carried out in two ways; the model is either calibrated to market instruments such as money-market products and interest-rate swaps, which are used to construct the yield curve, or the yield curve is constructed from market-instrument rates and the model is calibrated to this constructed curve. If the latter approach is preferred, there are a number of non-parametric methods that may be used. We will consider these later.

The academic literature contains a good deal of research into the empirical estimation of the term structure, the object of which is to fit a zero-coupon curve[1] that is a reasonably accurate fit to the market prices *and* is a smooth function. There is an element of trade-off between these two

---

[1] The zero-coupon or spot curve, or equivalently the forward-rate curve or the discount function: all would be describing the same thing.

objectives. The second objective is as important as the first, however, in order to derive a curve that makes economic sense. (It would be possible to fit the curve perfectly at the expense of smoothness, but this would be almost meaningless).

In this chapter, we present an overview of some of the methods used to fit the yield curve. An excellent account of the approaches we discuss in this chapter is given in Anderson *et al* (1996). Unfortunately, this book is now out of print, but an excellent working paper that formed part of the input to this book is still available, which is Deacon and Derry (1994). A selection of other useful references is given as usual in the bibliography.

Yield-curve smoothing

Introduction

An approach that has been used to estimate the term structure was described by Carleton and Cooper (1976) and which assumed that default-free bond cash flows are payable on specified discrete dates, with a set of unrelated discount factors that apply to each cash flow. These discount factors were then estimated as regression coefficients, with each bond cash flow acting as the independent variables, and the bond price for that date acting as the dependent variable.[2] Using simple linear regression in this way produces a discrete discount function, not a continuous one, and forward rates that are estimated from this function are very jagged. An approach more readily accepted by the market was described by McCulloch (1971), who fitted the discount function using polynomial splines. This method produces a continuous function, and one that is linear so that the ordinary least-squares regression technique can be employed. In a later study, Langetieg and Smoot (1981)[3] use an extended McCulloch method, fitting cubic splines to zero-coupon rates instead of the discount function, and using non-linear methods of estimation.

That is the historical summary of early efforts. But let's get back to the beginning. We know that the term structure can be described as the complete set of discount factors, the discount function, which can be extracted from the price of default-free bonds trading in the market. The bootstrapping technique described in an earlier chapter may be used to extract the relevant discount factors. However, there are a number of reasons why this approach is problematic in practice. First, it is unlikely that the complete set of bonds

---

[2] The basics of regression are summarised briefly in Appendix 5.1.
[3] Reference in Vasicek and Fong (1982).

in the market will pay cash flows at precise six-month intervals every six months from today to 30 years or longer. An adjustment is made for cash flows received at irregular intervals, and for the lack of cash flows available at longer maturities. Another issue is the fact that the technique presented earlier allowed practitioners to calculate the discount factor for six-month maturities, whereas it may be necessary to determine the discount factor for non-standard periods, such as four-month or 14.2-year maturities. This is often the case when pricing derivative instruments.

A third issue concerns the market price of bonds. These often reflect specific investor considerations, which include:

• the liquidity or lack thereof of certain bonds, caused by issue sizes, market-maker support, investor demand, non-standard maturity, and a host of other factors.
• the fact that bonds do not trade continuously, so that some bond prices will be "newer" than others.
• the tax treatment of bond cash flows, and the effect that this has on bond prices.
• the effect of the bid-offer spread on the market prices used.

The statistical term used for bond prices subject to these considerations is error. It is also common to come across the statement that these effects introduce noise into market prices.

To construct a fit to the yield curve that better handles the above considerations, smoothing techniques are used to derive the complete set of discount factors – known as the discount function – from market bond prices. Using the simple technique presented in Chapter 1, we graph the discount function for the UK gilt prices as at 12th June 2000. This is shown in Figure 5.2. The yield curve plotted from gilt redemption yields is shown in Figure 5.1. Figure 5.3 shows the zero-coupon yield curve and forward-rate curve that correspond to the discount function from the date.

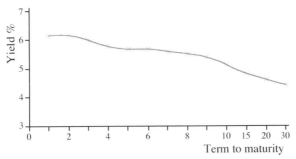

Figure 5.1 Gilt gross-redemption yields, 12th June 2000

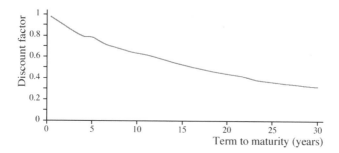

Figure 5.2 Discount factors from gilt prices, 12th June 2000

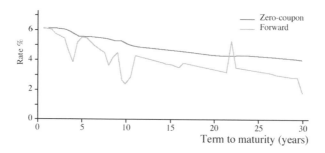

Figure 5.3 Zero-coupon (spot) and forward rates obtained from gilt yields, 12th June 2000

From Figure 5.2 we see that the discount function is quite smooth, while the zero-coupon curve is also relatively smooth, although not as smooth as the discount function. The forward rate curve is distinctly unsmooth, if the reader will permit such as an expression, and there is obviously something wrong. In fact, the jagged nature of implied forward rates is one of the main concerns of the fixed-income analyst, and indicates in the first instance that the discount function and zero-coupon curve are not as smooth as they appear. Using the naïve estimation method here, the main reason why the forward rates oscillate wildly[4] is that minor errors at the discount-factor stage are magnified many times over when translated into the forward rate. That is, any errors in the discount factors (which errors may stem from any of the reasons given above) are compounded when spot rates are calculated from them, and these are compounded into larger errors when calculating forward rates.

---

[4] I've been looking for an excuse to use this expression, for the most obscure reason which we can finally reveal: see Goddard (2002), page 140.

Smoothing techniques

A common technique that may be used, but which is not accurate and so not recommended, is linear interpolation. In this approach, the set of bond prices are used to graph a redemption yield curve (as in the previous section), and where bonds are not available for the required maturity term, the yield is interpolated from actual yields. Using gilt yields for 26th June 1997, we plot this as shown at Figure 5.4. The interpolated yields are those that are not marked by a cross. Figure 5.4 looks reasonable for any practitioner's purpose. However, spot and forward yields that are obtained from this curve are apt to behave in unrealistic fashion, as shown in Figure 5.5. The forward curve is very bumpy, and each bump will correspond to a bond used in the original set. The spot rate has a kink at 21.5 years, and so the forward curve jumps significantly at this point. This curve would appear to be particularly unrealistic.

For this reason, market analysts do not bother with linear interpolation and instead use multiple regression or spline-based methods. One approach might be to assume a functional form for the discount function and estimate parameters of this form from the prices of bonds in the market. We consider these approaches next.

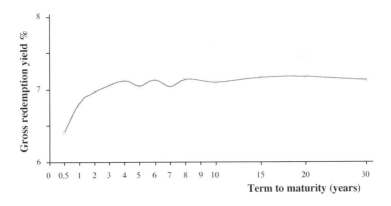

Figure 5.4 Linear interpolation of bond yields, 26th June 1997

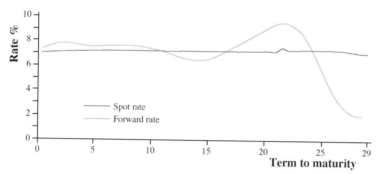

Figure 5.5 Spot and forward rates implied from Figure 5.4

Using a cubic polynomial

A simple functional form for the discount function is a cubic polynomial. This approach consists of approximating the set of discount factors using a cubic function of time. If we say that $d(t)$ is the discount factor for maturity t, we approximate the set of discount factors using the following cubic function.

$$\hat{d}(t) = a_0 + a_1(t) + a_2(t)^2 + a_3(t)^3$$

(5.1)

In some texts, the coefficients sometimes are written as a, b, and c rather than a_1 and so on.

The discount factor for $t = 0$, that is at time now, is 1. Therefore $a_0 = 1$, and (5.1) can then be re-written as:

$$\hat{d}(t) - 1 = a_1(t) + a_2(t)^2 + a_3(t)^3$$

(5.2)

The market price of a traded coupon bond can be expressed in terms of discount factors. So at (5.3) we show the expression for the price of an N-maturity bond paying identical coupons C at regular intervals and redeemed at maturity at M.

$$P = d(t_1)C + d(t_2)C + \ldots\ldots + d(t_N)(C + M)$$

(5.3)

Using the cubic polynomial equation (5.2), expression (5.3) is transformed into:

$$P = C[1 + a_1(t_1) + a_2(t_1)^2 + a_3(t_1)^3] + \ldots + (C + M)[1 + a_1(t_N) + a_2(t_N)^2 + a_3(t_N)^3]$$

(5.4)

We require the coefficients of the cubic function in order to start describing the yield curve, so we re-arrange (5.4) in order to express it in terms of these coefficients. This is shown at (5.5).

$$P = M + \sum C + a_1[C(t_1) + ... + (C + M)(t_N)] + a_2[C(t_1)^2 + ... + (C + M)(t_N)^2]$$
$$a_3[C(t_1)^3 + ... + (C + M)(t_N)^3]$$

$$(5.5)$$

In the same way, we can express the pricing equation for each bond in our data set in terms of the unknown parameters of the cubic function. From (5.5) we may write

$$P - (M + \sum C) = a_1 X_1 + a_2 X_2 + a_3 X_3 \qquad (5.6)$$

where X_i is the appropriate expression in square brackets in (5.5); this is the form in which the expression is encountered commonly in text books.

EXAMPLE 5.1

A benchmark semi-annual coupon four-year bond with a coupon of 8% is trading at a price of 101.25. Assume the first coupon is precisely six months from now, so that $t_1 = 0.5$ and so $t_N = 4$. Set up the cubic function expression.

We have $C = 4$ and $M = 100$ so therefore:

$$100 + \sum C = 100 + (8 \times 4) = 132$$

$$P - (100 + \sum C) = 101.25 - 132 = -30.75$$

$$X_1 = (4 \times 0.5) + (4 \times 1) + (4 \times 1.5) + ... + (104 \times 4) = 472$$

$$X_2 = [4 \times (0.5)^2] + [4 \times (1)^2] + [4 \times (1.5)^2] + ... + [104 \times (4)^2] = 1,796$$

$$X_3 = [4 \times (0.5)^3] + [4 \times (1)^3] + [4 \times (1.5)^3] + ... + [104 \times (4)^3] = 7,528$$

This means that we now have an expression for the three coefficients, which is:

$$472a_1 + 1796a_2 + 7528a_3 = -30.75 .$$

The prices for all other bonds are expressed in terms of the unknown parameters. To calculate the coefficient values, we use a statistical technique such as linear regression, such as least squares to find the best fit values of the cubic equation. An introduction to this technique is given in Appendix 5.1.

In practice, the cubic polynomial approach is too limited a technique, requiring one equation per bond, and does not have the required flexibility to fit market data satisfactorily. The resulting curve is not really a curve but, rather, a set of independent discount factors that have been fit with a line of best fit. In addition, the impact of small changes in the data can be significant at the non-local level; so, for example, a change in a single data point at the early maturities can result in badly behaved longer maturities. Alternatively, a piecewise cubic polynomial approach is used, whereby $d(t)$ is assumed to be a different cubic polynomial over each maturity range. This means that the parameters a_1, a_2, and a_3 will be different over each maturity range. We will look at a special case of this use, the cubic spline, a little later.

Non-parametric methods

Outside of the cubic-polynomial approach described in the previous section there are two main approaches to fitting the term structure. These are usually grouped into *parametric* and *non-parametric* curves. Parametric curves are based on term-structure models such as the Vasicek model or the Longstaff and Schwartz model. Non-parametric curves are not derived from an interest-rate model and are general approaches, described using a set of parameters. They include spline-based methods.

Spline-based methods

A spline is a statistical technique and a form of linear-interpolation method. There is more than one way of applying them, and the most straightforward method to understand the process is the spline function fitted using regression techniques. For the purposes of yield-curve construction, this method can cause curves to jump wildly and is over-sensitive to changes in parameters.[5] However, we feel it is the most accessible method to understand and an introduction to the basic technique, as described in Suits *et al* (1978), is given in Appendix 5.2.[6]

---

[5] For instance, see James and Webber (2000), section 15.3.

[6] The original article by Suits *et al* (1978) is excellent and highly recommended.

An n-th order spline is a piecewise-polynomial approximation with n-degree polynomials that are differentiable n-1 times. Piecewise means that the different polynomials are connected at arbitrarily selected points known as knot points (see Appendix 5.2). A cubic spline is a three-order spline, and is a piecewise cubic polynomial that is differentiable twice along all its points.

The x-axis in the regression is divided into segments at arbitrary points known as knot points. At each knot point the slopes of adjoining curves are required to match, as must the curvature. Figure 5.6 is a cubic spline. The knot points are selected at 0, 2, 5, 10 and 25 years. At each of these points, the curve is a cubic polynomial, and with this function we could accommodate a high and low in each space bounded by the knot points.

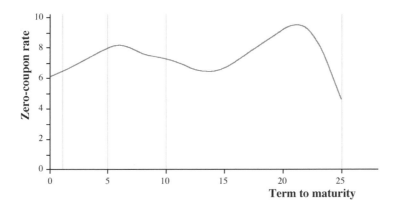

Figure 5.6 Cubic spline with knot points at 0, 2, 5, 10 and 25 years

Cubic-spline interpolation assumes that there is a cubic polynomial that can estimate the yield curve at each maturity gap. One can think of a spline as a number of separate polynomials of $y = f(X)$, where X is the complete range, divided into user-specified segments, which are joined smoothly at the knot points. If we have a set of bond yields $r_0, r_1, r_2, \ldots\ldots r_n$ at maturity points $t_0, t_1, t_2, \ldots\ldots t_n$, we can estimate the cubic-spline function in the following way:

- the yield on bond i at time t is expressed as a cubic polynomial of the form $r_i(t) = a_i + b_i t + c_i t^2 + d_i t^3$ for the interval over t_i and t_{i-1}.
- the coefficients of the cubic polynomial are calculated for all n intervals between the $n + 1$ data points, which results in $4n$ unknown coefficients that must be computed.

- these equations can be solved because they are made to fit the observed data. They are twice differentiable at the knot points, and these derivatives are equal at these points.
- the constraints specified are that the curve is instantaneously straight at the start of the curve (the shortest maturity) and instantaneously straight at the end of the curve, the longest maturity, that is $r''(0) = 0$.

An accessible and readable account of this technique can be found in Van Deventer and Imai (1997).

The general formula for a cubic spline is:

$$s(\tau) = \sum_{i=0}^{3} a_i \tau^i + \frac{1}{3!} \sum_{p=0}^{n-1} b_p (\tau - X_p)^3 \tag{5.7}$$

where τ is the time of receipt of cash flows and where X_p refers to the points where are joined and adjacent polynomials which are known as knot points, with $\{X_0, \ldots X_n\}$, $X_p < X_p + 1, p = 0, \ldots, n-1$. In addition $(\tau - X_p) = \max(\tau - X_p, 0)$. The cubic spline is twice differentiable at the knot points. In practice, the spline is written down as a set of basis functions with the general spline being made up of a combination of these. One way to do this is by using what are known as B-splines. For a specified number of knot points $\{X_0, \ldots, X_n\}$ this is given by (5.8),

$$B_p(\tau) = \sum_{j=p}^{p+4} \left[\prod_{i=p, i \neq i}^{p+4} \frac{1}{X_i - X_j} \right] (\tau - X_p)^3 \tag{5.8}$$

where $B_p(\tau)$ are cubic splines which are approximated on $\{X_0, \ldots, X_n\}$ with the following function:

$$\delta(\tau) = \delta(\tau \mid \lambda_{-3}, \ldots, \lambda_{n-1}) = \sum_{p=-3}^{n-1} \lambda_p B_p(\tau) \tag{5.9}$$

with $\lambda = (\lambda_{-3}, \ldots, \lambda_{n-1})$ the required coefficients. The maturity periods $\tau_1, \ldots, \tau_n$ specify the B-splines so that $B = \{B_p(\tau_j)\}_{p=-3, \ldots, n-1, j-1, \ldots, m}$ and $\delta = (\delta(\tau_1), \ldots, \delta(\tau_m))$. This allows us to set

$$\hat{\delta} = B'\lambda \tag{5.10}$$

and therefore the regression equation

$$\lambda^* = \arg \min_{\lambda} \{\varepsilon'\varepsilon \mid \varepsilon = P - D\lambda\} \tag{5.11}$$

with $D = CB'$.

$\varepsilon'\varepsilon$ are the minimum errors. The regression at (5.11) is computed using ordinary least-squares regression.

An illustration of the use of B-splines is given in Steeley (1991) and, more recently and with a complete methodology, by Didier Joannas in Choudhry *et al* (2001).

Appendix 5.2 provides background on splines fitted using regression methods.

Nelson and Siegel curves

The curve-fitting technique first described by Nelson and Siegel (1985) has since been applied and modified by other authors, which is why they are sometimes described as a "family" of curves. These curves provide a satisfactory rough fit of the complete term structure, with some loss of accuracy at the very short and very long end. In the original curve, the authors specify four parameters. The approach is not a bootstrapping technique but, rather, a method for estimating the zero-coupon rate function from the yields observed on T-Bills, under an assumed function for forward rates.

The Nelson and Spiegel curve states that the implied forward-rate yield curve may be modeled along the entire term structure using the following function:

$$rf(m,\beta) = \beta_0 + \beta_1\exp\left[\frac{-m}{t^1}\right] + \beta_2\left[\frac{m}{t^{1-}}\right]\exp\left[\frac{-m}{t^1}\right] \qquad (5.12)$$

where

$\beta = (\beta_0,\beta_1,\beta_2,t_1)'$ is the vector of parameters describing the yield curve, and m is the maturity at which the forward rate is calculated. There are three components; the constant term, a decay term and term reflecting the "humped" nature of the curve. The shape of the curve will gradually lead into an asymptote at the long end, the value of which is given by β_0, with a value of $\beta_0 + \beta_1$ at the short end.

A version of the Nelson and Siegel curve is the Svensson model (1994) with an adjustment to allow for the humped characteristic of the yield curve. This is fitted by adding an extension, as shown by (5.13).

$$rf(m,\beta) = \beta_0 + \beta_1\exp\left[\frac{-m}{t_1}\right] + \beta_2\left[\frac{m}{t_1}\right]\exp\left[\frac{-m}{t_1}\right] + \beta_3\left[\frac{m}{t_2}\right]\exp\left[\frac{-m}{t_2}\right] \quad (5.13)$$

The Svensson curve is modeled, therefore, using six parameters, with additional input of β_3 and t_2.

Nelson and Siegel curves are popular in the market because they are straightforward to calculate. Jordan and Mansi (2000) state that one of the advantages of these curves is that they force the long-date forward curve into an horizontal asymptote. Another is that the user is not required to specify knot points, the choice of which determines the effectiveness or otherwise of cubic spline curves. The disadvantage they note is that these curves are less flexible than spline-based curves and there is therefore a chance that they do not fit the observed data as accurately as spline models.[7] James and Webber (2000, p.444-445) also suggest that Nelson and Siegel curves are slightly inflexible due to the limited number of parameters, and are accurate for yield curves that have only one hump, but are unsatisfactory for curves that possess both a hump and trough. As they are only reasonable for approximations, Nelson and Siegel curves would not be appropriate for no-arbitrage applications.

Comparing curves

Whichever curve is chosen will depend on the user's requirements and the purpose for which the model is required. The choice of modelling methodology is usually a trade-off between simplicity and ease of computation and accuracy. Essentially. the curve chosen must fulfill the qualities of

- *accuracy*: Is the curve a reasonable fit of the market curve? Is it flexible enough to accommodate a variety of yield-curve shapes?

- *model consistency*: Is the curve-fitting method consistent with a theoretical yield-curve model such as Vasicek or Cox-Ingersoll-Ross?

- *simplicity*: Is the curve reasonably straightforward to compute; that is, is it *tractable*?

The different methodologies all fit these requirements to greater or lesser extent. A good summary of the advantages and disadvantages of some popular modelling methods can be found in James and Webber (2000, Chapter 15).

This is an excellent article, strongly recommended. A good overview introduction to curve fitting is given in the introduction, and the main body of the article gives a good insight into the type of research that is currently being undertaken in yield-curve analysis.

Appendices

APPENDIX 5.1 Linear regression: ordinary least squares

The main purpose of regression analysis is to estimate or predict the average value of a dependent variable given the known values of an independent or explanatory variable. In one way, it measures the relationship between two sets of data. This data might be the relationship between family income and expenditure; here the income would be the independent variable and expenditure the dependent variable. More relevant for our purposes, it could also be the relationship between the change in price of a corporate bond, priced off the benchmark yield curve, and changes in the price of a short-dated benchmark bond and the price of a long-term bond. In this case, the price of the corporate bond is the dependent variable, while the prices of the short- and long-term government bonds are independent variables. If there is a linear relationship between the dependent and independent variables, we may use a regression function to determine the relationship between them. In this appendix, we provide a basic overview and introduction to regression and ordinary least squares. Regression analysis is a key part of financial econometrics, and advanced econometric analysis is extensively used in fixed-income work. For a background in basic econometrics, we recommend the book of the same name by Damodar Gujarati, (1995), which is excellent. Gujarati's book is very accessible and readable, and provides a good grounding in the topic. Another excellent introduction to econometrics is Brooks (2002). For more advanced applications, we recommend *The Econometrics of Financial Markets* by Campbell, Lo and MacKinlay (Princeton, 1997).

If our data set consists of the entire population, rather than a statistical sample of the population, we estimate the relationship between two data sets using the population-regression function. Given an independent variable X and dependent variable Y it can be shown that the conditional mean $E(Y\,|\,X_i)$ is a function of X_i. This would be written

$$E(Y\,|\,X_i) = f(X_i) \qquad (A5.1.1)$$

where $f(X_i)$ is a function of the independent variable X_i. Equation (A5.1.1) is termed the two-variable population-regression function and states that average value of Y given X_i is a linear function of X_i. It can further be shown that

$$E(Y\,|\,X_i) = \alpha + \beta X_i \qquad (A5.1.2)$$

where α and β are the regression coefficients; they are unknown but fixed parameters. The α term is the intercept coefficient and β is the slope coefficient. These are shown in Figure 5.7. The objective of regression analysis is to estimate the values of the regression coefficients using observations of the values of X and Y.

Equation (A5.1.2) is a two-variable regression; it is sometimes written as

$$Y = \beta_1 + \beta_2 X_i \qquad (A5.1.3)$$

Where there are more than two variables, we use a multi-variable regression.

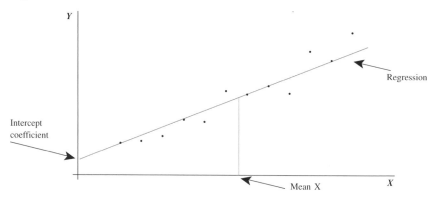

Figure 5.7 Regression line passing through values of X and Y

It can further be shown that given a value for X_i, the independent variable value will be clustered around the average value for Y at that X_i; in other words, around the conditional expectation. The deviation of an individual Y_i around its expected value is defined as

$$u_i = Y_i - E(Y \mid X_i) \,. \qquad (A5.1.4)$$

This is re-arranged to give

$$Y_i = E(Y \mid X_i) + u_i \qquad (A5.1.5)$$

where the term u_i is an unknown random variable and is known as the stochastic disturbance or stochastic error term or simply error term. It is written as ε in some text books.

The value of the dependent variable is the sum of two elements; the systematic or deterministic element, which is given by the regression function above, and a random or non-systematic element which is the error term. Essentially, the error term captures all those elements that have been missed out or left out of the regression model.

In practice it is most unlikely that we will have data sets available for the entire population, so we use statistical sample data instead. When regression is carried out on sample data we use the sample regression function (SRF), which is (A5.1.6) below.

$$Y_i = \hat{\alpha} + \hat{\beta} X_i + \hat{u}_i \qquad (A5.1.6)$$

where

$\hat{\alpha}$ is the *estimator* of α
$\hat{\beta}$ is the estimator of β

The SRF is determined using a statistical technique known as ordinary least squares or OLS. This approach is covered in any number of statistics and econometrics text books. We suggest Chapter 3 in Gujarati (1995). A very brief description is given here.

Let us expand our regression model. Assume we have N observations and m independent variables. Say that Y_i be the ith observation on the dependent variable and X_{it} be the ith observation on the tth independent variable. The regression function of the relationship between the dependent and independent variables is given by

$$Y_i = \beta_1 X_{1i} + \beta_2 X_{2i} + \ldots\ldots + \beta_m X_{mi} + \varepsilon_i \qquad (A5.1.7)$$

and where we must estimate the $\beta_1, \beta_2, \ldots\ldots \beta_m$ regression coefficients. This is done using OLS. From (A5.1.7) ε_i is the error in the model, the random element that is left out in predicting the ith value of the dependent variable. From our earlier description we know that

$$\varepsilon_i = Y_i - \beta_1 X_{1i} - \beta_2 X_{2i} - \ldots\ldots - \beta_m X_{mi} \qquad (A5.1.8)$$

We require the sum of squared errors, which is given by $\varepsilon_1^2 + \varepsilon_2^2 + \ldots\ldots + \varepsilon_i^2$, and OLS is determining the coefficients that minimize this sum of squared errors.

Earlier in the chapter we illustrated a bond pricing equation, which was $472a_1 + 1796a_2 + 7528a_3 = -30.75$.

What this expression tells us is that -30.75 is the value of the dependent variable. There are three independent variables with values of 472, 1796 and 7528. As there are three unknowns, we require only four such bond price equations and we can solve for a_1, a_2 and a_3. This may appear slightly daunting if it is to be carried out by hand, and in fact software applications are used to speed the process. Using such a package, we can calculate the values that minimize the sum of squared errors on the model.

If we say that the values are $\hat{a}_1$, $\hat{a}_2$ and $\hat{a}_3$, then the OLS estimate of the discount function, given the market bond prices used to derive the coefficient equations, is given by

$$\hat{d}(t) = 1 + \hat{a}_1 t + \hat{a}_2 t^2 + \hat{a}_3 t^3 .$$
(A5.1.9)

APPENDIX 5.2 Regression splines

This appendix is adapted from Suits *et al* (1978), an excellent account of how a spline function may be fitted using regression methods. The article is very accessible and strongly recommended.

A standard econometric approach is that of piecewise linear regression. This method is not suitable for fitting a relationship that is not purely linear, however (such as a term structure), as illustrated by Figure 5.8.

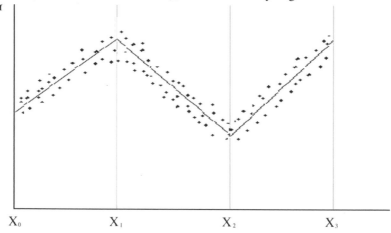

Figure 5.8

To get around this problem, one approach would be to join a series of linear regressions, at arbitrary points specified by the user. This is described by

$$Y = [a_1 + b_1(X - X_0)]D_1 + [a_2 + b_2(X - X_1)]D_2 + [a_3 + b_3(X - X_2)]D_3 + u$$
$$\text{(A5.2.1)}$$

In (A5.2.1) D_i is what is known as a dummy variable, with a value of 1 for all observations whenever $X_{i-1} \leq X \leq X_i$ and a value of 0 at other times. As it stands, (A5.2.1) is discontinuous at X_1 and X_2 but this can be removed by imposing the following constraints:

$$a_2 = a_1 + b_1(X_1 - X_0) \qquad \text{(A5.2.2)}$$
$$a_3 = a_2 + b_2(X_2 - X_1)$$

If (A5.2.2) is substituted into (A5.2.1), the following is obtained:

$$Y = \quad a_1 + b_1[(X - X_0)D_1 + (X_1 - X_0)D_2 + (X_2 - X_1)D_3] + b_2[(X - X_1)D_2$$
$$+ (X_2 - X_1)D_3] + b_3[(X - X_2)D_3] + u$$
$$\text{(A5.2.3)}$$

The expression at (A5.2.3) has converted a piecewise linear regression into a multiple regression. Y is the dependent variable and is regressed on three composite variables, the values for which are obtained from:
- the X data sets
- the values for X_i at the points at which the curve is required to "bend"
- the widths of the selected intervals
- the three dummy variables.

As Suits et al state it would be possible to calculate the coefficients by hand (!) but there are a number of standard software packages that the user can employ to solve the regression.

The disadvantages of piecewise linear regression if used for a number of applications, including yield-curve fitting, are two-fold; first, the derivatives of the function are not continuous, and this discontinuity can seriously distort the curve at the derivative points, which would make curve meaningless at these points. Secondly, and more crucial for yield-curve applications, it may not be obvious where the linear segments should be placed as the scatter diagram of observations may indicate several possibilities. This situation may make it desirable to specify X_i at user-specified (arbitrary) points, and this makes linear regression unsuitable.

To get around these problems we use a spline function. For this the linear function described by (A5.1.1) is replaced with a set of piecewise polynomial functions. It would be possible to use polynomials of any degree, but the most common approach is to use cubic polynomials. The x-axis is divided into three intervals, at the points X_0, X_1, X_2 and X_3. These points are known as knot points and are illustrated in Figure 5.9.

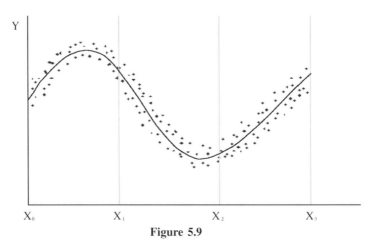

Figure 5.9

In Figure 5.9, the segments chosen, following Suits et al, are at equal intervals. This is not essential to the procedure, however, and for applications, including yield-curve modelling, is not undertaken. Instead, the knots are placed at points where the user thinks the relationship changes most. For example, for the term structure the knots may be placed at 0, 2-, 5- and 10-year maturities. If more than four knots are required – for instance, to go beyond to 20- and 30-year maturities – then the analyst will require a greater number of composite variables, as discussed later. The downside associated with a greater number of intervals is that, as more composite variables are required to fit the curve, additional degrees of freedom are lost.

The regression relationship now becomes

$$Y = [a_1 + b_1(X - X_0) + c_1(X - X_0)^2 + d_1(X - X_0)^3]D_1$$
$$+ [a_2 + b_2(X - X_1) + c_2(X - X_1)^2 + d_2(X - X_1)^3]D_2$$
$$+ [a_3 + b_3(X - X_2) + c_3(X - X_2)^2 + d_3(X - X_2)^3]D_3 + u$$

$$(A5.2.4)$$

where D_i is a dummy variable specified by the interval i.

This time, both the function described by (A5.2.4) and its derivatives are discontinuous at the knot points, but this feature can be removed by applying constraints to the coefficients. The constraints ensure the following:
- for a_i the values of the very short end and the very long end are equal at the start and end knot points
- for b_i the first derivatives, the slope of the left- and right-hand sides of each knot point, are equal
- for c_i the second derivatives are equal.

The constraints are given by (A5.2.5).

$$a_2 = a_1 + b_1(X - X_0) + c_1(X - X_0)^2 + d_1(X - X_0)^3$$
$$a_3 = a_2 + b_2(X - X_1) + c_2(X_2 - X_1)^2 + d_2(X_2 - X_1)^3$$
$$b_2 = b_1 + 2c_1(X_1 - X_0) + 3d_1(X_1 - X_0)^2$$
$$b_3 = b_2 + 2c_2(X_2 - X_1) + 3d_2(X_2 - X_1)^2$$
$$c_2 = c_1 + 3d_1(X_1 - X_0)$$
$$c_3 = c_2 + 3d_2(X_2 - X_1) \qquad \text{(A5.2.5)}$$

Using the expression above, a spline function becomes a multiple regression of the dependent variable Y on five composite variables and Suits et al show this to be

$$Y = a_1 + b_1(X - X_0) + c_1(X - X_0)^2 + d_1(X - X_0)^3 + (d_2 - d_1)(X - X_1)^3 D_1^*$$
$$+ (d_3 - d_2)(X - X_2)^3 D_2^*$$
$$\text{(A5.2.6)}$$

where D_1^* and D_2^* are dummy variables where $D_i^* = 1$ if $X \geq X_i$, at other times the dummy variable is equal to 0. To compute the coefficients of the regression we can use the least-squares procedure, available on standard software packages.

Finally, if we wish to select more than three intervals, that is more than four knot points, which is common in yield-curve applications, we can use (A5.2.7) below, derived in Suits et al (1978). This is a multiple regression, a fitted spline function with $n + 1$ intervals, with knot points at $X_0, X_1, X_2, \ldots, X_{n+1}$ and corresponding dummy variables $D_1^*, D_2^*, \ldots, D_n^*$.

$$Y = a_1 + b_1(X - X_0) + c_1(X - X_0)^2 + d_1(X - X_0)^3 + \sum_{i=1}^{n}(d_{i+1} - d_i)(X - X_i)^3 D_1^*$$
$$\text{(A5.2.7)}$$

With each extra interval, an extra composite variable is required and this results in the loss of one more degree of freedom.

Selected Bibliography and References

Questa (1999) is a good general introduction, see part two in his book. Chapter 2 of Van Deventer and Imai (1997) is also an excellent introduction to yield-curve smoothing, and the book itself is a good general text. James and Webber (2000) is an overview account of the main developments in yield-curve modelling, but assumes a good grounding in calculus and econometrics. For a readable introduction to econometric techniques, see Guajarati (1995). Choudhry et al (2001) is accompanied by a CD-ROM that contains a yield-curve calculator that allows users to calculate spot and forward-yield curves from observed bond-redemption yields. The journal articles we strongly recommend are Deacon and Derry (1994) and Jordan and Mansi (2000) for their accessibility and readability; both are very good accounts.

Anderson, N., Breedon, F., Deacon, M., Derry, A. and Murphy, M., *Estimating and Interpreting the Yield Curve*, Wiley, 1996.

Brennan, M., Schwartz, E., "A Continuous Time Approach to the Pricing of Bonds", *Journal of Banking and Finance* 3, 1979, pp. 133-155

Brooks. C., *Introductory Econometrics for Finance*, Cambridge University Press 2002

Campbell J., Lo A. and MacKinlay C., *The Econometrics of Financial Markets*, Princeton, 1997.

Carleton, W. and Cooper, I., "Estimation and Uses of the Term Structure of Interest Rates", *Journal of Finance*, September 1976, p.1067-1083.

Choudhry, M., Joannas, D., Pereira, R. and Pienaar, R., *Capital Market Instruments: Valuation and Analysis*, FT Prentice Hall, 2001.

Cox, J., Ingersoll, J., and Ross S., "A Theory of the Term Structure of Interest Rates", *Econometrica* 53, 1985, pp. 385-407

Deacon, M. and Derry, A., "Estimating the Term Structure of Interest Rates", Bank of England Working Paper No 24, July 1994.

Goddard, S., *The Smiths: Songs That Saved Your Life*, Reynolds and Hearn 2002

Gujarati, D., *Basic Econometrics*, (3rd edition), McGraw-Hill, 1995.

James, J. and Webber, N., *Interest Rate Modelling*, Wiley, 2000.

Jordan, J. and Mansi, S., "How Well do Constant-Maturity Treasuries Approximate the On-The-Run Term Structure?", *Journal of Fixed Income* 10:2, September 2000, p.35-45.

Langetieg, T.C., Smoot, S.J., *An Appraisal of Alternative Spline Methodologies for Estimating the Term Structure of Interest Rates*, Working Paper, University of Southern California, December 1981

McCulloch, J.H., "Measuring the Term Structure of Interest Rates", *Journal of Business*, January 1971, p.19-31.

Nelson, C. R., and Siegel, A. F., "Parsimonious Modelling of Yield Curves", *Journal of Business* 60, 1985, pp. 473-490

Questa, G., *Fixed Income Analysis for the Global Financial Market*, Wiley, 1999.

Steeley, J.M., "Estimating the Gilt-Eedged Term Structure: Basis Splines and Confidence Intervals", *Journal of Business Finance and Accounting* 18, 1991, p.513-530.

Suits, D., Mason, A. and Chan, L., "Spline Functions Fitted by Standard Regression Methods", *Review of Economics and Statistics* 60, 1978, p.132-139.

Svensson, L., "Estimating and Interpreting Forward Interest Rates: Sweden 1992-1994", Working Paper 114, International Monetary Fund, 1994

Van Deventer, D. and Imai, K., *Financial Risk Analytics*, Irwin, 1997.

Vasicek, O., "An equilibrium characterisation of the term structure", *Journal of Financial Economics* 5, 1977, pp. 177–188.

Vasicek, O. and Fong, H.G., "Term Structure Modelling Using Exponential Splines", *Journal of Finance* 37(2), May 1982, p.339-348

PART

II

Selected Market Instruments

The second part of the book reviews selected instruments traded in the debt capital markets. The products have been chosen to give the reader an idea of the depth of variety in the market. So we consider money market instruments, followed by hybrid securities, mortgage-backed bonds and callable bonds. We also consider index-linked bonds and a specific type of structured product known as a Collateralised Debt Obligation (CDO). Some of the techniques used to analyse these more complex products are also described and explained.

6

The Money Markets

In terms of trading volumes the money markets are the largest and most active market in the world. Money-market securities are securities with maturities of up to 12 months, so they are short-term debt obligations. Money-market debt is an important part of the global financial markets, and facilitates the smooth running of the banking industry as well as providing working capital for industrial and commercial corporate institutions. The market allows issuers, who are financial organisations as well as corporates, to raise funds for short-term periods at relatively low interest rates. These issuers include sovereign governments, who issuer Treasury bills, corporates issuing commercial paper and banks issuing bills and certificates of deposit. At the same time, investors are attracted to the market because the instruments are highly liquid and carry relatively low credit risk. Investors in the money market include banks, local authorities, corporations, money market investment funds and individuals, however the money market essentially is a wholesale market and the denominations of individual instruments are relatively large.

Although the money market has traditionally been defined as the market for instruments maturing in one year or less, frequently the money-market desks of banks trade instruments with maturities of up to two years, both cash and off-balance-sheet.[1] In addition to the cash instruments that go to make up the market, the money markets also consists of a wide range of over-the-counter off-balance-sheet derivative instruments. These instruments are used mainly to establish future borrowing and lending rates, and to hedge

---

[1] The author has personal experience in market-making on a desk that combined cash and derivative instruments of up to two years maturity as well as government bonds of up to three years maturity.

or change existing interest-rate exposure. This activity is carried out by banks, central banks and corporates. The main derivatives are short-term interest-rate futures, forward rate agreements, and short-dated interest-rate swaps.

In this chapter, we review the cash instruments traded in the money market as well as the two main money-market derivatives; interest-rate futures and forward-rate agreements.

Overview

The cash instruments traded in the money market include the following:
- Treasury bill
- Time deposit
- Certificate of Deposit
- Commercial Paper
- Bankers Acceptance
- Bill of exchange.

We can also add the market in repurchase agreements or repo, which are essentially secured cash loans, to this list.

A Treasury bill is used by sovereign governments to raise short-term funds, while certificates of deposit (CDs) are used by banks to raise finance. The other instruments are used by corporates and, occasionally, banks. Each instrument represents an obligation on the borrower to repay the amount borrowed on the maturity date together with interest if this applies. The instruments above fall into one of two main classes of money-market securities: those quoted on a yield basis and those quoted on a discount basis. These two terms are discussed below.

The calculation of interest in the money markets often differs from the calculation of accrued interest in the corresponding bond market. Generally the day-count convention in the money market is the exact number of days that the instrument is held over the number of days in the year. In the sterling market, the year base is 365 days, so the interest calculation for sterling money market instruments is given by (6.1).

$$i = n/365 \qquad (6.1)$$

Money markets that calculate interest based on a 365-day year are listed at Appendix 6.1. However, the majority of currencies, including the US dollar and the euro, calculate interest based on a 360-day base.

Settlement of money-market instruments can be for value today (generally only when traded in before mid-day), tomorrow or two days forward, known as spot.

Securities quoted on a yield basis

Two of the instruments in the list above are yield-based instruments.

Money-market deposits.

These are fixed-interest term deposits of up to one year with banks and securities houses. They are also known as time deposits or clean deposits. They are not negotiable so cannot be liquidated before maturity. The interest rate on the deposit is fixed for the term and related to the London Interbank Offer Rate (LIBOR) of the same term. Interest and capital are paid on maturity.

LIBOR

The term LIBOR or "Libor" comes from London Interbank Offered Rate and is the interest rate at which one London bank offers funds to another London bank of acceptable credit quality in the form of a cash deposit. The rate is "fixed" by the British Bankers Association at 1100 hours every business day morning (in practice the fix is usually about 20 minutes late) by taking the average of the rates supplied by member banks. The term LIBID is the bank's "bid" rate, that is the rate at which it pays for funds in the London market. The quote spread for a selected maturity is therefore the difference between LIBOR and LIBID. The convention in London is to quote the two rates as LIBOR-LIBID, thus matching the yield convention for other instruments. In some other markets the quote convention is reversed. EURIBOR is the interbank rate offered for euros as reported by the European Central Bank. Other money centers also have their rates fixed; so, for example, STIBOR is the Stockholm banking rate, while pre-euro the Portuguese escudo rate fixing out of Lisbon was LISBOR.

Libor fixes are reported each day on a number of newswire services. Figure 6.1 shows screen BBAM from Bloomberg, which is the Libor fixing page, as at 2 March 2004.

```
GRAB                                                    Govt   BBAM

BRITISH BANKERS'
ASSOCIATION                                           Page 1 of 4
03/02    16:27 GMT  [BRITISH BANKERS ASSOCIATION LIBOR RATES]              3750
[02/03/04]      RATES AT 11:00 LONDON TIME 02/03/2004        02/03 11:55 GMT
  CCY   |   USD   |   GBP   |   CAD   |   EUR   |   JPY    |  EUR 365
  O/N   | 1.05500 | 4.03125 | 2.31167 | 2.04875 |SNO.03250 | 2.07720
  1WK   | 1.07375 | 4.09188 | 2.30833 | 2.04863 | 0.03375  | 2.07708
  2WK   | 1.07875 | 4.12250 | 2.30333 | 2.04750 | 0.03625  | 2.07594
  1MO   | 1.10000 | 4.15625 | 2.29667 | 2.05163 | 0.04125  | 2.08012
  2MO   | 1.11000 | 4.19125 | 2.26667 | 2.05150 | 0.04688  | 2.07999
  3MO   | 1.12000 | 4.23500 | 2.24667 | 2.05025 | 0.05250  | 2.07873
  4MO   | 1.13000 | 4.27875 | 2.23000 | 2.04888 | 0.05663  | 2.07734
  5MO   | 1.15000 | 4.32750 | 2.21833 | 2.04663 | 0.05875  | 2.07506
  6MO   | 1.17250 | 4.37250 | 2.20667 | 2.04863 | 0.06500  | 2.07708
  7MO   | 1.19875 | 4.41500 | 2.20333 | 2.05600 | 0.07025  | 2.08456
  8MO   | 1.22750 | 4.45625 | 2.20333 | 2.06300 | 0.07225  | 2.09165
  9MO   | 1.25625 | 4.49875 | 2.20333 | 2.07363 | 0.07800  | 2.10243
 10MO   | 1.29625 | 4.54000 | 2.21333 | 2.09000 | 0.08250  | 2.11903
 11MO   | 1.33625 | 4.58000 | 2.22333 | 2.10150 | 0.08438  | 2.13069
 12MO   | 1.37625 | 4.62000 | 2.23333 | 2.11613 | 0.09000  | 2.14552

Australia 61 2 9777 8600     Brazil 5511 3048 4500      Europe 44 20 7330 7500      Germany 49 69 920410
Hong Kong 852 2977 6000 Japan 81 3 3201 8900 Singapore 65 6212 1000 U.S. 1 212 318 2000 Copyright 2004 Bloomberg L.P.
                                                                    G926-802-2 02-Mar-04 16:27:32
```

Figure 6.1 Page BBAM on Bloomberg.
©Bloomberg L.P. Used with permission.

The effective rate on a money-market deposit is the annual equivalent interest rate for an instrument with a maturity of less than one year.

Certificates of Deposit

Certificates of Deposit (CDs) are receipts from banks for deposits that have been placed with them. They were first introduced in the sterling market in 1958. The deposits themselves carry a fixed rate of interest related to LIBOR and have a fixed term to maturity, so cannot be withdrawn before maturity. However, the certificates themselves can be traded in a secondary market; that is, they are negotiable.[2] CDs are therefore very similar to negotiable money market deposits, although the yields are about 0.15% below the equivalent deposit rates because of the added benefit of liquidity. Most CDs issued are of between one and three months maturity, although they do trade in maturities of one to five years. Interest is paid on maturity except for CDs lasting longer than one year, where interest is paid annually or, occasionally, semi-annually.

Banks, merchant banks and building societies issue CDs to raise funds to finance their business activities. A CD will have a stated interest rate and

---

[2] A small number of CDs are non-negotiable.

fixed maturity date and can be issued in any denomination. On issue, a CD is sold for face value, so the settlement proceeds of a CD on issue always equal its nominal value. The interest is paid, together with the face amount, on maturity. The interest rate is sometimes called the coupon, but unless the CD is held to maturity this will not equal the yield, which is of course the current rate available in the market and varies over time. In the United States, CDs are available in smaller denomination amounts to retail investors.[3] The largest group of CD investors, however, are banks themselves, money-market funds, corporates and local-authority treasurers. Unlike coupons on bonds, which are paid in rounded amounts, CD coupon is calculated to the exact day.

CD yields. The coupon quoted on a CD is a function of the credit quality of the issuing bank, and its expected liquidity level in the market and, of course, the maturity of the CD, as this will be considered relative to the money-market yield curve. As CDs are issued by banks as part of their short-term funding and liquidity requirement, issue volumes are driven by the demand for bank loans and the availability of alternative sources of funds for bank customers. The credit quality of the issuing bank is the primary consideration, however. In the sterling market, the lowest yield is paid by "clearer" CDs, which are CDs issued by the clearing banks such as Royal Bank of Scotland, HSBC and Barclays plc. In the US market, "prime" CDs, issued by highly-rated domestic banks, trade at a lower yield than non-prime CDs. In both markets CDs issued by foreign banks such as French or Japanese banks will trade at higher yields.

Euro-CDs, which are CDs issued in a different currency from the home currency, also trade at higher yields in the US because of reserve and deposit-insurance restrictions.

If the current market price of the CD including accrued interest is P and the current quoted yield is r, the yield can be calculated given the price, using (6.2).

$$r = \left\{ \frac{M}{P} \times \left[1 + C\left(\frac{N_{im}}{B}\right) \right] - 1 \right\} \times \left(\frac{B}{N_{sm}} \right) \qquad (6.2)$$

The price can be calculated given the yield using (6.3).

$$P = M \times \left[1 + C\left(\frac{N_{im}}{B}\right) \right] / \left[1 + r\left(\frac{N_{sm}}{B}\right) \right] \qquad (6.3)$$

---

[3] This was first introduced by Merrill Lynch in 1982.

where

C is the quoted coupon on the CD
M is the face value of the CD
B is the year day-basis (365 or 360)
F is the maturity value of the CD
N_{im} is the number of days between issue and maturity
N_{sm} is the number of days between settlement and maturity
N_{is} is the number of days between issue and settlement.

After issue, a CD can be traded in the secondary market. The secondary market in CDs in the UK is very liquid, and CDs will trade at the rate prevalent at the time, which will invariably be different from the coupon rate on the CD at issue. When a CD is traded in the secondary market, the settlement proceeds will need to take into account interest that has accrued on the paper and the different rate at which the CD has now been dealt. The formula for calculating the settlement figure is given at (6.4), which applies to the sterling market and its 365-day count basis.

$$\text{Proceeds} = \frac{M \times \text{Tenor} \times C \times 100 + 36500}{\text{Days remaining} \times r \times 100 + 36500} \qquad (6.4)$$

The tenor of a CD is the life of the CD in days, while days remaining is the number of days left to maturity from the time of trade. The return on holding a CD is given by (6.5).

$$\text{Return} = \left[\frac{1 + \text{purchase yield} \times \frac{\text{days from purchase to maturity}}{B}}{1 + \text{sale yield} \times \frac{\text{days from sale to maturity}}{B}} - 1\right] \times \frac{B}{\text{days held}}$$

$$(6.5)$$

Securities quoted on a discount basis

The remaining money-market instruments are all quoted on a discount basis, and so are known as "discount" instruments. This means that they are issued at a discount to face value, and are redeemed on maturity at face value. Treasury bills, bills of exchange, bankers acceptances and commercial paper are examples of money-market securities that are quoted on a discount basis; that is, they are sold on the basis of a discount to par. The difference between the price paid at the time of purchase and the redemption value (par) is the interest earned by the holder of the paper. Explicit interest is not paid on discount instruments. Rather, interest is reflected implicitly in the difference between the discounted issue price and the par value received at maturity. Note that in some markets CP is quoted on a yield basis, but not in the UK or in the US, where they are discount instruments.

Treasury bills

Treasury bills or T-bills are short-term government "IOUs" of short duration, often three-month maturity. For example, if a bill is issued on 10th January, it will mature on 10th April. Bills of one-month and six-month maturity are also issued, but only rarely in the UK market. On maturity, the holder of a T-bill receives the par value of the bill by presenting it to the Central Bank. In the UK,
  A sterling T-bill with £10 million face value issued for 91 days will most such bills are denominated in sterling but issues are also made in euros. In a capital market, T-bill yields are regarded as the risk-free yield, as they represent the yield from short-term government debt. In emerging markets, they are often the most liquid instruments available for investors.be redeemed on maturity at £10 million. If the three-month yield at the time of issue is 5.25%, the price of the bill at issue is:

$$P = \frac{10m}{(1 + 0.0525 \times \frac{91}{365})} = £9,870,800.69 \ .$$

In the UK and US markets the interest rate on discount instruments is quoted as a discount rate rather than a yield. This is the amount of discount expressed as an annualised percentage of the face value, and not as a percentage of the original amount paid. By definition, the discount rate is always lower than the corresponding yield. If the discount rate on a bill is d, then the amount of discount is given by (6.6) below.

$$d_{value} = M \times d \times \frac{n}{B} \qquad (6.6)$$

The price P paid for the bill is the face value minus the discount amount, given by (6.7).

$$P = 100 \times \left[1 - \frac{d \cdot \left(\frac{N_{sm}}{365} \right)}{100} \right] \qquad (6.7)$$

If we know the yield on the bill, then we can calculate its price at issue by using the simple present-value formula, as shown at (6.8).

$$P = M \, / \left[1 + r\left(\frac{N_{sm}}{365}\right) \right] \tag{6.8}$$

The discount rate d for T-bills is calculated using (6.9).

$$d = (1 - P) \times \frac{B}{n} \tag{6.9}$$

The relationship between discount rate and true yield is given by (6.10).

$$d = \frac{r}{(1 + r \times \frac{n}{B})}$$

$$r = \frac{d}{1 - d \times \frac{n}{B}} \tag{6.10}$$

If a T-bill is traded in the secondary market, the settlement proceeds from the trade are calculated using (6.11).

$$\text{Proceeds} = M - \left(\frac{M \times \text{days remaining} \times d}{B \times 100} \right) \tag{6.11}$$

Bond equivalent yield. In certain markets, including the UK and US markets, the yields on government bonds that have a maturity of less than one year are compared to the yields of Treasury bills. However, before the comparison can be made, the yield on a bill must be converted to a "bond equivalent" yield. Therefore, the bond-equivalent yield of a US Treasury bill is the coupon of a theoretical Treasury bond trading at par that has an identical maturity date. If the bill has 182 days or less until maturity, the calculation required is the conventional conversion from discount rate to yield, with the exception that it is quoted on a 365-day basis (in the UK market, the quote basis is essentially the same unless it is a leap year. So the conversion element in (6.12) is not necessary). The calculation for the US market is given by (6.12).

$$r = \frac{d}{(1 - d \times \frac{days}{360})} \times \frac{365}{360} \tag{6.12}$$

where r is the bond-equivalent yield that is being calculated.

Note that if there is a bill and a bond that mature on the same day in a period under 182 days, the bond-equivalent yield will not precisely the same as the yield quoted for the bond in its final coupon period, although it is a very close approximation. This is because the bond is quoted on actual/actual basis, so its yield is actually made up of two-times the actual number of days in the interest period.

Bankers acceptances

A bankers acceptance is a written promise issued by a borrower to a bank to repay borrowed funds. The lending bank lends funds and in return accepts the bankers acceptance. The acceptance is negotiable and can be sold in the secondary market. The investor who buys the acceptance can collect the loan on the day that repayment is due. If the borrower defaults, the investor has legal recourse to the bank that made the first acceptance. Bankers acceptances are also know as bills of exchange, bank bills, trade bills or commercial bills.

Essentially, bankers acceptances are instruments created to facilitate commercial trade transactions. The instrument is called a bankers acceptance because a bank accepts the ultimate responsibility to repay the loan to its holder. The use of bankers acceptances to finance commercial transactions is known as acceptance financing. The transactions for which acceptances are created include the import and export of goods, the storage and shipping of goods between two overseas countries, where neither the importer nor the exporter is based in the home country,[4] and the storage and shipping of goods between two entities based as home. Acceptances are discount instruments and are purchased by banks, local authorities and money-market investment funds. The rate that a bank charges a customer for issuing a bankers acceptance is a function of the rate at which the bank thinks it will be able to sell it in the secondary market. A commission is added to this rate. For ineligible bankers acceptances (see below) the issuing bank will add an amount to offset the cost of the additional reserve requirements.

Eligible bankers acceptance. An accepting bank that chooses to retain a bankers acceptance in its portfolio may be able to use it as collateral for a loan obtained from the central bank during open-market operations – for example, from the Bank of England in the UK and the Federal Reserve in the US. Not all acceptances are eligible to be used as collateral in this way, as they must meet certain criteria set by the central bank. The main requirement for eligibility is that the acceptance must be within a certain maturity band (a maximum of six months in the US and three months in the UK), and that it must have been created to finance a self-liquidating

---

[4] A bankers acceptance created to finance such a transaction is known as a third-party acceptance.

commercial transaction. In the US, eligibility is also important because the Federal Reserve imposes a reserve requirement on funds raised via bankers acceptances that are ineligible. Bankers acceptances sold by an accepting bank are potential liabilities of the bank, but reserve imposes a limit on the amount of eligible bankers acceptances that a bank may issue. Bills eligible for deposit at a central bank enjoy a finer rate than ineligible bills, and also act a benchmark for prices in the secondary market.

Commercial paper

Commercial paper (CP) is a short-term money-market funding instrument issued by corporates. In the UK and US, it is a discount instrument, with sterling paper being dealt with on a 365-day basis. They trade essentially as T-bills but with higher yields as they are unsecured corporate obligations. CP is an important part of the US money market and began as a US instrument before being introduced in other money centers around the world. The instrument ranges in maturity from 30 to 270 days (although typical maturities are 30 to 90 days) and is usually issued in response to investor demand or for short-term working-capital considerations. As the paper is unsecured, investor sentiment usually requires that any issue be rated by a rating agency such as Moody's Investors Services or Standard & Poor's, although high-yield CP also exists.

Another significant market exists in Euro-commercial paper (ECP), which is similar in concept to CP but is not restricted to the 270-day maturity.[5] The market in ECP exists in money centers globally. Standard settlement of ECP is for spot value (which is two business days forward), whereas standard settlement of US and UK settlement is on a same-day basis. ECP can be issued both as a discount instrument or a yield-bearing instrument, although the latter is rarer.

For yield-bearing ECP, the calculation of settlement proceeds in the secondary market is given by (6.13).

$$\text{Proceeds} = M \times \left[\frac{1 + \frac{C \times T}{36000}}{1 + \frac{r \times N}{36000}} \right] \qquad (6.13)$$

where

---

[5] In the US market this is a Securities and Exchange Commission requirement.

M is the face amount
C is the coupon
r is the yield
T is the paper's original maturity or tenor
N is the time from settlement to maturity.

For paper issued on a discount basis, the proceeds are given by

$$\text{Proceeds} = \left[\frac{M}{1 + \frac{r \times N}{36000}} \right] \qquad (6.14)$$

The majority of ECP is issued in US dollars, although euro, sterling and Japanese yen are also popular currencies.

Asset-backed commercial paper

During the 1980s and 1990s the rise in popularity in the use of securitisation as a means of diversifying bank liquidity led to the introduction of short-term money market paper backed by the cash flows from other assets, known as *asset-backed commercial paper* (ABCP). Vehicles through which ABCP is issued are usually called *conduits*. Securitisation is looked at in greater detail elsewhere in this book, here we discuss the basic concept of ABCP and Conduit vehicles.

Generally securitisation is used as a funding instrument by companies for three main reasons: it offers lower-cost funding compared with than traditional bank loan or bond financing; it is a mechanism by which assets such as corporate loans or mortgages can be removed from the balance sheet, thus improving the lenders return on assets or return on equity ratios; and it increases a borrowers funding options. When entering into securitisation, an entity may issue term securities against assets into the public or private market, or it may issue commercial paper via a specially incorporated legal entity known as a special vehicle (this is the conduit). These conduits are usually sponsored by commercial banks.[6] The assets that may be securitised range from corporate loans, mortgages and office rents to equipment lease receivables and other receivables.

Entities usually access the commercial paper market in order to secure permanent financing, rolling over individual issues as part of a longer-term *programme* and using interest-rate swaps to arrange a fixed rate if required.

---

[6] A conduit is essentially an SPV through which asset-backed paper is issued. There does not seem to be any real reason why "conduit" is reserved for the ABCP market and "SPV" for the ABS market. Both terms mean essentially the same thing.

Conventional CP issues are typically supported by a line of credit from a commercial bank, and so this form of financing is in effect a form of bank funding.

Evolution of ABCP programmes

Once the basic premise that assets may be securitised to provide cash flow backing for an issue of liabilities (debt financing) is accepted, there is in principle no significant difference between this process being used to originate short-term paper in the form of CP or long-term paper in the form of bonds such as ABS. A key difference between CP and ABS is of course the shorter time required for refinancing with the former: a CP issuer must roll-over paper every a maximum of every 270 days (or 364 days with euro-CP). As with conventional CP programmes, as paper matures it is redeemed with the proceeds of a roll-over issue. If for any reason a roll-over issue cannot be placed in the market (for example there is a market correction and investor confidence disappears, or the Issuer suffers a credit rating downgrade), the Issuer will need to call on a bank lone of credit to repay investors. This line of credit is known as a *liquidity facility*. The liquidity facility acts as a form of credit enhancement to investors, providing comfort that in the last resort, there will be sufficient funds available to repay them. Another form of credit enhancement is over-collateralisation, which is when (say) 115% worth of assets are used as securitisation backing for issue of 100% nominal of paper.

ABCP conduits have followed the evolutionary path thus:

■ First generation: A fully-supported programme backed by 100% Letters-of-Credit (LOC) from sponsor banks

■ Second generation: Partially-supported programmes with multi-asset backing, with 100% bank LOC and 10-15% credit enhancement

■ Third generation: Security arbitrage vehicles that are unsupported by bank LOCs and have minimal credit enhancement. These conduits issue both CP and medium-term notes (MTNs), so are also known as Structured Investment Vehicles (SIVs)

■ Fourth generation: Multi-asset conduits also viewed as finance companies in their own right, with credit ratings based on quality of underlying assets. There is no bank LOC and the companies invest in high-quality assets and project finance programmes. Credit enhancement in SIV-type structures may take the form of subordinated notes and capital notes or "equity".

Figure 6.2 shows a single-seller ABCP structure.

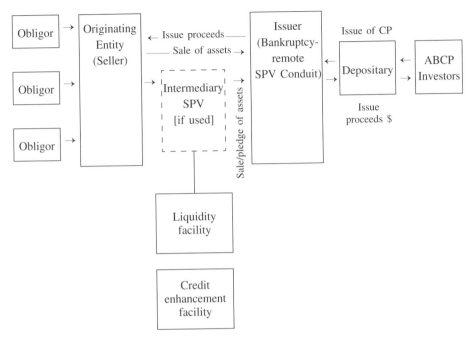

Figure 6.2 AB1 Single-seller ABCP Conduit structure

A single-seller conduit is established for the sale of assets originated by one entity. Typically it is 100% supported by a bank liquidity facility and by 10% credit enhancement. The liquidity provided is usually required by the credit ratings agencies to have a short-term rating of A-1/P-1/F-1.

A multi-seller conduit would have more than one seller into the conduit SPV.

Liquidity and credit enhancement

ABCP conduits require liquidity support to cover 100% of their outstanding CP for 364 days. A liquidity facility will guarantee timely repayment of CP as it matures, and is vital because most conduits do not match the term structure of their assets and liabilities. Facilities are typically required to purchase assets, in accordance with a pre-specified formula. Generally the facility will be called upon in the event of bankruptcy occurring with respect to the conduit, if it otherwise unable to honour its liabilities as they fall due, or if the underlying assets become rated at Caa1 or lower by Moodys and CCC+ or lower by Standard & Poor's and Fitch.

Liquidity support can be in the form of either a Liquidity Asset Purchase agreement (LAPA) or a Liquidity Loan agreement (LLA), which differ as follows:

- LAPA: the liquidity provider(s) purchase non-defaulted assets when called upon;
- LLA: the liquidity provider(s) lend money to the conduit in return for security pledge over the underlying asset cash flows.

A liquidity facility also covers other risks such as dilution, hedging and legal issues.

Other forms of credit enhancement are also set in place. If it is transaction-specific, credit enhancement provides the first layer of protection against shortfalls from the underlying collateral on specific asset pools, typically in the form of over-collateralisation, excess spread, a bank LOC or surety bond. The main features are that they are maintained as protection against delinquencies, losses or dilution, and that reserves are generally based on a multiple of the seller's historical delinquency, net losses and dilutions of the pool of assets.

If it is programme-wide, credit enhancement provides the second-layer of protection coverage for repurchase of cash receivables or guarantee of losses on the receivables. It supplements the seller's reserves, and will be used only after the seller's reserves are depleted. Its main features are:

- it is calculated as a percentage of the entire ABCP conduit;
- it is mainly in the form of a LOC, surety bond, subordinated notes, cash collateral bank account, or a total return swap;
- traditional receivables and loan programmes are sized at a minimum 5% of the total size and fluctuates in accordance with the credit quality of the asset pool.

Note that the enhancement for security arbitrage conduits and SIVs is usually at 0%, provided that the underlying assets are rated at AA-/Aa3/AA- or better.

Structural development

During 2001 and 2002 new structures were observed in the market that built on the first- and second-generation conduits first introduced. These focused on arrangements that reduced the need for bank liquidity support, and set up alternative sources of liquidity and credit enhancement. This was a response to the increasing difficulty in arranging traditional liquidity: for instance, the number of banks rated A-1/P-1 was in decline, banks were conserving their liquidity lines, investors were demanding higher return to reflect the true level of risk involved in these vehicles, and the growing popularity of conduits themselves made liquidity more expensive.

The newer generation of conduits featured alternative sources of liquidity including:

- capturing liquidity from the underlying assets, through matching asset/liability profiles, and capturing the excess spread between assets and liabilities;
- using non-bank liquidity providers, such as highly-rated entities;
- using investors as proxy liquidity providers, through issue of extendible notes and structured liquidity notes, and through issue of long-dated MTNs;
- use of derivative structures, such as total return swaps, credit default swaps and credit–linked notes;
- using monoline insurance firms to provide support backing to the conduit.

Vehicles such as arbitrage conduits and SIVs have much lower levels of credit enhancement, typically ranging from 0%-4% rather than to 10%-15%.

Another development in the US and euro-CP market is floating-rate CP. Unlike traditional CP which is discount paper, this is issued as interest-bearing CP at par. The paper is rolled typically at one-month or three-month Libor reset dates. Interest is paid to investors at each Libor reset date. Floating-rate paper is preferred by issuers to discount CP if they are expecting short-term interest rates to fall.

The newer vehicles securitise a wider range of assets, including equities and synthetic structures. We consider the synthetic ABCP conduit next.

The synthetic ABCP conduit

The latest development in conduits is the synthetic structure. Exactly as with synthetic structured credit products, this uses credit derivatives to make an economic transfer of risk and exposure between the originator and the issuer, so that there is not necessarily a sale of assets from the originator to the Issuer. We describe synthetic conduits by means of an hypothetical transaction, "Golden Claw Funding", which is a total return swap-backed ABCP structure.

Hypothetical case study: Golden Claw Funding

Figure 6.3 is a structure diagram for a synthetic ABCP vehicle that uses total return swaps (TRS) in its structure. It illustrates an hypothetical conduit, Golden Claw Funding Ltd, which issues paper into both the US CP market and the Euro CP market. It has been set up as a funding vehicle, with the originator accessing the CP market to fund assets that it holds on its balance sheet. The originator can be a bank, non-bank financial institution such as a hedge fund, or a corporate. In our case study the originator is a Hedge Fund called ABC Fund Limited.

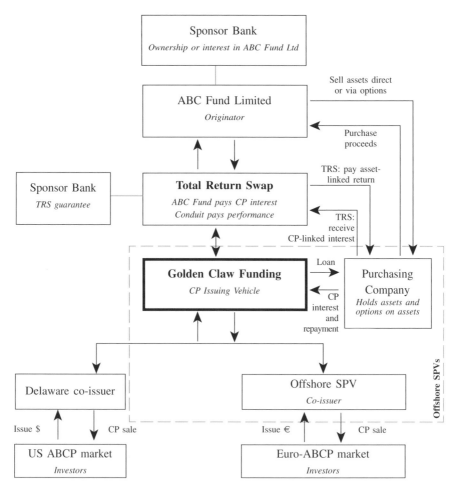

Figure 6.3 Synthetic ABCP conduit, hypothetical deal "Golden Claw Funding"

The structure shown at figure 6.3 has the following features:
- the CP issuance vehicle and the Purchase Company (PC) are based off-shore at a location such as Jersey, Ireland or Cayman Islands;
- the conduit issues CP in the USD market via a co-issuer based in Delaware. It also issues euro-CP via an off-shore SPV;
- proceeds of the CP issue are loaned to the PC, which uses these funds to purchase assets from the Originator. It also acquires an "interest" in assets that are held by ABC Fund Limited via an option called a zero-strike call (ZSC). (We describe ZSCs in the box). If assets are purchased directly onto the balance sheet of the PC, this is akin to what happens in a conventional ABCP structure. If interests in the assets are acquired via a ZSC then they are not actually sold to the PC, and remain on the balance sheet of ABC Fund Limited. Assets can be bonds, structured finance bonds, equities, mutual funds, hedge fund shares, convertible bonds, synthetic products and private equity;
- simultaneously as it purchases assets or ZSCs on assets, the PC enters into a TRS contract with ABC Fund Limited, under which it pays the performance on the assets and receives interest on the CP proceeds it has used to purchase assets and ZSCs. The TRS is the means by which ABC Fund retains the economic interest in the assets it is funding, and the means by which PC receives the interest it needs to pay back to Golden Claw as CP matures.
- the issue vehicle itself may also purchase assets and ZSCs, so we show at figure 6.3 that it also has a TRS between itself and ABC Fund Limited

We reproduce the term sheet for the TRS contract below. This states that the notional value and maturity of the TRS matches those of the CP issue.

The Golden Claw structure is a means by which funds can be raised without a true sale structure. The TRS is guaranteed by the sponsor bank, so will ensure that the conduit is rated at the short-term rating of the sponsor bank. As CP matures, it will be repaid with a roll-over issue of CP, with interest received via the TRS contract. If CP cannot rolled over, then the PC or the Issuer will need to sell assets or exercise ZSCs in assets to repay principal, or otherwise the TRS guarantor will need to cover the repayment.

Zero-strike calls

A zero-strike call (ZSC) is a call option with strike price set at zero. It is written on an underlying asset such as a bond or shares in a hedge fund, and is sold at par. It is essentially a means by which an interest in illiquid assets can be transferred to a customer. Consider the two following examples showing how ZSCs might be used:

- Buying a ZSC: a hedge fund of funds wishes to acquire an interest in assets that are not on its balance sheet. It buys a ZSC from a hedge fund that holds the assets, who writes the ZSC. If the asset appreciates in value, the gain is realised by the hedge fund of funds.
- Selling a ZSC: a hedge fund of funds holds assets on its books, which a client (investor) wishes to acquire an interest in. The fund of funds writes a ZSC to the investor, enabling the investor to acquire an interest in the assets.

These examples are illustrated below.

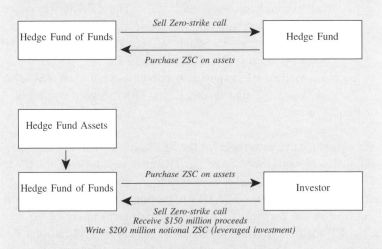

Frequently the ZSC is transacted as part of a leveraged investment play, so that in the example above described as "selling a ZSC", the fund of funds will invest its own funds in a leveraged proportion to those of the client. For example, for every $25 invested by the client, the fund of funds will invest $75, as part of a notional $100 investment in a ZSC option.

Synthetic ABCP conduit: example TRS term sheet

To illustrate the terms of the TRS used in the Golden Claw Funding Limited hypothetical case study, we produce below an example of what the term sheet for the TRS contract might look like. This describes the terms of the TRS used in the structure and has been produced for the Sponsoring Bank that is the guarantor to the TRS.

ABC Fund Limited
Golden Claw FUNDING LIMITED
TOTAL RETURN SWAP TERM SHEET

Programme summary
Golden Claw will raise money in the US CP and Euro CP market. It will lend this money to Golden Claw Purchase Company (PC). PC will buy assets such as bonds or equity from ABC Fund Limited. Golden Claw PC simultaneously enters into a Total Return Swap (TRS) contract with ABC Fund Limited. The TRS contract is the means by which ABC Fund Limited retains the price risk of the assets. Via the TRS, Golden Claw PC will transfer the return on the assets to ABC Fund Limited, and receive sufficient interest from ABC Fund Limited to pay Golden Claw the interest on maturing CP. The mark-to-market on the TRS will be set in line with CP repayment dates, and is guaranteed by the Sponsor Bank.

General Terms   A Total Return Swap (TRS) is entered into between Golden Claw PC and ABC Fund Limited. One leg of the TRS pays the performance of the underlying assets, while the other leg will pay the maturing CP interest. These payments are made two days after the TRS reset dates, which coincide with the CP issue maturity date.

A TRS is entered into simultaneously each time CP is issued. The notional value of each TRS will be equivalent to the outstanding nominal value of each CP issue. The maturity of the TRS will match the maturity of the CP issue.

Assets   Each of the Issuer and each PC will own a portfolio of assets of a particular type. Initially, the types of assets will include debt securities; equity securities; and hedge fund investments (including zero strike calls relating to such investments).

Total Return Swaps The Issuer and the PC will enter into a TRS ("Swap") with the Swap Counterparty (as defined below). The aggregate amount paid to the Issuer or PC under the Swap shall be sufficient to pay: (a) the interest payable on the CP issued to fund the related Assets through maturity and (b) expenses of the Issuer or the PC, including the fees of the Issuer's or PC's agents, taxes, rating agency and legal fees. All payments received in relation to the Assets held by the Issuer or the PC, will be paid to the related Swap Counterparty. Each Swap Agreement may also provide for periodic transfer (a) by the Issuer or the PC to the Swap Counterparty of market value increases of the related Assets and (b) by the Swap Counterparty to the Issuer or the PC, of market value decreases of the related Assets.

Swap counterparty Sponsor bank.

TRS Bookings The Issuer or PC will enter into a TRS with ABC Fund Limited under which the Issuer or PC will (a) pay the performance on the TRS reference asset to KBC Bank and (b) receive proceeds equivalent to maturing CP interest and costs. ABC Fund Limited will enter into a TRS with Issuer or PC under which it will (b) pay proceeds equivalent to maturing CP interest and other costs and (a) receive the performance on the TRS reference assets. The notional value of the Swap will be equal to the nominal value of outstanding CP. A Swap will be written each time there is an issue of CP. Net payments will be exchanged on Swap payment dates (value two days after Swap reset date), which will coincide with CP maturity payment date and Swap maturity.

Issue mechanics Golden Claw will issue CP on Trade date for settlement on T+2. Simultaneously, on T+0 PC will (a) enter into a loan with Golden Claw for the CP settlement proceeds, value date T+2, loan to expire on CP maturity date (b) will transact to purchase assets to the value of the loan from ABC Fund Limited, or ZSCs written on assets held by ABC Fund Limited, for asset delivery to PC on T+2 (c) will enter into a TRS agreement with ABC Fund Limited, for value date T+2, for the nominal value of the CP issue. The TRS reset date will be two days prior to CP maturity. ABC Fund Limited will pay CP interest and receive asset performance on this Swap.On T+0 ABC Fund Limited will enter into a TRS with PC for nominal value of CP issue, for value T+2. PC will pay asset performance and receive CP maturing interest on this Swap.

The synthetic ABCP conduit is a good example of the flexibility of structures that combine securitisation techniques and credit derivatives.

US Treasury bills

The Treasury-bill market in the United States is one of the most liquid and transparent debt markets in the world. Consequently, the bid-offer spread on these bills is very narrow. The Treasury issues bills at a weekly auction each Monday, made up of 91-day and 182-day bills. Every fourth week, the Treasury also issues 52-week bills as well. As a result there are large numbers of Treasury bills outstanding at any one time. The interest earned on Treasury bills is not liable to state and local income taxes.

Federal funds

Commercial banks in the US are required to keep reserves on deposit at the Federal Reserve. Banks with reserves in excess of required reserves can lend these funds to other banks, and these interbank loans are called federal funds or fed funds and are usually overnight loans. Through this market, commercial banks with excess funds are able to lend to banks that are short of reserves, thus facilitating liquidity. The transactions are very large denominations, and are lent at the fed funds rate, which is a very volatile interest rate because it fluctuates with market shortages.

Prime rate

The prime interest rate in the US is often said to represent the rate at which commercial banks lend to their most creditworthy customers. In practice, many loans are made at rates below the prime rate, so the prime rate is not the best rate at which highly rated firms may borrow. Nevertheless, the prime rate is a benchmark indicator of the level of US money-market rates, and is often used as a reference rate for floating-rate instruments. As the market for bank loans is highly competitive, all commercial banks quote a single prime rate, and the rate for all banks changes simultaneously.

Market rates and prices

Money market yields and prices can be determined from a number of sources. Here we show some key Bloomberg screens, which are MMR, MMCV and BTMM, as at 20th October 2003.

Figure 6.4 shows US money-market deposit rates. These are cash rates for overnight to 11-month terms. Figure 6.5 shows the same page for the Philippines money market, in this case prime bank-offered rates.

GRAB   Govt   MMR

8:23   USD Money Market Rates   Page 1 / 4
94<GO> View News.

SECURITY	TIME	BID	ASK	CHANGE	HIGH	LOW	PRV CLS
Fed Funds							
2)FDFD	10/17	.9375	1.0000	--	1.0000	1.0000	1.0000
Depo (Non-Japanese							
4)O/N	8:05	.9400	1.0600	+.0400	1.0650	.9500	.9900
5)USD Depo 2 Day	8:05	.9300	1.0500	+.0150	1.0250	.9950	1.0100
6)USD Depo 3 Day	8:05	.9300	1.0500	+.0150	1.0250	1.0050	1.0100
7)USD Depo 1 Wk	8:05	.9600	1.0800	+.0200	1.0500	1.0250	1.0300
8)USD Depo 2 Wk	8:05	.9800	1.1000	+.0200	1.0700	1.0500	1.0500
9)USD DEPO 3 Wk	8:05	.9800	1.1000	+.0200	1.0750	1.0600	1.0550
10)USD Depo 1 Mo	8:05	.9800	1.1000	+.0150	1.0750	1.0100	1.0600
11)USD Depo 2 Mo	8:05	.9900	1.1100	+.0150	1.0850	1.0200	1.0700
12)USD Depo 3 Mo	8:05	1.0400	1.1600	+.0200	1.1400	1.0450	1.1200
13)USD Depo 4 Mo	8:05	1.0700	1.1900	+.0575	1.1650	1.1050	1.1075
14)USD Depo 5 Mo	8:05	1.0900	1.2100	+.0625	1.1850	1.1275	1.1225
15)USD Depo 6 Mo	8:05	1.1300	1.2500	+.0725	1.2200	1.1475	1.1475
16)USD Depo 7 Mo	8:05	1.1600	1.2800	+.0350	1.2550	1.2050	1.2150
17)USD Depo 8 Mo	8:05	1.2000	1.3200	+.0200	1.2950	1.2550	1.2650
18)USD Depo 9 Mo	8:05	1.2400	1.3600	+.0150	1.3400	1.2850	1.3150
19)USD Depo 10 Mo	8:03	1.3500	1.3800	--	1.3950	1.3550	1.3650
20)USD Depo 11 Mo	8:03	1.4000	1.4300	+.0100	1.4350	1.3950	1.4050

Australia 61 2 9777 8600   Brazil 5511 3048 4500   Europe 44 20 7330 7500   Germany 49 69 920410
Hong Kong 852 2977 6000 Japan 81 3 3201 8900 Singapore 65 6212 1000 U.S. 1 212 318 2000 Copyright 2003 Bloomberg L.P.
G926-802-0 20-Oct-03 8:23:33

Figure 6.4 US money market rates
©Bloomberg L.P. Used with permission

GRAB   Govt   BIL

8:24   PRIME RATES BY BANKS   Page 1 / 3
94<GO> View News.

SECURITY	TICKER	CUR VAL	DATE	PREVIOUS	DATE	CHANGE	PCT CHN
1)GENERAL AVE	PLNDAVE	8.6134	10/17	8.6134	10/16	--	--
Local Banks							
3)ASIA UNITED	PLNDAUB	9.6290	10/17	9.6290	10/16	--	--
4)BNK OF COMMERCE	PLNDCOM	8.6290	10/17	8.6290	10/16	--	--
5)EAST WEST	PLNDEWB	10.5060	10/17	10.5060	10/16	--	--
6)EXPORT & INDS	PLNDEXIN	8.6290	10/17	8.6290	10/16	--	--
7)I-BANK	PLNDIBAN	10.6290	10/17	10.6290	10/16	--	--
8)PBCOM	PLNDPCOM	9.5000	10/17	9.5000	10/16	--	--
9)PHILTRUST	PLNDPTC	8.6290	10/17	8.6290	10/16	--	--
10)VETERANS BANK	PLNDPVB	9.0000	10/17	9.0000	10/16	--	--
11)TA BANK	PLNDTAB	8.9120	10/17	8.9120	10/16	--	--
Subsidiary FB's							
13)UOB	PLNDUOB	10.3750	10/17	10.3750	10/16	--	--
14)SANTANDER	PLNDBSAN	7.7500	10/17	7.7500	10/16	--	--
15)CHINATRUST	PLNDCHIB	8.8790	10/17	8.8790	10/16	--	--
16)MAY BANK	PLNDMAYB	10.1290	10/17	10.1290	10/16	--	--
17)LOCAL BKS AVE	PLNDAVLS	9.3228	10/17	9.3228	10/16	--	--
Foreign Banks							
19)ANZ BANK	PLNDANZ	7.4000	10/17	7.4000	10/16	--	--
20)BANGKOK BANK	PLNDBKB	6.6290	10/17	6.6290	10/16	--	--

Australia 61 2 9777 8600   Brazil 5511 3048 4500   Europe 44 20 7330 7500   Germany 49 69 920410
Hong Kong 852 2977 6000 Japan 81 3 3201 8900 Singapore 65 6212 1000 U.S. 1 212 318 2000 Copyright 2003 Bloomberg L.P.
G926-802-0 20-Oct-03 8:24:44

Figure 6.5 Philippines money market prime rates
©Bloomberg L.P. Used with permission

The money-market equivalent of the Bloomberg "IYC" yield-curve menu is MMCV, which shows money-market yield curves. We show at Figure 6.6 the money-market curves for three countries; Australia, Singapore and Thailand. This screen is also available in table form, with the rates that are used to draw the curve listed in a table.

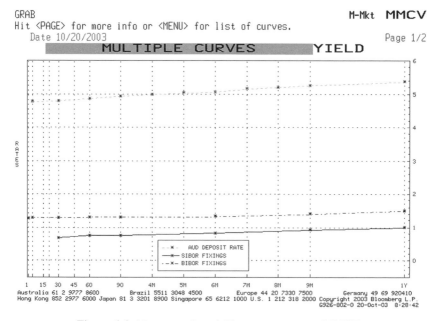

Figure 6.6 Money market yield curves on screen MMCV
©Bloomberg L.P. Used with permission

A useful summary screen for money-market rates on Bloomberg is BTMM. Figure 6.7 shows this page for the markets in Malaysia. This is a composite page that shows a range of sectors; for instance, government-bond yields, T-bills, cash-deposit rates, forward rates and bankers acceptances. Figure 6.8 shows the same page for the markets in Taiwan.

GRAB   M-Mkt BTMM

Change Country	MALAYSIA TSY & MONEY MARKETS			08:31:20

DEPOSIT RATES

1M	2.8250
3M	2.8550
6M	2.8850
9M	2.9250
12M	2.9750

LABUAN RATES

1M	1.14250
3M	1.24157
6M	1.28500
9M	1.41250
12M	1.58125

T-BILLS

3M	2.7700
6M	2.7700
12M	2.7700

SPOT FOREX

MYR	3.8000
SGD	1.7394
HKD	7.7512
JPY	109.4250
EUR	1.1677
GBP	1.6802

CROSS RATES

SGD/MYR	2.1844
JPY/MYR	3.4730
TWD/MYR	0.1121
HKD/MYR	0.4903
THB/MYR	0.0952
EUR/MYR	4.4384
GBP/MYR	6.3850
AUD/MYR	2.6387

KLIBOR

1M	3.0000
3M	3.0900
6M	3.1200
9M	3.1600
12M	3.2300

MYR SWAP

1Y	3.1200	3.1700
3Y	3.9800	4.0300
5Y	5.1200	5.2200
7Y	5.6500	5.7500

GOVT BONDS

3Y	3.3900	3.3900
5Y	4.2900	4.3200
7Y	4.1600	4.1600
10Y	4.2900	4.3900

INTERV RATE

| MAIR | 4.5000 |

PRIME RATE

| AVG | 6.0000 |

KLIBOR FUTURES

| KKA | 96.12 | -0.06 |

MGS FUTURES

| MGA | 0.00 | 0.00 |

STOCK INDICES

| KLCI | 781.09 | 0.04 |
| STI | 1779.76 | 7.58 |

NID

3M	2.85	2.83
6M	2.88	2.87
9M	2.95	2.90
12M	2.95	2.90

BA

1M	2.89	2.88
2M	2.90	2.88
3M	2.90	2.88
4M	2.91	2.89
5M	2.92	2.90
6M	2.92	2.90
9M	2.92	2.91

FORWARDS

1M	46.00	53.00
3M	135.00	147.00
6M	235.00	265.00
9M	260.00	290.00
12M	340.00	380.00

Date/Time		Indicator		BN Survey	Actual	Prior	Revised
10/22 10:00	MA 1)	Foreign Reserves	(OCT 15)	--	--	154801.0	--
10/28 10:00	MA 2)	Bank Negara releases money supply & bank lending data					
11/3 4:01	MA 3)	External Trade	(SEP)	--	--	6.13B	--
11/3 4:01	MA 4)	Exports YoY%	(SEP)	--	--		--

Australia 61 2 9777 8600   Brazil 5511 3048 4500   Europe 44 20 7330 7500   Germany 49 69 920410
Hong Kong 852 2977 6000 Japan 81 3 3201 8900 Singapore 65 6212 1000 U.S. 1 212 318 2000 Copyright 2003 Bloomberg L.P.
G926-802-0 20-Oct-03 8:31:20

Figure 6.7 Malaysian market rates on BTMM
©Bloomberg L.P. Used with permission

GRAB   M-Mkt BTMM

Change Country	TAIWAN - TSY & MONEY MARKETS			08:32:33

ONSHORE IRS

1Y	1.130	1.180
2Y	1.570	1.620
3Y	2.000	2.050
4Y	2.270	2.320
5Y	2.500	2.550
7Y	2.700	2.800
10Y	2.900	3.000

ONSHORE FWDS

0.000	0.000
0.000	0.000
0.000	0.000
0.000	0.000
0.000	0.000
0.000	0.000
0.000	0.000

ONSHORE OUTRT

1M	33.892
2M	33.862
3M	33.832
4M	33.802
5M	33.779
6M	33.739
9M	33.667
1Y	33.572

2ND CP FIX

10D	0.8958
20D	0.8958
30D	0.8958
60D	0.9295
90D	0.9500
120D	0.9670
150D	0.9750
180D	0.9795

NDF OUTRT

1M	33.866
2M	33.811
3M	33.736
4M	0.000
5M	0.000
6M	33.556
9M	33.435
1Y	33.306

NDF SWAP

1Y	-0.40
2Y	0.00
3Y	0.60
4Y	0.70
5Y	1.10
7Y	1.45
10Y	1.65

SPOT FOREX

TWD	33.9060	HKD	7.7512
EUR	1.1685	KRW	1174.0500
GBP	1.6809	SGD	1.7396
JPY	109.4200	THB	39.9050
CAD	1.3169	IDR	8437.5000
AUD	.6944		
CNY	8.2770	NTJY	0.3099
PHP	54.6500	NTEU	39.5954

CROSSES

PRIM RT	6.500
O/N RT	1.021
REDISC	1.375
TWD 11.00 FIX	
	33.896

GOLD

| SPOT | 371.65 |
| BRENT | 29.76 |

GOVT BONDS

1Y	33.306
2Y	0.9012
5Y	1.9220
10Y	2.7798
15Y	2.8972
20Y	3.0243
30Y	3.0492

REPOS

10D	1.150
20D	1.150
1M	0.675
2M	0.850
3M	0.850

INDICES

TWS	6077.89
TWOT	114.63
TWI	271.66
TAFI	11083.50

INDEX FUTURES

| FTA | 6072.000 |
| TWA | 5.990 |

Date/Time		Indicator		BN Survey	Actual	Prior	Revised
10/22 9:00	TA 1)	Unemployment Rate - sa	(SEP)	--	--	4.96%	--
10/22 9:00	TA 2)	Unemployment Rate (NSA)	(SEP)	--	--	5.21%	--
10/23 9:00	TA 3)	Export Orders (YoY)	(SEP)	--	--	10.70%	--
10/23 9:00	TA 4)	Industrial Production (YoY)	(SEP)	--	--	5.31%	--

Australia 61 2 9777 8600   Brazil 5511 3048 4500   Europe 44 20 7330 7500   Germany 49 69 920410
Hong Kong 852 2977 6000 Japan 81 3 3201 8900 Singapore 65 6212 1000 U.S. 1 212 318 2000 Copyright 2003 Bloomberg L.P.
G926-802-0 20-Oct-03 8:32:33

Figure 6.8 Taiwan money market rates on BTMM
©Bloomberg L.P. Used with permission

Repo Instruments

Repo is a short-term secured cash instrument that should always be labelled as part of the money markets. There is a wide range of uses to which repo might be put. Structured transactions that are very similar to repo include total return swaps, and other structured repo trades include floating-rate repo which contains an option to switch to a fixed rate at a later date. In the equity market repo is often conducted in a basket of stocks, which might be constituent stocks in an index such as the FTSE100 or CAC40 or user-specified baskets. Market makers borrow and lend equities with differing terms to maturity, and generally the credit rating of the institution involved in the repo transaction is of more importance than the quality of the collateral. Central banks' use of repo also reflects its importance; it is a key instrument in the implementation of monetary policy in many countries. Essentially then, repo markets have vital links and relationships with global money markets, bond markets, futures markets, swap markets and over-the-counter (OTC) interest rate derivatives.

In this section we discuss key features of the repo instrument.

Key features

Repo is essentially a secured loan. The term comes from *sale and repurchase agreement*; however, this is not necessarily the best way to look at it. Although in a *classic repo* transaction legal title of an asset is transferred from the "seller" to the "buyer" during the term of the repo, in the author's opinion this detracts from the essence of the instrument: a secured loan of cash. It is therefore a money market instrument.

There are a number of benefits in using repo, which concurrently have been behind its rapid growth. These include the following:

- market makers generally are able to finance their long bond and equity positions at a lower interest cost if they repo out the assets; equally they are able to cover short positions;
- there is greater liquidity in specific individual bond issues;
- greater market liquidity lowers the cost of raising funds for capital market borrowers;
- central banks are able to use repo in their open market operations;
- repo reduces *counterparty risk* in money market borrowing and lending, because of the security offered by the collateral given in the loan;
- investors have an added investment option when placing funds;

- institutional investors and other long-term holders of securities are able to enhance their returns by making their inventories available for repo trading.

The maturity of the majority of repo transactions are between overnight and three months, although trades of six months and one year are not uncommon. It is possible to transact in longer term repo as well. Because of this, repo is best seen as a money market product.[6] However, because of the nature of the collateral, repo market participants must keep a close eye on the market of the asset collateral, whether this is the government bond market, Eurobonds, equity or other asset.[7] The counterparties to a repo transaction will have different requirements, for instance to "borrow" a particular asset against an interest in lending cash. For this reason it is common to hear participants talk of trades being *stock-driven* or *cash-driven*. A corporate treasurer who invests cash while receiving some form of security is driving a cash-driven repo, whereas a market maker that wishes to cover a short position in a particular stock, against which she lends cash, is entering into a stock-driven trade.

There is a close relationship between repo and both the bond and money markets. The use of repo has contributed greatly to the liquidity of government, Eurobond and emerging market bond markets. Although it is a separate and individual market itself, operationally repo is straightforward to handle, in that it generally settles through clearing mechanisms used for bonds.

Financial institutions will engage in both repo and reverse repo trades. Investors also, despite their generic name, will be involved in both repo and reverse repo. Their money market funds will be cash-rich and engage in investment trades; at the same time they will run large fixed interest portfolios, the returns for which can be enhanced through trading in repo. Central banks are major players in repo markets and use repo as part of daily liquidity or *open market* operations and as a tool of monetary policy.

---

[6] The textbook definition of a "money market" instrument is of a debt product issued with between one day and one year to maturity, while debt instruments of greater than one year maturity are known as capital market instruments. In practice the money market desks of most banks will trade the yield curve to up to two years maturity, so it makes sense to view a money market instrument as being of up to two years maturity.

[7] This carries on to bank organisation structure. In most banks, the repo desk for bonds is situated in the money markets area, while in others it will be part of the bond division (the author has experience of banks employing each system). Equity repo is often situated as part of the back office settlement or Treasury function.

Repo itself is an over-the-counter market conducted over the telephone, with rates displayed on screens. These screens are supplied by both brokers and market makers themselves. Increasingly, electronic dealing systems are being used, with live dealing rates displayed on screen and trades being conducted at the click of a mouse button.

There are three main basic types of repo: the *classic* repo, the *sell/buy-back* and *tri-party repo*. A sell/buy-back, referred to in some markets as a *buy-sell*, is a spot sale and repurchase of assets transacted simultaneously. It does not require a dealing and settlement system that can handle the concept of a classic repo and is often found in emerging markets. A classic repo is economically identical but the repo rate is explicit and the transaction is conducted under a legal agreement that defines the legal transfer of ownership of the asset during the term of the trade. Classic repo, the type of transaction that originated in the USA, is a sale and repurchase of an asset where the repurchase price is unchanged from the "sale" price. Hence the transaction is better viewed as a loan and borrow of cash. In a tri-party repo a third party acts as an agent on behalf of both seller and buyer of the asset, but otherwise the instrument is identical to classic repo.

Figure 6.9 illustrates the variety of assets used in repo transactions during 2002.

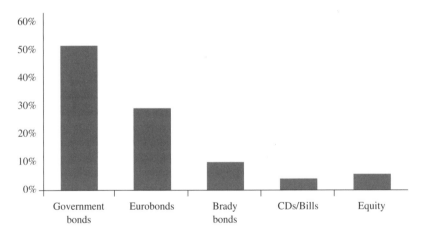

Figure 6.9 Assets used in repo transactions during 2002.
Source: ISMA.

Repo instruments

A repo agreement is a transaction in which one party sells securities to another, and at the same time and as part of the same transaction commits to repurchase identical securities on a specified date at a specified price. The seller delivers securities and receives cash from the buyer. The cash is supplied at a predetermined rate of interest – *the repo rate* – that remains constant during the term of the trade. On maturity the original seller receives back collateral of equivalent type and quality, and returns the cash plus repo interest. One party to the repo requires either the cash or the securities and provides *collateral* to the other party, as well as some form of compensation for the temporary use of the desired asset. Although legal title to the securities is transferred, the seller retains both the economic benefits and the market risk of owning them. This means that the "seller" will suffer loss if the market value of the collateral drops during the term of the repo, as they still retain beneficial ownership of the collateral. The "buyer" in a repo is not affected in profit/loss account terms if the value of the collateral drops, although as we shall see later, there will be other concerns for the buyer if this happens.

We have given here the legal definition of repo. However, the purpose of the transaction as we have described above is to borrow or lend cash, which is why we have used inverted commas when referring to sellers and buyers. The "seller" of stock is really interested in borrowing cash, on which they will pay interest at a specified interest rate. The "buyer" requires security or *collateral* against the loan they have advanced, and/or the specific security to borrow for a period of time. The first and most important thing to state is that repo is a secured loan of cash, and would be categorised as a money market yield instrument.[8]

We now look at the main repo instruments in turn.

The classic repo

The *classic repo* is the instrument encountered in the US, UK and other markets. In a classic repo one party will enter into a contract to sell securities, simultaneously agreeing to pur-chase them back at a specified future date and price. The securities can be bonds or equities but also money market instruments such as T-bills. The buyer of the securities is handing

---

[8] That is, a money market product quoted as a yield instrument, similar to a bank deposit or a Certificate of Deposit. The other class of money market products are *discount* instruments such as a Treasury Bill or Commercial Paper.

over cash, which on the termination of the trade will be returned to them, and on which they will receive interest.

The seller in a classic repo is selling or *offering* stock, and therefore receiving cash, whereas the buyer is buying or *bidding* for stock, and consequently paying cash. So if the one-week repo interest rate is quoted by a market-making bank as "$5^1/_2$ - $5^1/_4$", this means that the market maker will bid for stock, that is, lend the cash, at 5.50% and offers stock or pays interest on borrowed cash at 5.25%. In some markets the quote is reversed.

Illustration of classic repo

There will be two parties to a repo trade, let us say Bank A (the seller of securities) and Bank B (the buyer of securities). On the trade date the two banks enter into an agreement whereby on a set date, the *value* or *settlement* date Bank A will sell to Bank B a nominal amount of securities in exchange for cash.[9] The price received for the securities is the market price of the stock on the value date. The agreement also demands that on the termination date Bank B will sell identical stock back to Bank A at the previously agreed price; consequently, Bank B will have its cash returned with interest at the agreed repo rate.

In essence a repo agreement is a secured loan (or *collateralised* loan) in which the repo rate reflects the interest charged on the cash being lent.

On the value date, stock and cash change hands. This is known as the start date, *on-side* date, *first leg* or *opening leg*, while the termination date is known as the *second leg*, *off-side leg* or *closing leg*. When the cash is returned to Bank B, it is accompanied by the interest charged on the cash during the term of the trade. This interest is calculated at a specified rate known as the *repo rate*. It is important to remember that although in legal terms the stock is initially "sold" to Bank B, the economic effects of ownership are retained with Bank A. This means that if the stock falls in price it is Bank A that will suffer a capital loss. Similarly, if the stock involved is a bond and there is a coupon payment during the term of the trade, this coupon is to the benefit of Bank A, and although Bank B will have received it on the coupon date, it must be handed over on the same day or immediately after to Bank A. This reflects the fact that although legal title to the collateral passes to the repo buyer, economic costs and benefits of the collateral remain with the seller.

---

[9] The two terms are not necessarily synonymous. The value date in a trade is the date on which the transaction acquires value; for example, the date from which accrued interest is calculated. As such it may fall on a non-business day such as a weekend or public holiday. The settlement date is the day on which the transaction settles or *clears*, and so can only fall on a business day.

A classic repo transaction is subject to a legal contract signed in advance by both parties. A standard document will suffice; it is not necessary to sign a legal agreement prior to each transaction.

Note that although we have called the two parties in this case "Bank A" and "Bank B", it is not only banks that get involved in repo transactions, and we have used these terms for the purposes of illustration only.

The basic mechanism is illustrated in Figure 6.10.

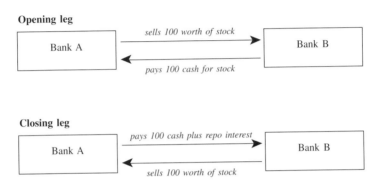

Figure 6.10 Classic repo transaction for 100-worth of collateral stock.

A seller in a repo transaction is entering into a repo, whereas a buyer is entering into a *reverse repo*. In Figure 6.10 the repo counterparty is Bank A, while Bank B is entering into a reverse repo. That is, a reverse repo is a purchase of securities that are sold back on termination. As is evident from Figure 6.10 every repo is a reverse repo, and the name given to a deal is dependent on whose viewpoint one is looking at the transaction.

Examples of classic repo

The basic principle is illustrated with the following example. This considers a *specific* repo, that is, one in which the collateral supplied is specified as a particular stock, as opposed to a *general collateral* (GC) trade in which a basket of collateral can be supplied, of any particular issue, as long as it is of the required type and credit quality.

We consider first a classic repo in the United Kingdom gilt market between two market counterparties, in the 5.75% Treasury 2009 gilt stock. The terms of the trade are given in Table 6.1 and illustrated in Figure 6.11. Note that the terms of a classic repo trade are identical, irrespective of which market the deal is taking place in. So the basic trade, illustrated in Table 6.1, would be recognisable for bond repo in European and Asian markets.

Trade date	5 July 2000
Value date	6 July 2000
Repo term	1 week
Termination date	13 July 2000
Collateral (stock)	UKT 5.75% 2009
Nominal amount	£10,000,000
Price	104.60
Accrued interest (29 days)	0.4556011
Dirty price	105.055601
Settlement proceeds (*wired amount*)	£10,505,560.11
Repo rate	5.75%
Repo interest	£11,584.90
Termination proceeds	£10,517,145.01

Table 6.1 Terms of classic repo trade.

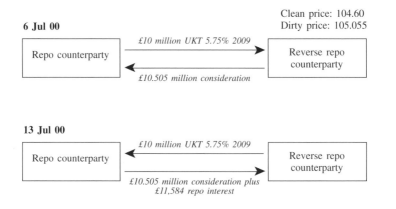

Figure 6.11 Diagram of Classic repo trade.

The repo counterparty delivers to the reverse repo counterparty £10 million nominal of the stock, and in return receives the purchase proceeds. The clean market price of the stock is £104.60. In this example no *margin* (called haircut) has been taken so the start proceeds are equal to the market value of the stock which is £10,505,560.11. It is common for a rounded sum to be transferred on the opening leg. The repo interest is 5.75%, so the repo interest charged for the trade is

$$10,505,560 \times 5.75\% \times 7/365$$

or £11,584.01. The sterling market day-count basis is actual/365, and the repo interest is based on a seven-day repo rate of 5.75%. Repo rates are agreed at the time of the trade and are quoted, like all interest rates, on an annualised basis. The settlement price (dirty price) is used because it is the market value of the bonds on the particular trade date and therefore indicates the cash value of the gilts. By doing this the cash investor minimises credit exposure by equating the value of the cash and the collateral.

On termination the repo counterparty receives back its stock, for which it hands over the original proceeds plus the repo interest calculated above.

Market participants who are familiar with the Bloomberg trading system will use screen RRRA for a classic repo transaction. For this example the relevant screen entries are shown in Figure 6.9. This screen is used in conjunction with a specific stock, so in this case it would be called up by entering

UKT 5.75 09 <GOVT> RRRA <GO>

where "UKT" is the ticker for UK gilts. Note that the date format for Bloomberg screens is the US style, which is mm/dd/yy. The screen inputs are relatively self-explanatory, with the user entering the terms of the trade that are detailed in Table 6.1. There is also a field for calculating margin, labelled "collateral" on the screen. As no margin is involved in this example, it is left at its default value of 100.00%. The bottom of the screen shows the opening leg cash proceeds or "wired amount", the repo interest and the termination proceeds.

If we wanted to use screen RRRA for other securities we would enter the relevant bond ticker, for example "T" for US Treasuries, "B" for German Bunds and so on. The principles are the same for classic repo trades whatever the jurisdiction, and the screen may be used for all markets that undertake classic repo.

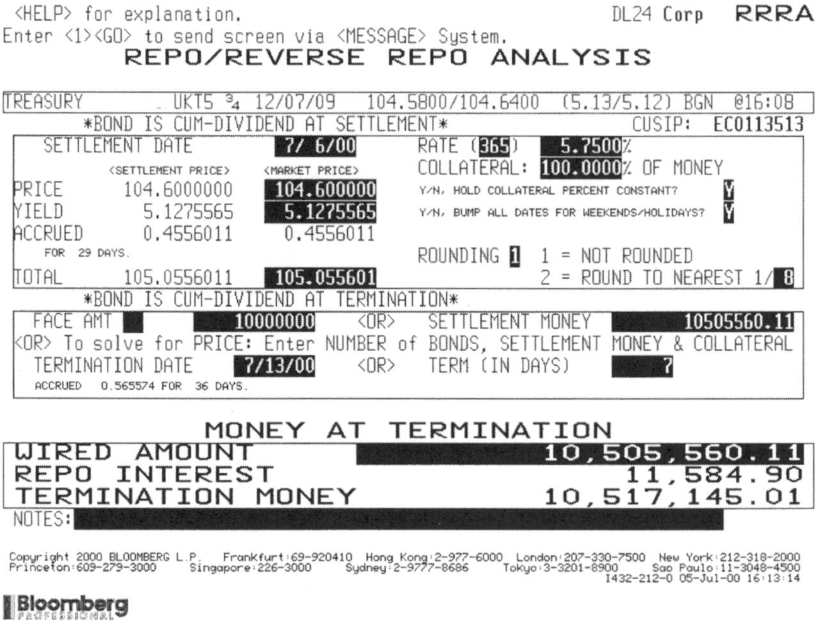

```
<HELP> for explanation.                            DL24 Corp    RRRA
Enter <1><GO> to send screen via <MESSAGE> System.
            REPO/REVERSE REPO ANALYSIS
┌─────────────────────────────────────────────────────────────────────┐
│TREASURY     _ UKTS ³₄ 12/07/09   104.5800/104.6400  (5.13/5.12) BGN  @16:08│
│      *BOND IS CUM-DIVIDEND AT SETTLEMENT*            CUSIP:  EC0113513 │
│  SETTLEMENT DATE         7/ 6/00    RATE (365)    5.7500%             │
│         <SETTLEMENT PRICE>   <MARKET PRICE>   COLLATERAL: 100.0000% OF MONEY │
│ PRICE     104.6000000    104.600000   Y/N, HOLD COLLATERAL PERCENT CONSTANT?  Y │
│ YIELD       5.1275565      5.1275565  Y/N, BUMP ALL DATES FOR WEEKENDS/HOLIDAYS? Y │
│ ACCRUED     0.4556011      0.4556011                                   │
│   FOR  29 DAYS.                       ROUNDING 1   1 = NOT ROUNDED     │
│ TOTAL     105.0556011    105.055601       2 = ROUND TO NEAREST 1/ 8   │
│      *BOND IS CUM-DIVIDEND AT TERMINATION*                            │
│  FACE AMT █        10000000   <OR>   SETTLEMENT MONEY █       10505560.11 │
│ <OR> To solve for PRICE: Enter NUMBER of BONDS, SETTLEMENT MONEY & COLLATERAL │
│  TERMINATION DATE      7/13/00   <OR>   TERM (IN DAYS)       7        │
│  ACCRUED  0.565574 FOR  36 DAYS.                                      │
└─────────────────────────────────────────────────────────────────────┘
            MONEY AT TERMINATION
┌──────────────────────────────────────────────────────────┐
│ WIRED AMOUNT                        10,505,560.11         │
│ REPO INTEREST                           11,584.90         │
│ TERMINATION MONEY                   10,517,145.01         │
└──────────────────────────────────────────────────────────┘
 NOTES:

Copyright 2000 BLOOMBERG L.P.   Frankfurt:69-920410  Hong Kong:2-977-6000  London:207-330-7500  New York:212-318-2000
Princeton:609-279-3000    Singapore:226-3000    Sydney:2-9777-8686    Tokyo:3-3201-8900    Sao Paulo:11-3048-4500
                                                               I432-212-0 05-Jul-00 16:13:14
```

▌Bloomberg

Figure 6.12 Bloomberg screen RRRA for classic repo transaction,
trade date 5 July 2000.
©Bloomberg L.P. Reproduced with permission.

What if a counterparty is interested in investing £10 million against gilt collateral? Let us assume that a corporate treasury function with surplus cash wishes to invest this amount in repo for a one-week term. It invests this cash with a bank that deals in gilt repo. We can use Bloomberg screen RRRA to calculate the nominal amount of collateral required. Figure 6.13 shows the screen for this trade, again against the 5.75% Treasury 2009 stock as collateral. We see from Figure 6.13 that the terms of the trade are identical to that in Table 6.1, including the bond price and the repo rate; however, the opening leg wired amount is entered as £10 million, which is the cash being invested. Therefore the nominal value of the gilt collateral required will be different, as we now require a market value of this stock of £10 million. From the screen we see that this is £9,518,769. The cash amount is different from the example in Figure 6.12 so of course the repo interest charged is different, and is £11,027 for the seven-day term. The diagram at Figure 6.14 illustrates the transaction details.

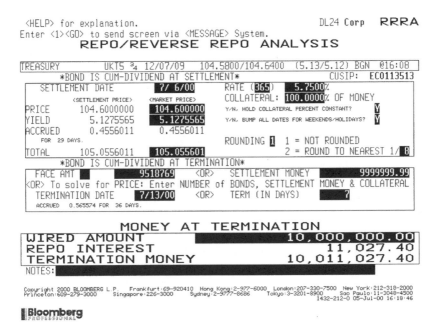

```
<HELP> for explanation.                                    DL24 Corp   RRRA
Enter <1><GO> to send screen via <MESSAGE> System.
              REPO/REVERSE REPO ANALYSIS
TREASURY         UKT5 ³₄ 12/07/09   104.5800/104.6400  (5.13/5.12) BGN  @16:08
        *BOND IS CUM-DIVIDEND AT SETTLEMENT*              CUSIP:   EC0113513
  SETTLEMENT DATE         7/ 6/00      RATE (365)   5.7500%
          <SETTLEMENT PRICE>  <MARKET PRICE>   COLLATERAL: 100.0000% OF MONEY
 PRICE      104.6000000      104.600000    Y/N, HOLD COLLATERAL PERCENT CONSTANT?   Y
 YIELD        5.1275565        5.1275565   Y/N, BUMP ALL DATES FOR WEEKENDS/HOLIDAYS? Y
 ACCRUED      0.4556011        0.4556011
         FOR  29 DAYS.                       ROUNDING 1   1 = NOT ROUNDED
 TOTAL     105.0556011      105.055601              2 = ROUND TO NEAREST 1/ 8
        *BOND IS CUM-DIVIDEND AT TERMINATION*
  FACE AMT             9518769    <OR>   SETTLEMENT MONEY          9999999.99
 <OR> To solve for PRICE: Enter NUMBER of BONDS, SETTLEMENT MONEY & COLLATERAL
  TERMINATION DATE       7/13/00    <OR>   TERM (IN DAYS)             ?
   ACCRUED   0.565574 FOR  36 DAYS.

              MONEY AT TERMINATION
 WIRED AMOUNT                        10,000,000.00
 REPO INTEREST                          11,027.40
 TERMINATION MONEY                   10,011,027.40
NOTES:
```

Copyright 2000 BLOOMBERG L.P.   Frankfurt:69-920410 Hong Kong:2-977-6000 London:207-330-7500 New York:212-318-2000
Princeton:609-279-3000   Singapore:226-3000   Sydney:2-9777-8686   Tokyo:3-3201-8900   Sao Paulo:11-3048-4500
                                                                    1432-212-0 05-Jul-00 16:18:46

Bloomberg

Figure 6.13 Bloomberg screen for the classic repo trade illustrated in Figure 6.14.
©Bloomberg L.P. Reproduced with permission.

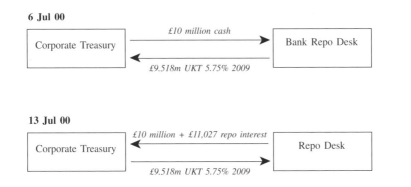

6 Jul 00

£10 million cash

Corporate Treasury → Bank Repo Desk

£9.518m UKT 5.75% 2009

13 Jul 00

£10 million + £11,027 repo interest

Corporate Treasury ← Repo Desk

£9.518m UKT 5.75% 2009

Figure 6.14 Corporate treasury classic repo.

The sell/buy-back

We next consider the sell/buy back which is economically identical to the classi repo but is described under different cashflow terms.

Definition

In addition to classic repo there exists *sell/buy-back*. A sell/buy-back is defined as an outright sale of a bond on the value date, and an outright repurchase of that bond for value on a *forward* date. The cash flows therefore become a sale of the bond at a *spot* price, followed by repurchase of the bond at the *forward* price. The forward price calculated includes the interest on the repo, and is therefore a different price to the spot price.[5] That is, repo interest is realised as the difference between the spot price and forward price of the collateral at the start and termination of the trade. The sell/buy-back is entered into for the same reasons as a classic repo, but was developed initially in markets where no legal agreement existed to cover repo transactions, and where the settlement and IT systems of individual counterparties were not equipped to deal with repo. Over time, sell/buy-backs have become the convention in certain markets, most notably Italy, and so the mechanism is still used. In many markets therefore, sell/buy-backs are not covered by a legal agreement, although the standard legal agreement used in classic repo now includes a section that describes them.[6]

A sell/buy-back is a spot sale and forward repurchase of bonds transacted simultaneously, and the repo rate is not explicit, but is implied in the forward price. Any coupon payments during the term are paid to the seller; however, this is done through incorporation into the forward price, so the seller will not receive it immediately, but on termination. This is a disadvantage when compared to classic repo. However there will be compensation payable if a coupon is not handed over straight away, usually at the repo rate used in the sell/buy-back. As sell/buy-backs are not subject to a legal agreement in most cases, in effect the seller has no legal right to any coupon, and there is no provision for marking-to-market and *variation margin*. This makes the sell/buy-back a higher-risk transaction when compared to classic repo, even more so in volatile markets.

---

[10] The "forward price" is calculated only for the purpose of incorporating repo interest; it should not be confused with a forward interest rate, which is the interest rate for a term starting in the future and which is calculated from a spot interest rate. Nor should it be taken to be an indication of what the market price of the bond might be at the time of trade termination, the price of which could differ greatly from the sell/buy-back forward price.

[11] This is the TBMA/ISMA Global Master Repurchase Agreement.

Note that in some markets the term "repo" is used to describe what are in fact sell/buy-backs. The Italian market is a good example of where this convention is followed.

A general diagram for the sell/buy-back is given in Figure 6.15.

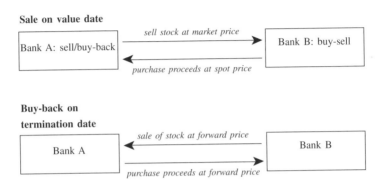

Figure 6.15 Sell/buy-back transaction.

Examples of sell/buy-back

We use the same terms of trade given in Figure 6.12 earlier but this time the trade is a sell/buy-back.[12] In a sell/buy-back we require the forward price on termination, and the difference between the spot and forward price incorporates the effects of repo interest. It is important to note that this forward price has nothing to with the actual market price of the collateral at the time of forward trade. It is simply a way of allowing for the repo interest that is the key factor in the trade. Thus in sell/buy-back the repo rate is not explicit (although it is the key consideration in the trade) rather, it is implicit in the forward price.

In this example, one counterparty sells £10 million nominal of the UKT 5.75% 2009 at the spot price of 104.60, this being the market price of the bond at the time. The consideration for this trade is the market value of the stock, which is £10,505,560 as before. Repo interest is calculated on this amount at the rate of 5.75% for one week, and from this the termination

---

[12] The Bank of England discourages sell/buy-backs in gilt repo and it is unusual, if not unheard of, to observe them in this market. However, we use these terms of trade for comparison purposes with the classic repo example given in the previous section. The procedure and the terms of the trade would be identical in other markets such as Italy and Portugal where sell/buy back trades are the norm.

proceeds are calculated. The termination proceeds are divided by the nominal amount of stock to obtain the forward dirty price of the bond on the termination date. For various reasons, the main one being that settlement systems deal in clean prices, we require the forward clean price, which is obtained by subtracting from the forward dirty price the accrued interest on the bond on the termination date. At the start of the trade the 5.75% 2009 had 29 days' accrued interest, therefore on termination this figure will be 29 + 7 or 36 days.

Bloomberg users access a different screen for sell/buy-backs, which is BSR. This is shown in Figure 6.16. Entering in the terms of the trade, we see from Figure 6.16 that the forward price is 104.605876. However the fundamental nature of this transaction is evident from the bottom part of the screen: the settlement amount ("wired amount"), repo interest and termination amount are identical for the classic repo trade described earlier. This is not surprising; the sell/buy-back is a loan of £10.505 million for one week at an interest rate of 5.75%. The mechanics of the trade do not differ on this key point.

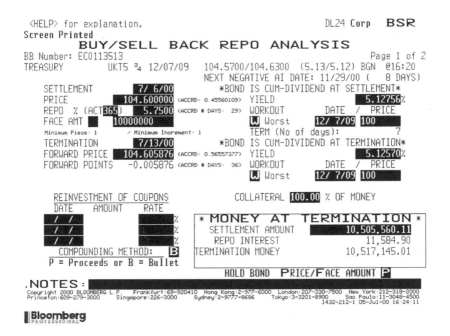

Figure 6.16 Bloomberg screen BSR for sell/buy-back trade in 5.75% 2009, trade date 5 July 2000.
©Bloomberg L.P. Used with permission.

Screen BSR on Bloomberg has a second page, which is shown at Figure 6.17. This screen summarises the cash proceeds of the trade at start and termination. Note how the repo interest is termed "funding cost". This is because the trade is deemed to have been entered into by a bond trader who is funding his book. This will be considered later, but we can see from the screen details that during the one week of the trade the bond position has accrued interest of £10,997. This compares unfavourably with the repo funding cost of £11,584.

If there is a coupon payment during a sell/buy-back trade and it is not paid over to the seller until termination, a compensating amount is also payable on the coupon amount, usually at the trade's repo rate. When calculating the forward price on a sell/buy-back where a coupon will be paid during the trade, we must subtract the coupon amount from the forward price. Note also that sell/buy-backs are not possible on an open basis, as no forward price can be calculated unless a termination date is known.

```
<HELP> for explanation.                            DL24 Corp  BSR
Screen Printed
              BUY/SELL  BACK  REPO  ANALYSIS
BB Number: EC0113513                                    Page 2 of 2
TREASURY          UKT5 ¾ 12/07/09   104.5700/104.6300  (5.13/5.12) BGN  @16:20
```

BOND INCOME		FUNDING COST	
AT SETTLEMENT DATE:	7/ 6/00		
PRINCIPAL	10,460,000.00		
ACCRUED INTEREST	45,560.11		
TOTAL:	10,505,560.11	---> 10,505,560.11 @	5.7500
		for 7 day(s)	
AT TERMINATION DATE:	7/13/00		
PRINCIPAL	10,460,000.00		
COUPON(S)	0.00		
ACCRUED INTEREST	56,557.38		
INTEREST ON CPNS	0.00		
TOTAL:	10,516,557.38		
NET INCOME:	10,997.27	COST:	11,584.90

```
DIFFERENCE            -587.63 TERMINATION
PER  100  NOM:    -0.00587633 AMOUNT              10,460,587.60
Copyright 2000 BLOOMBERG L.P.  Frankfurt:69-920410  Hong Kong:2-977-6000  London:207-330-7500  New York:212-318-2000
Princeton:609-279-3000         Singapore:226-3000  Sydney:2-9777-8686    Tokyo:3-3201-8900  Sao Paulo:11-3048-4500
                                                                           1432-212-1 05-Jul-00 16:25:39
```

Figure 6.17 Bloomberg screen BSR page 2 for sell/buy-back trade in 5.75% 2009 gilt shown at Figure 6.16.
©Bloomberg L.P. Reproduced with permission.

Comparing classic repo and sell/buy-back

Fundamentally both classic repo and sell/buy-backs are money market instruments that are a means by which one party may lend cash to another party, secured against collateral in the form of stocks and bonds. Both transactions are a contract for one party to sell securities, with a simultaneous agreement to repurchase them at a specified future. They also involve:

- in economic terms, an exchange of assets, usually bonds but also money market paper or equities as collateral against cash;
- the supplier of cash being compensated through the payment of interest, at an explicit (repo) or implicit (sell/buy-back) rate of interest;
- short-covering of positions by market makers or speculative sellers, when they are stock-driven trades.

In certain respects however, there are significant differences between the two instruments. A classic repo trade is carried out under formal legal documentation, which sets out the formal position of each counterparty in the event of default. Sell/buy-backs have traditionally not been covered by this type of documentation, although this is no longer the case as standard documentation now exists to cater for them. There is no provision for *marking-to-market* and variation margining in sell/buy-backs, issues we shall look at shortly.

A summary of the main features of both types of trade is given in Table 6.2.

Classic repo	Sell/buy-back
"Sale" and repurchase	Outright sale; forward buy-back
Bid at repo rate: bid for stock, lend the cash (Offer at repo rate: offer the stock, take the cash)	Repo rate implicit in forward buy-back price
Sale and repurchase prices identical	Forward buy-back price different
Return to cash lender is repo interest on cash	Return to cash lender is difference between sale price and forward buy-back price (the "repo" interest!)
Bond coupon received during trade is returned to seller	Coupon need not be returned to bond seller until termination (albeit with compensation)

Standard legal agreement (TBMA/ISMA GMRA)	No standard legal agreement (but may be traded under the GMRA)
Initial margin may be taken	Initial margin may be taken
Variation margin may be called	No variation margin unless transacted under a legal agreement
Specific repo dealing systems required	May be transacted using existing bond and equity dealing systems

Table 6.2 Summary of highlights of classic repo and sell/buy-back.

Basket repo

Banks, securities houses and hedge funds often repo out entire portfolios of bonds with a repo market maker. This is known as a *basket repo* and is operationally more convenient because it is treated as one repo trade rather than a large number of individual bond repo trades. The mechanics of a basket repo are identical to that for a single-name bond classic repo. In a basket repo the market maker may set a margin level for each security or assign a uniform margin level for the whole basket.

Figure 6.18 shows a portfolio of five structured finance bonds, a mix of ABS, MBS and CDO notes. Imagine that these are held by a securities house, ABC Securities Limited, that wishes to fund them using repo. It arranges a basket repo with an investment bank, with the following terms.

Basket repo trade terms

Trade date	13 February 2004
Value date	17 February 2004
Maturity date	17 February 2005
Interest reset	Three months
Wired proceeds	USD 45,564,607.50
Rate	1.18188
	[3-month Libor fix of 12 February 2004 plus 6 bps]
Interest	USD 134,629.75
Maturity proceeds	USD 45,699,237.25

These are quite favourable terms. The securities house has arranged funding of this portfolio at a rate of Libor plus 6 basis points. Given that most of the bonds are rated at A, this a good funding rate. In our example there are only five bonds; basket repo trades involving 50 or even 100

189

different securities are not uncommon. Each security in the basket will be delivered to the reverse repo counterparty, just like single-name classic repo trades.

Note that the investment bank that is entering into a basket reverse repo has applied a margin or haircut to each security, depending on what credit rating the security is assigned. The following margin levels can be assumed for haircut levels in this market:

AAA to AA	3.5%
A	5%
BBB	7%
Sub-investment grade	10%

The repo is booked as one trade, even though the securities house is repo-ing out five different bonds. It has a one-year formal term, but its interest rate is reset every quarter. The first interest period rate is set as three-month Libor plus a spread of 6 basis points. The trade can be "broken" at that date, or rolled for another three months. Figure 6.19 shows the trade ticket.

During the term of the trade, the market maker will make a margin call at pre-agreed intervals, say weekly or every fortnight. This is done by revaluing the entire basket and, if the portfolio has declined in value, a margin call will be made to restore the balance of the haircut. Figure 6.20 shows a margin call statement for one week after initial value date, we assume the portfolio has declined in value and hence a margin payment will need to be made by ABC Securities Limited.

As the trade is conducted under the GMRA agreement, the securities house will be able to substitute bonds out of the basket if it wishes, provided securities of equivalent quality are sent in the place of any bonds taken out of the basket. If a substitute is not available, the value of the loan can be reduced with the market maker to reflect the lower value of the basket once a bond is taken out.

Bond	CUSIP	Type	Asset Type	Original Face Amount	Pool Factor	Current Face	Credit Rating	Price	Market Value	Haircut	Loan Value USD
ABCMT 2003-B B	00761HAU5	ABS	Credit Card	10,000,000	1.0000	10,000,000	A	102.125	10,212,500	5.00%	9,701,875.00
ACAS 2002-2A B	00080AAL4	ABS	Small Business Loans	5,000,000	1.0000	5,000,000	A	102.25	5,112,500	5.00%	4,856,875.00
AMSI 2003-1 M2	03072SEZ4	MBS	Home Equity	8,500,000	1.0000	8,500,000	A	102.25	8,691,250	5.00%	8,256,687.50
AMSI 2003-IA1 M2	03072SLH6	ABS	Residential B/C	4,000,000	0.99999	3,999,960	A	102.50	4,099,959	5.00%	3,894,961.05
Indosuez Capital Funding III	45578YAA0	CLO	Commercial bank loans	20,000,000	1.0000	20,000,000	AA	97.69	19,538,000	3.50%	18,854,170.00
									47,654,209		**45,564,568.55**
											Repo basket amount

Figure 6.18 Hypothetical portfolio of ABS bonds, securities house basket repo trade.
Price source: Bloomberg L.P. Prices as at 12 Feb 2004.

Reverse Repo (RR)	Contract
Customer ID	123456789 ABC Securities Limited
Contract amount	$45,564,607.50
Rate (fixed)	1.18188%
Settle date	17-Feb-04
Lock-up date	17-May-04
Total repo principal	$45,564,607.50
Total repo interest	$134,629.75
Due at maturity	$45,699,237.25
Number of pieces	5

Figure 6.19 Basket repo trade ticket, investment bank market maker

Fixed Income Financing Margin Call

Date	24-Feb-04
Valuation date	23-Feb-04
Due date	24-Feb-04
Positive number =	Amount receivable
Negative number =	Amount payable
Exposure	(45,564,607.50)
Haircut amount	2,089,640.45
Portfolio revaluation	47,224,291.50
Margin call	429,917.50

Figure 6.20 Margin call statement

Repo variations

In the earlier section we described the standard classic repo trade, which has a fixed term to maturity and a fixed repo rate. Generally, classic repo trades will range in maturity from overnight to one year, however it is possible to transact longer maturities than this if required. The overwhelming majority of repo trades are between overnight and three months in maturity, although longer-term trades are not uncommon. A fixed-maturity repo is sometimes called a *term repo*. One could call this the "plain vanilla" repo. It is usually possible to terminate a vanilla repo before its stated maturity date if this is required by one or both of the counterparties.[13]

A repo that does not have a specified fixed maturity date is known as an *open repo*. In an open repo the borrower of cash will confirm each morning that the repo is required for a further overnight term. The interest rate is also fixed at this point. If the borrower no longer requires the cash, or requires the return of his collateral, the trade will be terminated at one day's notice.

In the remainder of this section we present an overview of the most common variations on the vanilla repo transaction that are traded in the markets.

Tri-party repo

The tri-party repo mechanism is designed to make the repo arrangement accessible to a wider range of market counterparties. Essentially it introduces a third-party agent in between the two repo counterparties, who can fulfil a number of roles from security custodian to cash account manager. The tri-party mechanism allows bond and equity dealers full control over their inventory, and incurs minimal settlement cost to the cash investor, but gives the investor independent confirmation that their cash is fully collateralised. Under a tri-party agreement, the securities dealer delivers collateral to an independent third-party custodian, such as Euroclear or Clearstream,[14] who will place it into a segregated tri-party account. The securities dealer maintains control over which precise securities are in this account (multiple substitutions are permitted) but the custodian undertakes to confirm each day to the investor that their cash remains fully collateralised by securities of suitable quality. A tri-party agreement needs to be in place with all three parties before trading can commence. This arrangement reduces the administrative burden for the cash-investor, but is not, in theory, as secure as a conventional delivery-versus-payment structure. Consequently the yield on the investor's cash (assuming collateral of identical credit quality) should be slightly higher. The structure is shown in Figure 6.21.

---

[13] The term *delivery repo* is sometimes used to refer to a vanilla classic repo transaction where the supplier of cash takes delivery of the collateral, whether in physical form or as a book-entry transfer to his account in the clearing system (or his agent's account).

[14] Clearstream was previously known as Cedel Bank. Other tri-party providers include JPMorgan Chase and Bank of New York.

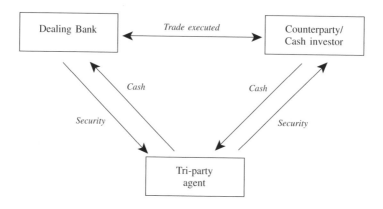

Figure 6.21 Tri-party repo structure.

The first tri-party repo deal took place in 1993 between the European Bank for Reconstruction and Development (EBRD) and Swiss Bank Corporation.[15]

A tri-party arrangement is, in theory, more attractive to smaller market participants as it removes the expense of setting up in-house administration facilities that would be required for conventional repo. This is mainly because the delivery and collection of collateral is handled by the tri-party agent. Additional benefits to cash-rich investors include:

- no requirement to install repo settlement and monitoring systems;
- no requirement to take delivery of collateral, or to maintain an account at the clearing agency;
- independent monitoring of market movements and margin requirements;
- in the event of default, a third-party agent that can implement default measures.

Set against the benefits is of course the cost of tri-party repo, essentially the fee payable to the third-party agent. This fee will include a charge for setting up accounts and arrangements at the tri-party agent, and a custodian charge for holding securities in the clearing system.

---

[15] Stated in Corrigan *et al* , *Repo: the ultimate guide*, London: Pearls of Wisdom publishinhg, (1999), p. 27.

As well as being attractive to smaller banks and cash-rich investors, the larger banks will also use tri-party repo, in order to be able to offer it as a service to their smaller-size clients. The usual arrangement is that both dealer and cash investor will pay a fee to the tri-party agent based on the range of services that are required, and this will be detailed in the legal agreement in place between the market counterparty and the agent. This agreement will also specify, among other detail, the specific types of security that are acceptable as collateral to the cash lender; the repo rate that is earned by the lender will reflect the nature of collateral that is supplied. In every other respect however, the tri-party mechanism offers the same flexibility of conventional repo, and may be transacted from maturities ranging from overnight to one year.

The tri-party agent is an agent to both parties in the repo transaction. It provides a collateral management service overseeing the exchange of securities and cash, and managing collateral during the life of the repo. It also carries out daily marking-to-market, and substitution of collateral as required. The responsibilities of the agent can include:

- the setting up of the repo account;
- monitoring of cash against purchased securities, both at inception and at maturity;
- initial and ongoing testing of *concentration* limits;
- the safekeeping of securities handed over as collateral;
- managing the substitution of securities, where this is required;
- monitoring the market value of the securities against the cash lent out in the repo;
- issuing margin calls to the borrower of cash.

The tri-party agent will issue close-of-business reports to both parties. The contents of the report can include some or all of the following:

- tri-party repo cash and securities valuation;
- corporate actions;
- pre-advice of expected income;
- exchange rates;
- collateral substitution.

The extent of the duties performed by the tri-party agent is dependent of the sophistication of an individual party's operation. Smaller market participants who do not wish to invest in extensive infrastructure may outsource all repo-related functions to the tri-party agent.

Tri-party repo was originally conceived as a mechanism through which repo would become accessible to smaller banks and non-bank counterparties. It is primarily targeted at cash-rich investors. However users of the instrument range across the spectrum of market participants, and include, on the investing side, cash-rich financial institutions such as banks, fund managers including life companies and pension funds, and savings institutions such as UK building societies. On the borrowing side users include bond and equity market makers, and banks with inventories of high-quality assets such as government bonds and highly-rated corporate bonds.[16]

Tri-party repo: deal mechanics

The process of cash and collateral flow in a tri-party repo trade is illustrated in Figures 6.22 and 6.23.

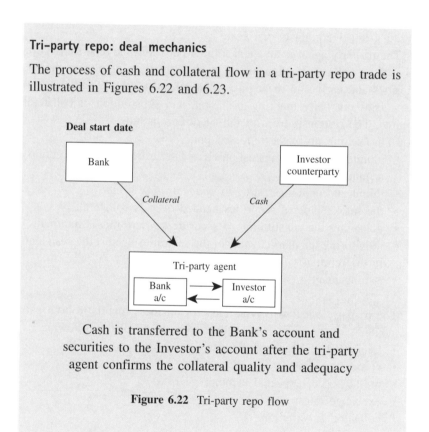

Figure 6.22 Tri-party repo flow

---

[16] Fabozzi (2001) also refers to *four-party repos*. The difference between tri-party and four-party repo is given as follows: "in a four-party repo there is a sub-custodian that is the custodian for the lender." This might occur because of legal considerations; for instance, local regulations stating that the custodian in a repo transaction must be a financial institution or must be based in a particular location.

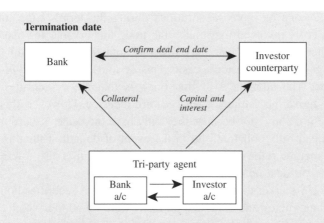

The tri-party agent effects a simultaneous transfer of cash (original capital plus repo interest) versus securities

Figure 6.23 Tri-party repo flow

Table 6.3 shows the acceptable collateral types as advised by the institutional trust arm of a US investment bank.

Government bonds	Cash
Government guaranteed/	Certificate of Deposits
local authority bonds	Delivery by Value (DBV)
Supranational bonds	Letters of credit
Eurobonds	Equities
Corporate bonds	American Depositary Receipts
ABS/MBS	Warrants
Convertible bonds	

Table 6.3 Tri-party acceptable collateral: US Investment bank counterparty

Hold-in-custody repo

This is part of the general collateral (GC) market, and is more common in the United States than elsewhere. Consider the case of a cash-rich institution investing in GC as an alternative to deposits or commercial paper. The better the quality of collateral, the lower the yield the institution can expect, while the mechanics of settlement may also affect the repo rate. The most secure procedure is to take physical possession of the collateral. However if the dealer needs one or more substitutions during the term of the trade, the settlement costs involved may make the trade unworkable for one or both parties. Therefore, the dealer may offer to hold the securities in his own custody against the investor's cash. This is known as a *hold-in-custody* (HIC) repo. The advantage of this trade is that since securities do not physically move, no settlement charges are incurred. However, this carries some risk for the investor because they only have the dealer's word that their cash is indeed fully collateralised in the event of default. Thus this type of trade is sometime referred to as a "Trust Me" repo; it is also referred to as a *due-bill repo* or a *letter repo*.

In the US market there have been cases in which securities houses that went into bankruptcy and defaulted on loans were found to have pledged the same collateral for multiple HIC repo trades. Investors dealing in HIC repo must ensure:

- they only invest with dealers of good credit quality, since an HIC repo may be perceived as an unsecured transaction;
- they receive a higher yield on their cash in order to compensate them for the higher credit risk involved.

A *safekeeping repo* is identical to an HIC repo whereby the collateral from the repo seller is not delivered to the cash lender but held in "safe keeping" by the seller. This has advantages in that there is no administration and cost associated with the movement of stock. The risk is that the cash lender must entrust the safekeeping of collateral to the counterparty, and has no means of confirming that the security is indeed segregated, and only being used for one transaction.

Due to the counterparty risk inherent in an HIC repo, it is rare to see it transacted either in the US market or elsewhere. Certain securities are not suitable for delivery; for example, the class of mortgage securities known as *whole loans* in the US, and these are often funded using HIC repo (termed *whole-loan repo*).

Borrow/loan vs cash

This is similar in almost all respects to a classic repo/reverse repo. A legal agreement between the two parties is necessary, and trades generally settle *delivery-versus-payment*. The key difference is that under a repo agreement legal title over the collateral changes hands. Under a securities lending agreement this is not necessarily the case. The UK standard securities lending agreement does involve transfer of title, but it is possible to construct a securities lending agreement where legal title does not move. This can be an advantage for customers who may have accounting or tax problems in doing a repo trade. Such institutions will opt to transact a *loan versus cash*. The UK standard lending agreement also covers items such as dividends and voting rights, and is therefore the preferred transaction structure in the equity repo market.

Bonds borrowed/collateral pledged

In the case of a bonds borrowed/collateral pledged trade the institution lending the bonds does not want or need to receive cash against them, as it is already cash-rich and would only have to re-invest any further cash generated. As such this transaction only occurs with *special collateral*. The dealer borrows the special bonds and pledges securities of similar quality and value (general collateral). The dealer builds in a fee payable to the lending institution as an incentive to do the trade.

EXAMPLE 6.1 Bonds borrowed/collateral pledged

■ ABC Bank plc wishes to borrow DKK 300 million of the Danish government bond 8% 2001. ABC owns the Danish government bond 7% 2007. ABC is prepared to pay a customer a 40 basis point fee in order to borrow the 8% 2001 for one month.

The market price of the 8% 2001 (including accrued interest) is 112.70. The total value of DKK 300 million nominal is therefore DKK 338,100,000.

The market price of the 7% 2007 (including accrued interest) is 102.55.

In order to fully collateralise the customer ABC needs to pledge (338,100,000/1.0255) which is 329,692,832.76; when rounded to the nearest DKK 1 million this becomes DKK 330 million nominal of the 7% 2007.

In a bonds borrowed/collateral pledged trade, both securities are delivered free of payment and ABC Bank plc would pay the customer a 40bp borrowing fee upon termination. In our example the fee payable would be:

$$338,100,000 \times (31/360) \times (0.4/100) = \text{DKK } 112,700.$$

Borrow versus letter of credit

This instrument is used when an institution lending securities does not require cash, but takes a third-party bank letter of credit as collateral. However, since banks typically charge 10–20 basis points for this facility, transactions of this kind are relatively rare.

Cross-currency repo

All of the examples of repo trades discussed so far have used cash and securities denominated in the same currency, for example gilts trading versus sterling cash, and so on. In fact there is no requirement to limit oneself to single-currency transactions. It is possible to trade say, gilts versus US dollar cash (or any other currency), or pledge Spanish government bonds against borrowing Japanese government bonds. A cross-currency repo is essentially a plain vanilla transaction, but where collateral that is handed over is denominated in a different currency to that of the cash lent against it. Other features of cross-currency repo include:

- possible significant daylight credit exposure on the transaction if securities cannot settle versus payment;
- a requirement for the transaction to be covered by appropriate legal documentation;
- fluctuating foreign exchange rates, which mean that it is likely that the transaction will need to be marked-to-market frequently in order to ensure that cash or securities remain fully collateralised.

It is also necessary to take into account the fluctuations in the relevant exchange rate when marking securities used as collateral, which are obviously handed over against cash that is denominated in a different currency.

EXAMPLE 6.2 Cross-currency repo

■ On 4 January 2000 a hedge fund manager funds a long position in US Treasury securities against sterling, for value the following day. It is offered a bid of 4.90% in the one-week, and the market maker also requires a 2% margin. The one-week Libor rate is 4.95% and the exchange rate at the time of trade is £1/$1.63. The terms of the trade are given below.

Trade date	4 January 2000
Settlement date	5 January 2000
Stock (collateral)	US Treasury 6.125% 2001

Nominal amount	$100 million
Repo rate	4.90% (sterling)
Term	7 days
Maturity date	12 January 2001
Clean price	99-19
Accrued interest	5 days (0.0841346)
Dirty price	99.6778846
Gross settlement amount	$99,677,884.62
Net settlement amount (after 2% haircut)	$97,723,416.29
Net wired settlement amount in sterling	£59,953,016.13
Repo interest	£56,339.41
Sterling termination money	£60,009,355.54

The repo market has allowed the hedge fund to borrow in sterling at a rate below the cost of unsecured borrowing in the money market (4.95%). The repo market maker is "overcollateralised" by the difference between the value of the bonds (in £) and the loan proceeds (2%). A rise in USD yields or a fall in the USD exchange rate value will adversely affect the value of the bonds, causing the market maker to be undercollateralised.

Repo-to-maturity

A *repo-to-maturity* is a classic repo where the termination date on the repo matches the maturity date of the bond in the repo. We can discuss this trade by considering the Bloomberg screen used to analyse repo-to-maturity, which is REM. The screen used to analyse a reverse repo-to-maturity is RRM.

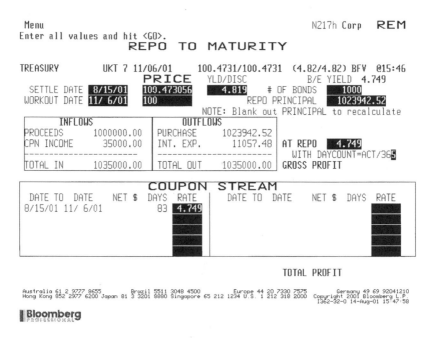

Figure 6.24 Bloomberg screen REM; used for repo-to-maturity analysis, for UK Treasury 7% 2001 on 14 August 2001.
©Bloomberg L.P. Reproduced with permission.

Screen REM is used to analyse the effect of borrowing funds in repo to purchase a bond, where the bond is the collateral security. This is conventional and we considered this earlier. In essence, the screen will compare the financing costs on the borrowed funds to the coupons received on the bond up to and including maturity. The key determining factor is the repo rate used to finance the borrowing. From Figure 6.24 we see that the screen calculates the break-even rate, which is the rate at which the financing cost equals the bond return. The screen also works out cash flows at start and termination, and the borrowed amount is labelled as the "repo principal". This is the bond total consideration. Under "outflows" we see the repo interest at the selected repo rate, labelled as "Int. Exp". Gross profit is the total inflow minus total outflow, which in our example is zero because the repo rate entered is the break-even rate. The user will enter the actual repo rate payable to calculate the total profit.

A reverse repo-to-maturity is a reverse repo with matching repo termination and bond expiry dates. This shown at Figure 6.25.

Repo-to-maturity is a low-risk trade as the financing profit on the bond position is known with certainty to the bond's maturity. For financial institutions that operate on an accruals basis rather mark-to-market basis, the trade can guarantee a profit and not suffer any losses in the interim while they hold the bond.

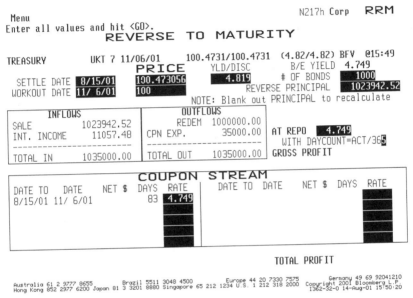

Figure 6.25 Bloomberg screen RRM, used for reverse repo-to-maturity analysis, for UK Treasury 7% 2001 on 14 August 2001.
©Bloomberg L.P. Used with permission.

Margin

To reduce the level of risk exposure in a repo transaction it is common for the lender of cash to ask for a margin, which is where the market value of collateral is higher than the cash value of cash lent out in the repo. This is a form of protection should the cash-borrowing counter-party default on the loan. Another term for margin is *overcollateralisation* or *haircut*. There are two types of margin: an *initial margin* taken at the start of the trade, and *variation margin* which is called if required during the term of the trade.

Initial margin

The cash proceeds in a repo are typically no more than the market value of the collateral. This minimises credit exposure by equating the value of the cash to that of the collateral. The market value of the collateral is calculated at its *dirty* price, not clean price – that is, including accrued interest. This is referred to as *accrual pricing*. To calculate the accrued interest on the (bond) collateral we require the day-count basis for the particular bond.

The start proceeds of a repo can be less than the market value of the collateral by an agreed amount or percentage. This is known as the *initial margin* or *haircut*. The initial margin protects the buyer against:

*   a sudden fall in the market value of the collateral;
*   illiquidity of collateral;
*   other sources of volatility of value (for example, approaching maturity);
*   counterparty risk.

The margin level of repo varies from 0–2% for collateral such as US Treasuries or German Bonds, to 5% for cross-currency and equity repo, to 10–35% for emerging market debt repo.

In both classic repo and sell/buy-back, any initial margin is given to the supplier of cash in the transaction. This remains true in the case of specific repo. For initial margin the market value of the bond collateral is reduced (or given a *"haircut"*) by the percentage of the initial margin and the nominal value determined from this reduced amount. In a stock loan transaction the lender of stock will ask for margin.

There are two methods for calculating the margin; for a 2% margin this could be one of the following:

*   (dirty price of the bonds) × 0.98
*   ((dirty price of the bonds)/1.02)

The two methods do not give the same value! The RRRA repo page on Bloomberg uses the second method for its calculations and this method is turning into something of a convention.

For a 2% margin level the BMA/ISMA GMRA defines a "margin ratio" as:

$$\text{collateral value/cash} = 102\%.$$

The size of margin required in any particular transaction is a function of the following:

- the credit quality of the counterparty supplying the collateral; for example, a central bank counterparty, interbank counterparty and corporate will all suggest different margin levels;
- the term of the repo; an overnight repo is inherently lower risk than a one-year risk;
- the duration (price volatility) of the collateral; for example, a T-bill compared to the long bond;
- the existence or absence of a legal agreement; repo traded under a standard agreement is considered lower risk.

Certain market practitioners, particularly those that work on bond research desks, believe that the level of margin is a function of the volatility of the collateral stock. This may be either, say, one-year historical volatility or the implied volatility given by option prices. Given a volatility level of say, 10%, suggesting a maximum expected price movement of −10% to +10%, the margin level may be set at, say, 5% to cover expected movement in the market value of the collateral. This approach to setting initial margin is regarded as onerous by most repo traders, given the differing volatility levels of stocks within GC bands. The counterparty credit risk and terms of trade remain the most influential elements in setting margin, followed by quality of collateral.[17]

In the final analysis margin is required to guard against market risk – the risk that the value of collateral will drop during the course of the repo. Therefore the margin call must reflect the risks prevalent in the market at the time; extremely volatile market conditions may call for large increases in initial margin.

Variation margin

The market value of the collateral is maintained through the use of *variation margin*. So if the market value of the collateral falls, the buyer calls for extra cash or collateral. If the market value of the collateral rises, the seller calls for extra cash or collateral. In order to reduce the administrative burden, margin calls can be limited to changes in the market value of the collateral in excess of an agreed amount or percentage, which is called a *margin maintenance limit*.

---

[17] In his years dealing repo, during 1992-1997 and again in 2003-2004, the author never once came across a repo market maker who set margin levels in line with collateral volatility levels. So much for certain bank research desks...

The standard market documentation that exists for the three structures covered so far includes clauses that allow parties to a transaction to call for variation margin during the term of a repo. This can be in the form of extra collateral (if the value of the collateral has dropped in relation to the asset exchanged) or a return of collateral, if the value has risen. If the cash-borrowing counterparty is unable to supply more collateral where required, they will have to return a portion of the cash loan. Both parties have an interest in making and meeting margin calls, although there is no obligation. The level at which variation margin is triggered is often agreed beforehand in the legal agreement put in place between individual counterparties. Although primarily viewed as an instrument used by the supplier of cash against a fall in the value of the collateral, variation margin can of course also be called by the repo seller if the value of the collateral has risen in value.

An illustration of variation margin being applied during the term of a trade is given in Exhibit 6.3.

EXAMPLE 6.3 Variation margin

■ Figure 6.26 shows a 60-day repo in the 5% Treasury 2004, a UK gilt, where a margin of 2% is taken. The repo rate is 5°%. The start of the trade is 5 January 2000. The clean price of the gilt is 95.25.

Nominal amount	1,000,000
Principal	£952,500.00
Accrued interest (29 days)	£3961.75
Total consideration	**£956,461.75**

The consideration is divided by 1.02, the amount of margin, to give £937,707.60. Assume that this is rounded up to the nearest pound.

Loan amount	£937,708.00
Repo interest at 5°%	£8477.91
Termination proceeds	£946,185.91

Assume that one month later there has been a catastrophic fall in the bond market and the 5% 2004 gilt is trading down at 92.75. Following this drop, the market value of the collateral is now:

Principal   £927,500
Accrued interest (59 days)   £8082.19
Market value   £935,582.19

However, the repo desk has lent £937,708 against this security, which exceeds its market value. Under a variation margin arrangement it can call margin from the counterparty in the form of general collateral securities or cash.

The formula used to calculate the amount required to restore the original margin of 2% is given by:

Margin adjustment =
((original consideration + repo interest charged to date)
× (1 + initial margin)) − (new all-in price × nominal amount)

This therefore becomes:
((937,708 + 4238.96) × (1 + 0.02)) − (0.93558219 × 1,000,000)
= £25,203.71.

The margin requirement can be taken as additional stock or cash. In practice, margin calls are made on what is known as a portfolio basis, based on the net position resulting from all repos and reverse repos in place between the two counterparties, so that a margin delivery may be made in a general collateral stock rather than more of the original repo stock. The diagrams below show the relevant cash flows at the various dates.

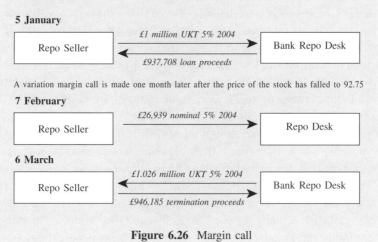

5 January

Repo Seller   *£1 million UKT 5% 2004* →   Bank Repo Desk
  ← *£937,708 loan proceeds*

A variation margin call is made one month later after the price of the stock has fallen to 92.75

7 February

Repo Seller   *£26,939 nominal 5% 2004* →   Repo Desk

6 March

Repo Seller   ← *£1.026 million UKT 5% 2004*
  £946,185 termination proceeds →   Bank Repo Desk

Figure 6.26 Margin call

Money-market derivatives

The market in short-term interest-rate derivatives is a large and liquid one, and the instruments involved are used for a variety of purposes. Here we review the two main contracts used in money-markets trading; the short-term interest-rate future and the forward-rate agreement. In a previous chapter we introduced the concept of the forward rate. Money-market derivatives are priced on the basis of the forward rate, and are flexible instruments for hedging against or speculating on forward interest rates. The FRA and the exchange-traded interest-rate future both date from around the same time, and although initially developed to hedge forward interest-rate exposure, they now have a range of uses. The instruments are introduced and analysed, and there is a review of the main uses that they are put to. Readers interested in the concept of convexity bias in swap and futures pricing may wish to refer to the chapter listed in the bibliography, which is by the author and is an accessible introduction.

Forward-rate agreements

A forward-rate agreement (FRA) is an OTC derivative instrument that trades as part of the money markets. It is essentially a forward-starting loan, but with no exchange of principal, so that only the difference in interest rates is traded. Trading in FRAs began in the early 1980s and the market now is large and liquid; turnover in London exceeds $5 billion each day. So an FRA is a forward-dated loan, dealt at a fixed rate, but with no exchange of principal – only the interest applicable on the notional amount between the rate dealt at and the actual rate prevailing at the time of settlement changes hands. That is, FRAs are off-balance-sheet (OBS) instruments. By trading today at an interest rate that is effective at some point in the future, FRAs enable banks and corporates to hedge interest-rate exposure. They are also used to speculate on the level of future interest rates.

An FRA is an agreement to borrow or lend a notional cash sum for a period of time lasting up to 12 months, starting at any point over the next 12 months, at an agreed rate of interest (the FRA rate). The "buyer" of a FRA is borrowing a notional sum of money while the "seller" is lending this cash sum. Note how this differs from all other money-market instruments. In the cash market, the party buying a CD or bill, or bidding for stock in the repo market, is the lender of funds. In the FRA market, to "buy" is to "borrow". We use the term "notional" because with an FRA no borrowing or lending of cash actually takes place, as it is an OBS product. The notional sum is simply the amount on which interest payment is calculated.

So when a FRA is traded, the buyer is borrowing (and the seller is lending) a specified notional sum at a fixed rate of interest for a specified period, the "loan" to commence at an agreed date in the future. The *buyer* is the notional borrower and so, if there is a rise in interest rates between the date that the FRA is traded and the date that the FRA comes into effect, she will be protected. If there is a fall in interest rates, the buyer must pay the difference between the rate at which the FRA was traded and the actual rate, as a percentage of the notional sum. The buyer may be using the FRA to hedge an actual exposure, that is an actual borrowing of money, or simply speculating on a rise in interest rates. The counterparty to the transaction, the *seller* of the FRA, is the notional lender of funds, and has fixed the rate for lending funds. If there is a fall in interest rates the seller will gain, and if there is a rise in rates the seller will pay. Again, the seller may have an actual loan of cash to hedge or be a speculator.

In FRA trading, only the payment that arises as a result of the difference in interest rates changes hands. There is no exchange of cash at the time of the trade. The cash payment that does arise is the difference in interest rates between that at which the FRA was traded and the actual rate prevailing when the FRA matures, as a percentage of the notional amount. FRAs are traded by both banks and corporates and between banks. The FRA market is very liquid in all major currencies and rates are readily quoted on screens by both banks and brokers. Dealing is over the telephone or over a dealing system such as Reuters.

The terminology quoting FRAs refers to the borrowing time period and the time at which the FRA comes into effect (or matures). Hence, if a buyer of a FRA wished to hedge against a rise in rates to cover a three-month loan starting in three months' time, she would transact a "three-against-six month" FRA, or more usually a 3 × 6 or 3-vs-6 FRA. This is referred to in the market as a "threes-sixes" FRA, and means a three-month loan in three months' time. So a "ones-fours" FRA (1 v 4) is a three-month loan in one month's time, and a "three-nines" FRA (3 v 9) is six-month money in three months' time.

EXAMPLE 6.4

A company knows that it will need to borrow £1 million in three months' time for a 12-month period. It can borrow funds today at Libor +50 basis points. Libor rates today are at 5% but the company's treasurer expects rates to go up to about 6% over the next few weeks. So the company will be forced to borrow at higher rates unless some sort of hedge is transacted to protect the borrowing requirement. The treasurer decides to buy a 3x15 ("threes-fifteens") FRA to cover the 12-month period beginning three months from now. A bank quotes 5°% for the FRA which the company buys for a notional £1 million. Three months from now rates have indeed gone up to 6%, so the treasurer must borrow funds at $6\frac{1}{2}\%$ (the Libor rate plus spread). However, she will receive a settlement amount which will be the difference between the rate at which the FRA was bought and today's 12-month Libor rate (6%) as a percentage of £1 million, which will compensate for some of the increased borrowing costs.

In virtually every market, FRAs trade under a set of terms and conventions that are identical. The British Bankers' Association (BBA) drew up standard legal documentation to cover FRA trading. The following standard terms are used in the market.

Notional sum: The amount for which the FRA is traded.

Trade date: The date on which the FRA is dealt.

Settlement date: The date on which the notional loan or deposit of funds becomes effective; that is, is said to begin. This date is used, in conjunction with the notional sum, for calculation purposes only as no actual loan or deposit takes place.

Fixing date; This is the date on which the reference rate is determined; that is, the rate to which the FRA dealing rate is compared.

Maturity date: The date on which the notional loan or deposit expires.

Contract period: The time between the settlement date and maturity date.

FRA rate: The interest rate at which the FRA is traded.

Reference rate: This is the rate used as part of the calculation of the settlement amount, usually the Libor rate on the fixing date for the contract period in question.

Settlement sum: The amount calculated as the difference between the FRA rate and the reference rate as a percentage of the notional sum, paid by one party to the other on the settlement date.

These terms are illustrated in Figure 6.27.

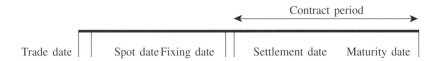

Figure 6.27 Key dates in a FRA trade

The spot date is usually two business days after the trade date; however, it can by agreement be sooner or later than this. The settlement date will be the time period after the spot date referred to by the FRA terms. For example, a 1×4 FRA will have a settlement date one calendar month after the spot date. The fixing date is usually two business days before the settlement date. The settlement sum is paid on the settlement date, and as it refers to an amount over a period of time that is paid up front, at the start of the contract period, the calculated sum is discounted. This is because a normal payment of interest on a loan/deposit is paid at the end of the time period to which it relates; because an FRA makes this payment at the *start* of the relevant period, the settlement amount is a discounted figure.

With most FRA trades the reference rate is the LIBOR fixing on the fixing date.

The settlement sum is calculated after the fixing date, for payment on the settlement date. We may illustrate this with a hypothetical example. Consider a case where a corporate has bought £1 million notional of a 1 v 4 FRA, and dealt at 5.75%, and that the market rate is 6.50% on the fixing date. The contract period is 90 days. In the cash market, the extra interest charge that the corporate would pay is a simple interest calculation, and is:

$$\frac{6.50 - 5.75}{100} \times 1,000,000 \times \frac{91}{365} = £1869.86$$

This extra interest that the corporate is facing would be payable with the interest payment for the loan, which (as it is a money-market loan) is when the loan matures. Under an FRA, then, the settlement sum payable should, if it was paid on the same day as the cash-market interest charge, be exactly equal to this. This would make it a perfect hedge. As we noted above, though, FRA settlement value is paid at the start of the contract period; that is, the beginning of the underlying loan and not the end. Therefore, the settlement sum has to be adjusted to account for this, and the amount of the adjustment is the value of the interest that would be earned if the unadjusted cash value was invested for the contract period in the money market. The amount of the settlement value is given by (6.15).

$$Settlement = \frac{(r_{ref} - r_{FRA}) \times M \times \frac{n}{B}}{1 + (r_{ref} \times \frac{n}{B})} \tag{6.15}$$

where

r_{ref} is the reference interest fixing rate
r_{FRA} is the FRA rate or contract rate
M is the notional value
n is the number of days in the contract period
B is the day-count base (360 or 365).

The expression at (6.15) simply calculates the extra interest payable in the cash market, resulting from the difference between the two interest rates, and then discounts the amount because it is payable at the start of the period and not, as would happen in the cash market, at the end of the period.

In our hypothetical illustration, as the fixing rate is higher than the dealt rate, the corporate buyer of the FRA receives the settlement sum from the seller. This then compensates the corporate for the higher borrowing costs that he would have to pay in the cash market. If the fixing rate had been lower than 5.75%, the buyer would pay the difference to the seller, because the cash market rates will mean that he is subject to a lower interest rate in the cash market. What the FRA has done is hedge the corporate, so that whatever happens in the market, it will pay 5.75% on its borrowing.

A market-maker in FRAs is trading short-term interest rates. The settlement sum is the value of the FRA. The concept is exactly as with trading short-term interest-rate futures; a trader who buys a FRA is running a long position, so that if on the fixing date $r_{ref} > r_{FRA}$, the settlement sum is positive and the trader realises a profit. What has happened is that the trader, by buying the FRA, "borrowed" money at an interest rate, which subsequently rose. This is a gain, exactly like a short position in an interest-rate future, where if the price goes down (that is, interest rates go up), the trader realises a gain. Equally a "short" position in a FRA, put on by selling a FRA, realises a gain if on the fixing date $r_{ref} < r_{FRA}$.

FRA pricing

As their name implies, FRAs are forward-rate instruments and are priced using the forward-rate principles we established earlier. Consider an investor who has two alternatives; either a six-month investment at 5% or a one-year investment at 6%. If the investor wishes to invest for six months and then roll the investment over for a further six months, what rate is required for the roll-over period such that the final return equals the 6% available from the one-year investment? If we view a FRA rate as the break-even forward rate between the two periods, we simply solve for this forward rate and that is our approximate FRA rate. This rate is sometimes referred to as the interest rate "gap" in the money markets (not to be confused with an interbank desk's gap risk, the interest-rate exposure arising from the net maturity position of its assets and liabilities).

We can use the standard forward-rate break-even formula to solve for the required FRA rate. We established this relationship earlier when discussing the calculation of forward rates that are arbitrage-free. The relationship given at (6.16) connects simple (bullet) interest rates for periods of time up to one year, where no compounding of interest is required. As FRAs are money-market instruments we are not required to calculate rates for periods in excess of one year[18], where compounding would need to be built into the equation.

$$(1 + r_2 t_2) = (1 + r_1 t_1)(1 + r_f t_f) \tag{6.16}$$

where

r_2 is the cash-market interest rate for the long period
r_1 is the cash-market interest rate for the short period
r_f is the forward rate for the gap period
t_2 is the time period from today to the end of the long period
t_1 is the time period from today to the end of the short period
t_f is the forward-gap time period, or the contract period for the FRA

This is illustrated diagrammatically in Figure 6.28.

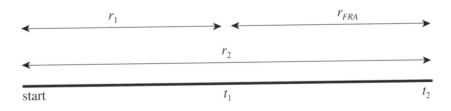

Figure 6.28 Rates used in FRA pricing

---

[18] Although it is, of course, possible to trade FRAs with contract periods greater than one year, for which a different pricing formula must be used.

The time period t_1 is the time from the dealing date to the FRA settlement date, while t_2 is the time from the dealing date to the FRA maturity date. The time period for the FRA (contract period) is t_2 minus t_1. We can replace the symbol "t" for time period with "n" for the actual number of days in the time periods themselves. If we do this and then re-arrange the equation to solve for r_{fra} the FRA rate, we obtain (6.17) below.

$$r_{FRA} = \frac{r_2 n_2 - r_1 n_1}{n_{fra}\left[1 + r_1 \dfrac{n_1}{365}\right]} \qquad (6.17)$$

where

n_1 is the number of days from the dealing date or spot date to the settlement date

n_2 is the number of days from dealing date or spot date to the maturity date

r_1 is the spot rate to the settlement date

r_2 is the spot rate from the spot date to the maturity date

n_{fra} is the number of days in the FRA contract period

r_{FRA} is the FRA rate.

If the formula is applied to, say, the US money markets, the 365 in the equation is replaced by 360, the day-count base for that market.

In practice, FRAs are priced off the exchange-traded short-term interest-rate future for that currency, so that sterling FRAs are priced off LIFFE short sterling futures. Traders normally use a spreadsheet pricing model that has futures prices directly fed into it. FRA positions are also usually hedged with other FRAs or short-term interest-rate futures.

FRA prices in practice

The dealing rates for FRAs are possibly the most liquid and transparent of any non-exchange-traded derivative instrument. This is because they are calculated directly from exchange-traded interest-rate contracts. The key consideration for FRA market-makers, however, is how the rates behave in relation to other market interest rates. The forward rate calculated from two period spot rates must, as we have seen, be set such that it is arbitrage-free. If, for example, the six-month spot rate was 8.00% and the nine-month spot rate was 9.00%, the 6 v 9 FRA would have an approximate rate of 11%. What would be the effect of a change in one or both of the spot rates? The same arbitrage-free principle must apply. If there is an increase in the short-rate period, the FRA rate must decrease, to make the total return unchanged. The extent of the change in the FRA rate is a function of the ratio of the contract period to the long period. If the rate for the long period increases, the FRA rate will increase, by an amount related to the ratio between the total period to the contract period. The FRA rate for any term is generally a function of the three-month LIBOR rate generally, the rate traded under an interest-rate future. A general rise in this rate will see a rise in FRA rates.

Short-term interest-rate futures

Description

A futures contract is a transaction that fixes the price today for a commodity that will be delivered at some point in the future. Financial futures fix the price for interest rates, bonds, equities and so on, but trade in the same manner as commodity futures. Contracts for futures are standardised and traded on exchanges. In London, the main futures exchange is LIFFE, although commodity futures are also traded on, for example, the International Petroleum Exchange and the London Metal Exchange. The money markets trade short-term interest-rate futures, which fix the rate of interest on a notional fixed-term deposit of money (usually for 90 days or three months) for a specified period in the future. The sum is notional because no actual sum of money is deposited when buying or selling futures; the instrument is off-balance-sheet. Buying such a contract is equivalent to making a notional deposit, while selling a contract is equivalent to borrowing a notional sum.

The three-month interest-rate future is the most widely used instrument for hedging interest-rate risk.

The LIFFE exchange in London trades short-term interest-rate futures for major currencies including sterling, euros, yen and Swiss franc. Table 6.3 summarises the terms for the short sterling contract as traded on LIFFE.

Name	90-day sterling Libor future
Contract size	£500,000
Delivery months	March, June, September
Delivery date	First business day after last trading day
Last trading day	Third Wednesday of delivery month
Price	100 minus yield
Tick size	0.005
Tick value	£6.25
Trading hours	0825 – 1830 LIFFE Connect (electronic screen trading)

Table 6.3 Description of LIFFE short sterling future contract

Figure 6.29 shows Bloomberg screen DES for the Eurodollar contract, traded on CBOT but actually available for trading 24 hours a day electronically across various global exchanges.

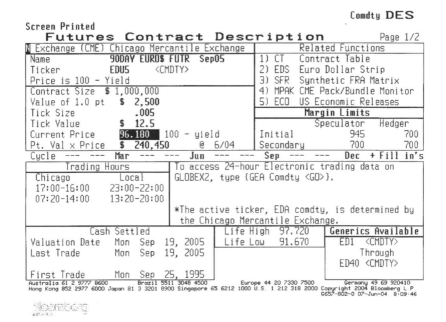

Figure 6.29 Bloomberg screen DES showing Eurodollar contract terms.
©Bloomberg L.P. Used with permission.

The original futures contracts related to physical commodities, which is why we speak of *delivery* when referring to the expiry of financial futures contracts. Exchange-traded futures such as those on LIFFE are set to expire every quarter during the year. The short sterling contract is a deposit of cash; so, as its price refers to the rate of interest on this deposit, the price of the contract is set as :

$$P = 100 - r$$

where P is the price of the contract and r is the rate of interest at the time of expiry implied by the futures contract. This means that if the price of the contract rises, the rate of interest implied goes down, and vice versa. For example, the price of the June 2004 short sterling future (written as Jun04 or M04, from the futures identity letters of H, M, U and Z for contracts expiring in March, June, September and December, respectively) at the start of trading when this contract become the front month on 1st March 2004 was 95.52, which implied a three-month Libor rate of 4.48% on expiry of the contract in June. If a trader bought 20 contracts at this price and then sold them just before the close of trading that day, when the price had risen to 95.55, an implied rate of 4.45%, she would have made 6 ticks profit or £1500. That is, a 6-tick upward price movement in a long position of 20 contracts is equal to £1500. This is calculated as follows:

Profit = ticks gained × tick value × number of contracts
Loss = ticks lost × tick value × number of contracts

The tick value for the short sterling contract is straightforward to calculate, since we know that the contract size is £500,000, there is a minimum price movement (tick movement) of 0.005% and the contract has a three month "maturity".

Tick value = 0.005% × £500,000 × 3/12
= £ 6.25

The profit made by the trader in our example is logical because if we buy short sterling futures we are depositing (notional) funds; if the price of the futures rises, it means the interest rate has fallen. We profit because we have "deposited" funds at a higher rate beforehand. If we expected sterling interest rates to rise, we would sell short sterling futures, which is equivalent to borrowing funds and locking in the loan rate at a lower level.

Note how the concept of buying and selling interest-rate futures differs from FRAs: if we buy an FRA we are borrowing notional funds, whereas if we buy a futures contract we are depositing notional funds. If a position in an interest-rate futures contract is held to expiry, cash settlement will take place on the delivery day for that contract.

Short-term interest-rate contracts in other currencies are similar to the short sterling contract and trade on exchanges such as Eurex in Frankfurt and CBOT in Chicago.

Bloomberg users can calculate the futures strip required to hedge a holding of a short-dated bond using screen TED. Figure 6.30 shows the strip required to hedge a holding on 24 March 2004 of £10 million nominal of a UK gilt, the 6$^3/_4$% 2004 gilt, that matures on 26 November 2004. A total of 54 contracts are required, spread between the June, September and December 2004 short sterling contracts.

<HELP> for explanation.   P174 Corp   **TED**

Euro-Future Strip Hedge   P 1/2

| TREASURY | UKT6 ³₄ | 11/26/04 | 101.6800/101.7400 | (4.17/4.08) BGN | @13:17 |

Price	101.740000	Settlement	3/25/04	Implied Yield TED	43.3
Yield	4.08051%	Face £	10000000	Spread Adjusted TED	43.3
*Implied Yld	4.51396%	Risk	0.67	Implied Price TED	44.0

(*-Compounded, Freq=2, ACT/ACT)

               A Worst //Maturity   Sign Conv N Curve-Security

Stub Period: 84 days   (11/26/04) (11/26/04)   Total Hedge: 54 contracts

Contract to strip L   RATES FROM 3/24/04

| 1-Mth | 2-Mth | 3-Mth | 4-Mth | 5-Mth | 6-Mth | 9-Mth | 12-Mt |
| 4.1719 | 4.2312 | 4.3263 | 4.3700 | 4.4125 | 4.4675 | 4.5738 | 4.6737 |

Price/Rate Quoted? R   Spread Adjusted Hedge? N   Bid/Mid/Ask/Last/Best B

	Rate	Cntrcts	Rate	Cntrcts	Rate	Cntrcts	Rate	Cntrcts
STUB	4.3017	19						
L M4	4.5000	20						
L U4	4.6400	15						

Figure 6.30   Bloomberg page TED, showing futures strip hedge for £10 million
position in UK gilt 6.75% 2004, as at 24 March 2004
©Bloomberg L.P. Used with permission.

Pricing interest-rate futures

The price of a three-month interest-rate futures contract is the implied
interest rate for that currency's three-month rate at the time of expiry of the
contract. Therefore, there is always a close relationship and correlation
between futures prices, FRA rates (which are derived from futures prices)
and cash-market rates. On the day of expiry, the price of the future will be
equal to the Libor rate as fixed that day. This is known as the Exchange
Delivery Settlement Price (EDSP) and is used in the calculation of the
delivery amount. During the life of the contract its price will be less closely
related to the actual three-month Libor rate *today*, but closely related to the
forward rate for the time of expiry.

Equation (3.25) was our basic forward-rate formula for money-market
maturity forward rates, which we adapted to use as our FRA price equation.
If we incorporate some extra terminology to cover the dealing dates involved
it can also be used as our futures price formula. Let us say that:

T_0 is the trade date

T_M is the contract expiry date

T_{CASH} is the value date for cash market deposits traded on T_0

T_1 is the value date for cash market deposits traded on T_M

T_2 is the maturity date for a three-month cash market deposit traded on T_M

We can then use equation (3.25) as our futures price formula to obtain P_{fut}, the futures price for a contract up to the expiry date.

$$P_{fut} = 100 - \left[\frac{r_2 n_2 - r_1 n_1}{n_f \left(1 + r_1 \frac{n_1}{365}\right)} \right] \qquad (6.18)$$

where

P_{fut} is the futures price

r_1 is the cash-market interest rate to T_1

r_2 is the cash-market interest rate to T_2

n_1 is the number of days from T_{CASH} to T_1

n_2 is the number of days from T_{CASH} to T_2

n_f is the number of days from T_1 to T_2.

The formula uses a 365 day-count convention which is applies in the sterling money markets; where a market uses a 360-day base this must be used in the equation instead.

In practice, the price of a contract at any one time will be close to the theoretical price that would be established by 6.18 above. Discrepancies will arise for supply-and-demand reasons in the market, as well as because Libor rates are often quoted only to the nearest sixteenth or 0.0625. The price between FRAs and futures are correlated very closely. In fact, banks will often price FRAs using futures, and use futures to hedge their FRA books. When hedging a FRA book with futures, the hedge is quite close to being exact, because the two prices track each other almost tick for tick. However, the tick value of a futures contract is fixed, and uses (as we saw above) a 3/12 basis, while FRA settlement values use a 360 or 365 day-base. The FRA trader will be aware of this when putting on her hedge.

In our discussion of forward rates in Chapter 3, we emphasized that they were the market's view on future rates using all information available today. Of course, a futures price today is very unlikely to be in line with the actual three-month interest rate that is prevailing at the time of the contract's expiry. This explains why prices for futures and actual cash rates will differ on any particular day. Up until expiry, the futures price is the implied forward rate; of course, there is always a discrepancy between this forward rate and the cash market rate *today*. The gap between the cash price and the futures price is known as the basis. This is defined as:

$$\text{Basis} = \text{Cash price} - \text{Futures price}$$

At any point during the life of a futures contract prior to final settlement – at which point futures and cash rates converge – there is usually a difference between current cash-market rates and the rates implied by the futures price. This is the difference we've just explained. In fact, the difference between the price implied by the current three-month interbank deposit and the futures price is known as simple basis, but it is what most market participants refer to as the basis. Simple basis consists of two separate components, theoretical basis and value basis. Theoretical basis is the difference between the price implied by the current three-month interbank deposit rate and that implied by the theoretical fair futures price based on cash-market forward rates, given by (6.18). This basis may be either positive or negative, depending on the shape of the yield curve.

Futures contracts do not, in practice, provide a precise tool for locking into cash-market rates today for a transaction that takes place in the future, although this is what they are, in theory, designed to do. Futures do allow a bank to lock in a rate for a transaction to take place in the future, and this rate is the forward rate. The basis is the difference between today's cash-market rate and the forward rate on a particular date in the future. As a futures contract approaches expiry, its price and the rate in the cash market will converge (the process is given the name convergence). As we noted earlier, this is given by the EDSP and the two prices (rates) will be exactly in line at the exact moment of expiry.

Hedging using interest-rate futures

Banks use interest-rate futures to hedge interest-rate risk exposure in cash and OBS instruments. Bond-trading desks also often use futures to hedge positions in bonds of up to two or three years' maturity, as contracts are traded up to three years' maturity. The liquidity of such "far month" contracts is considerably lower than for near-month contracts and the "front month" contract (the current contract, for the next maturity month). When hedging a bond with a maturity of, say, two years' maturity, the trader will put on a strip of futures contracts that matches as nearly as possible the expiry date of the bond. The purpose of a hedge is to protect the value of a current or anticipated cash market or OBS position from adverse changes in interest rates. The hedger will try to offset the effect of the change in interest rate on the value of his cash position with the change in value of her hedging instrument. If the hedge is an exact one, the loss on the main position should be compensated by a profit on the hedge position. If the trader is expecting a fall in interest rates and wishes to protect against such a fall she will buy futures, known as a long hedge, and will sell futures (a short hedge) if wishing to protect against a rise in rates.

Bond traders also use three-month interest-rate contracts to hedge positions in short-dated bonds. For instance, a market-maker running a short-dated bond book would find it more appropriate to hedge his book using short-dated futures rather than the longer-dated bond futures contract. When this happens it is important to accurately calculate the correct number of contracts to use for the hedge. To construct a bond hedge it will be necessary to use a strip of contracts, thus ensuring that the maturity date of the bond is covered by the longest-dated futures contract. The hedge is calculated by finding the sensitivity of each cash flow to changes in each of the relevant forward rates. Each cash flow is considered individually and the hedge values are then aggregated and rounded to the nearest whole number of contracts.

EXAMPLE 6.5 Forward rate calculation for money–market term

Consider two positions:
- a repo of £250 million gilts GC from 2nd January 2000 for 30 days at 6.500%,
- a reverse repo of £250 million gilts GC from 2nd January 2000 for 60 days at 6.625%.

The two positions generate a 30-day forward 30-day interest-rate exposure (a 30 versus 60 day forward rate). This exposure can be hedged by buying a FRA that matches the gap, or by selling a strip of futures. What forward rate must be used if the trader wished to hedge this exposure, assuming no bid-offer spreads and a 365 day-count base?

The 30-day by 60-day forward rate can be calculated using the forward-rate formula at 6.19.

$$rf = \left[\left(\frac{1 + \left(rs_2 \times \frac{L}{M}\right)}{1 + \left(rs_1 \times \frac{S}{M}\right)} \right) - 1 \right] \times \frac{M}{L - S} \qquad (6.19)$$

where
rf is the forward rate
rs_2 is the long-period rate
rs_1 is the short-period rate
L is the long-period days
S is the short-period days
M is the day-count base

Using this formula, we obtain a 30 v 60 day forward rate of 6.713560%. This assumes no bid-offer spread, which will of course apply.

This interest-rate exposure can be hedged using interest-rate futures or Forward Rate Agreements (FRAs). Either method is an effective hedging mechanism, although the trader must be aware of:

• basis risk that exists between Repo rates and the forward rates implied by futures and FRAs

• date mismatch between expiry of futures contracts and the maturity dates of the repo transactions.

Therefore, a FRA will probably be preferred.

APPENDIX 6.1

Currencies using money market year base of 365 days
• Sterling
• Hong Kong dollar
• Malaysian ringgit
• Singapore dollar
• South African rand
• Taiwan dollar
• Thai baht

In addition the domestic markets, but not the international markets, of the following currencies also use a 365-day base:
• Australian dollar
• Canadian dollar
• Japanese yen
• New Zealand dollar

To convert an interest rate i quoted on a 365-day basis to one quoted on a 360-day basis ($i*$) use the expressions given at A6.1.

$$i = i^* \times \frac{365}{360}$$

$$i^* = i \times \frac{360}{365}$$

(A6.1)

Selected Bibliography and References

Blake, D., *Financial Market Analysis*, Wiley, 2000.

Chicago Board of Trade, *Interest rate Futures for Institutional Investors*, CBOT, 1987.

Fabozzi, F., Mann, S., and Choudhry, M., *The Global Money Markets*, Wiley 2003.

Figlewski, F., *Hedging with Financial Futures for Institutional Investors*, Probus Publishing, 1986.

French, K., "A Comparison of Futures and Forwards Prices", *Journal of Financial Economics* 12, November 1983, p. 311-342.

Hull, J., *Options, Futures and Other Derivatives* (4th edition), Prentice-Hall Inc., 1999.

Jarrow, R. and Oldfield, G., "Forward Contracts and Futures Contracts", *Journal of Financial Economics* 9, December 1981, p.373-382.

Stigum, M. and Robinson, F., *Money Market and Bond Calculations*, Irwin, 1996.

7

Hybrid Securities and Structured Securities

In this chapter, we describe in generic format some of the more exotic or structured notes that have been introduced into the fixed-income market. The motivations behind the development and use of these products are varied, but include the desire for increased yield without additional credit risk, as well as the need to alter, transform or transfer risk exposure and risk-return profiles. Certain structured notes were also developed as hedging instruments. The instruments themselves have been issued by banks, corporate institutions and sovereign authorities. By using certain types of notes, investors can gain access to different markets, sometimes synthetically, that were previously not available to them. For instance, by purchasing a structured note an investor can take on board a position that reflects her views on a particular exchange rate and anticipated changes in yield curve but in a different market. The investment instrument can be tailored to suit the investor's particular risk profile.

We describe a number of structured notes that are currently available to investors today, although often investors will seek particular features that suit their needs, and so there are invariably detail variations in each note. We stress that this is only the tip of the iceberg, and many different types of notes are available. Indeed, if any particular investor or issuer requirement has not been met, it is often a relatively straightforward process whereby an investment bank can structure a note that meets one or both specific requirements.

Floating-rate notes

Floating-rate notes are not structured notes! However, we describe them here as a prelude to a discussion on inverse floating-rate notes.

Floating-rate notes (FRNs) are bonds that have variable rates of interest; the coupon rate is linked to a specified index and changes periodically as the index changes. An FRN is usually issued with a coupon that pays a fixed spread over a reference index; for example, the coupon may be 50 basis points over the six-month interbank rate. An FRN whose spread over the reference rate is not fixed is known as a variable rate note. Since the value for the reference benchmark index is not known, it is not possible to calculate the redemption yield for an FRN. Additional features have been added to FRNs, including floors (the coupon cannot fall below a specified minimum rate), caps (the coupon cannot rise above a maximum rate) and callability. There also exist perpetual FRNs. As in other markets, borrowers frequently issue paper with specific or even esoteric terms in order to meet particular requirements or meet customer demand. For example, during 2002 Citibank issued US dollar-denominated FRNs with interest payments indexed to the Euribor rate, and another FRN with its day-count basis linked to a specified Libor range.

Generally the reference interest rate for FRNs is the London interbank rate; the offered rate – that is, the rate at which a bank will lend funds to another bank – is LIBOR. An FRN will pay interest at LIBOR plus a quoted margin (or spread). The interest rate is fixed for a three-month or six-month period and is reset in line with the LIBOR fixing at the end of the interest period. Hence, at the coupon re-set date for a sterling FRN paying six-month Libor +0.50%, if the Libor fix is 7.6875%, then the FRN will pay a coupon of 8.1875%. Interest therefore will accrue at a daily rate of £0.0224315.

On the coupon reset date, an FRN will be priced precisely at par. Between reset dates, it will trade very close to par because of the way in which the coupon is reset. If market rates rise between reset dates an FRN will trade slightly below par; similarly, if rates fall the paper will trade slightly above. This makes FRNs very similar in behavior to money-market instruments traded on a yield basis, although FRNs have much longer maturities, of course. Investors can opt to view FRNs as essentially money-market instruments or as alternatives to conventional bonds. For this reason, one can use two approaches in analysing FRNs. The first approach is known as the margin method. This calculates the difference between the return on an FRN and that on an equivalent money-market security. There are two variations on this; simple margin and discounted margin.

The simple-margin method is sometimes preferred because it does not require the forecasting of future interest rates and coupon values. Simple margin is defined as the average return on an FRN throughout its life compared with the reference interest rate. It has two components: a quoted margin either above or below the reference rate, and a capital gain or loss element which is calculated under the assumption that the difference between the current price of the FRN and the maturity value is spread evenly over the remaining life of the bond. Simple margin is given by (7.1).

$$\text{Simple margin} = \frac{(M - P_d)}{(100 \times T)} + M_q \qquad (7.1)$$

where
P_d is $P + AI$, the dirty price
M is the par value
T is the number of years from settlement date to maturity
M_q is the quoted margin.

A quoted margin that is positive reflects yield for an FRN that is offering a higher yield than the comparable money-market security.

At certain times, the simple-margin formula is adjusted to take account of any change in the reference rate since the last coupon reset date. This is done by defining an adjusted price, which is either:

$$AP_d = P_d + (re + M) \times \frac{N_{sc}}{365} \times 100 - \frac{C}{2} \times 100$$

or $\qquad\qquad\qquad\qquad\qquad\qquad\qquad\qquad\qquad\qquad (7.2)$

$$AP_d = P_d + (re + M) \times \frac{N_{sc}}{365} \times P_d - \frac{C}{2} \times 100$$

where
AP_d is the adjusted dirty price
re is the current value of the reference interest rate (such as Libor)
$C/2$ is the next coupon payment (that is, C is the reference interest rate on the last coupon reset date plus M_q)
N_{sc} is the number of days between settlement and the next coupon date.

The upper equation in (7.2) ignores the current yield effect: all payments are assumed to be received on the basis of par, and this understates the value of the coupon for FRNs trading below par and overstates the value when they are trading above par. The lower equation in (7.2) takes account of the current yield effect.

The adjusted price AP_d replaces the current price P_d in 7.1 to give an adjusted simple margin. The simple-margin method has the disadvantage of amortising the discount or premium on the FRN in a straight line over the remaining life of the bond rather than at a constantly compounded rate. The discounted-margin method uses the latter approach. The distinction between simple margin and discounted margin is exactly the same as that between simple yield to maturity and yield to maturity. The discounted-margin method does have a disadvantage in that it requires a forecast of the reference interest rate over the remaining life of the bond.

The discounted margin is the solution to equation (7.3) shown below, given for an FRN that pays semi-annual coupons.

$$P_d = \left\{ \frac{1}{[1 + \frac{1}{2}(re + DM)]^{days/year}} \right\} \cdot \left\{ \frac{C}{2} + \sum_{t=1}^{N-1} \frac{(re^* + M) \times 100/2}{[1 + \frac{1}{2}(re^* + DM)]^t} + \frac{M}{[1 + \frac{1}{2}(re^* + DM)]^{N-1}} \right\}$$

(7.3)

where

DM is the discounted margin
re is the current value of the reference interest rate
re^* is the assumed (or forecast) value of the reference rate over the remaining life of the bond
M is the quoted margin
N is the number of coupon payments before redemption.

Equation (7.3) may be stated in terms of discount factors instead of the reference rate. The yield-to-maturity spread method of evaluating FRNs is designed to allow direct comparison between FRNs and fixed-rate bonds. The yield to maturity on the FRN (rmf) is calculated using (7.3) with both ($re + DM$) and ($re^* + DM$) replaced with rmf. The yield to maturity on a reference bond (rmb) is calculated using 1.11. The yield-to-maturity spread is defined as:

$$\text{Yield-to-maturity spread} = rmf - rmb.$$

If this is positive, the FRN offers a higher yield than the reference bond.

In addition to plain-vanilla FRNs, some of the other types of floating-rate bonds that have traded in the market are:

Collared FRNs: these offer caps and floors on an instrument, thus establishing a maximum and minimum coupon on the deal. Effectively, these securities contain two embedded options – the issuer buying a cap and selling a floor to the investor.

228

Step-up recovery FRNs: where coupons are fixed against comparable longer maturity bonds, thus providing investors with the opportunity to maintain exposure to short-term assets while capitalising on a positive sloping yield curve.

Corridor FRNs: these were introduced to capitalise on expectations of comparative interest-rate inactivity. A high-risk/high-reward instrument, it offers investors a very substantial uplift over a chosen reference rate. But rates have to remain within a relatively narrow corridor if the interest payment is not to be forfeited entirely.

Inverse floating-rate note

Description

The inverse floating-rate note or inverse floater is an instrument that offers enhanced returns to investors that believe the market outlook for bonds generally is positive. An inverse floater pays a coupon that increases as general market rates decline. In other words, it is an instrument for those who have an opposite view to the market consensus. They are suitable in an economic environment of low inflation and a positive yield curve, factors which would, in a conventional analysis, suggest rising interest rates in the medium term. It is also possible to link the inverse floater's coupon to rates in an environment of a negative yield curve. Such a note would suit an investor who agreed with the market consensus.

The coupon on an inverse floater may be determined in a number of ways. The most common approach involves a formula that quotes a fixed interest rate, minus a variable element that is linked to an index. Coupons are usually set at a floor level, which in the absence of a floor will be 0%.

Issuers of inverse floaters are usually corporates, although specialised investment vehicles also issue such notes to meet specific client demand.[1]

Table 7.1 illustrates the coupon arrangement on a typical inverse floater and, particularly, how changes in the Libor rate affect the coupon that is payable on the note.

---

[1] By specialised investment vehicles, we mean funds set up to invest in particular areas or sectors. For example, wholly-owned subsidiaries of Citigroup such as Centauri or Dorada Corporation issue notes, backed by a AAA-rating, specifically to suit investor demand. As such, notes issued by such bodies assume a wide variety of forms, often linked with a currency or interest-rate swap element, and in a wide variety of currencies. As they have an ongoing requirement for funds, notes may be issued at any time, especially when a particular investor requirement is identified. Such vehicles are also known as Structured Investment Vehicles (SIVs).

Nominal value	£100,000,000
Issue date	5 Jan 2000
Maturity date	5 Jan 2003
Note coupon	15.75% − (2 × Libor)
Day-count basis	act/365
Index	6-month Libor
Current Libor rate	5.15%
Rate fixing	Semi-annual
Initial coupon	5.45%
Minimum coupon	0%

GBP Libor	Coupon payable
1.00%	14.75%
1.50%	12.75%
2.00%	11.75%
2.50%	10.75%
3.00%	9.75%
3.50%	8.75%
4.00%	7.75%
4.50%	6.75%
5.00%	5.75%
5.50%	4.75%
6.00%	3.75%
6.50%	2.75%
7.00%	1.75%

Table 7.1 Terms of an hypothetical inverse floater bond

The inverse floater provides investors with a slightly above-market initial coupon in a yield-curve environment that is positive.[2] The above-market initial coupon results from the swap bank paying this in return for a Libor income, in a swap structure that matches the maturity of the note. The Libor level will be lower than the longer-term swap rate because we assume a positive-sloping yield-curve environment. Investors can benefit from an arrangement that provides them with a coupon sensitivity that is twice that of changes in the rate of Libor.

---

[2] The sterling yield curve was inverted at this time, but remained slightly positive at the money-market maturities, up to seven or eight months.

Another interesting feature of inverse-floater notes is their high duration, which results from the leveraged arrangement of the coupon. In our hypothetical example, the note has a calendar maturity of three years and thus its modified duration will be much higher. This is shown in Table 7.2. Inverse floaters have the highest duration values of any instrument traded in the fixed-income market. This makes them highly interest-rate-sensitive products.

Duration of 3-year note with 5.30% coupon	2.218 years
Duration of 3-year inverse floater ($\times$ 3)	6.654 years

Table 7.2 Duration of three-year inverse-floater note

A number of variations of the inverse floater described have been introduced. It is straightforward to link the notes to any quoted reference index, which would be of interest to investors who had a particular view of short- or long-term interest-rate indices – for example, the central bank repo rate, 10-year swap rates or a government benchmark. The leverage of the notes can also be altered to reflect the investor's risk preference, and the fixed element may be altered for the same reason. Equally, the fixed element can be set to move upwards or downwards as required. As another possibility, investors who have a particular view on a specific foreign interest-rate market, but who (for one reason or another) are not able to invest in that market's securities, can gain an exposure that reflects their views through the purchase of an inverse FRN that is linked to the foreign index but pays coupon in the domestic currency.

Hedging the note

Borrowers often issue notes in a different currency from the currency they require, and will typically swap the proceeds into the required currency by means of a currency swap. An interest-rate swap arrangement is used to hedge the interest-rate exposure on the inverse floater. The issuer will transact the swap structure with a swap bank, usually a high-rated institution. The swap bank will hedge its own exposure as part of its normal operations in the swap markets. The structure that would apply to the hypothetical note above is shown in Figure 7.1.

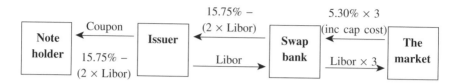

Figure 7.1 Inverse-floater hedge structure

The swap transacted with the issuer involves:
* paying fixed at the note coupon level
* receiving Libor.

The other side of this transaction for the swap bank is another swap where it pays floating and receives fixed. This is made up of the following:
* the swap bank pays Libor on the swap; and
* it receives 5.30%, which is the three-year swap rate.

However, the swap bank must also hedge the coupon rate on the note, as this is now his exposure (the issuer being fully hedged by the swap bank and paying Libor, its desired cost of funds). The coupon rate is 15.75% − (2 × Libor), which in effect means that the note holder is receiving 15.75% and paying 2 × Libor. Therefore, the swap bank, in order to hedge this cash flow, will pay 2 × Libor and receive two fixed rates of 5.30%. The three rates for the swap total 15.90%. This is higher than the fixed component of the coupon in the note, by 15 basis points. This difference is the cost of fixing a cap, as detailed below.

The inverse floater has a minimum coupon on 0%, and to hedge this element the swap bank will need to purchase an interest-rate cap on Libor with a strike rate of 7.875%. The strike rate is the note coupon on 15.75% divided by two. The cap element of the hedge protects the dealer against a rise in Libor over the set rate. The cap has a cost of 15 basis points, which explains the difference over the coupon rate in the swap structure.

Indexed amortising note

Description

Another type of hybrid note is the Indexed Amortising Note or IAN. They were introduced in the US domestic market in the early 1990s at the demand of investors in asset-backed notes known as collateralised mortgage obligations or CMOs. IANs are fixed-coupon unsecured notes issued with a nominal value that is not fixed. That is, the nominal amount may reduce in value ahead of the legal maturity according to the levels recorded by a specified reference index such as six-month Libor. If the reference remains static or its level decreases, the IAN value will amortise in nominal value. The legal maturity of IANs is short- to medium-term, with the five-year maturity being common. The notes have been issued by banks and corporates, although a large volume has been issued by US government agencies. The yield payable on IANs is typically at a premium above that of similar credit-quality conventional debt. The amortisation schedule on an IAN is linked to the movement of the specified reference index, which is easily understood. This is considered an advantage to certain mortgage-backed notes, which amortise in accordance with less clearly defined patterns such as a prepayment schedule.

An issuer of IANS will arrange a hedge that makes the funding obtained more attractive; for example, a straight Libor-type exposure. This is most commonly arranged through a swap arrangement that mirrors the note structure. A diagrammatic representation is shown in Figure 7.2. In fact, it is more common for the swap arrangement to involve a series of options on swaps. The coupon available on an IAN might be attractive to investors when the volatility on swaptions is high and there is a steep, positively sloping yield curve. Under such an environment the option-element of an IAN would confer greatest value.

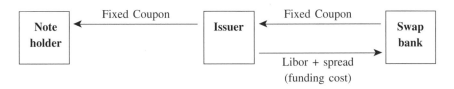

Figure 7.2 IAN hedge arrangement

The terms of a hypothetical IAN issue are given at Table 7.3.

Issuer	Mortgage agency
Nominal value	$250,000,000
Legal maturity	6 years
Coupon	2-year Treasury plus 100 bps
Interest basis	Monthly
"Lock-out period"	Three years
Reference index	6-month Libor
6m Libor fixing on issue	5.15%
Minimum level of note	20%

Average life sensitivity

Libor rate	Amortisation rate	Average life (years)
5.15%	100%	3
6.00%	100%	3
7.00%	21%	4.1
8.00%	7%	5.6
9.00%	0.00%	6

Table 7.3 Hypothetical IAN issue

Under the terms of issue of the note summarised in Table 7.3, the coupon payable is the current two-year government benchmark plus a fixed spread of 1%. The note has a legal maturity of six years. However, it will mature in three years if the six-month Libor rate is at a level of 6.00% or below two years from the date of issue. If the rate is above 6.00%, the maturity of the note will be extended. The "lock-out" of three years means that the note has a minimum life of three years, irrespective of what happens to Libor rates. Amortisation takes place if on subsequent rate-fixing dates after the lock-out period the Libor rate rises. The maximum maturity of the note is six years. If at any time there is less than 20% of the nominal value in issue, the note is cancelled in full.

Advantages to investors

The IAN structure offers advantages to investors under certain conditions. If the credit quality is acceptable, the notes offer a high yield over a relatively low term to maturity. The amortisation structure is easier to understand than that on mortgage-backed securities, which contain prepayment schedules that are based on assumptions that may not apply. This means that investors will know with certainty how the amortisation of the note will proceed, given the level of the reference index at any given time. The lock-out period of a note is usually set at a period that offers investor comfort, such as three years; during this time no amortisation can take place.

As with the other instruments described here, IANs can be tailored to meet individual investor requirements. The legal maturity and lock-out period are features that are most frequently subject to variation, with the yield premium decreasing as the lock-out period becomes closer to the formal maturity. The reference index can be a government benchmark or an interbank rate such as the swap rate. However, the most common reference is the Libor rate.

Synthetic convertible note

Description

Synthetic convertible notes are fixed-coupon securities whose total return is linked to an external source such as the level of an equity index, or the price of a specific security. The fixed-coupon element is typically at a low level, and the investor has greater exposure to the performance of the external index. A common arrangement has the note redeeming at par, but redeemable at a greater amount if the performance of the reference index exceeds a stated minimum. However, the investor has the safety net of redemption at par. Another typical structure is a zero-coupon note, issued at par and redeemable at par, but redeemable at a higher level if a specified equity index performs above a pre-specified level.

Table 7.4 lists the terms of a hypothetical synthetic convertible note issue that is linked to the FTSE-100 equity index. This note will pay par on maturity, but if the level of the FTSE-100 has increased by more than 10% from the level on note issue, the note will be redeemed at par plus this amount. Note, however, that this is an investment suitable only for someone who is very bullish on the prospects for the FTSE-100. If this index does not raise by the minimum level, the investor will have received a coupon of 0.5%, which was roughly five percentage points below the level for two-year sterling at this time.

Nominal value	£50,000,000
Term to maturity	Two years
Issue date	17-Jun-99
Maturity date	17-Jun-01
Issue price	£100
Coupon	0.50%
Interest basis	Semi-annual
Redemption proceeds	Min [100, Formula level]
Formula level	$100 + [100 \times (R(I) - (1.1 \times R(II)) / R(II)]$
Index	FTSE-100
R(I)	Index level on maturity
R(II)	Index level on issue

Hedge terms

Issuer pays	Libor
Swap bank pays	Redemption proceeds in accordance with formula

Table 7.4 Terms of a synthetic convertible note issue

Investor benefits

Similarly to a convertible bonds, a synthetic convertible note provides investors with a fixed coupon together with additional market upside potential if the level of the reference index performs above a certain level. Unlike the convertible, however, the payoff is in the form of cash.

The reference can be virtually any publicly quoted source, and notes have been issued whose payout is linked to the exchange rate of two currencies, the days on which Libor falls within a specified range, the performance of a selected basket of stocks (say, "technology stocks"), and so on.

Interest-differential notes

Interest-differential notes, or IDNs, are hybrid securities which are aimed at investors who wish to put on a position that reflects their view on the interest-rate differential between rates of two different currencies. Notes in the US market are usually denominated in US dollars, whereas Euromarket notes have been issued in a wide range of global currencies.

There are a number of variations of IDNs. Notes may pay a variable coupon and a fixed redemption amount, or a fixed coupon and a redemption amount that is determined by the level or performance of an external reference index. IDNs have also been issued with payoff profiles that are linked to the differentials in interest rates of two specified currencies, or between one currency across different maturities.

Example of IDN

Here, we discuss a five-year note that is linked to the differential between US dollar-Libor and euro-libor.

Term to maturity	Five years
Coupon	[(2 × USD Libor) − (2 × EUR Libor) − .50%]
Current USD Libor	6.15%
Current EUR Libor	3.05%
Rate differential	2.65%
First coupon fix	5.70%
Current five-year benchmark	4.75%
Yield spread over benchmark	0.95%

Change in Libor spread (bps p.a.)	Libor spread at rate reset	Spread over benchmark
75	4.78%	2.34%
50	3.90%	1.88%
25	3.15%	1.21%
0	2.65%	0.95%
−25	1.97%	0.56%
−50	1.32%	0.34%
−75	0.89%	0.12%
−100	0.32%	−0.28%

Table 7.5 IDN example

The return on this note is a function of the spread between the US dollar-Libor rate and euro-libor. An increase in the spread results in a higher coupon payable on the note, while a narrowing of the spread results in a lower coupon payable. Such a structure will appeal to an investor who has a particular view on the US-dollar and EUR yield curves. For instance, assume that the US-dollar curve is inverted and the euro curve is positively-sloping. A position in an IDN (structured as above) on these two currencies allows an investor to avoid outright yield-curve plays in each currency and, instead, put on a trade that reflects a view on the relative level of interest rates in each currency. An IDN in this environment would allow an investor to earn a high yield while taking a view that is different from the market consensus.

When analysing an IDN, an investor must regard the note to be the equivalent to a fixed-coupon bond together with a double indexation of an interest-rate differential. The effect of this double indexation on the differential is to create two long positions in a five-year US-dollar fixed-rate note and two short positions in a EUR fixed-rate note. The short position in the EUR note means that the EUR exchange-rate risk is removed and the investor has an exposure only to the EUR interest-rate risk, which is the desired position.

The issuer of the note hedges the note with a swap structure as with other hybrid securities. The arrangement involves both US-dollar and EUR interest-rate swaps. The swap bank takes the opposite position in the swaps.

Table 7.5 also illustrates the return profiles possible under different interest-rate scenarios. One possibility shows that the IDN provides a 95 basis point yield premium over the five-year government benchmark yield. However, this assumes, rather unrealistically, that the interest differential between the US-dollar and EUR interest rates remains constant through to the final coupon setting date. More significantly, though, we see that the yield premium available on the note increases as the spread differential between the two rates increases. In a spread-tightening environment, the note offers a premium over the government yield as long as the tightening does not exceed 100 basis points each year.

Benefits to investors

IDN-type instruments allow investors to put on positions that reflect their view on foreign interest-rate direction and/or levels, but without having to expose themselves to currency (exchange-rate) risk at the same time. The notes may also be structured in a way that allows investors to take a view on any maturity point of the yield curve. For instance, the coupon may be set in accordance with the differential between the 10-year government benchmark yields of two specified countries. As another approach, investors can arrange combinations of different maturities in the same currency, which is a straight yield curve or relative-value trade in a domestic or foreign currency.

The risk run by a note holder is that the interest-rate differential moves in the opposite direction from that sought, which reduces the coupon payable and may even result in a lower yield than that available on the benchmark bond.

Interest-spread and credit-linked notes

Yield-spread notes

An example of a yield-spread note is the so-called CMS spread note. In this structure, the coupon is linked to the spread between the short and long ends of the yield curve. For reasons of transparency, this is usually the swap-rate curve rather than the bond-yield curve. Some notes add this spread to the advertised (fixed) coupon of the bond. So, for instance, if the spread between the 30-year swap rate and the two-year swap rate at the start of the interest period is 2.4%, and the coupon element is 4%, the total coupon payable will be 6.40%.

The swap rate indices can be found on a media system such as Bloomberg, where the CMS (constant maturity swap) tickers for 30-year and two-year is CMS30Y and CMS20Y.

For illustration, we look at the terms of a 10-year callable, one-year CMS spread note below.

Issuer:	Banking entity (AA-rated)
Term:	10 years, subject to call provision
Issue price: 100%	
Coupon:	6.00% for year 1;
	Thereafter, Max [1.50 + 2.5*(CMS30Y −
CMS2Y); 0%]	
Redemption:	100%

Target-redemption note

A further variation on structured notes is the target-redemption note. This has a more esoteric risk/reward profile than most structured notes. It is terminated when the sum of all the coupons paid out reaches a specified target-redemption level at any coupon date, within the set life of the bond. So, in this case, only the maturity date of the bond is an unknown; both the total coupon and the principal are guaranteed.

Example terms of a target-redemption note are suggested below.

Issuer:	Banking entity (AA-rated)
Term:	10 years, subject to target redemption being reached earlier
Issue price:	100%
Coupon:	6.00% for year 1; Thereafter, max [10% − 2*(6m Libor in arrears);0]
Early redemption:	The note is redeemed at par on any coupon date on which the sum of the coupons paid to date reaches the lifetime coupon cap. The coupon paid on the last interest period shall be the lifetime coupon cap minus the sum of all paid coupons before that interest period
Lifetime coupon cap:	12.00%
Redemption:	100%

The attraction of this structure for investors is that it offers the potential of a higher return if the note is terminated ahead of schedule. So, for the bond illustrated above, if Libor moves upwards (something the forward curve or futures rates will imply), the note will terminate well ahead of schedule.

Principal-protected credit-linked notes

Principal-protected notes are observed frequently in the markets. Although they exist in many variations, typically these are notes that invest 100% of the principal on a highly rated credit, while conversely linking the interest payments to a riskier structure such as the lower-rated tranches of a synthetic CDO deal (see Chapter 12).

The interest element may be delivered in one of two ways: either paid as regular coupon or paid only on maturity. The latter arrangement will deliver a higher return because it carries a higher risk profile. Some notes have the credit-linking for only part of their life: for instance, a five-year credit-linked note where the coupon is indexed to credit events for the first three years only.[3]

---

[3] Credit events are discussed in Chapter 17 on credit derivatives.

An example of such a note is illustrated below.

Issuer:	Banking entity (AA-rated)
Term:	Five years
Issue price:	100%
Coupon:	Paid annually, indexed to the number of credit events to occur on a reference portfolio:
	6.5% for no credit event
	4.5% for one credit event
	2.5% for two credit events
	0% for three or more credit events
Credit events:	Bankruptcy, failure to pay, debt restructuring
Reference portfolio:	A basket of 50 investment-grade corporate names ("reference entities")

Warrants

Introduction

A warrant entitles its holder to purchase a specified asset at a set price at a specified date or dates. The terms defining a warrant usually remain unchanged during its entire life, and the asset may be bonds, equities, an index, commodities or other instruments. Hence a warrant is an option issued by a firm to purchase a given number of shares in that firm (*equity warrant*) or more of the firm's bonds (*bond warrant*), at a given exercise price at any time before the warrant expires. If the warrant is exercised, the firm issues new shares (or bonds) at the exercise price and so raises additional finance. Warrants generally have longer maturities than conventional options (five years or longer, although there is usually a liquid market in very long-dated over-the-counter equity options), and some warrants are perpetual.

Warrants are usually attached to bonds (*host bond*) to start with, in most cases such warrants are detachable and can be traded separately. Equity warrants do not carry any shareholders rights until they are exercised, for example they pay no dividends and have no voting rights. Bond warrants can either be exercised into the same class of bonds as the host bond or into a different class of bond. In valuing a warrant it is important to recognise that exercising the warrant (unlike exercising an ordinary call option) will increase the number of shares outstanding. This will have the effect of diluting earnings per share and hence reducing the share price. Hence although equity warrants are often valued in the same way as an American call option, the pricing must also take into account this dilution effect. Warrants are often used in conjunction with a new bond issue, to act as a "sweetener", and are common instruments in the Japanese bond and equity markets. If the issuing company performs well, the investor can eventually exercise the warrant purchase the company's equity at the exercise price fixed at the time the warrant was issued. During this time, in the same way as for a convertible bondholder, the investor has the security of holding the company's fixed interest debt, which acts as a type of security in the event that the company's share price declines.

In the UK some companies use warrants to obtain a steady flow of new investment. For example, every year from 1988 the London-listed company BTR has issued bonus warrants free to its shareholders, with the exercise price set just out-of-the-money. From the investor's viewpoint warrants may be used as a means of having an exposure to a company's shares but with a relatively low capital outlay at the start. They also allows the investor already holding shares to sell them while still maintaining an equity stake. This is known as *cash extraction* and is a straightforward strategy. The investor sells the shares, uses some of the proceeds to buy warrants representing the same number of shares, and invests the remaining cash in interest-bearing instruments. The price of warrants, just like convertibles, do not move one-for-one with the underlying equity unless they are deep in-the-money however, so a rise in the share price will not be matched by the same rise in the warrant price. In the short term therefore an investor following a cash extraction strategy may miss out on share price performance, in addition to any dividend payments.

A *put warrant* is similar to a put option in that it gives the holder to sell, rather than buy, a certain amount of underlying stock at a pre-specified strike price.

Analysis

As with vanilla call options the value of a warrant has two components, an intrinsic value (which in the warrant market is known as *formula value*) and a time value (*premium* over formula value). Although the term *premium* is used in the options market to refer to the price paid for an option, in the warrant market the conventional term *price* is used. The *warrant premium* is usually used to refer to the amount by which the warrant price plus the exercise price exceeds the current underlying share price.

The formula value is determined by Equation 20.1

Formula value = (Share price − Exercise price) × Number new shares issued
on exercise (7.4)

If the exercise price exceeds the share price, the formula value is zero
and the warrant is said to be "out-of-the-money". If the share price exceeds
the exercise price the warrant is in-the-money and the formula value is
positive. The time value is always positive up until expiry of the warrant. As
with options the time value declines as the expiry date approaches and on
the expiry date itself the time value is zero.

The fair price of a warrant is given by 20.2. below.

$$\text{Warrant value} = \frac{P_C}{1+q} \times \text{no. of new shares if warrant is exercised}$$
(7.5)

where q is the proportionate increase in the number of shares outstanding if
all the warrants were exercised, and P_C is the value of an American call
option with the same exercise price and expiry date as the warrant.

If a company issues new shares in a rights issue at a price below the
market price or issues convertible bonds or new warrants, the value of any
existing warrants already in issue will be affected. It is usual therefore for
companies to issue warrants with a provision that allows for the exercise
price to be reduced in the event of any corporate action that adversely affects
the current warrant price.

A warrant is attractive to investors because if the firm is successful and
its share price rises accordingly, the warrant can be exercised and the holder
can receive higher-value shares at the lower exercise price. Virtually all
warrants are issued by corporations and are equity warrants. In the late
1980's the Bank of England introduced *gilt warrants* which could be
exercised into gilts; however none are in existence at present. However it is
of course possible to trade in OTC call options on gilts with a number of
banks in the City of London.

Covered warrants are issued by a securities house or investment bank
rather than the company itself. The aim of the securities house is to create
an active and liquid market in the warrants, and to earn profit from making
a market in them. When covered warrants are exercised there is no recourse
to the company, and the company does not issue new shares. There is thus
no dilution effect. The securities house must settle the warrant holder's
application to subscribe for shares, either by providing shares already in
issue or by the payment of sufficient cash to allow the warrant holder to buy
shares in the market.

Bond warrants

Very occasionally bonds are issued with debt warrants attached. For example an issue of bonds with a coupon of 5% could be made with warrants that give the holder the right to subscribe at a future date for more 5% bonds at a fixed price. The warrants would be attractive to investors who expect interest rates to fall in the future; a fall in rates could result in the warrants being exercised or sold on at a profit, as the lower rates would now make them more valuable.

Say that a bond warrant entitles its holder to purchase bonds with a face value of M at a price of E. The bonds issued on exercise of the warrants may be either a further tranche of an existing issue or a new issue. The exercise cost of purchasing the underlying bond via the warrant is given by Equation (7.6).

$$Cost = \left\{ P_W + \frac{E \times M}{100} \right\} \times \frac{100}{M} \qquad (7.6)$$

where
P_W is the price of the warrant
E is the exercise price
M is the par value of the underlying bonds which may be purchased per warrant
When a bond warrant is exercised, the cost to the purchaser includes the accrued interest up to the exercise date.

If the warrant entitles the holder to the right to purchase a bond which is already in existence, a premium or discount resulting from purchasing the bond via the warrant, as opposed to directly in the market, may be calculated using 7.7 below.

$$Premium \ \% = \left\{ \frac{Exercise \ cost}{P_{bond}} - 1 \right\} \times 100 \qquad (7.7)$$

where P_{bond} is the clean price of the underlying bond.

EXAMPLE 7.1 ABC plc bond warrant

ABC plc warrant with the right to subscribe for 8% 2009 bonds. Each warrant gives the holder the right to subscribe for £1,000 nominal amount of the company's 8% bond due 2009, at the exercise price of 100 per cent of the nominal amount plus accrued interest from the previous coupon date (payable 7 June and 7 December each year). The warrants are exercisable up to and including 7 June 2005.

If the price of the warrant is £24, the exercise cost of purchasing the £1,000 nominal amount of the 8% bonds is:

$$(24 + (100 \times 1000) / 100) \times 100 / 1000$$

which is 102.4% in addition to any accrued interest.

If the bonds are trading in the market at 98.00, as the exercise cost of the bonds via the warrant is 102.4%, the premium is:

$$(102.4 / 98) - 1$$

which is 4.490%.

Comparison of warrants and convertibles

Warrants and convertibles are both hybrid instruments, both are issued by companies in the international markets. They are essentially similar in many respects, including:

- **valuation:** the theoretical value for a warrant is often calculated using the Black-Scholes or a similar model. In practice however investors are willing to pay only a fraction of the theoretical price of a warrant compared to convertibles, which trade near to or at fair value. Investors often pay more for the conversion premium on an issue of convertibles than they will pay for warrants in an issue of bonds with warrants attached. It is often the case therefore that companies are able to raise more capital by issuing convertibles rather than by issuing bonds with warrants attached;

- **investor base:** although warrants can have a long term to maturity, often they are held by short-term investors who buy them in the expectation of re-selling them at a profit when the company's share price rises by a sufficient amount. Until the exercise date approaches, many investors do not intend to hold the warrants in order to subscribe for shares in the future. The opposite is usually true for convertible bonds, whose investors are more likely to hold convertibles until conversion or redemption;

- **call flexibility:** bonds with warrants attached are often non-callable. The company cannot therefore force warrant holders into an immediate decision whether or not to subscribe for shares. A call option is only rarely a feature of a warrant bond;

- **maturity:** the maturity of a bond with warrants attached is predictable (unless a call feature is also included), as the bond portion remains outstanding until maturity. In contrast a convertible could remain outstanding for a proportionately much shorter time of its life, and be converted into equity. It is more common for convertibles to have call and/or put features attached. If a company required certainty of redemption dates for its financial planning, warrant bonds would be preferable to convertibles for this reason.

Generally however warrants are issued as a "sweetener" attached to a main issue, whereas convertibles are important corporate finance instruments in their own right. In certain markets though, for example in Japan, warrants are also an important corporate funding instrument.

Warrants on Bloomberg[4]

Practitioners in banks that use Bloomberg can access a number of pages on the system for analysis. We illustrate three screens here.

Screen WSRC is a search page that investors can use to find specific warrants.

This function allows you to search for warrants using a number of selected criteria such as put or call, exchange traded, currency, and underlying stock. Figure 7.4 below shows where a user has already specified

---

[4] This section was co-authored with Abukar M. Ali.

a few basic criteria as part of a search for UK-listed put warrants, as at 2nd March 2004. The search results are shown at Figure 7.3. A detailed description of the first warrant on the list, the Anglo-American put warrant, is shown at Figure 7.5, the standard Bloomberg description page.

It is possible to undertake a more advanced search on WSRC by using risk parameters; for example, one can search for warrants that have or trade on specific volatility levels.

Screen OV, which is the vanilla options calculator, can also to price warrants. Figure 7.6 shows this page being used to price the Anglo-American put warrant on 2 March 2004.

Sample UK listed warrants

BB Ticker	WRT SHORT NAME	Expiration Date	Strike Price	Uderlying Type	Warrent Per Share	Warrent Excercise Type
S065 LN Equity	ANGLO AMERI-PW04	02/06/2004	850	Equity	0.1	European
S068 LN Equity	BAE SYSTEMS-PW04	03/03/2004	125	Equity	1	European
S072 LN Equity	BARCLAYS PL-PW04	02/06/2004	350	Equity	0.1	European
S078 LN Equity	GLAXOSMITHK-PW04	02/06/2004	1100	Equity	0.1	European
S082 LN Equity	LLOYDS TSB -PW04	03/03/2004	400	Equity	0.1	European
S086 LN Equity	PRUDENTIAL -PW04	03/03/2004	350	Equity	0.1	European
S090 LN Equity	ABBEY NATIO-PW04	02/06/2004	350	Equity	0.1	European
S094 LN Equity	AVIVA PLC-PW04	02/06/2004	400	Equity	0.1	European
S098 LN Equity	HBOS PLC-PW04	02/06/2004	600	Equity	0.1	European
S102 LN Equity	LEGAL & GEN-PW04	02/06/2004	70	Equity	1	European
S108 LN Equity	ROYAL BANK -PW04	02/06/2004	1400	Equity	0.1	European
S130 LN Equity	VODAFONE GR-PW04	01/12/2004	130	Equity	1	European
S132 LN Equity	ANGLO AMERI-PW04	02/06/2004	1200	Equity	0.1	European
S134 LN Equity	BARCLAYS PL-PW04	02/06/2004	500	Equity	0.1	European
S137 LN Equity	BRITISH AIR-PW04	01/12/2004	200	Equity	1	European
S140 LN Equity	BRITISH SKY-PW04	01/12/2004	600	Equity	0.1	European
S141 LN Equity	BRITISH SKY-PW04	01/12/2004	800	Equity	0.1	European

Warrent   Warrent

Fixed Income Markets

WRT SHORT NAME		Warr. Price	Underlying Price	% Premium
S065 LN Equity	ANGLO AMERI-PW04	1	1411	40.15946
S068 LN Equity	BAE SYSTEMS-PW04	1	197.5	37.09367
S072 LN Equity	BARCLAYS PL-PW04	0.15	489	28.69565
S078 LN Equity	GLAXOSMITHK-PW04	5.5	1122	6.91964
S082 LN Equity	LLOYDS TSB -PW04	0.02	437.75	8.66933
S086 LN Equity	PRUDENTIAL -PW04	0.75	500.5	30.04
S090 LN Equity	ABBEY NATIO-PW04	0.4	465	26.88172
S094 LN Equity	AVIVA PLC-PW04	1	574	31.32782
S098 LN Equity	HBOS PLC-PW04	1	735	19.83696
S102 LN Equity	LEGAL & GEN-PW04	0.5	100.75	31.08685
S108 LN Equity	ROYAL BANK -PW04	1	1727	19.32213
S130 LN Equity	VODAFONE GR-PW04	11	136.75	12.61426
S132 LN Equity	ANGLO AMERI-PW04	2	1411	16.19419
S134 LN Equity	BARCLAYS PL-PW04	3.25	489	4.34783
S137 LN Equity	BRITISH AIR-PW04	12	321.75	41.45963
S140 LN Equity	BRITISH SKY-PW04	2.5	729.5	21.57534
S141 LN Equity	BRITISH SKY-PW04	12	729.5	7.53425

Figure 7.3 Search results for UK put warrants, 2 March 2004
© Abukar M. Ali. Used with permission

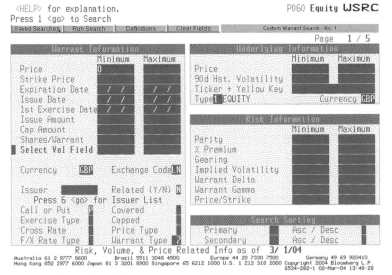

Figure 7.4 Bloomberg page WSRC, warrants search page
© Bloomberg L.P. Used with permission

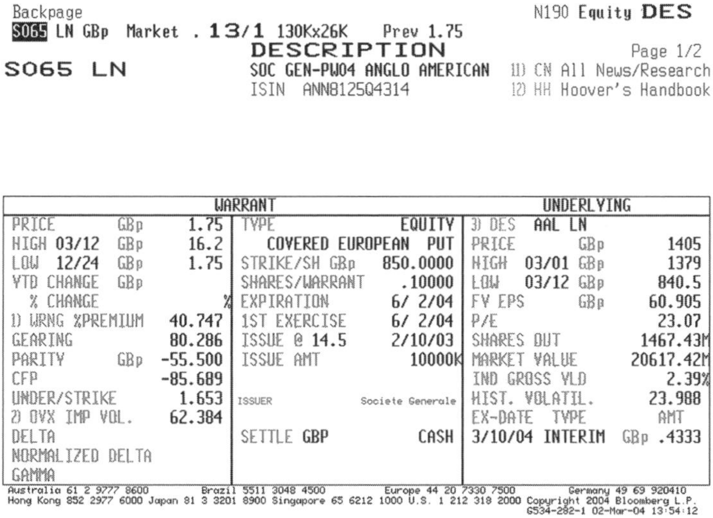

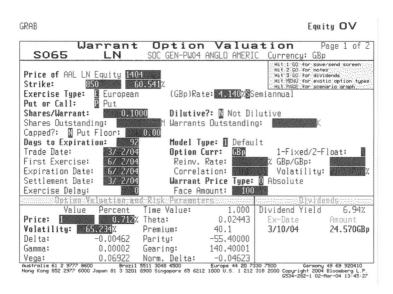

Figure 7.5 Description of key characteristics of the Anglo-American put warrant listed in Figure 7.3.

© Bloomberg L.P. Used with permission

Figure 7.6 Bloomberg screen OV used to price Anglo-American put warrant, 2 March 2004

© Bloomberg L.P. Used with permission

EXAMPLE 7.2 Term sheet for a "reverse kick-in note"

Below we show an example of a Termsheet for another type of hybrid security, known as a reverse kick-in note. The hypothetical bond we describe below pays a return that is linked to an equity index, and is issued by the hypothetical ABC Securities Limited.

The bond is a zero-coupon equity-linked note, issued at HKD 99 to par. It is linked to the Hang Seng Investment Index. While investors in the note benefit if the Index performs, their upside is capped at 123% of par value. There is a bonus return of an additional 3% of the Index never trades above 200% of the initial level at issue (termed the Initial Spot Level).

In other words, this note performs the best if the Index trades within a set barrier level during the life of the Note. The exact terms on redemption value are set out below.

FINAL TERMS AND CONDITIONS FOR
9 Month Reverse Kick-in Notes due 2004
Redemption proceeds linked to the
Hang Seng Investment Index Shares Index ETF

Issuer:	ABC Securities Ltd.
Issuer Rating:	Moodys Aa3
	Standard & Poor's AA-
Principal Amount:	HKD 100,000,000.00
	In Denomination of HKD 10,000 each
	(the "Note")
Underlying Shares:	Hang Seng Investment Index Funds Series H-Shares Index ETF, as quoted on the Hong Kong Stock Exchange (Reuters code 2828.HK) (the "Shares")
Issue Price:	99.00%
No. of Shares:	Each Note represents 200 Shares
Initial Spot Level:	HKD 51.17
Strike Level	HKD 51.17 (100% of Initial Spot Level)
Barrier:	HKD 40.94 (80% of Initial Spot Level)
Payout Cap	123% of Par Value

Bonus Return 3.0% per annum, subject to the condition that the Shares has never traded above 200% of Initial Spot Level

Reference Spot The arithmetic mean of official closing spot of 2828.HK as of 15 December 2004, 16 December 2004, 17 December 2004

Redemption: If the Shares has never traded below HKD 40.94 ("Barrier"); or

If the Shares trade at any time at a level below HKD 40.94 ("Barrier"), and the Reference Spot of the Shares is quoted at or above HKD 51.17, the Note will redeem in cash amount of:

Max $(100\%, \text{Shares }_{Final}/ \text{Shares }_{Initial})$ subject to cap of 123% plus Bonus Return

where:

Shares $_{Initial}$: HKD 51.17 ("Initial Spot Level")

Shares $_{Final}$: The Reference Spot

If the Shares trade at any time at a level below HKD 40.94 and the Reference Spot of the Shares is quoted below HKD 51.17, the Redemption for each Note shall be calculated as follows:

HKD $10,234 - 200 * (\text{HKD } 51.70 - \text{Shares }_{Final})$

Provided that the Redemption Amount shall not be less than zero

Exchange Rate: All currencies in HKD

Trade Date: 02 March 2004

Issue Date: 16 March 2004

Valuation Date: 15 December 2004

Maturity Date: 22 December 2004

Form: Notes are in Bearer form and settled in Euroclear and Clearstream

Governing Law: English

Bonds with Embedded Options and Option-Adjusted Spread Analysis

In a previous chapter we reviewed the yield-to-maturity calculation, the main measure of bond return used in the fixed-income markets. For conventional bonds, the yield calculation is relatively straightforward because the issue's redemption date is fixed. This means that the future cash flows that make up the total cash flows of the bond are known with certainty. As a result, data required to calculate the yield to maturity is known with certainty. Callable, put-able and sinking-fund bonds, generally termed bonds with embedded options, are not as straightforward to analyse. This is because some aspect of their cash flows, such as the timing or the value of their future payments, are not uncertain. The term "embedded" is used because the option element cannot be separated from the bond itself. Since callable bonds have more than one possible redemption date, the collection of future cash flows contributing to their overall return is not clearly defined. If we wish to calculate the yield to maturity for such bonds, we must assume a particular redemption date and calculate the yield to this date. The market convention is to assume the first possible maturity date as the one to be used for yield calculation if the bond is priced above par, and the last possible date if the bond is priced below par. The term "yield-to-worst" is sometimes used to refer to a redemption-yield calculation made under this assumption; this is the Bloomberg term. If the actual redemption date of a bond is different from the assumed redemption date, the measurement of return will be meaningless and irrelevant.

The market therefore prefers to use other measures of bond return for callable bonds. The most common method of return calculation is something known as option-adjusted spread analysis, or OAS analysis, a very good account of which can be found in Windas (1994). In this chapter we present one of the main methods by which callable bonds are priced. Although the discussion centers on callable bonds, the principles apply to all bonds with embedded-option elements in their structure.

Understanding embedded-option elements in a bond

Consider a hypothetical sterling corporate bond issued by ABC plc[1] with a 6% coupon on 1st December 1999 and maturing on 1st December 2019. The bond is callable after five years, under the schedule shown at Table 8.1. We see that the bond is first callable at a price of 103.00, after which the call price falls progressively until December 2014, after which the bond is callable at par.

Date	Call Price
01-Dec-2004	103.00
01-Dec-2005	102.85
01-Dec-2006	102.65
01-Dec-2007	102.50
01-Dec-2008	102.00
01-Dec-2009	101.75
01-Dec-2010	101.25
01-Dec-2011	100.85
01-Dec-2012	100.45
01-Dec-2013	100.25
01-Dec-2014	100.00

Table 8.1 Call schedule for "ABC plc" 6% bond due December 2019

Although our example is hypothetical, this form of call provision is quite common in the corporate-debt market. In the rest of this chapter we review the price behavior of callable bonds. The basic case can be stated quite easily, though; in our example the ABC plc bond pays a fixed semi-annual coupon of 6%. If the market level of interest rates rises after the bonds are issued, ABC plc effectively gains because it is paying below-market financing costs on its debt. If rates decline, however, investors gain from a rise in the capital value of their investment. But in this instance their upside is capped by the call provisions attached to the bond.

---

[1] After writing this chapter, I found that there really was a company called "ABC plc"! Of course we refer here to a hypothetical corporate entity.

The difference between the value of a callable bond and that of an (otherwise identical) non-callable bond of similar credit quality is the value attached to the option element of the callable bond. This is an important relationship and one that we will consider. But first, a word on the basics of option instruments.

Basic features of options

An option is a contract between two parties. The buyer of an option has the right, but not the obligation, to buy or sell an underlying asset at a specified price during a specified period or at a specified time (usually the expiry date of the option contract). The price of an option is known as the premium, which is paid by the buyer to the seller or writer of the option. An option that grants the holder the right to buy the underlying asset is known as a call option; one that grants the right to sell the underlying asset is a put option. The option writer is short the contract; the buyer is long. If the owner of the option elects to exercise her option and enter into the underlying trade, the option writer is obliged to execute under the terms of the option contract. The price at which an option specifies that the underlying asset may be bought or sold is known as the exercise or strike price. The expiry date of an option is the last day on which it may be exercised. Options that can be exercised anytime from the time they are struck up to and including the expiry date are called American options. Those that can be exercised only on the expiry date are known as European options.[2]

The profit/loss profiles for option buyers and sellers are quite different. The buyer of an option has her loss limited to the price of that option, while her profit can, in theory, be unlimited. The seller of an option has her profit limited to the option price, while her loss can, in theory, be unlimited, or at least potentially very substantial. The profit/loss profiles for the four main type of option positions are abundantly covered in existing literature.

The value or price of an option comprises two elements; its *intrinsic value* and its time value. The intrinsic value of an option is the value to the holder of an option if it were exercised immediately. That is, it is the difference between the strike price and the current price of the underlying asset. The holder of an option will only exercise it if there is underlying intrinsic value. For this reason, the intrinsic value is never less than zero. To illustrate, if a call option on a bond has a strike price of £100 and the underlying bond is currently trading at £103, the option has an intrinsic

---

[2] There are also Bermudan options, and Asian options, but these needn't concern us here.

value of £3. An option with intrinsic value greater than zero is said to be *in-the-money*. An option where the strike price is equal to the price of the underlying is said to be *at-the-money*, while one whose strike price is above (call) or below (put) the underlying is said to be *out-of-the-money*.

The time value of an option is the difference between the intrinsic value of an option and its total value. An option with zero intrinsic value has value composed solely of time value. That is,

Time value of an option = Option price − Intrinsic value

The time value reflects the potential for an option to move into the money during its life, or move a higher level of being in-the-money, before expiry. Time value diminishes steadily for an option up to its expiry date, when it will be zero. The price of an option on expiry is composed solely of intrinsic value.

Later in this chapter, we will illustrate how the price of a bond with an embedded option is calculated by assessing the value of the "underlying" bond and the value of its associated option. The basic issues behind the price of the associated option are considered here.[3] The main factors behind the price of an option on an interest-rate instrument such as a bond are:

- the strike price of the option
- the current price of the underlying bond, and its coupon rate
- the time to expiry
- the short-term risk-free rate of interest during the life of the option
- the expected volatility of interest rates during the life of the option.

The effect of each of these factors will differ for call and put options and American and European options. There are a number of option-pricing models used in the market, the most well-known of which is probably the Black-Scholes model. Market participants often use their own variations of models or varieties developed in-house. The fundamental principle behind the Black-Scholes model is that a synthetic option can be created and valued by taking a position in the underlying asset and borrowing or lending funds in the market at the risk-free rate of interest. Although it is the basis for certain subsequent option models and is still used widely in the market, it is not necessarily appropriate for certain interest-rate instruments. For instance, Fabozzi (1997) points out the unsuitability of the Black-Scholes model for

---

[3] For a technical review of option pricing, see the references cited in the bibliography.

certain bond options, based on its underlying assumptions. As a result, a number of other models have been developed for the analysis of callable bonds.

The call provision

A bond with early-redemption provisions essentially is a portfolio containing an underlying conventional bond, with the coupon and maturity date of the actual bond, and a put or call option on this underlying issue. Analysis therefore is interest-rate dependent; it must consider the possibility of the option being exercised when valuing the bond. The value of a bond with an option feature is the sum of the values of the individual elements; that is, the underlying bond and the option component. This is expressed at (8.1).

$$P_{bond} = P_{underlining} + P_{option} \qquad (8.1)$$

Expression (8.1) states simply that the value of the actual bond is composed of the value of the underlying conventional bond together with the value of the embedded option(s). The relationship would hold for a true conventional bond, as the option-component value would be zero. For a put-able bond, an embedded put option is an attractive feature for investors as the put feature contributes to its value by acting as a floor on the bond's price. Thus the greater the value of the put, the greater the value of the actual bond. We can express this by re-writing (8.1) as (8.2).

$$P_{bond} = P_{underlining} + P_{put} \qquad (8.2)$$

The expression at (8.2) states that the value of a put-able bond is equal to the sum of the values of the underlying conventional bond and the embedded put option. If any of the components of the total price were to increase in value, then so would the value of the put-able bond itself.

A callable bond is viewed as a conventional bond together with a short position in a call option, which acts as a cap on the actual bond's price. This "short" position in a call option reduces the total value of the actual bond, so we present the bond price in the form (8.3)

$$P_{cbond} = P_{underlining} - P_{call} \qquad (8.3)$$

Equation (8.3) states that the price of a callable bond is equal to the price of the underlying conventional bond less the price of the embedded call option. Therefore, if the value of the call option were to increase, the value of the callable bond would decrease. That is, when a bondholder of such a bond sells a call option, she receives the option price. The difference between the price of the option-free bond and the callable bond at any time is the price of the embedded call option. The precise nature of the behavior of the attached option element will depend on the terms of the callable bond issue. If the issuer of a callable bond is entitled to call the issue at any time after the first call date, the bondholder has effectively sold the issuer an American call option. However, the call-option price may vary with the date the option is exercised. This occurs when the call schedule for a bond has different call prices according to which date the bond is called. The underlying bond at the time the call is exercised comprises the remaining coupon payments that would have been received by the bondholder had the issue not been called. However, for ease of explanation the market generally analyses a callable bond in terms of a long position in a conventional bond and a short position in a call option, as stated by (8.3). Note, of course, that the option is embedded; it does not trade in its own right. Nevertheless, it is clear that embedded options are important elements not only in the behavior of a bond but in its valuation as well.

The binomial tree of short-term interest rates

In an earlier chapter, we illustrated how a coupon-bond yield curve could be used to derive spot (zero-coupon) and implied forward rates. A forward rate is defined as the one-period interest rate for a term beginning at a forward date and maturing one period later. Forward rates form the basis upon which a binomial interest-rate tree is built. For an introduction to a binomial process, see Appendix 15.1 of Choudhry (2001).

An option model that used implied forward rates to generate a price for an option's underlying bond on a future date would implicitly assume that interest rates implied by the yield curve today for a date in the future would occur with certainty. Such an assumption would essentially repeat the errors associated with yield-to-worst analysis, which would be inaccurate because interest rates do not remain unchanged from a future today to a future pricing date. To avoid this inaccuracy, a binomial-tree model assumes that interest rates do not remain fixed but fluctuate over time. This is done by treating implied forward rates, sometimes referred to as short rates, as outcomes of a binomial process. In a binomial interest-rate process, we construct a binomial tree of possible short rates for each future time period.

In the binomial tree, we model two interest rates as the possible outcomes of a previous time period, when the interest rate was known.

An introduction to arbitrage-free pricing

Consider a hypothetical situation. Assume that the short-term yield curve describes the following environment:

Six-month rate: 5.00%
One-year rate: 5.15%

Assume further that in six months' time the then six-month rate will be either 5.01% or 5.50%, and that the probability of either new rate is equal at 50% each. Our capital market is a semi-annual one (the convention is for bonds to pay a semi-annual coupon, as in the US and UK domestic markets). We can illustrate this state in the following way:

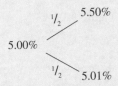

Figure 8.1

Figure 8.1 is a binomial interest-rate tree or lattice for the six-month interest rate. The tree is called "binomial" because there are precisely two possibilities for the future level of the interest rate. Using this lattice, we can calculate the tree for the prices of six-month and one-year zero-coupon bonds. The six-month zero-coupon bond price today is given by 100/(1 + [0.05/2]) or 97.56098. The price tree is given at Figure 8.2.

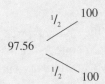

Figure 8.2

Period 0 is today; period 1 is the point precisely six months from today. Given that we are dealing with a six-month zero-coupon bond, it is apparent that there is only one state of the world whatever the interest rate is in period 1; the maturity value of the bond, which is 100.

The binomial lattice for the one-year zero-coupon bond is given in Figure 8.3.

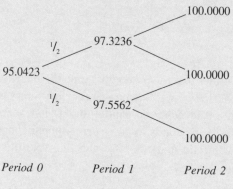

Period 0   Period 1   Period 2

Figure 8.3

At period 0, the price of the one-year zero-coupon bond is $100/(1 + [0.0515/2]^2)$ or 95.0423. The price of the bond at period 1, at which point it is now a six-month piece of paper, is dependent on the six-month rate at the time, shown in the diagram. At period 2 the bond matures and its price is 100. The model at Figure 8.3 demonstrates that the average or expected value of the price of the one-year bond at period 1 is $[(0.5 \times 97.3236) + (0.5 \times 97.5562)]$ or 97.4399. This is the expected price at period 1. Therefore, using this, the price at period 0 is:

$$97.4399/(1 + 0.05/2))$$
or 95.06332.

However, we know that the market price is 95.0423. This demonstrates a very important principle in financial economics, that markets do not price derivative instruments on the basis of their expected future value. At period 0, the one-year zero-coupon bond is a more risky investment than the shorter-dated bond; in the last six months of its life it will be worth either 97.32 or 97.55 depending on the direction of six-month rates. Investors' preference is for a bond that has a price of 97.4399 at period 1 with certainty. The price of such a bond at period 0 would be 97.4399/(1 + (0.05/2)) or 95.0633. In fact, the actual price of the one-year bond at that date, 95.0423, indicates the *risk premium* that the market places on the bond.

We can now consider the pricing of an option. What value should be given to a six-month call option maturing in six months' time (period 1) written on 100 nominal of the six-month zero-coupon bond "(zero-coupon bond)" at a strike price of 97.40? The binomial tree for this option is given at Figure 8.4. This shows that at period 1, if the six-month rate is 5.50% the call option has no value, because the price of the bond is below the strike price. If, on the other hand, the six-month rate is at the lower level, the option has a value of 97.5562 – 94.40 or 0.1562.

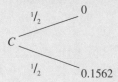

Figure 8.4

How do we calculate the price of the option? Option-pricing theory states that to do this one must construct a *replicating portfolio* and find the value of this portfolio. In our example, we must set up a portfolio of six-month and one-year zero-coupon bonds today that will have no value at period 1 if the six-month rate rises to 5.50%, but will have a value of 0.1562 if the rate at that time is 5.01%. If we let the value of the six-month and one-year bonds in the replicating portfolio be C_1 and C_2 respectively at period 1, we may set the following equations:

$$C_1 + 0.973236C_2 = 0 \tag{8.4}$$

$$C_1 + 0.975562C_2 = 0.1562 \tag{8.5}$$

The value of the six-month zero-coupon bond in the replicating portfolio at period 1 is 100 when it matures. In the case of an interest-rate rise, the value of the one-year bond (now a six-month bond) at period 1 is 97.3236. The total value of the portfolio is given by the first expression above, which states that this value must also be equal to the value of the option. The second expression gives the value of the replicating portfolio in the event that rates decrease, when the option value is 0.1562.

Solving the expressions above gives us $C_1 = -65.3566$ and $C_2 = 67.1539$. What does this mean? Basically, to construct the replicating portfolio we purchase 67.15 of one-year zero-coupon bonds and sell short 65.36 of the six-month zero-coupon bond. However, the original intention behind the replicating portfolio was to price the option: the portfolio and the option have equal values. The value of the portfolio is a known quantity, as it is equal to the price of the six-month bond at period 0 multiplied by C_1 together with the price of the one-year bond multiplied by C_2. This is given by

$$(0.9756 \times -65.3566) + (0.950423 \times 67.1539) = 0.0627$$

That is, the price of the six-month call option is 0.06. This is the *arbitrage-free* price of the option; below this price a market participant could buy the option and simultaneously sell short the replicating portfolio and would be guaranteed a profit. If the option was quoted at a price above this, a trader could write the option and buy the portfolio. Note how the probability of the six-month rate increasing or decreasing was not part of the analysis. This reflects the arbitrage pricing logic. That is, the replicating portfolio must be equal in value to the option whatever direction interest rates move in. This means probabilities do not have an impact in the construction of the portfolio. This is not to say that probabilities do not have an impact on the option price; far from it. For example, if there is a very high probability that rates will increase (in our example), intuitively we can see that the value of an option to an investor will fall. However, this is accounted for by the market in the value of the option or callable bond at any one time. If probabilities change, the market price will change to reflect this.

Let us now turn to the concept of risk-neutral pricing. Notwithstanding what we have just noted about how the market does not price instruments using expected values, there exist risk-neutral probabilities for which the discounted expected value does give the actual price at period 0. If we let p be the risk-neutral probability of an interest-rate increase and $(1 - p)$ be the probability of a rate decrease, we may set p such that

$$\frac{97.3236p + 97.5562(1 - p)}{1 + \frac{1}{2}0.05} = 95.0423 \ .$$

That is, we can calculate a value for p such that the discounted expected value, using the probability p rather than the actual probability of $\frac{1}{2}$, provides the true market price. The above expression solves to give $p=0.5926$.

In our example from the option price tree in figure 8.4, given the risk-neutral probability of 0.5926, we can calculate the option price to be

$$\frac{(0.5926 \times 0) + (0.4074 \times 0.1562)}{1 + \frac{1}{2}0.05} = 0.0621 \ .$$

This is virtually identical to the 0.062 option price calculated above. Put very simply, risk-neutral pricing works by first finding the probabilities that produce prices of the replicating or *underlying* security equal to the discounted expected value. An option on the security is valued by discounting this expected value under the risk-neutral probability.

We can now turn to binomial trees. In the description above we had a two-period tree. Moving to period 2, we might have Figure 8.5.

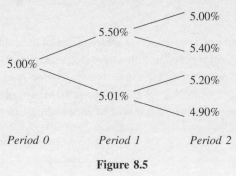

		5.00%
	5.50%	
		5.40%
5.00%		
		5.20%
	5.01%	
		4.90%

Period 0   *Period 1*   *Period 2*

Figure 8.5

This binomial tree is known as a non-recombining tree, because each node branches out to two further nodes. This might seem more logical, and such trees are used in practice in the market. However, implementing it requires a considerable amount of computer processing power, and it is easy to see why. In period 1, there are two possible levels for the interest rate, and at period 2 there are four possible levels. After N interest periods, there will be 2^N possible values for the interest rate. If we wished to calculate the current price of a 10-year callable bond that paid semi-annual coupons, we would have over one million possible values for the last period set of nodes. For a 20-year bond we would have over one trillion possible values. (Note also that in practice binomial models are not used with a six-month time step between nodes, but have much smaller time steps, further increasing the number of nodes).

For this reason certain market practitioners prefer to use a recombining binomial tree, where the upward-downward state has the same value as the downward-upward state. This is shown in Figure 8.6 below.

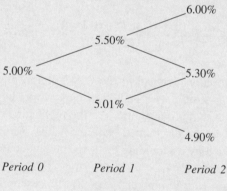

Figure 8.6

The number of nodes and possible values at the latest time step is much reduced in a recombining tree. For example, the number of nodes used to price a 20-year bond that was being priced with one-week time steps would be 52 x 20 + 1, or 1041. Implementation is therefore more straightforward with a recombining tree.

Pricing callable bonds

We can now consider a simple pricing method for callable bonds. We will assume a binomial term-structure model. It is well worth reading the box above beforehand, especially if one is not familiar with binomial models or the principle of the arbitrage-free pricing of financial instruments. Using the binomial model, we can derive a risk-neutral binomial lattice, where each lattice carries an equal probability of upward or downward moves, for the evolution of the six-month interest rate. The time step in the lattice is six months. This model is then used to price a hypothetical semi-annual coupon bond with the following terms:

Coupon	6%
Maturity	Three years
Call schedule	
Year 1	103.00
Year 1.5	102.00
Year 2	101.50
Year 2.5	101.00
Year 3	100.00

Table 8.2

The tree is shown at Figure 8.7.

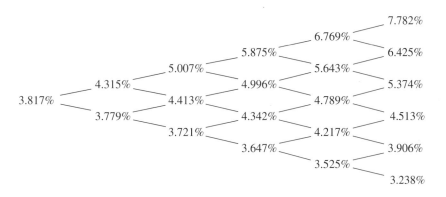

Figure 8.7

In the first instance, we construct the binomial tree that describes the price process followed by the bond itself, if we ignore its call feature. This is shown at Figure 8.8. Note that the maturity value of the bond on the redemption date is given as 100.00; that is, we perform the analysis on the basis of the bond's ex-coupon value. The final cash flow would, of course, be 103.00.

We construct the tree from the final date backwards. At each of the nodes at year 3, the price of the bond will be 100.00, the (ex-coupon) par value. At year 2.5, the price of the bond at the highest yield will be that at which the yield of the bond is 7.782%. At this point, the price of the bond after six months will be 103.00 in both the "up" state and the "down" state. Following risk-neutral pricing, therefore, the price of the bond at this node is

$$P_{bond} = \frac{0.5 \times 103 + 0.5 \times 103}{1 + \frac{0.07782}{2}} = 99.14237 \ .$$

The same process is used to obtain the prices for every node at year 2.5. Once all these prices have been calculated, we repeat the process for the prices at each node in year 2. At the highest yield, 6.769%, the two possible future values are

$$99.14237 + 3.0 = 102.14237$$

and

$$99.79411 + 3.0 = 102.79411.$$

Therefore, the price of the bond in this state is given by

$$P_{bond} = \frac{0.5 \times 102.14237 + 0.5 \times 102.79411}{1 + \frac{0.06769}{2}} = 99.14237 \ .$$

The same procedure is repeated until we have populated every node in the lattice. At each node the ex-coupon bond price is equal to the sum of the expected value and coupon, discounted at the appropriate six-month interest rate. The completed lattice is shown at Figure 8.8.

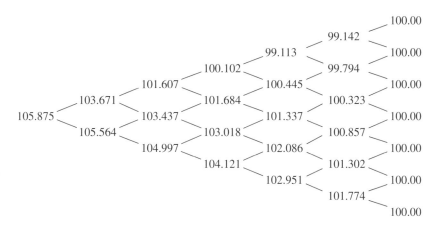

Figure 8.8

Once we have calculated the prices for the conventional element of the bond, we can calculate the value of the option element on the callable bond. This is shown in Figure 8.9. On the bond's maturity date, the option is worthless, because it is an option to call at 100, which is the price the bond is redeemed at in any case. At all other node points, a valuation analysis is called for.

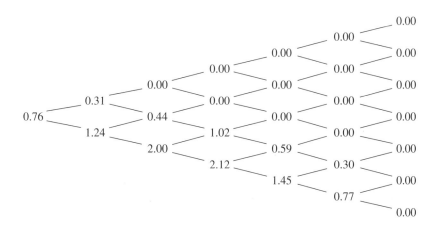

Figure 8.9

The holder of the option in the case of a callable bond is the issuing company. At any time during the life of the bond, the holder will either exercise the option on the call date or elect to hold it to the next date. The option holder must consider:

- the value of holding the option for an extra period, denoted by P_{Ct}
- the value of exercising the option straight away, denoted P_C.

If the value of the former exceeds that of the latter, the holder will elect to not exercise, and if the value at the exercise date is higher the holder will exercise immediately. At year 2.5 call date, for example, there is no value in holding the option because it will be worthless at year 3. Therefore, at any point where the option is in-the-money the holder will exercise.

We can express the general valuation as follows. The value of the option for immediate exercise is V_t. The value if one is holding on to the option for a further period is V_T. Additionally, let P be the value of the bond at any particular node, S the call option price, and V_h and V_l the values of the option in the up-state and down-state, respectively. The value of the option at any specified node is V. The six-month interest rate at any specified node point is r. We have

$$V_T = \frac{0.5V_h + 0.5V_l}{1 + \frac{1}{2}r} \qquad (8.6)$$

$$V_t = \max\,(0,\, P - S)$$

while the expression for V is $V = \max\,(V_t . V_t)$.

The rule is as demonstrated above; to work backwards in time and apply the expression at each node, which produces the option-value binomial lattice tree.

The general rule with an option is that they have more value "alive than dead". This means that sometimes it is optimal to run an in-the-money option rather than exercising straight away. The same is true for callable bonds. There are a number of factors that dictate whether an option should be exercised or not. The first is the asymmetric profile resulting when the price of the "underlying" asset rises; option holders gain if the price rises, but will only lose the value of their initial investment if the price falls. Therefore, it is optimal to run with the option position. There is also time value, which is lost if the option is exercised early. With callable bonds, it is often the case that the call price decreases as the bond approaches maturity. This is an incentive to delay exercise until a lower exercise price is available. The issue that may influence the decision to exercise sooner is coupon payments, as interest is earned sooner.

To return to our hypothetical example, we can now complete the price tree for the callable bond. Remember that the option in the case of a callable bond is held by the issuer, so the value of the option is subtracted from the price of the bond to obtain the actual value. We see from Figure 8.10 that the price of the callable bond today is 105.875 – 0.76 or 105.115. The price of the bond at each node in the lattice is also shown. By building a tree in this way, which can be programmed into a spreadsheet or as a front-end application, we are able to price a callable or put-able bond.

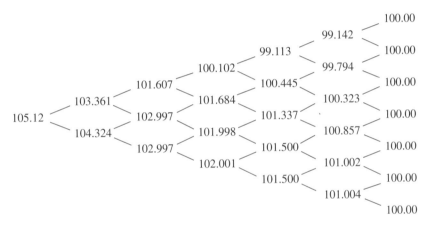

Figure 8.10

Price and yield sensitivity

As we saw in an earlier chapter, the price/yield relationship for a conventional vanilla bond is essentially convex in shape, while for a bond with an option feature attached this relationship changes as the price of the bond approaches par, at which the bond is said to exhibit negative convexity. This means that the rise in price will be lower than the fall in price for a large change in yield of a given number of basis points. We summarise the price/yield relationship for both conventional and option-feature bonds in Table 8.3.

	Value of price change for	
Change in yield	**Positive convexity**	**Negative convexity**
Fall of 100 bp	X%	Lower than Y%
Rise of 100 bp	Lower than X%	Y%

Table 8.3

The price/yield relationship for a callable bond exhibits negative convexity as interest rates fall. Option-adjusted spread analysis is used to highlight this relationship for changes in rates. This is done by effecting a parallel shift in the benchmark yield curve, holding the spread level constant and then calculating the theoretical price along the nodes of the binomial price tree. The average present value then becomes the projected price for the bond. General results for a hypothetical callable bond compared to a conventional bond are shown at Figure 8.11. In our example, once the market rate falls below the 10% level, the bond exhibits negative convexity. This is because it then becomes callable at that point, which acts as an effective cap on the price of the bond.

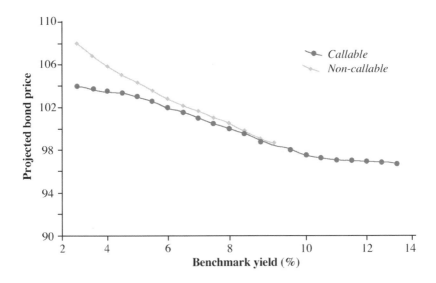

Figure 8.11 Projected prices for callable and conventional bonds with identical coupon and final maturity dates

The market analyses bonds with embedded options in terms of a yield spread, with a "cheap" bond trading at a higher yield spread and a "dear" bond trading at a lower yield spread. The usual convention is to quote yield spreads as the difference between the redemption yield of the bond being analysed and the equivalent-maturity government bond. This is not accurate because the redemption yield is, in effect, a meaningless number – there is not a single rate at which all the cash flows comprising either bond should be discounted but a set of spot or forward rates that are used for each successive interest period. The correct procedure for discounting, therefore, is to determine the yield spread over the spot or forward-rate curve. With regard to the binomial tree, what we require then is the constant spread that, when added to all the short-rates on the binomial tree, makes the theoretical (model-derived) price equal to the observed market price. The constant spread that satisfies this requirement is known as the *option-adjusted spread* (OAS). The spread is referred to as an "option-adjusted" spread because it reflects the option feature attached to the bond. The OAS will depend on the volatility level assumed in running the model. For any given bond price, the higher the volatility level specified, the lower will be the OAS for a callable bond, and the higher for a put-able bond. Since the OAS is usually calculated relative to a government spot or forward-rate curve, it reflects the credit risk and any liquidity premium between the corporate bond and the government bond. Note that OAS analysis reflects the valuation model being used, and its accuracy is a reflection of the accuracy of the model itself.

Measuring bond yield spreads

The binomial model evaluates the return of a bond by measuring the extent to which its return exceeds the returns determined by the risk-free short rates in the tree. The difference between these returns is expressed as a spread and may be considered the incremental return of a bond at a specified price. Determining the spread involves the following steps:

- the binomial tree is used to derive a theoretical price for the specified bond
- the theoretical price is compared with the bond's observed market price
- if the two prices differ, the rates in the binomial model are adjusted by a user-specified amount, which is the estimate of the spread
- using the adjusted rates, a new theoretical price is derived and compared with the observed price
- the last two steps are repeated until the theoretical price matches the observed price.

This process is programmed into the normal binomial pricing process used at banks.

Price volatility of bonds with embedded options

We have reviewed traditional duration and modified duration measures for bond interest-rate risk. Modified duration is essentially a predictive measure, used to describe the expected percentage change in bond price for a 1% change in yield. The measure is a snapshot in time, based on the current yield of the bond and the structure of its expected cash flows. In analysing a bond with an embedded option, the bondholder must assume a fixed maturity date, based on the current price of the bond, and calculate modified duration based on this assumed redemption date. However, under circumstances where it is not exactly certain what the final maturity is, modified duration may be calculated to the first call date and to the final maturity date. This would be of little use to bondholders in these circumstances, since it may be unclear which measure is appropriate. The problem is more acute for bonds that are continuously callable (or put-able) from the first call date up to maturity.

Effective duration

To recap, the duration for any bond is calculated using (8.7) which assumes annualised yields.

$$D = \frac{\sum_{t=1}^{n} \frac{tC_t}{(1 + rm)^t}}{P} \tag{8.7}$$

Following Fabozzi (1997), the measure can be approximated using (8.8) below.

$$D_{\text{approx}} = \frac{P_- - P_+}{2P_0(\Delta rm)} \tag{8.8}$$

where

P_0 is the initial price of the bond
P_- is the estimated price of the bond if the yield falls by Δrm
P_+ is the estimated price of the bond if the yield rises by Δrm
Δrm is the change in the yield of the bond.

The drawbacks of the traditional measure are overcome to a certain extent when OAS analysis is used to measure the *effective duration* of a bond. Whereas traditional duration seeks to predict a bond's price changes based on a given price and assumed redemption date, effective duration is solved from actual price changes resulting from specified shifts in interest rates. Applying the analysis to a bond with an embedded option means that the new prices resulting from yield changes reflect changes in the cash flow. Effective duration may be thought of as a duration measure which recognizes that yield changes may change the future cash flow of the bond. For bonds with embedded options, the difference between traditional duration and effective duration can be significant. For example, for a callable bond the effective duration is sometimes half that of its traditional duration measure. For mortgage-backed securities the difference is sometimes greater still.

To calculate effective duration using the binomial model and (8.8), we employ the following procedure:

- calculate the OAS spread for the bond
- change the benchmark yield through a downward parallel shift
- construct an adjusted binomial tree using the new yield curve
- add the OAS adjustment to the short rates at each of the node points in the tree
- use the modified binomial tree constructed above to calculate the new value of the bond, which then becomes P_+ for use in equation (8.8).

To determine the lower price resulting from a rise in yields, we follow the same procedure but effect an upward parallel shift in the yield curve.

Effective duration for bonds that contain an embedded option is often referred to as option-adjusted spread duration. There are two advantages associated with using this measure. These are that, by incorporating the binomial tree into the analysis, the interest-rate-dependent nature of the cash flows is taken into account. This is done by holding the bond's OAS constant over the specified interest-rate shifts, in effect maintaining the credit spread demanded by the market at a constant level. This takes into account the behavior of the embedded option as interest rates change. The second, and possibly more significant, advantage is that OAS duration is calculated on a parallel shift in the benchmark yield curve, which gives us an indication of the change in bond price with respect to changes in market interest rates rather with respect to changes in its own yield.

Effective convexity

In the same way that we calculate an effective-duration measure for bonds with embedded options, the standard measure of bond convexity we reviewed earlier may not be appropriate for such bonds. This is because the measure does not take into account the impact of a change in market interest rates on a bond's future cash flows. As shown in Fabozzi (*ibid*), the convexity measure for any bond may be approximated using (8.9).

$$CV = \frac{P+ + P- - 2P_0}{P_0(\Delta rm)^2} \qquad (8.9)$$

If prices input to (8.9) are those assuming that remaining cash flows for the bond do not change when market rates change, the convexity value is that for an option-free bond. To calculate a more meaningful value for bonds with embedded options, the prices used in the equation are derived by changing the cash flows when interest rates change, based on the results obtained from the binomial model. This measure is called effective convexity or option-adjusted convexity.

Sinking funds

In some markets, corporate-bond issuers set up *sinking-fund* provisions. For example, consider the following hypothetical bond issue:

Issuer	ABC plc
Issue date	1-Dec-99
Maturity date	1-Dec-19
Nominal	£100 million
Coupon	8%
Sinking fund provision	£5 million 1 December, 2009 to 2018

Table 8.4

In the example of the ABC plc 8% 2019 bond, a proportion of the principal is paid out over a period of time. This is the formal provision. In practice, the actual payments made may differ from the formal requirements.

A sinking fund allows the bond issuer to redeem the nominal amount using one of two methods. The issuer may purchase the stipulated amount in the open market, and then deliver these bonds to the Trustee[4] for cancellation. Alternatively, the issuer may call the required amount of the bonds at par. This is in effect a partial call, similar to a callable bond for which only a fraction of the issue may be called. Generally the actual bonds called are selected randomly by certificate serial numbers. Readers will have noticed, however, that the second method by which a portion of the issue is redeemed is actually a call option, which carries value for the issuer. Therefore, the method by which the issuer chooses to fulfill its sinking-fund requirement is a function of the level of interest rates. If interest rates have risen since the bond was issued, so that the price of the bond has fallen, the issuer will meet its sinking-fund obligation by direct purchase in the open market. However, if interest rates have fallen, the issuing company will call the specified amount of bonds at par. In the hypothetical example given at Table 8.4, in effect ABC plc has 10 options embedded in the bond, each relating to £5 million nominal of the bonds. The options each have different maturities, so the first expires on 1st December 2009 and subsequent options maturing on 1st December each following year until 2018.[5] The decision to exercise the options as they fall due is made using the same binomial-tree method that we discussed earlier.

Option–adjusted spread analysis

The modified duration and convexity methods we described earlier are only suitable for use in the analysis of conventional fixed income instruments with known fixed cash flows and maturity date. They are not satisfactory for use with bonds that contain embedded options, such as callable bonds, or instruments with unknown final redemption dates, such as mortgage-backed bonds.[6] For these and other bonds that exhibit uncertainties in their cash flow pattern and redemption date, so-called option-adjusted measures are used. The most common of these is option-adjusted spread (OAS) and

---

[4] Bond issuers appoint a Trustee that is responsible for looking after the interests of bondholders during the life of the issue. In some cases, the Trustee is appointed by the underwriting investment bank or the issuer's solicitors. Specialised arms of commercial and investment banks carry out the Trustee function; for example, JPMorgan Chase, Deutsche Bank, Bank of New York, Citibank and others.

[5] The "options" are European options, in that they can only be exercised on the expiry date.

[6] The term 'embedded' is used because the option element of the bond cannot be stripped out and traded separately, for example the call option inherent in a callable bond.

option-adjusted duration (OAD). The techniques were developed to allow for the uncertain cash flow structure of non-vanilla fixed income instruments, and to model the effect of the option element of such bonds.

A complete description of option-adjusted spread is outside the scope of this book; here we present an overview of the basic concepts. Accessible accounts of this technique are given in Wilson and Fabozzi (1990); another excellent introduction is Windas (1993).

Introduction

Option-adjusted spread analysis uses simulated interest rate paths as part of its calculation of bond yield and convexity. Therefore an OAS model is a *stochastic* model. The OAS refers to the yield spread between a callable or mortgage-backed bond and a government benchmark bond. The government bond chosen ideally will have similar coupon and duration values. Thus the OAS is an indication of the value of the option element of the bond, as well as the premium required by investors in return for accepting the default risk of the corporate bond. When OAS is measured as a spread between two bonds of similar default risk, the yield difference between the bonds reflects the value of the option element only. This is rare, and the market convention is to measure OAS over the equivalent benchmark government bond. OAS is used in the analysis of corporate bonds that incorporate call or put provisions, as well as mortgage-backed securities with prepayment risk. For both applications the spread is calculated as the number of basis points over the yield of the government bond that would equate the price of both bonds.

The essential components of the OAS technique are as follows:

- a simulation method such as Monte Carlo is used to generate sample interest rate paths, and a cash flow pattern generated for each interest rate path;
- the value of the bond for each of the future possible rate paths is found, by discounting in the normal manner each of the bond's cash flows at the relevant interest rate (plus a spread) along the points of each path. This produces a range of values for the bond, and for a given price the OAS is the spread at which the average of the range of values equates the given price.

Thus OAS is a general stochastic model, with discount rates derived from the standard benchmark term structure of interest rates. This is an advantage over more traditional methods in which a single discount rate is used. The calculated spread is a spread over risk-free forward rates, accounting for both interest rate uncertainty and the price of default risk. As with any methodology, OAS has both strengths and weaknesses; however it provides more realistic analysis than the traditional yield-to-maturity approach. It has been widely adopted by investors since its introduction in the late 1980s.

A theoretical framework

All bond instruments are characterised by the promise to pay a stream of future cash flows. The term structure of interest rates and associated discount function is crucial to the valuation of any debt security, and underpins any valuation framework.[7] Armed with the term structure we can value any bond, assuming it is liquid and default-free, by breaking it down into a set of cash flows and valuing each cash flow with the appropriate discount factor. Further characteristics of any bond, such as an element of default risk or embedded option, are valued incrementally over its discounted cash flow valuation.

Valuation under known interest rate environments

We showed in Chapter 3 how forward rates can be calculated using the no-arbitrage argument. We use this basic premise to introduce the concept of OAS. Consider the spot interest rates for two interest periods:

Term (interest periods)	Spot rate
1	5%
2	6%

From Chapter 3 can determine that the one-period interest rate starting one period from now is 7.009%. This is the implied one-period forward rate.

We may use the spot rate term structure to value a default-free zero-coupon bond, so for example a two-period bond would be priced at $89.[8] Using the forward rate we obtain the same valuation, which is exactly what we expect.[9]

---

[7] The term structure of interest rates is the spot rate yield curve; spot rates are viewed as identical to zero-coupon bond interest rates where there is a market of liquid zero-coupon bonds along regular maturity points. As such a market does not exist anywhere, the spot rate yield curve is considered a theoretical construct, which is most closely equated by the zero-coupon term structure derived from the prices of default-free liquid government bonds (see Chapter 4).

[8] $100/(1.06)2 = $88.9996.

[9] $100/(1.05) x (1.07009) = $89.

This framework can be used to value other types of bonds. Let us say we wish to calculate the price of a two-period bond that has the following cash flow stream:

Period 1 $5
Period 2 $105

Using the spot rate structure in Table 8.5, the price of this bond is calculated to be $98.21.[5] This would be the bond's fair value if it were liquid and default-free. Assume, however, that the bond is a corporate bond and carries an element of default risk, and is priced at $97. What spread over the risk-free price does this indicate? We require the spread over the implied forward rate that would result in a discounted price of $97. Using iteration, this is found to be 67.6 basis points.[11] The calculation is:

$$P = \frac{5}{1 + (0.005 + 0.00676)}$$

$$+ \frac{105}{[1 + (0.005 + 0.00676) \times [1 + (0.07009 + 0.00676)]}$$

$$= 97.00$$

The spread of 67.6 basis points is implied by the observed market price of the bond, and is the spread over the expected path of interest rates. Another way of considering this is that it is the spread premium earned by holding the corporate bond instead of a risk-free bond with identical cash flows.

This framework can be used to evaluate relative value. For example, if the average sector spread of bonds with similar credit risk is observed to be 73 basis points, a fairer value for the example bond might be:

$$P = \frac{5}{1 + (0.005 + 0.0073)}$$

$$+ \frac{105}{[1 + (0.005 + 0.0073) \times [1 + (0.07009 + 0.0073)]}$$

$$= 96.905$$

which would indicate that our bond is overvalued.

---

[10] [$5/1.05 + $105/(1.05) x (1.07009)] = $98.21.
[11] For students, problems requiring the use of iteration can be found using the 'Goal Seek' function in Microsoft Excel, under the 'Tools' menu.

The approach just described is the OAS methodology in essence. However, it applies only in an environment in which the future path of interest rates is known with certainty. The spread calculated is the OAS spread under conditions of no uncertainty. We begin to appreciate though that this approach is preferable to the traditional one of comparing redemption yields; whereas the latter uses a single discount rate, the OAS approach uses the correct spot rate for each period's cash flow.

However, our interest lies with conditions of interest rate uncertainty. In practice, the future path of interest rates is not known with certainty. The range of possible values of future interest rates is a large one, although the probability of higher or lower rates that are very far away from current rates is low. For this reason the OAS calculation is based on the most likely future interest rate path among the universe of possible rate paths. This is less relevant for vanilla bonds, but for securities whose future cash flow is contingent on the level of future interest rates, such as mortgage-backed bonds, it is very important. The first step, then, is to describe the interest rate process in terms that capture the character of its dynamics.[12]

Ideally the analytical framework under conditions of uncertainty would retain the arbitrage-free character of our earlier discussion. But by definition the evolution of interest rates will not match the calculated forward rate, thus creating arbitrage conditions. This is not surprising. For instance, if the calculated one-period forward rate shown above actually *turns out to be* 7.50%, the maturity value of the bond at the end of period 2 would be $100.459 rather than $100. This means that there was an arbitrage opportunity at the original price of $89. For the bond price to have been arbitrage-free at the start of period 1, it would have been priced at $88.59.[13]

This is a meaningless argument, short of advocating the employment of a clairvoyant. However, it illustrates how different eventual interest rate paths correspond to different initial fair values. As interest rates can follow a large number of different paths, of varying possibility, so bond prices can assume a number of fair values. The ultimate arbitrage-free price is as unknown as future interest rate levels! Let us look then at how the OAS

---

[12] This is interest rate modelling, an extensive and complex, not to mention heavily researched, subject. We present it here in accessible, intuitive terms. Chapter 4 introduced it in more formal fashion.

[13] The price of the bond at the start of period is $89, shown earlier. This is worth (89 x 1.05) or $93.45 at the end of period 1, and hence $100 at the end of period 2 (93.45 x 1.07009). However if an investor at the time of rolling over the one-period bond can actually invest at 7.50%, this amount will mature to (83.45 x 1.075) or $100.459. In this situation, *in hindsight* the arbitrage-free price of the bond at the start of period 1 would be 100/(1.05 x 1.075) or $88.59.

methodology uses the most likely interest rate path when calculating fair values.

Valuation under uncertain interest rate environments

We begin by assuming that the current spot rate term structure is consistent with bond prices of zero option-adjusted spread, so that their price is the average expected for all possible evolutions of the future interest rate. By assuming this we may state that the most likely future interest rate path, which lies in the centre of the range of all possible interest rate paths, will be a function of interest rate volatility. Here we use volatility to mean the average annual percentage deviation of interest rates around their mean value. So an environment of 0% volatility would be one of interest rate certainty and would generate only one possible arbitrage-free bond price. This is a worthwhile scenario, since it enables us to generalise the example in the previous section as the arbitrage-free model in times of uncertainty, but when volatility is 0%.

A rise in volatility generates a range of possible future paths around the expected path. The actual expected path that corresponds to a zero-coupon bond price incorporating zero OAS is a function of the dispersion of the range of alternative paths around it. This dispersion is the result of the dynamics of the interest rate process, so this process must be specified for the current term structure. We can illustrate this with a simple binomial model example. Consider again the spot rate structure shown early on. Assume that there are only two possible future interest rate scenarios, outcome 1 and outcome 2, both of equal probability. The dynamics of the short-term interest rate are described by a constant drift rate a, together with a volatility rate σ. These two parameters describe the evolution of the short-term interest rate. If outcome 1 occurs, the one-period interest rate one period from now will be:

$$5\% \times \exp(a + \sigma)$$

while if outcome 2 occurs, the period one rate will become:

$$5\% \times \exp(a - \sigma)$$

In Figure 8.12 we present the possible interest rate paths under conditions of 0% and 25% volatility levels, and maintain our assumption that the current spot rate structure price for a risk-free zero-coupon bond is identical to the price generated using the structure to obtain a zero option-adjusted spread. To maintain the no-arbitrage condition, we know that the price of the bond at the start of period 1 must be $89, so we calculate the implied drift rate by an iterative process. This is shown in Figure 8.12.

At 0% volatility the prices generated by the up and down moves are equal, because the future interest rates are equal. Hence the forward rate is the same as before: 7.009%. When there is a multiple interest rate path scenario, the fair value of the bond is determined as the average of the discounted values for each rate path. Under conditions of certainty (0% volatility), the price of the bond is, not surprisingly, unchanged at both paths. The average of these is obviously $89. Under 25% volatility the up-move interest rate is 7.889% and the down-move rate is 6.144%. The average of these rates is 7.017%. We can check the values by calculating the value of the bond at each outcome (or 'node') and then obtaining the average of these values; this is shown to be $89. Beginners can view the simple spreadsheet used to calculate the rates in Appendix 8.1, with the iterative process undertaken using the Microsoft Excel 'Goal Seek' function.

Term (interest periods)	Spot Rate
1	5.00%
2	6.00%
1v1 fwd rate	7.009%

0% volatility
Implied drift rate 33.776%

Expected future rate under zero volatility is 7.009%

Probability of up-move and down-move is identical at 50%

25% volatility
Implied drift rate 20.61%

Expected future rate under zero volatility is 7.017%

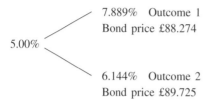

5.00%

7.889%   Outcome 1
Bond price £88.274

6.144%   Outcome 2
Bond price £89.725

Probability of up-move and down-move is identical at 50%

Figure 8.12   Expected interest rate paths under conditions of uncertainty

We now consider the corporate bond with $5 and $105 cash flows at the end of periods 1 and 2 respectively. In an environment of certainty, the bond price of $97 implied an OAS of 67.6 basis points (bps). In the uncertain environment we can use the same process as above to determine the spread implied by the same price. The process involves discounting the cash flows across each path with the spread added, to determine the price at each node. The price of the bond is the average of all the resulting prices; this is then compared to the observed market price (or required price). If the calculated price is lower than the market price, then a higher spread is required, and if the calculated price is higher than the market price, then the spread is too high and must be lowered.

Applying this approach to the model in Figure 8.12, under the 0% volatility the spread implied by the price of $97 is, unsurprisingly, 67.6 bps. In the 25% volatility environment however, this spread results in a price of $97.296, which is higher than the observed price. This suggests the spread is too low. By iteration we find that the spread that generates a price of $97 is 89.76 bps, which is the bond's option-adjusted spread. This is shown below.

Outcome 1:

$$P = \frac{5}{1 + (0.05 + 0.00897)}$$

$$+ \frac{105}{[1 + (0.05 + 0.00897) \times [1 + (0.07887 + 0.00897)]}$$

$$= \text{£}95.865$$

Outcome 2:

$$P = \frac{5}{1 + (0.05 + 0.00897)}$$

$$+ \frac{105}{[1 + (0.05 + 0.00897) \times [1 + (0.06144 + 0.00897)]}$$

$$= \text{£}98.135$$

The calculated price is the average of these two values and is [(95.87 + 98.13)/2] or $97 as required. The OAS of 89.76 bps in the binomial model is a measure of the value attached to the option element of the bond at 25% volatility.

The final part of this discussion introduces the value of the embedded option in a bond. Our example bond from earlier is now semi-annually paying and carries a coupon value of 7%. It has a redemption value of $101.75. Assume that the bond is callable at the end of period 1, and that it is advantageous for the issuer to call the bond at this point if interest rates fall below 7%. We assume further that the bond is trading at the fair value implied by the discounting calculation earlier. With a principal nominal amount of $101.75, this suggests a market price of (101.75/97.00) or $104.89. We require the OAS implied by this price now that there is an embedded option element in the bond. Under conditions of 0% volatility the value of the call is zero, as the option is out-of-the-money when interest rates are above 7%. In these circumstances the bond behaves exactly as before, and the OAS remains 67.6 bps. However, in the 25% volatility environment it becomes advantageous to the issuer to call the bond in the down-state environment, as rates are below 7%. In fact we can calculate that the spread over the interest rate paths that would produce an average price of 104.89 is 4 bps, which means that the option carries a cost to the bondholder of (67.6 – 4) or 63.6 bps. We illustrate this property in general terms in Figure 8.13. A conventional bond has a convex price/yield profile, but the introduction of a call feature limits the upside price performance of a bond, since there is a greater chance of it being called as market yields fall.

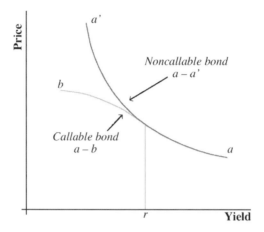

Figure 8.13 Impact of a call option on the price/yield (convexity) profile of a corporate bond
Reproduced with permission from Frank J Fabozzi, *Fixed Income Mathematics*, McGraw-Hill 1997.

The methodology in practice

In practice, the forward rate term structure is extracted using regression methods from the price of default-free government coupon bonds. Generally, OAS models used in the market are constructed so that they generate government prices that are identical to the prices observed in the market, because they assume that government bonds are fair value. This results in an implied forward rate yield curve that is the 'expected' path of future interest rates around which other rate possibilities are dispersed. Under this assumption then, an OAS value is a measure of the return over the government yield that an investor can expect to achieve by holding the option-embedded bond that is being analysed. Banks generally employ a simulation model such as Monte Carlo to generate the 'tree' of possible interest rate scenarios. This is a series of computer-generated random numbers that are used to derive interest rate paths. To generate the paths, the

284

simulation model runs using the two parameters introduced earlier: the deterministic drift term and the volatility term. Interest rates are assumed to be lognormally distributed.

When conducting relative value analysis, we strip a security down into the constituent cash flows relevant to each interest rate path. This is straightforward for vanilla bonds; however, for bonds such as mortgage-backed securities the cash flows are determined after assuming a level of prepayment. The results generated from the prepayment model are themselves based on interest rate scenarios. The OAS is then calculated by discounting the cash flows corresponding to each node on the interest rate tree, and is the spread that equates the calculated average price to the observed market price. In practice the model is run the other way: assuming a fair value spread over government bonds, the fair value price of a bond is the average price that is obtained by discounting all the cash flows at each relevant interest rate, together with the fair value spread.

OAS analysis for an hypothetical corporate callable bond and Treasury bond

We conclude this chapter with an illustration of the OAS technique. Consider a five-year semi-annual corporate bond with a coupon of 8%. The bond incorporates a call feature that allows the issuer to call it after two years, and is currently priced at $104.25. This is equivalent to a yield to maturity of 6.979%. We wish to measure the value of the call feature to the issuer, and we can do this using the OAS technique. Assume that a five-year Treasury security also exists with a coupon of 8%, and is priced at $109.11, a yield of 5.797%. The higher yield of the corporate bond reflects the market-required premium, due to the corporate bond's default risk and call feature.

The valuation of both securities is shown in Table 8.5.

Bond	Price	Yield
Corporate bond	104.25	6.979%
Treasury 8% 2006	109.11	5.797%

OAS Spread	110.81 bps

Period	YTM	Date	Spot rate	Discount Factor	Cash flow	Present Value	OAS adjusted spot rate	PV of OAS-adjusted cash flows
0	5.000	25-Feb-2001	5.000	1				
1	5.000	27-Aug-2001	5.069	0.97521333	4	3.901125962	6.177	3.88016
2	5.150	25-Feb-2002	5.225	0.95034125	4	3.798913929	6.333	3.75822
3	5.200	26-Aug-2002	5.277	0.92582337	4	3.699381343	6.385	3.64011
4	5.250	25-Feb-2003	5.329	0.90137403	4	3.600632571	6.437	3.52394
5	5.374	25-Aug-2003	5.463	0.87567855	4	3.495761898	6.571	3.40300
6	5.500	25-Feb-2004	5.597	0.84928019	4	3.389528778	6.705	3.28196
7	5.624	25-Aug-2004	5.734	0.82277146	4	3.281916075	6.842	3.16080
8	5.750	25-Feb-2005	5.870	0.79585734	4	3.173623771	6.978	3.04022
9	5.775	25-Aug-2005	5.895	0.77285090	4	3.079766213	7.003	2.93453
10	5.800	27-Feb-2006	5.920	0.74972455	104	77.6869373	7.028	73.62754
						109.1075878		104.25049

Table 8.5 OAS analysis for corporate callable bond and Treasury bond

Our starting point is the redemption yield curve, from which we calculate the current spot rate term structure. This was done using RATE software and is shown in column 4. Using the spot rate structure, we calculate the present value of the Treasury security's cash flows, which is shown in column 7. We wish to calculate the OAS that equates the price of the Treasury to that of the corporate bond. By iteration, this is found to be 110.81 bps. This is the semi-annual OAS spread. The annualised OAS spread is double this. With the OAS spread added to the spot rates for each period, the price of the Treasury matches that of the corporate bond, as shown in column 9. The adjusted spot rates are shown in column 8.

Figure 8.14 illustrates the yield curve for the Treasury security and the corporate bond.

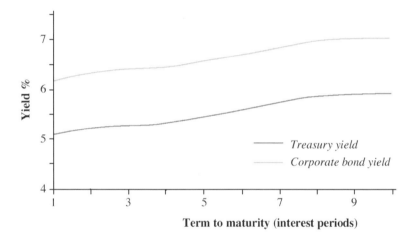

Figure 8.14 Yield curves illustrating OAS yield spread

Appendix 8.1 Calculating interest rate paths using Microsoft Excel

The table below shows the cell references when using Microsoft Excel to calculate interest rate paths.

Price 89
Period 1 rate 1.05
Volatility 0.25
Drift 0.206054017

| Up state | 0.078891779 | 1.078892 | Bond price | 88.2740022 | Average 88.9996 |

| Down state | 0.061440979 | 1.061441 | 89.72528584 | |
| | | | Fwd rate % | 0.070166379 |

	F	G		H	I	J		K	L
17									
18	Price	89							
19	Period 1 rate	1.05							
20	Volatility	0.25							
21	Drift	0.206054017							
22									
23									
24	Up state	=0.05*EXP(G21+G20)	=1+G24	Bond price	=100/(G19*H24)	Average =(J24+J25)/2			
25	Down state	=0.05*EXP(G21-H19)	=1+G25	=100/(G19*H25)					
26									
27					Fwd rate %	=(G24+G25)/2			

Selected Bibliography and References

For a good introduction on callable bonds, we recommend the Fabozzi titles, Questa (1999) and Livingstone (1993). Martellini et al (2003) is also excellent.

Bodie, Z. and Taggart, R., "Future Investment Opportunities and the Value of the Call Provision on a Bond", *Journal of Finance* 33, 1978, p.1187–2000.

Choudhry, M., *The Bond and Money Markets*, Butterworth-Heinemann, 2001.

Fabozzi, F.J., *Fixed Income Mathematics: Analytical and Statistical Techniques* (3rd edition), McGraw-Hill, 1997, Chapter 16.

Kalotay, A., Williams, G.O. and Fabozzi, F.J., " A model for the Valuation of Bonds and Embedded Options", *Financial Analysts Journal*, May-June 1993, p.35–46.

Kish, R. and Livingstone, M., "The Determinants of the Call Feature on Corporate Bonds", *Journal of Banking and Finance* 16, 1992, p.687–703.

Livingstone, M., *Money and Capital Markets* (2nd edition), NYIOF, 1993.

Martellini, L., P. Priaulet and S. Priaulet, *Fixed Income Securities*, John Wiley & Sons 2003.

Mitchell, K., "The Call, Sinking Fund, and Term-to-Maturity Features of Corporate Bonds: An Empirical Investigation", *Journal of Financial and Quantitative Analysis* 26, June 1991, p.201–222.

Narayanan, M.P. and Lim, S.P., "On the Call Provision on Corporate Zero-Coupon Bonds", *Journal of Financial and Quantitative Analysis* 24, March 1989, p.91–103.

Questa, G., *Fixed Income Analysis for the Global Financial Market*, Wiley, Chapter 8.

Si Chen, 'Understanding option-adjusted spreads: the implied prepayment hypothesis', *Journal of Portfolio Management*, summer 1996, pp. 104–13.

Tuckman, B., *Fixed Income Securities*, Wiley, 1996, Chapter 17.

Van Horne, J.C., *Financial Management and Policy*, Prentice Hall, 1986.

Wilson, R., Fabozzi, F., *The New Corporate Bond Market*, Probus Publishing 1990, Chapter 11.

Windas, T., *An Introduction to Option-Adjusted Spread Analysis*, Bloomberg Publications, 1993.

9

Inflation-indexed Bonds and Derivatives

In certain countries, there is a market in bonds whose return, both coupon and final redemption payment, is linked to the consumer price index. Investors' experience with inflation-indexed bonds differs across countries, as they were introduced at different times and, as a result, the exact design of index-linked bonds varies across the different markets. This, of course, makes the comparison of issues such as yield difficult and has in the past acted as a hindrance to arbitrageurs seeking to exploit real yield differentials. In this chapter, we will highlight the basic concepts behind the structure of indexed bonds and how this may differ from that employed in another market. Not all index-linked bonds link both coupon and maturity payments to a specified index; in some markets only the coupon payment is index-linked. Generally the most liquid market available will be the government-bond market in index-linked dent instruments.

The structure of index-linked bond markets across the world differs in various ways, including those noted below. Appendix 9.1 lists those countries that currently issue public-sector indexed securities.

Introduction and basic concepts

There are a number of reasons why investors and issuers alike are interested in inflation-indexed bonds. Before considering these, we look at some of the factors involved in security design.

Choice of index. In principle, bonds can be indexed to any number of variables, including various price indices, earnings, output, specific commodities or foreign currencies. Although ideally the chosen index would reflect the hedging requirements of both parties, these may not coincide. For instance, the overwhelming choice of retail investors is for indexation to consumer prices, whereas pension funds prefer linking to earnings levels, to offset earnings-linked pension liabilities. In practice, most bonds have been linked to an index of consumer prices such as the UK Retail Price Index, since this is usually widely circulated and well understood and issued on a regular basis.

Indexation lags. In order to provide practically precise protection against inflation, interest payments for a given period would need to be corrected for actual inflation over the same period. However, for two important reasons, there are unavoidable lags between the movements in the price index and the adjustment to the bond cash flows as they are paid. This reduces the inflation-proofing properties of indexed bonds. Deacon and Derry (1998) state two reasons why indexation lags are necessary. First, inflation statistics can only be calculated and published with a delay. The data for one month is usually known well into the next month, and there may be delays in publication. This calls for a lag of at least one month. Secondly, in some markets the size of the next coupon payment must be known before the start of the coupon period in order to calculate the accrued interest; this leads to a delay equal to the length of time between coupon payments.[1]

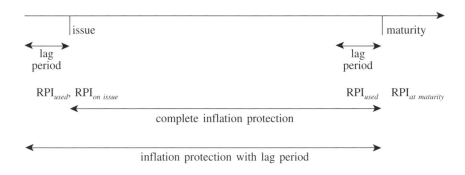

Figure 9.1 The indexation lag

---

[1] The same source cites various methods by which the period of the lag may be minimized; for example, the accrued-interest calculation for Canadian Real Return Bonds is based on cumulative movements in the consumer price index, which run from the last coupon date. This obviates the need to know with certainty the nominal value of the next coupon, unlike the arrangement for UK index-linked gilts. (See Deacon and Derry (1998), p.30–31).

Coupon frequency. Index-linked bonds often pay interest on a semi-annual basis, but long-dated investors such as fund managers whose liabilities may well include inflation-indexed annuities are also, at least in theory, interested in indexed bonds that pay on a quarterly or even monthly basis.

Indexing the cash flows. There are four basic methods of linking the cash flows from a bond to an inflation index. These are :

* Interest-indexed bonds: these pay a fixed real coupon and aindexation of the fixed principal every period; the principal repayment at maturity is not adjusted. In this case, all the inflation adjustment is fully paid out as it occurs and does not accrue on the principal. This type of bond has been issued in Australia, although the most recent issue was in 1987.
* Capital-indexed bonds: the coupon rate is specified in real terms. Interest payments equal the coupon rate multiplied by the inflation adjusted principal amount. At maturity, the principal repayment is the product of the nominal value of the bond multiplied by the cumulative change in the index. Compared with interest-indexed bonds of similar maturity, these bonds have higher duration and lower reinvestment risk. This type of bond has been issued in Australia, Canada, New Zealand, the UK and the USA.
* Zero-coupon indexed bonds: as their name implies these pay no coupons but the principal repayment is scaled for inflation. These have the highest duration of all indexed bonds and have no reinvestment risk. This type of bond has been issued in Sweden.
* Indexed-annuity bonds: the payments consist of a fixed annuity payment and a varying element to compensate for inflation. These bonds have the lowest duration and highest reinvestment risk of all index-linked bonds. They have been issued in Australia, although not by the central government.
* Current pay bond: as with interest-indexed bonds, the principal cash flow on maturity is not adjusted for inflation. The difference with current pay bonds is that their term cash flows are a combination of an inflation-adjusted coupon and an indexed amount that is related to the principal. Thus, in effect, current pay bonds are an inflation indexed floating-rate note. They have been issued in Turkey.

The choice of instrument will reflect the requirements of investors and issuers. Deacon and Derry (1998) cite duration, tax treatment and reinvestment risk as the principal factors that influence instrument design.

Although duration for an indexed bond measures something slightly different from that for a conventional bond, being an indication of the bond price sensitivity due to changes in the real interest rate, as with a conventional bond it is higher for zero-coupon indexed bonds than coupon bonds. Indexed annuities will have the shortest duration. Longer-duration instruments will (in theory) be demanded by investors that have long-dated hedging liabilities. Again, similarly to conventional bonds, investors holding indexed bonds are exposed to reinvestment risk, which means that the true yield earned by holding a bond to maturity cannot be determined when it is purchased, as the rate at which interim cash flows can be invested is not known. Hence, bonds that pay more of their return in the form of coupons are more exposed to this risk, which would be indexed annuities. Indexed zero-coupon bonds, like their conventional counterparts, do not expose investors to reinvestment risk. The tax regime in individual markets will also influence investor taste. For instance, some jurisdictions tax the capital gain on zero-coupon bonds as income, with a requirement that any tax liability be discharged as current income. This is unfavorable treatment as the capital is not available until maturity, which would reduce demand from institutional investors for zero-coupon instruments.

It should be noted also that in three countries – Canada, New Zealand and the United States – there exists a facility for investors to strip indexed bonds, thus enabling separate trading of coupon and principal cash flows.[2] Such an arrangement obviates the need for a specific issue of zero-coupon indexed securities, as the market can create them in response to investor demand.

Coupon stripping feature. Allowing market practitioners to strip indexed bonds enables them to create new inflation-linked products that are more specific to investors' needs, such as indexed annuities or deferred-payment indexed bonds. In markets which allow stripping of indexed government bonds, a strip is simply an individual uplifted cash flow. An exception to this is in New Zealand, where the cash flows are separated into three components; the principal, the principal-inflation adjustment and the set of inflation-linked coupons (that is, an indexed annuity).The US Tips market

---

[2] In the United Kingdom, the facility of "stripping" exists for conventional gilts but not index-linked gilts. The term originates in the US market, being an acronym for Separate Trading of Registered Interest and Principal.

EXAMPLE 9.1 The US Tips market

"Tips" is the term for what were first referred to as Treasury inflation-indexed securities. They were introduced in 1997 by the US Treasury, to increase investment options for investors but also to diversify its funding sources and risk exposure. They are similar to UK index-linked gilts in that they have a fixed coupon on issue, but one that is then adjusted to account for changes in the level of inflation. At the time of writing, Tips are issued only at 10-year maturities, through an auction held in January and July each year.[3] During 2003, Tips issuance represented over 25% of the total 10-year Treasury security issue.

Interest on Tips securities can be viewed as a mix of the fixed coupon and a floating coupon. The fixed coupon is known on issue. The "floating" coupon is the issued nominal amount, which is made up on coupon payments rising as the amount of principal increases. The bond principal amount increases because it is linked to the US Consumer Price Index (CPI).[4] The inflation-adjusted principal amount is paid out on maturity.

A general market convention is to measure Tips performance on the basis of break-even yields, which is the nominal Treasury yield minus the Tips yield. The lower the break-even yield, then the cheaper Tips are relative to conventional Treasuries of identical maturity.

As at December 2003 the market in Tips stood at over $160 billion.

Index-linked bond yields

Calculating index-linked yields

Inflation-indexed bonds have either or both of their coupon and principal linked to a price index such as the retail price index (RPI), a commodity price index (for example, wheat) or a stock market index. In the UK, the reference is to the RPI, whereas in other markets the price index is the

---

[3] At the start of the Tips programme the Treasury also issued five-year and 30-year Tips, but these have since been discontinued.

[4] Obviously this assumes that the economy experiences inflation. If it experienced deflation, the principal amount would of course decrease. In the event of deflation, Tips are redeemed at a minimum of par. This is known as the deflation floor and is a safety net for investors.

consumer price index (CPI). If we wish to calculate the yield on such bonds, it is necessary to make forecasts of the relevant index, which are then used in the yield calculation. In the UK, both the principal and coupons on UK index-linked government bonds are linked to the RPI and are therefore designed to give a constant real yield. Most of the index-linked stocks that have been issued by the UK government have coupons of 2 or $2°\%$. This is because the return from an index-linked bond represents, in theory, real return, as the bond's cash flows rise in line with inflation. Historically, real rate of return on UK market debt stock over the long-term has been roughly $2°\%$.

Indexed bonds differ in their make-up across markets. In some markets only the principal payment is linked, whereas other indexed bonds link only their coupon payments and not the redemption payment. In the case of the former, each coupon and the final principal are scaled up by the ratio of two values of the RPI. The main RPI measure is the one reported for eight months before the issue of the gilt, and is known as the base RPI. The base RPI is the denominator of the index measure. The numerator is the RPI measure for eight months prior to the month coupon payment, or eight months before the bond maturity date.

The coupon payment of an index-linked gilt is given by (9.1) below.

$$\text{Coupon payment} = (C/2) \times \frac{RPI_{C-8}}{RPI_0} \qquad (9.1)$$

Expression (9.1) shows the coupon divided by two before being scaled up, because index-linked gilts pay semi-annual coupons. The formula for calculating the size of the coupon payment for an annual-paying indexed bond is modified accordingly.

The principal repayment is given by (9.2).

$$\text{Principal payment} = 100 \times \frac{RPI_{M-8}}{RPI_0} \qquad (9.2)$$

where

C is the annual coupon payment

RPI_0 is the RPI value eight months prior to the issue of the bond (the base RPI)

RPI_{C-8} is the RPI value eight months prior to the month in which the coupon

        is paid

RPI_{M-8} is the RPI value eight months prior to the bond redemption.

Price indices are occasionally "re-based", which means that the index is set to a base level again. In the UK, the RPI has been re-based twice, the last occasion being in January 1987, when it was set to 100 from the January 1974 value of 394.5.

EXAMPLE 9.2

An index-linked gilt with coupon of 4.625% was issued in April 1988 and matured in April 1998. The base measure required for this bond is the RPI for August 1987, which was 102.1. The RPI for August 1997 was 158.5. We can use these values to calculate the actual cash amount of the final coupon payment and principal repayment in April 1998, as shown below.

$$\text{Coupon payment} = (4.625/2) \times \frac{158.5}{102.1} = £3.58992$$

$$\text{Principal payment} = 100 \times \frac{158.5}{102.1} = £155.23996$$

We can determine the accrued interest calculation for the last six-month coupon period (October 1987 to April 1998) by using the final coupon payment, given below.

$$3.58992 \times \frac{\text{No. of days accrued}}{\text{actual days in period}}$$

The markets use two main yield measures for index-linked bonds, both of which are a form of yield-to-maturity. These are the *money* (or nominal) *yield*, and the *real yield*.

In order to calculate a money yield for an indexed bond, we require forecasts of all future cash flows from the bond. Since future cash flows from an index-linked bond are not known with certainty, we require a forecast of all the relevant future RPIs, which we then apply to all the cash flows. In fact, the market convention is to take the latest available RPI and assume a constant inflation rate thereafter, usually $2\frac{1}{2}\%$ or 5%. By assuming a constant inflation rate we can set future RPI levels, which in turn allow us to calculate future cash-flow values.

We obtain the forecast for the first relevant future RPI using (9.3).

$$RPI_1 = RPI_0 \times (1 + \tau)^{m/12} \qquad (9.3)$$

where

RPI_1 is the forecast RPI level
RPI_0 is the latest available RPI
τ is the assumed future annual inflation rate
m is the number of months between RPI_0 and RPI_1

Consider an indexed bond that pays coupons every June and December. For analysis we require the RPI forecast value for eight months prior to June and December, which will be for October and April. If we are now in February, we require a forecast for the RPI for the next April. This sets $m = 2$ in our equation at (9.3). We can then use (9.4) to forecast each subsequent relevant RPI required to set the bond's cash flows.

$$RPI_{j+1} = RPI_1 \times (1 + \tau)^{j/2} \qquad (9.4)$$

where j is the number of semi-annual forecasts after RPI_1 (which was our forecast RPI for April). For example, if the February RPI was 163.7 and we assume an annual inflation rate of 2.5%, then we calculate the forecast for the RPI for the following April to be:

$$
\begin{aligned}
RPI_1 &= 163.7 \times (1.025)^{2/12} \\
&= 164.4
\end{aligned}
$$

and for the following October it would be:

$$
\begin{aligned}
RPI_3 &= 164.4 \times (1.025) \\
&= 168.5
\end{aligned}
$$

Once we have determined the forecast RPIs, we can calculate the yield. Under the assumption that the analysis is carried out on a coupon date, so that accrued interest on the bond is zero, we can calculate the money yield (ri) by solving equation (9.5).

$$P_d = \frac{(C/2)(RPI_1/RPI_0)}{(1 + \frac{1}{2}ri)} + \frac{(C/2)(RPI_2/RPI_0)}{(1 + \frac{1}{2}ri)^2} + \cdots\cdots + \frac{([C/2] + M)(RPI_N/RPI_0)}{(1 + \frac{1}{2}ri)^N}$$

$$(9.5)$$

where

ri is the semi-annualised money yield-to-maturity
N is the number of coupon payments (interest periods) up to maturity.

Equation (9.5) is for semi-annual paying indexed bonds such as index-linked gilts. The equation for annual coupon indexed bonds is given at (9.6).

$$P_d = \frac{C(RPI_1/RPI_0)}{(1 + ri)} + \frac{C(RPI_2/RPI_0)}{(1 + ri)^2} + \ldots\ldots + \frac{(C + M)(RPI_N/RPI_0)}{(1 + ri)^N}$$

(9.6)

The real yield ry is related to the money yield through equation (9.7), as it applies to semi-annual coupon bonds, which was first described by Fisher in *Theory of Interest* (1930).

$$(1 + \tfrac{1}{2}ry) = (1 + \tfrac{1}{2}ri) \,/\, (1 + \tau)^{1/2}$$

(9.7)

To illustrate this, if the money yield is 5.5% and the forecast inflation rate is 2.5%, then the real yield is calculated using (9.7) as shown below.

$$ry = \left\{ \frac{[1 + \tfrac{1}{2}(0.055)]}{[1 + (0.025)]^{1/2}} - 1 \right\} \times 2$$

$$= 0.0297 \text{ or } 2.97\%$$

We can re-arrange equation (9.5) and use (9.7) to solve for the real yield, shown at (9.8) and applicable to semi-annual coupon bonds. Again, we use (9.8) where the calculation is performed on a coupon date.

$$P_d = \frac{RPI_a}{RPI_0} \left[\frac{(C/2)(1 + \tau)^{1/2}}{(1 + \tfrac{1}{2}ri)} + \frac{(C/2)(1 + \tau)}{(1 + \tfrac{1}{2}ri)^2} + \ldots + \frac{([C/2] + M)(1 + \tau)^{N/2}}{(1 + \tfrac{1}{2}ri)^N} \right]$$

$$= \frac{RPI_a}{RPI_0} \left[\frac{(C/2)}{(1 + \tfrac{1}{2}ry)} + \ldots\ldots + \frac{(C/2) + M}{(1 + \tfrac{1}{2}ry)^N} \right]$$

(9.8)

where

$$RPI_a = \frac{RPI_1}{(1 + \tau)^{1/2}} \quad .$$

RPI_0 is the base index level as initially described. RPI_a/RPI_0 is the rate of inflation between the bond's issue date and the date the yield calculation is carried out.

It is best to think of the equations for money yield and real yield by thinking of which discount rate to employ when calculating a redemption yield for an indexed bond. Equation (9.5) can be viewed as showing that the money yield is the appropriate discount rate for discounting money or nominal cash flows. We then re-arrange this equation as given in (9.8) to show that the real yield is the appropriate discount rate to use when discounting real cash flows.

The yield calculation for a US TIPS security is given at Appendix 9.2.

Assessing yield for index-linked bonds

Index-linked bonds do not offer *complete* protection against a fall in real value of an investment. That is, the return from index-linked bonds (including index-linked gilts) is not in reality a guaranteed real return, in spite of the cash flows being linked to a price index such as the RPI. The reason for this is the lag in indexation, which for index-linked gilts is eight months. The time lag means that an indexed bond is not protected against inflation for the last interest period of its life, which for gilts is the last six months. Any inflation occurring during this final interest period will not be reflected in the bond's cash flows and will reduce the real value of the redemption payment and hence the real yield. This can be a worry for investors in high-inflation environments. The only way to effectively eliminate inflation risk for bondholders is to reduce the time lag in indexation of payments to something like one or two months.

Bond analysts frequently compare the yields on index-linked bonds with those on conventional bonds, as this implies the market's expectation of inflation rates. To compare returns between index-linked bonds and conventional bonds, analysts calculate the break-even inflation rate. This is the inflation rate that makes the money yield on an index-linked bond equal to the redemption yield on a conventional bond of the same maturity. Roughly speaking, the difference between the yield on an indexed bond and a conventional bond of the same maturity is what the market expects inflation during the life of the bond to be. Part of the higher yield available on the conventional bond is therefore the inflation premium. In August 1999, the redemption yield on the $5^3/_4\%$ Treasury 2009, the 10-year benchmark gilt, was 5.17%. The real yield on the $2°\%$ index-linked 2009 gilt, assuming a constant inflation rate of 3%, was 2.23%. Using (9.5), this gives us an implied break-even inflation rate of:

$$\tau = \left\{ \frac{[1 + \frac{1}{2}(0.0517)]}{[1 + \frac{1}{2}(0.0223)]} \right\}^2 - 1$$

$$= 0.029287 \text{ or } 2.9\%.$$

If we accept that an advanced, highly developed and liquid market such as the gilt market is of at least semi-strong form, if not strong form, then the inflation expectation in the market is built into these gilt yields. However, if this implied inflation rate understated what was expected by certain market participants, investors will start holding more of the index-linked bond rather than the conventional bond. This activity will then force the indexed yield down (or the conventional yield up). If investors had the opposite view and thought that the implied inflation rate overstated inflation expectations, they would hold the conventional bond. In our illustration above, the market is expecting long-term inflation to be at around 2.9% or less, and the higher yield of the $5\frac{3}{4}\%$ 2009 bond reflects this inflation expectation. A fund manager will take into account her view of inflation, amongst other factors, in deciding how much of the index-linked gilt to hold compared to the conventional gilt. It is often the case that investment managers hold indexed bonds in a portfolio against specific index-linked liabilities, such as pension contracts that increase their payouts in line with inflation each year.

The premium on the yield of the conventional bond over that of the index-linked bond is therefore compensation against inflation to investors holding it. Bondholders will choose to hold index-linked bonds instead of conventional bonds if they are worried by unexpected inflation. An individual's view on expected inflation will depend on several factors, including the current macroeconomic environment and the credibility of the monetary authorities, be they the central bank or the government. In certain countries such as the UK and New Zealand, the central bank has explicit inflation targets and investors may feel that, over the long-term, these targets will be met. If the track record of the monetary authorities is proven, investors may feel further that inflation is no longer a significant issue. In these situations the case for holding index-linked bonds is weakened.

The real-yield level on indexed bonds in other markets is also a factor. As capital markets around the world have become closely integrated in the last 20 years, global capital mobility means that high-inflation markets are shunned by investors. Therefore, over time, expected returns, certainly in developed and liquid markets, should be roughly equal, so that real yields are at similar levels around the world. If we accept this premise, we would then expect the real yield on index-linked bonds to be at approximately similar levels, whatever market they are traded in. For example, we would expect indexed bonds in the UK to be at a level near to that in, say, the US market. In fact, in May 1999 long-dated index-linked gilts traded at just over 2% real yield, while long-dated indexed bonds in the US were at the higher real-yield level of 3.8%. This was viewed by analysts as reflecting that international capital was not as mobile as had previously been thought, and that productivity gains and technological progress in the US economy had boosted demand for capital there to such an extent that real yield had had to rise. However, there is no doubt that there is considerable information content in index-linked bonds and analysts are always interested in the yield levels of these bonds compared to conventional bonds.

The Bloomberg YA page used for yield calculation shows the nominal and real yield analysis for inflation-linked bonds. Figure 9.2 shows this page for the US TIPS security the 2% of 2014, which was issued in January 2004, as at 15 March 2004. We see that the nominal or money yield was 1.462%, against a real yield of 3.485%, assuming an inflation rate of 2.00%. We also see that the base CPI at issue was 184.77.

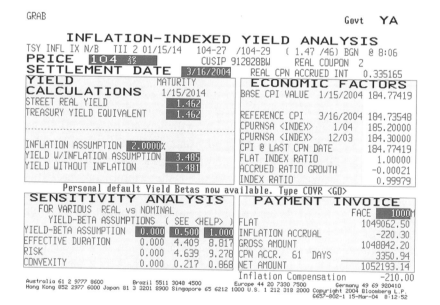

Figure 9.2 Bloomberg page YA showing yield calculation for US 2% 2014 TIP security, as at 15 March 2004.
© Bloomberg L.P. Used with permission

Further views on index-linked yields

The market analyses the trading patterns and yield levels of index-linked (I-L) gilts for their information content. The difference between the yield on I-L gilts and conventional gilts of the same maturity is an indication of the market's view on future inflation. Where this difference is historically low, it implies that the market considers that inflation prospects are benign. So the yield spread between index-linked gilts and the same maturity conventional gilt is roughly the market's view of expected inflation levels over the long term. For example, on 3rd November 1999 the 10-year benchmark, the 5³/₄% Treasury 2009, had a gross redemption yield of 5.280%. The 10-year index-linked bond, the 2¹/₂% I-L Treasury 2009[5], had a money yield of 5.046% and a real yield of 2.041%, the latter assuming an inflation rate of 3%. Roughly speaking, this reflects a market view on inflation of approximately 3.24% in the 10 years to maturity. Of course, other factors drive both conventional and I-L bond yields, including supply and demand, and liquidity. Generally, conventional bonds are more liquid than I-L bonds. An increased demand will depress yields for the conventional bond as well.[6] However, the inflation expectation will also be built into the conventional bond yield and it is reasonable to assume the spread to be an approximation of the market's view on inflation over the life of the bond. A higher inflation expectation will result in a greater spread between the two bonds, this reflecting a premium to holders of the conventional issue as a compensation against the effects of inflation. This spread has declined slightly from May 1997 onwards, the point at which the government gave up control over monetary policy and the Monetary Policy Committee (MPC) of the Bank of England became responsible for setting interest rates.

---

[5] This bond was issued in October 1982; as at October 1999 there was £2.625 billion nominal outstanding.

[6] For example, two days later, following a rally in the gilt market, the yield on the conventional gilt was 5.069%, against a real yield on the index-linked gilt of 1.973%, implying that the inflation premium had been reduced to 3.09%. This is significantly lower than the premium just two days later, which may reflect the fact that the MPC had just raised interest rates by ˜% the day before, but the rally in gilts would have a greater impact on the conventional bond than on the linker.

	Yields (%)							
Bonds	Feb-97	Jun-97	Feb-98	Jun-98	Feb-99	Jun-99	Sep-99	Nov-99
2.5% I-L 2009*	3.451	3.707	3.024	2.880	1.937	1.904	2.352	2.041
7.25% 2007	7.211	7.021	-	-	-	-	-	-
9% 2008	-	-	5.959	5.911	-	-	-	-
5.75% 2009	-	-	-	-	4.379	4.907	5.494	5.280
Spread	3.760	3.314	2.935	3.031	2.442	3.003	3.142	3.239

* Real yield, assuming 3% rate of inflation

Table 9.1 Real yield on the $2^1/_2\%$ I-L 2009 versus the 10-year benchmark
Source: Bloomberg

Table 9.1 shows the real yield of the $2^1/_2\%$ I-L 2009 bond at selected points since the beginning of 1997, alongside the gross redemption yield of the 10-year benchmark conventional bond at the time (we use the same I-L bond because there was no issue that matured in 2007 or 2008). Although the market's view on expected inflation rate over the 10-year period is, on the whole, stuck around the 3% level, there has been a downward trend in the period since the MPC became responsible for setting interest rates. As the MPC has an inflation target of 2.5%, the spread between the real yield on the 10-year linker and the 10-year conventional gilt implies that the market believes that the MPC will achieve its goal.[7]

The yield spread between I-L and conventional gilts fluctuates over time and is influenced by a number of factors and not solely by the market's view of future inflation (the implied forward inflation rate). As we discussed in the previous paragraph, however, the market uses this yield spread to gauge an idea of future inflation levels. The other term used to describe the yield spread is breakeven inflation, that is the level of inflation required that would equate nominal yields on I-L gilts with yields on conventional gilts. Figure 9.1 shows the implied forward inflation rate for the 15-year and 25-year terms to maturity as they fluctuated during 1998/1999. The data is from the Bank of England. For both maturity terms, the implied forward rate

---

[7] In fact, the MPC target centers on the RPIX measure of inflation, the "underlying" rate. This is the RPIX measure but with mortgage interest payments stripped out. During 2004 the MPC replaced its RPIX target with HICP, an EU harmonised measure of inflation.

decreased significantly during the summer of 1998. Analysts, however, ascribed this to the rally in the conventional gilts, brought on by the "flight to quality" after the emerging-markets fallout beginning in July that year. This rally was not matched by I-L gilts performance. The 25-year implied forward inflation rate touched 1.66% in September 1999, which was considered excessively optimistic given that that BoE was working towards achieving a 2.5% rate of inflation over the long term! This suggested then that conventional gilts were significantly overvalued.[8] As we see in Figure 9.1, this implied forward rate for both maturity terms returned to more explainable levels later during the year, slightly above 3%. This is viewed as more consistent with the MPC's target, and can be expected to fall to just over 2.5% over the long term.

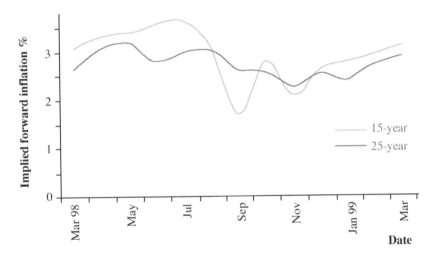

Figure 9.3 UK implied forward inflation rates during 1998/99

---

[8] As we have noted, the yield spread between I-L and conventional gilts reflects other considerations in addition to the forward inflation rate. As well as specific supply-and-demand issues, considerations include inflation risk premium in the yield of conventional gilts, and distortions created when modelling the yield curve. There is also a liquidity premium priced into I-L gilt yields that would not apply to benchmark conventional gilts. The effect of these is to generally overstate the implied forward inflation rate. Note also that the implied forward inflation rate applies to RPI, whereas the BoE's MPC inflation objective targets the RPIX measure of inflation, which is the headline inflation rate minus the impact of mortgage interest payments.

Analysis of real interest rates

Observing trading patterns in a liquid market in inflation-indexed bonds enables analysts to draw conclusions on nominal versus real interest indicators, and the concept of an inflation term structure. However, such analysis is often problematic as there is usually a significant difference between liquidity levels of conventional and indexed bonds. Nevertheless, as we discussed in the previous section, it is usually possible to infer market estimates of inflation expectations from the yields observed on indexed bonds, when compared to conventional yields.

Inflation expectations

Where an indexed bond incorporates an indexation lag, there is an imperfect indexation and the bond's return will not be completely inflation-proof. Deacon and Derry (1998) suggest that this means an indexed bond may be regarded as a combination of a true indexed instrument (with no lag) and an un-indexed bond. Where the lag period is exactly one coupon period the price/yield relationship is given by

$$P = \sum_{n:t_n>t}^{N} \frac{C\prod_{n=0}^{j-1}(1 + ri_i)}{(1 + rm_j)^j \prod_{i=1}^{j}(1 + ri_i)} + \frac{M\prod_{i=0}^{n-1}(1 + ri_i)}{(1 + rm_n)^n \prod_{i=1}^{n}(1 + ri_i)} \qquad (9.9)$$

where

ri is the rate of inflation between dates i-1 and i
rm is the redemption yield
and C and M are coupon and redemption payments, as usual. If the bond has just paid the last coupon ahead of its redemption date, (9.9) reduces to

$$P = \frac{C}{(1 + rm)(1 + ri)} + \frac{M}{(1 + rm)(1 + ri)} . \qquad (9.10)$$

In this situation, the final cash flows are not indexed and the price/yield relationship is identical to that of a conventional bond. This fact enables us to quantify the indexation element, as the yields observed on conventional bonds can be compared to that on the non-indexed element of the indexed bond. This implies a true real-yield measure for the indexed bond.

The Fisher identity is used to derive this estimate. Essentially, this describes the relationship between nominal and real interest rates, and in one form is given as

$$1 + y = (1 + r)(1 + i)(1 + \rho) \qquad (9.11)$$

where y is the nominal interest rate, r the real interest rate and i the expected rate of inflation. ρ is a premium for the risk of future inflation. Using (9.11), assuming a value for the risk premium ρ, we can link the two bond price equations, which can, as a set of simultaneous equations, be used to obtain values for the real interest rate and the expected inflation rate.

If they exist, one approach is to use two bonds of identical maturity, one conventional and one indexed, and, ignoring lag effects, use the yields on both to determine the expected inflation rate, given by the difference between the redemption yields of each bond. In fact, as we noted in the previous section, this measures the average expected rate of inflation during the period from now to the maturity of the bonds. This is at best an approximation. It is a flawed measure because an assumption of the expected inflation rate has been made when calculating the redemption yield of the indexed bond in the first place. As Deacon and Derry (1998, p.91) state, this problem is exacerbated if the maturity of both bonds is relatively short, because impact of the un-indexed element of the indexed bond is greater the shorter its maturity. To overcome this flaw, a breakeven rate of inflation is used. This is calculated by first calculating the yield on the conventional bond, followed by the yield on the indexed bond using an assumed initial inflation rate. The risk premium ρ is set to an assumed figure; say, 0. The Fisher identity is used to calculate a new estimate of the expected inflation rate i. This new estimate is then used to recalculate the yield on the indexed bond, which is then used to produce a new estimate of the expected inflation rate. The process is repeated iteratively until a consistent value for i is obtained.

The main drawback with this basic technique is that it is necessary for there to exist a conventional and an index-linked bond of identical maturity, so approximately similar maturities have to be used, further diluting the results. The yields on each bond will also be subject to liquidity, taxation, indexation and other influences. There is also no equivalent benchmark (or on-the-run) indexed security. The bibliography cites some recent research that has investigated this approach.

An inflation term structure

Where a liquid market in indexed bonds exists, across a reasonable-maturity term structure, it is possible to construct a term structure of inflation rates. In essence, this involves fitting the nominal and real interest rate term structures, the two of which can then be used to infer an inflation term structure. This, in turn, can be used to calculate a forward expected inflation rate for any future term, or a forward inflation curve, in the same way that a forward interest-rate curve is constructed.

The Bank of England uses an iterative technique to construct a term structure of inflation rates.[9] First, the nominal interest rate term structure is fitted using a version of the Waggoner model (1997, also described in James and Webber (2000)). An initial assumed inflation term structure is then used to infer a term structure of real interest rates. This assumed inflation curve is usually set flat at 3% or 5%. The real interest rate curve is then used to calculate an implied real interest rate forward curve. Second, the Fisher identity is applied at each point along the nominal and real interest rate forward curves, which produces a new estimate of the inflation term structure. A new real interest rate curve is calculated from this curve. The process is repeated until a single consistent inflation term structure is produced.

Inflation derivatives: introduction

One of the latest developments in derivatives markets are inflation-linked derivatives, or, simply, inflation derivatives. The first examples were introduced into the market in 2001. They arose out of the desire of investors for real, inflation-linked returns and hedging rather than nominal returns. Although index-linked bonds are available for those wishing to have such returns, as we've observed in other asset classes, inflation derivatives can be tailor-made to suit specific requirements. Volume growth has been rapid during 2003, as shown in Figure 9.4 for the European market.

---

[9] This is a term structure of *expected* inflation rates.

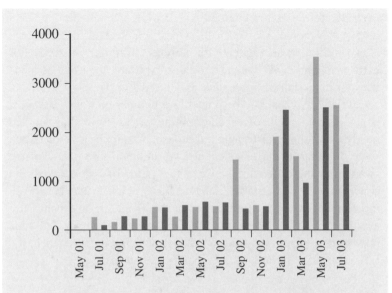

Figure 9.4 Inflation derivatives volumes, 2001-2003
Source: ICAP

The UK market, which features a well-developed index-linked cash market, has seen the largest volume of business in inflation derivatives. They have been used by market-makers to hedge inflation-indexed bonds, as well as by corporates who wish to match future liabilities. For instance, the retail company Boots plc added to its portfolio of inflation-linked bonds when it wished to better match its future liabilities in employees' salaries, which were assumed to rise with inflation. Hence, it entered into a series of inflation derivatives with Barclays Capital, in which it received a floating-rate, inflation-linked interest rate and paid nominal fixed-rate interest rate. The swaps ranged in maturity from 18 to 28 years, with a total notional amount of £300 million.

While this is an example of a pension fund that wishes to *receive* inflation-linked returns, corporates that receive revenues linked to inflation often wish to hedge this by *paying* inflation. For instance, utility companies often have pricing structures dictated by regulatory authorities, who may cap price increases that can be passed to customers. Such companies are natural issuers of index-linked bonds, and may therefore be interested in paying inflation in exchange for a fixed-rate return. Another UK-market corporate deal involved National Air Traffic Services, which paid inflation in a £200 million swap (again with Barclays Capital) in 2002. For market-making banks who take on this exposure, the usual hedge is with an index-linked bond such as UK gilts or Treasury TIPS.

Inflation swaps may be priced in a number of ways. The most common method involves determining prices from index-linked bonds using the bootstrapping approach. Assuming a zero-coupon swap, the market-maker calculates the inflation rate to use in the swap from the difference between the yields of index-linked and conventional bonds of the same maturity. This is the breakeven inflation rate we discussed earlier in the chapter. Some banks use asset-correlation models to price the swaps, such as the type presented in Jarrow and Yildirim (2003), which uses three stochastic factors to price inflation-linked bonds and swaps.

Inflation-indexed derivatives

Inflation-indexed derivatives, also known as inflation-linked derivatives *or inflation derivatives*, have become widely traded instruments in the capital markets in a relatively short space of time. They are traded generally by the same desks in investment banks that trade inflation-linked sovereign bonds, who use these instruments for hedging as well as to meet the requirements of clients such as hedge funds, pension funds and corporates. They are a natural development of the inflation-linked bond market.

Inflation derivatives are an additional means by which market participants can have an exposure to inflation-linked cash flows. They can also improve market liquidity in inflation-linked products, as an earlier generation of derivatives did for interest-rates and credit risk. As flexible OTS products, inflation derivatives offer advantages over cash products in certain circumstances. They provide:

- an ability to tailor cash flows to meet investors' requirements;
- a means by which inflation-linked exposures can be hedged;
- an instrument via which relative value positions can be put on across cash and synthetic markets;
- a building block for the structuring of more complex and hybrid products.

The inflation derivatives market in the UK was introduced after the introduction of the gilt repo market in 1996. In most gilt repo trades, index-linked (IL) gilts could be used as collateral; this mean that both IL and conventional gilts could be used as hedging tools against positions in inflation derivatives. In the euro area, IL derivatives were introduced later but experienced significant growth during 2002-2003. The existence of a sovereign IL bond market can be thought of as a necessary precursor to the development of IL derivatives, and although there is no reason why this should be the case, up to now this has been the case. The reason for this is probably because such a cash market suggests that investors are aware of the attraction of IL products, and wish to invest in them. From a market in IL bonds then develops a market in IL swaps, which are the most common IL derivatives. The IL bond market also provides a ready reference point form which IL derivatives can be priced.

Market instruments

We describe first some common inflation derivatives, before considering some uses for hedging and other purposes. We then consider IL derivatives pricing.

Inflation-linked bond swap

This is also known as a *synthetic index-linked bond*. It is a swap with the following two cashflow legs:

* pay (receive) the cashflows on a government IL bond;
* receive (pay) a fixed or floating cashflow.

This converts am existing conventional fixed- or floating-rate investments into inflation-linked investments. An example of such a swap is given below.

IL bond swap

Nominal	100,000,000
Start date	15 March 2004
Maturity term	15 March 2009

Bank receives   Six-month Euribor flat [+ spread], semi-annual, act/360
or
Fixed rate coupon $x\%$, annual 30/360

Bank pays   Real coupon of $y\%$
$y *$ [HICP $(p - 3)$ / (HICP $(s - 3))$] * daycount * notional
annual 30/360

On maturity:
Notional $* \max \{0\%, [\text{HICP } (m - 3) / \text{HICP } (s - 3) - 1]\}$

The symbols in the formulae above are
p payment date
s start date
m maturity date
HCIP   Harmonised Index of Consumer Prices

The "minus 3" in the formula for HCIP refers to a three-month lag for indexation, common in euro sovereign IL bond markets.
The swap is illustrated at Figure 9.5.

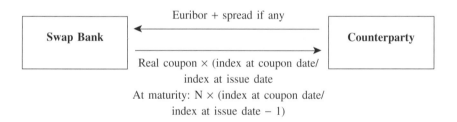

Figure 9.5 Synthetic index-linked bond

Year-on-year inflation swap

This swap is commonly used to hedge issues of IL bonds. The swap is comprised of:

- pay (receive) an index-linked coupon, which is a fixed rate component plus the annual rate of change in the underlying index
- receive (pay) Euribor or Libor, plus a spread if necessary.

With these swaps, IL leg is usually set at a floor of 0% for the annual change in the underlying index. This guarantees the investor a minimum return of the fixed rate coupon.

This swap is also known as a *pay-as-you-go swap*. It is shown at Figure 9.6.

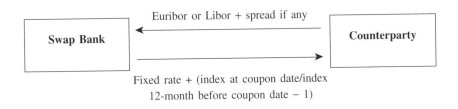

Euribor or Libor + spread if any

Fixed rate + (index at coupon date/index
12-month before coupon date − 1)

Figure 9.6 Year-on-year inflation swap

Tips swap

The Tips swap is based on the structure of US Tips securities. It pays a periodic fixed rate on an accreting notional amount, together with an additional one-off payment on maturity. This payout profile is identical to many government IL bonds. They are similar to synthetic IL bonds described above.

Tips swaps are commonly purchased by pension funds and other long-dated investors. They may prefer the added flexibility of the IL swap market compared to the cash IL bond market. Figure 9.7 shows the Tips swap.

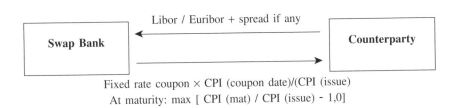

Libor / Euribor + spread if any

Fixed rate coupon × CPI (coupon date)/(CPI (issue)
At maturity: max [CPI (mat) / CPI (issue) − 1,0]

Figure 9.7 Illustration of a Tips swap

Breakeven swap

This is also known as a zero-coupon inflation swap or zero-coupon swap. It allows the investor to hedge away a breakeven exposure. Compared to IL swaps such as the synthetic bond swap, which hedge a real yield exposure, the breakeven swap has both cashflow legs paying out on maturity. The legs are:

- the total return on the inflation index
- a compounded fixed breakeven rate.

This structure enables IL derivative market makers to hedge their books. It is illustrated at Figure 9.8.

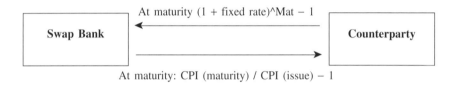

Figure 9.8 Breakeven inflation swap

Real annuity swap

A real-annuity swap is used to hedge inflation-linked cashflows where this applies for payments such as rental streams, lease payments, project finance cashflows and so on. It enables market participants who pay or receive such payments to replace the uncertainty of the future level of these cashflows with a fixed rate of growth. The swap is written on the same notional amount for both legs, but payout profiles differ as follows:

- the index-linked leg of the swap compounds its payments with the rate of change of the index
- the fixed leg of the swap compounds its payments at a pre-specified fixed rate.

These swaps are one of the most commonly traded. The fixed rate quoted for the swap provides a ready reference point against which to compare expected future rates of inflation. So for instance, if a bank is quoting for a swap with a fixed rate of 3.00%, and an investor believes that inflation rates will not rise above 3.00% for the life of the swap, then it will receive "fixed" (here meaning a fixed rate of growth) and pay inflation-linked on the swap.

The inflation term structure and pricing inflation derivatives

An inflation term structure is a necessary prerequisite to the pricing of inflation derivatives. It is constructed using the same principles we discussed in chapters 3 and 4. Previously, to construct this curve we would have used IL bond prices as the set of market yields used as inputs to the curve. Now however we can also use the prices of IL derivatives. As with other markets, the derivative prices are often preferred to cash prices for two reasons; one, we can use a continuous set of prices rather than have to rely on available bond maturities, and secondly, there is usually greater liquidity in the OTC market.

In the case of IL products, the indexation element is not in fact a true picture, but rather a picture based on a lag of three, six or seven months. This lag needs to be taken into account when constructing our curve.

The forward index value I at time T from time t ($t < T$) is given by

$$I(t,T) = \frac{I(t)P_r\,(t,T)}{P_r\,(t,T)} \qquad (9.12)$$

where

$I(t)$ is the index value at time t

$P_r(t,T)$ is the price at time t of a real zero-coupon bond of par value 1 maturing at T

$P_n(t,T)$ is the price at time t of a nominal zero-coupon bond of par value 1 maturing at T

Using Equation 9.12 we can build a forward inflation curve provided we have the values of the index at present, as well as a set of zero-coupon bond prices of required credit quality. Following standard yield curve analysis, we may build the term structure from forward rates and therefore imply the real yield curve, or alternatively we may construct the real curve and project the forward rates. However if we are using inflation swaps for the market price inputs, the former method is preferred because IL swaps are usually quoted in terms of a forward index value.

The curve can be constructed using standard bootstrapping techniques.

Inflation derivatives can be priced reasonably accurately once the inflation term structure is constructed. However some practitioners use stochastic models in pricing such products to account for the volatility surfaces. That is, they model the volatility of inflation as well. The recent literature describes such methods. For instance, Bezooyen *et al* (1997), Hughston (1998) and Jarrow and Yildirm (2003) suggest an approach based on that described by Amin and Jarrow (1991). This assumes that suitable proxies for the real and nominal term structures are those of foreign and the domestic economies. In other words, the foreign exchange rate captures the information required to model the two curves. We describe this approach here.

We assume that the index follows a lognormal distribution, and we use normal models for the real and nominal forward rates. For the index we then have

$$dI(t) = I(t)[\mu_1(t)dt + \sigma(t)dW(t)] \qquad (9.13)$$

and we have

$$dF_n(t,T) = a_n(t,T)dt + \sigma_n(t,T)dW(t) \qquad (9.14)$$

$$dF_r(t,T) = a_r(t,T)dt + \sigma_r(t,T)dW(t) \qquad (9.15)$$

for the nominal and real forward rate processes.

The dynamics of the zero-coupon bonds introduced earlier for Equation 9.13 are given by

$$d(\log P_k(t,T)) = \left[r_k(t) - \int_t^T \alpha_k(t,u)du \right]dt + \sum_k(t,T)dW(t)$$

$$k = n,r \qquad (9.16)$$

and where

$$\sum_k(t,T) = -\int \alpha_k(t,u)du$$

$$k = n,r$$

describes the zero-coupon bond volatilities. We use a one-factor model (see chapter 4) for each of the term structures and one for the index. Therefore $dW(t)$ is a combined three-dimensional vector of three correlated Brownian or Weiner or processes, with a correlation of ρ. The volatility of each bond and the index is therefore also a three-element vector.

From the above, the price at time t of an option on the index struck at X and expiring at time T is given by

$$V_\phi^{Index}(t,T) = \phi[I(t)P_r(t,T)N(\phi h_1) - XP_n(t,T)N(\phi h_2)] \qquad (9.17)$$

where

$\phi = 1$ for a call option and $\phi = -1$ for a put option, and where

$$h_1 = \left(\log\left(\frac{I(t)P_r(t,T)}{P_n(t,T)X}\right) + \frac{V(t,T)^2}{2}\right)/V(t,T)$$

$$h_2 = h_1 - V(t,T)$$

and where

$$V(t,T)^2 = \int_t^T \sum_I(u,t) \cdot \rho \cdot \sum_I(u,T)du$$

and where we define

$$\sum_I(t,T) = \sum_n(t,T) - \sum_r(t,T) - \sigma_I(u) \quad .$$

The result above has been derived, in different forms, in all three references noted above. As with other options pricing models, it needs to be calibrated to the market before it can be used. Generally this will involve using actual and project forward inflation rates to fit the model to market prices and volatilities.

Applications

We now describe some common applications of IL derivatives.

Hedging pension liabilities

This is perhaps the most obvious application. Assume a life assurance company or corporate pension fund wishes to hedge its long-dated pension liabilities, which are linked to the rate of inflation. It may invest in sovereign IL bonds such as IL gilts, or in IL corporate bonds that are hedged (for credit risk purposes) with credit derivatives. However the market in IL bonds is not always liquid, especially in IL corporate bonds. The alternative is to buy a synthetic IL bond. This is structured as a combination of a conventional government bond and an IL swap, in which the pension fund pays away the bond coupon and receives inflation-linked payments.

The net cashflow leaves the pension fund receiving a stream of cash flow that are linked to inflation. The fund is therefore hedged against its liabilities. In addition, because the swap structure can be tailor-made to the pension fund's requirements, the dates of cashflows can be set up exactly as needed. This is an added advantage over investing in the IL bonds directly.

Portfolio restructuring using inflation swaps

Assume that a bank or corporate has an income stream that is linked to inflation. Up to now, it has been funded by a mix of fixed- and floating-rate debt. Say that these are floating-rate bank loans and fixed-rate bonds. However from an asset-liability management (ALM) point of view this is not optimal, because of the nature of a proportion of its income. It makes sense, therefore, to switch a part of its funding into an inflation-linked segment. This can be done using either of the following approaches:

- issue an IL bond;
- enter into an IL swap, with a notional value based on the optimum share of its total funding that should be inflation-linked, in which it pays inflation-linked cash flows and receives fixed-rate income.

The choice will depend on which approach provides cheapest funding and most flexibility.

Hedging a bond issue

Assume that a bank or corporate intends to issue an IL bond, and wishes to hedge against a possible fall in government IL bond prices, against which its issue will be priced. It can achieve this hedge using a IL gilt-linked derivative contract.

The bank or corporate enters into cash-settled contract for difference (CFD), which pays out in the event of a rise in government IL bond yields. The CFD has a term to maturity that ties in with the issue date of the IL bond. The CFD market maker has effectively shorted the government bond, from the CFD trade date until maturity. On the issue date, the market maker will provide a cash settlement if yields have risen. If yields have fallen, the IL bond issuer will pay the difference. However, this cost is netted out by the expected "profit" from the cheaper funding when the bond is issued. Meanwhile, if yields have risen and the bank or corporate issuer does have to fund at a higher rate, it will be compensated by the funds received by the CFD market maker.

Appendices

APPENDIX 9.1 Current issuers of public-sector indexed securities

Country	Date first issued	Index linking
Australia	1983	Consumer prices
	1991	Average weekly earnings
Austria	1953	Electricity prices
Brazil	1964 - 1990	Wholesale prices
	1991	General prices
Canada	191	Consumer prices
Chile	1966	Consumer prices
Colombia	1967	Wholesale prices
	1995	Consumer prices
Czech Republic	1997	Consumer prices
Denmark	1982	Consumer prices
France	1956	Average value of French securities
Greece	1997	Consumer prices
Hungary	1995	Consumer prices
Iceland	1964-1980	Cost of Building Index
	1980-1994	Credit Terms Index
	1995	Consumer prices
Ireland	1983	Consumer prices
Italy	1983	Deflator of GDP at factor cost
Mexico	1989	Consumer prices
New Zealand	1977-1984	Consumer priceS
	1995	Consumer prices
Norway	1982	Consumer prices
Poland	1992	Consumer prices
Sweden	1952	Consumer prices
	1994	Consumer prices
Turkey	1994-1997	Wholesale prices
	1997	Consumer prices
United Kingdom	1981	Consumer prices
United States	1997	Consumer prices

Table A9.1 Current issuers of public-sector inflation-indexed securities
Source: Deacon and Derry (1998).
Used with permission of Prentice Hall Europe.

APPENDIX 9.2 US Treasury Inflation-Indexed Securities (TIPS)

■ **Indexation calculation**

United States Treasury inflation-indexed securities link their coupon and principal to an Index Ratio of the Consumer Prices Index. The index ratio is given by

$$IR = \frac{CPI_{Settlement}}{CPI_{Issue}}$$

where "settlement" is the settlement date and "issue" is the issue date of the bond. The actual CPI used is that recorded for the calendar month three months earlier than the relevant date, this being the lag time. For the first day of any month, the reference CPI level is that recorded three months earlier; so, for example, on 1st May the relevant CPI measure would be that recorded on 1st February. For any other day in the month, linear interpolation is used to calculate the appropriate CPI level recorded in the reference month and the following month.

■ **Cash-flow calculation**

The inflation adjustment for the security cash flows is given as the principal multiplied by the index ratio for the relevant date, minus the principal (P). This is termed the Inflation Compensation (IC), given as

Inflation Compensation$_{Set\ Date}$ = (Principal × Index Ratio$_{SetDate}$) − Principal.

Coupon payments are given by

$$Interest_{DivDate} = C/2 \times (P + IC_{DivDate}) \ .$$

The redemption value of a TIPS is guaranteed by the Treasury to be a minimum of $100, whatever value has been recorded by the CPI during the life of the bond.

■ **Settlement price**

The price/yield formula for a TIPS security is given by the following expressions:

Price = Inflation − Adjusted price + Inflation − Adjuted accrued interest

Inflation − Adjusted price = Real price × Index ratio$_{SetDate}$.

The real price is given by

$$\text{Real Price} = \left[\frac{1}{1 + \frac{f}{d}\frac{r}{2}}\right]\left(\frac{C}{2} + \frac{C}{2}\sum_{j=1}^{n}\phi_j + 100\phi^n\right) - RAI \qquad (A9.2.1)$$

where

$$\text{Inflation} - \text{Adjusted accrued interest} = RAI \times IR_{SetDate}$$

and where

$$\phi = \left[\frac{1}{1 + \frac{r}{2}}\right]$$

r	is the annual real yield
RAI	is the unadjusted accrued interest, which is {symbol}
f	is the number of days from the settlement date to the next coupon date
d	is the number of days in the regular semi-annual coupon period ending on the next coupon date
n	is the number of full semi-annual coupon periods between the next coupon date and the maturity date

Selected Bibliography and References

Amin, K., and Jarrow, R., "Pricing foreign currency options under stochastic interest rates", *Journal of International Money and Finance* 10, 1991, pp.310-329

Anderson, N., Breedon, F., Deacon, M., Derry, A. and Murphy, J., *Estimating and Interpreting the Yield Curve*, Wiley, 1996.

Arak, M. and Kreicher, L., "The real rate of interest: inferences from the new UK indexed gilts", *International Economic Review* (26) 2, 1985, p.399-408.

Bootle, R., *Index-Linked Gilts: A Practical Investment Guide* (2nd edition), Woodhead-Faulkner, 1991.

Brown, R. and Schaefer, S., "The term structure of real interest rates and the Cox, Ingersoll and Ross model", *Journal of Financial Economics*, 35:1, 1994, p.3-42.

Brynjolfsson, J., Fabozzi, F., *Handbook of Inflation Indexed Bonds*, FJF Associates 1999

Deacon, M. and Derry, A., "Deriving estimates of inflation expectations from the prices of UK Government bonds", Bank of England working paper no.23, July 1994.

Deacon, M. and Derry, A., *Inflation Indexed Securities*, Prentice Hall, 1998.

Deacon, M., Derry, A. and Mirfendereski, J., *Inflation-linked Securities: bonds, swaps and other derivatives*, John Wiley and Sons 2004.

Foresi, S., Penati, A. and Pennacchi, G., "Reducing the cost of government debt: the role of index-linked bonds", in de Cecco, M., Pecchi, L. and Piga, G., (editors), *Public Debt: Index-Linked Bonds in Theory and Practice*, Edward Elgar, 1997.

Hughston, L., *Inflation Derivatives*, Merrill Lynch International 1998

James, J. and Webber, N., *Interest Rate Modelling*, Wiley, 2000.

Jarrow, R. and Yildirim, Y., "Pricing Treasury Inflation Protected Securities and Derivatives using an HJM Model", *Journal of Financial and Quantitative Analysis* 38, June 2003.

Van Bezooyen, J., Exley, C., Smith, A., A *market-based approach to valuing LPI liabilities*, Group for Economic and Market Value based Studies 1997

Waggoner, D., "Spline methods for extracting interest rate curves from coupon bond prices", Federal Reserve Bank of Atlanta working paper, 97-10, 1997.

Wojnilower, A., *Inflation-Indexed Bonds: Promising the Moon*, Clipper Group, 1997.

10

Securitisation and Mortgage-backed Securities

The asset-based markets represent a large and diverse group of securities which are suited to a varied group of investors. Often, they are the only way for institutional investors to pick up yield while retaining assets with high credit ratings. They are popular with issuers because they represent a cost-effective means of removing assets off the balance sheet, thus freeing up lending lines, and enabling them to have access to lower-cost funding. Depending on the nature of the underlying asset-backing, there are instruments available that cover the entire term of the yield curve. They are also available paying fixed- or floating-rate coupon. Although the market was developed in the United States, there are liquid markets in the United Kingdom, Europe, Asia and Latin America. The flexibility of the securitisation is its key advantage for both issuers and investors. For instance, in the UK it is common for mortgage-backed bonds to have a floating coupon, reflecting the interest basis of UK mortgages, although there have been structures paying fixed-rate coupon to suit investors' requirements. To arrange this, the transaction will include a swap arrangement.

We would suggest that perhaps the best illustration of the flexibility, innovation, and simple user-friendliness of the debt-capital markets is the rise in the use and importance of securitisation. For a definition of this technique let us turn to Sundaresan, who says that the approach

"...simply stated...is a framework in which some illiquid assets of a corporation or a financial institution are transformed into a package of securities backed by these assets, through careful packaging, credit enhancements, liquidity enhancements and structuring." (Sundaresan 1997, p.359)

The process of securitisation creates asset-backed bonds. These are debt instruments that have been created from a package of loan assets on which interest is payable, usually on a floating basis. The asset-backed market was developed in the United States and is a large, diverse market containing a wide range of instruments. The characteristics of asset-backed securities (ABS) present additional features in their analysis, which are introduced in this chapter. Financial engineering techniques employed by investment banks today enable an entity to create a bond structure from any type of cash flow. The typical forms are high-volume loans such as residential mortgages, car loans, and credit-card loans. The loans form assets on a bank or finance house balance sheet, which are packaged together and used as backing for an issue of bonds. The interest payments on the original loans form the cash flows used to service the new bond issue. The development of the market in securitised bonds is such that these days an investment bank will not think it unusual to underwrite a bond issued secured against any type of cash flow; from the more traditional mortgages and loan assets to cash flows received by leisure and recreational facilities such as heath clubs, public houses and other entities such as nursing homes. The asset class behind a securitised bond issue is significant, and there are distinct classes, each calling for their own methods of analysis and valuation. Traditionally, mortgage-backed bonds are grouped in their own right as mortgage-backed securities (MBS) while all other securitisations are known as asset-backed bonds or ABS.

In this chapter, we present an introduction to the basic technique of securitisation. The market is large and diverse, and stretches across a large number of markets and currencies. Readers who need to specialise should consult the bibliography. Two good overview titles are the Fabozzi-edited books on structured products and mortgage-backed securities.

Introduction

Reasons for undertaking securitisation

The driving force behind the growth the securitisation was the need for banks to realise value from the assets on their balance sheet. Typically, these assets were residential and commercial mortgages, corporate loans, and retail loans such as credit-card debt. What factors might lead a financial institution to securitise a part of its balance sheet?

A bank may wish to reduce the size of its balance sheet for the following reasons:

- if revenues received from assets remain roughly unchanged but the size of assets has decreased; this will lead to an increase in the return on equity ratio.
- the level of capital required to support the balance sheet will be reduced, which again can lead to cost savings or allows the institution to allocate the capital to other, perhaps more profitable, business.
- to obtain cheaper funding. Frequently the interest payable on ABS securities is considerably below the level payable on the underlying loans. This creates a cash surplus for the originating entity.

By entering into securitisation a lower-rated entity can access debt-capital markets that would otherwise be the preserve of higher-rated institutions. The growth of the so-called credit-card banks in the US, such as MBNA, would have been severely restricted if a market for the securitised debt of these firms had not been in place.

Market participants

The securitisation process involves a number of participants. In the first instance, there is the originator, the firm whose assets are being securitised. The most common process involves an issuer acquiring the assets from the originator. The issuer is usually a company that has been specially set up for the purpose of the securitisation and is known as a special-purpose vehicle, or SPV, and is usually domiciled offshore. The creation of an SPV ensures that the underlying asset pool is held separate from the other assets of the originator. This is done so that in the event that the originator is declared bankrupt or insolvent, the impact on the original assets is minimized.

This last is often the responsibility of a trustee. The issue trustee is responsible for looking after the interests of bondholders. Its roles include:

- representing the interests of investors (note holders).
- monitoring the transaction and issuer to see if any violation of the deal covenants has occurred.
- enforcing the rights of the note holders in the event of bankruptcy.

The security trustee is responsible for undertaking the following duties:
- holding the security interest in the underlying collateral pool
- liaising with the manager of the underlying collateral
- acting under the direction of the note trustee in the event of default.

By holding the assets within an SPV framework, defined in formal legal terms, the financial status and credit rating of the originator becomes almost irrelevant to the bondholders. The process may also involve credit enhancements, in which a third-party guarantee of credit quality is obtained, so that notes issued under the securitisation are often rated at investment grade and up to triple-A grade.

Figure 10.1 illustrates in simple fashion the process of securitisation.

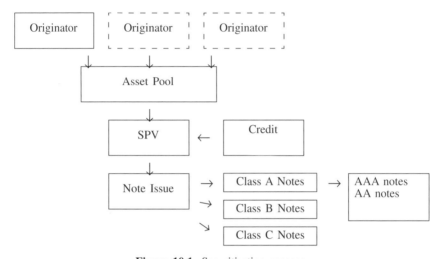

Figure 10.1 Securitisation process

Securitising mortgages

Introduction

A mortgage is a loan made for the purpose of purchasing property which, in turn, is used as the security for the loan itself. It is defined as a debt instrument giving conditional ownership of an asset, and secured by the asset that is being financed. The borrower provides the lender a mortgage in exchange for the right to use the property during the term of the mortgage, and agrees to make regular payments of both principal and interest. The mortgage lien is the security for the lender, and is removed when the debt is paid off. A mortgage may involve residential property or commercial property and is a long-term debt, normally 25 to 30 years. However, it can be drawn up for shorter periods if required by the borrower. If the borrower or mortgagor defaults on the interest payments, the lender or mortgagee has the right to take over the property and recover the debt from the proceeds of selling the property. Mortgages can be either fixed-rate or floating-rate interest. Although in the US mortgages are generally amortising loans, known as repayment mortgages in the UK, there are also interest-only mortgages where the borrower only pays the interest on the loan. On maturity, the original loan amount is paid off by the proceeds of a maturing investment contract taken out at the same time as the mortgage. These are known as endowment mortgages and are popular in the UK market, although their popularity has been waning in recent years.

A lending institution may have many hundreds of thousands of individual residential and commercial mortgages on its book. If the total loan book is pooled together and used as collateral for the issue of a bond, the resulting instrument is a mortgage-backed security. This process is known as securitisation, which is the pooling of loan assets in order to use them as collateral for a bond issue. Sometimes an SPV is set up specifically to serve as the entity representing the pooled assets. This is done for administrative reasons and also sometimes to enhance the credit rating that may be assigned to the bonds. In the UK, some SPVs have a triple-A credit rating (although the majority are below this), while retaining investment-grade status. In the US market, certain mortgage-backed securities are backed, either implicitly or explicitly, by the government, in which case they trade essentially as risk-free instruments and are not rated by the credit agencies. In the US, a government agency, the Government National Mortgage Association (GNMA, known as "Ginnie Mae") and two government-sponsored agencies, the Federal Home Loan Corporation and the Federal National Mortgage Association ("Freddie Mac" and "Fannie Mae", respectively), purchase mortgages for the purpose of pooling them and holding them in their portfolios. They may then be securitised. Bonds that are not issued by government agencies are rated in the same way as other corporate bonds. On the other hand, non-government agencies sometimes obtain mortgage insurance for their issue, in order to boost its credit quality. When this happens, the credit rating of the mortgage insurer becomes an important factor in the credit standing of the bond issue.

Growth of the market

One study[1] has suggested the following advantages of mortgage-backed bonds:

---

[1] Hayre, L., Mohebbi, C. and Zimmermann, T., "Mortgage Pass-Through Securities", in Fabozzi, F. (editor) *The Handbook of Fixed Income Securities* (5th edition), McGraw-Hill, 1998.

- although many mortgage bonds represent comparatively high-quality assets and are collateralised instruments, the yields on them are usually higher then corporate bonds of the same credit quality. This is because of the complexity of the instruments and the uncertain nature of the mortgage cash flows. In the mid 1990s, mortgage-backed bonds traded at yields of around 100–200 basis points above Treasury bonds.

- the wide range of products offers investors a choice of maturities, cash flows and security to suit individual requirements.

- agency mortgage-backed bonds are implicitly backed by the government and therefore represent a better credit risk than triple-A rated corporate bonds; the credit ratings for non-agency bonds is often triple-A or double-A rated.

- the size of the market means that it is very liquid, with agency mortgage-backed bonds having the same liquidity as Treasury bonds.

- the monthly coupon frequency of mortgage-backed bonds make them an attractive instrument for investors who require frequent income payments; this feature is not available for most other bond-market instruments.

In the UK, the asset-backed market has also witnessed rapid growth, and many issues are triple-A rated because issuers create a special-purpose vehicle that is responsible for the issue. Various forms of insurance are also used. Unlike the US market, most bonds are floating-rate instruments, reflecting the variable-rate nature of the majority of mortgages in the UK.

Mortgages

In the US market, the terms of a conventional mortgage, known as a level-payment fixed-rate mortgage, will state the interest rate payable on the loan, the term of the loan and the frequency of payment. Most mortgages specify monthly payment of interest. These are, in fact, the characteristics of a level-payment mortgage, which has a fixed interest rate and fixed term to maturity. This means that the monthly interest payments are fixed; hence the term "level-pay".

The singular feature of a mortgage is that, even if it charges interest at a fixed rate, its cash flows are not known with absolute certainty. This is because the borrower can elect to repay any or all of the principal before the final maturity date. This is a characteristic of all mortgages, and although some lending institutions impose a penalty on borrowers who retire the loan early, this is a risk for the lender, known as repayment risk. The uncertainty of the cash-flow patterns is similar to that of a callable bond and, as we shall see later, this feature means that we may value mortgage-backed bonds using a pricing model similar to that employed for callable bonds.

The monthly interest payment on a conventional fixed-rate mortgage is given by (10.3), which is derived from the conventional present-value analysis used for a annuity. Essentially, the primary relationship is:

$$M_{m0} = I\left[\frac{1 - \left[\frac{1}{(1 + r)^n}\right]}{r}\right] \tag{10.1}$$

from which we can derive:

$$I = \frac{M_{m0}}{\left[\frac{1 - \left[\frac{1}{(1 + r)^n}\right]}{r}\right]} \tag{10.2}$$

This is simplified to:

$$I = M_{m0}\left[\frac{r(1 + r)^n}{[(1 + r)^n - 1]}\right] \tag{10.3}$$

where

M_{m0} is the original mortgage balance (the cash amount of loan)
I is the monthly cash mortgage payment
r is the simple monthly interest rate, given by (annual interest rate/12)
n is the term of the mortgage in months.

EXAMPLE 10.1 Mortgage contract calculations

A mortgage borrower enters into a conventional mortgage contract, in which he borrows £72,200 for 22 years at a rate of 7.99%. What is the monthly mortgage payment?

This gives us n equal to 264 and r equal to (0.0799 / 12) or 0.0066583. Inserting the above terms into 10.3 we have:

$$I = 72,200\left[\frac{0.0066583(1.0066583)^{264}}{[(1.0066583)^{264} - 1]}\right]$$

or I equal to £581.60

The mortgage balance after ten years is given below, where t is 120:

$$M_{m120} = 72,200 \left[\frac{(1.0066583) - (1.0066583)^{120}}{[(1.0066583)^{264} - 1]} \right]$$

or a remaining balance of £53,756.93.

In the same month the scheduled principal repayment amount is:

$$P_{120} = 72,200 \left[\frac{0.0066583(1.0066583)^{120-1}}{[(1.0066583)^{264} - 1]} \right]$$

or £222.19.

The interest only payable in month 120 is shown below:

$$i_{120} = 72,200 \left[\frac{0.0066583[(1.0066583)^{264} - (1.0066583)^{120-1}]}{[(1.0066583)^{264} - 1]} \right]$$

and is equal to £359.41. The combined mortgage payment is £581.60, as calculated before.

The monthly repayment includes both the interest servicing and a repayment of part of the principal. In example 10.1, after the 264th interest payment, the balance will be zero and the mortgage will have been paid off. Since a portion of the original balance is paid off every month, the interest payment reduces by a small mount each month; that is, the proportion of the monthly payment dedicated to repaying the principal steadily increases. The remaining mortgage balance for any particular month during the term of the mortgage may be calculated using (10.4).

$$M_{mt} = M_{m0} \left[\frac{[(1 + r)^n - (1 + r)^n]}{[(1 + r)^n - 1]} \right] \tag{10.4}$$

where M_{mt} is the mortgage cash balance after t months and n remains the original maturity of the mortgage in months.

The level of interest payment and principal re-payment in any one month during the mortgage term can be calculated using the equations below. If we wish to calculate the value of the principal re-payment in a particular month during the mortgage term, we may use (10.5).

$$P_t = M_{m0} \left[\frac{[r(1 + r)^{t-1}]}{[(1 + r)^n - 1]} \right] \tag{10.5}$$

where p_t is the scheduled principal repayment amount for month t, while the level of interest payment in any month is given by (10.6).

$$i_t = M_{m0}\left[\frac{[r(1 + r)^n - (1 + r)^{t-1}]}{[(1 + r)^n - 1]}\right]$$ (10.6)

where i_t is the interest payment only in month t.

Some mortgage contracts incorporate a servicing fee. This is payable to the mortgage provider to cover the administrative costs associated with collecting interest payments, sending regular statements and other information to borrowers, chasing overdue payments, maintaining the records and processing systems, and other activities. Mortgage providers also incur costs when re-possessing properties after mortgagors have fallen into default. Mortgages may be serviced by the original lender or another third-party institution that has acquired the right to service it, in return for collecting the fee. When a servicing charge is payable by a borrower, the monthly mortgage payment comprises the interest costs, the principal repayment and the servicing fee. The fee incorporated into the monthly payment is usually stated as a percentage, say 0.25%. This is added to the mortgage rate.

Another type of mortgage in the US market is the adjustable-rate mortgage (ARM). These loans allow interest payments to be reset at periodic intervals to a short-term interest-rate index that has been specified beforehand. The re-sets are at periodic intervals depending on the terms of the loan, and can be on a monthly, six-monthly or annual basis, or even longer. The interest rate is usually fixed at a spread over the reference rate. The reference rate that is used can be a market-determined rate such as the prime rate, or a calculated rate based on the funding costs for US savings and loan institutions or thrifts. The cost of funds for thrifts is calculated using the monthly average funding cost on the thrifts' activities, and there are "thrift indexes" that are used to indicate to the cost of funding. The two most common indices are the Eleventh Federal Home Loan Bank Board District Cost of Funds Index (COFI) and the National Cost of Funds Index. Generally, borrowers prefer to fix the rate they pay on their loans to reduce uncertainty, and this makes fixed-rate mortgages more popular than variable-rate mortgages. A common incentive used to entice borrowers away from fixed-rate mortgages is to offer a below-market interest rate on an ARM mortgage, usually for an introductory period. This comfort period may be from two to five years or even longer. ARM mortgages are usually issued with additional features such as an interest-rate cap specified beforehand;

such a cap limits the maximum rate that the borrower would have to pay in the event that market rates increase dramatically. ARMs make up more than half the market share in the US domestic mortgage business.[2]

Mortgages in the UK are predominantly variable-rate mortgages, in which the interest rate moves in line with the clearing-bank base rate. It is rare to observe fixed-rate mortgages in the UK market, although short-term fixed-rate mortgages are more common (the rate reverts to a variable basis at the termination of the fixed-rate period).

A balloon mortgage entitles a borrower to long-term funding, but under its terms, at a specified future date the interest rate payable is re-negotiated. This effectively transforms a long-dated loan into a short-term borrowing. The balloon payment is the original amount of the loan, minus the amount that is amortised. In a balloon mortgage, therefore, the actual maturity of the bonds is below that of the stated maturity.

A graduated-payment mortgage (GPM) is aimed at lower-earning borrowers, as the mortgage payments for a fixed initial period, say the first five years, are set at lower than the level applicable for a level-paying mortgage with an identical interest rate. The later mortgage payments are higher as a result. Hence, a GPM mortgage will have a fixed term and a mortgage rate, but the offer letter will also contain details on the number of years over which the monthly mortgage payments will increase and the point at which level payments will take over. There will also be information on the annual increase in the mortgage payments. As the initial payments in a GPM are below the market rate, there will be little or no repayment of principal at this time. This means that the outstanding balance may actually increase during the early stages, a process known as negative amortisation. The higher payments in the remainder of the mortgage term are designed to pay off the entire balance in maturity. The opposite to the GPM is the growing-equity mortgage (GEM). This mortgage charges fixed-rate interest but the payments increase over time. This means that a greater proportion of the principal is paid off over time, so that the mortgage itself is repaid in a shorter time than the level-pay mortgage.

In the UK market, it is more common to encounter hybrid mortgages, which charge a combination of fixed-rate and variable-rating interest. For example, the rate may be fixed for the first five years, after which it will vary with changes in the lender's base rate. Such a mortgage is known as a fixed/adjustable hybrid mortgage.

---

[2] Sundaresan (2000), p.366.

Mortgage risk

Although mortgage contracts are typically long-term loan contracts, running usually for 20 to 30 years or even longer, there is no limitation on the amount of the principal that may be repaid at any one time. In the US market, there is no penalty for repaying the mortgage ahead of its term, which is known as a mortgage prepayment. In the UK, some lenders impose a penalty if a mortgage is prepaid, although this is more common for contracts that have been offered at special terms, such as a discounted loan rate for the start of the mortgage's life. The penalty is often set as extra interest; for example, six months' worth of mortgage payments at the time when the contract is paid off. As a borrower is free to prepay a mortgage at a time of her choosing, the lender is not certain of the cash flows that will be paid after the contract is taken out. This is known as *prepayment risk*.

A borrower may pay off the principal ahead of the final termination date for a number of reasons. The most common reason is when the property on which the mortgage is secured is subsequently sold by the borrower, which results in the entire mortgage being paid off at once. The average life of a mortgage in the UK market is eight years, and mortgages are most frequently prepaid because the property has been sold.[3] Other actions that result in the prepayment of a mortgage are when a property is repossessed after the borrower has fallen into default, if there is a change in interest rates making it attractive to refinance the mortgage (usually with another lender), or if the property is destroyed as a result of accident or natural disaster.

An investor acquiring a pool of mortgages from a lender will be concerned at the level of prepayment risk, which is usually measured by projecting the level of expected future payments using a financial model. Although it would not be possible to evaluate meaningfully the potential of an individual mortgage to be paid off early, it is tenable to conduct such analysis for a large number of loans pooled together. A similar activity is performed by actuaries when they assess the future liability of an insurance provider who has written personal pension contracts. Essentially, the level of prepayment risk for a pool of loans is lower than that of an individual mortgage. Prepayment risk has the same type of impact on a mortgage pool's performance and valuation as a call feature does on a callable bond. This is understandable because a mortgage is essentially a callable contract, with the "call" at the option of the borrower of funds.

The other significant risk of a mortgage book is the risk that the

---

[3] Source: HBOS plc

borrower will fall into arrears, or be unable to repay the loan on maturity (in the UK). This is known as default risk. Lenders take steps to minimize the level of default risk by assessing the credit quality of each borrower, as well as the quality of the property itself. A study has also found that the higher the deposit paid by the borrower, the lower the level of default.[4] Therefore, lenders prefer to advance funds against a borrower's equity that is deemed sufficient to protect against falls in the value of the property. In the UK, the typical deposit required is 25%, although certain lenders will advance funds against smaller deposits such as 10% or 5%.

EXAMPLE 10.2 Mortgage pass-through security

An investor purchases a book consisting of 1000 individual mortgages, with a total repayable value of $100,000,000. The loans are used as collateral against the issue of a new bond, and the cash flows payable on the bond are the cash flows that are received from the mortgages. The issuer sells 500 bonds, with a face value of $200,000. Each bond is therefore entitled to 1/500 or 0.2% of the cash flows received from the mortgages.

The prepayment risk associated with the original mortgages is unchanged, but any investor can now purchase a bond with a much lower value than the mortgage pool but with the same level of prepayment risk, which is lower than the risk of an individual loan. This would have been possible if an investor buying all 100 mortgages, but by buying a bond that represents the pool of mortgages, a smaller cash value is needed to achieve the same performance. The bonds will also be more liquid than the loans, and the investor will be able to realise her investment ahead of the maturity date is she wishes. For these reasons the bonds will trade at higher prices than would an individual loan. A mortgage pass-through security therefore is a way for mortgage lenders to realise additional value from their loan book, and if it is sold to another investor (who issues the bonds), the loans will be taken off the original lender's balance sheet, thus freeing up lending lines for other activities.

---

[4] Brown, S., et al., *Analysis of Mortgage Servicing Portfolios*, Financial Strategies Group, Prudential-Bache Capital Funding, 1990.

Mortgage-backed securities

Mortgage-backed securities are bonds created from a pool of mortgages. They are formed from mortgages that are for residential or commercial property or a mixture of both. Bonds created from commercial mortgages are known as commercial mortgage-backed securities. There are a range of different securities in the market, known in the US as mortgage pass-though securities. There also exist two related securities known as collateralised mortgage securities and stripped mortgage-backed securities. Bonds that are created from mortgage pools that have been purchased by government agencies are known as agency mortgage-backed securities, and are regarded as risk-free in the same way as Treasury securities.

A collateralised mortgage obligation (CMO) differs from a pass-through security in that the cash flows from the mortgage pool are distributed on a prioritized basis, based on the class of security held by the investor. In example 10.2 this might mean that three different securities are formed, with a total nominal value of $100 million, each entitled to a pro-rate amount of the interest payments but with different priorities for the repayment of principal. For instance, $60 million of the issue might consist of a bond known as "class A" and may be entitled to receipt of all the principal repayment cash flows, after which the next class of bonds is entitled to all the repayment cash flow. This bond would be "class B" bonds, of which, say, $25 million was created, and so on. If 300 class A bonds are created, they would have a nominal value of $200,000 and each would receive 0.33% of the total cash flows received by the class A bonds. Note that all classes of bonds receive an equal share of the interest payments; it is the principal repayment cash flows received that differ. What is the main effect of this security structure? The most significant factor is that, in our illustration, the class A bonds will be repaid earlier than any other class of bond that is formed from the securitisation. It therefore has the shortest maturity. The last class of bonds will have the longest maturity. There is still a level of uncertainty associated with the maturity of each bond, but this is less than the uncertainty associated with a pass-through security.

Let us consider another type of mortgage bond, the stripped mortgage-backed security. As its name suggests, this is created by separating the interest and principal payments into individual distinct cash flows. This allows an issuer to create two very interesting securities, the IO-bond and the PO-bond. In a stripped mortgage-backed bond the interest and principal are divided into two classes, and two bonds are issued that are each entitled to receive one class of cash flow only. The bond class that receives the interest payment cash flows is known as an interest-only or IO class, while the bond receiving the principal repayments is known as a principal-only or PO class. The PO bond is similar to a zero-coupon bond in that it is issued at a discount to par value. The return achieved by a PO-bond holder is a function of the rapidity at which prepayments are made; if prepayments are received in a relatively short time, the investor will realise a higher return. This would be akin to the buyer of a zero-coupon bond receiving the maturity payment ahead of the redemption date, and the highest possible return that a PO-bond holder could receive would occur if all the mortgages were prepaid the instant after the PO bond was bought! A low return will be achieved if all the mortgages are held until maturity, so that there are no prepayments. Stripped mortgage-backed bonds present potentially less advantage to an issuer than a pass-through security or a CMO. However, they are liquid instruments and are often traded to hedge a conventional mortgage bond book.

The price of a PO-bond fluctuates as mortgage interest rates change. As we noted earlier, in the US market the majority of mortgages are fixed-rate loans, so that if mortgage rates fall below the coupon rate on the bond, the holder will expect the volume of prepayments to increase as individuals refinance loans in order to gain from lower borrowing rates. This will result in a faster stream of payments to the PO-bond holder as cash flows are received earlier than expected. The price of the PO rises to reflect this, and also because cash flows in the mortgage will now be discounted at a lower rate. The opposite happens when mortgage rates rise and the rate of prepayment is expected to fall, which causes a PO bond to fall in price. An IO bond is essentially a stream of cash flows and has no par value. The cash flows represent interest on the mortgage principal outstanding; therefore, a higher rate of prepayment leads to a fall in the IO price. This is because the cash flows cease once the principal is redeemed. The risk for the IO-bond holder is that prepayments occur so quickly that interest payments cease before the investor has recovered the amount originally paid for the IO-bond. The price of an IO is also a function of mortgage rates in the market, but exhibits more peculiar responses. If rates fall below the bond coupon, again the rate of prepayment is expected to increase. This would cause the cash flows for the IO to decline, as mortgages were paid off more quickly. This would cause the price of the IO to fall as well, even though the cash flows themselves would be discounted at a lower interest rate. If mortgage rates rise, the outlook for future cash flows will improve as the prepayment rate falls. However, there is also a higher discounting rate for the cash flows themselves, so the price of an IO may move in either direction. Thus IO bonds exhibit a curious characteristic for a bond instrument in that their price moves in the same direction as market rates. Both versions of the stripped mortgage bond are interesting instruments, and they have high volatilities during times of market rate changes. Note that PO and IO bonds could be created from the hypothetical mortgage pool described above. Therefore, the combined modified duration of both instruments must equal the modified duration of the original pass-through security.

The securities described so far are essentially plain-vanilla mortgage-backed bonds. There are more complicated instruments currently trading in the market.

Cash-flow patterns

We stated that the exact term of a mortgage-backed bond cannot be stated with accuracy at the time of issue, because of the uncertain frequency of mortgage prepayments. This uncertainty means that it is not possible to analyse the bonds using the conventional methods used for fixed-coupon bonds. The most common approach used by the market is to assume a fixed prepayment rate at the time of issue and use this to project the cash flows and, hence, the life span of the bond. The choice of prepayment selected therefore is significant, although it is recognized also that prepayment rates are not stable and will fluctuate with changes in mortgage rates and the economic cycle. In this section we consider some of the approaches used in evaluating the prepayment pattern of a mortgage-backed bond.

Prepayment analysis

Some market analysts assume a fixed life for a mortgage pass-through bond based on the average life of a mortgage. Traditionally a "12-year prepaid life" has been used to evaluate the securities, as market data suggested that the average mortgage has paid off after the twelfth year. This is not generally favored because it does not take into account the effect of mortgage rates and other factors. A more common approach is to use a constant prepayment rate (CPR) This measure is based on the expected number of mortgages in a pool that will be prepaid in a selected period, and is an annualised figure. The measure for the monthly level of prepayment is known as the constant monthly repayment, and measures the expected amount of the outstanding balance, minus the scheduled principal, that will be prepaid in each month. Another name for the constant monthly repayment is the single monthly mortality rate or SMM. The SMM is given by (10.7) and is an expected value for the percentage of the remaining mortgage balance that will be prepaid in that month.

$$SMM = 1 - (1 - CPR)^{1/12} \qquad (10.7)$$

Constant prepayment rate

The constant prepayment rate for a pool of mortgages is 2% each month. The outstanding principal balance at the start of the month is £72,200, while the scheduled principal payment is £223. This means that 2% of £71,977, or £1,439 will be prepaid in that month. To approximate the amount of principal prepayment, the constant monthly prepayment is multiplied by the outstanding balance.

In the US market, the convention is to use the prepayment standard developed by the Public Securities Association,[5] which is the domestic bond-market trade association. The PSA benchmark, known as 100%PSA, assumes a steadily increasing constant prepayment rate each month until the 30th month, when a constant rate of 6% is assumed. The starting prepayment rate is 0.2%, increasing at 0.2% each month until the rate levels off at 6%.

For the 100%PSA benchmark we may set, if t is the number of months from the start of the mortgage, that

if $t < 30$, the CPR = $6\% . t / 30$

while if t > 30,

then CPR is equal to 6%.

This benchmark can be altered if required to suit changing market conditions. So, for example, the 200%PSA has a starting prepayment rate and an increase that is double the 100%PSA model; so the initial rate is 0.4%, increasing by 0.4% each month until it reaches 12% in the 30th month, at which point the rate remains constant. The 50%PSA has a starting (and increases by a) rate of 0.1%, remaining constant after it reaches 3%.

The prepayment level of a mortgage pool will have an impact on its cash flows. If the amount of prepayment is nil, the cash flows will remain constant during the life of the mortgage. In a fixed-rate mortgage, the proportion of principal and interest payment will change each month as more

---

[5] Since re-named the Bond Market Association.

and more of the mortgage amortises. That is, as the principal amount falls each month, the amount of interest decreases. If we assume that a pass-through security has been issued today so that its coupon reflects the current market level, the payment pattern will resemble the bar chart shown at Figure 10.2.

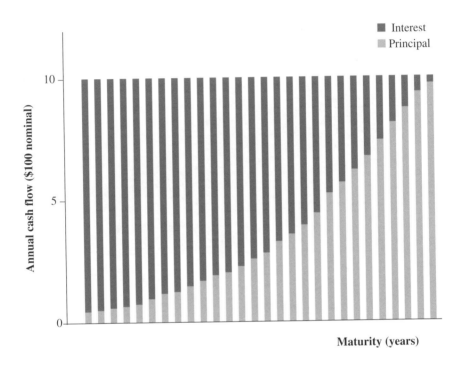

Figure 10.2 Mortgage pass-through security with 0% constant prepayment rate

When there is an element of prepayment in a mortgage pool – for example, as in the 100%PSA or 200%PSA model – the amount of principal payment will increase during the early years of the mortgages and then becomes more steady, before declining for the remainder of the term. This is because the principal balance has declined to such an extent that the scheduled principal payments become less significant. The example for a prepayment of a single loan at 100%PSA (for a 9% rate 30-year maturity loan) is shown at Figure 10.3.

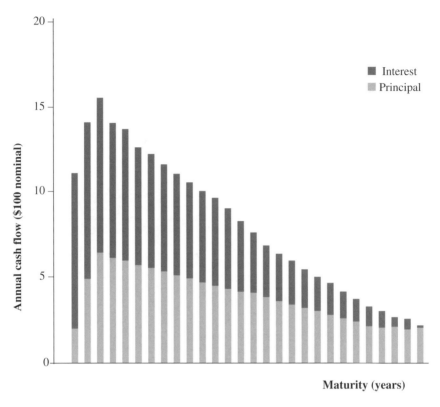

Figure 10.3 100%PSA model

The prepayment volatility of a mortgage-backed bond will vary according to the interest rate of the underlying mortgages. It has been observed that where the mortgages have interest rates of between 100 and 300 basis points above current mortgage rates, the prepayment volatility is the highest. At the bottom of the range, any fall in interest rates often leads to a sudden increase in refinancing of mortgages, while at the top of the range, an increase in rates will lead to a decrease in the prepayment rate. The actual cash flow of a mortgage pass-through, of course, is dependent on the cash-flow patterns of the mortgages in the pool. The projected monthly mortgage payment for a level-paying fixed-rate mortgage in any month is given by (10.8) [below]

$$\overline{I}_t = \overline{M}_{mt-1} \left[\frac{r(1+r)^{n-t+1}}{(1+r)^{n-t+1} - 1} \right] \tag{10.8}$$

where

$\overline{I}_t$ is the projected monthly mortgage payment for month t

$\overline{M}_{mt-1}$ is the projected mortgage balance at the end of month t assuming that prepayments have occurred in the past.

To calculate the interest proportion of the projected monthly mortgage payment we use (10.9) where $\overline{i}_t$ is the projected monthly interest payment for month t.

$$\overline{i}_t = \overline{Mm}_{t-1} \cdot i \tag{10.9}$$

Formula (10.9) states that the projected monthly interest payment can be obtained by multiplying the mortgage balance at the end of the previous month by the monthly interest rate. In the same way, the expression for calculating the projected monthly scheduled principal payment for any month is given by (10.10), where $\overline{p}_t$ is the projected scheduled principal payment for the month t.

$$\overline{p}_t = \overline{I}_t - \overline{i}_t \tag{10.10}$$

The projected monthly principal prepayment, which is an expected rate only and not a model forecast, is given by (10.11).

$$\overline{pp}_t = SMM_t(\overline{Mm}_{t-1} - \overline{p}_t) \tag{10.11}$$

where $\overline{pp}_t$ is the projected monthly principal prepayment for month t.
The above relationships enable us to calculate values for:
- the projected monthly interest payment;
- the projected monthly scheduled principal payment;
- and the projected monthly principal prepayment.

These values may be used to calculate the total cash flow in any month that a holder of a mortgage-backed bond receives, which is given by (10.12) below, where cf_t is the cash-flow receipt in month t.

$$cf_t = i_t + p_t + pp_t \tag{10.12}$$

The practice of using a prepayment rate is a market convention that enables analysts to evaluate mortgage-backed bonds. The original PSA prepayment rates were arbitrarily selected, based on the observation that prepayment rates tended to stabilise after the first 30 months of the life of a mortgage. A linear increase in the prepayment rate is also assumed. However, this is a market convention only, adopted by the market as a standard benchmark. The levels do not reflect seasonal variations in prepayment patterns, or the different behavior patterns of different types of mortgages.

The PSA benchmarks can be (and are) applied to default assumptions to produce a default benchmark. This is used for non-agency mortgage-backed bonds only, as agency securities are guaranteed by the one of the three government or government-sponsored agencies. Accordingly the PSA standard default assumption (SDA) benchmark is used to assess the potential default rate for a mortgage pool. For example, the standard benchmark, 100 SDA assumes that the default rate in the first month is 0.02% and increases in a linear fashion by 0.02% each month until the 30th month, at which point the default rate remains at 0.60%. In month 60, the default rate begins to fall from 0.60% to 0.03% and continues to fall linearly until month 120. From that point, the default rate remains constant at 0.03%. The other benchmarks have similar patterns.

Prepayment models

The PSA standard benchmark reviewed in the previous section uses an assumption of prepayment rates and can be used to calculate the prepayment proceeds of a mortgage. It is not, strictly speaking, a prepayment *model* because it cannot be used to estimate actual prepayments. A prepayment model, on the other hand, does attempt to predict the prepayment cash flows of a mortgage pool, by modelling the statistical relationships between the various factors that have an impact on the level of prepayment. These factors are the current mortgage rate, the characteristics of the mortgages in the pool, seasonal factors and the general business cycle. Let us consider them in turn.

The prevailing mortgage interest rate is probably the most important factor in the level of prepayment. The level of the current mortgage rate and its spread above or below the original contract rate will influence the decision to refinance a mortgage; if the rate is materially below the original rate, the borrower will prepay the mortgage. As the mortgage rate at any time reflects the general bank base rate, the level of market interest rates has the greatest effect on mortgage prepayment levels. The current mortgage rate also has an effect on housing prices, since if mortgages are seen as "cheap" the general perception will be that now is the right time to purchase: this affects housing-market turnover. The pattern is followed by mortgage rates since the original loan also has an impact, a phenomenon known as refinancing burnout.

Observation of the mortgage market has suggested that housing-market and mortgage activity follows a strong seasonal pattern. The strongest period of activity is during the spring and summer, while the market is at its quietest in the winter. The various factors may be used to derive an expression that can be used to calculate expected prepayment levels. For example, a US investment bank uses the following model to calculate expected prepayments:[6]

Monthly prepayment rate =
(Refinancing incentive) × (Season multiplier) × (Month multiplier) x (Burnout)

Collateralised mortgage securities

In this section, we review some of the newer structures of these instruments. A large number of the instruments in the US market are collateralised mortgage obligations (CMOs), the majority of which are issued by government-sponsored agencies and so offer virtual Treasury-bond credit quality but at significantly higher yields. This makes the paper attractive to a range of institutional investors, as does the opportunity to tailor the characteristics of a particular issue to suit the needs of a specific investor. The CMO market in the US experienced rapid growth during the 1990s, with a high of $324 billion issued in 1993; this figure had fallen to just under $100 billion during 1998.[7] The growth of the market has brought with it a range of new structures. For example, bondholders who wished to have a lower exposure to prepayment risk have invested in planned-amortisation classes (PACs) and targeted-amortisation classes (TACs). The uncertain term to maturity of mortgage-backed bonds has resulted in the creation of bonds that were guaranteed not to extend beyond a stated date, which are known as very accurately defined maturity (VDAM) bonds. In the United Kingdom and certain overseas markets, mortgage-backed bonds pay a floating-rate

---

[6] Fabozzi (1997)
[7] The source for statistical data in this section is *Asset-Backed Alert*. Used with permission.

coupon, and the interest from foreign investors in the US domestic market led to the creation of bonds with coupons linked to the LIBOR rate. Other types of instruments in the market include interest-only (IO) and principal-only (PO) bonds, also sometimes called Strips, and inverse floating-rate bonds, which are usually created from an existing fixed-rate bond issue.

The primary features of US-market CMOs are summarised as follows:

Credit quality. CMOs issued by US government agencies have the same guarantee as agency pass-through securities, so may be considered risk-free. These bonds therefore do not require any form of credit insurance or credit enhancement. Whole-loan CMOs do not carry any form of government guarantee, and are rated by credit-rating agencies. Most bonds carry a triple-A rating, either because of the quality of the mortgage pool or issuing vehicle or because a form of credit enhancement has been used.

Interest frequency. CMOs typically pay interest on a monthly basis, which is calculated on the current outstanding nominal value of the issue.

Cash-flow profile. The cash-flow profile of CMOs is based on an assumed prepayment rate. This rate is based on the current market expectation of future prepayment levels and expected market interest rates, and is known as the pricing speed.

Maturity. Most CMOs are long-dated instruments, and originally almost all issues were created from underlying mortgage collateral with a 30-year stated maturity. During the 1990s, issues were created from shorter-dated collateral, including five–seven-year and 15–20-year mortgages.

Market convention. CMOs trade on a yield – as opposed to a price – basis and are usually quoted as a spread over the yield of the nearest maturity Treasury security. The yields are calculated on the basis of an assumed prepayment rate. Agency CMOs are settled on a T+3 basis via an electronic book-entry system known as "Fedwire", the clearing system run by the Federal Reserve. Whole-loan CMOs also settle on a T+3 basis, and are cleared using either physical delivery or by electronic transfer. New issues CMOs settle from one to three months after the initial offer date.

Originally, mortgage-backed bonds were created from individual underlying mortgages. Agency CMOs are created from mortgages that have already been pooled and securitised, usually in the form of a pass-through security. Issuers of whole-loan CMOs do not, therefore, need to create a pass-through security from a pool of individual mortgages, but are structured according to cash flows from the entire pool. In the same as for agency pass-through securities, the underlying mortgages in a whole-loan pool are generally of the same risk type, maturity and interest rate. The other difference between whole-loan CMOs and agency pass-throughs is that the latter comprise mortgages of up to a stated maximum size, while larger loans are contained in CMOs. There are essentially two CMO structures; those issues that re-direct the underlying pool interest payments and issues re-directing both interest and principal. The main CMO instrument types pay out both interest and principal and are described below.

Whole-loan CMO structures also differ from other mortgage-backed securities in terms of what is known as compensating interest. Virtually all mortgage securities pay principal and interest on a monthly basis, on a fixed coupon date. The underlying mortgages, however, may be paid off on any day of the month. Agency mortgage securities guarantee their bondholders an interest payment for the complete month, even if the underlying mortgage has been paid off ahead of the coupon date (and so has not attracted any interest). Whole-loan CMOs do not offer this guarantee, and so any payment interest shortfall will be lost, meaning that a bondholder would receive less than one month's worth of interest on the coupon date. Some issuers, but not all, will pay a compensating interest payment to bondholders to make up this shortfall

CMO structure

CMOs are usually rated AAA by rating agencies, and this is because, in practice, the cash flows generated by the underlying mortgages or agency securities are well in excess of what is required to service the interest obligations of all tranches of the notes. As summarised in Sundaresan (1997, p.389), the general characteristics of CMO structures include the following:

- the high credit rating is ensured by arranging credit insurance via a third-party provider, such as a specialist credit-guarantee firm.
- there is always considerable excess of underlying collateral as against the nominal value of notes issued; this leads to a significant level of over-collateralisation.
- notes issued usually pay coupon on a semi-annual or quarterly basis, although the underlying mortgages pay interest more frequently, say monthly or almost daily. This surplus cash is reinvested in between coupon dates at a money-market rate of interest. Issuers usually

prefer a guaranteed-investment contract (GIC) for their surplus cash, but these are only provided by a few banks and insurance companies, so most issuers have to settle for a money-market account. However, the providers will usually accept funds at a much lower level than is usual for interbank deposits, sometimes down to $100,000.

The cash flows that originate from the underlying collateral are separated and allocated to more than one class of notes, known as tranches. Typically these tranches will pay different rates of interest to appeal to different classes of investors. The two basic CMO structures are sequential structure and planned-amortisation class (PAC) structure.

Sequential structure

One of the requirements that CMOs were designed to meet was the demand for mortgage-backed bonds with a wider range of maturities. Most CMO structures re-direct principal payments *sequentially* to individual classes of bonds within the structure, in accordance with the stated maturity of each bond. That is, principal payments are first used to pay off the class of bond with the shortest stated maturity, until it is completely redeemed, before being re-allocated to the next maturity-band class of bond. This occurs until all the bonds in the structure are retired. Sequential-pay CMOs are attractive to a wide range of investors, particularly those with shorter-term investment horizons, as they are able purchase only the class of CMO whose maturity terms meet their requirements. In addition, investors with more traditional longer-dated investment horizons are protected from prepayment risk in the early years of the issue, because principal payments are used to pay off the shorter-dated bonds in the structure.

The typical generic CMO sequential structure would have, say, four tranches, as suggested in Table 10.1. The collateral cash flows are allocated to each tranche in specified order, and the first tranche is allotted both its coupon and any prepayments. The remaining tranches do not receive any payments until the first one is fully retired, with the exception of their coupon payments. Essentially, each tranche receives successive payments as soon as its immediate predecessor is redeemed. The last tranche is usually known as a Z-bond and will receive no cash flows until all preceding tranches have been repaid. In the interim, the face amount of this note will accrue at the stated coupon.

Tranche	Principal	Coupon	Average life (years)	Yield
A	100	7.00%	2.5	2-year benchmark plus 80 bps
B	250	7.00%	5	5-year benchmark plus 100 bps
C	75	7.00%	10	10-year benchmark plus 120 bps
Z	75	7.00%	20	30-year benchmark plus 150 bps

Table 10.1 Generic CMO sequential structure

Planned-amortisation class

The first issue of PACs was in 1986, after a period of sustained falls in the market interest rates led to a demand for less interest-rate volatile mortgage-backed structures. PAC structures are designed to reduce prepayment risk and also the volatility of the weighted average life measure, which is related to the prepayment rate. The securities have a principal payment schedule that is maintained irrespective of any change in prepayment rates. The process is similar to a corporate bond sinking-fund schedule, and is based on the minimum amount of principal cash flow that is produced by the underlying mortgage pool at two different prepayment rates, known as PAC bands. The PAC bands are set as a low and high PSA standard; for example, 50%PSA and 250%PSA. This has the effect of constraining the amount of principal repayment, so that in the early years of the issue the minimum of principal received is at the level of the lower of the two bands, while later in the bond's life the payment is schedule is constrained by the upper PAC band. The total principal cash flow under the PAC schedule will determine the value of PACs in a structure.

A PAC schedule follows an arrangement whereby cash-flow uncertainty of principal payment is directed to another class of security known as companions, or support classes. When prepayment rates are high, companion issues support the main PACs by absorbing any principal prepayments that are in excess of the PAC schedule. When the prepayment rate has fallen, the companion amortisation rates are delayed as the level of principal prepayment is not sufficient to reach the minimum level stipulated by the PAC bands. Essentially, then, the structure of PACs results in the companion issues carrying the prepayment uncertainty, since when prepayment rates are high the average life of the companions will be reduced as they are paid off, and when prepayment rates are low the companions will see their measure of average life increase as they remain outstanding for a longer period.

The principal cash flows of PACs and companions can be divided sequentially, similar to a sequential-pay structure, which is reviewed in the next section. PACs have a lower price volatility than other mortgage securities, the level of which is relatively stable when the prepayment rates are within the PAC bands. When prepayment rates move outside the bands, the volatility increases by a lower amount than they otherwise would, because the prepayment risk is transferred to the companions. For this reason, PAC issues trade at lower spreads to the Treasury yield curve than other issues of similar average life. The companion bonds are always priced at a higher spread than the PACs, reflecting their higher prepayment risk.

PAC bonds that have a lower prepayment risk than standard PACs are known as Type II and Type III PACs. A Type II PAC is created from an existing PAC/companion structure, and has a narrower band than the original PAC. This reduces the prepayment risk. If prepayment rates remain within the bands, Type II PACs trade as PACs. If prepayment rates move outside the narrower band, the extra cash flow is redirected to the companion. Type II PACs are second in priority to the PACs and so carry a higher yield. If prepayment rates remain high over a period of time such that all the companions are redeemed, the Type II PACs take over the function of companion, so that they then carry higher prepayment risk. A further PAC with yet narrower bands, created from the same structure, is known as a Type III PAC.

The upper and lower bands in a PAC may "drift" during the life of the CMO, irrespective of the level that actual prepayment rates are at. This drift arises because of the interaction between actual cash prepayments and the bands, and changes in collateral balance and the ratio between the PAC and companion nominal values. The impact of this drift differs according to where the prepayment rate is. The three possible scenarios are:

prepayment level lies within the current bands: in this case the PAC will receive principal in line with the payment schedule, while any prepayments above the schedule amount will be re-directed to the companion issue. The effect of this if it continues is that both the lower and upper bands will drift upwards, because any prepayment that occurs is within the bands. This causes the upper band to rise, the rationale being that as prepayments have been below it, they have been received at a slower rate than expected, leaving more companion issues to receive future prepayments. The lower band rises as well, the reasoning being that prepayments have been received faster than expected (as they have been above the minimum level) so that a lower amount of collateral is available to generate future principal payments.

It has been observed that upper bands tend to rise at a higher rate than the lower rate, so that prepayment levels lying within the bands causes them to widen over time.

prepayment level lies above the upper band: where prepayment rates are above the upper band, the PAC will receive principal in line with the payment schedule until it is paid off. If the prepayment rates stay above the upper band, the two bands will begin to narrow, because the number of companions available to receive faster prepayments will fall. The two bands will converge completely once all the companion bonds have been redeemed, and the PAC will trade as a conventional sequential-pay security after that until it is paid off.

prepayment level lies below the lower band: if prepayment rates lie below the lower PAC band, the upper band will drift upwards as more companion bonds are available to receive a greater level of prepayments in the future. The lower band may also rise by a small amount. This situation is relatively rare, however, as PAC have the highest priority of all classes in a CMO structure until the payment schedule is back on track.

The band-drift process occurs over a long time period and is sometimes not noticeable. Significant changes to the band levels only take place if the prepayment rate is outside the band for a long period. Prepayment rates that move outside the bands over a short time period do not have any effect on the bands.

Targeted-amortisation class

These bonds were created to cater for investors who require an element of prepayment protection but at a higher yield than would be available with a PAC. Targeted-amortisation class bonds (TAC) offer a prepayment principal in line with a schedule, providing that the level of prepayment is within the stated range. If the level of principal prepayment moves outside of the range, the extra principal amounts are used to pay off TAC companion bonds, just as with PACs. The main difference between TACs and PACs is that TACs have extra prepayment risk if the level of prepayments falls below the amount required to maintain the payment schedule; this results in the average life of the TAC being extended. Essentially, a TAC is a PAC but with a lower "PAC band" setting. The preference to hold TACs over PACs is a function of the prevailing interest-rate environment; if current rates are low and/or are expected to fall, there is a risk that increasing prepayments will reduce the average life of the bond. In this scenario, investors may be willing to do without the protection against an increase in the average life (deeming it unlikely to be required), and take the extra yield over PACs as a result. This makes TACs attractive compared to PACs under certain conditions and, because one element of the "PAC band" is removed, TACs trade at a higher yield.

Z-class bonds

We have already alluded to these securities. This type of bond is unique to the domestic US market, and has a very interesting structure. The Z-class bond (or Z-bond) is created from a CMO structure and has re-allocation of both principal and interest payments. It is essentially a coupon-bearing bond that ranks below all other classes in the CMO's structure, and pays no cash flows for part of its life. When the CMO is issued, the Z-bond has a nominal value of relatively small size, and at the start of its life it pays out cash flows on a monthly basis as determined by its coupons. However, at any time that the Z-bond itself is receiving no principal payments, these cash flows are used to retire some of the principal of the other classes in the structure. This results in the nominal value of the bond being increased each month that the coupon payments are not received, so that the principal amount is higher at the end of the bond's life than at the start. This process is known as accretion. At the point when all classes of bond ahead of the Z-bond are retired, the Z-bond itself starts to pay out principal-and-interest cash flows.

In the conventional sequential-pay structure, the existence of a Z-bond will increase the principal prepayments in the CMO structure. The other classes in the structure receive some of their principal prepayments from the Z-bond, which lowers their average life volatility. Creating a Z-bond in a CMO structure therefore reduces the average life volatility of all the classes in the structure. Z-bonds are an alternative to investors who might otherwise purchase Treasury zero-coupon bonds, with a similar feature of no reinvestment risk. They also offer the added attraction of higher yields than those available on Treasury strips with a similar average life.

Interest-only and principal-only class

Stripped-coupon mortgage securities are created when the coupon cash flows payable by a pool of mortgages are split into interest-only (IO) and principal-only (PO) payments. The cash flows will be a function of the prepayment rate, since this determines the nominal value of the collateral pool. IO issues, also known as IO strips, gain whenever the prepayment rate falls, as interest payments are reduced as the principal amount falls. If there is a rise in the prepayment rate, PO bonds benefit because they are discount securities and a higher prepayment rate results in the redemption proceeds being received early. Early strip issues were created with an unequal amount of coupon and principal, resulting in a synthetic coupon rate that was different from the coupon on the underlying bond. These instruments were known as synthetic coupon pass-throughs. Nowadays, it is more typical for all the interest to be allocated to one class, the IO issue, and all the principal to be allocated to the PO class. The most common CMO structures have a portion of their principal stripped into IO and PO bonds, but in some structures the entire issue is made up of IO and PO bonds. The amount of principal used to create stripped securities will reflect investor demand. In certain cases, IO issues created from a class of CMO known as real-estate mortgage-investment conduits (REMICs) have quite esoteric terms. For example, the IO classes might be issued with an amount of principal attached known as the nominal balance. The cash flows for bonds with this structure are paid through a process of amortising and prepaying the nominal balance. The balance itself is a small amount, resulting in a very high coupon, so that the IO has a multi-digit coupon and very high price (such as 1183% and 3626-12).[8]

Strips created from whole-loan CMOs trade differently from those issued out of agency CMOs. Agency CMOs pay a fixed coupon, whereas whole-loan CMOs pay a coupon based on a weighted average of all the individual mortgage coupons. During the life of the whole-loan issue, this coupon value will alter as prepayments change the amount of principal. To preserve the coupon payments of all issues within a structure, therefore, a portion of the principal-and-interest cash flows are stripped from the underlying mortgages, leaving collateral that has a more stable average life. This is another reason that IOs and POs may be created.

IO issue prices exhibit the singular tendency of moving in the same direction as interest rates under certain situations. This reflects the behavior of mortgages and prepayment rates: when interest rates fall below the mortgage coupon rate, prepayment rates will increase. This causes the cash flow for an IO strip to fall, as the level of the underlying principal declines, which causes the price of the IO to fall as well. This is despite the fact that the issue's cash flows are now discounted at a lower rate. Figure (10.4) shows the price of a sensitivity of a 7% pass-through security compared to

---

[8] Ames 1997

the prices of a IO and a PO that have been created from it. Note that the price of the pass-through is not particularly sensitive to a fall in the mortgage rate below the coupon rate of 7%. This illustrates the negative-convexity property of pass-through securities. The price sensitivity of the two strip issues is very different. The PO experiences a dramatic fall in price as the mortgage rate rises above the coupon rate. The IO, on the other hand, experiences a rise in price in the same situation, while its price falls significantly if mortgage rates fall below the coupon rate.

Both PO and IO issues are extremely price volatile at times of moves in mortgage rates, and have much greater interest rate sensitivity than the pass-through securities form which they are created.

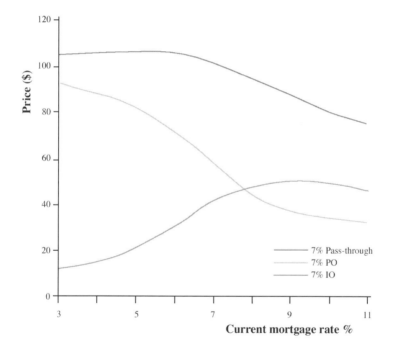

Figure 10.4 Price sensitivity of pass-through security, IO and PO to changes in mortgage rate

Non-agency CMO bonds

There are no significant differences in the structure and terms of non-agency CMOs and agency CMOs. The key feature of non-agency CMOs, however, is that they are not guaranteed by government agencies, and so carry an element of credit risk, in the same way that corporate bonds expose investors to credit risk. To attract investors, therefore, most non-agency CMOs incorporate an element of credit enhancement designed to improve the credit standing of the issue. The use of credit enhancement usually results in a triple-A rating; indeed a large majority of non-agency CMOs are triple-A rated, with very few falling below a double-A rating. All of the four main private credit-rating agencies are involved in credit analysis and rating of non-agency CMOs. The rating granted to a particular issue of CMOs is dependent on a range of factors, which include:

- the term of the underlying loans
- the size of the loans, whether conforming or jumbo (agency mortgages do not include mortgages above a certain stated size, whereas non-agency issues often comprise larger-size loans known as "jumbo loans")
- the interest basis for the loans, whether level-pay fixed-rate, variable or other type
- the type of property
- the geographical area within which the loans have been made
- the purpose behind the loans – whether a first purchase or a refinancing.

In this section, we discuss the credit-enhancement facility that is used in non-agency CMOs.

Credit enhancements

CMOs are arranged with either an external or internal credit enhancement. An external credit enhancement is a guarantee made by a third party to cover losses on the issue. Usually a set amount of the issue is guaranteed, such as 25%, rather than the entire issue. The guarantee can take the form of a letter of credit, bond insurance or pool insurance. A pool-insurance policy would be written to insure against losses that arose as a result of default, usually for a cash amount of cover that would remain in place during the life of the pool. Certain policies are set up so that the cash coverage falls in value during the life of the bond. Pool insurance is provided by specialised agencies. Note that only defaults and foreclosures are included in the policy, which forces investors to arrange further cover if they wish to be protected against any other type of loss. A CMO issue that obtains credit enhancement from an external party still has an element of credit risk, but now linked to the fortunes of the provider of insurance. That is, the issue is at risk from a deterioration in the credit quality of the provider of insurance. Investors who purchase non-agency CMOs must ensure that they are satisfied with the credit quality of the third-party guarantor, as well as the quality of the underlying mortgage pool. Note that an external credit enhancement has no impact on the cash-flow structure of the CMO.

Internal credit enhancements generally have more complex arrangements and sometimes also affect the cash-flow structures of the instruments themselves. The two most common types of internal credit enhancement are reserve funds and a senior/subordinated structure.

Reserve funds: There are two types of reserve funds. A cash-reserve fund is a deposit of cash that has been built up from payments arising from the issue of the bonds. A portion of the profits made when the bonds were initially issued is placed in a separate fund. The fund in turn places this cash in short-term bank deposits. The cash-reserve fund is used in the event of default to compensate investors who have suffered capital loss. It is often set up in conjunction with another credit-enhancement product, such as a letter of credit. An *excess servicing spread account* is also a separate fund, generated from excess spread after all the payments of the mortgage have been made; that is, the coupon, servicing fee and other expenses. For instance, if an issue has a gross weighted-average coupon of 7.50%, and the service fee is 0.10% and the net weighted-average coupon is 7.25%, then the excess servicing amount is 0.15%. This amount is paid into the spread account, and will grow steadily during the bond's life. The funds in the account can be used to pay off any losses arising from the bond that affect investors.

Senior/subordinated structure: This is the most common type of internal credit-enhancement method encountered in the market. Essentially, it involves a bond ranking below the CMO that absorbs all the losses arising from default, or other cause, leaving the main issue unaffected. The subordinated bond clearly has the higher risk attached to it, so it trades at a higher yield. Most senior/subordinated arrangements also incorporate a "shifting interest structure". This arranges for prepayments to be re-directed from the subordinated class to the senior class. Hence, it alters the cash-flow characteristics of the senior notes, irrespective of the presence of defaults or otherwise.

Commercial mortgage-backed securities

The mortgage-backed bond market includes a sector of securities that are backed by commercial, as opposed to residential, mortgages. These are known as commercial mortgage-backed securities (CMBS). They trade, essentially, as other mortgage securities but there are differences of detail in their structure, which are summarised in this section.

Issuing a CMBS

As with a residential-mortgage security, a CMBS is created from a pool or "trust" of commercial mortgages, with the cash flows of the bond backed by the interest and principal payments of the underlying mortgages. A commercial mortgage is a loan made to finance or refinance the purchase of a commercial (business) property. There is a market in direct purchase of a commercial loan book in addition to the more structured CMBS transaction. An issue of CMBS is rated in the same way as a residential-mortgage security and usually has a credit-enhancement arrangement to raise its credit rating. The credit rating of a CMBS takes into account the size of the issue as well as the level of credit-enhancement support.

Classes of bonds in a CMBS structure are usually arranged in a sequential-pay series, and bonds are retired in line with their rating in the structure; the highest-rated bonds are paid off first.

Commercial mortgages impose a penalty on borrowers if they are redeemed early, usually in the form of an interest charge on the final principal. There is no such penalty in the US residential-mortgage market, although early-retirement fees are still a feature of residential loans in the UK. The early payment protection in a commercial loan can have other forms as well, such as a prepayment "lockout", which is a contractual arrangement that prevents early retirement. This prepayment protection is repeated in a CMBS structure, and may be in the form of call protection of the bonds themselves. There is already a form of protection in the ratings of individual issues in the structure, because the highest-rated bonds are paid off first. That is, the triple-A rated bonds will be retired ahead of the double-A rated bonds, and so on. The highest-rated bonds in a CMBS structure also have the highest protection from default of any of the underlying mortgages, which means that losses of principal arising from default will affect the lowest-rated bond first.

As well as the early-retirement protection, commercial mortgages differ from residential loans in that many of them are balloon mortgages. A balloon loan is one on which only the interest is paid, or only a small amount of the principal is paid as well as the interest, so that all or a large part of the loan remains to be paid off on the maturity date. This makes CMBSs potentially similar to conventional vanilla bonds (which are also sometimes called "bullet" bonds) and so attractive to investors who prefer less uncertainty on a bond's term to maturity.

Types of CMBS structures

In the US market, there are currently five types of CMBS structures. They are:

- liquidating trusts
- multi-property single borrower
- multi-property conduit
- multi-property non-conduit
- single-property single borrower.

We briefly describe the three most common structures here.

Liquidating trusts: This sector of the market is relatively small by value and represents bonds issued against non-performing loans, hence the other name of non-performing CMBS. The market is structured in a slightly different way from regular commercial mortgage securities. The features include a fast-pay structure, which states that all cash flows from the mortgage pool be used to redeem the most senior bond first, and over-collateralisation, which is when the value of bonds created is significantly lower than the value of the underlying loans. This over-collateralisation results in bonds being paid off sooner. Due to the nature of the asset backing for liquidating CMBSs, bonds are usually issued with relatively short average lives, and will receive cash flows on only a portion of the loans. A target date for paying off is set and in the event that the target is not met, the bonds usually have a provision to raise the coupon rate. This acts as an incentive for the borrower to meet the retirement target.

Multi-property single borrower: The single borrower/multi-property structure is an important and substantial part of the CMBS market. The special features of these bonds include cross-collateralisation, which is when properties that are used as collateral for individual loans are pledged against each loan. Another feature known as cross-default allows the lender to call each loan in the pool if any one of them defaults. Since cross-collateralisation and cross-default link all the properties together, sufficient cash flow is available to meet the collective debt on all of the loans. This influences the grade of credit rating that is received for the issue. A property-release provision in the structure is set up to protect the investor against the lender removing or prepaying the stronger loans in the book. Another common protection against this risk is a clause in the structure terms that prevents the issuer from substituting one property for another.

Multi-borrower/conduit: A conduit is a commercial lending entity that has been set up solely to generate collateral to be used in securitisation deals. The major investment banks have all established conduit arms. Conduits are responsible for originating collateral that meets requirements on loan type (whether amortising or balloon, and so on), loan term, geographic spread of the properties and the time that the loans were struck. Generally, a conduit will want to have a diversified range of underlying loans, known as pool diversification, with a wide spread of location and size. A diversified pool reduces the default risk for the investor. After it has generated the collateral, the conduit then structures the deal, on terms similar to CMOs but with the additional features described in this section.

Covered bonds

Covered bonds are similar in most economic aspects to residential MBS instruments but have detail differences in their structure and legal definition. The longest-established covered bond market is that in German Pfandbriefe; there are also covered bond markets in other European markets such as the Netherlands, Ireland, Spain and the United Kingdom. In this section we describe UK covered bonds, which represent a new market for issuers and investors alike.

Covered bond markets and securitisation

The low profile of covered bonds in the financial literature is surprising, given that some of the earliest bond market instruments were in the form of covered bonds, including German *Pfandbriefe*, Danish *Realkreditobligationer* and French *Obligations Foncieres*. More recently covered bonds have been introduced in Spain (*Cedulas Hipotecarias*) and Ireland. At the end of 2003 it was estimated that over €1.5 trillion of covered bonds was in issue in Europe.[9]

---

[9] Source: HBOS plc

A covered bond may be defined as a full recourse debt issue secured against a pool of mortgages or public-sector assets. In certain countries such as Germany the central authorities have enacted specific legislation that govern covered bonds. In countries where no specific legislation exists, such as the UK, originators have used traditional securitisation structuring techniques to create an identical instrument, the *structured covered bond*. With a covered bond, investors continue to have recourse to the originator, but it is only upon default that the assigned underlying collateral pool is used to repay the principal. Otherwise the cashflows from the collateral are not used to service the debt. In a traditional securitisation, investors would have only the cashflows from the assigned collateral pool to repay their amount owed on the debt.

Hence, the key difference between an RMBS and a mortgage-backed covered bond is that an SPV is not created and assets are not transferred to an SPV. Instead, a wholly-owned subsidiary is created within the originating bank or financial institution and assets are transferred to this legal entity. Hence, these assets are not taken off the originating entity's balance sheet, as they remain part of the group structure assets.

Issuer and investor factors

Covered bonds in the euro and sterling markets present new attractions for investors. For instance they:

- offer a diversified alternative for investors' funds, away from traditional issuers;
- offer access to the residential mortgage market but outside of RMBS securities;
- present a structure that provides potentially a greater ability to repay liabilities on a stand-alone basis;
- are rated AAA/Aaa;
- are issued in large size and hence offer liquidity;
- are risk-weighted at 20% for Basel I capital purposes.

Covered bonds also present certain advantages for originators, these include:

- a potential new investor base that may not have been tapped previously;
- due to rating and collateral security, a lower cost of funds than a traditional (unsecured) MTN programme, as well as more longer-

term funding;[10] also a lower-cost and longer-term funding than securitised securities;

- potential ease of reissue under the programme structure.

These points would suggest strong future growth potential in this market.

HBOS plc covered bond

As an example, consider the mortgage covered bond issued by Halifax plc (a former UK building society and part of the HBOS group). It is illustrated in figure 10.5. This was created as follows:

- the arm of HBOS responsible for funding activity, HBOS Treasury, issued covered bonds to investors. It is legally obliged to pay the interest and principal on the bonds;
- funds raised by this issue were loaned to a new Group company, Halifax LLP, a wholly-owned subsidiary of HBOS group. The LLP guarantees the covered bonds;
- the Group sold a pool of residential mortgages to Halifax LLP, at an overcollateralisation of 15%;
- Halifax LLP placed these assets under a security trust and guarantee which was placed in favour of the investors.

Unlike a traditional securitisation, the liabilities on the issues notes were held by HBOS Treasury, not the new legal entity. It funded the liabilities out of its normal activities, not out of the cash flows represented by the mortgages transferred to Halifax LLP. Only in the event of default on the issued notes would investors have recourse to the assets held by Halifax LLP. This structure presented certain advantages over traditional RMBS issues as it was operated as a programme of rolling issues, and also appealed to a wider investor base.

The bonds were rated at AAA/Aaa/AAA. The initial pool was comprised entirely of Halifax plc, although there is freedom to include any mortgage (provided certain criteria are met) from within the HBOS group.

The covered bonds are part of a €14 billion MTN programme set up by HBOS plc. For investor comfort, various tests are performed on the portfolio

---

[10] During Jan 2004 the covered bond yield in the UK ranged around 5-10 basis points lower compared to MTN yields from the same issuer.

to ensure that it maintains minimum quality levels during the bonds life. This process is similar to the quality tests performed on CDO structures. The Halifax bond test is called the Asset Coverage Test; it is designed to protect investors and aims to ensure that the value of the underlying assets (mortgages, substitute assets and cash reserves) is equal to the outstanding principal. It includes:

- portfolio revaluation: the value of the portfolio is updated every quarter and is overcollateralised by 15% (that is, its value is calculated using 85% of the Halifax house price index);
- defaulted mortgages: any mortgage in the collateral pool that is over 90 days in arrears is designated a defaulted mortgage and for asset valuation purposes is assigned a zero value;
- repurchase and substitution: to satisfy the asset coverage test, Halifax must repurchase defaulted mortgages from the LLP company at principal value, and either assign replacement mortgages or supply cash collateral until the asset coverage test is passed.

The asset coverage test is

$$AALA \geq \sum PAO$$

where
$AALA$ is the adjusted aggregate loan amount and which is comprised as follows

$AALA$ = outstanding loan value + cash + substitute assets − (set-off risk + redraws + negative carry)

and where
PAO is the principal amount outstanding.

Other tests and triggers in the structure include the following:
- if the issuer's rating falls below a certain level than Halifax must repurchase sufficient mortgages and/or inject cash into the LLP to cover the next maturing bond;
- if the issuer short-term rating falls below A−1+/P−1/F1+ then the LLP must establish a reserve fund, which will then accumulate interest to cover the coupon on the covered bond as it falls due;
- the LLP bank accounts must be maintained at an A-1+/P-1/F1+ rated bank.

The HBOS covered bond was a ground-breaking deal in the UK covered bond market. It established a precedent that subsequently attracted interest from other UK mortgage banks.

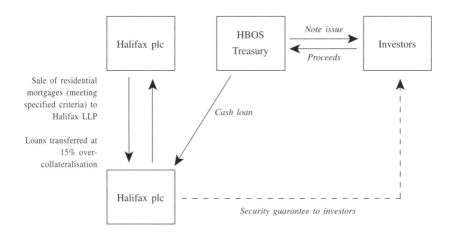

Figure 10.5 Halifax mortgage covered bond, July 2003
© HBOS. Reproduced with permission

Introduction to the evaluation and analysis of mortgage-backed bonds[11]

Term to maturity

The term to maturity cannot be given with any certainty for a mortgage pass-through security, since the cash flows and prepayment patterns cannot be predicted. To evaluate such a bond, therefore, it is necessary to estimate the term for the bond, and use this measure for any analysis. The maturity measure for any bond is important as, without it, it is not possible to assess over what period of time a return is being generated. Also, it will not be possible to compare the asset to any other bond. The term to maturity of a bond also gives an indication of its sensitivity to changes in market interest rates. If comparisons with other securities such as government bonds are

---

[11] The pricing and hedging of mortgage-backed securities is a complex one and space here does not allow a detailed treatment of it. Interested readers should consult Chapter 9 of Sundaresan (1997) or the other relevant references cited in the bibliography. Tuckman (1996) is also a good introduction to pricing models for mortgage securities; see his Chapter 18.

made, we cannot use the stated maturity of the mortgage-backed bond because prepayments will reduce this figure. The convention in the market is to use to other estimated values, which are average life and the more traditional duration measure.

The average life of a mortgage-pass through security is the weighted-average time to return of a unit of principal payment, made up of projected scheduled principal payments and principal prepayments. It is also known as the weighted-average life. It is given by (10.13).

$$\text{Average life} = \frac{1}{12} \sum_{t=1}^{n} \frac{t(\text{Principal received at } t)}{\text{Total principal received}} \qquad (10.13)$$

where n is the number of months remaining. The time from the term measured by the average life to the final scheduled principal payment is the bond's tail.

We've seen that to calculate duration (or Macaulay's duration) for a bond we required the weighted present values of all its cash flows. To apply this for a mortgage-backed bond, therefore, it is necessary to project the bond's cash flows, using an assumed prepayment rate. The projected cash flows, together with the bond price and the periodic interest rate may then be used to arrive at a duration value. The periodic interest rate is derived from the yield. This calculation for a mortgage-backed bond produces a periodic duration figure, which must be divided by 12 to arrive at a duration value in years (or by four in the case of a quarterly-paying bond).

Calculating yield and price: static cash–flow model

There are a number of ways that the yield on a mortgage-backed bond can be calculated. One of the most common methods employs the static cash-flow model. This assumes a single prepayment rate to estimate the cash flows for the bond, and does not take into account how changes in market conditions might affect the prepayment pattern.

The conventional yield measure for a bond is the discount rate at which the sum of the present values of all the bond's expected cash flows will be equal to the price of the bond. The convention is usually to compute the yield from the clean price; that is, excluding any accrued interest. This yield measure is known as the bond's redemption yield or yield-to-maturity. However, for mortgage-backed bonds it is known as a *cash-flow yield* or mortgage yield. The cash flow for a mortgage-backed bond is not known with certainty, due to the effect of prepayments, and so must be derived using an assumed prepayment rate. Once the projected cash flows have been calculated, it is possible to calculate the cash-flow yield. The formula is given as (10.14) below.

$$P = \sum_{n=1}^{N} \frac{C(t)}{(1 + ri / 1200)^{t-1}} \tag{10.14}$$

Note, however, that a yield so computed will be for a bond with monthly coupon payments,[12] so it is necessary to convert the yield to an annualised equivalent before any comparisons are made with conventional bond yields. In the US and UK markets, the bond-equivalent yield is calculated for mortgage-backed bonds and measured against the relevant government bond yield, which (in both cases) is a semi-annual yield. Although it is reasonably accurate to simply double the yield of a semi-annual coupon bond to arrive at the annualised equivalent,[13] to obtain the bond equivalent yield for a monthly paying mortgage-backed bond we use (10.15), as shown below.

$$rm = 2[(1 + ri_M)^6 - 1] \tag{10.15}$$

where rm is the bond equivalent yield (we retain the designation that was used to denote yield to maturity in Chapter 4) and ri_M is the interest rate that will equate the present value of the projected monthly cash flows for the mortgage-backed bond to its current price. The equivalent semi-annual yield is given by (10.16).

$$rm_{s/a} = (1 + ri_M)^6 - 1 \tag{10.16}$$

The cash-flow yield calculated for a mortgage-backed bond in this way is essentially the redemption yield, using an assumption to derive the cash flows. In this, the measure suffers from the same drawbacks as when it is used to measure the return of a plain-vanilla bond; that is, that the calculation assumes a uniform reinvestment rate for all the bond's cash flows and that the bond will be held to maturity. The same weakness will apply to the cash-flow yield measure for a mortgage-backed bond. In fact, the potential inaccuracy of the redemption-yield measure is even greater with a mortgage-backed bond because the frequency of interest payments is higher, which makes the reinvestment risk greater. The final yield that is returned by a mortgage-backed bond will depend on the performance of the mortgages in the pool, specifically the prepayment pattern.

---

[12] The majority of mortgage-backed bonds pay interest on a monthly basis, since individual mortgages usually do as well; certain mortgage-backed bonds pay on a quarterly basis.

[13] See Chapter 2 for the formulae used to convert yields from one convention basis to another.

Given the nature of a mortgage-backed bond's cash flows, the exact yield cannot be calculated. However, it is common for market practitioners to use the cash-flow yield measure and compare this to the redemption yield of the equivalent government bond. The usual convention is to quote the spread over the government bond as the main measure of value. When measuring the spread, the mortgage-backed bond is compared to the government security that has a similar duration, or a term to maturity similar to its average life.

As we noted in Chapter four, it is possible to calculate the price of a mortgage-backed bond once its yield is known (or vice-versa). As with a plain-vanilla bond, the price is the sum of the present values of all the projected cash flows. It is necessary to convert the bond-equivalent yield to a monthly yield, which is then used to calculate the present value of each cash flow. The cash flows of IO and PO bonds are dependent on the cash flows of the underlying pass-through security, which is itself dependent on the cash flows of the underlying mortgage pool. Again, to calculate the price of an IO or PO bond, a prepayment rate must be assumed. This enables us to determine the projected level of the monthly cash flows of the IO and the principal payments of the PO. The price of an IO is the present value of the projected interest payments, while the price of the PO is the present value of the projected principal payments, comprising the scheduled principal payments and the projected principal prepayments.

Bond price and option-adjusted spread

The concept of option-adjusted spread (OAS) and its use in the analysis and valuation of bonds with embedded options was considered briefly in Chapter 9, when OAS in discussed in the context of callable bonds. The behavior of mortgage securities often resembles that of callable bonds, because effectively there is a call feature attached to them, in the shape of the prepayment option of the underlying mortgage holders. This option feature is the principal reason why it is necessary to use average life as the term to maturity for a mortgage security. It is frequently the case that the optional nature of a mortgage-backed bond, and the volatility of its yield, have a negative impact on the bond holders. This is for two reasons: the actual yield realised during the holding period has a high probability of being lower than the anticipated yield, which was calculated on the basis of an assumed prepayment level, and mortgages are frequently prepaid at the time when the bondholder will suffer the most. That is, prepayments occur most often when rates have fallen, leaving the bondholder to reinvest repaid principal at a lower market interest rate.

These features combined represent the biggest risk to an investor of holding a mortgage security, and market analysts attempt to measure and quantify this risk. This is usually done using a form of OAS analysis. Under this approach, the value of the mortgagor's prepayment option is calculated in terms of a basis-point penalty that must be subtracted from the expected yield spread on the bond. This basis-point value is calculated using a binomial model or a simulation model to generate a range of future interest-rate paths, only some of which will cause a mortgagor to prepay her mortgage. The interest-rate paths that would result in a prepayment are evaluated for their impact on the mortgage bond's expected yield spread over a government bond.[14] As OAS analysis takes account of the option feature of a mortgage-backed bond, it will be less affected by a yield change than the bond's yield spread. Assuming a flat yield-curve environment, the relationship between the OAS and the yield spread is given by:

$$OAS = \text{Yield spread} - \text{Cost of option feature.}$$

This relationship can be observed occasionally when yield spreads on current coupon mortgages widen during upward moves in the market. As interest rates fall, the cost of the option feature on a current coupon mortgage will rise, as the possibility of prepayment increases. Put another way, the option feature begins to approach being in-the-money. To adjust for the increased value of the option, traders will price in higher spreads on the bond, which will result in the OAS remaining more or less unchanged.

Effective duration and convexity

The modified duration of a bond measures its price sensitivity to a change in yield; the calculation is effectively a snapshot of one point in time. It also assumes that there is no change in expected cash flows as a result of the change in market interest rates. Therefore, it is an inappropriate measure of interest-rate risk for a mortgage-backed bond, whose cash flows would be expected to change after a change in rates, due to the prepayment effect. Hence, mortgage-backed bonds react differently to interest-rate changes compared to conventional bonds, because when rates fall, the level of

---

[14] The yield spread from OAS analysis is based on the discounted value of the expected cash flow using the government bond-derived forward rate. The yield spread of the cash-flow yield to the government bond is based on yields-to-maturity. For this reason, the two spreads are not strictly comparable. The OAS spread is added to the entire yield curve, whereas a yield spread is a spread over a single point on the government-bond yield curve.

prepayments is expected to rise (and vice-versa). Therefore, when interest rates fall, the duration of the bond may also fall, which is opposite to the behavior of a conventional bond. This feature is known as negative convexity and is similar to the effect displayed by a callable bond. The prices of both these types of security react to interest-rate changes differently from the price of conventional bonds.

For this reason, the more accurate measure of interest-rate sensitivity to use is effective duration. To recap from Chapter 9, effective duration is the approximate duration of a bond when, as given by (10.17) below,

$$D_{app} = \frac{P_- - P_+}{2P_0(\Delta rm)} \quad (10.17)$$

where

P_0 is the initial price of the bond
P_- is the estimated price of the bond if the yield decreases by Δrm
P_+ is the estimated price of the bond if the yield increases by Δrm
Δrm is the change in the yield of the bond.

The approximate duration is the effective duration of a bond when the two values P_- and P_+ are obtained from a valuation model that incorporates the effect of a change in the expected cash flows (from prepayment effects) when there is a change in interest rates. The values are obtained from a pricing model such as the static cash-flow model, the binomial model or the simulation model. The calculation of effective duration uses higher and lower prices that are dependent on the prepayment rate that is assumed. Generally, analysts will assume a higher prepayment rate when the interest rate is at the lower level of the two.

Figure 10.6 illustrates the difference between modified duration and effective duration for a range of agency mortgage pass-through securities, where the effective duration for each bond is calculated using a 20 basis point change in rates. This indicates that the modified-duration measure effectively overestimates the price sensitivity of lower-coupon bonds. This factor is significant when hedging a mortgage-backed bond position, because using the modified-duration figure to calculate the nominal value of the hedging instrument will not prove effective for anything other than very small changes in yield.

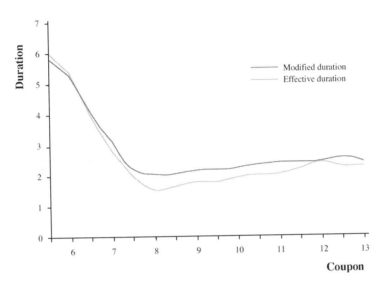

Figure 10.6 Modified duration and effective duration for
agency mortgage-backed bonds

The formula to calculate approximate convexity (or effective convexity) is given below as (10.18). Again, if the values used in the formula allow for the cash flow to change, the convexity value may be taken to be the effective convexity. The effective convexity value of a mortgage pass-through security is invariably negative.

$$CV_{app} = \frac{P_+ + P_- - 2P_0}{P_0(\Delta rm)^2}$$ (10.18)

Total return

To assess the value of a mortgage-backed bond over a given investment horizon, it is necessary to measure the return generated during the holding period from the bond's cash flows. This is done using what is known as the total return framework. The cash flows from a mortgage-backed bond consist of (1) the projected cash flows of the bond (which are the projected interest payments and principal repayments and prepayments); (2) the interest earned on the reinvestment of all the payments; and (3) the projected price of the bond at the end of the holding period. The first sum can be estimated using an assumed prepayment rate during the period the bond is held, while the second cash flow requires an assumed reinvestment rate. To obtain (3) the bondholder must assume, first, what the bond-equivalent yield of the mortgage bond will be at the end of the holding period and, second, what prepayment rate the market will assume at this point. The second rate is a function of the projected yield at the time. The total return during the time the bond is held, on a monthly basis, is then given by (10.19).

$$\left[\frac{\text{Total future cash flow amount}}{P_m}\right]^{1/n} - 1 \qquad (10.19)$$

which can be converted to an annualised bond-equivalent yield using (10.15) or (10.16).

Note that the return calculated using (10.19) is based on a range of assumptions, which render it almost academic. The best approach is to calculate a yield for a range of different assumptions, which then give some idea of the likely yield that may be generated over the holding period, in the form of a range of yields (that is, an upper and lower limit).

Price-yield curves of mortgage pass-through, PO and IO securities

In this section, we present an introduction to the yield behavior of selected mortgage-backed securities under conditions of changing interest rates. To recap, in an environment of high interest rates the holders of mortgage-backed bonds prefer prepayments to occur. This is because the mortgage will be paying at a low interest rate relative to market conditions, and the likelihood of mortgage prepayment at par results in a higher value for the bond. In the same way, when interest rates are low, note holders would prefer that there not be any prepayment, as the bond will be paying interest at a relatively high rate and will therefore bex price-valuable.

Figure 10.7 illustrates the price behavior of pass-through securities, with nominal coupon of 7%.

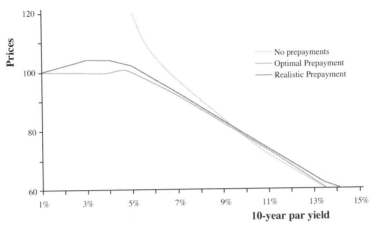

Figure 10.7

Under conditions of no prepayments, the bond cash flows are certain and the price-yield behavior resembles that of a conventional bond. Under optimal prepayment, the bond will behave similarly to a callable bond: in a high-interest-rate environment the bond behaves much like a vanilla bond, while under lower rates the price of the bond is capped at par. However, under what Tuckman (1996) calls "realistic payment" conditions the price behavior is somewhat different, as illustrated in Figure 10.6. In an environment of very low rates, bond value is higher with the realistic payments assumption than the other two scenarios. This is because there are always a number of mortgage borrowers who will repay their loans irrespective of the level of interest rates, whether rates are low or high. Remember that note holders desire prepayments when interest rates are high, and the bond value under the realistic-payments model is higher than those of the other two, which predict no prepayments under high-interest-rate conditions.

As interest rates decline, certain mortgage borrowers will prepay their loans, but by no means all. As prepayment decreases the value of a mortgage under low interest rates, the fact that not all borrowers prepay under the "optimal" scenario results in an increase in value of a mortgage to a level greater than its optimal prepaid value. This non-prepayment behavior can lead to an increase in bond value above par. This is something of an anomaly, as the bond is then priced above the level at which it can theoretically be called. The scenario concludes when eventually all borrowers redeem their mortgages as rates have fallen far enough. This is why the realistic-prepayments curve moves down to par at very low levels of rates. The graph shows the existence of negative convexity as bond prices fall as interest rates decline, which reflects the behavior of mortgage borrowers after a long enough period of very low rates. However, this does not mean that investors should not buy mortgage-backed bonds at that range of yields when negative convexity applies: as Tuckman notes, the mortgages will be earning rates at above-market levels. It is the total return of the bond over the holding period that is relevant, rather than its price behavior.[15]

It is also worth commenting on the behavior of IO and PO securities, which we described earlier. To recap, an IO receives the interest payments of the underlying collateral while the PO receives principal payments. Figure 10.8 illustrates the price behavior of these instruments, based on a $100 nominal amount for both the underlying mortgage and the IO/PO.

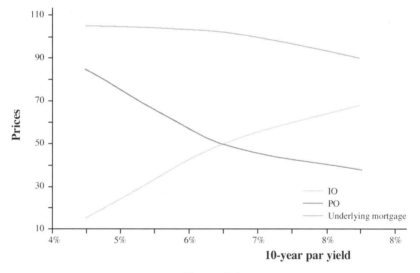

Figure 10.8

Under very high interest rates and where prepayments are unlikely, a PO will act as is repayable at par on maturity, similar to a zero-coupon bond. As interest rates decline and the level of prepayments increases, the value of the PO will increase. However, other forces are at work that, as rates change further, make PO securities more interesting than vanilla strips. These are:

---

[15] This is especially true when compared to the performance of other debt-market investments. Investment reasoning on price behaviour alone is "as bad as concluding that premium Treasuries should never be purchased because they will eventually decline in price to par"! (author's exclamation mark; Tuckman 1996, p 256).

- the conventional price/yield effect, as lower interest rates cause higher prices
- that the PO, again similarly to vanilla strips, is very sensitive to the price/yield effect
- as the level of prepayments increases, with the expectation of higher levels still, the effective maturity of the PO declines. The effect of this lower maturity is to raise the price of the PO even higher.

The impact of these factors is that PO securities are highly volatile.

The price/yield relationship of the IO is a function of that for the PO, and is obtained by subtracting the value of the latter from that of the underlying mortgage. A significant feature is the high price volatility of the IO under conditions of lower and falling interest rates. This is explained as follows: in an high-interest-rate environment, with very low prepayment levels, IOs act as vanilla bonds, with cash flows known with certainty. This changes as interest rates start to fall, and the cash flows of the IO effectively disappear. This is because as more principal is repaid, the nominal amount of the mortgage on which interest is charged decreases in amount. However, unlike pass-through or other mortgage securities, which receive some principal payment when interest payments decline or cease, IOs receive no cash flow. The impact of a vanishing cash flow is that, as interest rates fall, the price of the IO declines dramatically.

As well as purchases by investors, this negative-duration property of IOs makes them of use as interest-rate hedging instruments by market-makers in mortgage-backed securities.

CASE STUDY 1 Shipshape Residential Mortgages No 1

Bristol & West plc is a former UK building society that is now part of the Bank of Ireland group. In October 2000, it issued £300 million of residential mortgage-backed securities through ING Barings. It was the third time that Bristol & West had undertaken a securitisation of part of its mortgage book. The Shipshape Residential Mortgages No 1 was structured in the following way:
- a £285 million tranche senior note, rated Aaa by Moody's and Fitch IBCA, with an average life of 3.8 years and paying 25 basis points over three-month Libor
- a class "B" note of £9 million, rated A1 by Moody's and paying a coupon on 80 basis points over three-month Libor. These

notes had an average life of 6.1 years
- a junior note of £6 million nominal, rated triple-B by Moody's and with an average life of 6.8 years. These notes paid a coupon of 140 basis points over Libor.

CASE STUDY 2   Fosse Securities No 1 plc

This was the first securitisation undertaken by Alliance & Leicester plc, another former UK building society which converted into a commercial bank in 1997. The underlying portfolio was approximately 6,700 loans secured by first mortgages on property in the UK. The transaction was a £250 million securitisation via the SPV, named Fosse Securities No 1 plc. The underwriter was Morgan Stanley Dean Witter, which placed the notes in November 2000. The transaction structure was:
- a senior class "A" note with AAA/Aaa rating by Standard & Poor's and Moody's, which represented £235 million of the issue, with a legal maturity of November 2032
- a class "B" note rated Aa/Aa3 of nominal £5 million
- a class "C" note rated BBB/Baa2 of nominal £10 million.

The ratings agencies cited the strengths of the issue as follows:[16] the loans were prime quality; there was a high level of seasoning in the underlying asset pool, with average age of 35 months; the average level of the loan-to-value ratio (LTV) was considered low, at 73.5%; and there were low average loan-to-income multiples amongst underlying borrowers.

CASE STUDY 3   SRM Investment No 1 Limited

Sveriges Bostadsfinansieringsaktiebolag (SBAB) is the Swedish state-owned national housing-finance corporation. Its second-ever securitisation issue was the EUR1 billion SRM Investment No 1 Limited, issued in October 2000. The underlying asset backing was Swedish residential-mortgage loans, with properties being mainly detached and semi-detached single-family properties. The issue was structured and underwritten by Nomura International.

---

[16] Source: ISR, November 2000

As reported in *International Securitisation Report*, the underlying motives behind the deal were that it allowed SBAB to:
- reduce capital allocation, thereby releasing capital for further lending
- remove part of its mortgage loan-book off the balance sheet
- obtain a more diversified source for its funding.

The transaction was structured into the following notes:
- senior class "A1" floating-rate note rated AAA/Aaa by S&P and Moody's, issue size EUR755 million, with a legal maturity date in 2057
- senior class "A2" fixed coupon note, rated AAA/Aaa and denominated in Japanese yen, incorporating a step-up facility, legal maturity 2057; issue size JPY 20 billion
- class "M" floating-rate note rated A/A2, due 2057; issue size EUR20 million
- class "B" floating-rate note, rated BBB/Baa2, issue size EUR10 million.

The yen tranche reflects the targeting of a Japanese domestic investor base. On issue, the class A1 notes paid 26 basis points over euribor. The structure is illustrated in Figure 10.8.

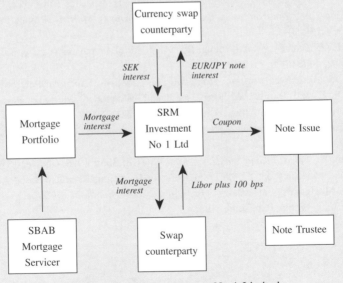

Figure 10.9 SRM Investment No 1 Limited

Selected Bibliography and References

For a good introduction, we recommend the two Fabozzi-edited books, while a good technical introduction is provided in the two articles noted from the June 2000 issue of the *Journal of Fixed Income*. The chapter in Sundaresan (1997), like the rest of his book, is excellent and well worth reading. For a general introduction to the principles of securitisation, see Morris (1990).

Anderson, G., Barber, J. and Chang, C., "Prepayment Risk and the Duration of Default-Free Mortgage-Backed Securities", *Journal of Financial Research* 16, 1993, p.1-9.

Arora, A., Heike, D. and Mattu, R., "Risk and Return in the Mortgage Market: Review and Outlook", *Journal of Fixed Income*, June 2000, p.5-18.

Bear Stearns, *Asset-Backed Securities Special Report*, 5th December 1994.

Bhattacharya, A. and Fabozzi, F. (editors.), *Asset-Backed Securities*, FJF Associates, 1996.

Deacon, J., *Global Securitisation and CDOs*, John Wiley & Sons, 2004

Fabozzi, F., *The Handbook of Mortgage-Backed Securities*, FJF Associates, 2000.

Fabozzi, F. (editor), *The Handbook of Structured Financial Products*, FJF Associates, 1998.

Fabozzi, F. (editor), *Mortgage-Backed Securities: New Strategies, Applications and Research*, Probus Publishing, 1987.

Fabozzi, F. and Jacob, D., *The Handbook of Commercial Mortgage-Backed Securities*, FJF Associates, 1996.

Fabozzi, F., Ramsey, C. and Ramirez, F., *Collateralised Mortgage Obligations*, FJF Associates, 1994.

Hayre, L. and Mohebbi, C., "Mortgage Pass-Through Securities", in Fabozzi, F., (ed), *Advances and Innovations in the Bond and Mortgage Markets*, Probus Publishing, 1989, p.259-304.

Hayre, L., Chaudhary, S. and Young, R., "Anatomy of Prepayments", *Journal of Fixed Income*, June 2000, p.19-49.

Morris, D., *Asset Securitisation: Principles and Practices*, Executive Enterprise, 1990.

Schwartz, E. and Torous, W., "Prepayment and Valuation of Mortgage Pass-Through Securities", *Journal of Business* 15(2), 1992, p.221-240.

Sundaresan, S., *Fixed Income Markets and Their Derivatives*, South-Western Publishing, 1997, Chapter 9.

Tuckman, B., *Fixed Income Securities*, John Wiley & Sons, 1996, Chapter 18Waldman, M. and Modzelewski, S., "A Framework for Evaluating Treasury-Based Adjustable Rate Mortgages", in Fabozzi, F. (editor), *The Handbook of Mortgage-Backed Securities*, Probus Publishing, 1985.

Collateralised Debt Obligations[1]

Introduction

The market in collateralised-bond obligations (CBOs) and collateralised-loan obligations (CLOs), which together make up collateralised-debt obligations (CDOs) is one of the newest and most exciting developments in securitisation. The origins of the market are generally held to be the repackaging of high-yield debt or loans into higher-rated bonds, which began in the late 1980s. Today, there is great diversity in the different CDO transactions, and the market has expanded into Europe and Asia from its origin in the US. Both CBOs and CDOs are notes or securities issued against an underlying collateral of assets, almost invariably a diverse pool of corporate bonds or loans, or a combination of both. A transaction with a corporate- or sovereign-bond asset pool is a CBO, while a CLO is backed by a portfolio of secured and/or unsecured corporate and commercial bank loans. Cash flow CBOs/CDOs fall into two types; these are arbitrage and balance-sheet CDOs. Some analysts also categorize a third variety known as emerging-market CDOs.

A typical CDO structure involves the transfer of credit risk from an underlying asset pool to a special-purpose vehicle and this credit risk is then transferred to investors via the issue of credit-linked notes by the special-purpose vehicle. The objectives behind CDO transactions include:

- Optimisation of returns on regulatory capital by reducing the need for capital to support assets on the balance sheet
- Improvement of return on economic capital by managing risk effectively

---

[1] This chapter was co-authored with Richard Pereira.

- Manage risk (for example, purchasing or transferring credit risk) and balance sheet
- Issue of securities as a means of funding
- Provision of funding for the acquisition of assets
- Increasing funds under management.

Figure 11.1 shows CDO issue volumes in the years to 2003, while Figure 11.2 shows the country of origin of underlying assets during 2003. The "family tree" of CDOs is shown at Figure 11.3. A typical conventional CDO structure is shown in Figure 11.4.

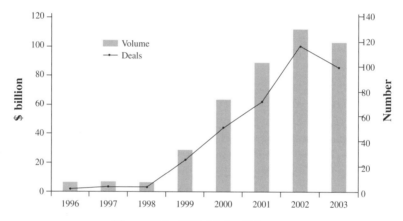

Figure 11.1 CDO Market Volume.
Source: Moody's.

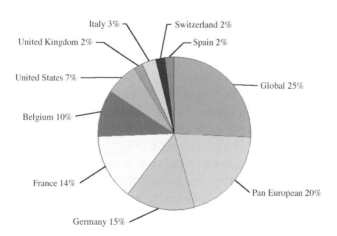

Figure 11.2 Origin of assets

The main distinction between a CLO and CBO is the dominant investment class in the underlying asset pool. With a CLO, the underlying asset pool is a portfolio of bank loans, while a CBO series is issued against an underlying asset pool of a portfolio of bonds. So although they are grouped into a single generic form, there are key differences between CBOs and CLOs. In the first instance, assets such as bank loans have different features to bonds; the analysis of the two will therefore differ. Note also the following:

- loans are less uniform instruments, and their terms vary widely. This includes terms such as interest dates, amortisation schedules, reference rate indices, reset dates, terms to maturity and so on, which affect the analysis of cash flows.
- the legal documentation for loans is less standardised, in part reflecting the observation above, and this calls for more in-depth legal review.
- it is often possible to restructure a loan portfolio to reflect the changed or changing status of borrowers (for example, their ability to service the debt), a flexibility not usually afforded to participants in a CBO.
- the market in bank loans is far less liquid than that in bonds.

These issues, among others, mean the analysis of CBOs often presents considerable differences from that used for CLOs.

This chapter briefly introduces CDOs, describes the motivation for an originator such as a commercial bank, and some of the issues relating to the CDO structures.

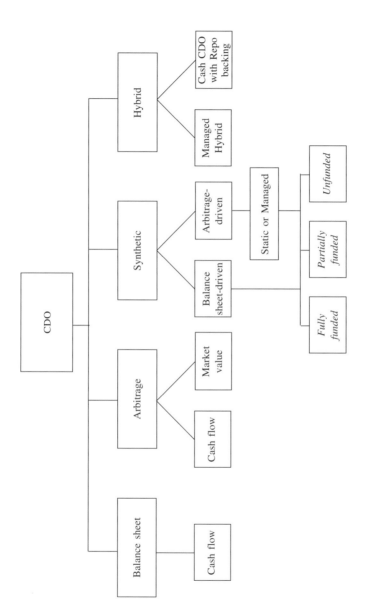

Figure 11.3 The CDO family

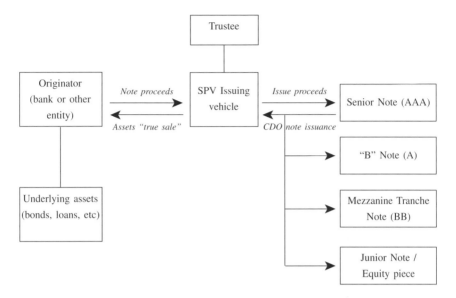

Figure 11.4 Generic Cash flow CDO

Bonds and loans

Until the mid 1990s there was a distinct separation between bonds and loans in the capital market. The key difference was that the latter did not really trade in a liquid secondary market. This factor was a key driver in the origination of CLOs, as banks sought to extract value from and reduce the capital burden of their loan books. The rise and acceptance of CLOs has partly then been behind the development of a secondary market in syndicated loans.

Many loans are now priced, evaluated and traded in a secondary market. Certain syndicated loans can be sold to investors who desire a safer haven than the corporate bond market, or who wish to enter into relative value positions by taking advantage of the spread differential between loans and bonds issued by the same borrower. Syndicated loans are classified as senior debt, so they have a higher priority over corporate bonds in the event of a winding-up of the issuer.

It can be problematic to value a syndicated loan, as it may have a repayment schedule, as well as a floating interest rate that may step up or down depending on changes in (say) the credit rating of the issuer. This is a key issued addressed whenever loans are evaluated for a CLO portfolio.

Bloomberg's YA page can also be used for syndicated loan analysis. Any loan must be found on the system first by typing

LOAN <Go>

which brings up the syndicated bank loan menu function. This includes a loan finder function. Once the loan is found, it can be evaluated using screen YA.

Figure 11.5 shows the page being used to assess a USD loan issued by Singapore Aircraft Leasing, which is part of the Singapore Airlines group. At the time it was evaluated the loan had approximately six years left to maturity, having been issued originally in 1998 at a spread of 70 basis points over Libor.

Figure 11.6 shows the yield analysis function for the same loan, as at 17 March 2004. The screen is split into four parts that include:

- loan information data;
- curve information about the yield curve selected to analyse this loan;
- the calculator which shows the internal rate of return and the current spread over the Libor forward curve ("Z-DM" field).

The Zero-Discount Margin field is the main measure of return on the loan. It shows the current spread on the loan over the Libor forward curve, in this case 71.341 basis points. The evaluation is carried out against the USD swap curve, on a 30/360 and semi-annual basis (the same terms as the loan). The internal rate of return loan is shown to be 1.87%.

The discount margin assumes that that day's Libor is unchanged for the life of the loan (a necessary, but unrealistic, assumption). This spread can be used to compare the return on the loan compared to that on a bond. If there is a similar maturity floating-rate bond available from the same issuer, then the comparison is easily made. Otherwise we can compare the asset swap spread for a fixed-coupon bond. To do that we can call up a similar maturity bond for the same issuer on page ASW on Bloomberg. The ASW page calculates the swap market's value of a fixed-rate bond as a spread over Libor. This spread can be compared to the spread for the loan to assess relative value. At any time that the loan pays a higher spread, it might be deemed an attractive investment compared to the bond, especially since it has a repayment priority on default over the bond.

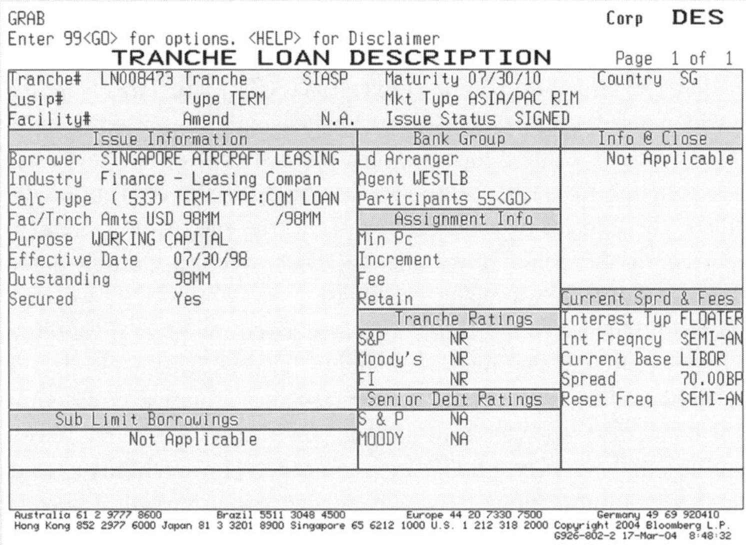

```
GRAB                                                     Corp   DES
Enter 99<GO> for options.  <HELP> for Disclaimer
          TRANCHE  LOAN  DESCRIPTION            Page  1 of  1
Tranche# LN008473 Tranche      SIASP   Maturity 07/30/10   Country  SG
Cusip#            Type TERM             Mkt Type ASIA/PAC RIM
Facility#         Amend        N.A.    Issue Status  SIGNED
          Issue Information              Bank Group          Info @ Close
Borrower  SINGAPORE AIRCRAFT LEASING  Ld Arranger          Not Applicable
Industry  Finance - Leasing Compan    Agent WESTLB
Calc Type  ( 533) TERM-TYPE:COM LOAN  Participants 55<GO>
Fac/Trnch Amts USD 98MM      /98MM       Assignment Info
Purpose  WORKING CAPITAL              Min Pc
Effective Date     07/30/98           Increment
Outstanding        98MM               Fee
Secured            Yes                Retain              Current Sprd & Fees
                                        Tranche Ratings   Interest Typ FLOATER
                                      S&P       NR        Int Freqncy  SEMI-AN
                                      Moody's   NR        Current Base LIBOR
                                      FI        NR        Spread       70.00BP
                                        Senior Debt Ratings Reset Freq  SEMI-AN
      Sub Limit Borrowings            S & P     NA
        Not Applicable                MOODY     NA


Australia 61 2 9777 8600      Brazil 5511 3048 4500      Europe 44 20 7330 7500      Germany 49 69 920410
Hong Kong 852 2977 6000 Japan 81 3 3201 8900 Singapore 65 6212 1000 U.S. 1 212 318 2000 Copyright 2004 Bloomberg L.P.
                                                                  G926-802-2 17-Mar-04  8:48:32
```

Figure 11.5 Loan information data on Bloomberg for loan
issued by Singapore Aircraft Leasing
© Bloomberg L.P. Used with permission

```
GRAB                                                     Corp   YA

               TERM  LOAN  CALCULATOR
SINGAP AIRCRAFT       (SIASP  L  7/30/10)    Not Priced
   Loan  Information   |  Curve  Information

    Tranche#:LN008473      Price Date: 3/17/04  Crv Settle: 3/19/04

  Effective Date: 7/30/98   Curve: S 23 ASK US USD Swaps(30/360,S/A)
      First Cpn: 1/30/99    2<GO> Curve Update
  Next to Last Cpn: 1/30/10    Spread  Scenario
    Maturity Date: 7/30/10   Scenario:                    FLAT
                            3<GO> Scenario Update  4<GO> Scenario List
      Day Count: ACT/360      Calculator
      Month End: Y
  Business Day Adj: 0        Settle: 3/27/04      Floater: 95.7360
     Payment Freq: S  Fix Freq: S  Workout: 7/30/10  Margin Value: 4.2140
                            Price: 99.9500 USD   Avg Life: 6.3427
  Benchmark Index: 6M US LIBOR   Z-DM: 71.341 bp
     Last Reset: 1.214% 1/30/04    DM:  71.11 bp  Sensitivity Analysis
   Current Index: 1.159%          IRR:  1.870            Z-DM    Curve
  Current Spread: 70.00 bp                      Mod Dur: 5.71    0.48
  Current Coupon: 1.914%                           Risk: 5.73    0.48
                                                    BPV: 0.06    0.00
1<GO> Repayment Schedule   5<GO> Projected CashFlows
Australia 61 2 9777 8600      Brazil 5511 3048 4500      Europe 44 20 7330 7500      Germany 49 69 920410
Hong Kong 852 2977 6000 Japan 81 3 3201 8900 Singapore 65 6212 1000 U.S. 1 212 318 2000 Copyright 2004 Bloomberg L.P.
                                                                  G926-802-2 17-Mar-04  9:02:45
```

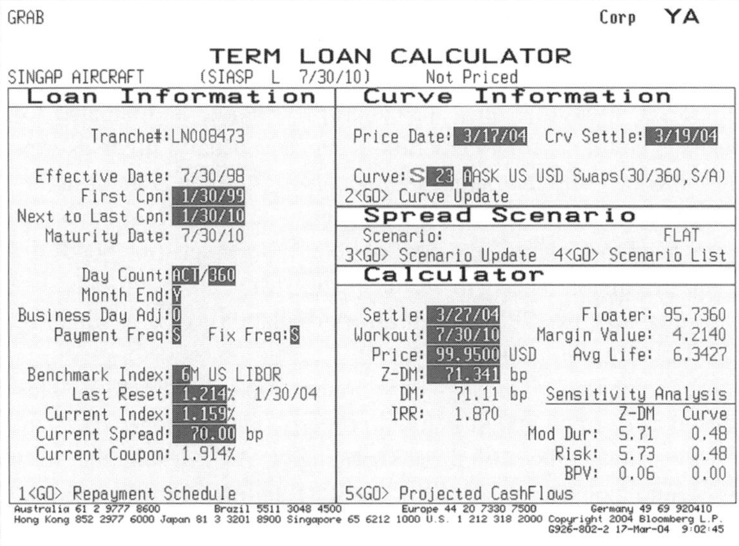

Figure 11.6 Bloomberg page YA used to evaluate
the Singapore Aircraft Leasing syndicated loan, as at 17 March 2004
© Bloomberg L.P. Used with permission

CDO structures

CDO structures are classified into conventional CDO structures and synthetic CDO structures. While conventional CDO structures were the first to be widely used, synthetic CLOs have increasingly been used from the late 1990s onwards. The difference between these structures lies in the method of risk transfer from the originator to the SPV. In conventional CDO structures, the transfer of assets, known as a true sale, is how credit risk is transferred to the SPV. In synthetic CDO structures, credit-derivative instruments are used to transfer credit risk.

In practice, the two structures are categorized by the motivation behind their issue. There are two main motivations: issuer- or balance-sheet-driven transactions and investor-driven or market-value arbitrage transactions. To date, balance-sheet-driven transactions have been the main reason for structuring the majority of CDOs in Europe. However, investor-driven arbitrage CDO transactions have experienced strong growth as investment managers increase funds under management and release value through management expertise of the underlying asset portfolio.

The two structures are described in more detail below.

Conventional CDO structure

Conventional collateralised-debt obligations (CDOs) issue notes from a special-purpose vehicle (SPV) to investors. Special-purpose vehicles are created to enable the effective transfer of risk from the originator. Most SPVs are set up so that they are bankruptcy-remote and isolated from the originator's credit risk. The creation of an SPV usually involves a nominal amount of equity and the main funding comes from the issue of notes. SPVs may be set up and registered in a tax haven. The funds from the issue of the notes are used to "acquire" the pool of underlying assets (the bonds or loans) from the originator. This will result in the "true sale" of the assets to the SPV. In this way, the SPV has an asset-and-liability profile which must be managed during the term of the CDO.

The ownership of the assets is transferred into the SPV. This asset transfer, if performed and structured properly, may remove assets from the regulatory balance sheet of a bank originator. As a result, the securitised assets would not be included in the calculation of capital ratios. This provides regulatory-capital relief and is the main motivation for some of the CDO structures in the market today.

The typical liability structure would include a senior tranche rated in the Aaa/Aa category, a junior tranche rated in the Ba category and an un-rated equity tranche. The equity tranche is the most risky, as first losses in the underlying portfolio are absorbed by the equity tranche. For this reason, the equity tranche is often referred to as the "first-loss" tranche. The losses on the notes are said to "indemnify" the SPV.

In the case of bank CLOs, the bank will continue to service the loans in the portfolio and usually also retains the first-loss interest.

Structuring a conventional CDO may give rise to significant other issues. The transfer of assets into the SPV in practice may have adverse tax, legal and regulatory implications. The impact will depend on the jurisdiction in which the transfer of assets takes place and the detailed legislation of that jurisdiction. Another practical issue is that the conventional CDO is a funded transaction as the originator receives cash. However, if the originator's main intention is to transfer credit risk or to acquire protection for credit risk, then the conventional CDO structure introduces reinvestment risk, as the cash received would need to be reinvested in other assets.

The SPV which issues the notes is generally an offshore bankruptcy-remote entity to isolate the underlying assets from the default risk of the originator. In most structures, the transfer of credit risk to the investors is via the notes issued by the SPV. The return to investors in the issued notes will be dependent on the performance of the underlying asset pool.

Credit enhancement is provided via subordination (prioritization of cash-flow payments to investors) of the tranches issued by the SPV. However, in addition to a multi-tranche structure, the bank may also use other mechanisms to credit-enhance the senior notes. An example might include credit insurance on the underlying portfolio, known as a credit wrap, and the use of reserve accounts which assume a loss before the equity tranche.

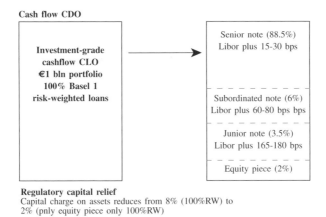

Figure 11.7 Conventional CDO hypothetical mechanics

Synthetic CDO structure

In a synthetic CDO, no transfer of assets takes place; therefore, the underlying reference pool of assets remains on the balance sheet of the originator. The originator buys credit protection from the SPV by entering into a credit-default swap with the SPV and this covers any losses in the underlying asset pool on the originator's balance sheet.[2] In this way the credit-default swap transfers the credit risk of the underlying asset portfolio to the SPV and this may allow the bank to release regulatory and economic capital, if the offset to the credit risk of the bank is recognized by its regulatory authority. The originator bank pays a premium, typically in the form of a regular fee, to the SPV for the credit protection and this contributes to the extra return to the investors for assuming the credit risk.

The SPV issues notes to investors, and the funds received are used to purchase high-quality (AAA) liquid securities which act as collateral. Examples of the type of collateral purchased include US Treasuries and triple-A rated German bonds such as Pfandbriefe. The collateral will provide the "Libor-related" interest and principal cash flows into the SPV and the credit-default swap premium pays the additional credit spread on the notes. The notes issued are linked to the credit risk of the portfolio via the credit-default swap and to the credit-derivative counterparty. Usually, the notes issued and the credit-default swap will have the same term to maturity. The notes are therefore credit linked.

Any mismatch between the cash flows on the collateral and the payments on the issued notes – for example, fixed receipts on the collateral versus floating payments on the notes issued – are usually managed by the use of a swap agreement between the SPV and a swap counterparty. The swap counterparty may also sell other derivative instruments, such as interest-rate caps, to the SPV to manage possible cash-flow risk. The management of the risk exposure in a SPV requires careful attention since the risk profile of the SPV is an important factor that may impact on the credit risk of notes issued. The value of notes issued by the SPV to the investors will be equivalent to the credit protection it is offering on the reference pool of assets in an "unleveraged" transaction. For example, if the credit-default swap is on a nominal of $300 million, then the nominal value of the notes issued will be $300 million.

The payout from the credit-default swap will take place upon the occurrence of a credit event. A credit event is usually defined as bankruptcy

---

[2] See Chapters 17 and 18 for discussion of credit derivatives.

or failure to pay of the underlying credit. The "failure to pay" definition may include a period of grace so that default is not triggered if the payment is delayed for technical reasons such as information technology issues. A precise definition of the credit event is important. Investors should understand the definition, as it may affect the return on the notes. The ISDA definitions for a credit-derivative transaction refer to "restructuring" as a credit event. Whether this will be included in the credit definitions of default swaps in synthetic CDO transactions will depend on whether the inclusion would affect the regulatory-capital relief treatment of the underlying asset pool.

If a credit event occurs, then the SPV would usually make a payout of the cash amount equal to the par value of the underlying assets less the post-default price. The alternative (which is less common) is for the SPV to physically settle the credit-default swap payment, by purchasing the defaulted assets and paying par value. The credit loss is then passed onto the notes according to the priority of the notes.

The main motivation behind the issue of synthetic CDO structures remains the desire to hedge or transfer credit risk, in order to achieve regulatory-capital relief or to effectively obtain credit protection on an underlying asset pool.

The generic hypothetic CDO structure is shown at Figure 11.8. Further details on synthetic CDOs are given in Chapter 12.

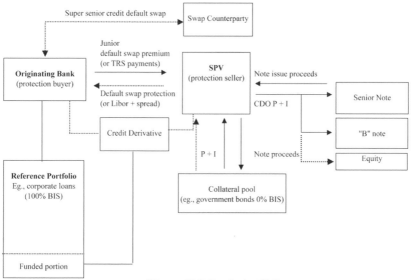

Figure 11.8 Synthetic CLO

Motivation behind CDO issue

Balance-sheet-driven transactions

In a balance-sheet CDO, the motivation for the originator is usually to obtain capital relief through the transfer of credit risk on the pool of underlying assets. The transaction is intended to obtain off-balance-sheet treatment for existing on-balance-sheet assets to which bank capital has been allocated. The regulatory off-balance-sheet treatment enables an originator bank to manage capital constraints and to improve the return on capital for the bank.

The originators of bank balance-sheet CLOs are mainly commercial banks. The underlying asset pool may include commercial loans, both secured and unsecured, guarantees and revolving credits. The originator of the underlying assets usually acts as investment advisor so as to maintain the quality of the underlying asset pool. Although there is usually no trading intention for the underlying asset pool, over the life of the structure there may be changes, such as substitutions or replenishments to the underlying asset pool. A form of protection to the note holders from these changes is usually that the quality of the underlying pool of assets does not significantly deteriorate. This may be via the maintenance of an average credit quality of the asset pool. Such a restriction is often required by the rating agencies.

The equity tranche in a CDO structure is commonly held by the originator for the following reasons:

- the bank has detailed information on the loans which will allow it to effectively manage the risk it retains.
- the bank retains economic interest in the performance of the loan portfolio and remains motivated to service the asset pool.
- the return required by a potential purchaser of the equity tranche may be too high, and this tranche may therefore be difficult to place if the risk/reward profile is not attractive to investors.

In some cases, the lowest-rated debt tranche is also held by the originator.

Investor-driven arbitrage transactions

In an arbitrage CDO, the underlying asset pool is more actively managed. The investment advisor is usually the manager of the CDO. The type of structure is driven by the opportunity to actively manage the portfolio with the intention of generating arbitrage profits from the spread differential between the investment- and sub-investment-grade markets. The underlying asset pool includes investments which not only provide investment income but may provide the opportunity to generate value from active trading strategies. The opportunity to generate arbitrage profits is often dependent on the quality and expertise of the manager of the CDO.

The underlying assets may be existing positions that are being managed or may be acquired for the CDO. In practice, when structuring the transaction the profitability of the transaction will depend on factors such as:

- the required return to the note-holders of the issued tranches;
- the portfolio return of the underlying asset pool; and
- the expenses (for example, management fee) of managing the SPV.

If the underlying portfolio performs well and the loss-in-the-event-of-default profile is lower than expected, due to lower than expected default levels and higher levels of recovery, the required return to investors in the tranches of the CDO will be achieved and the return to the equity holder will be higher than expected. However, if the underlying portfolio performs poorly and the loss in the event of default is higher than expected (due to higher-than-expected default levels and lower levels of recovery rate, perhaps due to adverse economic conditions), then the return on the tranches issued will be lower than expected. Poor investment-management performance will also have an adverse impact on the return to investors.

Fund managers use arbitrage CDOs in higher-yielding markets since the CDO structure may allow the manager to achieve a large size of funds under management for a comparatively small level of equity. This has been used effectively in the US in the past few years. The objective is to set up the CDO so that the returns produced by the underlying pool of high-yielding assets will be enough to pay off investors and provide the originator/fund manager with a profit from the management fee and the return on the equity tranche.

Analysis and evaluation

Here, we introduce a number of important factors that are relevant when analysing, evaluating or rating a CDO. The list is not an exhaustive one; rather, we address some of the basic concepts.

Portfolio characteristics

Credit quality

The credit quality of the underlying asset pool is critical as this is a source of credit risk in the structure. It is common to allocate an average rating to the initial reference asset pool. A constraint in the structuring of the transaction may be that any future changes to the asset pool that the structure allows should not reduce the average rating below the initial rating. The analysis of the portfolio's credit and the possible variability of the credit quality is used to determine the default frequency and the loss rates which may be experienced by the underlying asset pool. In some cases, the originator's internal credit-scoring system is a key part of the rating process. In particular, for un-rated assets the rating process should involve a mapping process between the internal rating system and the agency's rating system to determine accuracy.

Diversity

The level of diversity within the reference portfolio directly influences the level of credit risk in the portfolio. Broadly, we would expect that the greater the level of diversification, the lower the level of credit risk. Diversity may be determined by considering concentrations by industry group, obligor and sovereign country. The level of diversity in the portfolio may be quantified by attributing a single diversity score to reflect the level of diversification of the underlying asset pool.

Broadly, the diversity score is a weighted-average credit score for a portfolio of credit exposures. The marginal score allocated to each marginal credit exposure in the underlying asset pool depends on the existing credit portfolio. For example, if the portfolio has a concentration in a category – for example, in an industry group – the marginal score attributed to the marginal credit is reduced to reflect this concentration (or lack of diversity). This has the effect that a higher diversity score is attributed to an asset pool where the range of credit exposure is wide. The higher the score, the better the level of diversification.

A constraint may be placed on the level of change in the diversity as a result of a change to the underlying asset pool. For example, a minimum required diversity score for a transaction may need to be maintained.

Cash-flow analysis and stress testing

The cash-flow profile of a CDO structure depends on the following issues:
- the spread between the interest earned on the loans/collateral and the coupon paid on the securities issued by the CDO
- the impact of default events – for example, default frequency and severity (level of recovery rates) in the underlying asset pool – and the impact of losses on the principal of investors

- the principal repayment profile/expected amortisation
- the contingent payments in the event of default under any the credit-default swap which may be used to transfer credit risk from the originator to another party (such as the SPV or an OECD bank)
- contingent cash flows on any credit wrap or credit insurance on the underlying asset pool;
- cash-flows receivable/payable with the hedge counterparty; for example, under swap agreements or derivative contracts
- premium received from the credit-default swap counterparty
- fees and expenses.

The sensitivity of these cash flows is tested to obtain an understanding of the impact on the cash-flow profile under stressed and normal scenarios. The relevant stress scenarios that are tested are dependent on the underlying asset pool.

Originator's credit quality

The impact of the credit quality of the originator on the rating of the notes issued is dependent upon the structure. For example, where the underlying assets are transferred to the SPV (which is bankruptcy-remote) from the originator, the credit quality of the CDO notes is only dependent on the portfolio performance and the credit enhancement. The credit performance of the CDO notes can be said to be "de-linked" from the credit quality of the originator.

However, in some structures the underlying asset pool remains on the balance sheet of the originator; for instance, as with credit-linked CDOs, as shown in Figure 11.9. In this case, the notes issued by the SPV remain "linked" to the credit of the originator.

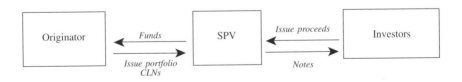

Figure 11.9 Credit linked CDO

Here, an investor in the CDO has exposure to both the credit quality of the bank and the portfolio performance. The rating of the credit-linked CDO is capped by the rating of the originator, because payment of interest and principal depends on the originator's ability to pay.

However, for the senior tranches of a synthetic de-linked CDO, the portfolio may remain on the originator's balance sheet, but the senior tranches may be collateralised and de-linked from the bank's rating by using AAA-rated collateral and default swaps. The final rating is influenced by the credit rating of the default-swap provider, the extent to which the cash flows to investors are exposed to the risk of default by the originator.

Operational aspects

In market-value transactions, the abilities of the manager are a key aspect to consider, since the performance of the underlying portfolio is critical to the success of the structure. The review of the credit-approval and monitoring process of the originator is another factor which may provide further comfort on the integrity and quality of the underlying asset portfolio. Better credit assessment and monitoring processes will lead to higher levels of comfort.

Review of credit-enhancement mechanisms

Credit enhancement may include the use of reserve accounts, subordinated tranches, credit wraps and liquidity facilities. These are briefly defined below. The impact of any credit-enhancement methods should be considered and understood. This will usually be observed via stress scenarios, which are developed to determine the impact on the cash flows.

Subordination

The rights and priority of each tranche to interest and principal is set out in the offering circular for the issue. This is a detailed description of the notes, together with the legal structure. The cash flows are allocated according to priority of the notes. Typically, fees and expenses are paid first. The most senior tranches are then serviced, followed by the junior tranches and, finally, the equity tranche. The method by which excess cash flows can be allocated to remaining subordinated tranches is sometimes referred to as a cash-flow *waterfall*. This is illustrated at Figure 11.10.

Credit wrap

This is a credit protection of a debt instrument by an insurer or bank to improve the credit quality of the portfolio.

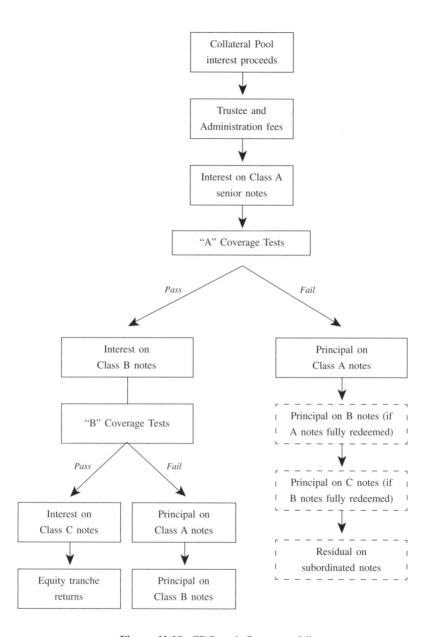

Figure 11.10 CDO cash flow waterfall

Reserve accounts

Reserve accounts are cash reserves set up at the outset from note proceeds, which provide first-loss protection to investors. Such surplus funds are usually invested by the servicing agent or specialised cash-management provider.

Liquidity facility

A liquidity facility may exist to ensure that short-term funding is available to pay any interest or principal obligations on the notes if there is a temporary cash shortfall.

Legal structure of the transaction

A typical CDO structure is described in a number of legal agreements. For example, the offering circular is the legal document that presents the transaction in detail to investors.

The various legal agreements formalise the roles played in the CDO structure by the various counterparties to the deal. The documentation includes:

- Trustee agreements: the provision of administrative duties and maintenance of books and records
- Manager/servicer agreement: describes management of the underlying portfolio and provides market expertise
- Sale agreement or credit-default swap agreements used to transfer credit risk
- Hedging agreements: for example, interest-rate or cross-currency swaps and other derivative contracts
- Guarantees or insurance: for example, credit wraps on the underlying asset pool.

Prior to the closure of the deal, the SPV incorporation documents are also reviewed to ensure that it is bankruptcy-remote and that it is established in a tax-neutral jurisdiction.

Expected loss

The rating process for each transaction involves a detailed analysis of the CDO structure, including the points noted above. However, the actual process of assigning a rating to the notes issued in the CDO will include a quantitative assessment. Often this is based on the expected loss (EL) to note holders, which is an important statistic when deciding on the quality of a tranche.

The expected loss may be defined as:

$$EL_x = \sum_x P*L_x \tag{11.1}$$

where

L_x is the loss on the notes under scenario 'x'
P_x is the probability of the scenario 'x' occurring.

The calculated expected-loss statistic will be mapped to a table of ratings and their corresponding expected losses. In this way, the rating can be allocated to each tranche.

The loss to note holders is determined by considering the impact of credit losses on the cash flows to note holders which would occur under the various possible scenarios. This would involve the allocation of any credit loss to the various tranches in issue.

The cash flows to the note holders depend on whether or not a default has occurred, and the size of the loss in the event of default. The severity of the loss will depend on the par value of the note less the recovery rate. The calculated probability of default may be inferred from the rating of the underlying credit exposures. In practice, the calculation of the expected loss may be based on Monte Carlo simulation techniques in which thousands of scenarios and cash flows are simulated. This requires sophisticated computational models.

The expected losses on the tranches should be in line with the level of subordination. The expected losses on the tranche will be a key factor in the process of assigning a credit rating to the tranche. The credit rating of the tranche is a key determinant in the ultimate pricing and marketability of the tranche.

Case study: H2 Finance Ltd.[3]

To conclude this discussion of CDOs we describe a structure that incorporates elements of previous transactions. H2 Finance Limited is an arbitrage CDO of ABS, that is, a cash CDO with underlying assets of asset-backed securities. The underlying securities are purchased through the issuance of both long-dated notes and short-term liabilities. As such it

---

[3] The author thanks Serj Walia at KBC Financial Products in London for assistance with providing information for this section.

combines elements of a cash CDO as well as investment entities known as Structured Investment Vehicles (SIVs).[4] H" Finance is the name of the SPV, a private company with limited liability incorporated in the Cayman Islands. As with other CDO SPVs, it was incorporated on behalf of the sponsor, Wharton Asset Management, for the sole purpose of acquiring the portfolio and issuing notes and short-term liabilities.

An innovative aspect of this transaction is the repo feature. The majority of the portfolio is financed via a short-term repo arrangement with a number of counterparties, with the portfolio itself acting as collateral for the repo. As such, H" issues two types of liabilities:

- medium-term tranched notes;
- repo agreements using eligible collateral.

The terms of the structure are shown below.

Name	H2 Finance Ltd.
	€105 million senior secured floating-rate notes
Sponsor and manager	Wharton Asset Management Bermuda Ltd
Arranger and underwriter	Nomura International
Trustee	Deutsche Trustee Co. Ltd.
Pay agent, account bank, and Administrator	Deutsche Bank AG, London
Custodian	HSBC Bank plc
Repo counterparties	Multiple counterparties rated at A-1 or above by S&P
Closing date	March 2004

The structure is shown at Figure 11.11, while Table 11.1 shows the note tranching.

H2 Finance is a CDO of high-rated ABS securities. It is fully-funded, that is the complete value of the portfolio is purchased through the issue of notes and via the repo facility. The underlying portfolio has an average maturity of 3.5 years and weighted-average rating of AAA from S&P, so it a high-quality portfolio.

---

[4] We have not considered SIVs in this book. They are essentially CDOs that issue both AB-CP and MTNs. There is much more to them that that of course, but space does not permit a discussion here.

Repo arrangement

The repo facility in H2 Finance is one of more unusual features of the transaction. The majority of securities purchased by H2 Finance are repo'd out to repo counterparties. Counterparties pay the market value of the securities to H2 Finance minus the haircut, which is around 1% of the purchase price.[5] Repo trades are put on for a one-year maturity, at a rate of Libor flat.

During the term of the trade, variation margin will be called if the value of the securities plus the margin level drops outside the 1% threshold. Margin payments are paid out of the cash reserve account that is held by the CDO account bank on behalf of the vehicle. On repo maturity date, the securities are rolled over in a new repo, at the prevailing market price for the securities.

Repo securities are ABS bonds, made up of credit card, consumer loans, auto loans, trade receivables, whole business, sovereign and public sector ABS, RMBS and CMBS bonds. A minimum of 95% of the securities must be rated at AAA. The portfolio must also meet other specified requirements, laid out by S&P as part of its criteria for rating the vehicle liabilities. Among these are:

- a maximum portfolio amount of €1.5 billion;
- only a maximum of 10% of securities have coupon frequencies of greater than quarterly.

In addition no CDO notes or aviation securities (aircraft leasing ABS, etc) are allowed in the portfolio.

Portfolio management

The portfolio is actively managed by the manager, Wharton Asset Management Bermuda Ltd. The manager is permitted to sell and repurchase portfolio securities, in accordance with specified criteria, during the reinvestment period for the deal. It is also permitted to sell and substitute portfolio securities under the following conditions:

- if the security is in default;
- if the security is deemed a credit risk;

---

[5] This is a very low level of haircut and reflects the quality of the collateral. Usual haircut levels for repo of ABS assets ranges from 3% to 15% depending on collateral quality; see chapter 6 in this book or the author's book *The Global Repo Markets* (Wiley 2004).

- if the security is rated below AA- and the amount of securities below AAA exceeds the 5% level;
- if the security is rated A or below.

Under these circumstances the manager may bring in replacement assets of acceptable quality.

The ability of the asset manager to manage the CDO is what will attract investors to the notes. The D note holder, in particular, is expecting the vehicle to generate excess spread on its portfolio, after allowing for vehicle liabilities, that will be an attractive return for its investment. The rated note investors are attracted to the risk/return profile of the notes, which, given the high quality of the underlying assets, presents a high return for comparatively low risk.

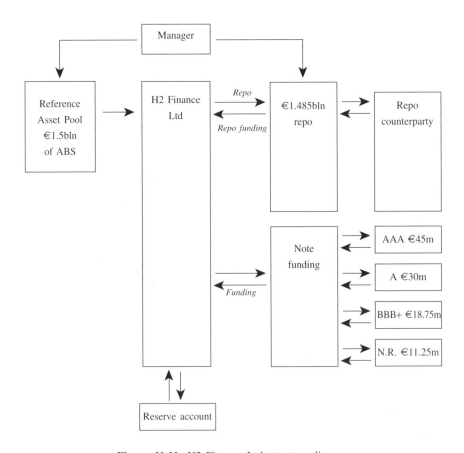

Figure 11.11 H2 Finance Ltd structure diagram

Class	Rating	Nominal amount (m)	Weighted-average life (years)	Libor spread (bps)	Legal final maturity
Senior Repo Programme	A-1+	1,485.00	n/a	0	2052
A	AAA	45.00	5.4	22	2052
B	AA	30.00	6.7	40	2052
C	BBB+	18.75	7.1	120	2052
D	NR	11.25	n/a	Excess	2052

Table 11.1 H2 Finance Ltd note tranching
Source: Standard & Poor's. Reproduced with permission.

Selected Bibliography and References

Goodman, L., Fabozzi, F., *Collaterised Debt Obligation*, John Wiley 2003.
Gregory, J., *Credit Derivatives: The Definitive Guide*, RISK Publishing 2003

12

Structured Credit Products

The previous chapter was a brief introduction to the concept of the collateralised-debt obligation, a progressive development of well-established securitisation techniques. This chapter is an analysis of the synthetic collateralised-debt obligation, or collateralised-synthetic obligation. We focus on the key drivers of this type of instrument, from both an issuer's and an investor's point of view, before assessing the mechanics of the structures themselves. This takes the form of a case study-type review of two innovative transactions.

Readers may wish to familarise themselves on credit derivatives first, covered in chapters 17 and 18.

The synthetic CDO

Synthetic CDOs were introduced to meet differing needs of originators, where credit-risk transfer is of more importance than funding considerations. Compared with conventional cash-flow deals, which feature an actual transfer of ownership or true sale of the underlying assets to a separately incorporated legal entity, a synthetic securitisation structure is engineered so that the credit risk of the assets is transferred by the sponsor or originator of the transaction, from itself, to the investors by means of credit derivative instruments. The originator is therefore the credit-protection buyer and investors are the credit-protection sellers. This credit-risk transfer may be undertaken either directly or via an SPV. Using this approach, underlying or reference assets are not necessarily moved off the originator's balance sheet, so it is adopted whenever the primary objective is to achieve risk transfer rather than balance-sheet funding. The synthetic structure enables removal of credit exposure without asset transfer, so may be preferred for risk management and regulatory-capital relief purposes. For banking institutions, it also enables loan risk to be transferred without selling the loans themselves, thereby allowing customer relationships to remain unaffected.

Assessing the genesis of the synthetic CDO

The original cash-flow-style CDO was a tool for intermediation. In this respect, it can be viewed as a (mini-) bank, albeit a more efficient tool for intermediation than a bank. Where a CDO-type structure differs from a bank is in the composition of its asset pool: unlike a bank, it's asset pool is not diverse, but will have been tailored to meet the specific requirements of both the originator and the customer (investor). It is this tailoring that generates the economic efficiencies of the CDO. In an institutional scenario, as exists in a bank, assets are, in effect, priced at their lowest common denominator. Hence, a bank that had 10% of its assets held in the form of emerging-market debt would be priced at a lower value than an equivalent institution that did not hold such risky assets. The CDO-structure's liabilities will also be more tailored to specific needs, with a precise mix of equity holders, AAA-liabilities and so on.

Thus far, then, we may view the CDO-type entity as being similar to a banking institution and a tool for the intermediation of risk. A synthetic CDO may be viewed in similar terms, but in its case the analogy is more akin to that of an insurance company than a bank. This reflects the separation of funding from credit risk that is facilitated by the synthetic approach, and the resulting ability to price pure credit – a risk-management mechanism that is analogous to how an insurance company operates in comparison to a bank. The investors in a synthetic CDO do not purchase the assets that are referenced in a vehicle; they merely wish an economic exposure to it. This is made possible through the use of credit derivatives in the CDO structure.

Combining securitisation technology with credit derivatives into synthetic structures, was particularly suited to the European market, with its myriad of legal and securitisation jurisdictions. The traditional method of securitisation, which involves selling assets into a special-purpose vehicle and is used for balance-sheet and risk-management purposes, was seen as being less efficient than it had proved in the North American market. This was due to the differing circumstances prevailing in each market:

- In the US market, commercial banks were traditionally lower-rated than their counterparts in Europe. Hence, the funding element of a cash-flow securitisation was a key motivating factor behind a deal, as the originator could secure lower funding costs by means of the securitisation.

- European banks, being higher-rated than US banks, had less need of the funding side in a securitisation deal – compared to US banks, they obtained a greater share of their funding from their retail customer base. A significant portion of their funding was obtained at Libor-minus, compared to the Libor-flat funding of US banks.

So while European banks had an interest in wanting to transfer risk from their balance sheet, they had less need of the funding associated with a traditional securitisation. A cash-flow CDO would not be as economic for originators in the European market because they did not have a need for funding, and so this approach had little or no benefit for them. However, banks still had a requirement to reduce regulatory-capital requirements and transfer-credit risk. This led to the first static balance-sheet synthetic CDO, known as BISTRO and originated by JPMorgan in 1997.

The first synthetic CDOs were balance-sheet-driven: banks structured deals for regulatory-capital management purposes. These deals reflected a desire by banks to shift their credit risk and, by so doing, manage capital more efficiently. Later deals followed an arbitrage model: they were originated by fund managers, who were recognized by investors as being more specialised at managing risk. Hence, the "second generation" of CDO structures, which reflected the comparative advantage generated as insurance companies were able to split up an overall "pool" of risk and break this into a separate pieces, which were tailored to specific investor preferences. Compared to cash-flow structures, synthetic structures separate the risk-transfer element from the funding element. This mirrors what occurred with interest-rate swaps shortly after these were introduced in the early 1980s,. Interest-rate swaps also split the interest-rate risk from the funding risk, as they were off-balance-sheet instruments with no exchange of principal. This is the same case with credit derivatives and is precisely what has also happened in the credit-derivatives market.

Deal motivations

Differences between synthetic and cash CDOs are perhaps best reflected in the different cost-benefit economics of issuing each type. The motivations behind the issue of each type usually also differ. A synthetic CDO can be seen as being constructed out of the following:

- a short position in a credit-default swap (bought protection), by which the sponsor transfers its portfolio credit risk to the issuer
- a long position in a portfolio of bonds or loans, the cash flow from which enables the sponsor to pay liabilities of overlying notes.

The originators of the first synthetic deals were banks who wished to manage the credit-risk exposure of their loan books without having to resort to the administrative burden of true-sale cash securitisation. Such deals are a natural progression in the development of credit-derivative structures, with single-name credit-default swaps being replaced by portfolio default swaps. Synthetic CDOs can be "de-linked" from the sponsoring institution, so that investors do not have any credit exposure to the sponsor itself. The first deals were introduced (in 1998) at a time when widening credit spreads and the worsening of credit quality among originating firms meant that investors were sellers of cash CDOs which had retained a credit linkage to the sponsor. A synthetic arrangement also means that the credit risk of assets that are otherwise not suited to conventional securitisation may be transferred, while assets are retained on the balance sheet. Such assets include bank guarantees, letters of credit, or cash loans that have some legal or other restriction against being securitised. For this reason, synthetic deals are more appropriate for assets that are described under multiple legal jurisdictions.

The economic advantage of issuing a synthetic rather than a cash CDO can be significant. Put simply, the net benefit to the originator is the gain in regulatory capital cost, minus the cost of paying for credit protection on the credit-default swap side. In a partially funded structure, which we describe shortly, a sponsoring bank will obtain full capital relief when note proceeds are invested in 0% risk-weighted collateral such as Treasuries or gilts. The portfolio credit default swap portion will carry a 20% risk weighting.[1] In fact, a moment's thought should make clear to us that a synthetic deal would be cheaper: where credit default swaps are used, the sponsor pays a basis-point fee, which for AAA security might be in the range 10–30 bps, depending on the stage of the credit cycle. In a cash structure where bonds are issued, the cost to the sponsor would be the benchmark yield plus the credit spread, which would be considerably higher than the default-swap premium. This is illustrated in the example shown in Figure 12.1, where we assume certain spreads and premiums in comparing a partially funded synthetic deal with a cash deal. The assumptions are:

- that the super-senior credit-swap cost is 15 bps, and carries a 20% risk weighting
- the equity piece retains a 100% risk-weighting
- the synthetic CDO invests note proceeds in sovereign collateral that pays sub-Libor.

---

[1] This is as long as the counterparty is an OECD bank, which is invariably the case.

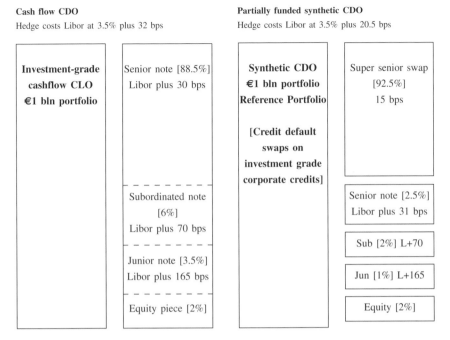

Cash flow CDO
Hedge costs Libor at 3.5% plus 32 bps

Partially funded synthetic CDO
Hedge costs Libor at 3.5% plus 20.5 bps

Regulatory capital relief
Cash CDO
Capital charge on assets reduces from 8% (100%RW) to 2% (equity piece only now 100% RW)
Regulatory capital relief is 6%.

Synthetic CDO
Capital charge on assets reduces from 8% (100%RW) to 3.48% (equity piece plus super senior swap at 20% RW)
Regulatory capital relief is 4.52%.

Figure12.1 Hypothetical generic cash flow CDO and synthetic CDO comparative deal economics

Synthetic deals can be *unfunded, partially funded* or *fully funded*. An unfunded CDO would be composed wholly of credit-default swaps, while fully funded structures would be arranged so that the entire credit risk of the reference portfolio was transferred through the issue of credit-linked notes. We discuss these shortly.

Within the Asian market, static synthetic balance-sheet CDOs are the most common structure. The reasons that banks originate them are two-fold:

• *capital relief*: banks can obtain regulatory-capital relief by transferring lower-yield corporate credit risk such as corporate bank loans off their balance sheet. Under Basel I rules, all corporate debt carries an identical

100% risk-weighting. Therefore, with banks having to assign 8% of capital for such loans, higher-rated (and hence lower-yielding) corporate assets will require the same amount of capital but will generate a lower return on that capital. A bank may wish to transfer such higher-rated, lower-yield assets from its balance sheet, and this can be achieved via a CDO transaction. The capital requirements for a synthetic CDO are lower than for corporate assets. For example, the funded segment of the deal wouldl be supported by high-quality collateral such as government bonds and, via a repo arrangement with an OECD bank, would carry a 20% risk weighting, as does the super-senior element.

• *transfer of credit risk*: the cost of servicing a fully funded CDO, and the premium payable on the associated credit-default swap, can be prohibitive. With a partially funded structure, the issue amount is typically a relatively small share of the asset portfolio. This lowers substantially the default swap premium. Also, as the CDO investors suffer the first-loss element of the portfolio, the super-senior default swap can be entered into at a considerably lower cost than that on a fully funded CDO.

Deal mechanics

A synthetic CDO is so called because the transfer of credit risk is achieved "synthetically" via a credit derivative, rather than by a "true sale" to an SPV. Thus, in a synthetic CDO, the credit risk of the underlying loans or bonds is transferred to the SPV using credit-default swaps and/or total-return swaps (TRS). However, the assets themselves are not legally transferred to the SPV, and they remain on the originator's balance sheet. Using a synthetic CDO, the originator can obtain regulatory-capital relief[2] and manage the credit risk on its balance sheet, but will not be receiving any funding. In other words, a synthetic CDO structure enables originators to separate credit-risk exposure and asset-funding requirements. The credit risk of the asset portfolio, now known as the reference portfolio, is transferred, directly or to an SPV, through credit derivatives. The most common credit derivative contracts used are credit-default swaps. A portion of the credit risk may be sold on as credit-linked notes. Typically a large majority of the credit risk is transferred via a "super-senior" credit-default swap,[3] which is dealt with a

---

[2] This is because reference assets that are protected by credit-derivative contracts, and which remain on the balance sheet, will, under Basel rules, attract a lower regulatory capital charge.

[3] So called because the swap is ahead of the most senior of any funded (note) portion, which latter being "senior" means the swap must be "super-senior". This super-senior swap represents catastrophe risk protection, as it statistically highly unlikely to experience default.

swap counterparty but usually sold to monoline insurance companies at a significantly lower spread over Libor than the senior AAA-rated tranche of cash-flow CDOs. This is a key attraction of synthetic deals for originators. Most deals are structured with mezzanine notes sold to a wider set of investors, the proceeds of which are invested in risk-free collateral such as Treasury bonds or Pfandbriefe securities. The most junior note, known as the "first-loss" piece, may be retained by the originator. When a credit event occurs among the reference assets, the originating bank receives funds remaining from the collateral after they have been used to pay the principal on the issued notes, less the value of the junior note.

A generic synthetic-CDO structure is shown at figure 12.2. In this generic structure, the credit risk of the reference assets is transferred to the issuer SPV and ultimately the investors, by means of the credit-default swap and an issue of credit-linked notes. In the default-swap arrangement, the risk transfer is undertaken in return for the swap premium, which is then paid to investors by the issuer. The note issue in invested in risk-free collateral rather than passed on to the originator, in order to de-link the credit ratings of the notes from the rating of the originator. If the collateral pool was not established, a downgrade of the sponsor could result in a downgrade of the issued notes. Investors in the notes expose themselves to the credit risk of the reference assets, and if there are no credit events they will earn returns at least the equal of the collateral assets and the default-swap premium. If the notes are credit-linked, they will also earn excess returns based on the performance of the reference portfolio. If there are credit events, the issuer will deliver the assets to the swap counterparty and will pay the nominal value of the assets to the originator out of the collateral pool. Credit-default swaps are unfunded credit derivatives, while CLNs are funded credit derivatives where the protection seller (the investors) funds the value of the reference assets up front, and will receive a reduced return of principal on occurrence of a credit event.

Funding mechanics

As the super-senior piece in a synthetic CDO does not need to be funded, this provides the key advantage of the synthetic mechanism over a cash-flow arbitrage CDO. During the first half of 2002, the yield spread for the AAA-note piece averaged 45–50 basis points over Libor,[4] while the cost of the super-senior swap was around 10–12 basis points. This means that if the

---

[4] Averaged from the yield spread on seven synthetic deals closed during Jan–Jun 2002. Yield spread at issue; rates data from Bloomberg.

CDO manager can reinvest in the collateral pool risk-free assets at Libor minus five basis points, it is able to gain from a saving of 28–35 basis points on each nominal $100 of the structure that is not funded. This is a considerable gain. If we assume that a synthetic CDO is 95% unfunded and 5% funded, this is equivalent to the reference assets trading at approximately 26–33 basis points cheaper in the market. There is also an improvement to the return-on-capital measure for the CDO manager. Since typically the manager retains the equity piece, if this is 2% of the structure and the gain is 33 basis points, the return on equity will be improved by [.36/.02] or 16.5%.

Another benefit of structuring CDOs as synthetic deals is their potentially greater attraction for investors (protection sellers). Often, selling credit-default swap protection on a particular reference credit generates a higher return than going long of the underlying cash bond. In general, this is because the credit-default swap price is greater than the asset-swap price for the same name, for a number of reasons (see Choudhry 2001). For instance, during 2001 the average spread of the synthetic price over the cash price was 16-18 basis points in the five-year maturity area for BBB-rated credits.[5] The main reasons why default-swap spreads tend to be above cash spreads are:

- while the bondholder is aware of the exact issue that they are holding in the event of default, default-swap sellers may receive potentially any bond from a basket of deliverable instruments that rank *pari passu* with the cash asset. This is the delivery option afforded the long-swap holder.
- the borrowing rate for a cash bond in the repo market may differ from Libor if the bond is to any extent special. This does not impact the default-swap price which is fixed at inception.
- certain bonds rated AAA (such as US agency securities) sometimes trade below Libor in the asset-swap market. However, a bank writing protection on such a bond will expect a premium (positive spread over Libor) for selling protection on the bond.
- depending on the precise reference credit, the default swap may be more liquid than the cash bond, resulting in a lower default-swap price, or less liquid than the bond, resulting in a higher price.

---

[5] Source: Merrill Lynch, *CDO Monitor*, 15 April 2002.

- default swaps may be required to pay out on credit events that are technical defaults, and not the full default that affects a cash bondholder. Protection sellers may demand a premium for this additional risk.
- for assets trading below par, the protection seller is covering a greater loss than is the cash bondholder. This is because credit-default swaps are "par products" and pay out the par value of the reference asset, minus the market value at time of termination. This means that for an asset trading below par, the protection seller is protecting a greater value than the actual loss suffered by someone who is holding the cash bond.

This difference in pricing between the cash and synthetic markets for credit feeds through into structured product economics.

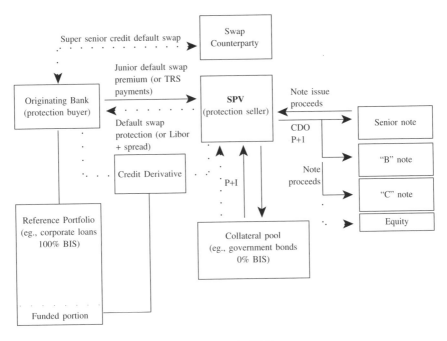

Figure 12.2 Synthetic CDO structure

Synthetic–CDO deal structures

We now look in further detail at the various types of synthetic CDO structures.

Generic concept

Synthetic CDOs have been issued in a variety of forms, labeled in generic form as arbitrage CDOs or balance-sheet CDOs. Structures can differ to a considerable degree from one another, having only the basics in common. The latest development is the managed synthetic CDO.

A synthetic arbitrage CDO is originated generally by collateral managers who wish to exploit the difference in yield between that obtained on the underlying assets and that payable on the CDO, both in note interest and servicing fees. The generic structure is as follows: a specifically-created SPV enters into a total-return swap with the originating bank or financial institution, referencing the bank's underlying portfolio (the reference portfolio). The portfolio is actively managed and is funded on the balance sheet by the originating bank. The SPV receives the "total return" from the reference portfolio and, in return, it pays Libor plus a spread to the originating bank. The SPV also issues notes that are sold into the market to CDO investors, and these notes can be rated as high as AAA as they are backed by high-quality collateral, which is purchased using the note proceeds. A typical structure is shown at figure 12.3.

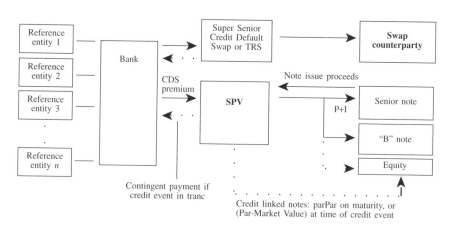

Figure 12.3 Synthetic arbitrage CDO structure

A balance-sheet synthetic CDO is employed by banks that wish to manage regulatory capital. As before, the underlying assets are bonds, loans and credit facilities originated by the issuing bank. In a balance-sheet CDO, the SPV enters into a credit-default swap agreement with the originator, with the specific collateral pool designated as the reference portfolio. The SPV receives the premium payable on the default swap, and thereby provides credit protection on the reference portfolio. There are three types of CDO within this structure. A fully synthetic CDO is a completely unfunded structure which uses credit-default swaps to transfer the entire credit risk of the reference assets to investors who are protection sellers. In a partially funded CDO, only the highest credit-risk segment of the portfolio is transferred. The cash flow that would be needed to service the synthetic CDO overlying liability is received from the AAA-rated collateral that is purchased by the SPV with the proceeds of an overlying note issue. An originating bank obtains maximum regulatory-capital relief by means of a partially funded structure, through a combination of the synthetic CDO and what is known as a super-senior swap arrangement with an OECD banking counterparty. A super-senior swap provides additional protection to that part of the portfolio, the senior segment, that is already protected by the funded portion of the transaction. The sponsor may retain the super-senior element or may sell it to a monoline insurance firm or credit-default swap market-making bank.

Synthetic deals may be either static or managed. Static deals hold the following advantages:

- there are no ongoing management fees to be borne by the vehicle
- the investor can review and grant approval to credits that are to make up the reference portfolio.

The disadvantage is that if there is a deterioration in credit quality of one or more names, there is no ability to remove or offset this name from the pool and the vehicle continues to suffer from it. During 2001, a number of high-profile defaults in the market meant that static pool CDOs performed below expectation. This explains partly the rise in popularity of the managed synthetic deal, which we consider in a later section.

Funded and unfunded deals

Synthetic deal structures are arranged in a variety of ways, with funded and unfunded elements to meet investor and market demand. A generic partially funded synthetic transaction is shown in figure 12.4. It shows an arrangement whereby the issuer enters into two credit-default swaps; the first with an SPV that provides protection for losses up to a specified amount of the reference pool[6], while the second swap is set up with the OECD bank or, occasionally, an insurance company.[7]

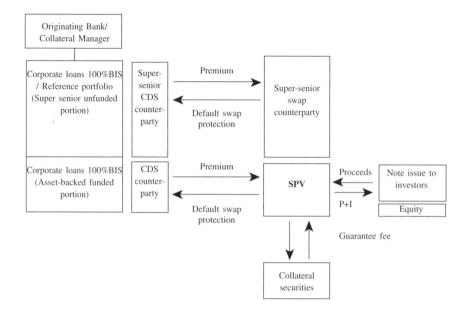

Figure 12.4 Partially funded synthetic CDO structure

A fully funded CDO is a structure where the credit risk of the entire portfolio is transferred to the SPV via a credit-default swap. In a fully funded (or just "funded") synthetic CDO, the issuer enters into the credit-default swap with the SPV, which itself issues credit-linked notes (CLNs) to the entire value of the assets on which the risk has been transferred. The proceeds from the notes are invested in risk-free government or agency debt such as gilts, bunds or Pfandbriefe, or in senior unsecured bank debt. Should there be a default on one or more of the underlying assets, the required amount of the collateral is sold and the proceeds from the sale are paid to the issuer to recompense for the losses. The premium paid on the credit-

---

[6] In practice, to date this portion has been between 5% and 15% of the reference pool.

[7] An "OECD" bank, thus guaranteeing a 20% risk weighting for capital-ratio purposes, under Basel I rules.

default swap must be sufficiently high to ensure that it covers the difference in yield between that on the collateral and that on the notes issued by the SPV. The generic structure is illustrated in figure 12.5.

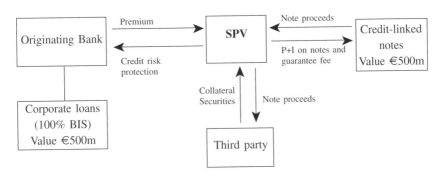

Figure 12.5 Fully funded synthetic balance-sheet CDO structure

Fully funded CDOs are relatively uncommon. One of the advantages of the partially funded arrangement is that the issuer will pay a lower premium than for a fully funded synthetic CDO, because it is not required to pay the difference between the yield on the collateral and the coupon on the note issue (the unfunded part of the transaction). The downside is that the issuer will receive a reduction in risk weighting for capital purposes to 20% for the risk transferred via the super-senior default swap.

The fully unfunded CDO uses only unfunded credit derivatives in its structure. The swaps are rated in a similar fashion to notes, and there is usually an "equity" piece that is retained by the originator. The reference portfolio will again be commercial loans, usually 100% risk-weighted, or other assets. The credit rating of the swap tranches is based on the rating of the reference assets, as well as other factors such as the diversity of the assets and ratings performance correlation. The typical structure is illustrated in figure 12.6. As well as the equity tranche, there will be one or more junior tranches, one or more senior tranches and a super-senior tranche. The senior tranches are sold on to AAA-rated banks as a portfolio credit-default swap, while the junior tranche is usually sold to a an OECD bank. The ratings of the tranches will typically be:

- super-senior: AAA
- senior: AA to AAA
- junior: BB to A
- equity: unrated.

The credit-default swaps are not single-name swaps, but are written on a class of debt. The advantage for the originator is that it can name the reference asset class to investors to investors without having to disclose the name of specific loans. Default swaps are usually cash-settled and not physically settled, so that the reference assets can be replaced with other assets if desired by the sponsor.

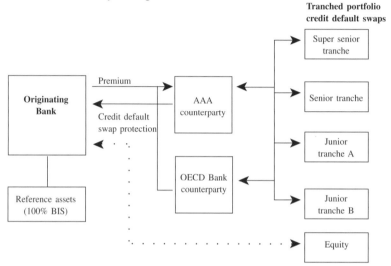

Figure 12.6 The fully synthetic or unfunded CDO

The managed synthetic CDO

Managed synthetic CDOs are the latest variant of the synthetic CDO structure.[8] They are similar to the partially funded deals we described earlier except that the reference asset pool of credit derivatives is actively traded by the sponsoring investment manager. It is the maturing market in credit-default swaps, resulting in good liquidity in a large number of synthetic corporate credits, that has facilitated the introduction of the managed synthetic CDO. With this structure, originators can use credit derivatives to arbitrage cash and synthetic liabilities, as well as leverage off their expertise in credit trading to generate profit. The advantages for investors are the same

---

[8] These are also commonly known as "collateralised synthetic obligations", or CSOs, within the market. *RISK* magazine has called them "collateralised swap obligations", which handily also shortens to CSOs. Boggiano et al (2002) refer to these structures as "managed variable synthetic CDOs", although the author has not come across this term in other literature.

as with earlier generations of CDOs, except that with active trading they are gaining a still-larger exposure to the abilities of the investment manager. The underlying asset pool is, again, a portfolio of credit-default swaps. However, these are now managed dynamically and traded actively under specified guidelines. Thus, there is greater flexibility afforded to the sponsor, and the vehicle will record trading gains or losses as a result of credit-derivative trading. In most structures, the investment manager can only buy protection (short credit) in order to offset an existing sold protection-default swap. For some deals, this restriction is removed and the investment manager can buy or sell credit derivatives to reflect its view.

Structure

The structure of the managed synthetic is similar to the partially funded synthetic CDO, with a separate legally incorporated SPV. On the liability side, there is an issue of notes, with note proceeds invested in collateral or eligible investments, which is one or a combination of the following:

- a bank deposit account or guaranteed-investment contract (GIC) which pays a pre-specified rate of interest[9]
- risk-free bonds such as US Treasury securities, German Pfandbriefe or AAA-rated bonds such as credit-card ABS securities
- a repo agreement with risk-free collateral
- a liquidity facility with a AA-rated bank
- a market-sensitive debt instrument, often enhanced with the repo or liquidity arrangement described above.

On the asset side, the SPV enters into credit-default swaps and/or total-return swaps, selling protection to the sponsor. The investment manager (or "collateral manager") can trade in and out of credit-default swaps after the transaction has closed in the market.[10] The SPV enters into credit derivatives via a single basket credit-default swap to one swap counterparty, written on a portfolio of reference assets, or via multiple single-name credit swaps with a number of swap counterparties. The latter arrangement is more common and is referred to as a multiple-dealer CDO. A percentage of the reference

---

[9] A GIC has been defined either as an account that pays a fixed rate of interest for its term or, more usually, as an account that pays a fixed spread below Libor or euribor, usually three-month floating rolled over each interest period.

[10] This term is shared with other securitisation structures: when notes have been priced and placed in the market, and all legal documentation signed by all named participants, the transaction has *closed*. In effect, this is the start of the transaction and, all being well, the noteholders will receive interest payments during the life of the deal and principal repayment on maturity.

portfolio will be identified at the start of work on the transaction, with the remainder of the entities being selected during the ramp-up period ahead of closing. The SPV enters into the other side of the credit-default swaps by selling protection to one of the swap counterparties on specific reference entities. Thereafter, the investment manager can trade out of this exposure in the following ways:

- buying credit protection from another swap counterparty on the same reference entity. This offsets the existing exposure, but there may be residual risk exposure unless premium dates are matched exactly or if there is a default in both the reference entity and the swap counterparty.
- unwinding or terminating the swap with the counterparty.
- buying credit protection on a reference asset that is outside the portfolio. This is uncommon as it will leave residual exposures and may affect premium spread gains.

The SPV actively manages the portfolio within specified guidelines, the decisions being made by the investment manager. Initially, the manager's opportunity to trade may be extensive, but this will be curtailed if there are losses. The trading guidelines will extend to both individual credit-default swaps and at the portfolio level. They may include:

- parameters under which the investment manager (in the guise of the SPV) may actively close out, hedge or substitute reference assets using credit derivatives.
- guidelines under which the investment manager can trade credit derivatives to maximize gains or minimize losses on reference assets that have improved or worsened in credit quality or outlook.

Credit-default swaps may be cash-settled or physically settled[11], with physical settlement being more common in a managed synthetic deal. In a multiple-dealer CDO, the legal documentation must be in place with all names on the counterparty dealer list, which may add to legal costs as standardisation may be difficult.

Investors who are interested in this structure are seeking to benefit from the following advantages it offers over vanilla synthetic deals:

- active management of the reference portfolio and the trading expertise of the investment manager in the corporate credit market.
- a multiple-dealer arrangement, so that the investment manager can obtain the most competitive prices for default swaps.

---

[11] See chapters 17-18 on credit derivatives

- under physical settlement, the investment manager (via the SPV) has the ability to obtain the highest recovery value for the reference asset.

A generic managed synthetic CDO is illustrated in Figure 12.7.

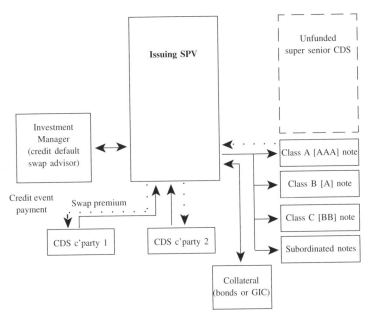

Figure 12.7 Generic managed synthetic CDO

The single-tranche synthetic CDO

One of the advantages offered to investors in the synthetic market is the ability to invest at maturities required by the investor, rather than at maturities selected by bind issuers. For instance, figure 12.8 illustrates how, while the bond market provides assets at only selected points on the credit curve, synthetic products allow investors access to the full curve.

The flexibility of the CSO, enabling deal types to be structured to meet the needs of a wide range of investors and issuers, is well illustrated with the tailor-made or "single-tranche CDO" structure.[12] This structure has been

---

[12] These deals have been arranged by a number of investment banks, including JPMorgan Chase, Bank of America and Credit Agricole Indosuez. They are known variously as "tailor-made CDOs", "tranche-only CDOs", "on-demand CDOs", "iCDOs" and "investor-driven CDOs". The author prefers "single-tranche CDOs".

developed in response to investor demand for exposure to a specific part of a pool of reference credits. With this structure, an arranging bank creates a tailored portfolio that meets specific investor requirements with regard to:

- portfolio size and asset class
- portfolio concentration, geographical and industry variation
- portfolio diversity and rating
- investment term-to-maturity.

The structure is illustrated at figures 12.9 and 12.10, with and without an SPV issuer respectively. Under this arrangement, there is only one note tranche. The reference portfolio, made up of credit-default swaps, is dynamically hedged by the originating bank itself. The deal has been arranged to create a risk/reward profile for one investor only, who buys the single tranche note. This also creates an added advantage that the deal can be brought to market very quickly. The key difference with traditional CSOs is that the arranging bank does not transfer the remainder of the credit risk of the reference pool. Instead, this risk is dynamically managed, and hedged in the market using derivatives.

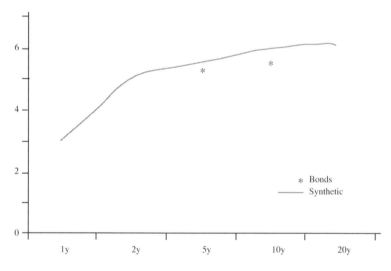

Figure12.8 Credit term structure

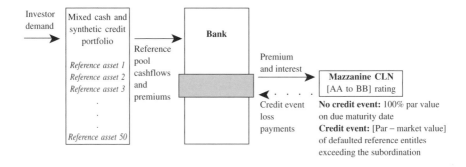

Figure 12.9 Single-tranche CDO, issued direct from arranging bank

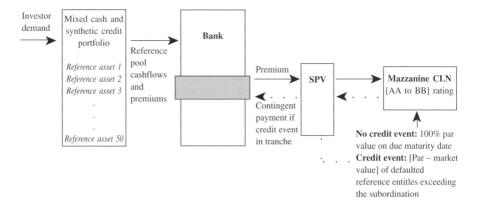

Figure 12.10 Single-tranche CDO, issued via SPV

Deal structure

The investor in a single-tranche CDO will decide on the criteria of assets in the portfolio, and the subordination of the issued tranche. Typically, this will be at the mezzanine level; so, for example, covering the 4% –9% loss level in the portfolio. This enables a very favorable risk return profile to be set up: a CDO tranche that is exposed to 4%–9% losses has a very low historical risk of default (approximately equivalent to a Moody's A2 rating) and a high relative return given its tranching, around Libor plus 200 basis points as at May 2003. This is the risk/return profile of the mezzanine piece.

Figure 12.11 shows the default-probability distribution for credit events in a CDO. Figure 12.12 shows the more specific distribution as applicable to the mezzanine tranche.

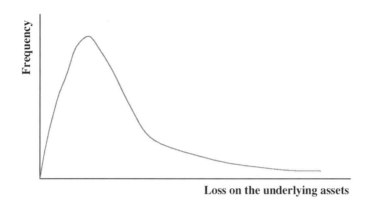

Figure 12.11 Credit-loss distribution

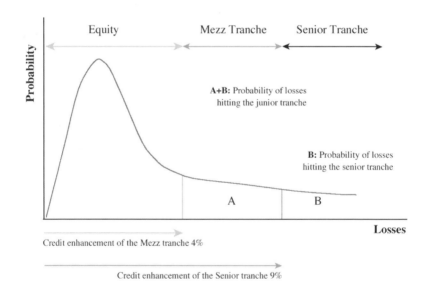

Figure 12.12 Expected-loss distribution for tranched notes

Unlike a traditional CDO, a single-tranche CDO has a very simple cash-flow "waterfall". Compared with figure 11.10, which showed the waterfall for a cash CDO, a single-tranche waterfall will consist of only agency service and hedge costs, and the coupon of the single tranche note itself.

Some of the issues the investor will consider when working with the arranging bank to structure the deal include:

- the number of names in the credit portfolio; usually this ranges from 50 to 100.
- the geographical split of the reference names.
- the required average credit rating and average interest spread of the portfolio.
- the minimum credit rating required in the portfolio.

If the deal is being rated, as with any CDO type, the mix of assets will need to meet ratings-agency criteria for diversity and average rating. The *diversity score* of a portfolio is a measure of the diversity of a portfolio based on qualities such as industrial and geographical concentration. It can be defined as the number of equivalent uncorrelated assets in the pool.[13] We illustrate a hypothetical portfolio in figure 12.13, which shows the composition of a generic portfolio for a single-tranche CDO.

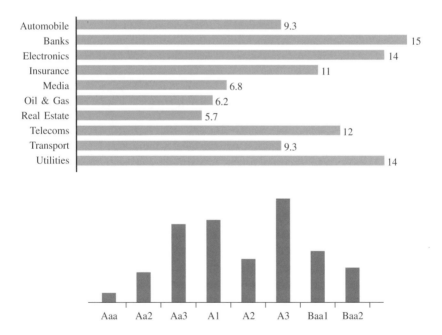

Figure 12.13 Hypothetical portfolio composition for generic single-tranche CDO: industry sector and rating distribution

---

[13] Further background on Moody's diversity score is given in Appendix 12.1.

The position and rating of the issued single tranche is as required by the investor. The subordination of the note follows from the required rating of the investor. For instance, the investor may require an A2 rating for the note. The process followed involves:

- targeting the required rating on the issued tranche
- setting the required return on the note, and hence determining where the tranche will lie
- defining the percentage of first loss that must occur before the issued tranche is affected by further losses
- setting the size of the note issue, in line with investor requirements. For instance, if the investor wishes to place $20 million in the note, and the reference pool is $800 million nominal value, this will imply a 2.5% tranche.

As with the previous synthetic CDOs, a single-tranche CDO can be either a static or a managed deal. In a managed deal, the investor can manage the portfolio and effect substitutions if this is part of its requirement. To facilitate this, the deal may be set up with one or more fund managers in place to deal with the investor when substitutions are required by the investor. Alternatively, an investor may leave trading decisions to a fund manager.

Advantages of the single-tranche structure

For certain investors, the single-tranche CDO presents a number of advantages over the traditional structure. These include:

- Flexibility: the features of the investment can be tailor-made to suit the investor's needs precisely. The investor can select the composition of the portfolio, the size of the tranche and its subordination level.
- Note terms exactly as required: the coupon and maturity of the note are tailor-made for the investor.
- Shorter time frame: the deal can be brought to market relatively quickly, and in as little as four weeks compared to anything from two months to one year for a conventional CSO.
- Lower cost of issue: including lower legal costs because of short time to issue and no protracted marketing effort by the arranger.

The flexibility of the single-tranche structure means that the market can expect to see more variations in their arrangement, as more investors evaluate it as an asset class.

Repackaging structures

Repackaging structures or "repacks" were introduced in the cash securitisation market first, before also becoming a feature of the synthetic markets. In its simplest form, a repack is an underlying security or group of securities that have been packaged-up and transformed into a new note or class of notes that are more attractive to investors than the original securities. This may have been done because the original security has become illiquid or otherwise not tradeable.[14] Repacks were originally classed as "single-asset" or "multi-asset" repacks according to how many underlying securities they represented. Multi-asset repacks may be considered prototype CDOs.

In the synthetic market, investment banks have also structured repacks using credit derivatives. Often this will be to transform a particular feature of an existing bond (or bonds) in ways other than to make it more attractive to new investors, for example to transfer an existing credit exposure or to reduce balance sheet capital requirement. In other words, synthetic market repacks make use of the credit derivatives market to hedge out risk exposure on other bonds, which are frequently also structured products.

Synthetic repack motivations

A synthetic repack uses funded or unfunded credit derivatives in its structure. It may be originated for the following reasons:

- by an investment bank that is tasked with making an asset "tradeable" again;
- by a broker-dealer to transform a current interest-rate or credit risk exposure;
- by a portfolio manager looking to extract value from assets currently held on the balance sheet or assets in the market that are trading below fair value.

The assets in question are often existing structured finance securities, such as CDO notes or CLNs. Hence if the repack vehicle SPV issues securities this will be a repacj of securities issued by another SPV. Hence a repack structure is usually similar in certain respects to a synthetic CDO and often targeted at the same class of investors.

---

[14] For instance, one of the first repacks was of Japanese convertible bonds. With the bear market in Japanese equities during the 1990s, these became illiquid as they no longer were attractive to investors. Individual convertibles or groups of convertibles were packaged up, often with an enhanced coupon or additional new feature of attraction, and sold on to new investors.

Example deal structure

To illustrate the mechanics of a synthetic repack, we present an hypothetical transaction that is a repack of a synthetic CDO. The repack has been structured by an investment bank, ABC Securities Limited, to hedge a position it holds in the junior tranche of a CDO. Through this transaction the bank hedges the credit risk exposure in its existing holding while also meeting the needs of client investors who seek an exposure to the risk-reward profile the repack represents.

It is necessary to describe first the original synthetic CDO deal. We then consider the motivation behind and structure of the repack.

All names and situations quoted are of course fictitious.

Synthetic CDO: Black Island Finance Ltd

The underlying CDO is a fully unfunded synthetic CDO ("Black Island Finance Ltd). This is a CDO originated on a pool of 100% risk-weighted bank assets, with the credit risk and regulatory capital requirements of the assets transferred via a tranched series of credit default swaps to investors. Figure 12.14 shows the structure of Black Island Finance Ltd.

The liabilities of the CDO are split into a series of credit default swaps, which pay a premium based on their seniority. If there are any credit events amongst reference assets then the nominal amounts of the CDS contracts is reduced (thereby reducing the interest receivable by protection sellers) in order of priority. On issue ABC Securities invests in the junior tranche of Black Island CDO. This represents the 2.5% to 10% tranche of risk in the reference pool. Assume it is at BBB level and so would represent this level of risk-return for the investor.

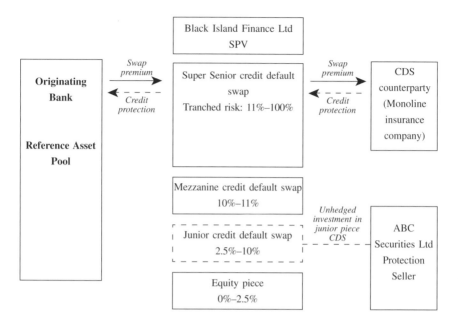

Figure 12.14 Black Island Finance Ltd, hypothetical unfunded synthetic CDO

Later on in the deal life, ABC Securities Ltd decides to hedge its unhedged position in the 2.5%-10% risk piece of Black Island CDO. It also identifies a client requirement for a funded investment at a BBB-rated risk-return level. It therefore structures a repackage vehicle, let us call it Red Sea Finance Limited to meet this client requirement while simultaneously hedging its exposure in Black Island CDO.

Synthetic repackage vehicle: Red Sea Finance Ltd

The purpose of Red Sea Finance Ltd is to hedge out the ABC Securities Ltd exposure in Black Island Finance CDO, which is a position in the junior CDS of that deal. The client order however, is for a funded position. Red Sea Finance Ltd is set up to repackage the exposure, thus transforming it from a credit default swap into a credit-linked note. An SPV is set up to issue the CLN to the investor. The liabilities of Red Sea CDO are the single CLN, that is, there is no tranching. This is placed with the client investor. The proceeds of the note issue are invested in eligible investments, which are risk-free securities. These are repo'd out with a bank and act as a reservce against losses suffered due to credit events in Black Island CDO.

The structure diagram for Red Sea Finance Ltd CDO is shown at figure 12.15.

By structuring its holding via a synthetic repack, ABC Securities has transferred its credit risk exposure in its initial investment, whilst also meeting the needs of its client.

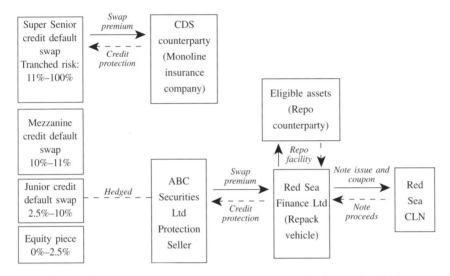

Figure 12.15 Red Sea Finance Ltd, hypothetical synthetic repack vehicle

Case studies

We now consider two specific deals to illustrate the progressive development of the synthetic-CDO market since inception. These are:

- ALCO1: a balance-sheet deal arranged for credit-risk management and regulatory capital purposes
- Jazz I CDO: a managed synthetic "hybrid" CDO.

The latest manifestation of synthetic securitisation technology is the managed synthetic CDO or CSO. In Europe, these have been originated by fund managers, with the first example being issued in 2001. Although they are, in effect, investment vehicles, the disciplines required to manage what is termed a "structured credit product" is not necessarily identical to those required for a corporate bond fund. Investment bank arrangers are apt to suggest that a track record in credit-derivatives trading is an essential prerequisite to being a successful CSO manager. There is an element of reputational risk at stake if a CDO suffers a downgrade; for example, during 2001 Moody's downgraded elements of 83 separate CDO deals, across 174 tranches, as underlying pools of investment-grade and high-yield corporate bonds experienced default.[15] Thus, managing a CDO presents a high-profile record of a fund manager's performance.

The two deals discussed below are innovative structures and a creative combination of securitisation technology and credit derivatives. They show how a portfolio manager can utilise vehicles of this kind to exploit its expertise in credit trading as well as provide attractive returns for investors. Managed synthetic CDOs also present fund managers with a vehicle to build on their credit-derivatives experience. As the market in synthetic credit is, in Europe at least, frequently more liquid than the cash market for the same reference names, it is reasonable to expect more developments of this type in the near future.

ALCO 1 Limited

The ALCO 1 CDO is described as the first rated synthetic balance-sheet CDO from a non-Japanese bank.[16] It is a S$2.8 billion structure sponsored and managed by the Development Bank of Singapore (DBS). The structure diagram is shown in Figure 12.16.

The structure allows DBS to shift the credit risk on a S$2.8 billion reference portfolio of mainly Singapore corporate loans to a special-purpose vehicle, ALCO 1, using credit-default swaps. As a result, DBS can reduce the risk capital it has to hold on the reference loans, without physically moving the assets from its balance sheet. The structure is S$2.45 billion super-senior tranche – an unfunded credit-default swap – with S$224 million notes issue and S$126 million first-loss piece retained by DBS. The notes are issued in six classes, collateralised by Singapore government T-bills and a reserve bank account known as a "GIC" account. There is also a currency and interest-rate swap structure in place for risk hedging, and a put option that covers purchase of assets by arranger if the deal terminates before expected maturity date. The issuer enters into credit-default swaps with specified list of counterparties. The default swap pool is static, but there is a substitution facility for up to 10% of the portfolio. This means that under certain specified conditions, up to 10% of the reference loan portfolio may be replaced by loans from outside the vehicle. Other than this, though, the reference portfolio is static.

---

[15] Source: CreditFlux, April 2002.
[16] Source: Moody's.

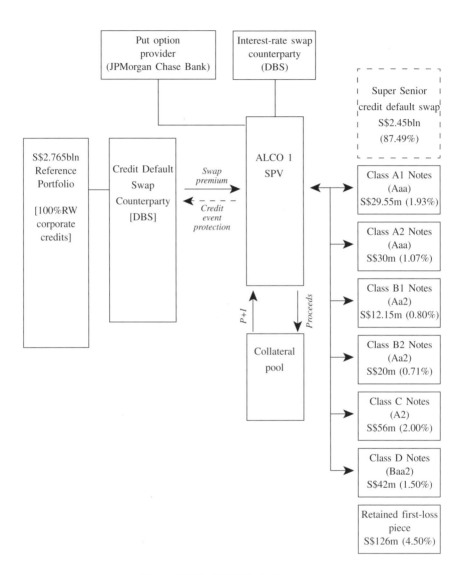

Figure 12.16 ALCO 1 deal structure

Name:	ALCO 1 Limited
Originator:	Development Bank of Singapore Ltd
Arrangers:	JPMorgan Chase Bank
	DBS Ltd
Trustee:	Bank of New York
Closing date:	15 December 2001
Maturity:	March 2009
Portfolio:	S$2.8 billion of credit-default swaps
Reference assets:	199 reference obligations (136 obligors)
Portfolio Administrator:	JPMorgan Chase Bank Institutional Trust Services

Table 12.1 ALCO 1 terms

Class	Amount	Per cent	Rating	Interest rate
Super-senior swap	S$2.45m	87.49%	NR	N/A
Class A1	US$29.55m	1.93%	AAA	3m USD Libor + 50 bps
Class A2	S$30m	1.07%	AAA	3m SOR + 45 bps
Class B1	US$12.15m	0.80%	AA2	3m USD Libor + 85 bps
Class B2	$20m	0.71%	AA2	3m SOR + 80 bps
Class C	S$56m	2.00%	A2	5.20%
Class D	S$42m	1.50%	BAA2	6.70%

Table 12.2 ALCO 1 note tranching
Source: Moody's. Used with permission.

ALCO 1-type structures have subsequently been adopted by other commercial banks in the region. The principal innovation of the vehicle is the method by which the reference credits are selected. The choice of reference credits on which swaps are written must, as expected with a CDO, follow a number of criteria set by the ratings agency, including diversity score, rating factor, weighted-average spread, geographical and industry concentration, among others.

Structure and mechanics

The issuer enters into a portfolio credit-default swap with DBS as the CDS counterparty to provide credit protection against losses in the reference portfolio. The credit-default swaps are cash-settled. In return for protection premium payments, after aggregate losses exceeding the S$126 million "threshold" amount, the issuer is obliged to make protection payments to DBS. The maximum obligation is the S$224 million note-proceeds value. In standard fashion associated with securitised notes, further losses above the threshold amount will be allocated to overlying notes in their reverse order of seniority. The note proceeds are invested in a collateral pool comprising, initially, Singapore Treasury bills.

During the term of the transaction, DBS as the CDS counterparty is permitted to remove any eliminated reference obligations that are fully paid, terminated early or otherwise no longer eligible. In addition, it has the option to remove up to 10% of the initial aggregate amount of the reference portfolio, and substitute new or existing reference names.

For this structure, credit events are defined specifically as failure to pay or bankruptcy.

Note how this differs from European market CDOs where the list of defined credit events is invariably longer, frequently including restructuring and credit-rating downgrade. Another unusual feature is the fixed coupon of the C and D notes.

The reference portfolio is an Asian corporate portfolio, but with a small percentage of loans originated in Australia. The portfolio is concentrated in Singapore (80%). The weighted-average credit quality is Baa3/Ba1, with an average life of three years. The Moodys' diversity score is low (20), reflecting the concentration of loans in Singapore. There is a high industrial concentration. The total portfolio at inception was 199 reference obligations amongst 136 reference entities (obligors). By structuring the deal in this way, DBS obtains capital relief on the funded portion of the assets, but at lower cost and less administrative burden than a traditional cash-flow securitisation, and without having to have a true sale of the assets.

Jazz CDO I B.V.

Jazz CDO I BV is an innovative CDO structure and one of the first hybrid CDOs introduced in the European market. A hybrid CDO combines elements of a cash-flow arbitrage CDO and a managed synthetic CDO. Hence, the underlying assets are investment-grade bonds and loans, and synthetic assets such as credit-default swaps and total-return swaps. The Jazz vehicle comprises a total of €1.5 billion of referenced assets, of which €210 million is made up of a note issue. Its hybrid arrangement enables the portfolio manager to take a view on corporate and bank credits in both cash and synthetic markets. Thus, a structure like Jazz bestows the greatest flexibility for credit trading on CDO originators. The vehicle is illustrated in figure 12.17.

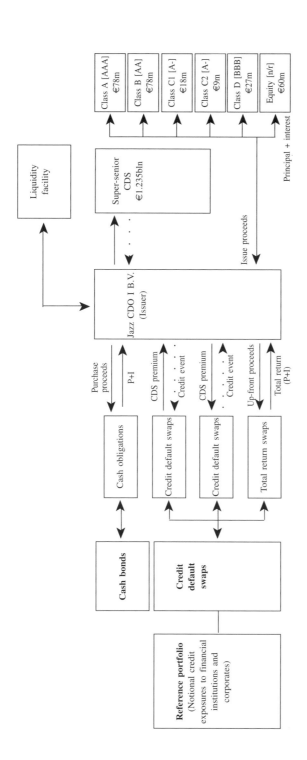

Figure 12.17 Jazz 1 B.V. structure diagram

The main innovation of the structure is a design that incorporates both funded and unfunded assets as well as funded and unfunded liabilities. This arrangement means that the portfolio manager is free to trade both cash and derivative instruments, thereby exploiting its experience and knowledge across the markets. At a time of increasing defaults in CDOs, during 2001 and 2002, static pool deals began to be viewed unfavorably by certain investors, because of the inability to offload deteriorating or defaulted assets. Jazz CDO I is an actively managed deal, and its attraction reflects to a great extent the perception with which the portfolio manager is viewed by investors. So the role of the portfolio manager was critical to the ratings analysis of the deal. This covered:

- experience in managing cash and synthetic assets
- its perceived strength in credit research
- previous experience in managing CDO vehicles
- infrastructure arrangements, such as settlement and processing capability.

These factors, together with the traditional analysis used for static pool cash CDOs, were used by the ratings agencies when assessing the transaction.

Name:	Jazz CDO I B.V.
Manager:	Axa Investment Managers S.A.
Arrangers:	Deutsche Bank AG
Closing date:	8 March 2002
Maturity:	February 2011
Portfolio:	€1.488 billion
Reference assets:	Investment-grade synthetic and cash securities
Portfolio Administrator:	JPMorgan Chase Bank Institutional Trust Services

Table 12.3 Jazz CDO I B.V. terms
Source: S&P. Reproduced with permission

Structure

The assets in Jazz CDO I may comprise credit-default swaps, total-return swaps, bonds and loans, at the manager's discretion. The asset mix is set up by:

- purchase of cash assets, funded by the proceeds of the note issue and the liquidity facility

- selling protection via credit-default swaps
- buying protection via credit-default swaps
- entering into total-return swaps, whereby the total return of the reference assets is received by the vehicle in return for a payment of Libor plus spread (on the notional amount). This is funded via the liquidity facility.

The liability side of the structure is a combination of:
- the super-senior credit-default swap;
- issued notes and equity piece (see figure 12.17).

However, the asset and liability mix can be varied by the portfolio manager at its discretion, and can be expected to change over time. In theory, the asset pool can comprise 100% cash bonds or 100% credit-default swaps; in practice, we should expect to see a mixture as shown in figure 12.17.

Liquidity facility

A liquidity facility of €1.7 billion is an integral part of the structure. It is used as a reserve to cover losses arising from credit-default swap trading, the occurrence of credit events, and to fund any purchases when the mix of cash and synthetic assets is altered by the manager. This can include the purchase of bonds and the funding of total-return swaps. The facility is similar to a revolving credit facility and is provided by the arrangers of the transaction.

If the manager draws on the liquidity facility, this is viewed as a funded liability, similar to an issue of notes, and is in fact senior in the priority of payments to the overlying notes and the super-senior credit-default swap.

Trading arrangements

Hybrid CDOs are the latest development in the arena of managed synthetic CDOs. The Jazz CDO structure enables the portfolio manager to administer credit risk across cash and synthetic markets. The cash-market instruments that may be traded include investment-grade corporate bonds, structured finance securities such as ABS or MBS, and corporate loans. The portfolio manager may buy and sell both types of assets; that is, it may short credit in accordance with its view. In other words, the restriction that exists with some similar deals is removed in Jazz CDO. Therefore, the portfolio manager can buy protection in the credit-derivative market as it wishes, and not only to offset an existing long-credit position (sold protection). The only rules that must be followed when buying protection are that:

- the counterparty risk is of an acceptable level
- there are sufficient funds in the vehicle to pay the credit-derivative premiums.

The manager may trade where existing assets go into default, or where assets have either improved or worsened in credit outlook (to take or cut a trading profit/loss). Another significant innovation is the ability of the vehicle to enter into basis trades in the credit market. An example of such a trade would be to buy a cash bond and simultaneously purchase protection on that bond in the credit-default swap market. Similar to trades undertaken in the exchange-traded government-bond futures market, this is an arbitrage-type strategy where the trader seeks to exploit price mismatches between the cash and synthetic markets.

The various combinations of trades that may be entered into are treated in different ways for counterparty risk and regulatory capital. For an off-setting position in a single name, the options are:

- using only credit-default swaps to cancel out an exposure, both credit default swaps traded with the same counterparty. This is netted out for risk purposes.
- using credit-default swaps only, but with different counterparties. There will be a set-aside for counterparty risk-requirement exposure.
- using credit-default swap and cash bond, which is regarded as a AAA-rated asset for capital purposes.

The Offering Circular for the deal lists a number of trading guidelines that must be followed by the manager. These include a limit of 20% by volume annual-turnover level.

APPENDIX 12.1 The Moody's diversity score

The diversity score for a CDO is Moody's measure for the number of uncorrelated assets in a portfolio. A CDO portfolio must meet a minimum diversity score for its required credit rating. The strict definition of diversity score is "the number of independent assets with identical nominal amount which as a portfolio have the same total notional amount, expected loss and variance as the portfolio itself". Moody's divides assets in accordance with their industry sector and assigns a default correlation among assets in each industry.

The diversity score D is given by

$$D = \frac{\left\{\sum_{j=1}^{T}(N_j * p_j)\right\} * \left\{\sum_{j=1}^{T}(N_j(1 - p_j))\right\}}{\sum_{j=1}^{T}\left\{\left(\sum_{k=1}^{T}\left(r_{jk} * N_k * \sqrt{(p_k * (1 - p_k)))}\right)\right) * N_j * \sqrt{(p_j * (1 - p_j))}\right\}}$$

where

N_j is the outstanding principal balance of collateral-debt security j
N_k is the outstanding principal balance of collateral-debt security k
p_j is the default probability of security j
p_k is the default probability of security k
T is the total number of collateral-debt securities in the portfolio
r_{jk} is the correlation of security j with security k.

The default correlations are assigned by Moody's to each industry sector that it classifies. The default probability is the cumulative probability that a collateral-debt security defaults during its life. It is given by

$$p_j = \frac{E}{(1 - R)}$$

where

E is the expected loss
R is the Moody's recovery rate.

The expected loss is assigned to a security based as shown on a standard table supplied by Moody's, and is based on its credit rating and term-to-maturity. The recovery rate is assigned to each class of security by Moody's, in accordance with its credit rating.

Selected Bibliography and References

Anson M., *Credit Derivatives*, FJF Associates, 1999, Chapter 3.
Boggiano, K., Waterson, K., and Stein, C., "Four forms of synthetic CDOs", *Derivatives Week*, Euromoney Publications, Volume XI, No 23, 10 June 2002.
Bomfim, A., "Credit Derivatives and Their Potential to Synthesize Riskless Assets", *Journal of Fixed Income*, December 2002, p.6–16.
Choudhry, M., "Some issues in the asset-swap pricing of credit default swaps", *Derivatives Week*, Euromoney Publications, 2 December 2001.

Choudhry, M., "Trading credit spreads: the case for a specialised exchange-traded credit futures contract", *Journal of Derivatives Use, Trading and Regulation*, Volume 8, No 1, June 2002.

Choudhry, M., "Combining securitisation and trading in credit derivatives: an analysis of the managed synthetic collateralised debt obligation", *Euromoney Debt Capital Markets Yearbook*, London: Euromoney Publications, 2002.

Choudhry, M., *Credit Derivatives and Synthetic Securitisation*, Singapore: John Wiley & Son 2004

Das, S., *Structured Products and Hybrid Securities*, John Wiley, 2001, Chapter 12.

Fabozzi, F. and Goodman, L. (editors), *Investing in Collateralised Debt Obligations*, FJF Associates, 2001.

Gregory, J., *Credit Derivatives: The Definitive Guide*, RISK Publishing 2003

Kasapi, A., *Mastering Credit Derivatives*, FT Prentice Hall, 1999.

McPherson, N., Remeza H. and Kung D., *Synthetic CDOs and Credit Default Swaps*, CSFB, 2002.

In the third part of the book, we consider the primary derivative instruments. These are *not* securities, and it is incorrect to refer to them as such. Hence, we have fixed-income securities in the cash markets and fixed-income derivatives (or interest-rate derivatives) in the synthetic markets. We look here at their application in the bond markets.

We concentrate on interest-rate swaps, and how they are used by bond-market participants for, say, hedging purposes (essentially, vanilla options), and an exciting new development of the 1990s – credit derivatives. There is also a chapter on the theory of forward and futures pricing, with a case study featuring the price history and implied repo rate for the LIFFE exchange's long gilt future.

Readers who wish to learn more about derivative instruments have a large selection of titles to choose from. We recommend Blake (2000) as an introductory-level text. This book does a good job of placing all capital-market instruments within an integrated context, including the analysis and use of options. Marshall and Bansall (1992) and Levy (1999) are also very good introductory texts that cover a wide range of instruments, including options. Another excellent title is Jarrow and Turnbull (1999), while the author's personal favorite on options and other derivatives is Galitz (1995); this book is well worth purchasing. For an intermediate- to advanced-level treatment, the standard text is Hull (2000), but this is not immediately accessible unless one has at least an A-level in mathematics (and has taken the exam recently!). Rubinstein (1999) is at the same level, and is very accessible and readable; it is highly recommended. An excellent advanced text on derivatives is Briys et al (1998), which presents the concepts in a way that practitioners will appreciate, whilst remaining academically rigorous. Other advanced treatments that are written in clear and readable style are Pliska (1997) and Elliott and Kopp (1999). An excellent introduction to the mathematics contained in these two texts is given in Ross (1999).

Finally, two references cited elsewhere but worth mentioning again because of their high readability are Questa (1999) and Sundaresan (1997). These are introductory- and intermediate-level treatments, respectively, which discuss derivatives and price processes within the context of the fixed-income markets. The latter especially is an excellent all-round text.

Recommended reading

Blake, D., *Financial Market Analysis* (2nd edition), Wiley, 2000.

Briys, E., Bellalah, M., Mai, H. and de Varenne, F., *Options, Futures and Exotic Derivatives*, Wiley, 1998.

Elliot, R. and Kopp, P., *Mathematics of Financial Markets*, Springer, 1999.

Galitz, L., *Financial Engineering*, FT Pitman, 1995.

Hull, J., *Options, Futures and Other Derivatives*, 4th edition, Prentice Hall 2000

Jarrow, R. and Turnbull, S., *Derivative Securities* (2nd edition), South-Western Publishing, 2000.

Joshi, M., *The concepts and practice of mathematical finance*, Cambridge U.P. 2004.

Kolb, R., *Futures, Options and Swaps* (3rd edition), Blackwell, 2000.

Levy, H., *Introduction to Investments* (2nd edition), South-Western Publishing, 1999.

Marshall, J. and Bansal, V., *Financial Engineering*, New York Institute of Finance, 1992.

Pliska, S., *Introduction to Mathematical Finance*, Blackwell, 1997.

Questa, G., *Fixed Income Analysis for the Global Financial Market*, Wiley, 1999.

Ross, S., *An Introduction to Mathematical Finance*, Cambridge UP, 1999.

Rubinstein, M., *Rubinstein on Derivatives*, RISK Books, 1999.

Sundaresan, S., *Fixed Income Markets and their Derivatives*, South-Western Publishing, 1997.

13

Forwards and Futures Valuation

To begin our discussion of derivative instruments, we discuss the valuation and analysis of forward and futures contracts. A description of interest-rate futures was given in Chapter 6. Here we develop basic valuation concepts.

Introduction

A forward contract is an agreement between two parties in which the buyer contracts to purchase from the seller a specified asset, for delivery at a future date, at a price agreed today. The terms are set so that the present value of the contract is zero. For the forthcoming analysis we use the following notation:

P is the current price of the underlying asset, also known as the spot price
P_T is the price of the underlying asset at the time of delivery
X is the delivery price of the forward contract
T is the term-to-maturity of the contract in years, also referred to as the time-to-delivery
r is the risk-free interest rate
R is the return of the payout or its yield
F is the current price of the forward contract.

The payoff of a forward contract is therefore given by

$$P_T - X \qquad (13.1)$$

with X set at the start so that the present value of $(P_T - X)$ is zero. The payout yield is calculated by obtaining the percentage of the spot price that is paid out on expiry.

Forwards

When a forward contract is written, its delivery price is set so that the present value of the payout is zero. This means that the forward price F is then the price on delivery which would make the present value of the payout, on the delivery date, equal to zero. That is, at the start $F = X$. This is the case only on day 1 of the contract, however. From then on until the contract expiry the value of X is fixed, but the forward price F will fluctuate continuously until delivery. It is the behavior of this forward price that we wish to examine. For instance, generally as the spot price of the underlying asset increases, so the price of a forward contract written on the asset also increases; and vice versa.

At this stage, it is important to remember that the forward price of a contract is not the same as the value of the contract, and the terms of the agreement are set so that at inception the value is zero. The relationship given above is used to show that an equation can be derived which relates F to P, T, r and R.

Consider first the profit/loss profile for a forward contract. This is shown in Figure 13.1. The price of the forward can be shown to be related to the underlying variables as

$$F = S(r/R)^T \qquad (13.2)$$

and for the one-year contract highlighted in Figure 13.1 is 52.5, where the parameters are

$$S = 50, \ r = 1.05 \text{ and } R = 1.00.$$

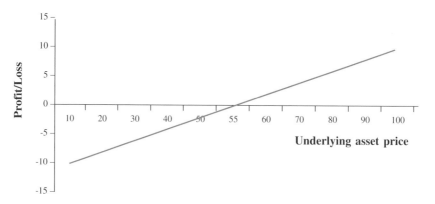

Figure 13.1 Forward contract profit/loss profile

Futures

Forward contracts are tailor-made instruments designed to meet specific individual requirements. Futures contracts, on the other hand, are standardised contracts that are traded on recognized futures exchanges. Apart from this, the significant difference between them, and the feature that influences differences between forward and futures prices, is that profits or losses that are gained or suffered in futures trading are paid out at the end of the day. This does not occur with forwards. The majority of trading in futures contracts are always closed out; that is, the position is netted out to zero before the expiry of the contract. If a position is run into the delivery month, depending on the terms and conditions of the particular exchange, the investor that is long the future may be delivered into (the asset). Settlement is by physical delivery in the case of commodity futures or in cash in the case of certain financial futures. Bond futures are financial futures where any bond that is in the delivery basket for that contract will be delivered to the holder of the long. With both physical and financial futures, only a very small percentage of contracts are actually delivered into, as the majority of trading is undertaken for hedging and speculative purposes.

With futures contracts, as all previous trading profits and losses have been settled, on the day of expiry only the additional change from the previous day needs to be accounted for. With a forward contract, all loss or gain is rolled up until the expiry day and handed over as a total amount on this day.[1]

Forwards and futures

Cash-flow differences

We can now look at the cash-flow treatment of the two contracts in greater detail. This is illustrated in Table 13.1, which uses F to denote the price of the futures contract as well. The table shows the payoff schedule at the end of each trading day for the two instruments; assume that they have identical terms. With the forward, there is no cash flow on intermediate dates, whereas with the futures contract there is. As with the forward contract, the price of the future fixes the present value of the futures contract at zero.

---

[1] We assume the parties have traded only one forward contract between them. If, as is more accurate to assume, a large number of contracts have been traded across a number of different maturity periods and perhaps instruments, as contracts expire only the net loss or gain is transferred between counterparties.

Each day the change in price, which at the end of the day is marked-to-market at the close price, will have resulted in either a profit or gain[2], which is handed over or received each day as appropriate. The process of daily settlement of price movements means that the nominal delivery price can be reset each day so that the present value of the contract is always zero. This means that the future and nominal delivery prices of a futures contract are the same at the end of each trading day.

Time	Forward contract	Futures contract
0	0	0
1	0	$F_1 - F$
2	0	$F_2 - F_1$
3	0	$F_3 - F_2$
4	0	$F_4 - F_3$
5	0	$F_5 - F_4$
...	0	...
...	0	...
...	0	...
$T - 1$	0	$F_{T-1} - F_{T-2}$
T	$P_T - F$	$P_T - F_{T-1}$
Total	$P_T - F$	$P_T - F$

Table 13.1 Cash-flow process for forwards and futures contracts

We see in Table 13.1 that there are no cash flows changing hands between counterparties to a forward contract. The price of a futures contract is reset each day; after day 1, this means it is reset from F to F_1. The amount $(F_1 - F)$, if positive, is handed over by the short future to the long future. If this amount is negative, it is paid by the long future to the short. On the expiry day T of the contract the long future will receive a settlement amount equal to $(P_T - F_{T-1})$ which expresses the relationship between the price of the future and the price of the underlying asset. As significant, the daily cash flows transferred when holding a futures contract cancel each other out, so that on expiry the value of the contract is (at this stage) identical to that for a forward, that is $(P_T - F)$.

[2] Or no profit or gain if the closing price is unchanged from the previous day's closing price, a "doji" as technical traders call it.

With exchange-traded contracts, all market participants are deemed to conduct their trading with a central counterparty, the exchange's clearing house. This eliminates counterparty risk in all transactions, and the clearing house is able to guarantee each bargain because all participants are required to contribute to its clearing fund. This is by the process of margin, by which each participant deposits an initial margin and then, as its profits or losses are recorded, deposits further variation margin on a daily basis. The marking-to-market of futures contracts is an essential part of this margin process. A good description of the exchange clearing process is contained in Galitz (1995).

This is the key difference between future and forward contracts. If holding a futures position that is recording a daily profit, the receipt of this profit on a daily basis is advantageous because the funds can be reinvested while the position is still maintained. This feature is not available with a forward. Equally, losses are suffered on a daily basis that are not suffered by the holder of a loss-making forward position.

Relationship between forward and future price

Continuing with the analysis, we wish to illustrate that under certain specified assumptions, the price of futures and forwards written with identical terms must be the same.

This can be shown in the following way. Consider two trading strategies of identical term-to-maturity and written on the same underlying asset; one strategy uses forward contracts while the other uses futures. Both strategies require no initial investment and are self-financing. The assumptions are:
- the absence of risk-free arbitrage opportunities
- the existence of an economist's perfect market
- certainty of returns.

Under these conditions it can be shown that the forward and future price must be identical. In this analysis, the return r is the daily return (or instantaneous money-market interest rate) and T is the maturity term in days. Let's look further at the strategies.

For the strategy employing forwards, we buy r^T forward contracts. The starting forward price is $F = X$ but, of course, there is no cash outlay at the start, and the payoff on expiry is

$$r^T(P_T - F) .$$

The futures strategy is more involved, as a result of the daily margin cash flows that are received or paid during the term of the trade. On day 1, we buy r contracts each priced at F. After the close we receive $F_1 - F$. The position is closed out and the cash received is invested at the daily rate r up to the expiry date. The return on this cash is r^{T-1}, which means that on expiry we will receive an amount of

$$r(F_1 - F)r^{T-1}.$$

The next day we purchase r^2 futures contracts at the price of F_1 and at the close the cash flow received of $F_2 - F_1$, is invested at the close of trading at r^{T-2}. Again we will receive on expiry a sum equal to

$$r^2(F_2 - F_1)r^{T-2}.$$

This process is repeated until the expiry date, which we assume to be the delivery date. What is the net effect of following this strategy? We will receive on the expiry date a set of maturing cash flows that have been invested daily from the end of day 1. The cash sums will be

$$r^T(F_1 - F) + r^T(F_2 - F_1) + r^T(F_3 - F_2) + \ldots + r^T(P_T - F_{T-1})$$

which nets to

$$r^T(P_T - F)$$

which is also the payoff from the forward contract strategy. Both strategies have a zero cash outlay and are self-financing. The key point is that if indeed we are saying that

$$r^T(P_T - F)_{forward} = r^T(P_T - F)_{future} , \qquad (13.3)$$

for the assumption of no arbitrage to hold, then

$$F_{forward} = F_{future} .$$

The forward-spot parity

We can use the forward strategy to imply the forward price provided we know the current price of the underlying asset and the money-market interest rate. A numerical example of the forward strategy is given at Figure 13.2, with the same parameters given earlier. We assume no-arbitrage and a perfect, frictionless market.

	Cash flows	
	Start date	*Expiry*
Buy forward contract	0	$P_T - F$
Buy one unit of the underlying asset	-50	P_T
Borrow zero present-value of forward price	$F / 1.05$	F
Total	$-50 + F / 1.05$	$P_T - F$

Result
Set $-50 + F / 1.05$ equal to zero (no-arbitrage condition)
Therefore $F = 52.5$

Figure 13.2 Forward strategy

What Figure 13.2 is saying is that it is possible to replicate the payoff profile we observed in Figure 13.1 by a portfolio composed of one unit of the underlying asset, which purchase is financed by borrowing a sum that is equal to the present value of the forward price. This borrowing is repaid on maturity and is equal to $(F /1.05) \times 1.05$ which is, in fact, F. In the absence of any arbitrage opportunity, the cost of forming the portfolio will be identical to that of the forward itself. However, we have set the current cost of the forward contract at zero, which gives us

$$-50 + F/1.05 = 0.$$

We solve this expression to obtain F and this is 52.50.

So to recap, the price of the forward contract is 52.50 although the present value of the forward contract when it is written is zero. We prove this in Figure 13.3.

	Start date	Expiry date
Buy forward contract	0	$P_T - F$
Buy R^T units of the underlying asset	$-PR^T$	P_T
Borrow zero present-value of forward price	Fr^{-T}	$-F$
Total	$-PR^T + Fr^{-T}$	$P_T - F$

Set
$$-PR^T + Fr^T = 0$$
Therefore
$$F = P(r / R)^T$$

Figure 13.3 Algebraic proof of forward price

What Figure 13.3 states is that the payoff profile for the forward can be replicated precisely by setting up a portfolio that holds R^T units of the underlying asset, which is funded through borrowing a sum equal to the present value of the forward price. This borrowing is repaid at maturity, this amount being equal to

$$(Fr^{-T}) \times r^T = F .$$

The portfolio has an identical payoff profile (by design) to the forward, this being $(P^T - F)$. In a no-arbitrage environment, the cost of setting up the portfolio must be equal to the current price of the forward, as they have identical payoffs and, if one was cheaper than the other, there would be a risk-free profit for a trader who bought the cheap instrument and shorted the dear one. However, we set the current cost of the forward (its present value) as zero, which means the cost of constructing the duplicating portfolio must therefore be zero as well. This gives us

$$-PR^T \times Fr^{-T} = 0.$$

which allows us to solve for the forward price F.

The significant aspect for the buyer of a forward contract is that the payoff of the forward is identical to that of a portfolio containing an equivalent amount of the underlying asset, which has been constructed using borrowed funds. The portfolio is known as the *replicating portfolio*. The price of the forward contract is a function of the current underlying spot price, the risk-free or money-market interest rate, the payoff and the maturity of the contract.

To recap, then, the forward-spot parity states that

$$F = P(r \mathbin{/} R)^T . \qquad (13.4)$$

It can be shown that neither of the possibilities $F > P(r \mathbin{/} R)^T$ or $F < P(r \mathbin{/} R)^T$ will hold unless arbitrage possibilities are admitted. The only possibility is (13.4), at which the futures price is *fair value*.

The basis and implied repo rate

For later analysis, we introduce now some terms used in the futures markets.

The difference between the price of a futures contract and the current underlying spot price is known as the *basis*. For bond futures contracts, which are written not on a specific bond but on a notional bond that can in fact be represented by any bond that fits within the contract terms, the size of the basis is given by (13.5).

$$Basis = P_{bond} - (P_{fut} \times CF) \qquad (13.5)$$

where the basis is the *gross basis* and CF is the *conversion factor* for the bond in question. All delivery-eligible bonds are said to be in the *delivery basket*. The conversion factor equalises each deliverable bond to the futures price.[3] The size of the gross basis represents the cost of carry associated with the bond from today to the delivery date. The bond with the lowest basis associated with it is known as the cheapest-to-deliver bond.

The magnitude of the basis changes continuously and this uncertainty is termed basis risk. Generally, the basis declines over time as the maturity of the contract approaches, and converges to zero on the expiry date. The significance of basis risk is greatest for market participants who use futures contracts for hedging positions held in the underlying asset. The basis is positive or negative according to the type of market in question, and is a function of issues such as cost of carry. When the basis is positive, that is $F > P$, the situation is described as a *contango*, and is common in precious-

---

[3] For a description and analysis of bond futures contracts, the basis, implied repo and the cheapest-to-deliver bond, see Burghardt et al (1994), an excellent account of the analysis of the Treasury bond basis. Plona (1998) is also a readable treatment of the European government bond basis.

metals markets. A negative basis $P < F$ is described as *backwardation* and is common in oil contracts and foreign currency markets.

The hedging of futures and the underlying asset requires a keen observation of the basis. To hedge a position in a futures contract, one could run an opposite position in the underlying asset. However, running such a position incurs the cost of carry referred to above, which depending on the nature of the asset may include storage costs, opportunity cost of interest foregone, funding costs of holding the asset and so on. The futures price may be analysed in terms of the forward-spot parity relationship and the risk-free interest rate. If we say that the risk-free rate is

$$r - 1$$

and the forward-spot parity is

$$F = P(r \mid R)^T .$$

we can set

$$r - 1 = R(F \mid P)^{1/T} - 1 \tag{13.5}$$

which must hold because of the no-arbitrage assumption.

This interest rate is known as the *implied repo rate*, because it is similar to a repurchase agreement carried out with the futures market. Generally, a relatively high implied repo rate is indicative of high futures prices, and the same for low implied repo rates. The rates can be used to compare contracts with each other, when these have different terms to maturity and even underlying assets. The implied repo rate for the contract is more stable than the basis; as maturity approaches the level of the rate becomes very sensitive to changes in the futures price, spot price and (by definition) time to maturity.

We present a hypothetical illustration of the basis convergence at Figure 13.4. The implied repo rate is constant during this time. If we start with

$$F = P(r \mid R)^T$$

we can derive

$$r = R(F \mid P)^{1/T}$$

where r is the implied repo rate. The cost of carry is defined as the net cost of holding the underlying asset from trade date to expiry date (or delivery date).

The case study shows the price histories for the LIFFE[4] September 2000 long gilt futures contract.

CASE STUDY **LIFFE September 2000 long gilt future contract**

In theory, a futures contract represents the price for forward delivery of the underlying asset. Therefore, one should observe a convergence in the price of the future and the price of the underlying as the contract approaches maturity. The gilt price is for the UK Treasury $5\frac{3}{4}\%$ 2009, the cheapest-to-deliver gilt for the September 2000 contract throughout the contract's life. However, note that there is in fact no actual convergence of prices. For a bond futures contract, the convergence is best analysed using the basis, as Figure 13.4 shows (the x-axis lists the contract days to maturity, which is in fact the dates 29th June 2000 to 27th September 2000, the contract expiry date). The associated yields are shown at Figure 13.5, which do demonstrate slight convergence on the very last day of trading. However, the liquidity of bond futures is very low in the delivery month, and decreases further in the last three days of trading up to the expiry Wednesday.

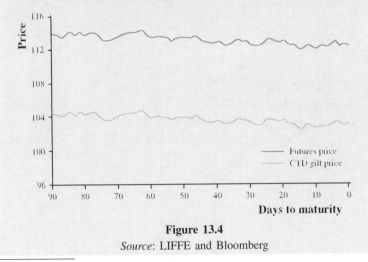

Figure 13.4

Source: LIFFE and Bloomberg

---

[4] The London International Financial Futures and Options Exchange (LIFFE), pronounced "life". The terms of this contract are available at the exchange's website, www.liffe.com, which also contains other useful information on contracts traded at the exchange.

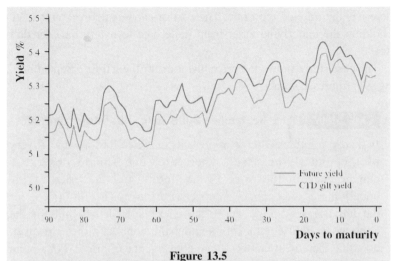

Figure 13.5
Source: LIFFE and Bloomberg

The basis history is shown at Figure 13.6, which confirms the convergence, as the contract approaches expiry; the dates match those used for Figure 13.4. Figure 13.7 shows the stability of the implied repo rate, confirming the analysis we suggested earlier. The spike towards maturity also illustrates the sensitivity of the implied repo rate to very small changes in cash or futures price.

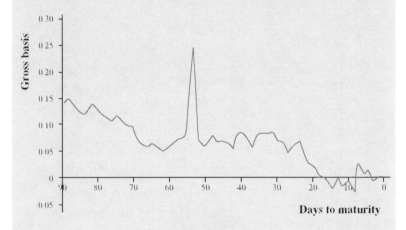

Figure 13.6
Source: LIFFE and Bloomberg

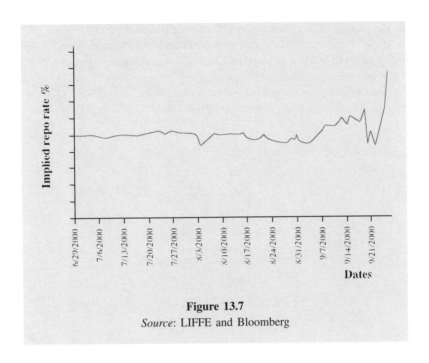

Figure 13.7
Source: LIFFE and Bloomberg

Selected Bibliography and References

See Rubinstein (1999) for the full treatment, very accessibly presented and highly recommended. One of the author's personal favorites is the chapter by Grinblatt and Jegadeesh in Jegadeesh and Tuckamn (2000), which is very insightful and well presented. It is quite technical, however. Chapter 3 of Kolb (2000) is a standard introductory treatment, while Chapter 3 of Hull (2000) is an oft-quoted text on futures and forwards and a more quantitative approach than Kolb.

The earlier-dated journal references are also well worth reading.

Burghardt, G., *The Treasury Bond Basis*, Irwin 1994

Choudhry, M., *The Futures Bond Basis*, YieldCurve Publishing 2003

French, K., "A Comparison of Futures and Forwards Prices", *Journal of Financial Economics* 12, November 1983, p.311-342.

Galitz, L., *Financial Engineering*, FT Pitman, 1995, Chapters 3, 4, 6-8.

Grinblatt, M. and Jegadeesh, N., "Futures vs. Forward Prices: Implications for Swap Pricing and Derivatives Valuation" in Jegadeesh, N. and Tuckman, B., *Advanced Fixed-Income Valuation Tools*, John Wiley & Sons, 2000.

Hull, J., *Options, Futures and Other Derivatives* (4th edition), Prentice Hall, 2000.

Jarrow, R. and Oldfield, G., "Forward Contracts and Futures Contracts", *Journal of Financial Economics* 9, December 1981, p.373-382.

Kolb, R., *Futures, Options and Swaps* (3rd edition), Blackwell, 2000.

Park, H. and Chen, A., "Differences between Futures and Forward Prices: A Further Investigation of Marking to Market Effects", *Journal of Futures Markets* 5, February 1985, p.77-88.

Plona, C., *The European Bond Basis*, McGraw-Hill 1998.

Rubinstein, M., *Rubinstein on Derivatives*, RISK 1999.

14

Bond Futures Contracts

The most widely used risk-management instrument in the bond markets is the government-bond futures contract. This is usually an exchange-traded standardised contract that fixes the price today at which a specified quantity and quality of a bond will be delivered at a date during the expiry month of the futures contract. Unlike short-term interest-rate futures, which only require cash settlement, and which we encountered in the section on money markets, bond futures require the actual physical delivery of a bond when they are settled.

In this chapter we review bond futures contracts and their use for trading and hedging purposes.

Introduction

The concept of a bond futures contract is probably easier to grasp intuitively than a short-dated interest-rate future. This reflects the fact that a bond futures contract represents an underlying physical asset, the bond itself, and a bond must be delivered on expiry of the contract. In this way, bond futures are similar to commodity futures, which also require physical delivery of the underlying commodity.

A futures contract is an agreement between two counterparties that fixes the terms of an exchange that will take place between them at some future date. They are standardised agreements as opposed to OTC ones, when traded on an exchange, so they are also referred to as exchange-traded futures. In the UK, financial futures are traded on LIFFE, which opened in 1982. There are four classes of contract traded on LIFFE: short-term interest-rate contracts; long-term interest-rate contracts (bond futures); currency contracts; and stock-index contracts. We discussed interest-rate futures contracts, which generally trade as part of the money markets, in an earlier chapter. In this section we will look at bond futures contracts, which are an important part of the bond markets; they are used for hedging and speculative purposes. Most futures contracts on exchanges around the world trade at three-month maturity intervals, with maturity dates fixed at March, June, September and December each year. This includes the contracts traded on LIFFE. Therefore, at pre-set times during the year a contract for each of these months will expire, and a final settlement price is determined for it. The further out one goes, the less liquid the trading is in that contract. It is normal to see liquid trading only in the front month contract (the current contract, so that if we are trading in April 2004 the front month is the June 2004 future), and possibly one or two of the next contracts, for most bond futures contracts. The liquidity of contracts diminishes the further one trades out in the maturity range.

When a party establishes a position in a futures contract, it can either run this position to maturity or close out the position between trade date and maturity. If a position is closed out, the party will have either a profit or loss to book. If a position is held until maturity, the party who is long the future will take delivery of the underlying asset (bond) at the settlement price; the party who is short futures will deliver the underlying asset. This is referred to as physical settlement or sometimes, confusingly, as cash settlement.

There is no counterparty risk associated with trading exchange-traded futures, because of the role of the clearing house, such as the London Clearing House (LCH). This is the body through which contracts are settled. A clearing house acts as the buyer to all contracts sold on the exchange, and the seller to all contracts that are bought. So in the London market, the LCH acts as the counterparty to all transactions, so that settlement is effectively guaranteed. The LCH requires all exchange participants to deposit margin with it, a cash sum that is the cost of conducting business (plus broker's commissions). The size of the margin depends on the size of a party's net open position in contracts (an open position is a position in a contract that is held overnight and not closed out). There are two types of margin, maintenance margin and variation margin. Maintenance margin is the minimum level required to be held at the clearing house; the level is set by the exchange. Variation margin is the additional amount that must be deposited to cover any trading losses and as the size of the net open positions increases. Note that this is not like margin in, say, a repo transaction. Margin in repo is a safeguard against a drop in value of collateral that has been supplied against a loan of cash. The margin deposited at a futures exchange clearing house acts essentially as "good faith" funds, required to provide comfort to the exchange that the futures trader is able to satisfy the obligations of the futures contract that are being traded.

```
GRAB                                                      Govt   CTM
<PAGE> now scrolls 17 contracts.   Enter # <GO> to scroll contracts.
Session D          Contract  Table
US  LONG  BOND(CBT)
Exchange Web Page       Pricing Date: 3/19/04      Price Display: 2
Chicago Board of Trade                        --AS REPORTED 3/19 --      2
Grey date = options trading                   556509    18187 Previous
              Last   2Pct Chg  Time   High  2  Low    OpenInt TotVol  Close
1)USH4 Mar04  116-12s  -.35% Close  116-23   113-21   23157   2274   116-25
2)USM4 Jun04  114-29s  -.35% Close  115-10   114-25   520921  15753  115-10
3)USU4 Sep04  113-16s  -.36% Close  113-27b  113-13   12056   159    113-29
4)USZ4 Dec04  112-04s  -.36% Close                    194     0      112-17
5)USH5 Mar05  110-27s  -.37% Close                    181     1      111-08
```

```
Australia 61 2 9777 8600      Brazil 5511 3048 4500      Europe 44 20 7330 7500      Germany 49 69 920410
Hong Kong 852 2977 6000 Japan 81 3 3201 8900 Singapore 65 6212 1000 U.S. 1 212 318 2000 Copyright 2004 Bloomberg L.P.
                                                                     G926-802-0 22-Mar-04  8:45:33
```

Figure 14.1 Bond futures price quotes, Bloomberg page CTM, 22 March 2004.
© Bloomberg L.P. Used with permission.

Bond futures contracts

We have noted that futures contracts traded on an exchange are standardised. This means that each contract represents exactly the same commodity, and it cannot be tailored to meet individual customer requirements. In this section, we describe two very liquid and commonly traded contracts, starting with the US T-Bond contract traded on the Chicago Board of Trade (CBOT). The details of this contract are given at Figure 14.2.

Unit of Trading	US Treasury bond with notional value of $100,000 and a coupon of 8%
Deliverable grades	US T-bonds with a minimum maturity of 15 years from first day of delivery month
Delivery months	March, June, September, December
Delivery date	Any business day during the delivery month
Last trading day	12:00 noon, seventh business day before last business day of delivery month
Quotation	Percent of par expressed as points and thirty-seconds of a point, e.g., 108–16 is 108 16/32 or 108.50
Minimum price movement	1/32
Tick value	$31.25
Trading hours	07.20 – 14.00 (trading pit)
	17.20 – 20.05
	22.30 – 06.00 hours (screen trading)

Figure 14.2 CBOT US T-Bond futures contract specifications

The terms of this contract relate to a US Treasury bond with a minimum maturity of 15 years and a notional coupon of 8%. We introduced the concept of the notional bond in the chapter on repo markets. A futures contract specifies a notional coupon to prevent delivery and liquidity problems that would arise if there was shortage of bonds with exactly the coupon required, or if one market participant purchased a large proportion of all the bonds in issue with the required coupon. For exchange-traded futures, a short future can deliver any bond that fits the maturity criteria specified in the contract terms. Of course, a long future would like to be delivered a high-coupon bond with significant accrued interest, while the short future would want to deliver a low-coupon bond with low interest accrued. In fact, this issue does not arise because of the way the invoice amount (the amount paid by the long future to purchase the bond) is calculated. The invoice amount on the expiry date is given at (14.1) below.

$$Inv_{amt} = P_{fut} \times CF + AI \qquad (14.1)$$

where

Inv_{amt} is the invoice amount
P_{fut} is the price of the futures contract
CF is the conversion factor
AI is the bond accrued interest.

Any bond that meets the maturity specifications of the futures contract is said to be in the delivery basket, the group of bonds that are eligible to be delivered into the futures contract. Every bond in the delivery basket will have its own *conversion factor*, which is used to equalise coupon and accrued interest differences of all the delivery bonds. The exchange will announce the conversion factor for each bond before trading in a contract begins; the conversion factor for a bond will change over time, but remains fixed for one individual contract. That is, if a bond has a conversion factor of 1.091252, this will remain fixed for the life of the contract. If a contract specifies a bond with a notional coupon of 7%, like the long gilt future on LIFFE, then the conversion factor will be less than 1.0 for bonds with a coupon lower than 7% and higher than 1.0 for bonds with a coupon higher than 7%. A formal definition of conversion factor is given below.

Conversion Factor

The conversion factor (or price factor) gives the price of an individual cash bond such that its yield to maturity on the delivery day of the futures contract is equal to the notional coupon of the contract. The product of the conversion factor and the futures price is the forward price available in the futures market for that cash bond (plus the cost of funding, referred to as the gross basis).

Although conversion factors equalise the yield on bonds, bonds in the delivery basket will trade at different yields and, for this reason, they are not "equal" at the time of delivery. Certain bonds will be cheaper than others, and one bond will be the cheapest-to-deliver bond. The cheapest-to-deliver bond is the one that gives the greatest return from a strategy of buying a bond and simultaneously selling the futures contract, and then closing out positions on the expiry of the contract. This so-called cash-and-carry trading is actively pursued by proprietary trading desks in banks. If a contract is purchased and then held to maturity the buyer will receive, via the exchange's clearing house, the cheapest-to-deliver gilt. Traders sometimes try to exploit arbitrage price differentials between the future and the cheapest-to-deliver gilt, known as basis trading. This is discussed in Choudhry (2003). The mathematical calculation of the conversion factor for the gilt future is given at Appendix 14.1.

We summarise the contract specification of the long gilt futures contract traded on LIFFE at Figure 14.3. There is also a medium gilt contract on LIFFE, which was introduced in 1998 (having been discontinued in the early

1990s). This trades a notional five-year gilt, with eligible gilts being those of four to seven years maturity.

Unit of Trading	UK Gilt bond having a face value of £100,000, a notional coupon of 7% and a notional maturity of 10 years, changed from contract value of £50,000 from the September 1998 contract)
Deliverable grades	UK gilts with a maturity ranging from $8^3/_4$ to 13 years from the first day of the delivery month (changed from 10-15 years from the December 1998 contract)
Delivery months	March, June, September, December
Delivery date	Any business day during the delivery month
Last trading day	11:00 hours two business days before last business day of delivery month
Quotation	Percent of par expressed as points and hundredths of a point, for example 114.56 (changed from points and 1/32nds of a point, as in 11717 meaning 114 17/32 or 114.53125, from the June 1998 contract)
Minimum price movement	0.01 of one point (one tick)
Tick value	£10
Trading hours	08:00 - 16:15 hours
	16:22 - 18:00 hours
	All trading conducted electronically on LIFFE Connect

Figure 14.3 LIFFE Long Gilt future contract specifications

Futures pricing

The theoretical principle

Although it may not appear so on first sight, floor trading on a futures exchange is probably the closest one gets to an example of the economist's perfect and efficient market. The immediacy and liquidity of the market will ensure that at virtually all times the price of any futures contract reflects fair value. In essence because a futures contract represents an underlying asset, albeit a synthetic one, its price cannot differ from the actual cash-market price of the asset itself. This is because the market sets futures prices such they are arbitrage-free. We can illustrate this with a hypothetical example.

Let us say that the benchmark 10-year bond, with a coupon of 8% is trading at par. This bond is the underlying asset represented by the long bond futures contract; the front month contract expires in precisely three months. If we also say that the three-month Libor rate (the repo rate) is 6%, what is fair value for the front month futures contract?

For the purpose of illustration, let us start by assuming the futures price to be 105. We could carry out the following arbitrage-type trade:
- Buy the bond for £100
- Simultaneously sell the future at £105
- Borrow £100 for three months at the repo rate of 6%.

As this is a leveraged trade, we have borrowed the funds with which to buy the bond, and the loan is fixed at three months because we will hold the position to the futures contract expiry, which is in exactly three months' time. At expiry, as we are short futures we will deliver the underlying bond to the futures clearing house and close out the loan. This strategy will result in cash flows for us as shown below.

Futures settlement cash flows
    Price received for bond = 105.00
    Bond accrued =   2.00 (8% coupon for three months)
    Total proceeds =   107.00

Loan cash flows
    Repayment of principal = 100.00
    Loan interest =   1.500 (6% repo rate for three months)
    Total outlay =   101.50

The trade has resulted in a profit of £5.50, and this profit is guaranteed as we have traded the two positions simultaneously and held them both to maturity. We are not affected by subsequent market movements. The trade is an example of a pure arbitrage, which is risk-free. There is no cash outflow at the start of the trade because we borrowed the funds used to buy the bond. In essence, we have locked in the forward price of the bond by trading the future today, so that the final settlement price of the futures contract is irrelevant. If the situation described above were to occur in practice it would be very short-lived, precisely because arbitrageurs would buy the bond and sell the future to make this profit. This activity would force changes in the prices of both bond and future until the profit opportunity was removed.

So in our illustration, the price of the future was too high (and possibly the price of the bond was too low as well) and not reflecting fair value because the price of the synthetic asset was out of line with the cash asset. What if the price of the future was too low? Let us imagine that the futures contract is trading at 95.00. We could then carry out the following trade:

- Sell the bond at 100
- Simultaneously buy the future for 95
- Lend the proceeds of the short sale (100) for three months at 6%.

This trade has the same procedure as the first one, with no initial cash outflow, except that we have to cover the short position in the repo market, through which we invest the sale proceeds at the repo rate of 6%. After three months, we are delivered a bond as part of the futures settlement, and this is used to close out our short position. How has our strategy performed?

Futures settlement cash flows

Clean price of bond =	95.00
Bond accrued =	2.00
Total cash outflow =	97.00

Loan cash flows

Principal on loan maturity =	100.00
Interest from loan =	1.500
Total cash inflow =	101.500

The profit of £4.50 is again a risk-free arbitrage profit. Of course, our hypothetical world has ignored considerations such as bid-offer spreads for the bond, future and repo rates, which would apply in the real world and impact on any trading strategy. Yet again, however, the futures price is out of line with the cash market and has provided opportunity for arbitrage profit.

Given the terms and conditions that apply in our example, there is one price for the futures contract at which no arbitrage-profit opportunity is available. If we set the future price at 99.5, we would see that both trading strategies, buying the bond and selling the future or selling the bond and buying the future, yield a net cash flow of zero. There is no profit to be made from either strategy. So at 99.5 the futures price is in line with the cash market, and it will only move as the cash-market price moves; any other price will result in an arbitrage-profit opportunity.

Arbitrage-free futures pricing

The previous section demonstrated how we can arrive at the fair value for a bond futures contract provided we have certain market information. The market mechanism and continuous trading will ensure that the fair price *is* achieved, as arbitrage-profit opportunities are eliminated. We can determine the bond future's price given:

- the coupon of the underlying bond, and its price in the cash market
- the interest rate for borrowing or lending funds, from the trade date to the maturity date of the futures contract. This is known as the repo rate.

For the purpose of deriving this pricing model we can ignore bid-offer spreads and borrowing and lending spreads. If we set the following:

r is the repo rate

rc is the bond's running yield

P_{bond} is the price of the cash bond

P_{fut} is the price of the futures contract

t is the time to the expiry of the futures contract.

We can substitute these symbols into the cash-flow profile for our earlier trade strategy, that of buying the bond and selling the future. This gives us:

Futures settlement cash flows

     Clean price for bond = P_{fut}

     Bond accrued = $rc.t.P_{bond}$

     Total proceeds = $P_{fut} + (rc.t.P_{bond})$

Loan cash flows

     Repayment of loan principal = P_{bond}

     Loan interest = $r.t.P_{bond}$

     Total outlay = $P_{bond} + (r.t.P_{bond})$

The profit from the trade would be the difference between the proceeds and outlay, which we can set as follows:

$$\text{Profit} = P_{fut} + rc.t.P_{bond} - (P_{bond} + r.t.P_{bond})$$

We have seen how the futures price is at fair value when there is no profit to be gained from carrying out this trade, so if we set profit at zero, we obtain the following:

$$0 = P_{fut} + rc.t.P_{bond} - (P_{bond} + r.t.P_{bond})$$

Solving this expression for the futures price P_{fut} gives us:

$$P_{fut} = P_{bond} + P_{bond}\, t(r - rc)$$

Re-arranging this we get:

$$P_{fut} = P_{bond} + (1 + t[r - rc]) \tag{14.2}$$

If we repeat the procedure for the other strategy, that of selling the bond and simultaneously buying the future, and set the profit to zero, we will obtain the same expression for the futures price as given in (14.2) above.

It is the level of the repo rate in the market, compared to the running yield on the underlying bond, that sets the price for the futures contract. From the examples used at the start of this section we can see that it is the cost of funding compared to the repo rate that determines if the trade strategy results in a profit. The expression $[r - rc]$ from (14.2) is the net financing cost in the arbitrage trade, and is known as the *cost of carry*. If the running yield on the bond is higher than the funding cost (the repo rate) this is positive funding or *positive carry*. Negative funding (*negative carry*) is when the repo rate is higher than the running yield. The level of $[r - rc]$ will determine whether the futures price is trading above the cash-market price or below it. If we have positive carry (when $rc > r$) then the futures price will trade below the cash-market price, known as trading at a *discount*. Where $r > rc$ and we have negative carry then the futures price will be at a premium over the cash-market price. If the net funding cost was zero, such that we had neither positive or negative carry, then the futures price would be equal to the underlying bond price.

The cost of carry related to a bond futures contract is a function of the yield curve. In a positive yield-curve environment, the three-month repo rate is likely to be lower than the running yield on a bond so that the cost of carry is likely to be positive. As there is generally only a liquid market in long bond futures out to contracts that mature up to one year from the trade date, with a positive yield curve it would be unusual to have a short-term repo rate higher than the running yield on the long bond. So, in such an environment, we would have the future trading at a discount to the underlying cash bond. If there is a negative-sloping yield curve, the futures price will trade at a premium to the cash price. It is in circumstances of changes in the shape of the yield curve that opportunities for relative value and arbitrage trading arise, especially as the bond that is cheapest-to-deliver for the futures contract may change with large changes in the curve.

A trading strategy that involved simultaneous and opposite positions in the cheapest-to-deliver bond (CTD) and the futures contract is known as cash-and-carry trading or basis trading. However, by the law of no-arbitrage pricing, the payoff from such a trading strategy should be zero. If we set the profit from such a trading strategy as zero, we can obtain a pricing formula for the fair value of a futures contract, which summarises the discussion above, and states that the fair-value futures price is a function of the cost of carry on the underlying bond. This is given at (14.3).

$$P_{fut} = \frac{(P_{bond} + AI_0) \times (1 + rt) - \sum_{i=1}^{N} Ci(1 + rt_{i.del}) - AI_{del}}{CF} \qquad (14.3)$$

where

AI is the accrued interest on the underlying bond today
AI is the accrued interest on the underlying bond on the expiry or delivery date (assuming the bond is delivered on the final day, which will be the case if the running yield on the bond is above the money market rate)
C_i is the i'th coupon
N is the number of coupons paid from today to the expiry or delivery date.

Hedging using futures

The theoretical position

Bond futures are used for a variety of purposes. Much of one day's trading in futures will be speculative; that is, a punt on the direction of the market. Another main use of futures is to hedge bond positions. In theory, when hedging a cash-bond position with a bond futures contract, if cash and futures prices move together then any loss from one position will be offset by a gain from the other. When prices move exactly in lock-step with each other, the hedge is considered perfect. In practice, the price of even the cheapest-to-deliver bond (which one can view as being the bond being traded – implicitly – when one is trading the bond future) and the bond future will not move exactly in line with each other over a period of time. The difference between the cash price and the futures price is called the basis. The risk that the basis will change in an unpredictable way is known as *basis risk*.

The futures basis

The term "basis" is also used to describe the difference in price between the future and the deliverable cash bond. The basis is of considerable significance. It is often used to establish the fair value of a futures contract, as it is a function of the cost of carry. The gross basis is defined (for deliverable bonds only) as follows:

Gross basis = Clean bond price − (futures price × conversion factor).

Futures are a liquid and straightforward way of hedging a bond position. By hedging a bond position, the trader or fund manager is hoping to balance the loss on the cash position by the profit gained from the hedge. However, the hedge will not be exact for all bonds except the cheapest-to-deliver (CTD) bond, which we can assume is the futures contract underlying bond. The basis risk in a hedge position arises because the bond being hedged is not identical to the CTD bond. The basic principle is that if the trader is long (or net long, where the desk is running long and short positions in different bonds) in the cash market, an equivalent number of futures contracts will be sold to set up the hedge. If the cash position is short, the trader will buy futures. The hedging requirement can arise for different reasons. A market-maker will wish to hedge positions arising out of client business, when she is unsure when the resulting bond positions will be unwound. A fund manager may, for example, know that she needs to realise a cash sum at a specific time in the future to meet fund liabilities, and sell bonds at that time. The market-maker will want to hedge against a drop in value of positions during the time the bonds are held. The fund manager will want to hedge against a rise in interest rates between now and the bond sale date, to protect the value of the portfolio.

When putting on the hedge position, the key is to trade the correct number of futures contracts. This is determined by using the hedge ratio of the bond and the future, which is a function of the volatilities of the two instruments. The number of contracts to trade is calculated using the hedge ratio, which is given by :

$$\text{Hedge ratio} = \frac{\text{Volatility of bond to be hedged}}{\text{Volatility of hedging instrument}}$$

Therefore one needs to use the volatility values of each instrument. We can see from the calculation that if the bond is more volatile than the hedging instrument, then a greater amount of the hedging instrument will be required. Let us now look in greater detail at the hedge ratio.

There are different methods available to calculate hedge ratios. The most common ones are the conversion-factor method, which can be used for deliverable bonds (also known as the price-factor method) and the modified-duration method (also known as the basis-point value method).

Where a hedge is put on against a bond that is in the futures delivery basket it is common for the conversion factor to be used to calculate the hedge ratio. A conversion-factor hedge ratio is more useful as it is transparent and remains constant, irrespective of any changes in the price of the cash bond or the futures contract. The number of futures contracts required to hedge a deliverable bond using the conversion-factor hedge ratio is determined using the following equation:

$$Number\ of\ contracts = \frac{M_{bond} \times CF}{M_{fut}} \qquad (14.4)$$

where M is the nominal value of the bond or futures contract.

The conversion-factor method may only be used for bonds in the delivery basket. It is important to ensure that this method is only used for one bond. It is an erroneous procedure to use the ratio of conversion factors of two different bonds when calculating a hedge ratio. This will be considered again later.

Unlike the conversion-factor method, the modified-duration hedge ratio may be used for all bonds, both deliverable and non-deliverable. In calculating this hedge ratio the modified duration is multiplied by the dirty price of the cash bond to obtain the basis-point value (BPV). As we discovered in Chapter 2, the BPV represents the actual impact of a change in the yield on the price of a specific bond. The BPV allows the trader to calculate the hedge ratio to reflect the different price sensitivity of the chosen bond (compared to the CTD bond) to interest-rate movements. The hedge ratio calculated using BPVs must be constantly updated, because it will change if the price of the bond and/or the futures contract changes. This may necessitate periodic adjustments to the number of lots used in the hedge. The number of futures contracts required to hedge a bond using the BPV method is calculated using the following :

$$Number\ of\ contracts = \frac{M_{bond}}{M_{fut}} \times \frac{BPV_{bond}}{BPV_{fut}} \qquad (14.5)$$

where the BPV of a futures contract is defined with respect to the BPV of its CTD bond, as given by (14.6).

$$BPV_{fut} = \frac{BPV_{CTDbond}}{CF_{CTDbond}} \qquad (14.6)$$

The simplest hedge procedure to undertake is one for a position consisting of only one bond, the cheapest-to-deliver bond. The relationship between the futures price and the price of the CTD given by (14.3) indicates that the price of the future will move for moves in the price of the CTD bond; so, therefore, we may set:

$$\Delta P_{fut} \cong \frac{\Delta P_{bond}}{CF} \qquad (14.7)$$

where CF is the CTD conversion factor.

The price of the futures contract, over time, does not move tick-for-tick (although it may on an intra-day basis) but rather by the amount of the change divided by the conversion factor. It is apparent, therefore, that to hedge a position in the CTD bond we must hold the number of futures contracts equivalent to the value of bonds held multiplied by the conversion factor. Obviously, if a conversion factor is less than one, the number of futures contracts will be less than the equivalent nominal value of the cash position; the opposite is true for bonds that have a conversion factor greater than one. However, the hedge is not as simple as dividing the nominal value of the bond position by the nominal value represented by one futures contract (!); this error is frequently made by graduate trainees and those new to the desk.

To measure the effectiveness of the hedge position, it is necessary to compare the performance of the futures position with that of the cash-bond position, and to see how much the hedge instrument mirrored the performance of the cash instrument. A simple calculation is made to measure the effectiveness of the hedge, given by (14.8), which is the percentage value of the hedge effectiveness.

$$Hedge\ effectiveness = -\left[\frac{Fut\ p/l}{Bond\ p/l}\right] \times 100 \qquad (14.8)$$

Hedging a bond portfolio

The principles established above may be applied when hedging a portfolio containing a number of bonds. It is more realistic to consider a portfolio as holding not just bonds that are outside the delivery basket, but are also non-government bonds. In this case, we need to calculate the number of futures contracts to put on as a hedge based on the volatility of each bond in the portfolio compared to the volatility of the CTD bond. Note that, in practice, there is usually more than one futures contract that may be used as the hedge instrument. For example, in the sterling market it would be more sensible to use LIFEE's medium gilt contract, whose underlying bond has a notional maturity of four to seven years, if hedging a portfolio of short- to medium-dated bonds. However, for the purposes of illustration we will assume that only one contract, the long gilt, is available.

To calculate the number of futures contracts required to hold as a hedge against any specific bond, we use the expression at (14.9).

$$Hedge = \frac{M_{bond}}{M_{fut}} \times Vol_{bond/CTD} \times Vol_{CTD/fut} \qquad (14.9)$$

where

M is the nominal value of the bond or future

$Vol_{bond/CTD}$ is the relative volatility of the bond being hedged compared to that of the CTD bond

$Vol_{CTD/fut}$ is the relative volatility of the CTD bond compared to that of the future.

It is not necessarily straightforward to determine the relative volatility of a bond vis-à-vis the CTD bond. If the bond being hedged is a government bond, we can calculate the relative volatility using the two bonds' modified duration. This is because the yields of both may be safely assumed to be strongly positively correlated. If, however, the bond being hedged is a corporate bond and/or a non-vanilla bond, we must obtain the relative volatility using regression analysis, as the yields between the two bonds may not be strongly positively correlated. This is apparent when one remembers that the yield spread of corporate bonds over government bonds is not constant, and will fluctuate with changes in government-bond yields. To use regression analysis to determine relative volatilities, historical price date on the bond is required. The daily price moves in the target bond and the CTD bond are then analysed to assess the slope of the regression line. In this section, we will restrict the discussion to a portfolio of government bonds.

If we are hedging a portfolio of government bonds, we can use (14.10) to determine relative volatility values, which are based on the modified duration of each of the bonds in the portfolio.

$$Vol_{bond/CTD} = \frac{\Delta P_{bond}}{\Delta P_{CTD}} = \frac{MD_{bond} \times P_{bond}}{MD_{CTD} \times P_{CTD}} \qquad (14.10)$$

where MD is the modified duration of the bond being hedged or the CTD bond, as appropriate. This preserves the terminology we introduced in Chapter 2.[1]

Once we have calculated the relative volatility of the bond being hedged, equation (14.11) (obtained by re-arranging (14.7)) tells us that the relative volatility of the CTD bond to that of the futures contract is approximately the same as its conversion factor. We are then in a position to calculate the futures hedge for each bond in a portfolio.

$$Vol_{CTD/fut} = \frac{\Delta P_{CTD}}{\Delta P_{fut}} \approx CF_{CTD} \qquad (14.11)$$

Table 14.1 shows a portfolio of five UK gilts on 20th October 1999. The nominal value of the bonds in the portfolio is £200 million, and the bonds have a market value, excluding accrued interest, of £206.84 million. Only one of the bonds is a deliverable bond, the 5¾% 2009 gilt which is in fact the CTD bond. For the Dec99 futures contract the bond had a conversion factor of 0.9124950. The fact that this bond is the CTD explains why it has a relative volatility of 1. We calculate the number of futures contracts required to hedge each position, using the equations listed above. For example, the hedge requirement for the position in the 7% 2002 gilt was calculated as follows:

$$\frac{5,000,000}{100,000} \times \frac{2.245 \times 101.50}{7.235 \times 99.84} \times 0.9124950 = 14.39$$

The volatility of all the bonds is calculated relative to the CTD bond, and the number of futures contracts determined using the conversion factor for the CTD bond. The bond with the highest volatility is, not surprisingly, the 6% 2028, which has the longest maturity of all the bonds and hence the highest modified duration. We note from Table 14.1 that the portfolio

---

[1] In certain textbooks and research documents, it is suggested that the ratio of the conversion factors of the bond being hedged (if it is in the delivery basket) and the CTD bond can be used to determine the relative volatility of the target bond. This is a fallacious argument. The conversion factor of a deliverable bond is the price factor that will set the yield of the bond equal to the notional coupon of the futures contract on the delivery date, and it is a function mainly of the coupon of the deliverable bond. The price volatility of a bond, on the other hand, is a measure of its modified duration, which is a function of the bond's duration (that is, the term to maturity). Therefore, using conversion factors to measure volatility levels will produce erroneous results. It is important not to misuse conversion factors when arranging hedge ratios.

requires a hedge position of 2091 futures contracts. This illustrates how a "rough-and-ready" estimate of the hedging requirement, based on nominal values, would be insufficient as that would suggest a hedge position of only 2000 contracts.

		CTD	5.75% 2009		
		Modified duration	7.2345656		
		Conversion factor	0.9124950		
		Price	99.84		

Bond	Nominal amount (£m)	Price	Yield %	Duration	Modified duration	Relative volatility	Number of contracts
UKT 8% 2000	12	102.17	5.972	1.072	1.01158797	0.143090242	15.67
UKT 7% 2002	5	101.50	6.367	2.388	2.24505721	0.315483336	14.39
UKT 5% 2004	38	94.74	6.327	4.104	3.85979102	0.50626761	175.55
UKT 5.75% 2009	100	99.84	5.770	7.652	7.23456557	1	912.50
UKT 6% 2028	45	119.25	4.770	15.031	14.3466641	2.368603078	972.60
Total	200						2090.71

Table 14.1 Bond futures hedge for hypothetical gilt portfolio, 20 October 1999

The effectiveness of the hedge must be monitored over time. No hedge will be completely perfect, however, and the calculation illustrated above, as it uses modified-duration value, does not take into account the convexity effect of the bonds. The reason why a futures hedge will not be perfect is because, in practice, the price of the futures contract will not move tick-for-tick with the CTD bond, at least not over a period of time. This is the basis risk that is inherent in hedging cash bonds with futures. In addition, the calculation of the hedge is only completely accurate for a parallel shift in yields, as it is based on modified duration, so as the yield curve changes around pivots, the hedge will move out of line. Finally, the long gilt future is not the appropriate contract to use to hedge three of the bonds in the portfolio, or over 25% of the portfolio by nominal value. This is because these bonds are short- or medium-dated, and so their price movements will not track the futures price as closely as longer-dated bonds. In this case, the more appropriate futures contract to use would have been the medium gilt contract, or (for the first bond, the 8% 2000) a strip of short sterling contracts. Using shorter-dated instruments would reduce some of the basis risk contained in the portfolio hedge.

The margin process

Institutions buying and selling futures on an exchange deal with only one counterparty at all times, the exchange clearing house. The clearing house is responsible for the settlement of all contracts, including managing the delivery process. A central clearing mechanism eliminates counterparty risk for anyone dealing on the exchange, because the clearing house guarantees the settlement of all transactions. The clearing house may be owned by the exchange itself, such as the one associated with the Chicago Mercantile Exchange (the CME Clearinghouse) or it may be a separate entity, such as the London Clearing House, which settles transactions on LIFFE. The LCH is also involved in running clearing systems for swaps and repo products in certain currencies.

One of the key benefits to the market of the clearing-house mechanism is that counterparty risk, as it is transferred to the clearing house, is virtually eliminated. The mechanism that enables the clearing house to accept the counterparty risk is the margining process that is employed at all futures exchanges. A bank or local trader must deposit margin before commencing dealing on the exchange; each day a further amount must be deposited or returned, depending on the results of the day's trading activity.

The exchange will specify the level of margin that must be deposited for each type of futures contract that a bank wishes to deal in. The initial margin will be a fixed sum per lot. So, for example, if the margin was £1000 per lot, an opening position of 100 lots would require margin of £100,000. Once initial margin has been deposited, there is a mark-to-market of all positions at the close of business; exchange-traded instruments are the most transparent products in the market, and the closing price is not only known to everyone, it is also indisputable. The closing price is also known as the settlement price. Any losses suffered by a trading counterparty, whether closed out or run overnight, are entered as a debit on the party's account and must be paid the next day. Trading profits are credited and may be withdrawn from the margin account the next day. This daily process is known as variation margining. Thus, the margin account is updated on a daily basis and the maximum loss that must be made up on any morning is the maximum price movement that occurred the previous day. It is a serious issue if a trading party is unable to meet a margin call. In such a case, the exchange will order it to cease trading, and will also liquidate all its open positions; any losses will be met out of the firm's margin account. If the level of funds in the margin account is insufficient, the losses will be made good from funds paid out of a general fund run by the clearing house, which is maintained by all members of the exchange.

Payment of margin is made by electronic funds transfer between the trading party's bank account and the clearing house. Initial margin is usually paid in cash, although clearing houses will also accept high-quality securities, such as T-bills or certain government bonds, to the value of the margin required. Variation margin is always cash. The advantage of depositing securities rather than cash is that the depositing firm earns interest on its margin. This is not available on a cash margin, and the interest forgone on a cash margin is effectively the cost of trading futures on the exchange. However, if securities are used, there is effectively no cost associated with trading on the exchange (we ignore, of course, infrastructure costs and staff salaries).

The daily settlement of exchange-traded futures contracts, as opposed to when the contract expires or the position is closed out, is the main reason why futures prices are not equal to forward prices for long-dated instruments. This is known as the convexity bias and is discussed in Chapter 15.

Appendices

APPENDIX 14.1 The conversion factor for the long gilt future

In this appendix, we describe the process used for the calculation of the conversion factor or price factor for deliverable bonds of the long gilt contract. The contract specifies a bond of maturity $8^3/_4$–13 years and a notional coupon of 7%. For each bond that is eligible to be in the delivery basket, the conversion factor is given by the following expression:

$$\frac{P(7)}{100}$$

where the numerator $P(7)$ is equal to the price per £100 nominal of the deliverable gilt at which it has a gross redemption yield of 7%, calculated as at the first day of the delivery month, less the accrued interest on the bond on that day. This calculation uses the formulae given at (A14.1) and the expression used to calculate accrued interest.

The numerator $P(7)$ is given by A40.1 below.

$$P(7) = \frac{1}{1.035^{\frac{t}{s}}}\left[c_1 + \frac{c_2}{1.035} + \frac{C}{0.07}\left(\frac{1}{1.035} - \frac{1}{1.035^n}\right) + \frac{100}{1.035^n}\right] - AI$$

$$(A14.1)$$

where

c_1 is the cash flow due on the following quasi-coupon date, per £100 nominal of the gilt.

c_1 will be zero if the first day of the delivery month occurs in the ex-dividend period or if the gilt has a long first coupon period and the first day of the delivery month occurs in the first full coupon period.

c_1 will be less than $C/2$ if the first day of the delivery month falls in a short first coupon period. c_1 will be greater than $C/2$ if the first day of the delivery month falls in a long first coupon period and the first day of the delivery month occurs in the second full coupon period

c_2 is the cash flow due on the next-but-one quasi-coupon date, per £100 nominal of the gilt. c_2 will be greater than $C/2$ if the first day of the delivery month falls in a long first coupon period and in the first full coupon period. In all other cases, $c_2 = C/2$.

C is the annual coupon of the gilt, per £100 nominal

t is the number of calendar days from and including the first day of the delivery month up to but excluding the next quasi-coupon date

s is the number of calendar days in the full coupon period in which the first day of the delivery month occurs

n is the number of full coupon periods between the following quasi-coupon date and the redemption date

AI is the accrued interest per £100 nominal of the gilt.

The accrued interest used in the formula above is given according to the following procedures.

If the first day of the delivery month occurs in a standard coupon period, and the first day of the delivery month occurs on or before the ex-dividend date, then:

$$AI = \frac{t}{s} \times \frac{C}{2}$$

$$(14.2)$$

If the first day of the delivery month occurs in a standard coupon period, and the first day of the delivery month occurs after the ex-dividend date, then:

$$AI = \left(\frac{t}{s} - 1\right) \times \frac{C}{2} \qquad (A14.3)$$

where

t is the number of calendar days from and including the last coupon date up to but excluding the first day of the delivery month:

s is the number of calendar days in the full coupon period in which the first day of the delivery month occurs.

If the first day of the delivery month occurs in a short first coupon period, and the first day of the delivery month occurs on or before the ex-dividend date, then:

$$AI = \frac{t^*}{s} \times \frac{C}{2} \qquad (A14.4)$$

If the first day of the delivery month occurs in a short first coupon period, and the first day of the delivery month occurs after the ex-dividend date, then:

$$AI = \left(\frac{t^* - n}{s}\right) \times \frac{C}{2} \qquad (A14.5)$$

where

t^* is the number of calendar days from and including the issue date up to but excluding the first day of the delivery month

n is the number of calendar days from and including the issue date up to but excluding the next quasi-coupon date.

If the first day of the delivery month occurs in a long first coupon period, and during the first full coupon period, then:

$$AI = \frac{u}{s_1} \times \frac{C}{2} \qquad (A14.6)$$

If the first day of the delivery month occurs in a long first coupon period, and during the second full coupon period and on or before the ex-dividend date, then:

$$AI = \left(\frac{p_1}{s_1} + \frac{p_2}{s_2}\right) \times \frac{C}{2} \qquad\qquad (A14.7)$$

If the first day of the delivery month occurs in a long first coupon period, and during the second full coupon period and after the ex-dividend date, then:

$$AI = \left(\frac{p_2}{s_2} - 1\right) \times \frac{C}{2} \qquad\qquad (A14.8)$$

where

u is the number of calendar days from and including the issue date up to but excluding the first day of the delivery month

s_1 is the number of calendar days in the full coupon period in which the issue date occurs

s_2 is the number of days in the next full coupon period after the full coupon period in which the issue date occurs

p_1 is the number of calendar days from and including the issues date up to but excluding the next quasi-coupon date

p_2 is the number of calendar days from and including the quasi-coupon date after the issue date up to but excluding the first day of the delivery month which falls in the next full coupon period after the full coupon period in which the issue date occurs.

Selected Bibliography and References

Choudhry, M., *An Introduction to Bond Markets*, p.229–242, SI (Services) Publishing, 1999.

Choudhry, M., *The Bond and Money Markets,* Butterworth-Heinemann 2001

Choudhry, M., *The Futures Bond Basis,* YieldCurve publishing 2003

Fabozzi, F., *Fixed Income Mathematics*, Probus, 1993.

Figlewski, S., *Hedging with Financial Futures for Institutional Investors*, Ballinger, 1986.

Kolb, R., *Interest Rate Futures: A Comprehensive Introduction*, RF Dame, 1982.

Kolb, R., *Futures, Options and Swaps*, 4th edition, Blackwell, 2003

Resnick, B., "The Relationship between Futures Prices for US Treasury Bonds", *Review of Research in Futures Markets* 3, 1984, p.84–104.

Stultz, R., "Optimal Hedging Policies", *Journal of Financial and Quantitative Analysis*", 19, June 1984, p.127–140.

CHAPTER

15

Swaps

Swaps are off-balance-sheet instruments involving combinations of two or more basic building blocks. Most swaps currently traded in the market involve combinations of cash-market securities; for example, a fixed interest-rate security combined with a floating interest-rate security, possibly also combined with a currency transaction. However, the market has also seen swaps that involve a futures or forward component, as well as swaps that involve an option component. The market in, say, dollar, euro and sterling interest-rate swaps is very large and very liquid. The main types of swap are interest-rate swaps, asset swaps, basis swaps, fixed-rate currency swaps and currency-coupon swaps. The market for swaps is organised by the International Swaps and Derivatives Association (ISDA).

Swaps are now one of the most important and useful instruments in the debt-capital markets. They are used by a wide range of institutions, including banks, mortgage banks and building societies, corporates and local authorities. The demand for them has grown as the continuing uncertainty and volatility of interest rates and exchange rates has made it ever more important to hedge their exposures. As the market has matured, the instrument has gained wider acceptance, and is regarded as a "plain-vanilla" product in the debt-capital markets. Virtually all commercial and investment banks will quote swap prices for their customers, and as they are OTC instruments, dealt over the telephone, it is possible for banks to tailor swaps to match the precise requirements of individual customers. There is also a close relationship between the bond market and the swap market, and corporate finance teams and underwriting banks keep a close eye on the government yield curve and the swap yield curve, looking out for possibilities regarding new issue of debt.

In this chapter, we review the use of interest-rate swaps from the point of view of the bond-market participant; this includes pricing and valuation and its use as a hedging tool. The bibliography lists further reading on important topics such as pricing, valuation and credit risk. The following chapter looks at a new development in the swaps market, the exchange-traded interest-rate swap.

Interest–rate swaps

Introduction

Interest-rate swaps are the most important type of swap in terms of volume of transactions. They are used to manage and hedge interest-rate risk and exposure, while market-makers will also take positions in swaps that reflect their view on the direction of interest rates. An interest-rate swap is an agreement between two counterparties to make periodic interest payments to one another during the life of the swap, on a predetermined set of dates, based on a notional principal amount. One party is the fixed-rate payer, and this rate is agreed at the time of trade of the swap; the other party is the floating-rate payer, the floating rate being determined during the life of the swap by reference to a specific market index. The principal or notional amount is never physically exchanged; hence, the term "off-balance-sheet", but is used merely to calculate the interest payments. The fixed-rate payer receives floating-rate interest and is said to be "long" or to have "bought" the swap. The long side has conceptually purchased a floating-rate note (because it receives floating-rate interest) and issued a fixed coupon bond (because it pays out fixed interest at intervals); that is, it has in principle borrowed funds. The floating-rate payer is said to be "short" or to have "sold" the swap. The short side has conceptually purchased a coupon bond (because it receives fixed-rate interest) and issued a floating-rate note (because it pays floating-rate interest). So an interest-rate swap is :

- an agreement between two parties
- to exchange a stream of cash flows
- calculated as a percentage of a *notional* sum
- and calculated on different interest bases.

For example, in a trade between Bank A and Bank B, Bank A may agree to pay fixed semi-annual coupons of 10% on a notional principal sum of £1 million, in return for receiving from Bank B the prevailing six-month sterling Libor rate on the same amount. The known cash flow is the fixed payment of £50,000 every six months by Bank A to Bank B.

Interest-rate swaps trade in a secondary market, so their value moves in line with market interest rates, in exactly the same way as bonds. If a five-year interest-rate swap is transacted today at a rate of 5%, and five-year interest rates subsequently fall to 4.75%, the swap will have decreased in value to the fixed-rate payer, and correspondingly increased in value to the floating-rate payer, who has now seen the level of interest payments fall. The opposite would be true if five-year rates moved to 5.25%. Why is this? Consider the fixed-rate payer in an IR swap to be a borrower of funds; if she fixes the interest rate payable on a loan for five years, and then this interest rate decreases shortly afterwards, is she better off? No, because she is now paying above the market rate for the funds borrowed. For this reason, a swap contract decreases in value to the fixed-rate payer if there is a fall in rates. Equally a floating-rate payer gains if there is a fall in rates, as he can take advantage of the new rates and pay a lower level of interest; hence, the value of a swap increases to the floating-rate payer if there is a fall in rates.

A bank swaps desk will have an overall net interest-rate position arising from all the swaps it has traded that are currently on the book. This position is an interest-rate exposure at all points along the term structure, out to the maturity of the longest-dated swap. At the close of business each day, all the swaps on the book will be *marked-to-market* at the interest rate quoted for that day.

A swap can be viewed in two ways; either as a bundle of forward or futures contracts, or as a bundle of cash flows arising from the "sale" and "purchase" of cash-market instruments. If we imagine a strip of futures contracts, maturing every three or six months out to three years, we can see how this is conceptually similar to a three-year interest-rate swap. However, in the author's view it is better to visualise a swap as being a bundle of cash flows arising from cash instruments.

Let us imagine we have only two positions on our book:
- a long position in £100 million of a three-year FRN that pays six-month Libor semi-annually, and is trading at par
- a short position in £100 million of a three-year gilt with coupon of 6% that is also trading at par.

Being short, a bond is the equivalent to being a borrower of funds. Assuming this position is kept to maturity, the resulting cash flows are shown in Table 15.1

Cashflows resulting from long position in FRN and short position in gilt

Period (6mo)	FRN	Gilt	Net cashflow
0	−£100m	+£100m	£0
1	+(Libor × 100)/2	−3	+(Libor × 100)/2 - 3.0
2	+(Libor × 100)/2	−3	+(Libor × 100)/2 - 3.0
3	+(Libor × 100)/2	−3	+(Libor × 100)/2 - 3.0
4	+(Libor × 100)/2	−3	+(Libor × 100)/2 - 3.0
5	+(Libor × 100)/2	−3	+(Libor × 100)/2 - 3.0
6	+[(Libor × 100)/2] + 100	−103	+(Libor × 100)/2 - 3.0

The Libor rate is the six-month rate prevailing at the time of the setting, for instance the Libor rate at period 4 will be the rate actually prevailing at period 4.

Table 15.1 Three-year cash flows

There is no net outflow or inflow at the start of these trades, as the £100 million purchase of the FRN is netted with receipt of £100 million from the sale of the gilt. The resulting cash flows over the three-year period are shown in the last column of Table 15.1. This net position is exactly the same as that of a fixed-rate payer in an IR swap. As we had at the start of the trade, there is no cash inflow or outflow on maturity. For a floating-rate payer, the cash flow would mirror exactly a long position in a fixed-rate bond and a short position in an FRN. Therefore, the fixed-rate payer in a swap is said to be short in the bond market; that is, a borrower of funds. The floating-rate payer in a swap is said to be long the bond market.

Market terminology

Virtually all swaps are traded under the legal terms and conditions stipulated in the ISDA standard documentation. The trade date for a swap is, not surprisingly, the date on which the swap is transacted. The terms of the trade include the fixed interest rate, the maturity and notional amount of the swap, and the payment bases of both legs of the swap. The date from which floating interest payments are determined is the setting date, which may also be the trade date. Most swaps fix the floating-rate payments to Libor, although other reference rates that are used include the US Prime rate, the Fed Funds rate, euribor, the Treasury-bill rate and the commercial-paper rate. In the same way as for FRA and eurocurrency deposits, the rate is fixed two business days before the interest period begins. The second (and subsequent) setting date will be two business days before the beginning of the second (and subsequent) swap periods. The effective date is the date from which interest on the swap is calculated, and this is typically two business days after the trade date. In a forward-start swap, the effective date will be at some point in the future, specified in the swap terms. The floating interest rate for each period is fixed at the start of the period, so that the interest payment amount is known in advance by both parties (the fixed rate is known, of course, throughout the swap by both parties).

Although for the purposes of explaining swap structures, both parties are said to pay interest payments (and receive them), in practice only the net difference between both payments changes hands at the end of each interest period. This eases the administration associated with swaps and reduces the number of cash flows for each swap. The counterparty that is the net payer at the end of each period will make a payment to the other counterparty. The first payment date will occur at the end of the first interest period, and subsequent payment dates will fall at the end of successive interest periods. The final payment date falls on the maturity date of the swap. The calculation of interest is given by (15.1).

$$I = M \times r \times \frac{n}{B} \qquad (15.1)$$

where

I is the interest amount, M is the nominal amount of the swap and B is the interest day-base for the swap. Dollar and euro-denominated swaps use an actual/360 day-count, similar to other money-market instruments in those currencies, while sterling swaps use an actual/365 day-count basis.

The cash flows resulting from a vanilla interest-rate swap are illustrated in Figure 15.1, using the normal convention where cash inflows are shown as an arrow pointing up, while cash outflows are shown as an arrow pointing down. The counterparties in a swap transaction only pay across net cash flows, however, so at each interest payment date only one actual cash transfer will be made, by the net payer. This is shown as Figure 15.1(iii).

(i) Cash flows for fixed-rate payer

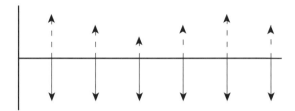

(ii) Cash flows for floating-rate payer

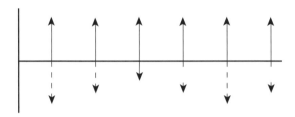

(iii) Net cash flows

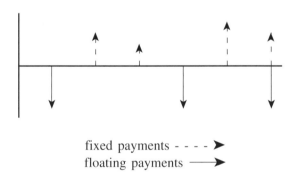

fixed payments - - - - ➤
floating payments ──────➤

Figure 15.1 Cash flows for typical interest-rate swap

Swap spreads and the swap yield curve

In the market, banks will quote two-way swap rates, on screens and on the telephone or via a dealing system such as Reuters. Brokers will also be active in relaying prices in the market. The convention in the market is for the swap market-maker to set the floating leg at Libor and then quote the fixed rate that is payable for that maturity. So for a five-year swap, a bank's swap desk might be willing to quote the following:

Floating-rate payer: pay 6-mo-Libor
                      receive fixed rate of 5.19%.
Fixed-rate payer: pay fixed rate of 5.25%
                      receive 6-mo Libor.

In this case, the bank is quoting an offer rate of 5.25%, which the fixed-rate payer will pay, in return for receiving Libor flat. The bid price quote is 5.19%, which is what a floating-rate payer will receive fixed. The bid-offer spread in this case is therefore 6 basis points. The fixed-rate quotes are always at a spread above the government bond yield curve. Let us assume that the five-year gilt is yielding 4.88%. In this case, then, the five-year swap bid rate is 31 basis points above this yield. So the bank's swap trader could quote the swap rates as a spread above the benchmark-bond yield curve, say 37–31, which is her swap spread quote. This means that the bank is happy to enter into a swap paying fixed 31 basis points above the benchmark yield and receiving Libor, and receiving fixed 37 basis points above the yield curve and paying Libor. The bank's screen on, say, Bloomberg or Reuters might look something like Table 15.2, which quotes the swap rates as well as the current spread over the government-bond benchmark.

1YR	4.50	4.45	+17
2YR	4.69	4.62	+25
3YR	4.88	4.80	+23
4YR	5.15	5.05	+29
5YR	5.25	5.19	+31
10YR	5.50	5.40	+35

Table 15.2 Swap quotes

The swap spread is a function of the same factors that influence the spread over government bonds for other instruments. For shorter-duration swaps of, say, up to three years, there are other yield curves that can be used in comparison, such as the cash-market curve or a curve derived from futures prices. For longer-dated swaps, the spread is determined mainly by the credit spreads that prevail in the corporate-bond market. Because a swap is viewed as a package of long and short positions in fixed- and floating-rate bonds, it is the credit spreads in these two markets that will determine the swap spread. This is logical; essentially, it is the premium for greater credit risk involved in lending to corporates that dictates that a swap rate will be higher than the same maturity government-bond yield. Technical factors will be responsible for day-to-day fluctuations in swap rates, such as the supply of corporate bonds and the level of demand for swaps, plus the cost to swap traders of hedging their swap positions.

We can summarise by saying that swap spreads over government bonds reflect the supply and demand conditions of both swaps and government bonds, as well as the market's view on the credit quality of swap counterparties. There is considerable information content in the swap yield curve, much like that in the government-bond yield curve. During times of credit concerns in the market, such as the corrections in Asian and Latin American markets in summer 1998, and the possibility of default by the Russian government regarding its long-dated US-dollar bonds, the swap spread will increase, more so at higher maturities. To illustrate this, let us consider the sterling swap spread in 1998/99. The UK swap spread widened from the second half of 1998 onwards, a reaction to bond market volatility around the world. At such times, investors embark on a "flight to quality" that results in yield spreads widening. In the swap market, the spread between two-year and 10-year swaps also increased, reflecting market concern with credit and counterparty risk. The spreads narrowed in the first quarter 1999, as credit concerns brought about by market corrections in 1998 declined. The change in swap spreads is shown in Figure 15.2

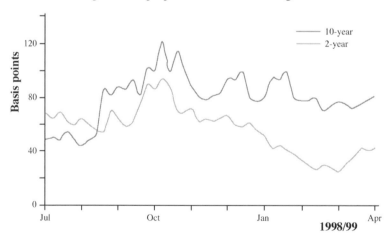

Figure 15.2 Sterling two-year and 10-year swap spreads during 1998/99

Generic swap valuation

Banks generally use par-swap (zero-coupon) swap pricing. We will look at this method in the next section. First, however, we will introduce an intuitive swap valuation method.

Intuitive swap pricing

Assume we have a vanilla interest-rate swap with a notional principal of N that pays n payments during its life, to a maturity date of T. The date of each payment is on t_i with $i=1,\ldots n$. The present value today of a future payment is denoted by $PV(0, t)$. If the swap rate is r, the value of the fixed-leg payments is given by (15.2) below.

$$PV_{fixed} = N\sum_{i=1}^{n} PV(0,t_i) \times \left[r \times \left(\frac{t_i - t_{i-1}}{B} \right) \right] \qquad (15.2)$$

where B is the money-market day base. The term {symbol} is simply the number of days between the ith and the i-1th payments.

The value of the floating-leg payments at the date t_1 for an existing swap is given by,

$$PV_{float} = N \times \left[rl \times \frac{t_1}{B} \right] + N - [N \times PV(t_1,t_n)] \qquad (15.3)$$

where rl is the LIBOR rate that has been set for the next interest payment. We set the present value of the floating-rate payment at time 0 as follows,

$$PV(0,t_1) = \frac{1}{1 + rl(t_1)(\frac{t_1}{B})} . \qquad (15.4)$$

For a new swap, the value of the floating payments is given by

$$PV_{float} = N\left[rl \times \frac{t_1}{B} + 1 \right] \times PV(0,t_1) - PV(0,t_n) . \qquad (15.5)$$

The swap valuation is then given by $PV_{fixed} - PV_{float}$. The swap rate quoted by a market-making bank is that which sets $PV_{fixed} = PV_{float}$ and is known as the par or zero-coupon swap rate. We consider this next.

Zero-coupon swap pricing

So far, we have discussed how vanilla swap prices are often quoted as a spread over the benchmark government-bond yield in that currency, and how this swap spread is mainly a function of the credit spread required by the market over the government (risk-free) rate. This method is convenient and also logical because banks use government bonds as the main instrument when hedging their swap books. However, because much bank swap trading is now conducted in non-standard, tailor-made swaps, this method can sometimes be unwieldy, as each swap needs to have its spread calculated to suit its particular characteristics. Therefore, banks use a standard pricing method for all swaps known as zero-coupon swap pricing.

In Chapter 3, we referred to zero-coupon bonds and zero-coupon interest rates. Zero-coupon or spot rates, are true interest rates for their particular term to maturity. In zero-coupon swap pricing, a bank will view all swaps, even the most complex, as a series of cash flows. The zero-coupon rates that apply now for each of the cash flows in a swap can be used to value these cash flows. Therefore, to value and price a swap, each of the swap's cash flows are present-valued using known spot rates; the sum of these present values is the value of the swap.

In a swap, the fixed-rate payments are known in advance and so it is straightforward to present-value them. The present value of the floating rate payments is usually estimated in two stages. First, the implied forward rates can be calculated using (15.6). We are quite familiar with this relationship from our reading of the earlier chapter.

$$rf_i = \left(\frac{df_i}{df_{i+1}} - 1\right)N \qquad (15.6)$$

where

rf_i is the one-period forward rate starting at time i
df_i is the discount factor for the maturity period i
df_{i+1} is the discount factor for the period $i + 1$
N is the number of times per year that coupons are paid.

By definition, the floating-payment interest rates are not known in advance, so the swap bank will predict what these will be, using the forward rates applicable to each payment date. The forward rates are those that are currently implied from spot rates. Once the size of the floating-rate payments have been estimated, these can also be valued by using the spot rates. The total value of the fixed and floating legs is the sum of all the present values, so the value of the total swap is the net of the present values of the fixed and floating legs.

While the term "zero-coupon" refers to an interest rate that applies to a discount instrument that pays no coupon and has one cash flow (at maturity), it is not necessary to have a functioning zero-coupon bond market in order to construct a zero-coupon yield curve. In practice, most financial pricing models use a combination of the following instruments to construct zero-coupon yield curves:

- money-market deposits
- interest-rate futures
- FRAs
- government bonds.

Frequently an overlap in the maturity period of all instruments is used. FRA rates are usually calculated from interest-rate futures so it is only necessary to use one of either FRA or futures rates.

Once a zero-coupon yield curve (term structure) is derived, this may be used to value a future cash flow maturing at any time along the term structure. This includes swaps: to price an interest-rate swap, we calculate the present value of each of the cash flows using the zero-coupon rates and then sum all the cash flows. As we noted above, while the fixed-rate payments are known in advance, the floating-rate payments must be estimated, using the forward rates implied by the zero-coupon yield curve. The net present value of the swap is the net difference between the present values of the fixed- and floating-rate legs.

Calculating the forward rate from spot-rate discount factors

Remember that one way to view a swap is as a long position in a fixed-coupon bond that was funded at Libor, or against a short position in a floating-rate bond. The cash flows from such an arrangement would be paying floating-rate and receiving fixed-rate. In the former arrangement, where a long position in a fixed-rate bond is funded with a floating-rate loan, the cash flows from the principals will cancel out, as they are equal and opposite (assuming the price of the bond on purchase was par), leaving a collection of cash flows that mirror an interest-rate swap that pays floating and receives fixed. Therefore, as the fixed-rate on an interest-rate swap is the same as the coupon (and yield) on a bond priced at par, calculating the fixed-rate on an interest-rate swap is the same as calculating the coupon for a bond that we wish to issue at par.

The price of a bond paying semi-annual coupons is given by (15.7), which may be re-arranged for the coupon rate r to provide an equation that enables us to determine the par yield, and hence the swap rate r, given by (15.8).

$$P = \frac{r_n}{2}df_1 + \frac{r_n}{2}df_2 + \ldots\ldots + \frac{r_n}{2}df_n + Mdf_n \qquad (15.7)$$

where r_n is the coupon on an n-period bond with n coupons and M is the maturity payment. It can be shown then that

$$
\begin{aligned}
r_n &= \frac{1 - df_n}{\dfrac{df_1}{2} + \dfrac{df_2}{2} + \ldots\ldots + \dfrac{df_n}{2}} \\[2mm]
&= \frac{1 - df_n}{\displaystyle\sum_{i=1}^{n} \frac{df_i}{2}}
\end{aligned}
\qquad (15.8)
$$

For annual coupon bonds there is no denominator for the discount factor, while for bonds paying coupons on a frequency of N we replace the denominator 2 with N.[1] The expression at (15.8) may be rearranged again, using F for the coupon frequency, to obtain an equation which may be used to calculate the nth discount factor for an n-period swap rate, given at (15.9).

$$df_n = \frac{1 - r_n \displaystyle\sum_{i=1}^{n-1} \frac{df_i}{N}}{1 + \dfrac{r_n}{N}} \qquad (15.9)$$

The expression at (15.9) is the general expression for the *bootstrapping* process that we first encountered in Chapter 1. Essentially, to calculate the n-year discount factor we use the discount factors for the years 1 to n-1, and the n-year swap rate or zero-coupon rate. If we have the discount factor for any period, we may use (15.9) to determine the same period zero-coupon rate, after re-arranging it, shown at (15.10).

$$rs_n = \sqrt[t_n]{\frac{1}{df_n}} - 1 \qquad (15.10)$$

Discount factors for spot rates may also be used to calculate forward rates. We know that

$$df_1 = \frac{1}{\left(1 + \dfrac{rs_1}{N}\right)} \qquad (15.11)$$

---

[1] The expression also assumes an actual/365 day-count basis. If any other day-count convention is used, the $1/N$ factor must be replaced by a fraction made up of the actual number of days as the numerator and the appropriate year base as the denominator.

where *rs* is the zero-coupon rate. If we know the forward rate we may use this to calculate a second discount rate, shown by (15.12).

$$df_2 = \frac{df_1}{\left(1 + \frac{rf_1}{N}\right)} \qquad (15.12)$$

where rf_1 is the forward rate. This is of no use in itself; however, we may derive from it an expression to enable us to calculate the discount factor at any point in time between the previous discount rate and the given forward rate for the period n to $n+1$, shown at (15.13), which may then be rearranged to give us the general expression to calculate a forward rate, given at (15.14).

$$df_{n+1} = \frac{df_n}{\left(1 + \frac{rf_n}{N}\right)} \qquad (15.13)$$

$$rf_n = \left(\frac{df_n}{df_{n+1}} - 1\right)N \qquad (15.14)$$

The general expression for an n-period discount rate at time n from the previous period forward rates is given by (15.15).

$$df_n = \frac{1}{\left(1 + \frac{rf_{n-1}}{N}\right)} \times \frac{1}{\left(1 + \frac{rf_{n-2}}{N}\right)} \times \ldots \ldots \times \frac{1}{\left(1 + \frac{rf_n}{N}\right)}$$

$$df_n = \prod_{i=0}^{n-1} \left[\frac{1}{\left(1 + \frac{rf_i}{N}\right)}\right] \qquad (15.15)$$

From the above, we may combine equations (15.8) and (15.14) to obtain the general expression for an n-period swap rate and zero-coupon rate, given by (15.16) and (15.17), respectively.

$$r_n = \frac{\displaystyle\sum_{i=1}^{n} \frac{rf_{i-1}df_i}{N}}{\displaystyle\sum_{i=1}^{n} \frac{df_i}{F}} \qquad (15.16)$$

$$1 + rs_n = \sqrt[t_n]{\prod_{i=0}^{n-1} \left(1 + \frac{rf_i}{N}\right)} \qquad (15.17)$$

The two expressions do not tell us anything new, as we have already encountered their results in Chapter 3. The swap rate, which we have denoted as r_n is shown by (15.16) to be the weighted average of the forward rates. If we consider that a strip of FRAs constitutes an interest-rate swap, then a swap rate for a continuous period could be covered by a strip of FRAs. Therefore, an average of the FRA rates would be the correct swap rate. As FRA rates are forward rates, we may be comfortable with (15.16), which states that the n-period swap rate is the average of the forward rates from rf_0 to rf_n. To be accurate, we must weight the forward rates, and these are weighted by the discount factors for each period. Note that although swap rates are derived from forward rates, interest payments under a swap are paid in the normal way at the end of an interest period, while payments for a FRA are made at the beginning of the period and must be discounted.

Equation (15.17) states that the zero-coupon rate is calculated from the geometric average of (one plus) the forward rates. The n-period forward rate is obtained using the discount factors for periods n and n-1. The discount factor for the complete period is obtained by multiplying the individual discount factors together, and exactly the same result would be obtained by using the zero-coupon interest-rate for the whole period to obtain the discount factor.

Illustrating interest–rate swap pricing

The rate charged on a newly-transacted interest-rate swap is the one that gives its net present value as zero. The term "valuation" of a swap is used to denote the process of calculating the net present value of an existing swap, when marking-to-market the swap against current market interest rates. Therefore, when we price a swap, we set its net present value to zero; while, when we value a swap, we set its fixed rate at the market rate and calculate the net present value.

To illustrate the basic principle, we price a plain-vanilla interest-rate swap with the terms set out below; for simplicity we assume that the annual fixed-rate payments are the same amount each year, although in practice there would be slight differences. Also assume we already have our zero-coupon yields as shown in Table 15.3.

We use the zero-coupon rates to calculate the discount factors, and then use the discount factors to calculate the forward rates. This is done using equation (15.14). These forward rates are then used to predict what the floating-rate payments will be at each interest period. Both fixed-rate and floating-rate payments are then present-valued at the appropriate zero-coupon rate, which enables us to calculate the net present value.

The fixed-rate for the swap is calculated using equation (15.8) to give us:

$$\frac{1 - 0.71298618}{4.16187950}$$

or 6.8963%.

The swap terms are:

Nominal principal	£10 million
Fixed rate	6.8963%
Day count fixed	Actual/365
Day count floating	Actual/365
Payment frequency fixed	Annual
Payment frequency floating	Annual
Trade date	31st January 2000
Effective date	2nd February 2000
Maturity date	2nd February 2005
Term	Five years

For reference, the Microsoft Excel® formulae are shown at Table 15.4. It is not surprising that the net present value is zero, because the zero-coupon curve is used to derive the discount factors which are then used to derive the forward rates, which are used to value the swap. As with any financial instrument, the fair value is its breakeven price or hedge cost, and in this case the bank that is pricing the five-year swap shown in Table 15.3 could hedge the swap with a series of FRAs transacted at the forward rates shown. If the bank is paying fixed and receiving floating, value of the swap to it will rise if there is a rise in market rates, and fall if there is a fall in market rates. Conversely, if the bank was receiving fixed and paying floating, the swap value to it would fall if there was a rise in rates, and vice versa.

This method is used to price any interest-rate swap, even an exotic one.

Valuation using final-maturity discount factor

A short-cut to valuing the floating-leg payments of an interest-rate swap involves using the discount factor for the final maturity period. This is possible because, for the purposes of valuation, an exchange of principal at the beginning and end of the swap is conceptually the same as the floating-leg interest payments. This holds because, in an exchange of principal, the interest payments earned on investing the initial principal would be

Period	Zero-coupon rate %	Discount factor	Forward rate %	Fixed payment	Floating payment	PV fixed payment	PV floating payment
1	5.50	0.94	5.50	689,625	550,000.00	653,672.98	521,327.01
2	6.00	0.88	6.50	689,625	650,236.96	613,763.79	578,708.58
3	6.25	0.83	6.75	689,625	675,177.02	574,944.84	562,899.47
4	6.50	0.77	7.25	689,625	725,353.49	536,061.43	563,834.02
5	7.00	0.71	9.02	689,625	902,358.47	491,693.09	643,369.11
		4.16				2870137.00	2870137.00

Table 15.3 Generic interest-rate swap

CELL C	D	E	F	G	H	I	J
21		10000000					
22							
23 Period	Zero-coupon rate %	Discount factor	Forward rate %	Fixed payment	Floating payment	PV fixed payment	PV floating payment
24 1	5.50	0.94	5.50	689,625	"(F24*10000000)/100	"G24/1.055	"H24/(1.055)
25 2	6.00	0.88	"((E24/E25)-1)*100	689,625	"(F25*10000000)/100	"G24/(1.06)^2	"H25/(1.06)^2
26 3	6.25	0.83	"((E25/E26)-1)*100	689,625	"(F26*10000000)/100	"G24/(1.0625)^3	"H26/(1.0625^3)
27 4	6.50	0.77	"((E26/E27)-1)*100	689,625	"(F27*10000000)/100	"G24/(1.065)^4	"H27/(1.065)^4
28 5	7.00	0.71	"((E27/E28)-1)*100	689,625	"(F28*10000000)/100	"G24/(1.07)^5	"H28/(1.07)^5
		"SUM(E24:E28)		2,870,137.00		2,870,137.00	2,870,137.00

Table 15.4 Generic interest-rate swap (Excel formulae)

uncertain, as they are floating rate, while on maturity the original principal would be returned. The net result is a floating-rate level of receipts, exactly similar to the floating-leg payments in a swap. To value the principals, then, we need only the final maturity discount rate.

To illustrate, consider Table 15.3, where the present value of both legs was found to be £2,870,137. The same result is obtained if we use the five-year discount factor, as shown below.

$$PV_{floating} = (10,000,000 \times 1) - (10,000,000 \times 0.71298618) = 2,870,137$$

The first term is the principal multiplied by the discount factor 1; this is because the present value of an amount valued immediately is unchanged (or rather, it is multiplied by the immediate-payment discount factor, which is 1.0000).

Therefore, we may use the principal amount of a swap if we wish to value the swap. This is, of course, for valuation only, as there is no actual exchange of principal in a swap.

Summary of IR Swap

Let us summarise the chief characteristics of swaps. A plain-vanilla swap has the following characteristics:

- one leg of the swap is fixed-rate interest, while the other will be floating-rate, usually linked to a standard index such as Libor..
- the fixed rate is fixed through the entire life of the swap.
- the floating rate is set in advance of each period (quarterly, semi-annually or annually) and paid in arrears.
- both legs have the same payment frequency.
- the maturity can be standard whole years up to 30 years, or set to match the customer's requirements.
- the notional principal remains constant during the life of the swap.

Of course, to meet customer demand banks can set up swaps that have variations on any or all of the above standard points. Some of the more common variations are discussed in the next section.

Non-vanilla interest-rate swaps

The swap market is very flexible and instruments can be tailor-made to fit the requirements of individual customers. A wide variety of swap contracts have been traded in the market. Although the most common reference rate for the floating-leg of a swap is six-month Libor, for a semi-annual paying floating leg, other reference rates that have been used include three-month Libor, the prime rate (for dollar swaps), the one-month commercial paper rate, the Treasury bill rate and the municipal bond rate (again, for dollar swaps). The term of a swap need not be fixed; swaps may be extendable or put-able. In an extendable swap, one of the parties has the right but not the obligation to extend the life of the swap beyond the fixed maturity date, while in a put-able swap one party has the right to terminate the swap ahead of the specified maturity date. It is also possible to transact options on swaps, known as swaptions. A swaption is the right to enter into a swap agreement at some point in the future, during the life of the option. Essentially, a swaption is an option to exchange a fixed-rate bond cash flow for a floating-rate bond cash-flow structure. As a floating-rate bond is valued on its principal value at the start of a swap, a swaption may be viewed as the value on a fixed-rate bond, with a strike price that is equal to the face value of the floating-rate bond.

Constant-maturity swap

A constant-maturity swap is a swap in which the parties exchange a Libor rate for a fixed swap rate. For example, the terms of the swap might state that six-month Libor is exchanged for the five-year swap rate on a semi-annual basis for the next five years, or for the five-year government bond rate. In the US market, the second type of constant-maturity swap is known as a constant-maturity Treasury swap.

Plain-vanilla swap

In a plain-vanilla swap the notional principal remains unchanged during the life of the swap. However, it is possible to trade a swap where the notional principal varies during its life. An accreting (or step-up) swap is one in which the principal starts off at one level and then increases in amount over time. The opposite, an amortising swap, is one in which the notional reduces in size over time. An accreting swap would be useful where, for instance, a funding liability that is being hedged increases over time. The amortising swap might be employed by a borrower hedging a bond issue that featured sinking-fund payments, where a part of the notional amount outstanding is paid off at set points during the life of the bond. If the principal fluctuates in amount – for example, increasing in one year and then reducing in another – the swap is known as a roller-coaster swap. Another application for an amortising swap is as a hedge for a loan that is itself an amortising one. Frequently, this is combined with a forward-starting swap, to tie in with the cash flows payable on the loan. The pricing and valuation of an amortising swap is no different in principle from a vanilla interest-rate swap; a single swap rate is calculated using the relevant discount factors, and at this rate the net present value of the swap cash flows will equal zero at the start of the swap.

Libor-in-arrears swap

In a Libor-in-arrears swap (also known as a back-set swap), the setting date is just before the end of the accrual period for the floating-rate setting and not just before the start. Such a swap would be attractive to a counterparty who had a different view on interest rates from the market consensus. For instance, in a rising yield-curve environment, forward rates will be higher than current market rates, and this will be reflected in the pricing of a swap. A Libor-in-arrears swap would be priced higher than a conventional swap. If the floating-rate payer believed that interest rates would, in fact, rise more slowly than forward rates (and the market) were suggesting, she may wish to enter into an arrears swap as opposed to a conventional swap.

Conventional swap

In a conventional swap, one leg comprises fixed-rate payments and the other floating-rate payments. In a basis swap, both legs are floating-rate but linked to different money-market indices. One leg is normally linked to Libor, while the other might be linked to the CD rate, say, or to the commercial-paper rate. This type of swap would be used by a bank in the US that had made loans that paid at the prime rate, and financed its loans at Libor. A basis swap would eliminate the basis risk between the bank's income and expense cash flows. Other basis swaps have been traded where both legs are linked to Libor, but at different maturities; for instance, one leg might be at three-month Libor and the other at six-month Libor. In such a swap, the basis is different and so is the payment frequency: one leg pays out semi-annually while the other would be paying on a quarterly basis. Note that where the payment frequencies differ, there is a higher level of counterparty risk for one of the parties. For instance, if one party is paying out on a monthly basis but receiving semi-annual cash flows, it would have made five interest payments before receiving one in return.

Margin swap

It is common to encounter swaps where there is a margin above or below Libor on the floating leg, as opposed to a floating leg of Libor flat. If a bank's borrowing is financed at Libor+25bps, it may wish to receive Libor+25bps in the swap so that its cash flows match exactly. The fixed rate quote for a swap must be adjusted correspondingly to allow for the margin on the floating side. This is known as a margin swap. In our example, if the fixed-rate quote is, say, 6.00%, it would be adjusted to around 6.25%; differences in the margin quoted on the fixed leg might arise if the day-count convention or payment frequency were to differ between fixed and floating legs. Another reason why there may be a margin is if the credit quality of the counterparty demanded it, so that highly rated counterparties may pay slightly below Libor, for instance.

When a swap is transacted, its fixed rate is quoted at the current market rate for that maturity. Where the fixed rate is different from the market rate, this is an off-market swap, and a compensating payment is made by one party to the other. An off-market rate may be used for particular hedging requirements, for example, or when a bond issuer wishes to use the swap to hedge the bond as well as to cover the bond's issue costs.

Differential swap

A differential swap is a basis swap but with one of the legs calculated in a different currency. Typically, one leg is floating-rate, while the other is floating-rate but with the reference index rate for another currency, but denominated in the domestic currency. For example, a differential swap may have one party paying six-month sterling Libor, in sterling, on a notional principal of £10 million, and receiving euro-Libor, minus a margin, payable in sterling and on the same notional principal. Differential swaps are not very common and are the most difficult for a bank to hedge. The hedging is usually carried out using what is known as a quanto option.

Forward-start swap

A forward-start swap is one where the effective date is not the usual one or two days after the trade date but a considerable time afterwards, for instance; say, six months after trade date. Such a swap might be entered into where one counterparty wanted to fix a hedge or cost of borrowing now, but for a point some time in the future. Typically, this would be because the party considered that interest rates would rise or the cost of hedging would rise. The swap rate for a forward-starting swap is calculated in the same way as that for a vanilla swap.

Swaptions

Description

Swaptions are options on swaps. The buyer of a swaption has the right but not the obligation to enter into an interest rate swap agreement during the life of the option. The terms of the swaption will specify whether the buyer is the fixed- or floating-rate payer; the seller of the option (the *writer*) becomes the counterparty to the swap if the option is exercised. The convention is that if the buyer has the right to exercise the option as the fixed-rate payer, he has traded a *call swaption*, also known as a *payer swaption*, while if by exercising the buyer of the swaption becomes the floating-rate payer he has bought a *put swaption,* also known as a *receiver swaption.* The writer of the swaption is the party to the other leg. In the sterling market swaptions are referred to in terms similar to FRA terminology, so that a 3/6 or 3-6 payer's swaption is a three-year option to pay fixed on a three-year interest-rate swap.

Swaptions are similar to forward start swaps up to a point, but the buyer has the *option* of whether or not to commence payments on the effective date. A bank may purchase a call swaption if it expects interest rates to rise, and will exercise the option if indeed rates do rise as the bank has expected. A company will use swaptions as part of an interest-rate hedge for a future exposure. For example, assume that a company will be entering into a five-year bank loan in three months time. Interest on the loan is charged on a floating-rate basis, but the company intend to swap this to a fixed-rate liability after they have entered into the loan. As an added hedge, the company may choose to purchase a swaption that gives it the right to receive Libor and pay a fixed rate, say 10%, for a five-year period beginning in three months time. When the time comes for the company to take out a swap and exchange its interest-rate liability in three months time (having entered into the loan), if the five-year swap rate is below 10%, the company will transact the swap in the normal way and the swaption will expire worthless. However if the five-year swap rate is above 10%, the company will instead exercise the swaption, giving it the right to enter into a five-year swap and paying a fixed rate of 10%. Essentially the company has taken out protection to ensure that it does not have to pay a fixed rate of more than 10%. Hence swaptions can be used to guarantee a maximum swap rate liability. They are similar to forward-starting swaps, but do not commit a party to enter into a swap on fixed terms. The swaption enables a company to hedge against unfavourable movements in interest rates but also to gain from favourable movements, although there is of course a cost associated with this, which is the premium paid for the swaption.

As with conventional put and call options, swaptions turn in-the-money under opposite circumstances. A call swaption increases in value as interest rates rise, and a put swaption becomes more valuable as interest rates fall. Consider a one-year European call swaption on a five-year semi-annual interest-rate swap, purchased by a bank counterparty. The notional value is £10 million and the "strike price" is 6%, against Libor. Assume that the price (premium) of the swaption is 25 basis points, or £25,000. On expiry of the swaption, the buyer will either exercise it, in which case she will enter into a five-year swap paying 6% and receiving floating-rate interest, or elect to let the swaption expire with no value. If the five-year swap rate for counterparty of similar credit quality to the bank is above 6%, the swaption holder will exercise the swaption, while if the rate is below 6% the buyer will not exercise. The principle is the same for a put swaption, only in reverse.

A company will use swaptions as part of an interest-rate hedge for a future exposure. For example, assume that a company will be entering into a five-year bank loan in three months time. Interest on the loan is charged on a floating-rate basis, but the company intend to swap this to a fixed-rate liability after they have entered into the loan. As an added hedge, the company may choose to purchase a swaption that gives it the right to receive Libor and pay a fixed rate, say 10%, for a five-year period beginning in three months time. When the time comes for the company to take out a swap and exchange its interest-rate liability in three months time (having entered into the loan), if the five-year swap rate is below 10%, the company will transact the swap in the normal way and the swaption will expire worthless. However if the five-year swap rate is above 10%, the company will instead exercise the swaption, giving it the right to enter into a five-year swap and paying a fixed rate of 10%. Essentially the company has taken out protection to ensure that it does not have to pay a fixed rate of more than 10%. Hence swaptions can be used to guarantee a maximum swap rate liability. They are similar to forward-starting swaps, but do not commit a party to enter into a swap on fixed terms. The swaption enables a company to hedge against unfavourable movements in interest rates but also to gain from favourable movements, although there is of course a cost associated with this, which is the premium paid for the swaption.

Valuation

Swaptions are typically priced using the Black-Scholes or Black 76 option pricing models. These are used to value a European option on a swap, assuming that the appropriate swap rate at the expiry date of the option is lognormal. Consider a swaption with the following general terms:

Swap rate on expiry	rs
Swaption strike rate	rX
Maturity	T
Start date	t
Pay basis	F (say quarterly, semi-annual or annual)
Notional Principal	M

If the actual swap rate on the maturity of the swaption is rs, the pay-off from the swaption is given by:

$$\frac{M}{F} \max(r-r_n,0) \ .$$

The value of a swaption is essentially the difference between the strike rate and the swap rate at the time it is being valued. If a swaption is exercised, the payoff at each interest date is given by $(rs - rX) \times M \times F$. As a call swaption is only exercised when the swap rate is higher than the strike rate (that is, $rs > rX$), the option payoff on any interest payment in the swap is given by

$$Swaption_{InterestPayment} = \text{Max}[0,(rs - rX) \times M \times F \qquad (15.18)$$

It can then easily be shown that the value of a call swaption on expiry is given by

$$PV_{Swaption} = \sum_{n=1}^{N} Df_{(0,n)}(rs - rX) \times M \times F \qquad (15.19)$$

where $Df_{(0, n)}$ is the spot rate discount factor for the term beginning now and ending at time t. By the same logic the value of a put swaption is given by the same expression except that $(rX - rs)$ is substituted at the relevant point above.

Consider then, that a swaption can be viewed as a collection of calls or puts on interest deposits or Libor, enabling us to use the Black model when valuing it. This means that we value each call or put on for a single payment in the swap, and then sum these payments to obtain the value of the swaption. The main assumption made when using this model is that the Libor rate follows a lognormal distribution over time, with constant volatility.

Consider a call swaption being valued at time t that matures at time T. We begin by valuing a single payment under the swap (assuming the option is exercised) made at time T_n. The point at time T_n is into the life of the swap, so that we have $T_n > T > t$. At the time of valuation, the option time to expiry is $T - t$ and there is $T_n - t$ until the nth payment. The value of this payment is given by

$$C_t = MFe^{-r(T_n-t)}[rsN(d1) - rXN(d2)]$$ (15.20)

where

C_t is the price of the call option on a single payment in the swap
r is the risk-free instantaneous interest rate
$N(.)$ is the cumulative normal distribution
σ is the interest-rate volatility

and where

$$d_1 = \frac{\ln(rs_t \,/\, rX) + \frac{\sigma^2}{2}(T - t)}{\sigma\sqrt{T - t}}$$

$$d2 = d1 - \sigma\sqrt{T - t}$$

The remaining life of the swaption $(T - t)$ governs the probability that it will expire in-the-money, determined using the lognormal distribution. On the other hand the interest payment itself is discounted (using $e^{-r(T_n-t)}$) over the period $T_n - t$ as it is not paid until time T_n.

Having valued a single interest payment, viewing the swap as a collection of interest payments, we value the call swaption as a collection of calls. Its value is given therefore by

$$PVSwaption_t = \sum_{n=1}^{N} MFe^{-r(T_n-t)}[rsN(d_1) - rXN(d_2)]$$ (15.21)

where t, T and n are as before.

If we substitute discrete spot rate discount factors instead of the continuous form given by (15.21) the expression becomes

$$PVSwaption_t = MF[rsN(d_1) - rXN(d_2)] \sum_{n=1}^{N} Df_{t,T_n} . \qquad (15.22)$$

Note that vanilla caps and floors are also priced using the Black 76 model, as are European swaptions. This leads to some interesting results.[2] For instance, given our basic assumption that a forward-starting swap is a linear function of forward interest rates, using the Black 76 model for caps or floors assumes that forward *interest rates* follow a lognormal distribution. Using the same model for swaptions means we are assuming that forward *swap* rates are lognormally distributed. This is a contradictory set of assumptions; nevertheless the market uses the same model to price both products.

If we consider a payer's swaption with strike rX and value of PV_F and PV_L for fixed and floating sides respectively, the swaption payoff is given by

$$\max[0, \ PV_L - PV_F \ ].$$

As the level of interest rates fluctuates during the life of the swaption, the values PV_F and PV_L will also move. This produces a payoff that does not follow the general form for the Black 76 model, which is a stochastic pattern in relation to the fixed level of rX. To counter this the market also uses a "spread option model",[3] which is given below.

$$PV_{Swaption} = PV_L \times N(d_1) - PV_F \times N(d_2) \qquad (15.23)$$

where

$d1 = [\ln(PV_L / PV_F) + \frac{1}{2}\sigma^2 t] / (\sigma \sqrt{t})$, etc

$\sigma^2 = (\sigma_L)^2 + (\sigma_F)^2 - 2\sigma_L\sigma_F\rho_{LF}$

and

σ_L and σ_F are the volatilities of the floating and fixed sides
ρ_{LF} is the correlation between the two sides.

---

[2] See, for example, Flavell, R., *Swaps and other Derivatives*, John Wiley 2002, chapter 7.
[3] Ibid., chapter 7

Fixed Income Markets

EXAMPLE 15.1 Swaption pricing[4]

We present an hypothetical term structure environment in this
example to illustrate the basic concepts. This is shown in table 15.5.
We wish to price a forward-starting annual interest swap starting in
two years for a term of three years. The swap has a notional of £10
million.

Date	Term (years)	Discount factor	Par yield	Zero-coupon rate	Forward rate
2/18/2001	0	1	5	5	5
2/18/2002	1	0.95238095	5.00	5	6.03015
2/18/2003	2	0.89821711	5.50	5.51382	7.10333
2/18/2004	3	0.83864539	6.00	6.04102	6.66173
2/18/2005	4	0.78613195	6.15	6.19602	6.71967
2/20/2006	5	0.73637858	6.25	6.30071	8.05230
2/19/2007	6	0.68165163	6.50	6.58946	8.70869
2/18/2008	7	0.62719194	6.75	6.88862	9.40246
2/18/2009	8	0.57315372	7.00	7.20016	10.1805
2/18/2010	9	0.52019523	7.25	7.52709	5.80396
2/18/2011	10	0.49165950	7.15	7.35361	6.16366

Table 15.5 Interest rate data for swaption valuation

The swap rate is given by

$$rs = \frac{\sum_{n=1}^{N} rf_{(t-1),t} \times Df_{0,t}}{\sum_{n=1}^{N} Df_{0,t}}$$

where rf is the forward rate.

Using the above expression, the numerator in this example is
$(0.0666 \times 0.8386) + (0.0672 \times 0.7861) + (0.0805 \times 0.7634)$ or
0.1701.

---

[4] This example follows an approach described in a number of other texts, for example Kolb, R.,
Futures, Options and Swaps, Blackwell (2000); although here we use discount factors in the
calculation whereas in Kolb for example the illustration uses zero-coupon factors which are (1 +
spot rate).

498

The denominator is
$$0.8386 + 0.7861 + 0.7634 \text{ or } 2.3881.$$

Therefore the forward-starting swap rate is $0.1701 / 2.3881$ or 0.071228 (7.123%).

We now turn to the call swaption on this swap, the buyer of which acquires the right to enter into a three-year swap paying the fixed-rate swap rate of 7.00%. If the volatility of the forward swap rate is 0.20, the d_1 and d_2 terms are

$$d_1 = \frac{\ln\left(\frac{rs}{rX}\right) + \frac{\sigma^2}{2}(T-t)}{\sigma\sqrt{T-t}} = \frac{\ln\left(\frac{0.071228}{0.07}\right) + \left(\frac{0.2^2}{2} \times 2\right)}{0.2\sqrt{2}}$$

or 0.2029068

$$d^2 = d^1 - \sigma\sqrt{T-t} = 0.20290618 - 0.2(1.4142)$$

or -0.079934.

The cumulative normal values are
$N(d_1) = N(0.2029)$ which is 0.580397
$N(d_2) = N(-0.079934)$ which is 0.468145.[5]

From above we know that $\Sigma Df_{t,T_n}$ is 2.3881. So using (15.22) we calculate the value of the call swaption to be

$$PVSwaption_t = MF[rsN(d_1) - rXN(d_2)] \sum_{n=1}^{N} Df_{t,T_n}.$$

$$\begin{aligned}
&= 10,000,000 \times 1 \times [0.07228 \times 0.580397 - 0.07 \times 0.468145] \\
&\quad \times 2.3881 \\
&= 219,250
\end{aligned}$$

or £219,250. Option premiums are frequently quoted as basis points of the notional amount, so in this case the premium is (219,250 / 10,000,000) or 219.25 basis points.

---

[5] These values may be found from standard normal distribution tables or using the Microsoft Excel formula =NORMSDIST().

Swaptions for risk management

A swaption is another instrument that may be used for interest-rate risk management purposes. Hence they are an alternative to swaps, caps and floors. In some cases, an institution will have the option of using any of these products. For instance, consider a situation where a corporate entity is aware that it must borrow funds at a future date, for a fixed period of time. The funds are only available at a floating rate. This requirement presents an interest-rate risk in that rates may rise between now and the start date of the loan, and then rise during the loan. If the Treasury desk of the entity wishes to remove uncertainty and nullify this risk, it may consider the following:

- trade in a forward-start swap, for the term of the loan, paying fixed and receiving floating. The swap will come into effect at the start of the loan. This removes uncertainty in that the company knows what it will be paying for the term of the loan, thus it's interest-rate exposure is known. The downside is that the company cannot benefit if interest rates fall;
- enter into a forward-start cap: the company can buy a cap, with start date for the start of the loan, and this fixes its upper borrowing rate. It also enables the company to gain if rates fall;
- buy a swaption. The company can purchase a payers swaption, with expiry date matching the start date of the loan, which if exercised kicks in a pay-fixed swap for the term of the loan. If rates were above the strike rate of the swaption on expiry, the swaption will be exercised, otherwise it would expire worthless.

Alternatively the company could leave the exposure intact and do nothing. It will suffer if rates, but it will benefit if rates fall, and it wouldn't have paid any money for the privilege! Shareholders prefer certainty over risk exposure however, so this strategy is rarely followed.

The choice between a cap and a swaption will be influenced by their relative cost. Cap premiums are significantly higher than swaption premiums, both at-the-money or out-of-the-money. This is not unexpected, because a cap provides a greater level of protection for its buyer. It last for the entire period of the exposure, and also enables its buyer to benefit from downward movements in rates. The swaption only provides protection for the period leading up the start of the loan, and then can be exercised only on expiry. If rates have fallen, it will expire un-exercised. The cap can be exercised at fixed times during the term of the loan (as each caplet approaches its exercise date). It thereofr incorporates more time value than a swaption. So it is a straightforward choice the company is faced with: the higher-priced cap that offers more insurance, or the lower-cost swaption. This is illustrated further in example 15.2

EXAMPLE 15.2 Swaption and cap premiums

A corporate will need to enter into a two-year sterling loan in one year's time. The loan rate will be a spread over three-month Libor. To hedge the future risk exposure, it can purchase a forward-start vanilla cap for the term of the loan, a mid-curve cap or a 1/3 payers swaption. We have the following terms:

Trade date	8 January 2001
Start date	9 January 2002
Terms	3-month Libor from 9 Jan 02 to 9 Jan 04
Strike	5.50%
Volatility	12% p.a.

In the sterling market as at January 2001 we observed the following premiums:

Two-year vanilla cap	44.7 bps
Two-year mid-curve cap	36.5 bps
1/3 payer swaption	32.9 bps

If the company exercises the swaption, it will be paying a fixed rate on its loan. This, being the swap rate, is in effect the average of the implied forward rates given by the zero-coupon curve as at January 2001. If Libor falls after the exercise date, the company will not benefit. The vanilla cap is the expensive approach, but it has eight exercise dates – every quarter for the two-year period of the loan. The mid-curve cap has one exercise date, but is made up of eight separate options. The swaption is the cheapest instrument because it is a single option on one exercise date.

Overnight interest–rate swaps and Eonia / SONIA swaps

This section could also have been placed in chapter 6, our chapter on money market securities and derivatives. Overnight-index swaps (OIS) are interest-rate swaps that are traded in the money markets.

We saw earlier in the chapter that an interest rate swap contract, which is generally regarded as a capital market instrument, is an agreement between two counterparties to exchange a fixed interest rate payment in return for a floating interest rate payment, calculated on a notional swap amount, at regular intervals during the life of the swap. A swap may be viewed as being equivalent to a series of successive FRA contracts, with each FRA starting as the previous one matures. The basis of the floating interest rate is agreed as part of the contract terms at the inception of the trade. Conventional swaps index the floating interest rate to Libor; however an exciting recent development in the money markets has been the OIS. In the sterling market they are known as sterling overnight interest rate average swaps or SONIA, while euro-currency OIS are known as Eonia. In this section we review OIS swaps, which are used extensively by commebrcial and investment banks.

SONIA swaps

SONIA is the average interest rate of interbank (unsecured) overnight sterling deposit trades undertaken before 1530 hours each day between members of the London Wholesale Money Brokers' Association. Recorded interest rates are weighted by volume. A SONIA swap is a swap contract that exchanges a fixed interest rate (the swap rate) against the geometric average of the overnight interest rates that have been recorded during the life of the contractd. Exchange of interest takes place on maturity of the swap. SONIA swaps are used to speculate on or to hedge against interest rates at the very short end of the sterling yield curve; in other words, they can be used to hedge an exposure to overnight interest rates.[6] The swaps themselves are traded in maturities of one week to one year, although two-year SONIA swaps have also been traded.

Conventional swap rates are calculated off the government bond yield curve and represent the credit premium over government yields of interbank default risk. Essentially they represent an average of the forward rates derived from the government spot (zero-coupon) yield curve. The fixed rate

---

[6] Traditionally overnight rates fluctuate in a very wide range during the day, depending on the day's funds shortage, and although volatility has reduced since the introduction of gilt repo, it is still unpredictable on occasion.

quoted on a SONIA swap represents the average level of the overnight interest rates expected by market participants over the life of the swap. In practice the rate is calculated as a function of the Bank of England's repo rate. This is the two-week rate at which the Bank conducts reverse repo trades with banking counterparties as part of its open market operations. In other words, this is the Bank's base rate. In theory one would expect the SONIA rate to follow the repo rate fairly closely, since the credit risk on an overnight deposit is low. However in practice, the spread between the SONIA rate and the Bank repo rate is very volatile, and for this reason the swaps are used to hedge overnight exposures.

The daily turnover in SONIA swaps is considerably lower than cash instruments such as gilt repo (£20 billion) or more established derivative instruments such as short sterling (£45 billion), however it is now a key part of the sterling market. Most trades are between one-week and three-month maturity, and the bid-offer spread has been reported by the BoE as around 2 basis points, which compares favourably with the 1 basis point spread of short sterling.

Figure 15.3 illustrates the monthly average of the SONIA index minus Bank's repo rate during 1999 and 2000, with the exaggerated spread in December 1999 reflecting millenium bug concerns.

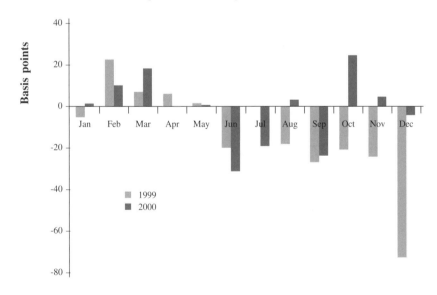

Figure 15.3 SONIA average rate minus BoE repo rate.
Source: Bank of England

EXAMPLE 15.3 Using an OIS swap to hedge a funding requirement

A structured hedge fund derivatives desk at an investment bank offers a leveraged investment product to a client in the form of a participating interest share in a fund of hedge funds. The client's investment is leveraged up by funds lent to it by the investment bank, for which the interest rate charged ins overnight Libor plus a spread. (In other words, for instance for each $25 invested by the client, the investment bank puts up $75 to make a total investment of $100. This gives the investor a leveraged investment in the hedge fund of funds. In most cases, the client would also bear the first $15 of loss of the $100 share of the investment).

Assume that this investment product has an expected life of at least two years, and possibly longer. As part of its routine asset-liability management operations, the bank's Treasury desk has been funding this requirement by borrowing overnight each day. It now wishes to match the funding requirement raised by this product by matching asset term structure to the liability term structure. Let us assume that this product creates a USD 1 billion funding requirement for the bank.

The current market deposit rates are shown in Figure 15.4 The Treasury desk therefore funds this requirement in the following way:

Assets $1 billion, > 1-year term
                Receiving overnight Libor + 130 bps

Liability $350 million, six-month loan
                Pay 1.22%
                $350 million, 12-month loan
                Pay 1.50%
                $300 million, 15-month loan
                Pay 1.70% (not shown in figure 15.4)

This matches the asset structure more closely to the term structure of the assets, however it opens up an interest rate basis mismatch in that the bank is now receiving an overnight-Libor based income but paying a term-based liability. To remove this basis mismatch, the Treasury desk transacts an OIS swap to match the amount and term of each of the loan deals, paying overnight floating-rate interest and receiving fixed-rate interest. The rates for OIS swaps of varying terms are shown in figure 15.5, which show two-way prices for OIS swaps up to two years in maturity. So for the six-month OIS the hedger is receiving fixed-interest at a rate of 1.085% and for the 12-month OIS he is receiving 1.40%. The difference between what it is receiving in the swap and what it is paying in the term loans is the cost of removing the basis mismatch, but more fundamentally reflects a key feature of OIS swaps versus deposit rates: deposit rates are Libor-related, whereas US dollar OIS rates are driven by the Fed Funds rate. On average, the Fed Funds rate lies approximately 8-10 bps below the dollar deposit rate, and sometimes as much as 15 bps below cash levels. Note that at the time of this trade, the Fed Funds rate was 1% and the market was not expecting a rise in this rate until at least the second half of 2004. This sentiment would have influenced the shape of the USD OIS curve.

The action taken above hedges out the basis mismatch and also enables the Treasury desk to match its asset profile with its liability profile. The net cost to the Treasury desk represents its hedging costs.

Figure 15.6 illustrates the transaction.

GRAB M-Mkt TTDE

11:37 TULLETT & TOKYO PAGE 1 / 1

USD Cash Deposits	Non-Japanese Bid	Ask	Time	USD Cash Deposits	Japanese Bid	Ask	Time
1) Spot	1.0000	1.0200	9:33	18) T/N	1.0000	1.0300	11/07
2) T/N	1.0100	1.0300	11/07	19) 1 Week	1.0400	1.0600	9:33
3) 1 Week	1.0300	1.0500	9:33	20) 2 Week	1.0500	1.0700	9:33
4) 2 Week	1.0300	1.0500	9:33	21) 3 Week	1.0600	1.0800	9:33
5) 3 Week	1.0300	1.0500	9:33	22) 1 Month	1.0800	1.1000	9:33
6) 1 Month	1.0400	1.0500	9:33	23) 2 Month	1.1800	1.2100	9:33
7) 2 Month	1.1200	1.1400	9:33	24) 3 Month	1.1900	1.2200	9:33
8) 3 Month	1.1300	1.1500	9:33	25) 4 Month	1.2000	1.2300	9:33
9) 4 Month	1.1400	1.1700	9:33	26) 5 Month	1.2100	1.2400	9:33
10) 5 Month	1.1600	1.1900	9:33	27) 6 Month	1.2300	1.2600	9:33
11) 6 Month	1.2000	1.2200	9:33	28) 7 Month	1.2700	1.3000	9:33
12) 7 Month	1.2300	1.2500	9:33	29) 8 Month	1.3100	1.3400	9:33
13) 8 Month	1.2700	1.2900	9:33	30) 9 Month	1.3800	1.4100	9:33
14) 9 Month	1.3300	1.3600	9:33	31) 10 Month	1.4600	1.4900	9:33
15) 10 Month	1.3800	1.4100	9:33	32) 11 Month	1.5300	1.5600	9:33
16) 11 Month	1.4500	1.4800	9:33	33) 12 Month	1.5500	1.5800	9:33
17) 12 Month	1.5000	1.5300	9:33				

Figure 15.4 Tullet US dollar deposit rates, 10 November 2003
© Bloomberg L.P. ©Tullett & Tokyo. Used with permission.

```
GRAB                                                  Corp   ICAU
11:34 USD  OIS  -  ICAU                              PAGE  1  /  1
    USD OIS       Ask      Bid     Time
 1)  1 Month     1.0190   0.9990    9:30
 2)  2 Month     1.0240   1.0040    9:30
 3)  3 Month     1.0310   1.0110    9:30
 4)  4 Month     1.0440   1.0240   10:59
 5)  5 Month     1.0710   1.0510   10:59
 6)  6 Month     1.1050   1.0850   11:04
 7)  7 Month     1.1420   1.1220   10:59
 8)  8 Month     1.1920   1.1720   11:00
 9)  9 Month     1.2420   1.2220   11:05
10) 10 Month     1.2930   1.2730   11:00
11) 11 Month     1.3580   1.3380   11:00
12) 12 Month     1.4210   1.4000   11:06
13) 15 Month     1.6250   1.6040   11:00
14) 18 Month     1.8090   1.7890   11:00
15) 21 Month     2.0080   1.9880   11:00
16) 24 Month     2.2030   2.1820   11:00


Australia 61 2 9777 8600      Brazil 5511 3048 4500      Europe 44 20 7330 7500      Germany 49 69 920410
Hong Kong 852 2977 6000 Japan 81 3 3201 8900 Singapore 65 6212 1000 U.S. 1 212 318 2000 Copyright 2003 Bloomberg L.P.
                                                          G657-802-0 10-Nov-03 11:34:17
```

Figure 15.5 Garban ICAP US dollar OIS rates, 10 November 2003
© Bloomberg L.P. Used with permission.

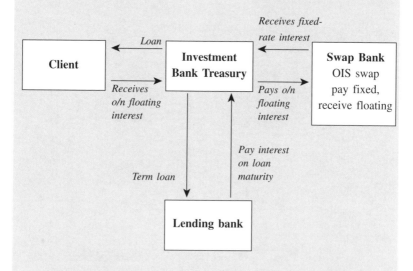

Figure 15.6 Illustration of interest basis mismatch hedging
using OIS instrument

OIS swap terms

To illustrate OISs further, we give here the terms of one of the OIS executed in example 15.3, the six-month swap. The counterparties to the trade are as labelled in figure 15.6.

Notional	$350 million
Trade date	10 November 2003
Effective date	12 November 2003
Termination date	12 May 2004
Payment terms	The net interest payment is paid as a bullet amount on maturity.

Fixed Amounts

Fixed rate payer	OIS swap bank
Fixed rate period end date	12 May 2004
Fixed rate	1.085%
Fixed rate day-count fraction	Act/360

Floating Amounts

Floating rate payer	Treasury desk
Floating rate period end date	12 May 2004
Floating rate option	USD-Fed Funds

The floating rate is calculated as follows:

$$F_{OIS} = \left[\prod\left(1 + \frac{FedFunds_i \times n_i}{360}\right) - 1\right] \times \frac{360}{d} \qquad (15.24)$$

where

d_0	is the number of New York banking days in the calculation period
i	is a series of whole numbers from 1 to d_0, each representing a New York banking day
$FedFunds_i$	is a reference rate equal to the overnight USD Federal Funds interest rate, as displayed on Telerate page 118 and Bloomberg page BTMM
n_i	is the number of calendar days in the calculation period on which the rate is $FedFunds_i$
d	is the number of days in the calculation period

Floating rate day-count	Act/360
Reset dates	The last day of each calculation period
Compounding	Inapplicable
Business day convention	Modified following business day
Calculation agent	OIS swap bank

An overview of interest-rate swap applications

In this section, we review some of the principal uses of swaps as a hedging tool for bond instruments and also how to hedge a swap book.

Corporate applications

Swaps are part of the over-the-counter (OTC) market and so they can be tailored to suit the particular requirements of the user. It is common for swaps to be structured so that they match particular payment dates, payment frequencies and Libor margins, which may characterise the underlying exposure of the customer. As the market in interest-rate swaps is so large, liquid and competitive, banks are willing to quote rates and structure swaps for virtually all customers, although it may be difficult for smaller customers to obtain competitive piece quotes as notional values below $10 million or $5 million.

Swap applications can be viewed as being one of two main types; asset-linked swaps and liability-linked swaps. Asset-linked swaps are created when the swap is linked to an asset such as a bond in order to change the characteristics of the income stream for investors. Liability-linked swaps are traded when borrowers of funds wish to change the pattern of their cash flows. Of course, just as with repo transactions, the designation of a swap in such terms depends on from whose point of view one is looking at the swap. An asset-linked swap hedge is a liability-linked hedge for the counterparty, except in the case of swap market-making banks who make two-way quotes in the instruments.

A straightforward application of an interest-rate swap is when a borrower wishes to convert a floating-rate liability into a fixed-rate one, usually in order to remove the exposure to upward moves in interest rates. For instance, a company may wish to fix its financing costs. Let us assume a company currently borrowing money at a floating rate, say six month Libor +100 basis points, fears that interest rates may rise in the remaining three years of its loan. It enters into a three-year semi-annual interest-rate swap with a bank, as the fixed-rate payer, paying say 6.75 per cent against receiving six-month Libor. This fixes the company's borrowing costs for three years at 7.75% (7.99 per cent effective annual rate). This is shown in Figure 15.7.

Figure 15.7 Changing liability from floating- to fixed-rate

EXAMPLE 15.4 **Liability-linked swap, fixed- to floating- to fixed-rate exposure**

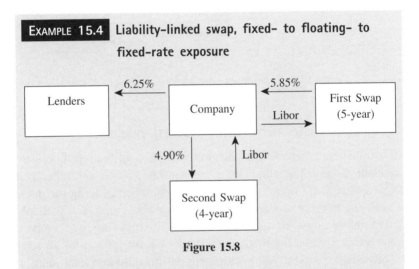

Figure 15.8

A corporate borrows for five years at a rate of $6\frac{1}{4}\%$ and shortly after enters into a swap paying floating-rate, so that its net borrowing cost is Libor + 40bps. After one year, swap rates have fallen such that the company is quoted four-year swap rates as 4.90 – 84%. The company decides to switch back into fixed-rate liability in order to take advantage of the lower interest rate environment. It enters into a second swap paying fixed at 4.90% and receiving Libor. The net borrowing cost is now 5.30%. The arrangement is illustrated in Figure 15.8 The company has saved 95 basis points on its original borrowing cost, which is the difference between the two swap rates.

Asset-linked swap structures might be required when, for example, investors require a fixed-interest security when floating-rate assets are available. Borrowers often issue FRNs, the holders of which may prefer to switch the income stream into fixed coupons. As an example, consider a local authority pension fund holding two-year floating-rate gilts. This is an asset of the highest quality, paying Libid minus 12.5bps. The pension fund wishes to swap the cash flows to create a fixed-interest asset. It obtains a quote for a tailor-made swap where the floating leg pays Libid, the quote being 5.55 – 50%. By entering into this swap, the pension fund has in place a structure that pays a fixed coupon of 5.375%. This is shown in Figure 15.9.

Figure 15.9 Transforming floating-rate asset to fixed-rate

Hedging bond instruments using interest–rate swaps

We illustrate here a generic approach to the hedging of bond positions using interest-rate swaps. The bond trader has the option of using other bonds, bond futures or bond options, as well as swaps, when hedging the interest-rate risk exposure of a bond position. However, swaps are particularly efficient instruments to use because they display positive convexity characteristics; that is, the increase in value of a swap for a fall in interest rates exceeds the loss in value with a similar magnitude rise in rates. This is exactly the price/yield profile of vanilla bonds.

The primary risk measure we require when hedging using a swap is its present value of a basis point or PVBP.[7] This measures the price sensitivity of the swap for a basis-point change in interest rates. The PVBP measure is used to calculate the hedge ratio when hedging a bond position. The PVBP can be given by

$$PVBP = \frac{\text{Change in swap value}}{\text{Rate change in basis points}} \qquad (15.25)$$

---

[7] This is also known as DVBP or dollar value of a basis point in the US market.

which can be written as

$$PVBP = \frac{dS}{dr} \qquad (15.26)$$

Using the basic relationship for the value of a swap, which is viewed as the difference between the values of a fixed-coupon bond and equivalent-maturity floating-rate bond (see Table 15.1) we can also write

$$PVBP = \frac{d\text{Fixed bond}}{dr} - \frac{d\text{Floating bond}}{dr} \qquad (15.27)$$

which essentially states that the basis-point value of the swap is the difference in the basis-point values of the fixed-coupon and floating-rate bonds. The value is usually calculated for a notional £1 million of swap. The calculation is based the duration and modified-duration calculations used for bonds[8] and assumes that there is a parallel shift in the yield curve.

Figure 15.10 illustrates how equations 15.26 and 15.27 can be used to obtain the PVBP of a swap. Hypothetical five-year bonds are used in the example. The PVBP for a bond can be calculated using Bloomberg or the MDURATION function on Microsoft Excel. Using either of the two equations above we see that the PVBP of the swap is £425.00. This is shown below.

Interest rate swap		
	Term to maturity	5 years
	Fixed leg	6.50%
	Basis	Semi-annual, act/365
	Floating leg	6-month Libor
	Basis	Semi-annual, act/365
	Nominal amount	£1,000,000

		Present value £	
	Rate change −10 bps	0 bps	Rate change +10 bps
Fixed coupon bond	1,004,940	1,000,000	995,171
Floating rate bond	1,000,640	1,000,000	999,371
Swap	4,264	0	4,236

Figure 15.10 PVBP for interest-rate swap

---

[8] See Chapter 2.

Calculating the PVBP using (15.27), we have

$$PVBP_{swap} = \frac{dS}{dr} = \frac{4264 - (-4236)}{20} = 425$$

while we obtain the same result using the bond values

$$PVBP_{swap} = PVBP_{fixed} - PVBP_{floating}$$

$$= \frac{1004940 - 995171}{20} - \frac{1000640 - 999371}{20}$$

$$= 488.45 - 63.45$$

$$= 425.00$$

The swap basis-point value is lower than that of the five-year fixed-coupon bond; that is, £425 compared to £488.45. This is because of the impact of the floating-rate bond risk measure, which reduces the risk exposure of the swap as a whole by £63.45. As a rough rule of thumb, the PVBP of a swap is approximately equal to that of fixed-rate bond that has a maturity similar to the period from the next coupon reset date of the swap through to the maturity date of the swap. This means that a 10-year semi-annual paying swap would have a PVBP close to that of a 9.5-year fixed-rate bond, and a 5.50-year swap would have a PVBP similar to that of a five-year bond.

When using swaps as hedge tools, we bear in mind that over time the PVBP of swaps behaves differently from that of bonds. Immediately preceding an interest reset date, the PVBP of a swap will be near-identical to that of the same-maturity fixed-rate bond, because the PVBP of a floating-rate bond at this time has essentially nil value. Immediately after the reset date, the swap PVBP will be near-identical to that of a bond that matures at the next reset date. This means that at the point (and this point only) right after the reset the swap PVBP will decrease by the amount of the floating-rate PVBP. In between reset dates, the swap PVBP is quite stable, as the effect of the fixed- and floating-rate PVBP changes cancel each other out. Contrast this with the fixed-rate PVBP, which decreases in value over time in stable fashion.[9] This feature is illustrated in Figure 15.11. A slight anomaly is that the PVBP of a swap actually increases by a small amount between reset dates; this is because the PVBP of a floating-rate bond decreases at a slightly faster rate than that of the fixed-rate bond during this time.

---

[9] This assumes no sudden large-scale yield movements.

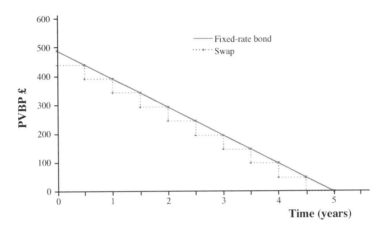

Figure 15.11 PVBP of a 5-year swap and fixed-rate bond

Hedging bond instruments with interest-rate swaps is conceptually similar to hedging with another bond or with bond futures contracts. If one is holding a long position in a vanilla bond, the hedge requires a long position in the swap: remember that a long position in a swap is to be paying fixed (and receiving floating). This hedges the receipt of fixed from the bond position. The change in the value of the swap will match the change in value of the bond, only in the opposite direction.[10] The maturity of the swap should match that of the bond as closely as possible. As swaps are OTC contracts, it should be possible to match interest dates as well as maturity dates. If one is short the bond, the hedge is to be short the swap, so the receipt of fixed matches the pay-fixed liability of the short bond position.

The correct nominal amount of the swap to put on is established using the PVBP hedge ratio. This is given as

$$\text{Hedge ratio} = \frac{PVBP_{bond}}{PVBP_{swap}} \qquad (15.28)$$

This technique is still used in the market but suffers from the assumption of parallel yield-curve shifts and can therefore lead to significant hedging error at times. More advanced techniques are used by banks when hedging books using swaps, which space does not permit any discussion here.

---

[10] The change will not be an exact mirror. It is very difficult to establish a precise hedge for a number of reasons, which include differences in day-count bases, maturity mismatches and basis risk.

Bloomberg screens

A number of screens on Bloomberg are of value to swaps users and traders. We highlight a selection of some of them here.

Broker rates screens

Swap rates can be viewed on a number of brokers pages. We show those from Tullett as at 9 February 2004.

Figure 15.12 is the USD swaps page SMKR. Rates for semi-annual and annual swaps are shown. This page also shows benchmark Treasury yields for selected maturities, and the swap spread over the benchmark. Figure 15.13 shows USD OIS and FRA rates.

```
GRAB                                                      Govt   SMKR
(c) 2003 Tullett Financial Information                     Page 1 of 1
                                                        09-Feb-04 12:27 GMT

          ---------------- Tullett plc USD Medium Term Swaps ----------------

        Price    Price    Mid    Swap Spread      IRS        IRS
        Bid      Ask      Yield  Bid    Ask      Semi-Bond   Ann-Actual  When Issued
2Y      100.070  100.076  1.756  32.50  36.50    2.081-121   2.062-102   2Y
3Y      101.06+  101.076  2.165  49.75  53.75    2.662-702   2.643-683   3Y    2.304
4Y                        2.624  49.25  53.25    3.117-157   3.098-139   5Y    3.107
5Y      100.230  100.240  3.087  39.50  43.50    3.482-522   3.463-503   10Y   4.102
6Y                        3.287  47.75  51.75    3.765-805   3.748-788   30Y
7Y                        3.488  50.25  54.25    3.990-030   3.975-015
8Y                        3.690  48.75  52.75    4.177-217   4.162-202
9Y                        3.890  44.75  48.75    4.337-377   4.323-363   Spread to 10Y
10Y     101.080  101.09+  4.090  38.50  42.50    4.475-515   4.462-502   Bid    Ask
11Y                       4.132  46.00  50.00    4.592-632   4.580-620   50.18  54.18
12Y                       4.174  52.25  56.25    4.696-736   4.685-726   60.61  64.61
13Y                       4.216  57.50  61.50    4.791-831   4.780-820   70.07  74.07
14Y                       4.257  62.00  66.00    4.877-917   4.868-908   78.74  82.74
15Y                       4.299  63.75  67.75    4.937-977   4.928-968   84.66  88.66
20Y                       4.508  63.25  67.25    5.141-181   5.134-174   105.08 109.0
25Y                       4.717  49.25  53.25    5.210-250   5.203-244   111.99 115.99
30Y     106.200  106.220  4.927  30.25  34.25    5.229-269   5.222-263
Australia 61 2 9777 8600      Brazil 5511 3048 4500      Europe 44 20 7330 7500      Germany 49 69 920410
Hong Kong 852 2977 6000 Japan 81 3 3201 8900 Singapore 65 6212 1000 U.S. 1 212 318 2000 Copyright 2004 Bloomberg L.P.
                                                                      G926-802-2 09-Feb-04 12:27:41
```

Figure 15.12 Screen SMKR on Bloomberg, Tullet USD swaps page,
9 February 2004

© Bloomberg L.P. © Tullet Financial Information. Reproduced with permission

```
GRAB                                             Govt  SMKP
(c) 2003 Tullett Financial Information           Page 1 of 1
                                                 09-Feb-04 12:27 GMT
              USD Overnight Index Swaps Composite
    OIS            FWD OIS           3M FRA          SHORT SWAPS
1M 0.994 1.024   1X2 0.992 1.022   1X4 1.141 1.171   IRS Vs 3 MONTH LIBOR
2M 0.993 1.023   2X3 1.007 1.037   3X6 1.229 1.259   6M 1.174 1.204
3M 0.998 1.028   3x4 1.050 1.080   6X9 1.446 1.476   9M 1.269 1.299
4M 1.012 1.042   4x5 1.091 1.121      6M FRA          12M 1.403 1.433
5M 1.029 1.059   1x4 1.017 1.047   1X7 1.217 1.247    18M 1.721 1.751
6M 1.040 1.070   2x5 1.051 1.081   3X9 1.340 1.370   IRS Vs 1MONTH LIBOR
7M 1.081 1.111   3x6 1.078 1.108   6X12 1.617 1.647   3M
8M 1.108 1.138   4x7 1.165 1.195                       4M
9M 1.130 1.160   1x7 1.093 1.123   ----------------    5M
10M 1.182 1.212  2x8 1.144 1.174                       6M
11M 1.221 1.251  3x9 1.191 1.221      IMM SWAPS        7M
12M 1.257 1.287  4x10 1.288 1.318      1 YEAR          8M
                                   Mar04 1.483-513      9M
USD LIBOR FIX    ON FED FUNDS      Jun04 1.779-809    10M
 Mon 09-Feb      Bid    Ask        Sep04 2.153-183    11M
1M  1.10000      0.9700 0.9800     Dec04 2.536-566    12M
2M  1.11625      High   Low          2 YEAR
3M  1.13000      0.9900 0.9700     Mar04 2.181-211    ----------------
6M  1.20000      Last   Close      Jun04 2.511-541    BASIS SWAPS (1M) / (3M)
9M  1.29250      0.9800 1.0000     Sep04 2.840-870    1Y 1M+ -0.250 3.750
                                   Dec04 3.163-193    2Y 1M+ -0.500 3.500
Australia 61 2 9777 8600   Brazil 5511 3048 4500   Europe 44 20 7330 7500   Germany 49 69 920410
Hong Kong 852 2977 6000 Japan 81 3 3201 8900 Singapore 65 6212 1000 U.S. 1 212 318 2000 Copyright 2004 Bloomberg L.P.
                                                                    G926-002-2 09-Feb-04 12:28:30
```

Figure 15.13 Screen SMKP on Bloomberg, Tullet USD OIS and FRA rates page, 9 February 2004

© Bloomberg L.P. © Tullet Financial Information. Reproduced with permission

Figures 15.14-16 shows the same broker's composite pages for AUD, SGD and TWD currencies. A composite page shows both cash and derivative rates.

```
GRAB                                                      Govt  SMKP
(c) 2003 Tullett Financial Information                    Page 1 of 1
                                                          09-Feb-04 12:29 GMT
                       AUSTRALIAN DOLLAR COMPOSITE
   IR SWAPS        BASIS SWAPS          FRA         CASH DEPOSITS    SPOT FX
1Y3 5.58 5.62   1Y 7.00   9.00    1X4 5.55 5.57   TN 5.1900 5.2600   AUD
2Y3 5.68 5.72   2Y 8.00  10.00    2X5 5.55 5.57   1W 5.2300 5.2800   0.7776/80
3Y3 5.75 5.79   3Y 9.00  11.00    3X6 5.58 5.60   1M 5.3700 5.4000   JPY
4Y6 5.87 5.91   4Y 9.50  11.50    4X7 5.58 5.60   2M 5.4300 5.4700   105.65/69
5Y6 5.92 5.96   5Y 11.00 13.00    5X8 5.60 5.62   3M 5.4600 5.5000   EUR
7Y6 5.97 6.01   6Y 11.00 13.00    6X9 5.61 5.63   4M 5.4900 5.5400   1.2741/43
10Y6 6.04 6.08  7Y 11.00 13.00    7X10 5.63 5.65  5M 5.5000 5.5700   GBP
                8Y 11.00 13.00    8X11 5.64 5.66  6M 5.5500 5.6000   1.8617/19
                9Y 11.00 13.00    9X12 5.65 5.67  9M 5.5900 5.6500   HKD
                10Y 11.00 13.00                   1Y 5.6600 5.7000   7.7680/82
-----------------------------INTEREST RATE OPTIONS-----------------------------
          SWAPTIONS                            CAPS              FLOORS
Ex  1Y    2Y    3Y    4Y    5Y    7Y   10Y   1Y 13.50 15.50   1Y 13.50 15.50
1M 15.50 16.60 17.60 17.50 17.40 17.20 17.00 2Y 14.90 16.90   2Y 14.90 16.90
2M 15.70 17.00 17.70 17.60 17.50 17.40 17.10 3Y 15.20 17.20   3Y 15.20 17.20
3M 15.70 17.40 17.80 17.70 17.60 17.50 17.30 4Y 14.90 16.90   4Y 14.90 16.90
6M 16.10 17.20 17.80 17.70 17.60 17.50 17.30 5Y 14.70 16.70   5Y 14.70 16.70
1Y 16.40 17.00 17.40 17.20 17.10 17.00 16.90 7Y 14.10 16.10   7Y 14.10 16.10
2Y 15.80 16.10 16.90 16.70 16.60 16.60 16.60 10Y 13.80 15.80  10Y 13.80 15.80
3Y 15.20 15.60 16.40 16.40 16.40 16.30 16.20
Australia 61 2 9777 8600   Brazil 5511 3048 4500   Europe 44 20 7330 7500   Germany 49 69 920410
Hong Kong 852 2977 6000 Japan 81 3 3201 8900 Singapore 65 6212 1000 U.S. 1 212 318 2000 Copyright 2004 Bloomberg L.P.
                                                                    G926-002-2 09-Feb-04 12:29:59
```

Figure 15.14 Tullett Australian dollar composite page

© Bloomberg L.P. © Tullet Financial Information. Reproduced with permission

Fixed Income Markets

```
                        SINGAPORE DOLLAR COMPOSITE

     IR SWAPS          OIS          SGD/USD SWAPS      CASH DEPOSITS      SPOT FX
1Y  0.98 1.00   1M 0.70 0.74    Sem Bnd/6M (L)     TN 0.6250 0.6250      SGD
2Y  1.49 1.52   2M 0.70 0.74    1Y -3.00  0.00     SW 0.6250 0.6250    1.6842/58
3Y  1.90 1.93   3M 0.70 0.74    2Y -3.00  0.00     1M 0.6250 0.6250
4Y  2.21 2.24   6M 0.78 0.82    3Y -3.00  0.00     2M 0.6250 0.6250      JPY
5Y  2.51 2.54   9M 0.85 0.89    4Y -3.00  0.00     3M 0.6250 0.6250    105.65/69
6Y  2.77 3.81   1Y 0.95 0.99    5Y -3.00  0.00     4M 0.6875 0.6875
7Y  3.05 3.08                   7Y -3.00 -1.00     5M 0.6875 0.6875      EUR
10Y 3.55 3.59                   10Y-3.00 -1.00     6M 0.6875 0.6875    1.2741/43
12Y 3.61 3.71                                      9M 0.7500 0.7500
15Y 3.72 3.82                                      1Y 0.8750 0.8750
-----------------------------------------------------------------------------
 SIBOR FIX         CAPS & FLOORS              SWAPTIONS (MID)
Mon 09-Feb        1Y 56.00 63.50    Ex  1Y    2Y    3Y    5Y    10Y
1M  0.75000       2Y 54.50 58.00    3M  #     #     #    44.00 34.50
2M  0.75000       3Y 49.00 52.50    6M  #     #     #    41.50 32.50
3M  0.75000       4Y 44.50 47.50    1Y 56.00 47.50 43.00 37.50   #
6M  0.81250       5Y 40.00 43.50    2Y 41.00 38.50 35.50 31.00   #
12M 1.00000       7Y 33.50 37.50    3Y 35.50 32.50 30.50 27.00   #
                  10Y 28.00 32.00   5Y 26.00 24.50 24.00 23.25   #
```

Figure 15.15 Tullett Singapore dollar composite page
© Bloomberg L.P. © Tullet Financial Information. Reproduced with permission

```
                        TAIWAN DOLLAR COMPOSITE

IR SWAPS      TWD/USD SWAPS      SPOT FX
 Act/365       Sem Mny/6M (L)     TWD
1.15 1.19   1Y  0.73  0.83     33.17/27
1.49 1.53   2Y  1.05  1.15
1.82 1.86   3Y  1.35  1.45      JPY
2.02 2.06   4Y  1.55  1.65     105.65/69
2.22 2.26   5Y  1.68  1.78
2.45 2.55   7Y  1.81  1.91      EUR
2.73 2.83   10Y 1.96  2.06     1.2741/43
```

Figure 15.16 Tullett Taiwan dollar composite page
© Bloomberg L.P. © Tullet Financial Information. Reproduced with permission

Calculation screens

A number of analytics pages are also used by swap traders and analysts. Figure 15.17 shows the vanilla swap calculator page, BCSW. We illustrate its use to price a five-year Singapore dollar swap where there the floating leg has a spread below Libor of 15 bps. As there is a spread, the fixed rate will differ from the standard interbank quote for five-year SGD swaps, which was 2.317% on the calculation date of 22 March 2004. The terms of the swap are:

Trade date	22 March 2004
Effective date	24 March 2004
Nominal	SGD 10,000,000
Floating rate	Libor minus 15 bps
Curve	Singapore government benchmark (Bloomberg number 44)
Floating pay	Semi-annual, act/365
Fixed pay	Semi-annual, act/365

Figure 15.17(a) shows the calculation and that the fixed rate for the swap was 2.16750%. This differs from the swap rate because of the spread under Libor on the floating side. The standard swap rate of 2.213% can be seen on the swap rate curve on the right-hand side of the screen. As the swap is being calculated as at its start date, the market value and accrued is zero. Figure 15.17(b) shows the cashflows for the swap; this is page 2 of the screen.

This screen can also be used to obtain the present-value of an existing swap, used when swaps are terminated ahead of maturity (and a one-off cash payment is made to close out the swap). The user selects the yield curve against which the swap is valued, usually the generic benchmark curve. For this particular swap the curve selected was number 44 on the Bloomberg menu, the Singapore government bond yield curve.

Screen SWPM, shown at figure 15.18(a), allows greater flexibility as more of the swap terms can be set by the user themselves. For comparison we have used the terms for the same Singapore dollar swap calculated using screen BCSW at figure 15.17. The one difference is that we have elected for the floating leg to pay quarterly, rather than semi-annual, payments; the fixed leg still pays semi-annually. We can see the difference this causes to the DV01 measure, which was SGD 4,738 in the first swap against SGD 4,507 in this one. The "Index" is also different, which is expected: the first swap seen at Figure 15.17(a) shows the six-month SGD fix, whereas the rate shown on Figure 15.18(a) is the three-month rate, since this swap pays floating-rate quarterly. All this can be observed on the screen.

Figure 15.18(b) is from the same screen, with the user selecting

2 <Go>

to view the swap curve.

Figure 15.19 is the swaption valuation page OVSW. We have input details for a one-year option on the same SGD swap analysed in Figure 15.17. The user must select the pricing model as well as other parameters such as the volatility level. We show the same swaption valuation using first the Black 76 model at figure 15.19(a) and the Black-Derman-Toy model at figure 15.19(b). As expected the option premium differs according to the model selected. The zero-yield volatilities are listed on the bottom right-hand of the screen.

Note how the fixed rate calculated for the swap is the five-year forward rate in one year's time.

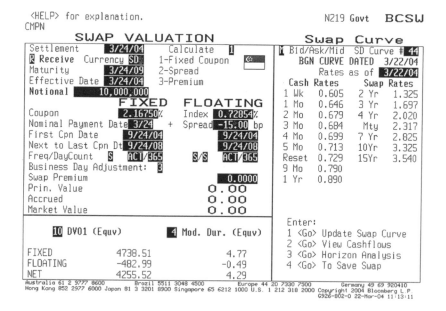

Figure 15.17(a) Bloomberg screen BCSW, swap valuation page, calculation on 22 March 2004

© Bloomberg L.P. Reproduced with permission

<HELP> for explanation.   N219 Govt   **BCSW**

SWAP VALIDATION SCREEN

                                                                    Page 1/ 1
Pay/Rec   **R**   Maturity   Effective Date   Settlement
                       3/24/2009   3/24/2004   3/24/2004
          Coupon   Spread   Pay Reset   Day Cnt   Notional
Fixed   2.16750%   S   ACT/365   10000000
Float   0.72854% + -15.0bp   S   S   ACT/365   10000000

Currency SD	Payments			Present	**3**	**5**
Date	Fixed	Float	Net	Value	FltIndex	SpotRate
9/24/04	109265.75	29164.76	80101.00	79807.89		0.728540
3/24/05	107484.25	44877.82	62606.42	62052.70	1.054995	0.892347
9/26/05	110453.42	71533.26	38920.16	38272.90	1.553744	1.120294
3/24/06	106296.58	90242.06	16054.51	15634.92	1.990131	1.341836
9/25/06	109859.59	108138.58	1721.00	1656.85	2.283545	1.544626
3/26/07	108078.08	124393.95	-16315.86	-15503.20	2.644714	1.744129
9/24/07	108078.08	136617.05	-28538.97	-26732.28	2.889847	1.928719
3/24/08	108078.08	151813.25	-43735.17	-40324.14	3.194606	2.113309
9/24/08	109265.75	167036.01	-57770.25	-52350.56	3.463486	2.297103
3/24/09	107484.25	177748.87	-70264.63	-62515.08	3.734439	2.477900

                                            Total   0.00
Australia 61 2 9777 8600   Brazil 5511 3048 4500   Europe 44 20 7330 7500   Germany 49 69 920410
Hong Kong 852 2977 6000 Japan 81 3 3201 8900 Singapore 65 6212 1000 U.S. 1 212 318 2000 Copyright 2004 Bloomberg L.P.
                                                                      G926-802-0 22-Mar-04 11:13:18

Figure 15.17(b) Bloomberg screen BCSW, page forward to show swap cashflows
© Bloomberg L.P. Reproduced with permission

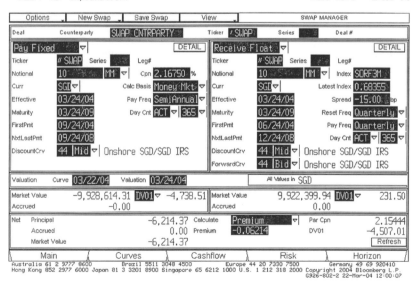

Figure 15.18(a) Bloomberg screen SWPM, user-selected swap calculator
on 22 March 2004 to analyse same swap shown in Figure 15.17
© Bloomberg L.P. Reproduced with permission

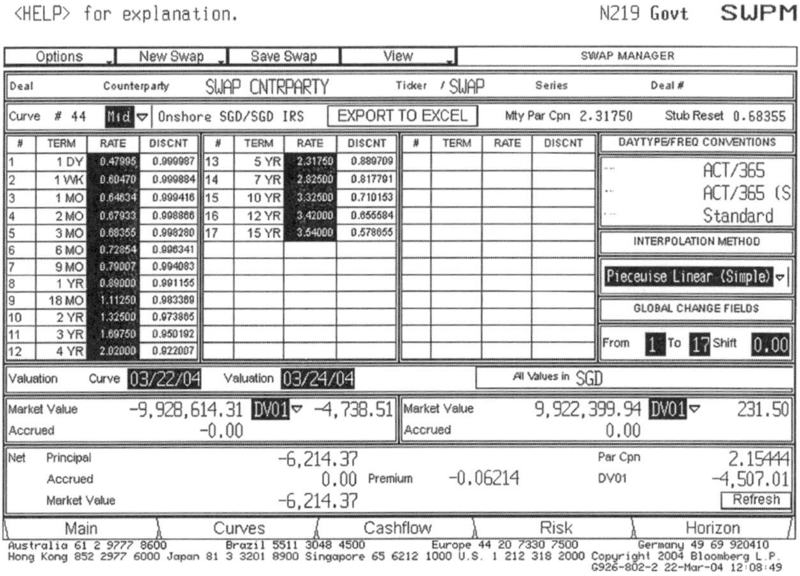

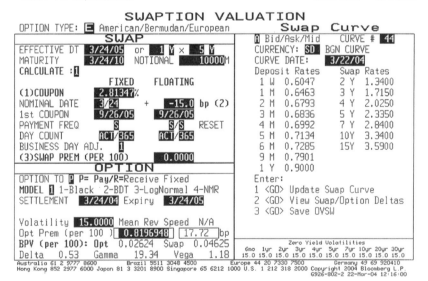

Figure 15.18(b) Bloomberg screen SWPM, page forward to show swap curve
© Bloomberg L.P. Reproduced with permission

Figure 15.19(a) Bloomberg screen OVSW, swaption valuation screen for SGD swap
on 22 March 2004, using Black 76 model
© Bloomberg L.P. Reproduced with permission

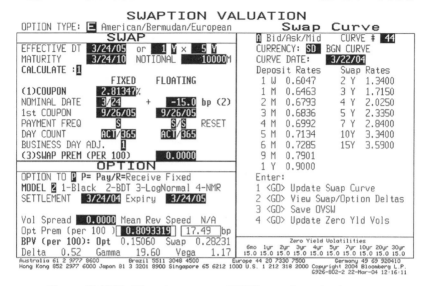

Figure 15.19(b)　Bloomberg screen OVSW, swaption valuation screen
using Black-Derman-Toy model
© Bloomberg L.P. Reproduced with permission

The convexity bias

It is common for swaps traders to calculate swaps prices from the prices of interest-rate futures contracts. The price of a futures contract is the implied three-month forward rate on expiry date of the contract. However there are differences in the way that futures contracts and swaps behave that means swap rates derived from futures prices, or a zero-coupon yield curve constructed from futures contracts and swap rates, will not be completely accurate. The main difference between the two instruments is that futures contracts move in minimum increments of a tick, which applies to the number of months covered by the contract. Swaps on the other hand have less discrete rate movements and accrue interest on a daily basis. These differences lead to swap rates exhibiting lower convexity than futures prices, which can lead to inaccuracies in pricing. In this section we review the impact of the *convexity bias* and how it should be accounted for in futures and swaps analysis. The convexity bias in interest rate futures contracts was first highlighted by Galen Burghardt in a research paper for Dean Witter Futures in 1994. This paper was later published in Burghardt (2003). The original paper was a ground-breaking piece of research and led to changes in the way futures are used to price swaps.

The convexity bias in futures contracts

Although in practice the rates implied by futures contracts are assumed to be equal to actual forward rates, for longer-dated futures contracts, differences in the way that forwards and exchange-traded futures are handled will result in futures rates not being equal to forward rates. In this section we review how the difference between rates implied by futures contracts and forward rates in practice must be taken into account when pricing long-dated forward instruments.

The convexity bias is the term used to explain the observation that the price of futures contracts such as the Eurodollar contract (traded on the Chicago Mercantile Exchange) should in fact be lower than their fair value, that is, the three-month interest rates implied by the contract should be higher than the three-month forward rates to which they are tied. The bias becomes more prominent for longer-dated contracts, but is negligible for contracts that have an expiry date of under two years. The presence of this bias however will influence the fair value for a swap; for example a five-year swap rate should be lower than the yield implied by the first five years of the Eurodollar contract. Where swap rates do not take the convexity bias into account, there would be an advantage to being short of the swap, against a hedge with futures contracts. Let us consider the main issues.

Interest-rate swaps and futures contracts such as Eurodollar futures are both priced under the same type of forward interest rate environment. The two instruments are fundamentally different in one key respect however; with an interest-rate swap, cash flows are exchanged (in fact a net cash payment) only once for each leg of a swap, and then only in arrears. With an exchange-traded futures contract though, profits and losses are settled every day. The difference in the way profit and loss are settled affects the values of swap and futures relative to each other. The resulting bias acts in favour of a short swap (paying floating, receiving fixed) against a long futures contract. It is therefore important to measure the extent of this bias when calculating swap rates. As first reported by Burghardt (2003), the bias is worth about 6 basis points for a five-year swap, when compared to the price implied by the Eurodollar futures contract. For a 10-year swap the bias is about 18 basis points.

Interest-rate swaps and futures

From our reading of the chapter to now, we are familiar with the structure of an interest-rate swap as being an exchange of fixed- versus floating-rate interest payments on a specified notional principal. The floating-leg may be on any required basis but is usually reset on a semi-annual or quarterly basis.

A five-year swap that paid fixed and received quarterly floating payments would require the floating-rate to be reset 20 times during its life, once when the swap was transacted and then every three months thereafter. We may therefore view the swap as being conceptually the same as the sum of 20 separate segments, with the value of each segment being dependent on the fixed rate of the swap and on the market's expectation of what the floating rate will be on the quarterly reset date.

The basis point value (BPV) of a swap is given by (15.29) and is the amount by which the swap changes value for every basis point that the closing day's same-maturity swap rate fixes above or below the swap fixed rate. A change in value given by a change in market rates is not realised on the day however,[11] but is realised on the maturity of the swap.

$$BPV = 0.00001 \times \frac{d}{B} \times M \qquad (15.29)$$

where
d is the number of days in the floating period
B is the year day base (360 or 365)
M is the notional principal of the swap.

The basis point value of a futures contract is fixed however, irrespective of the maturity of the contract, and is the "tick value" of the contract itself. For example the Eurodollar futures contract has a BPV of $25, while the short-sterling contract on LIFFE has a tick value of £6.25. In a combined position therefore, consisting of an interest-rate swap hedged with futures contracts, both instruments are sensitive to the same change in interest rates. If we wish to compare the effects of a change in the value of both instruments, the most straightforward way to do this is to use the present value for both price changes. As futures contracts are settled on a daily basis, the present value of its basis point value is unchanged, so $25 in the case of the Eurodollar contract. The present value of the BPV of an interest-rate swap can be determined using a set of futures rates from a strip of similar maturity. How could we obtain the discount rate used?

In his illustration, Burghardt (2003) assumed an hypothetical $100 million five-year swap, with quarterly floating coupons, with a BPV of $2 500, but with a forward start date five years away. We require a means of calculating the present value of the BPV. Ordinarily we would require the five-year discount rate. However the simplest way to calculate the present

___
[11] The mark-to-market is unrealised P/L.

value is to first calculate what $1 would grow to if we invested it at the successive rates given by the futures strip, out to five years (that is, invest for the first 91 days at the front month futures rate, then the next 91 days for the following contract's futures rate, and so on). Let us say that this resulted in a future value of $1.55 at the end of the five-year period. This would give us a present value of: $1/$1.55 = 0.645161. That is, $0.645161 is the present value of $1 to be received in five years' time. We may use this value to calculate the present value of our hypothetical five-year swap. We said that this had a BPV of $2500, so the present value of this sum is obtained as follows:

$$\$2\,500 \times 0.645161 = \$1\,612.90.$$

Given these values, we can determine the number of Eurodollar futures contracts that would be required to hedge our hypothetical swap, which is 1 612.90/25 = 64.516 or 65 contracts. That is, 65 Eurodollar futures would have the same exposure to a change in the five-year three-month forward rate as would the $100 million five-year swap. If a bank is short the swap, that is receiving fixed-rate and paying floating-rate, it could hedge the interest-rate exposure arising from a rise in the forward rate by selling 65 Eurodollar futures. Therefore we may set the hedge calculation for any leg of a swap whose floating rate is three-month Libor as (15.30):

$$Hedge\ ratio = \frac{M \times (0.00001 \times \frac{d}{B}) \times P_{zero\text{-}coupon}}{PV(BPV_{fut})} \tag{15.30}$$

where $P_{zero\text{-}coupon}$ is the price today of a bond that pays $1 on the same day when the swap settlement is paid. In the hypothetical example we discussed, the swap settlement is five years away, and the price of such a bond was given as 0.645161. The denominator of (15.30) requires the present value of the basis point value of the futures contract, however this is for a cash flow that is received on the same day so it is unchanged from the basis point value itself.

The basis point value of the future and the swap is a measure of their interest-rate risk. A swap contract has another type of interest-rate risk however. Since any gain or loss on a swap contract in unrealised, and realised only at the end of the term, a swap may have unrealised asset value. In particular the present value of a short position in the hypothetical swap we described may be calculated using (15.31):

$$PV_{swap} = M \times ((r_{swap} - rf) \times \frac{d}{B}) \times P_{zero\text{-}coupon} \tag{15.31}$$

where

r_{swap} is the swap fixed rate

rf is the current market same-maturity forward rate.

Equation (15.31) tells us that the unrealised asset value of a swap depends both on the difference between the swap fixed rate and the market swap rate, as well as on the present value of one dollar (or pound) to be received on the swap's maturity date. In effect (15.31) states that there are in fact two sources of interest-rate risk in a forward-starting swap. The first is the uncertainty surrounding the forward rate rf. The other concerns uncertainty about the zero-coupon bond price, which is a reflection of the term structure of forward rates from today to the swap cash settlement date. If the forward rate is below the fixed rate, for example the person who is receiving fixed and paying floating has an asset whose value is reduced by a general increase in interest rates. To protect against interest-rate risk then, the person hedging the swap must not only offset the exposure to changes in the forward rate, but also the exposure to changes in the term structure of the zero-coupon yield curve as well. This may be done by buying or selling an appropriate quantity of zero-coupon bonds whose maturity matches that of the swap.

This is the key difference between an interest-rate swap and a futures contract. With futures such as Eurodollar futures the only source of market risk is the forward or futures rate. When the futures rate changes, the holder of a futures contract experiences a profit or loss, and collects the profit or pays out the loss the next day. The holder of a swap however faces two types of risk, arising from a change in the forward rate and a change in the term rate. What is the impact of this?

The effect on the change in value of the swap contract will differ from interest rate moves in different direction, because of the convexity effect, while the futures will experience the same change whatever direction rates move in. Put another way, and alluding to our hypothetical example again, if the prices of all futures contracts from the front month out the five-year contract moved up or down by 10 basis points, the effect on the P/L of our 65 contracts would be the same. However, the swap would behave differently. If there was a parallel shift upwards of 10 basis points, the present value of the loss on the five-year swap would be lower than the present value of the profit of there was a parallel shift downwards of the same magnitude. The precise amounts will depend on the maturity and BPV of the swap; however for the purposes of our discussion, the hedge position of futures contracts makes a net gain if there is rise in forward rates and less if forward rates fall. Remember this is from the point of view of someone who is short the swap. The opposite will apply for someone long the swap. This relationship is illustrated graphically in Figure 15.20.

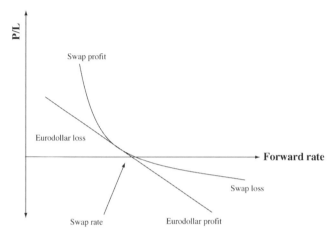

Figure 15.20 The convexity difference between swaps and futures.

As a result of the difference in convexities of the two instruments, a short swap hedged with a short position in Eurodollar futures benefits from changes in the level of interest rates. The difference in the performance of a swap and a futures contract is a function of:

- the magnitude of the change in the forward rate;
- the magnitude of the change in the term rate (or zero-coupon bond price);
- the correlation between the two rates.

As we might expect, there is a very close positive correlation between forward interest rates and zero-coupon rates, verging on unity. With virtually no exceptions, increases in the forward rate are accompanied by increases in the term rate, and vice-versa.

Calculating the convexity bias

Banks often calculate the value of the convexity bias by empirical analysis of their futures and swaps P/L history. There is a more systematic approach that may be used however, and this involves estimating the bias using three parameters, the volatility of the forward rate, the volatility of the corresponding term rate and the correlation between the two rates – the three factors we noted above. The extent of the bias can be measured using (15.32), first demonstrated by Burghardt (2003), which calculates the *drift* in the spread between the futures rates and the forward rates. This drift is the amount of bias that must be accounted for when say, pricing swaps or arranging a hedge.

$$CVbias = s_{rf} \times s_{rs} \times r_{rf/rs} \qquad (15.32)$$

where

$CVbias$ is the amount of drift

s_{rf} is the standard deviation of changes in the forward rate

s_{rs} is the standard deviation of changes in the zero-coupon rate

$r_{rf/rs}$ is the correlation coefficient between changes in the two rates.

The drift is the number of ticks that the swap rate spread has to fall during any given period to compensate for the convexity bias. The derivation of this expression is given at Appendix 15.1.

The value of the convexity bias is a function of the convexity of the forward swap that is associated with the futures contract. This depends in turn on the price sensitivity of the zero-coupon bond that corresponds to the swap maturity. Since the price of a zero-coupon bond with say, five-years to maturity is more interest-rate sensitive than the price of a bond with less than five years to maturity, (measured by the modified duration of the bond), the value of the bias is higher the longer the maturity of the futures contract. This is why the convexity bias effect is greatest for long-dated futures and swaps positions. The highlighting of the convexity bias is a relatively recent phenomenon for this reason; as the longest-dated futures contracts have extended out to 10 years, and very long-dated swaps are now fairly common, the impact of the convexity bias has been more pronounced.

Impact of the convexity bias

It is common practice for swaps traders to price forward-starting dollar swaps against Eurodollar futures contracts, and this is not surprising given the liquidity and transparency of the contract, as well as its narrow bid-offer spread. However the convexity bias that results from the inherent differences between the two instruments makes it important for traders to price in the effect of the bias for long-dated forward swaps. By adjusting the prices of futures contracts by the amount of the convexity bias before using them to calculate the implied swap rate, we will obtain a more accurate reflection of the forward rates implied by the futures prices. The extent of the bias is indicated in Table 15.6, which was calculated as the convexity bias to be applied for Eurodollar contracts used to price forward swaps during 1994 and is reproduced with permission from Burghardt (2003).

Swap term (years)

Years forward	1	2	3	4	5	6	7	8	9	10
Spot	0.23	1.08	2.32	3.83	5.58	7.57	9.77	12.189	14.79	17.58
1	1.99	3.49	5.23	7.21	9.44	11.88	14.55	17.42	20.48	
2	5.11	7.05	9.25	11.71	14.39	17.32	20.46	23.78		
3	9.16	11.58	14.31	17.24	20.43	23.85	27.47			
4	14.22	17.22	20.42	23.91	27.61	31.52				
5	20.48	23.94	27.71	31.73	35.95					
6	27.71	31.81	36.14	40.69						
7	36.28	40.91	45.77							
8	45.93	51.13								
9	56.76									

Table 15.6 Convexity bias in forward swaps (basis points).
Reproduced with permission from Burghardt, G.,
The Eurodollar Futures and Options Handbook, McGraw-Hill, 2003.

Any calculation of convexity bias is based on an assumption about the volatility of market interest rates. This assumption must be advertised before the values may be used. From Table 40.5 we see that the bias effect is greatest for long-dated long forward swaps. The effect is least for "spot swaps" or swaps that have an immediate effective date. Therefore at the time that these rates were effective, if we were pricing a five-year swap with a one-year forward start date, we would adjust the one-year futures contract by 9.44 basis points before using it to calculate the swap rate.

The other effect of the convexity bias concerns the marking-to-market of the swap book. The common practice is for the mark to be based on the closing prices of the futures contracts, and for dollar swaps this may go out to long-dated swaps. However the convexity bias means that Eurodollar futures prices produce forward rates that are higher than the forward rates that should ideally be used to value swaps. Therefore some banks make an allowance for the value of the bias, which enables a more accurate picture of the value of the swap book to be drawn. However such an adjustment is based on assumptions of interest-rate volatilities, which is one reason why many banks do not make the convexity adjustment.

Using Bloomberg to observe convexity bias in the Eurodollar contract

Figure 15.21 shows the Eurodollar futures analysis, page EDS on Bloomberg, as at 2 June 2004. This shows the implied three-month USD Libor rates from the futures prices, starting with the Jun04 contract, as well as the actual cash rates as at that date. Exchange-traded futures contracts including the Eurodollar trade at a fixed value per basis point, and hence have zero convexity. However the market uses these contracts to hedge other instruments that do possess a convexity effect, hence the impact on this when undertaking hedging, especially for longer-dated assets, needs to be known as well. Hitting

1 <Go>

at page EDS will bring up the convexity bias analysis for this contract. We see from Figure 15.22 that this is calculated as the

futures rate – the adjusted rate

and is shown under column 7 of Figure 15.22.

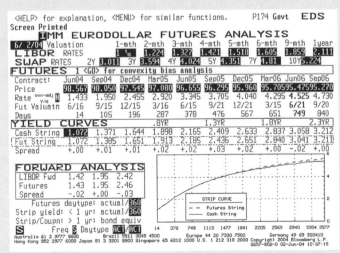

Figure 15.21 Eurodollar Futures analysis, Bloomberg page EDS, as at 2 June 2004.

© Bloomberg L.P. Used with permission

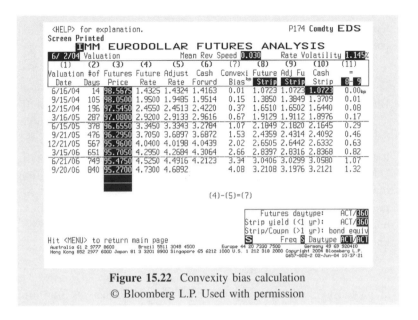

Figure 15.22 Convexity bias calculation
© Bloomberg L.P. Used with permission

Appendices

APPENDIX 15.1 | Calculating the convexity bias

Appendix 15.1 is reproduced with kind permission of McGraw-Hill from Burghardt (2003).

A method that is used to calculate the convexity bias in Eurodollar rates, the rate of *drift* relative to forward rates involves calculating the expected gain when a forward swap is hedged with Eurodollar futures, and assuming specified volatility levels for the change in forward rates and zero-coupon rates.

Swap value

The net present value of a forward swap that receives fixed and pays quarterly floating is given by (15.33):

$$PV_{swap} = M \times (r_{swap} - rf) \times \frac{d}{B} \times P_{zero\text{-}coupon} \qquad (15.33)$$

where r_{swap} and rf are expressed in basis points. Multiplying the expression by \$1 million and dividing by 90, and them rearranging gives us an expression setting the new present value in terms of the \$25 tick value of a Eurodollar futures contract, shown as (15.34):

$$PV_{swap} = (\frac{M}{\$1m}) \times (r^{c}_{swap} - rf\cent) \times \frac{d}{90} \times \$25 \times P_{zero\text{-}coupon} \quad (15.34)$$

At the time the forward swap is transacted the difference between the twp rates is zero as the net present value of the swap is zero. As interest rates change the rate rf and the value of $P_{zero\text{-}coupon}$ both change, which affects the present value of the swap.

Swap P/L and hedge ratio

For a change of Δrf in the forward rate and $\Delta P_{zero\text{-}coupon}$ in the price of the zero-coupon bond, the mark-to-market profit on a forward swap is given by (15.35):

$$\Delta PV = - (\frac{M}{\$1m}) \times (\frac{d}{90}) \times \$25 \times \Delta rf \times (P_{zero\text{-}coupon} + \Delta P_{zero\text{-}coupon}). \quad (15.35)$$

The change in the value of one Eurodollar futures contract is equal to the tick value multiplied by the change in the forward rate, therefore the number of contracts required to hedge against $1 million notional of the swap is given by (15.36):

$$HedgeRatio = - (\frac{M}{\$1m}) \times (\frac{d}{90}) \times P_{zero\text{-}coupon}. \quad (15.36)$$

The negative sign in (15.36) indicates that the hedge against the short swap position (receive fixed, pay floating) is a short sale of Eurodollar futures. Given this hedge ratio the profit on the short Eurodollar futures position is expressed as (15.37):

$$\text{profit or loss} = (\frac{M}{\$1m}) \times (\frac{d}{90}) \times P_{zero\text{-}coupon} \times (\Delta rf + drift) \times \$25 \quad (15.37)$$

where *drift* is the systematic change in the Eurodollar futures rate relative to the forward rate required to compensate for the convexity difference between the swap contract and the futures contract.

To preserve no-arbitrage pricing, the expected profit from such a hedge must be zero. That is, the expected profit on the swap must offset precisely the expected profit on the Eurodollar position. This principle enables us to calculate the drift. The expression $(M/\$1m) \times (d/90) \times \$25$ is used to calculate the profit for both swaps and futures, therefore it cancels out. Thus we may set the following expression, which recognises that there is no profit advantage (in theory) between the short swap and futures hedge, so if we arrange the profit expressions as equal to zero, we may rearrange to solve for drift. This is shown as (15.38):

$$E[\Delta rf \times (P_{zero\text{-}coupon} + \Delta P_{zero\text{-}coupon})] = E[P_{zero\text{-}coupon} \times (\Delta rf + drift)] \quad (15.38)$$

where $E[\ ]$ represents the market's expectation today of the value of profit. As $P_{zero\text{-}coupon}$ is known, we may solve for drift by dividing the expression by it, which gives us (15.39):

$$E(drift) = E\left(\Delta rf \times \left(\frac{\Delta P_{zero\text{-}coupon}}{P_{zero\text{-}coupon}}\right)\right) \quad (15.39)$$

This is the expression for the calculation of the convexity bias. Assuming that the average change in forward rates and zero-coupon rates is zero, we may combine the expression with the standard formula for correlation to give us an expression which may be used to approximate the amount of the convexity bias, shown as (15.40):

$$E(drift) = \sigma(\Delta rf) \times \sigma\left(\frac{\Delta P_{zero\text{-}coupon}}{P_{zero\text{-}coupon}}\right) \times \rho\left(\Delta rf, \frac{\Delta P_{zero\text{-}coupon}}{P_{zero\text{-}coupon}}\right) \quad (15.40)$$

No assumption is made about the distribution of rate changes. The drift is expressed in basis points per period.

APPENDIX 15.2 Calculating futures strip rates and implied swap rates

A futures strip is a position that contains one each of the futures contracts in a sequence of contract months. For example the one-year short sterling strip in August 2004 would consist of one each of the Sep04, Dec04, Mar05 and Jun05 contracts. The two-year strip would contain these but be followed by one each of the Sep05, Dec05, Mar06 and Jun06 contracts. The three-month forward rates that are implied by the prices of these contracts, together with the initial cash market deposit rate for the *stub* period may be used to obtain the future value of an investment made today. The expression to calculate this is given at (15.41):

$$FV_N = \left(1 + r_0 \times \left(\frac{d_0}{B}\right)\right) \times \left(1 + rf_1 \times \left(\frac{d_0}{B}\right)\right) \times L \times \left(1 + rf_n \times \left(\frac{d_n}{B}\right)\right)$$

$$(15.41)$$

where

FV_N is the future value of £1 invested today for N years

r_0 is the cash market deposit rate (Libor) for the period from today to the expiry

date of the first futures contract

rf_1 is the forward rate implied by the price of the front-month futures contract

rf_n is the forward rate implied by the price of the last futures contract in the strip

d_i is the number of days in each futures period, where $i = 0, 1, \ldots n$

B is the year day-base (360 or 365).

The future value of an investment made at futures rates can then be used to calculate implied zero-coupon bond yields. The continuously compounded yield r_{CC} is given by (15.42) while the price $P_{zero\text{-}coupon}$ of a zero-coupon bond of maturity N years is given by (15.43).

$$r_{CC} = \ln \left(\frac{FV_N}{N} \right) \qquad (15.42)$$

$$P_{zero\text{-}coupon} = \frac{1}{FV_N} . \qquad (15.43)$$

The forward rates implied by a strip of futures contracts may be used to calculate implied swap rates. As we saw in this chapter, a plain vanilla interest-rate swap is priced on the basis that it consists of conceptually a short position in a fixed-coupon bond and a long position in a floating-rate bond, that is, a pay fixed- and receive floating-rate swap. The theoretical swap rate is therefore the average of the forward rates given by the futures strip from rf_1 to rf_N where N is the maturity of the swap. The most straightforward way to calculate this is using the discount factors of each spot rate, rather than the forward rates, and this was described in the main body of the text in this chapter.

Selected Bibliography and References

The swaps market is extensively covered in the academic and practitioner literature. A good general introduction is in Decovny (1998), while another accessible and reader-friendly discussion is given in Eales (1995). A superlative overview treatment is given in Chapter 14 of Jarrow and Turnbull (2000), and this is a standard text in the market. Technical aspects are covered in the journal references.

Fixed Income Markets

A good account of hedging with swaps can be found in Chapter 11 of Fabozzi (1998), which is authored by Shrikant Ramamurthy. Chapter 6 in Gup and Brooks (1993) is a readable introduction to swaps in asset & liability management.

Bicksler, J. and Chen, A., "An Economic Analysis of Interest Rate Swaps", *Journal of Finance* 41, 3, 1986, p. 645-655.

Block, T., *Pricing and hedging interest-rate swaps*, Mars Business Associates, 1994.

Brotherton-Ratcliffe, R. and Iben, B., "Yield Curve Applications of Swap Products", in Schwartz, R. and Smith, C. (editors) , *Advanced Strategies in Financial Risk Management*, New York Institute of Finance, 1993.

Burghardt, G., *The Eurodollar Futures and Options Handbook*, McGraw-Hill 2003.

Das, S., *Swaps and Financial Derivatives* (2nd edition), IFR Publishing, 1994.

Decovny, S., *Swaps* (2nd edition), FT Prentice Hall, 1998.

Dunbar, N., "Swaps volumes see euro wane", *Risk*, September 2000.

Eales, B., *Financial Risk Management*, McGraw Hill, 1995, Chapter 3.

Fabozzi, F. (editor), *Perspectives on Interest Rate Risk Management for Money Managers and Traders*, FJF Associates, 1998.

Flavell, R., *Swaps and other derivatives*, Wiley 2003.

French, K., "A Comparison of Futures and Forwards Prices", *Journal of Financial Economics* 12, November 1983, pp. 311–342.

Gup, B. and Brooks, R., *Interest Rate Risk Management*, Irwin, 1993.

Henna, P., *Interest-rate Risk Management using Futures and Swaps*, Probus, 1991.

International Swaps and Derivatives Association, *Code of Standard Working, Assumptions and Provisions for Swaps*, New York, 1991.

Jarrow, R. and Turnbul, S., *Derivative Securities* (2nd edition), South-Western Publishing, 2000.

Jarrow, R., Oldfield, G., "Forward Contracts and Futures Contracts", *Journal of Financial Economics* 9, December 1981, pp. 373–382.

Khan, M., "Online platforms battle for business", *Risk*, September 2000.

Kolb, R., *Futures, Options and Swaps* (4th edition), Blackwell, 2004.

Li, A. and Raghavan, V.R., "LIBOR-In-Arrears Swaps", *Journal of Derivatives* 3, Spring 1996, p.44-48.

Lindsay, R., "High Wire Act", *Risk*, August 2000.

Marshall, J. and Kapner, K., *Understanding Swap Finance*, South-Western Publishing, 1990.

Park, H., Chen, A., "Differences between Futures and Forward Prices: A Further Investigation of Marking to Market Effects", *Journal of Futures Markets* 5, February 1985, pp. 77–88.

Turnbull, S., "Swaps: A Zero Sum Game", *Financial Management* 16, Spring 1987, p.15-21.

The Standardised Interest-rate Swap Contract: Assessing the LIFFE Swapnote® Contract

The interest-rate swap is arguably the most widely-traded derivative contract and has lent itself to constant development and application. Its flexibility derives in part from its over-the-counter (OTC) bespoke nature. Paradoxically, financial institutions have also considered that an exchange-traded swap contract, transacted along similar lines to exchange-traded futures, may present unique advantages in combining both the flexibility of the OTC swap *and* the usefulness of standardised contracts.

Thus, financial institutions have considered a new class of interest-rate futures products – the exchange-traded swap contract. On 20th March 2001, LIFFE launched Swapnote®. The Swapnote® contract is essentially a forward-starting swap contract that cash-settles on the start/effective date of the underlying swap. Following its introduction, trading volume in this instrument can now be considered liquid. The success of the Swapnote® is due to its simplicity in creating a standardised exchange-traded futures contract but combining the price sensitivity of an interest-rate swap. As such, it can be used for a variety of hedging and trading purposes.

In this chapter, we explore some methods of evaluating Swapnote® futures. First, we consider briefly the take-up of Swapnote®. We look at evaluating Swapnote® using one of the standard interest-rate models. We then consider briefly the standard method for computing the convexity adjustment necessary when using the contract for cash-market hedging.

This chapter was co-authored with Mohamoud Dualeh and Abukar Ali.

Swaps and a new benchmark

The Swapnote® has introduced a new dimension to the interest-rate swap market. Swapnote® is a family of futures contracts that allows institutions to access the euro interest-rate swaps market. It is valued off the euro-swap yield curve, usually simply called the swap curve. In terms of notional volume, the swap market is the largest fixed-income market in the world, being approximately six times the size of the bond market.[1] In an era of diminishing liquidity in government bond markets, and the advent of the euro, the swap market has become the benchmark for long-term interest rates. Hence, the swap curve has become the primary means of price discovery in the euro-denominated fixed-income market. The factors which contributed to this included the size and homogeneity of the swap market, compared to combined government-bond markets, and the decline in government-bond issuance, together with growing non-government and corporate bond issuance.[2] The turnover of the swap market, on the other hand, consistently trends upwards; for instance, it grew by 104% between 1998 and 2001.[3]

From a trader's point of view, the best hedges are achieved through vehicles that are highly liquid and as closely correlated with the underlying assets as possible. In Europe (and arguably in other markets), the interest-rate swaps market now appears to achieving this more than the government-debt markets. The efficacy of the swap curve as a benchmark reflects the fact that the euro-swaps market is now larger than the eurozone government-bond market.

Exchange-traded swap contracts are traded on the London International Financial Futures and Options Exchange (Liffe) and the Chicago Board of Trade (CBOT). Both are based on the future value of a swap rate. The Swapnote® futures contracts have grown rapidly since their introduction in March 2001. For traders and investors with exposure to credit risk based on the LIBOR, the Swapnote® contract has been accepted as an effective hedging tool as, for instance, the U.S. Treasury futures contract does not take credit risk into account. Hedging a swap portfolio with government bonds appears to work extremely well. However, the assumption that the bond-

---

[1] Source: ISDA, "Summary of OTC Derivative Market Data", www.isda.org/statistics/

[2] A number of other factors have contributed to this, resulting in greater use of the swap curve to as the euro Benchmark. For a general discussion of government-bond market illiquidity and the issues behind alternative benchmarks, see Choudhry (2003).

[3] Source: www.isda.org/statistics/. For a good discussion and related issues, see Eli M Remolona and Philip D Wooldridge, "The euro interest rate swap market", *BIS Quarterly Review*, March 2003.

swap spread remains constant is, in practice, not realistic. The spread often exhibits significant volatility.[4] In fact, hedging with government-bond futures presents significant basis risk. The Swapnote® is designed to both strengthen the benchmark status of the swap curve and provide an effective and accessible hedge for portfolios of securities. It should also reduce basis risk for practitioners looking to hedge (say) corporate-bond portfolios.

The Swapnote® contract

For readers' reference, we provide first an overview of the main features of the Swapnote® contract.

Swapnote® is essentially a forward-starting swap contract that cash-settles on the start or effective date of the underlying swap. The contract can also be regarded as a cash-settled bond futures contract with a single notional bond in the deliverable basket. The contract is essentially similar to a standardised exchange-traded futures contract but with the price sensitivity of an interest-rate swap. Each Swapnote® contract has a series of notional cash flows underlying it, comprising a fixed-coupon element together with a principal repayment such that it replicates a notional bond.

At first, the coupon level is set at 6% for each of the contracts, thereby facilitating spread trading between government bond futures contracts and Swapnote® contracts of related maturity. Similarly the contracts are timed on a quarterly expiry cycle for the months of March, June, September and December, the usual expiry months for futures exchanges, and denoted by the letters H, M, U and Z.

Figure 16.1 illustrates the 10-year Swapnote contract specification.

Unit of Trading	€100,000 notional principal amount
Notional Coupon	6.0%
Maturities	Notional principal amount due ten years from the delivery day
Delivery Months	March, June, September and December such that the nearest two delivery months are always available for trading
Delivery Day	Third Wednesday of the delivery month
Last Trading Day	11:00 Brussels time (10:00 London time). Two London business days prior to the delivery day

---

[4] See Flavell (2001), Chapter 9 for more discussion about how the optimal hedge effectiveness in this regard can be rather low.

Quotation	Per €100 nominal value
Minimum Price Movement	0.01
(Tick Size and Value)	(€10)
Trading hours	07:00 - 18:00 on LIFFE CONNECT™

Figure 16.1 10-year Swapnote® – contract specification
Source: Liffe

Swapnote® is a standardised exchange-traded futures contract. In other words, the 10-year swap futures will all be in the same contract month. With Swapnote®, if we assume that there is sufficient liquidity,[5] it may be easier to execute a buy or sale of 10-year swap futures than it currently is to buy or sell a 10-year strip of Eurodollar futures contracts.

We show trading volumes for the Swapnote® futures contract in Figure 16.2. During 2003, volumes experienced new highs, with the 10-year contract recording a daily volume high of 55,261 in June 2003 (13/06/03) and the five-year contract setting a new volume high record of 57,761 the same month.[6]

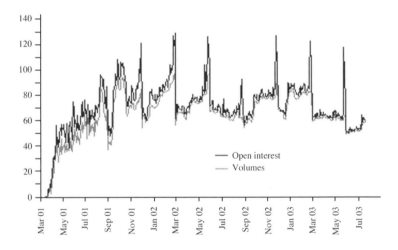

Figure 16.2 Swapnote® trading volumes and open interest
Source: Liffe. Reproduced with permission.

---

[5] From anecdotal evidence the authors conclude that there is sufficient liquidity in the market. However, given the relative youth of this instrument, this cannot be assumed to be permanent and continued observation would be prudent.

[6] The authors express thanks to Kumud Chavda from LIFFE for providing these figures.

Evaluating the Swapnote® contract

The price of the Swapnote® contract until its expiration date will reflect underlying supply and demand risk factors. At expiration, the contract settles based on the Exchange Delivery Settlement Price (EDSP) fixed by the exchange. The EDSP is defined as the sum of the discounted notional cash flows, each of which has been presently-valued using zero-coupon discount factors derived from the ISDA Benchmark Swap Rates on the last trading day. The discount factors are zero-coupon rates bootstrapped from the current par-swap curve. Cash-flow payment dates are defined as anniversary dates of the effective date. However, should any of these dates fall on a weekend or holiday, notional cash flows are moved to a business day.

Users of the Bloomberg system can use the Bloomberg Swapnote® Futures Analysis function, screen FVD, to evaluate the fair value of a Swapnote® contract, which is illustrated at Figure 16.3. It is obtained by typing

P A Cmdty FVD <GO>.

Page FVD shows the market value of the Swapnote® and its conventions such as the day count and valuation date. The Swapnote® can be priced as a forward-starting swap where the swap's effective date is set as the valuation date of the futures contract. The sensitivity measures from the FVD screen can be replicated by pricing a 10-year euro-denominated bond with a forward-settlement date of the futures valuation date and maturity date, day count, and frequency from the futures contract. Note from Figure 16.3 that a 6% notional coupon is used as the bond's fixed-coupon rate. In our example, we have evaluated the 10-year Swapnote®. Figure 16.4 is from the same screen, and lists the fixed-coupon and forward rates at each interest fixing date. The forward rates as at each fixing date are also shown.

GRAB   Comdty **FVD**

SWAPNOTE FUTURES ANALYSIS

Page 1 / 2

Future Contract		Swap Curve Info	
Name	10Y SWAPNOTE FUT Sep03	Currency	EU
Ticker	P U3	SWYC#	45
Last Trading Date	9/15/03	Curve Date	9/11/03
Current Price	113.27	Curve Settle	9/15/03
Valuation Date	9/17/03	Bid/Mid/Ask	M
Notional Maturity	9/17/13	1<Go> Update Swap Curve	
Notional Coupon	6.00 %	Bond Comparison	
Frequency	Annually	Ticker DBR 3 ¾ 07/04/13 Corp	
Day Count	30E/360	Price(Mid) 95.89	
		Yield(Mid) 4.271	

Forward Yield / Sensitivity		Parallel Swap Curve Based Fair Value					
Equivalent Yield	4.336 %	Shift:	-100	-50	0	50	100
Mod Duration	7.621	Price:	122.48	117.75	113.24	108.95	104.86
Risk	8.632	Chng:	+9.213	+4.478	-.029	-4.320	-8.405
Spread to selected bond	6.590	cRisk:	9.703	9.233	8.789	8.369	7.971

Forward Implied Par Rate	
Current Future Price Implied Forward Swap	4.369 %
Implied Forward Swap	4.360 %
Spread to spot swap	-11.588
Spread to selected bond	8.908

Australia 61 2 9777 8600   Brazil 5511 3048 4500   Europe 44 20 7330 7500   Germany 49 69 920410
Hong Kong 852 2977 6000 Japan 81 3 3201 8900 Singapore 65 6212 1000 U.S. 1 212 318 2000 Copyright 2003 Bloomberg L.P.
665-802-2 11-Sep-03 17:54:06

Figure 16.3 Bloomberg screen FVD for 10-year Swapnote® contract,
as at 11th September 2003
Source: Bloomberg L.P. Used with permission.

GRAB   Comdty **FVD**

SWAPNOTE EXPIRY DAY ANALYSIS

Page 2 / 2

Notional Value Dates	Notional Coupon amounts	Curve Derived Disc. Factors	Forward Swap Rates	Expiry Day Settle Price
				113.23
9/17/03		0.99988424		
9/17/04	6.00000000 %	0.97710051	2.332 %	
9/19/05	6.03333333 %	0.94657311	2.764 %	
9/18/06	5.98333333 %	0.91087056	3.137 %	
9/17/07	5.98333333 %	0.87262840	3.432 %	
9/17/08	6.00000000 %	0.83352702	3.663 %	
9/17/09	6.00000000 %	0.79426123	3.854 %	
9/17/10	6.00000000 %	0.75516532	4.018 %	
9/19/11	6.03333333 %	0.71682427	4.156 %	
9/17/12	5.96666667 %	0.68041108	4.267 %	
9/17/13	6.00000000 %	0.64520653	4.361 %	

Australia 61 2 9777 8600   Brazil 5511 3048 4500   Europe 44 20 7330 7500   Germany 49 69 920410
Hong Kong 852 2977 6000 Japan 81 3 3201 8900 Singapore 65 6212 1000 U.S. 1 212 318 2000 Copyright 2003 Bloomberg L.P.
665-802-1 11-Sep-03 17:58:42

Figure 16.4 Bloomberg screen FVD, page 2
Source: Bloomberg L.P. Used with permission.

The Swapnote® delivery method is cash settlement. The final settlement value will be determined as

$$X * [6 / r + (1 - 6 / r) * (1 + 0.01 * r / 2) - 20] . \qquad (16.1)$$

The underlying notional cash flows consist of a series of fixed notional coupons and a notional principal at maturity, the dates of which fall on anniversaries of the delivery day. Once the cash flows from futures contracts are implicit, any of the standard interest-rate models can be used[7] to price Swapnote® contracts.

Of course, it is not essential that a proper term-structure model should be used. Fundamentally, the Swapnote® quoted price corresponds to the forward value of a bond having a 6% coupon. At maturity, the settlement price is computed by discounting the 6% coupons plus principal using a zero-coupon curve derived from the official swap-rate fixings.

To illustrate, using linear interpolation we priced the two-year, five-year and 10- year Swapnote® Supernote contracts. First we constructed a zero curve off deposit and swap rates and discounted the coupons and the notional principal of the underlying swap. From Figure 16.5 we show the quoted prices and our theoretical prices. Note that we converted those into equivalent bond yields to get a difference in term of basis points. In fact, we can do the same analysis using Bloomberg.

	Two-year	Five-year	10-year
Quoted	106.06750	110.46000	113.52500
Theoretical	106.07138	110.46619	113.51066

Figure 16.5 Comparison of quoted and theoretical prices

As the Swapnote® contract is essentially a forward-starting swap contract that cash-settles on the start/effective date of the underlying swap, it can be interpreted as a package of forward/futures contracts. Future contracts are designed to remove the risk of default[8] inherent in forward contracts. Through the device of marking to market,[9] the value of the future

---

[7] For instance, the Black 76, Cox-Ingersoll-Ross, Black-Derman-Toy and Hull-White models, to mention a few.

[8] The default risk in a swap agreement is the counterparty risk.

[9] That is, at end of each trading day, the margin account is adjusted to reflect the investor's gain or loss.

contract is maintained at zero at all times. Thus, either party can close out his/her position at any time. This difference gives rise to the convexity bias. When hedging or pricing across futures and swaps markets, the issue of the convexity bias will lead to hedge risk.

If one is pricing the Swapnote® as a forward-starting swap using the swap curve, then there is no issue: the swap curve already exhibits a convex feature. Hence there is no need to adjust for the convexity effect. If, however, one wishes to price the swap off the Euribor futures contracts, then one will need to adjust the curve defaults for convexity bias. The Bloomberg Swapnote Futures calculator does not adjust for convexity because it uses the market swap curve (see Figure 16.3) and not the curve derived from futures contracts to calculate the implied forward rates needed when pricing swaps. Therefore, when using the Euribor futures, the back-month futures do not reflect the true Euribor forward rates and the volatility of rates required for valuing swaps. To overcome the imperfections in hedging that this will cause, one must adjust for this bias. The simplest approach is to use one of the standard interest-rate models but with a convexity adjustment.

In Figures 16.5 and 16.6 we are comparing the Swapnote® settlement prices with those of the Euribor futures which settle at around the same time. The main difference between these methods of evaluating the Swapnote is that the last method takes into account the convexity correction discussed below.

Figure 16.6 illustrates pricing Swapnote® off of the Eurodollar futures market, together with a convexity correction using the Kirikos & Novak equation. We look again at this issue in greater detail later.

	Two-year	Five-year	10-year
Uncorrected	105.697	107.094	104.386
Theoretical	105.702	107.505	106.273
Settle	105.720	107.52	106.26

Figure 16.6

Pricing framework

We can now formulate the framework that leads to the standard methodology for pricing the Swapnote® contract. Let us start first by defining the accumulation factor (i.e. the saving account) as

$$\beta(t) = \exp\left\{\int_0^t r(u)du\right\} \tag{16.2}$$

A zero-coupon, maturing at time T, pays \$1 at time T and nothing before time T[10]. Intuitively, equation (16.2) represents the price process of a risk-free security which continuously compounds in value at the rate r.

We first consider the situation with discrete trading dates
$$0 = t_0 < t_1 < \ldots\ldots < t_n = T$$

On each (t_j, t_{j+1}) r is constant, so

$$\beta(t_{k+1}) = \exp\left\{\int_0^{t_{k+1}} r(u)du\right\}$$
$$= \exp\left\{\sum_{j=0}^{k} r(t_j)(t_{j+1} - t_j)\right\} \tag{16.3}$$

is $I(t_k)$-measurable[11].

Suppose we enter a future contract at time t_k, taking the long position, when the future price is $\pi(t_k)$. At time t_{k+1}, when the future price is $\pi(t_{k+1})$, we receive a payment of $\pi(t_{k+1}) - \pi(t_k)$. We pay $-\pi(t_{k+1}) - \pi(t_k)$ if the future price has fallen. The process of paying and receiving these payments is the margin account held by the broker.[12]

By time $T = t_n$, we will received the sequences of payments

$$\pi(t_{k+1}) - \pi(t_k), \; \pi(t_{k+2}) - \pi(t_{k+1}), \ldots\ldots, \; \pi(t_n) - \pi(t_{n-1})$$

at times $t_{k+1}, t_{k+2}, \ldots, t_n$. The value of this sequence is

$$\beta(t)E\left[\sum \frac{1}{\beta(t_{j+1})}(\pi(t_{j+1}) - \pi(t_j)) \mid I(t)\right]. \tag{16.4}$$

The futures price for a contract is defined as the delivery price that makes the contract have zero value at the time that the contract is entered into. Because it costs nothing to enter the future contract at time t, the above expression must be zero almost surely.

---

[10] Our approach follows that of Steven Shreve (1997). There are number of sources on derivatives instruments that one can access on this issue; for instance, Hull (2000). For the mathematics of derivatives, we refer the reader to Steven Shreve, *Stochastic Calculus and Finance* (1997).

[11] Some authors write $I(t)$ as $F(t)$; it is a matter of choice!

[12] A good reference about the margin requirement is Frank J. Fabozzi, *Valuation of Fixed Income Securities and Derivatives* (3rd edition), FJF Associates, 1998.

Cash flows

As we mentioned earlier, once the cash flows from Swapnote® futures contract are known, any of the standard interest-rate models can be used. With a future contract, entered at time 0, the buyer receives a cash flow between times 0 and T. If we hold the contract at time T, then we pay $V(T)$ at time T for an asset valued at $V(T)$. Thus, the cash flow received between times 0 and T sums to

$$\int_0^T d\pi(u) = \pi(T) - \pi(0) = V(T) - \pi(0) \tag{16.5}$$

Therefore, if we take delivery at time T, we paid a total of

$$(\pi(0) - V(T)) + V(T) = \pi(0)$$

for an asset valued at $V(T)$.

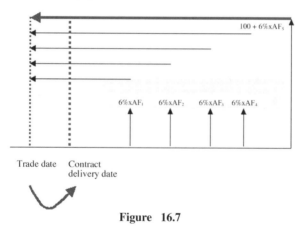

Figure 16.7

Figure 16.7 illustrates the arbitrage-free pricing of a five-year, 6% Swapnote®. The notional cash flows are present-valued to the contract trade date, summed and financed to delivery.

Forward–future spread

Earlier, we suggested an interpretation of a swap as a package of forward/futures contracts. Given that, we can now look at the forward/futures spread.[13] First let us define the future price and the forward price.[14]

---

[13] Basically we can view the swap spread as the futures/forward spread.

[14] It is important to keep in mind that futures affect the swap through both estimation and discounting process.

Future price: $\pi(t) = E[V(T) | (t)]$.

Forward price:

$$F(t) = \frac{V(t)}{B(t,T)} = \frac{V(t)}{\beta(t)E\left[\frac{1}{\beta(T)} | (t)\right]}$$

We can derive the difference between the forward bond price by using a zero-coupon curve and the future bond price.

Let $E\left[\frac{1}{\beta(T)}\right]$ be the discount factor until time T.[15]

The forward–future spread is

$$\pi(0) - F(0) = E\left[V(T)\right] - \frac{V(0)}{E\left[\frac{1}{\beta(T)}\right]}$$

(16.6)

$$= \frac{1}{E\left[\frac{1}{\beta(T)}\right]} \left\{E\left[\frac{1}{\beta(T)}\right]E(V(T)) - E\left[\frac{V(T)}{\beta(T)}\right]\right\}$$

If $\frac{1}{\beta(T)}$ and $V(T)$ are uncorrelated, then $\pi(0) = F(0)$.

Assuming that $V(T)$ and $\frac{1}{\beta(T)}$ are perfectly correlated, then we have, using last expression of equation (16.6) and rearranging,

$$E\left[\frac{V(T)}{\pi(T)}\right] = E\left[\frac{1}{\pi(T)}\right]E(VT) + \sigma V(T) * \sigma\left[\frac{1}{\pi(T)}\right]$$

(16.7)

Therefore, the forward–future spread is given by

$$Forward - Futures\ Spread = \left[\frac{1}{\beta(T)}\right] * \sigma V(T) * \sigma\left[\frac{1}{\beta(T)}\right]$$

(16.8)

$\beta(T)$ denotes the saving account value at time T (for \$1 invested at time 0) and $V(T)$ the value of the asset considered at time T.

To calculate the standard deviation of $\beta(T)$ and $V(T)$, it is best to use the one-factor Hull-White model because other standard interest-rate models such as Black-Karasinsky, Black-Derman-Toy and Cox-Ingersoll-Ross are

---

[15] Until expiry.

more knotty.[16] Basically the core difference between the models is skew, and the convexity correction is mainly an at-the-money phenomenon which is not very sensitive to skew.[17] Thus, the H-W model is less opaque and compute-intensive. In the next section, we consider the convexity correction.

Convexity adjustment estimation

A tailed hedge for the money-market swap possesses a very desirable property; namely, the net value of the swap plus hedge is positive irrespective of rates going up or down. Earlier, we derived the forward/futures spread to be zero. However, if the futures position is greater (i.e. gaining) than the forward position, then, as compensation, there must be an adjustment. There are several approaches to measuring the convexity effect (i.e. the convexity bias in futures),[18] but the Kirikos & Novak equation using Hull and White is a robust treatment for the convexity correction. For a rate that applies between time t and time T, under the Hull and White model the difference between the forward and futures rates is expressed as the z parameter of the popular Kirikos & Novak equation.[19]

Convexity adjustments for several futures markets are provided by brokers or can be obtained from market-data vendors. Estimating the convexity adjustment requires an estimation of the future path of interest rates up to the future contract maturity. In the Hull-White model, the continuously compounded forward rate, lasting between times t and T (denominated in years from current date), equals the continuously compounded future rate with the following adjustment factor e^z.

Of course this is the Kirikos & Novak factor,
where $Z = \Lambda + \Phi$

$$\Lambda = \sigma^2 \left(\frac{1 - e^{-2at}}{2a} \right) \left[\frac{1 - e^{-a(t-t)}}{a} \right]^2$$ adjusts for the fact that the underlying is an

interest rate, and

$$\Phi = \frac{\sigma^2}{2} \left(\frac{1 - e^{-a(T-t)}}{a} \right) \left[\frac{1 - e^{-at}}{a} \right]^2$$

---

[16] There is no closed-form solution for these models. You could use Monte Carlo simulation, for example, to calculate the payments along each path and discount them back.

[17] Thanks to Patrick Hagan for pointing this out. See Patrick Hagan's paper (2003) for more discussion.

[18] See Richard Flavell, *Swaps and Other Derivatives*, Wiley, 2000, pp.185–203.

[19] Kirikos, G. and Novak, D. "Convexity conundrums", RISK, March 1997, pp.60–61. This is also available at www.powerfinance.com/convexity.

where σ is the standard deviation of the change in short-term interest rates expressed annually, and a is the mean reversion rate.

Estimation of the convexity bias requires an estimate of the mean reversion rate (a) and the standard deviation (σ) of the change in short-term interest rates expressed annually. For simplicity, LIFFE assumes a constant default value for the mean reversion speed. The LIFFE US$ Swapnote® calculator assumes that the mean reversion parameter (a) remains at 0.03. Bloomberg does allow convexity adjustment for pricing swaps if the underlying interest-rate curve is based on traded futures contracts. There are two input parameters that are required in order to adjust futures contracts for convexity: the mean reversion speed, which has a default level of 0.03, and volatility parameters, which are fed from market-traded implied cap/floor rates.

There are various alternative methodologies for estimating the volatility parameters (σ and a). The two most popular methodologies are:
- estimate the volatility parameters from prices of traded securities
- a deposit/swap-derived curve could be used to estimate the volatility parameters, as discussed above.

Conclusion

Hedging a swap portfolio with government-bond curves presents significant basis risk. A futures contract referenced to the swap curve provides a far more effective hedging tool with appreciably reduced basis risk. To address the problem of basis risk, one can use a Swapnote® contract. The value of the Swapnote® as a hedging tool reflects the ability to match and hedge credit exposures with a derivative instrument that closely correlates with that exposure. The capacity to hedge swap-book exposures and the avoidance of convexity using Swapnote®, compares favourably with the problems that can be associated with using government-bond contracts under adverse market conditions.

The Swapnote® has allowed institutional investors to access the euro interest-rate swaps market in standardised fashion. It is simple to price, once the cash flows from futures contracts are known. Any of the standard interest-rate models can be used to evaluate the contract. The futures/forward spread can be adjusted using the Kirikos & Novak equation.

Finally, we have shown how the convexity-bias adjustment can be effected by following a straightforward approach and which will allow Swapnote® to be applied across futures and swaps markets for effective hedging.

Selected Bibliography and References

Choudhry, M., *Illiquidity in government bond markets and the search for alternative benchmarks*, PhD draft Working Paper, Birkbeck, University of London, 2003.

Fabozzi, F., *Valuation of Fixed Income Securities and Derivatives* (3rd Edition) John Wiley, 2003.

Flavell, R., *Swaps and other Derivatives*, John Wiley, 2001.

Hagan, P., "Convexity conundrums: Pricing CMS Swaps, Caps and Floors", *Wilmott Magazine*, March 2003, p.38-44.

Hull, J., *Options, Futures, and Other Derivatives* (4th Edition), FT Prentice Hall, 2000.

Kirikos, G. and Novak, D., "Convexity conundrums", RISK, March 1997.

Remolona, E. AND Wooldridge, P., *The euro interest rate swap market, BIS Quarterly Review*, March 2003.

Shreve, S., *Lectures on Stochastic Calculus and Finance* (1997), available at www-2.cs.cmu.edu/~chal./shreve.html.

17

Credit Derivatives I:
Instuments and Applications

Credit derivatives allow investors to manage the credit-risk exposure of their portfolios or asset holdings, essentially by providing insurance against a deterioration in credit quality of the borrowing entity.[1] If there is a technical default by the borrower[2] or an actual default on the loan itself, and the bond is marked down in price, the losses suffered by the investor can be recouped in part or in full through the payout made by the credit derivative.

Credit risk

Credit risk is the risk that a borrowing entity will default on a loan, either through inability to maintain the interest servicing or because of bankruptcy or insolvency leading to inability to repay the principal itself. When technical or actual default occurs, bondholders suffer a loss as the value of their asset declines, and the potential greatest loss is that of the entire asset. The extent of credit risk fluctuates as the fortunes of borrowers change in line with their own economic circumstances and the macroeconomic business cycle. The magnitude of risk is described by a firm's credit rating. Ratings agencies undertake a formal analysis of the borrower, after which a rating is announced. The issues considered in the analysis include:

- the financial position of the firm itself; for example, its balance-sheet position and anticipated cash flows and revenues
- other firm-specific issues such as the quality of the management and succession planning

---

[1] The simplest credit derivative works exactly like an insurance policy, with regular premiums paid by the protection-buyer to the protection-seller, and a payout in the event of a specified credit event.

[2] A technical default is a delay in timely payment of the coupon, or non-payment of the coupon altogether.

- an assessment of the firm's ability to meet scheduled interest and principal payments, both in its domestic and foreign currencies
- the outlook for the industry as whole, and competition within it
- general assessments for the domestic economy.

Another measure of credit risk is the credit-risk premium, which is the difference between yields on the same-currency government benchmark bonds and corporate bonds. This premium is the compensation required by investors for holding bonds that are not default-free. The credit premium required will fluctuate as individual firms and sectors are perceived to offer improved or worsening credit risk, and as the general health of the economy improves or worsens. For example, Figure 17.1 illustrates the yield curves for industrial-sector bonds of various ratings in the US-dollar market, as at January 2003, compared to the benchmark Treasury yield curve.

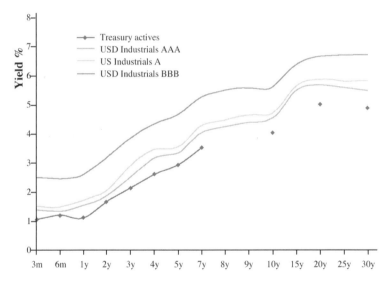

Figure 17.1 US-dollar bond yield curves, January 2003
Source: Bloomberg

Credit risk and credit derivatives

Credit derivatives are financial contracts designed to reduce or eliminate credit-risk exposure by providing insurance against losses suffered due to credit events. A payout under a credit derivative is triggered by a credit event. As banks define default in different ways, the terms under which a credit derivative is executed usually include a specification of what constitutes a credit event.

The principle behind credit derivatives is straightforward. Investors desire exposure to non-default-free debt because of the higher returns this offers. However, such exposure brings with it concomitant credit risk. This can be managed with credit derivatives. At the same time, the exposure itself can be taken on synthetically if, for instance, there are compelling reasons why a cash-market position cannot be established. The flexibility of credit derivatives provides users a number of advantages and as they are over-the-counter (OTC) products they can be designed to meet specific user requirements.

We focus on credit derivatives as instruments that may be used to manage risk exposure inherent in a corporate or non-AAA sovereign-bond portfolio. They may also be used to manage the credit risk of commercial-loan books. The intense competition amongst commercial banks, combined with rapid disintermediation, has meant that banks have been forced to evaluate their lending policy, with a view to improving profitability and return on capital. The use of credit derivatives assists banks with restructuring their businesses, because they allow banks to repackage and parcel out credit risk, while retaining assets on balance sheet (when required) and thus maintain client relationships. As the instruments isolate certain aspects of credit risk from the underlying loan or bond and transfer them to another entity, it becomes possible to separate the ownership and management of credit risk from the other features of ownership associated with the assets in question. This means that illiquid assets such as bank loans, and illiquid bonds, can have their credit-risk exposures transferred; the bank owning the assets can protect against credit loss even if it cannot transfer the assets themselves.

The same principles carry over to the credit-risk exposures of portfolio managers. For fixed-income portfolio managers the advantages of credit derivatives include the following:

- they can be tailor-made to meet the specific requirements of the entity buying the risk protection, as opposed to the liquidity or term of the underlying reference asset.
- they can be "sold short" without risk of a liquidity or delivery squeeze, as it is a specific credit risk that is being traded. In the cash market, it is not possible to "sell short" a bank loan, for example, but a credit derivative can be used to establish synthetically the economic effect of such a position.

- as they theoretically isolate credit risk from other factors such as client relationships and interest-rate risk, credit derivatives introduce a formal pricing mechanism to price credit issues only. This means a market can develop in credit only, allowing more efficient pricing, and it becomes possible to model a term structure of credit rates.
- they are off-balance-sheet instruments[3] and as such incorporate tremendous flexibility and leverage, exactly like other financial derivatives. For instance, bank loans are not particularly attractive investments for certain investors because of the administration required in managing and servicing a loan portfolio. However, an exposure to bank loans and their associated return can be achieved by, say, a total-return swap while simultaneously avoiding the administrative costs of actually owning the assets. Hence, credit derivatives allow investors access to specific credits while allowing banks access to further distribution for bank loan credit risk.

Thus, credit derivatives can be an important instrument for bond-portfolio managers as well as commercial banks, who wish to increase the liquidity of their portfolios, gain from the relative value arising from credit pricing anomalies, and enhance portfolio returns. Some key applications are summarised below.

Applications

Diversifying the credit portfolio

A bank or portfolio manager may wish to take on credit exposure by providing credit protection on assets that it already owns, in return for a fee. This enhances income on their portfolio. They may sell credit derivatives to enable non-financial counterparties to gain credit exposures, if these clients do not wish to purchase the assets directly. In this respect, the bank or asset manager performs a credit-intermediation role.

Reducing credit exposure

A bank can reduce credit exposure either for an individual loan or a sectoral concentration, by buying a credit-default swap. This may be desirable for assets in their portfolio that cannot be sold for client relationship or tax

---

[3] When credit derivatives are embedded in certain fixed-income products, such as structured notes and credit-linked notes, they are then off-balance-sheet but part of a structure that may have on-balance-sheet elements.

reasons. For fixed-income managers, a particular asset or collection of assets may be viewed as favorable holdings in the long term, but at risk from short-term downward price movement. In this instance, a sale would not fit in with long-term objectives; however, short-term credit protection can be obtained via credit swap.

Acting as a credit-derivatives market-maker

A financial entity may wish to set itself up as a market-maker in credit derivatives. In this case, it may or may not hold the reference assets directly and, depending on its appetite for risk and the liquidity of the market, it can offset derivative contracts as and when required.

Credit event

The occurrence of a specified credit event will trigger payment of the default payment by the seller of protection to the buyer of protection. Contracts specify physical or cash settlement. In physical settlement, the protection buyer transfers to the protection seller the deliverable obligation (usually the reference asset or assets), with the total principal outstanding equal to the nominal specified in the default-swap contract. The protection seller simultaneously pays to the buyer 100% of the nominal. In cash settlement, the protection seller hands to the buyer the difference between the nominal amount of the default swap and the final value for the same nominal amount of the reference asset. This final value is usually determined by means of a poll of dealer banks.

The following may be specified as credit events in the legal documentation between counterparties:

- downgrade in S&P and/or Moody's credit rating below a specified minimum level
- financial or debt restructuring; for example, occasioned under administration or as required under US bankruptcy protection
- bankruptcy or insolvency of the reference asset obligor
- default on payment obligations such as bond coupon and continued non-payment after a specified time period
- technical default; for example, the non-payment of interest or coupon when it falls due
- a change in credit spread payable by the obligor above a specified maximum level.

The 1999 ISDA credit-default swap documentation specifies bankruptcy, failure to pay, obligation default, debt moratorium and restructuring to be credit events. Note that it does not specify a rating downgrade to be a credit event.[4]

The precise definition of "restructuring" is open to debate and has resulted in legal disputes between protection buyers and sellers. Prior to issuing its 1999 definitions, ISDA had specified restructuring as an event or events that resulted in making the terms of the reference obligation "materially less favorable" to the creditor (or protection seller) from an economic perspective. This definition is open to more than one interpretation and caused controversy when determining if a credit event had occurred. The 2001 definitions specified more precise conditions, including any action that resulted in a reduction in the amount of principal. In the European market, restructuring is generally retained as a credit event in contract documentation, but in the US market it is less common to see it included. Instead, US contract documentation tends to include as a credit event a form of modified restructuring, the impact of which is to limit the options available to the protection buyer as to the type of assets it could deliver in a physically settled contract.

Restructuring, modified restructuring and modified–modified restructuring

The original 1999 ISDA credit definitions defined restructuring among the standard credit events. The five specified definitions included events such as a reduction in the rate of interest payable, a reduction in the amount of principal outstanding and a postponement or deferral of payment. Following a number of high-profile cases where there was disagreement or dispute between protection buyers and sellers on what constituted precisely a restructuring, the Supplement to the 1999 ISDA limited the term to maturity of deliverable obligations. This was modified restructuring or Mod-R, which was intended to reduce the difference between the loss suffered by a holder of the actual restructured obligation and the writer of a CDS on that reference name. In practice this has placed a maturity limit on deliverable obligations of 30 months.

---

[4] The ISDA definitions from 1999, restructuring supplement from 2001 and 2003 definitions are available at www.ISDA.org.

The 2003 Definitions presented further clarification and stated that the restructuring event had to be binding on all holders of the restructured debt. The modified-modified restructuring definition or Mod-Mod-R described in the 2003 ISDA defines the modified restructuring term to maturity date as the later of:
- the scheduled termination date, and
- 60 months following the restructuring date

in the event that a restructured bond or loan is delivered to the protection seller. If another obligation is delivered, the limitation on maturity is the scheduled maturity date and 30 months following the restructuring date.

Credit-derivative instruments

Credit-derivative instruments enable participants in the financial market to trade in credit as an asset, as they isolate and transfer credit risk. They also enable the market to separate funding considerations from credit risk. A number of instruments come under the category of credit derivatives. In this section, we consider the most commonly encountered credit-derivative instruments. Irrespective of the particular instrument under consideration, all credit derivatives can be described under the following characteristics:
- the reference entity, which is the asset or name on which credit protection is being bought and sold
- the credit event, or events, which indicate that the reference entity is experiencing or about to experience financial difficulty and which act as trigger events for payments under the credit-derivative contract
- the settlement mechanism for the contract, whether cash settled or physically settled;
- (under physical settlement) the deliverable obligation that the protection buyer delivers to the protection seller on the occurrence of a trigger event.

Credit derivatives are grouped into funded and unfunded instruments. In a funded credit derivative, typified by a credit-linked note (CLN), the investor in the note is the credit-protection seller and is making an upfront payment to the protection buyer when it buys the note. Thus, the protection buyer is the issuer of the note. If no credit event occurs during the life of the note, the redemption value of the note is paid to the investor on maturity.

If a credit event does occur, then on maturity a value less than par will be paid out to the investor. This value will be reduced by the nominal value of the reference asset that the CLN is linked to. The exact process will differ according to whether cash settlement or physical settlement has been specified for the note. We will consider this later.

In an unfunded credit derivative, typified by a credi-default swap, the protection seller does not make an upfront payment to the protection buyer. Credit-default swaps have a number of applications and are used extensively for flow trading of single reference-name credit risks or, in portfolio swap form, for trading a basket of reference credits. Credit-default swaps and CLNs are used in structured products, in various combinations, and their flexibility has been behind the growth and wide application of the synthetic collateralised-debt obligation and other credit hybrid products.

We now consider the key credit-derivative instruments.

Credit–default swap

The most common credit derivative is the credit-default swap, *credit swap* or default swap.[5] This is a bilateral contract in which a periodic fixed fee or a one-off premium is paid to a protection seller, in return for which the seller will make a payment on the occurrence of a specified credit event. The fee is quoted as a basis-point multiplier of the nominal value. It is usually paid quarterly in arrears.

The swap can refer to a single asset, known as the "reference asset" or "underlying asset", or a basket of assets. The default payment can be paid in whatever way suits the protection buyer or both counterparties. For example, it may be linked to the change in price of the reference asset or another specified asset; it may be fixed at a pre-determined recovery rate; or it may be in the form of actual delivery of the reference asset at a specified price. The basic structure is illustrated in Figure 17.2.

The credit-default swap enables one party to transfer its credit-risk exposure to another party. Banks may use default swaps to trade sovereign and corporate credit spreads without trading the actual assets themselves. For example, someone who has gone long a default swap (the protection buyer) will gain if the reference asset obligor suffers a rating downgrade or defaults, and can sell the default swap at a profit if he can find a buyer

---

[5] The author prefers the first term, but the other two terms are common. "Credit swap" does not, we feel, adequately describe the actual purpose of the instrument.

counterparty.[6] This is because the cost of protection on the reference asset will have increased as a result of the credit event. The original buyer of the default swap need never have owned a bond issued by the reference asset obligor.

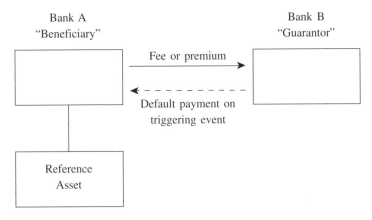

Figure 17.2 Credit-default swap

The maturity of the credit swap does not have to match the maturity of the reference asset and often does not. When a credit event occurs, the swap contract is terminated and a settlement payment is made by the protection seller or guarantor to the protection buyer. This termination value is calculated at the time of the credit event, and the exact procedure that is followed to calculate the termination value will depend on the settlement terms specified in the contract. This will be either cash settlement or physical settlement.

•   **Cash settlement:** the contract may specify a pre-determined pay-out value on occurrence of a credit event. This may be the nominal value of the swap contract. Such a swap is known in some markets as a digital credit derivative. Alternatively, the termination payment is calculated as the difference between the nominal value of the reference asset and its market

---

[6]   Be careful with terminology here. To "go long" of an instrument generally is to purchase it. In the cash market, going long the bond means one is buying the bond and so receiving coupon; the buyer has therefore taken on credit risk exposure to the issuer. In a credit-default swap, going long is to buy the swap, but the buyer is purchasing protection and therefore paying premium; the buyer has no credit exposure on the name and has in effect "gone short" on the reference name (the equivalent of shorting a bond in the cash market and paying coupon). So buying a credit-default swap is frequently referred to in the market as "shorting" the reference entity.

value at the time of the credit event. This arrangement is more common with cash-settled contracts.[7]

• **Physical settlement:** on occurrence of a credit event, the buyer delivers the reference asset to the seller, in return for which the seller pays the face value of the delivered asset to the buyer. The contract may specify a number of alternative assets that the buyer can deliver; these are known as deliverable obligations. This may apply when a swap has been entered into on a reference name rather than a specific obligation (such as a particular bond) issued by that name. Where more than one deliverable obligation is specified, the protection buyer will invariably deliver the asset that is the cheapest on the list of eligible assets. This gives rise to the concept of the cheapest-to-deliver, as encountered with government-bond futures contracts, and is in effect an embedded option afforded the protection buyer.

In theory, the value of protection is identical irrespective of which settlement option is selected. However, under physical settlement the protection seller can gain if there is a recovery value that can be extracted from the defaulted asset; or its value may rise as the fortunes of the issuer improve. Swap market-making banks often prefer cash settlement as there is less administration associated with it. It is also more suitable when the swap is used as part of a synthetic structured product, because such vehicles may not be set up to take delivery of physical assets. Another advantage of cash settlement is that it does not expose the protection buyer to any risks should there not be any deliverable assets in the market; for instance, due to shortage of liquidity in the market. Were this to happen, the buyer may find the value of its settlement payment reduced.

Nevertheless, physical settlement is widely used because counterparties wish to avoid the difficulties associated with determining the market value of the reference asset under cash settlement. Physical settlement also permits the protection seller to take part in the creditor negotiations with the reference entity's administrators, which may result in improved terms for them as holders of the asset.

For illustrative purposes, Figure 17.3 shows investment-grade credit-default swap levels during 2001 and 2002 for US dollar and euro reference entities (average levels taken).

---

[7] Determining the market value of the reference asset at the time of the credit event may be a little problematic: the issuer of the asset may well be in default or administration. An independent third-party Calculation Agent is usually employed to make the termination payment calculation.

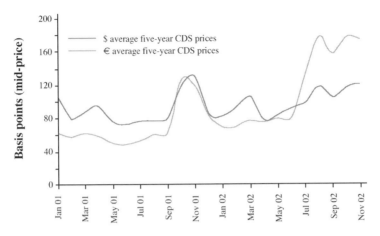

Figure 17.3 Investment-grade credit default swap levels
Source: Bloomberg

Credit-default swap: example

XYZ plc credit spreads are currently trading at 120 bps over government for five-year maturities and 195 bps over for 10-year maturities. A portfolio manager hedges a $10 million holding of 10-year paper by purchasing the following credit-default swap, written on the five-year bond. This hedge protects for the first five years of the holding and, in the event of XYZ's credit spread widening, will increase in value and may be sold on before expiry at profit. The 10-year bond holding also earns 75 bps over the shorter-term paper for the portfolio manager.

Term	Five years
Reference credit	XYZ plc five-year bond
Credit event	The business day following occurrence of specified credit event
Default payment	Nominal value of bond × [100 − price of bond after credit event]
Swap premium	3.35%

Assume now that midway into the life of the swap there is a technical default on the XYZ plc five-year bond, such that its price now stands at $28. Under the terms of the swap, the protection buyer delivers the bond to the seller, who pays out $7.2 million to the buyer.

The total-return swap

A total-return swap (TRS), sometimes known as a total rate of return swap or TR swap, is an agreement between two parties that exchanges the total return from a financial asset between them. This is designed to transfer the credit risk from one party to the other. It is one of the principal instruments used by banks and other financial instruments to manage their credit-risk exposure and, as such, is a credit derivative. One definition of a TRS is given in Francis *et al* (1999), which states that a TRS is a swap agreement in which the *total return* of a bank loan or credit-sensitive security is exchanged for some other cash flow, usually tied to Libor or some other loan or credit-sensitive security.

In some versions of a TRS, the actual underlying asset is actually sold to the counterparty, with a corresponding swap transaction agreed alongside; in other versions, there is no physical change of ownership of the underlying asset. The TRS trade itself can be to any maturity term; that is, it need not match the maturity of the underlying security. In a TRS, the total return from the underlying asset is paid over to the counterparty in return for a fixed or floating cash flow. This makes it slightly different from other credit derivatives, as the payments between counterparties to a TRS are connected to changes in the market value of the underlying asset, as well as changes resulting from the occurrence of a credit event.

Figure 17.4 illustrates a generic TR swap. The two counterparties are labeled as banks, but the party termed "Bank A" can be another financial institution, including cash-rich fixed-income portfolio managers such as insurance companies and hedge funds. Bank A has contracted to pay the "total return" on a specified reference asset, while simultaneously receiving a Libor-based return from Bank B. The reference or underlying asset can be a bank loan such as a corporate loan or a sovereign or corporate bond. The total return payments from Bank A include the interest payments on the underlying loan as well as any appreciation in the market value of the asset. Bank B will pay the Libor-based return; it will also pay any difference if there is a depreciation in the price of the asset. The economic effect is as if Bank B owned the underlying asset and, as such, TR swaps are synthetic loans or securities. A significant feature is that Bank A will usually hold the underlying asset on its balance sheet, so that if this asset was originally on Bank B's balance sheet, this is a means by which the latter can have the asset removed from its balance sheet for the term of the TR swap.[8] If we assume

---

[8] Although it is common for the receiver of the Libor-based payments to have the reference asset on its balance sheet, this is not always the case.

Bank A has access to Libor funding, it will receive a spread on this from Bank B. Under the terms of the swap, Bank B will pay the difference between the initial market value and any depreciation, so it is sometimes termed the "guarantor" while Bank A is the "beneficiary".

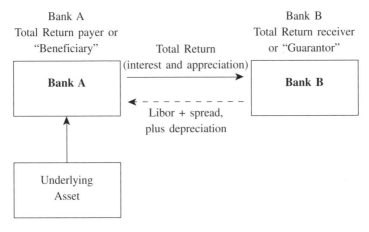

Figure 17.4 Total-return swap

The total return on the underlying asset is the interest payments and any change in the market value if there is capital appreciation. The value of an appreciation may be cash-settled or, alternatively, there may be physical delivery of the reference asset on maturity of the swap, in return for a payment of the initial asset value by the total-return "receiver". The maturity of the TR swap need not be identical to that of the reference asset and, in fact, it is rare for it to be so.

The swap element of the trade will usually pay on a quarterly or semi-annual basis, with the underlying asset being re-valued or marked-to-market on the re-fixing dates. The asset price is usually obtained from an independent third-party source such as Bloomberg or Reuters, or as the average of a range of market quotes. If the *obligor* of the reference asset defaults, the swap may be terminated immediately, with a net present-value payment changing hands according to what this value is, or it may be continued with each party making appreciation or depreciation payments as appropriate. This second option is only available if there is a market for the asset, which is unlikely in the case of a bank loan. If the swap is terminated, each counterparty is liable to the other for accrued interest plus any appreciation or depreciation of the asset. Commonly under the terms of the trade, the guarantor bank has the option to purchase the underlying asset from the beneficiary bank, and then deal directly with loan defaulter.

The total-return swap and the synthetic CDO

A variation on the generic TRS has been used in structured credit products such as synthetic collateralised-debt obligations (CDO). An example of this is the Jazz I CDO B.V., which was described in chapter 12. It is a vehicle that can trade in cash bonds as well as credit-default swaps and total-return swaps. It has been called a hybrid CDO for this reason. In the Jazz structure, the TRS is a funded credit derivative because the market price of the reference asset is paid upfront by the Jazz vehicle to the swap counterparty. In return, the swap counterparty pays the principal and interest on the reference asset to Jazz CDO. The Jazz CDO has therefore purchased the reference asset synthetically. If a credit event occurs, the swap counterparty delivers the asset to the CDO and the TRS is terminated. Because these are funded credit derivatives, a liquidity facility is needed by the vehicle, which it will draw on whenever it purchases a TRS. This facility is provided by the bank that arranges the structure.

The TRS arrangement in the Jazz structure is shown in Figure 17.5.

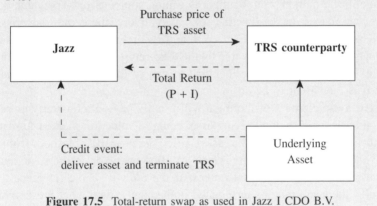

Figure 17.5 Total-return swap as used in Jazz I CDO B.V.

There are a number of reasons why portfolio managers may wish to enter into TR swap arrangements. One of these is to reduce or remove credit risk. Using TR swaps as a credit-derivative instrument, a party can remove exposure to an asset without having to sell it. In a vanilla TR swap, the total-return payer retains rights to the reference asset, although in some cases servicing and voting rights may be transferred. The total-return receiver gains an exposure to the reference asset without having to pay out the cash proceeds that would be required to purchase it. As the maturity of the swap rarely matches that of the asset, the swap receiver may gain from the positive funding or carry that derives from being able to roll over short-term funding of a longer-term asset.[9] The total-return payer, on the other hand, benefits from protection against market and credit risk for a specified period of time, without having to liquidate the asset itself. On maturity of the swap, the total-return payer may reinvest the asset if it continues to own it, or it may sell the asset in the open market. Thus, the instrument may be considered a synthetic repo. A TR-swap agreement entered into as a credit derivative is a means by which banks can take on unfunded off-balance-sheet credit exposure. Higher-rated banks that have access to Libid funding can benefit by funding on-balance-sheet assets that are credit protected through a credit derivative such as a TR swap, assuming the net spread of asset income over credit-protection premium is positive.

A TR swap conducted as a synthetic repo is usually undertaken to effect the temporary removal of assets from the balance sheet. This may be desired for a number of reasons; for example, if the institution is due to be analysed by credit-rating agencies or if the annual external audit is due shortly. Another reason a bank may wish to temporarily remove lower credit-quality assets from its balance sheet is if it is in danger of breaching capital limits in between the quarterly return periods. In this case, as the return period approaches, lower-quality assets may be removed from the balance sheet by means of a TR swap, which is set to mature after the return period has passed.

Banks have employed a number of methods to price credit derivatives and TR swaps. Essentially, the pricing of credit derivatives is linked to that of other instruments; however, the main difference between credit derivatives and other off-balance-sheet products such as equity, currency or bond derivatives is that the latter can be priced and hedged with reference to the underlying asset, which can be problematic when applied to credit derivatives. The pricing of credit products uses statistical data on likelihood of default, probability of payout, level of risk tolerance and a pricing model. With a TR swap, the basic concept is that one party "funds" an underlying asset and transfers the total return of the asset to another party, in return for a (usually) floating return that is a spread to Libor. This spread is a function of:

---

[9]   This assumes a positively-sloping yield curve.

- the credit rating of the swap counterparty
- the amount and value of the reference asset
- the credit quality of the reference asset
- the funding costs of the beneficiary bank
- any required profit margin
- the capital charge associated with the TR swap.

The TR swap counterparties must consider a number of risk factors associated with the transaction, which include:

- the probability that the TR beneficiary may default while the reference asset has declined in value
- the reference asset obligor defaults, followed by default of the TR swap receiver before payment of the depreciation has been made to the payer or "provider".

The first risk measure is a function of the probability of default by the TR swap receiver and the market volatility of the reference asset, while the second risk is related to the joint probability of default of both factors as well as the recovery probability of the asset.

The Total Return Swap as a funding tool

The TRS may be used as a funding tool, as a means of securing off-balance sheet financing for assets held (for example) on a market making book. It is most commonly used in this capacity by broker-dealers and securities houses that have little or no access to unsecured or Libor-flat funding. When used for this purpose the TRS is similar to a repo transaction, although there are detail differences. Often a TRS approach is used instead of classic repo when the assets that require funding are less liquid or indeed not really tradeable. These can include lower-rated bonds, illiquid bonds such as certain ABS, MBS and CDO securities and assets such as hedge fund interests.

Bonds that are taken on by the TRS provider must be acceptable to it in terms of credit quality. If no independent price source is available the TRS provider may insist on pricing the assets itself.

As a funding tool the TRS is transacted as follows:

- the broker-dealer swaps out a bond or basket of bonds that it owns to the TRS counterparty (usually a bank), who pays the market price for the security or security;
- the maturity of the TRS can be for anything from one week to one year or even longer. For longer-dated contracts, a weekly or monthly re-set is usually employed, so that the TRS is re-priced and cashflows exchanged each week or month;
- the funds that are passed over by the TRS counterparty to the broker-dealer have the economic effect of being a loan to cover the financing of the underlying bonds. This loan is charged at Libor plus a spread;
- at the maturity of the TRS, the broker-dealer will owe interest on funds to the swap counterparty, while the swap counterparty will owe the market performance of the bonds to the broker-dealer if they have increased in price. The two cashflows are netted out;
- for a longer-dated TRS that is re-set at weekly or monthly intervals, the broker-dealer will owe the loan interest plus any decrease in basket value to the swap counterparty at the reset date. The swap counterparty will owe any increase in value.

By entering into this transaction the broker-dealer obtains Libor-based funding for a pool of assets it already owns, while the swap counterparty earns Libor plus a spread on funds that are in effect secured by a pool of assets. This transaction takes the original assets off the balance sheet of the broker-dealer during the term of the trade, which might also be desirable.

The broker-dealer can add or remove bonds from or to the basket at each re-set date. When this happens the swap counterparty re-values the basket and will hand over more funds or receive back funds as required. Bonds are removed from the basket if they have been sold by the broker-dealer, while new acquisitions can be funded by being placed in the TRS basket.

We illustrate a funding TRS trade using an example. Figure 17.6 shows a portfolio of five hypothetical convertible bonds on the balance sheet of a broker-dealer. The spreadsheet also shows market prices. This portfolio has been swapped out to a TRS provider in a six-month, weekly re-set TRS contract. The TRS bank has paid over the combined market value of the portfolio at a lending rate of 1.14125%. This represents one-week Libor plus 7 basis points. We assume the broker-dealer usually funds at above this level, and that this rate is an improvement on its normal funding. It is not unusual for this type of trade to be undertaken even if the funding rate is not an improvement however, for diversification reasons.

We see from Figure 17.6 that the portfolio has a current market value of approximately USD 151,080,000. This value is lent to the broker-dealer in return for the bonds.

One week later the TRS is re-set. We see from Figure 17.7 that the portfolio has increased in market value since the last re-set. Therefore the swap counterparty pays this difference over to the broker-dealer. This payment is netted out with the interest payment due from the broker-dealer to the swap counterparty. The interest payment is shown as USD 33,526.

Figure 17.8 shows the basket after the addition of a new bonds, and the resultant change in portfolio value.

Market Rates
EUR/USD FX Rate   1.266550
US$ 1W Libor   1.4055

Name	Currency	Nominal Value	Price	Accrued	Amount	FX Rate	ISIN/ CUSIP Code	Market Price	Accrued Interest
ABC Telecom	EUR	16,000,000	111.671%	0.8169%	22,795,534.57	1.2666		111.6713875	0.81693989
XYZ Bank	USD	17,000,000	128.113%	1.7472%	22,076,259.03	1.0000		128.113125	1.74722222
XTC Utility	EUR	45,000,000	102.334%	0.3135%	58,845,000.00	1.2666		102.3337875	0.31352459
SPG Corporation	EUR	30,000,000	100.325		30,000,325.00	1.2666		100.325	0
Watty Exploited	USD	15,000,000	114.997%	0.7594%	17,363,503.13	1.0000		114.9973125	0.759375
					151,080,621.72				

Payments
Interest ($)
Rate   0.000000%
Principle   151,080,000.00
Interest Payable   +0.00

Performance ($)
New Portfolio Value   151,080,621.72
Old Portfolio Value   n/a
Performance Payment   n/a

Net Payment ($)
Broker-Dealer receives from swap counterparty   +0.00
New Loan
Portfolio Additions ($)   0.00
New Loan Amount ($)   151,080,621.72
New Interest Rate   1.141250% 1w Libor + 7 bps

Figure 17.6 Spreadsheet showing basket of bonds used in TRS funding trade

EUR/USD	1.2431								
Bond	Curr	Nominal Value	Price	Accrued	Amount	FX	ISIN/CUSIP	Market Price	Accrued
ABC Telecom	EUR	16,000,000	111.500%	0.78%	22,331,239	1.2431		111.5	0.77595628
XYZ Bank	USD	17,000,000	125.000%	1.58%	21,518,931	1		125	1.58194444
XTC Utility	EUR	45,000,000	113.000%	0.28%	63,369,825	1.2431		113	0.28278689
SPG Corporation	EUR	30,000,000	100.750		30,225,000	1.2431		100.75	
Watty Exploited	USD	15,000,000	113.062%	0.63%	17,053,518.2	1		113.0619965	0.628125
					154,498,511.95				

Payments
Interest

Rate	1.14125%	1W LIBOR + 7bps
Amount	151,080,000.00	151,113,526.12
Interest payable	33,526.12	

Performance

Old portfolio value	151,080,000.00		Old portfolio value:	+151,080,951.67 US$
New portfolio value	154,498,511.95		Interest rate:	1.14125%
Performance payment	**(3,418,511.95)**		Interest payable by broker-dealer	+33,526.33 US$

Swap ctpy pays	**(3,384,985.83)**		New portfolio value:	+154,498,511 US$
	[if negative, swap counterparty pays, if positive, broker-dealer pays]		Performance:	3,418,511 US$
			Net payment	

New loan

Additions	-
New loan amount	**154,498,511.95**
New interest rate	1.14875%

Figure 17.7 Spreadsheet showing basket of bonds at TRS re-set date plus performance and interest payments due from each TRS counterparty

EUR/USD 1.228

Name	Currency	Nominal	Price	Accrued	Amount	FX	Isin	Price	Accrued
ABC Telecom	EUR	16,000,000	111.500%	0.78%	22,331,239	1.2431		111.5	0.77595628
XYZ Bank	USD	17,000,000	125.000%	1.58%	21,518,931	1		125	1.58194444
XTC Utility	EUR	45,000,000	113.000%	0.28%	63,369,825	1.2431		113	0.28278689
SPG Corporation	EUR	30,000,000	100.750		30,225,000	1.2431		100.75	
Watty Exploited	USD	15,000,000	113.062%	0.00628125	17,053,518	1		113.061996	0.628125
Lloyd Cole Funding	USD	15,000,000	112.0923%	0.57%	16,899,628.1	1		112.092313	0.571875
					171,398,140.07				

Payments
Interest
Rate 1.14875% 1W LIBOR + 7bps
Amount 154,498,511.95
Interest payable 34,510.03

Performance
Old portfolio value 154,498,511.95
New portfolio value 171,398,140.07
Performance payment **(16,899,628.13)**

Swap ctpy pays (16,865,118.09)

New loan
Additions 16,899,628.13
New loan amount 171,398,140.07
New interest rate 1.22750%

Figure 17.8 TRS basket value after addition of new bond

Credit options

Credit options are also bilateral OTC financial contracts. A credit option is a contract designed to meet specific hedging or speculative requirements of an entity, which may purchase or sell the option to meet its objectives. A credit call option gives the buyer the right without the obligation to purchase the underlying credit-sensitive asset, or a credit spread, at a specified price and specified time (or period of time). A credit put option gives the buyer the right without the obligation to sell the underlying credit-sensitive asset or credit spread. By purchasing credit options, banks and other institutions can take a view on credit-spread movements for the cost of the option premium only, without recourse to actual loans issued by an obligor. The writer of credit options seeks to earn premium income.

Credit option terms are similar to those used for conventional equity options. A call option written on a stock grants the purchaser the right but not the obligation to purchase a specified amount of the stock at a set price and time. A credit option can be used by bond investors to hedge against a decline in the price of specified bonds, in the event of a credit event such as a ratings downgrade. The investor would purchase an option whose payoff profile is a function of the credit quality of the bond, so that a loss on the bond position is offset by the payout from the option.

As with conventional options, there are both vanilla credit options and exotic credit options. The vanilla credit option[10] grants the purchaser the right but not the obligation to buy (or sell if a put option) an asset or credit spread at a specified price (the strike price) for a specified period of time up to the maturity of the option. A credit option allows a market participant to take a view on credit only, and no other exposure such as interest rates. As an example, consider an investor who believes that a particular credit spread, which can be that of a specific entity or the average for a sector (such as "all AA-rated sterling corporates"), will widen over the next six months. She can buy a six-month call option on the relevant credit spread, for which a one-off premium (the price of the option) is paid. If the credit spread indeed does widen beyond the strike during the six months, the option will be in-the-money and the investor will gain. If not, the investor's loss is limited to the premium paid.[11]

Exotic credit options are options that have one or more of their parameters changed from the vanilla norm; the same terms are used as in

---

[10] Sometimes referred to as the standard credit option.
[11] Depending on whether the option is an American or European one will determine whether it can be exercised before its expiry date or on its expiry date only.

other option markets. Examples include the barrier credit option, which specifies a credit event that would trigger (activate) the option or inactivate it. A digital credit option would have a payout profile that would be fixed, irrespective of how much in-the-money it was on expiry, and a zero payout if out-of-the-money.

Credit-linked notes

Credit-linked notes are a form of credit derivative. Credit derivative instruments enable participants in the financial market to trade in credit as an asset, as they isolate and transfer credit risk. They also enable the market to separate funding considerations from credit risk. A number of instruments come under the category of credit derivatives. In this article we consider a commonly encountered credit derivative instrument, the credit-linked note.

Irrespective of the particular instrument under consideration, all credit derivatives can be described under the following characteristics:
- the *reference entity*, which is the asset or name on which credit protection is being bought and sold;
- the credit event, or events, which indicate that the reference entity is experiencing or about to experience financial difficulty and which act as trigger events for payments under the credit derivative contract;
- the settlement mechanism for the credit derivative instrument, whether cash settled or physically settled;
- (under physical settlement), the deliverable obligation that the protection buyer delivers to the protection seller on the occurrence of a trigger event.

Credit derivatives are grouped into *funded* and *unfunded* variants. In an unfunded credit derivative, typified by a *credit default swap*, the protection seller does not make an upfront payment to the protection buyer. Credit default swaps have a number of applications and are used extensively for flow trading of single reference name credit risks or, in *portfolio swap* form, for trading a basket of reference credits.

In a funded credit derivative, typified by a credit-linked note (CLN), the investor in the note is the credit-protection seller and is making an upfront payment to the protection buyer when it buys the note. Thus, the protection buyer is the issuer of the note. If no credit event occurs during the life of the note, the redemption value of the note is paid to the investor on maturity. If a credit event does occur, then on maturity a value less than par will be paid out to the investor. This value will be reduced by the nominal value of the reference asset that the CLN is linked to. The exact process will differ according to whether *cash settlement* or *physical settlement* has been specified for the note. We will consider this later.

Credit default swaps and CLNs are used in structured products, in various combinations, and their flexibility has been behind the growth and wide application of the synthetic collateralised debt obligation and other credit hybrid products.

We now consider the credit-linked note.

Description of CLNs

Credit-linked notes exist in a number of forms, but all of them contain a link between the return they pay and the credit-related performance of the underlying asset. A standard credit-linked note is a security, usually issued by an investment-graded entity, that has an interest payment and fixed maturity structure similar to a vanilla bond. The performance of the note however, including the maturity value, is linked to the performance of a specified underlying asset or assets as well as that of the issuing entity. Notes are usually issued at par. The notes are often used by borrowers to hedge against credit risk, and by investors to enhance the yield received on their holdings. Hence, the issuer of the note is the protection buyer and the buyer of the note is the protection seller.

Essentially credit-linked notes are hybrid instruments that combine a pure credit-risk exposure with a vanilla bond. The credit-linked note pays regular coupons, however the credit derivative element is usually set to allow the issuer to decrease the principal amount, and/or the coupon interest, if a specified credit event occurs.

Figure 17.9 shows screen Bloomberg screen SND and their definition of the CLN.

Page 11/ 12
Credit Linked Notes (CLN): A hybrid debt security that offers investors a
synthetic credit exposure to a specified Reference Entity or basket of
Reference Entities. This credit exposure can be gained through a variety of
methods including (but not limited to): a credit default swap, a credit
spread swap, a total return swap, or as a repackaged note where the issuer
passes through the risk of an underlying credit to the noteholder in exchange
for an enhanced return. For example, a note might provide for its principal
repayment to be reduced below par in the event that a reference obligation
defaults.
20) Example: EC771465 <CORP> DES. A note that is linked to the credit of
            Sodexho Alliance SA. Following a credit event on the underlying
            reference obligation, this note will be redeemed early at
            less than par.
Repackaged Notes: A debt instrument secured by an underlying asset where the
cashflows of that asset are reprofiled through a derivative contract while
the credit risk is passed through to the investor of the Repackaged Note.
21) Example: EC785183 <CORP> DES. A note that is secured by Roche Holdings
            convertible notes and a swap agreement. Following an event of
            default on all or part of the underlying, this note will be
            redeemed early at an amount based on the underlying.

Page <FWD> for FFIEC 034 Structured Note Call Reporting Revision

Australia 61 2 9777 8600   Brazil 5511 3048 4500   Europe 44 20 7330 7500   Germany 49 69 920410
Hong Kong 852 2977 6000 Japan 81 3 3201 8900 Singapore 65 6212 1000 U.S. 1 212 318 2000 Copyright 2003 Bloomberg L.P.
                                                                                          H021-57-0 30-May-03 11:38:24

Figure 17.9 Bloomberg screen SND: definition of credit-linked note
Source: Bloomberg L.P. Used with permission.

To illustrate a CLN, consider a bank issuer of credit cards that wants
to fund its credit card loan portfolio via an issue of debt. The bank is rated
AA–. In order to reduce the credit risk of the loans, it issues a two-year
CLN. The principal amount of the bond is 100 (par) as usual, and it pays a
coupon of 7.50%, which is 110 basis points above the two-year benchmark.
At the time of issue the equivalent spread for a vanilla bond issued by a bank
of this rating would be of the order of 65 bps. With the CLN though, if the
incidence of bad debt amongst credit card holders exceeds 10% then the
terms state that note holders will only receive back 85 per 100 par. The
credit card issuer has in effect purchased a credit option that lowers its
liability in the event that it suffers from a specified credit event, which in
this case is an above-expected incidence of bad debts. The cost of this credit
option is paid in the form of a higher coupon payment on the CLN. The
credit card bank has issued the CLN to reduce its credit exposure, in the
form of this particular type of credit insurance. If the incidence of bad debts
is low, the CLN is redeemed at par. However if there a high incidence of
such debt, the bank will only have to repay a part of its loan liability.

Investors may wish purchase the CLN because the coupon paid on it
will be above what the credit card bank would pay on a vanilla bond it

issued, and higher than other comparable investments in the market. In addition such notes are usually priced below par on issue. Assuming the notes are eventually redeemed at par, investors will also have realised a substantial capital gain.

As with credit default swaps, credit-linked notes may be specified under cash settlement or physical settlement. Specifically:

- under cash settlement, if a credit event has occurred, on maturity the protection seller receives the difference between the value of the initial purchase proceeds and the value of the reference asset at the time of the credit event;
- under physical settlement, on occurrence of a credit event, the note is terminated. At maturity the protection buyer delivers the reference asset or an asset among a list of deliverable assets, and the protection seller receives the value of the original purchase proceeds minus the value of the asset that has been delivered.

Figure 17.10 illustrates a cash-settled credit-linked note.

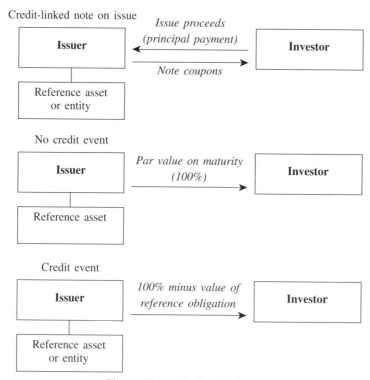

Figure 17.10 Credit-linked note

CLNs may be issued directly by a financial or corporate entity or via a Special Purpose Vehicle (SPV). They have been issued with the form of credit-linking taking on one or more of a number of different guises. For instance, a CLN may have its return performance linked to the issuer's, or a specified reference entity's, credit rating, risk exposure, financial performance or circumstance of default. Figure 17.11 shows Bloomberg screen CLN and a list of the various types of CLN issue that have been made. Figure 17.12 shows a page accessed from Bloomberg screen "CLN", which is a list of CLNs that have had their coupon affected by a change in the reference entity's credit rating.

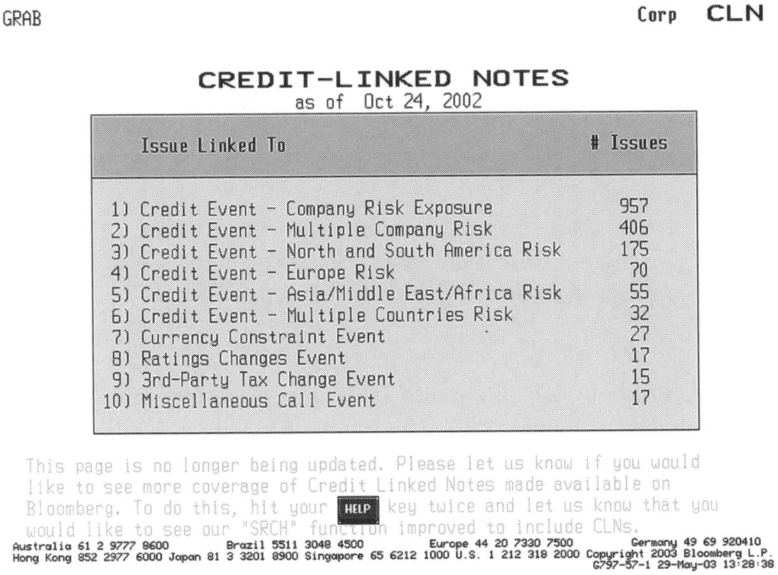

GRAB   Corp   **CLN**

CREDIT-LINKED NOTES
as of Oct 24, 2002

Issue Linked To	# Issues
1) Credit Event – Company Risk Exposure	957
2) Credit Event – Multiple Company Risk	406
3) Credit Event – North and South America Risk	175
4) Credit Event – Europe Risk	70
5) Credit Event – Asia/Middle East/Africa Risk	55
6) Credit Event – Multiple Countries Risk	32
7) Currency Constraint Event	27
8) Ratings Changes Event	17
9) 3rd-Party Tax Change Event	15
10) Miscellaneous Call Event	17

This page is no longer being updated. Please let us know if you would like to see more coverage of Credit Linked Notes made available on Bloomberg. To do this, hit your HELP key twice and let us know that you would like to see our "SRCH" function improved to include CLNs.

Australia 61 2 9777 9600   Brazil 5511 3048 4500   Europe 44 20 7330 7500   Germany 49 69 920410
Hong Kong 852 2977 6000 Japan 81 3 3201 8900 Singapore 65 6212 1000 U.S. 1 212 318 2000 Copyright 2003 Bloomberg L.P.
G797-57-1 29-May-03 13:28:38

Figure 17.11 Bloomberg screen CLN
Source: Bloomberg L.P. Used with permission.

RATINGS CHANGES EVENT

Issuer	Settle Date	Cpn	Crncy	Maturity Date	Rating Changes Exposure
1) BHFBK	04/28/1998	6.25	DEM	04/28/2006	Govt of Ukraine
2) BSPIR	03/21/2000	7.00	EUR	02/20/2010	B-Spires
3) CATTLE	10/21/1999	8.63	GBP	12/07/2007	Cattle PLC
4) CNTCNZ	09/14/2000	FRN	AUD	09/14/2007	Contact Energy
5) CNTCNZ	09/14/2000	FRN	USD	09/14/2007	Contact Energy
6) HI	11/13/1997	FRN	USD	11/13/2013	Household Fin Co
7) IFCTF	08/04/1997	7.88	USD	08/04/2002	Indust Fin Corp
8) IFCTF	08/04/1997	7.75	USD	08/04/2007	Indust Fin Corp
9) KPN	06/13/2000	FRN	EUR	06/13/2002	KPN NV
10) KPN	06/13/2000	FRN	EUR	06/13/2002	KPN NV
11) KPN	06/13/2000	6.05	EUR	06/13/2003	KPN NV
12) METALF	07/25/2000	6.75	EUR	07/25/2005	MetallGesell Fin
13) METALF	07/25/2000	6.75	EUR	07/25/2005	MetallGesell Fin
14) OSTDRA	02/16/2000	Var	EUR	02/16/2007	Oester Draukraft
15) SIRSTR	06/25/1998	FRN	USD	10/06/2006	Bk Tokyo-Mitsub
16) SOWLN	03/26/1998	6.89	GBP	03/26/2008	Southern Water
17) SPIRES	01/26/1998	FRN	DEM	10/24/2007	Greece

Australia 61 2 9777 8600   Brazil 5511 3048 4500   Europe 44 20 7330 7500   Germany 49 69 920410
Hong Kong 852 2977 6000 Japan 81 3 3201 8900 Singapore 65 6212 1000 U.S. 1 212 318 2000 Copyright 2003 Bloomberg L.P.
G797-57-1 29-May-03 13:29:32

Figure 17.12 Bloomberg screen showing a sample of CLNs impacted by change
in reference entity credit rating, October 2002
Source: Bloomberg L.P. Used with permission.

The majority of CLNs are issued by issuers direct. An example of such a bond is shown at Figure 17.13. This shows Bloomberg screen DES for a CLN issued by British Telecom plc, the 8.125% note due in December 2010. The terms of this note state that the coupon will increase by 25 basis points for each one-notch rating downgrade below A-/A3 suffered by the issuer during the life of the note. The coupon will decrease by 25 basis points for each ratings upgrade, with a minimum coupon set at 8.125%. In other words, this note allows investors to take on a credit play on the fortunes of the issuer.

Figure 17.14 shows Bloomberg screen YA for this note, as at 29 May 2003. We see that a rating downgrade meant that the coupon on the note was now 8.375%.

Chapter 17 Credit Derivatives I: Instruments and Applications

GRAB   Corp DES

SECURITY DESCRIPTION   Page 1/ 2
BRITISH TEL PLC BRITEL8 '₈ 12/10 125.1533/125.4033 (4.41/4.38) BGN @ 5/28

ISSUER INFORMATION	IDENTIFIERS	1) Additional Sec Info
Name BRITISH TELECOM PLC	Common 012168527	2) Multi Cpn Display
Type Telephone-Integrated	ISIN US111021AD39	3) Identifiers
Market of Issue GLOBAL	CUSIP 111021AD3	4) Ratings
SECURITY INFORMATION	RATINGS	5) Fees/Restrictions
Country GB Currency USD	Moody's Baa1	6) Sec. Specific News
Collateral Type NOTES	S&P A-	7) Involved Parties
Calc Typ(133)MULTI-COUPON	Fitch A	8) Custom Notes
Maturity 12/15/2010 Series	ISSUE SIZE	9) Issuer Information
MAKE WHOLE	Amt Issued	10) ALLQ
Coupon 8 '₈ FIXED	USD 3,000,000 (M)	11) Pricing Sources
S/A ISMA-30/360	Amt Outstanding	12) Related Securities
Announcement Dt 12/ 5/00	USD 3,000,000 (M)	
Int. Accrual Dt 12/12/00	Min Piece/Increment	
1st Settle Date 12/12/00	1,000.00/ 1,000.00	
1st Coupon Date 6/15/01	Par Amount 1,000.00	
Iss Pr 99.8370	BOOK RUNNER/EXCHANGE	
SPR @ ISS 265.0 vs T 5 ³₄ 08/10	ML,MSDW,CITI	65) Old DES
NO PROSPECTUS DTC	LONDON	66) Send as Attachment

CPN INC BY 25BP FOR EACH RTG DOWNGRADE BY 1 NOTCH BY S&P OR MOODYS BELOW A-/A3.
CPN DECREASE BY 25BP FOR EACH UPGRADE. MIN CPN=8'₈%. CALL @MAKE WHOLE+30BP.

Figure 17.13 Bloomberg screen DES for British Telecom plc
8.125% 2010 credit-linked note issued on 5 December 2000
Source: Bloomberg L.P. Used with permission.

GRAB   Corp YA
Enter all values and hit <GO>.
MULTI-CPN BOND PRICE/YIELD ANALYSIS

BRITISH TEL PLC BRITEL8 '₈ 12/10 125.1533/125.4033 (4.41/4.38) BGN @ 5/28

SETTLEMENT DATE   6/ 3/2003
PRICE   125.403279

COUPON SCHEDULE

RATE(%)	START	END	1ST CMPND
8.125	12/12/2000	6/15/2001	6/15/2001
8.375	6/15/2001	12/15/2010	

Worst
YIELD   MATURITY 12/15/2010
CALCULATIONS 12/15/2010 @ 100.000
STREET CONVENTN 4.3792   4.3792
EQUIV 1/YEAR   4.4272   4.4272
U.S. GOVT EQUIV 4.3795   4.3795
SENSITIVITY ANALYSIS
CNV DURATION   5.774 5.774
ADJ/MOD DUR   5.651 5.651
RISK   7.307 7.307
CONVEXITY   0.407 0.407

USING A REINVESTMENT RATE OF   4.38%
GIVES AN EFFECTIVE YIELD OF   4.38%
(@WORKOUT   )

PAYMENT	NUMBER OF BONDS 1000	INCOME	
PRINCIPAL	1254032.79	REDEMPTION VALUE	1000000.00
168 DAYS ACCRUED INT	39083.33	COUPON PAYMENTS	670000.00
TOTAL PAYMENT	1293116.12	INTEREST ON INTEREST	122114.62
GROSS PROFIT	498998.49	TOTAL INCOME	1792114.62

Figure 17.14 Bloomberg screen YA for British Telecom CLN, as at 29 May 2003
Source: Bloomberg L.P. Used with permission.

577

CLNs have been issued with a number of different types of credit linking.

Figure 17.15 is the Bloomberg DES page for a USD-denominated CLN issued directly by Household Finance Corporation.[12] Like the British Telecom bond, this is a CLN whose return is linked to the credit risk of the Issuer, but in a different way. The coupon of the HFC bond was issued as floating USD-Libor, but in the event of the bond not being called from November 2001, the coupon would be the Issuer's two-year "credit spread" over a fixed rate of 5.9%. In fact the issuer called the bond with effect from the coupon change date. Figure 17.16 shows the Bloomberg screen YA for the bond and how its coupon remained as at first issue until the call date.

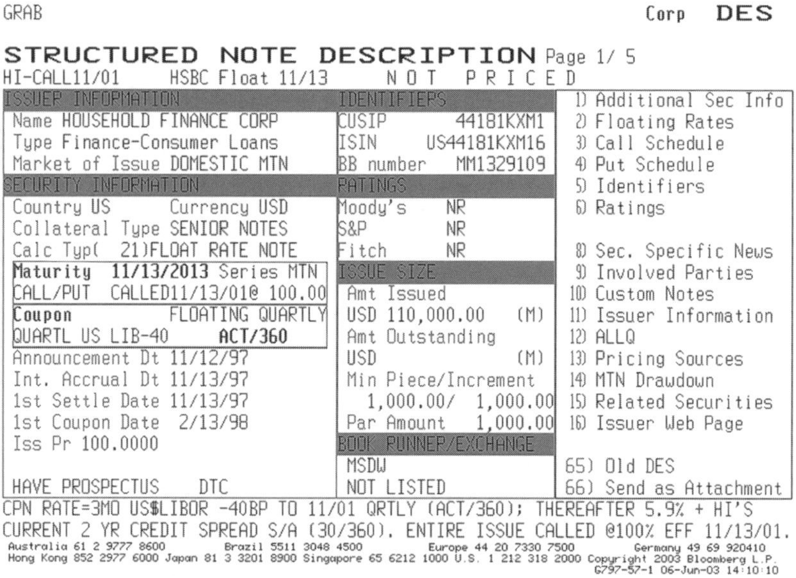

```
GRAB                                                   Corp  DES

STRUCTURED  NOTE  DESCRIPTION Page 1/ 5
HI-CALL11/01      HSBC Float 11/13      N O T    P R I C E D
ISSUER INFORMATION        IDENTIFIERS          1) Additional Sec Info
Name HOUSEHOLD FINANCE CORP  CUSIP    44181KXM1  2) Floating Rates
Type Finance-Consumer Loans  ISIN   US44181KXM16  3) Call Schedule
Market of Issue DOMESTIC MTN BB number  MM1329109  4) Put Schedule
SECURITY INFORMATION       RATINGS             5) Identifiers
Country US       Currency USD  Moody's    NR     6) Ratings
Collateral Type SENIOR NOTES  S&P       NR
Calc Typ( 21)FLOAT RATE NOTE  Fitch     NR      8) Sec. Specific News
Maturity  11/13/2013 Series MTN  ISSUE SIZE     9) Involved Parties
CALL/PUT   CALLED11/13/01@ 100.00  Amt Issued   10) Custom Notes
Coupon          FLOATING QUARTLY  USD 110,000.00  (M)  11) Issuer Information
QUARTL US LIB-40    ACT/360     Amt Outstanding   12) ALLQ
Announcement Dt 11/12/97       USD         (M)  13) Pricing Sources
Int. Accrual Dt 11/13/97       Min Piece/Increment  14) MTN Drawdown
1st Settle Date 11/13/97        1,000.00/  1,000.00  15) Related Securities
1st Coupon Date  2/13/98       Par Amount   1,000.00  16) Issuer Web Page
Iss Pr 100.0000               BOOK RUNNER/EXCHANGE
                              MSDW            65) Old DES
HAVE PROSPECTUS    DTC        NOT LISTED     66) Send as Attachment
CPN RATE=3MO US$LIBOR -40BP TO 11/01 QRTLY (ACT/360); THEREAFTER 5.9% + HI'S
CURRENT 2 YR CREDIT SPREAD S/A (30/360). ENTIRE ISSUE CALLED @100% EFF 11/13/01.
Australia 61 2 9777 8600     Brazil 5511 3048 4500     Europe 44 20 7330 7500     Germany 49 69 920410
Hong Kong 852 2977 6000 Japan 81 3 3201 8900 Singapore 65 6212 1000 U.S. 1 212 318 2000 Copyright 2003 Bloomberg L.P.
                                                              G797-57-1 06-Jun-03 14:10:10
```

Figure 17.15 HFC bond, screen DES on Bloomberg

Source: Bloomberg L.P. Used with permission.

---

[12] HFC was subsequently acquired by HSBC.

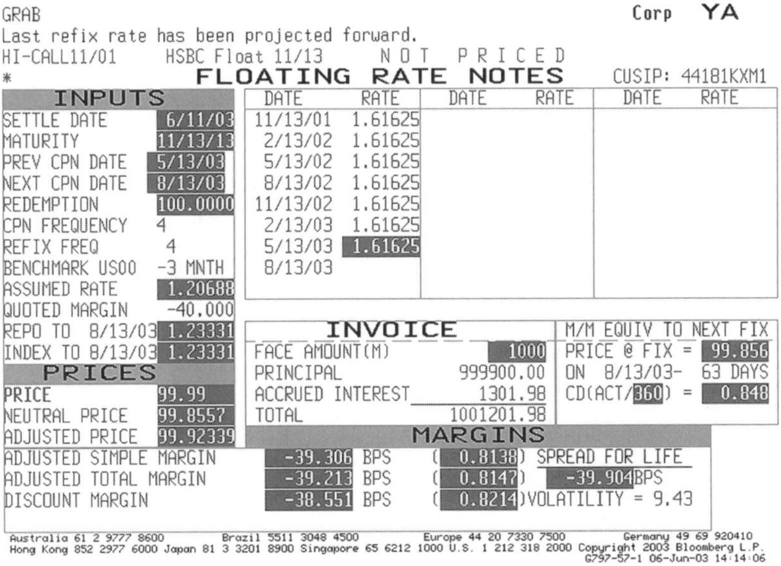

```
GRAB                                                    Corp  YA
Last refix rate has been projected forward.
HI-CALL11/01    HSBC Float 11/13     N O T   P R I C E D
  *                FLOATING  RATE  NOTES      CUSIP: 44181KXM1
╔══════INPUTS══════╗  DATE     RATE  │ DATE    RATE │ DATE    RATE
║SETTLE DATE  6/11/03║ 11/13/01 1.61625
║MATURITY    11/13/13║ 2/13/02  1.61625
║PREV CPN DATE 5/13/03║ 5/13/02  1.61625
║NEXT CPN DATE 8/13/03║ 8/13/02  1.61625
║REDEMPTION  100.0000║ 11/13/02 1.61625
║CPN FREQUENCY  4    ║ 2/13/03  1.61625
║REFIX FREQ     4    ║ 5/13/03  1.61625
║BENCHMARK US00 -3 MNTH║ 8/13/03
║ASSUMED RATE 1.20688║
║QUOTED MARGIN -40.000║╔═════INVOICE═════╗║M/M EQUIV TO NEXT FIX║
║REPO TO 8/13/03 1.23331║                  ║PRICE @ FIX = 99.856║
║INDEX TO 8/13/03 1.23331║FACE AMOUNT(M)  1000║ON 8/13/03- 63 DAYS║
╔══════PRICES══════╗  PRINCIPAL  999900.00║CD(ACT/360) = 0.848║
║PRICE        99.99║  ACCRUED INTEREST 1301.98║
║NEUTRAL PRICE 99.8557║ TOTAL     1001201.98║
║ADJUSTED PRICE 99.92339║      MARGINS
║ADJUSTED SIMPLE MARGIN  -39.306 BPS ( 0.8138) SPREAD FOR LIFE
║ADJUSTED TOTAL MARGIN   -39.213 BPS ( 0.8147)  -39.904 BPS
║DISCOUNT MARGIN         -38.551 BPS ( 0.8214) VOLATILITY = 9.43
```

Figure 17.16 HFC bond YA screen
Source: Bloomberg L.P. Used with permission.

Another type of credit-linking is evidenced from the details show at Figure 17.17. This is a JPY-denominated bond issued by Alpha-Spires, which is an MTN programme vehicle set up by Merrill Lynch. The note itself is linked to the credit quality of Ford Motor Credit. In the event of a default of the reference name, the note will be called immediately. Figure 17.18 shows the rate fixing for this note as at the last coupon date. The screen snapshot was taken on 6 June 2003.

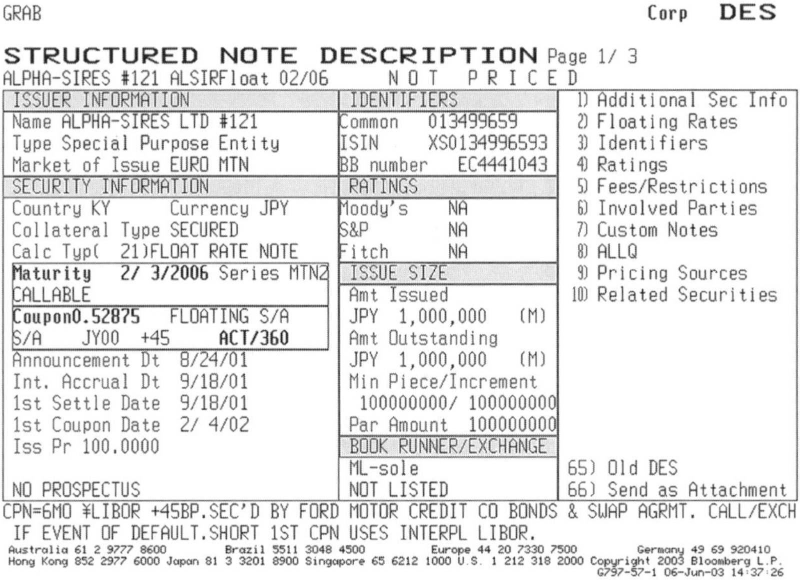

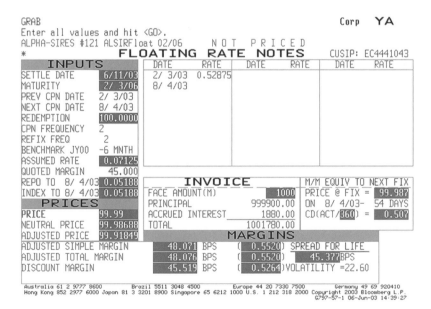

Figure 17.17 Ford CLN DES page
Source: Bloomberg L.P. Used with permission.

Figure 17.18 Ford CLN YA page
Source: Bloomberg L.P. Used with permission.

Structured products such as synthetic collateralised debt obligations (CDOs) may combine both CLNs and credit default swaps, to meet issuer and investor requirements. For instance, figure 17.19 shows a credit structure designed to provide a higher return for an investor on comparable risk to the cash market. An issuing entity is set up in the form of a special purpose vehicle (SPV) which issues CLNs to the market. The structure is engineered so that the SPV has a neutral position on a reference asset. It has bought protection on a single reference name by issuing a funded credit derivative, the CLN, and simultaneously sold protection on this name by selling a credit default swap on this name. The proceeds of the CLN are invested in risk-free collateral such as T-bills or a Treasury bank account. The coupon on the CLN will be a spread over Libor. It is backed by the collateral account and the fee generated by the SPV in selling protection with the credit default swap. Investors in the CLN will have exposure to the reference asset or entity, and the repayment of the note is linked to the performance of the reference entity. If a credit event occurs, the maturity date of the CLN is brought forward and the note is settled as par minus the value of the reference asset or entity.

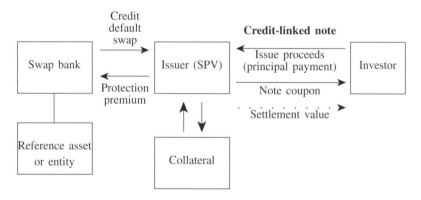

Figure 17.19 CLN and credit default swap structure on single reference name

The first-to-default credit-linked note

A standard credit-linked note is issued in reference to one specific bond or loan. An investor purchasing such a note is writing credit protection on a specific reference credit. A CLN that is linked to more than one reference credit is known as a *basket credit-linked note*. A development of the CLN as a structured product is the First-to-Default CLN (FtD), which is a CLN that is linked to a basket of reference assets. The investor in the CLN is selling protection on the first credit to default.[13] Figure 17.20 shows this progression in the development of CLNs as structured products, with the *fully-funded synthetic* collateralised debt obligation (CDO) being the vehicle that uses CLNs tied to a large basket of reference assets.

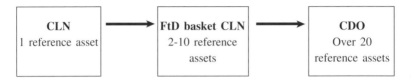

Figure 17.20 Progression of CLN development

An FtD CLN is a funded credit derivative in which the investor sells protection on one reference in a basket of assets, whichever is the first to default. The return on the CLN is a multiple of the average spread of the basket. The CLN will mature early on occurrence of a credit event relating to any of the reference assets. Note settlement can be either of the following:

- physical settlement, with the defaulted asset(s) being delivered to the noteholder;
- cash settlement, in which the CLN issuer pays redemption proceeds to the noteholder calculated as (principal amount × reference asset recovery value).[14]

Figure 17.21 shows a generic FtD credit-linked note.

To illustrate, consider an FtD CLN issued at par with a term-to-maturity of five years and linked to a basket of five reference assets with a face value (issued nominal amount) of $10 million. An investor purchasing this note will pay $10 million to the issuer. If no credit event occurs during the life of the note, the investor will receive the face value of the note on maturity. If a credit event occurs on any of the assets in the basket, the note will redeem early and the issuer will deliver a deliverable obligation of the reference entity, or a portfolio of such obligations, for a $10 million nominal amount. An FtD CLN carries a similar amount of risk exposure on default to a standard CLN, namely the recovery rate of the defaulted credit.

---

[13] "Default" here meaning a credit event as defined in the ISDA definitions.

[14] In practice, often it is not the "recovery value" that is used but the market value of the reference asset at the time the credit event is verified. Recovery of a defaulted asset follows a legal process of administration and/or liquidation that can take some years, the final recovery value may not be known for certainty for some time.

However its risk exposure prior to default is theoretically lower than a standard CLN, as it can reduce default probability through diversification. The investor can obtain exposure to a basket of reference entities that differ by industrial sector and by credit rating.

The matrix at Figure 17.22 illustrates how an investor can select a credit mix in the basket that diversifies risk exposure across a wide range – we show an hypothetical mix of reference assets to which an issued FtD could be linked. The precise selection of names will reflect investors' own risk/return profile requirements.

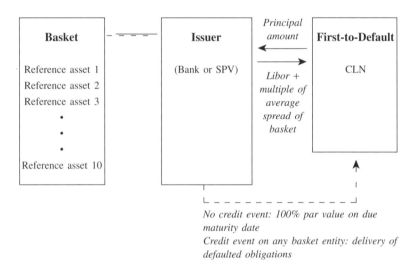

Figure 17.21 First-to-Default CLN structure

	Automobiles	Banks	Electronics	Insurance	Media	Telecoms	Utilities
AAA							
Aa1							
Aa2				SunAlliance			
Aa3		RBos					
A1							
A2							Powergen
A3	Ford					British Telecom	
Baa1			Philips				
Baa2							
Baa3							

Figure 17.22 Diversified credit exposure to basket of reference assets: hypothetical reference asset mix

The FtD CLN creates a synthetic credit entity that features a note return with enhanced spread. Investors receive a spread over Libor that is the average return of all the reference assets in the basket. This structure serves to diversify credit risk exposure while benefiting from a higher average return. If the pool of reference assets is sufficiently large, the structure becomes similar to a *single-tranche CDO*. This was considered in chapter 12.

The iBOXX Index Note

The details below are of a contract for a CDS written on the iBOXX index. The hypothetical bank "XYZ Securities" is the protection seller and the counterparty is an hypothetical hedge fund called "ABC Fund".

iBOXX is the name of a range of credit indices developed by a group of credit derivatives market makers. The other major group of indices is known as Trac-X. iBOXX was founded by a consortium comprised of ABN Amro, Citigroup, Deutsche Bank, Dresdner Kleinwort Wasserstein and Societe Generale. The index is available in funded form, as the iBOXX note, or in unfunded form as a CDS written on the index. The index can be traded in the following forms:

- a portfolio of 100 equally-weighted European corporate and financial entities. These were a selection of corporates and financial entities, with a Moody's diversity score of 61 and average rating of Baa1/Baa2. At launch in September 2003 the CLN paid quarterly Euribor plus 39 basis points;
- the top 100 €-denominated issuers weighted by market value and duration; at launch these notes paid Euribor plus 90 basis points, at an issue price of €99.87. The average rating was Baa1 and they had a Moodys diversity score of 33;
- the iBoxx 100 excluding financial entities. This note had a diversity score of 23 and paid Euribor plus 125 basis points on launch, issue price par. The average rating was Baa2 across 62 reference entities.

The first index is aimed at providing an index for investors who are seeking to access a diversified market exposure, whereas the second index is for investors who wish to track the market overall rather than diversify. The third index exhibits higher beta and volatility compared to the other two. The main advantage of these index products for investors is the standardisation they represent. Investors can now trade in a standard note across the market, and one that has a ready set of market makers available at all times supporting it.

The funded form of the indices are CLNs tied to the index level and are known as iBoxx notes. They are all 5.25-year notes, with quarterly coupon for the first index and semi-annual coupon for the other two indices. The bonds are issued by an entity incorporated in Ireland, iBond Securities plc.

Investors trading in the funded credit derivative for iBoxx, via the iBoxx note, can opt for a fixed coupon bond set at inception, whose price fluctuates as the value of the reference names fluctuate.

Figure 17.23 shows Bloomberg pages DES and YA for the top 100 companies index note.

```
GRAB                                                    Corp   DES

STRUCTURED  NOTE  DESCRIPTION  Page 1/ 4
IBOND - IBX 100A IBX Float 03/08        N O T   P R I C E D
┌─ISSUER INFORMATION────────┬─IDENTIFIERS──────────┬ 1) Additional Sec Info
│Name IBOND SECS PLC -IBX 100│Common    016346195   │ 2) Floating Rates
│Type Special Purpose Entity │ISIN      XS0163461956 │ 3) FRN Coupon Formula
│Market of Issue EURO MTN    │BB number    EC8616954 │ 4) Identifiers
├─SECURITY INFORMATION───────┼─RATINGS──────────────┤ 5) Ratings
│Country IE     Currency EUR │Moody's      Baa1      │ 6) Fees/Restrictions
│Collateral Type SECURED     │S&P          NA        │
│Calc Typ( 21)FLOAT RATE NOTE│Composite    BBB+      │ 8) Sec. Specific News
│Maturity    3/20/2008 Series 1A│ISSUE SIZE──────────┤ 9) Involved Parties
│NORMAL                      │Amt Issued             │10) Custom Notes
│Coupon2.94      FLOATING QUARTLY│EUR   600,000.00 (M)│11) ALLQ
│QUARTL EURIBO+90     ACT/360 │Amt Outstanding        │12) Pricing Sources
│Announcement Dt   2/20/03   │EUR   600,000.00 (M)   │13) Related Securities
│Int. Accrual Dt   3/20/03   │Min Piece/Increment    │
│1st Settle Date   3/20/03   │ 50,000.00/ 50,000.00  │
│1st Coupon Date   6/20/03   │Par Amount  50,000.00  │
│Iss Pr    99.8700           ├─BOOK RUNNER/EXCHANGE──┤
│                            │ABN,DB                 │65) Old DES
│NO PROSPECTUS               │DUBLIN                 │66) Send as Attachment
└────────────────────────────┴───────────────────────┘
CPN RATE=3MO EURIBOR +90BP. SEC BY AAA ASSETS & SWAP AGRMT. CREDIT LINKED TO A
BSKT OF 100 REF ENTITIES - IBOXX 100 NOTE. ADDL €100MM ISS'D @100% ON 6/9/03.
Australia 61 2 9777 8600      Brazil 5511 3048 4500      Europe 44 20 7330 7500       Germany 49 69 920410
Hong Kong 852 2977 6000 Japan 81 3 3201 8900 Singapore 65 6212 1000 U.S. 1 212 318 2000 Copyright 2004 Bloomberg L.P.
                                                              G657-802-0 23-Mar-04  8:57:22
```

Figure 17.23(a) Bloomberg screen DES for iBoxx note, 23 March 2004
© Bloomberg L.P. Used with permission.

Note that in June 2004 the iBoxx and Trac-X indices merged into a new single index, known as iTrax.

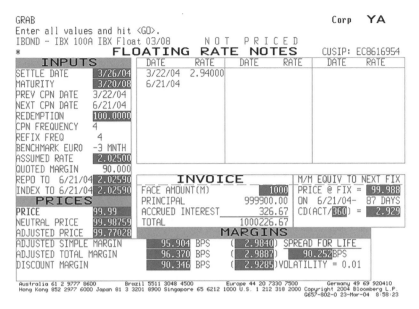

Figure 17.23(b) Bloomberg screen YA for iBoxx note, 23 March 2004
© Bloomberg L.P. Used with permission

Investors can also trade in the unfunded instrument tied to the Index. Details of a CDS traded on the iBoxx are shown on the iBoxx term sheet shown below.

The "fixed rate" refers to the coupon on the Index at its inception. There is a fixed coupon set at the start of trading in the index, this is set at "fair value" based on the aggregate value of all the single-name CDS prices for each reference entity in the index (100 names in all). Over the time the traded value of the Index fluctuates to reflect changes in the value of underlying names. The current price is calculated by taking the cashflows representing the underlying CDSs and discounting them at he risky rate.

To arbitrage between the Index and the underlying names, a trader will put on a position in the Index contract and the opposite position in single-name CDSs for each of the constituent names. This would be undertaken when the "traded value" of the Index CDS was felt to not reflect the fair value given the current price of each of the underlying names. Given that this would involve administration for 101 CDS contracts, as well as paying the bid-offer spread, the amount of divergence from fair value would need to be sufficiently high to make the trade worthwhile, say 10 bps or more.

iBOXX® CDX INDEX TERM SHEET

Counterparty:	ABC Fund LLC
Trade Date:	February 24, 2004
Effective Date:	February 25, 2004
Schedule Termination Date:	March 20, 2009
Floating Rate Payer (Seller)	Counterparty
Fixed Rate Payer (Buyer)	XYZ Securities Ltd
Calculation Agent:	XYZ Securities Ltd
Index:	iBoxx CDX.NA.HVOL ®
Traded Rate	107.5 bps
Fixed Rate	125 bps
XYZ Receives (Pays)	$256,517
Amount Traded	$25,000,000

Applications for portfolio managers

Applications overview

Credit derivatives have allowed market participants to separate and disaggregate credit risk, and thence to trade this risk in a secondary market.[15] Initially, portfolio managers used them to reduce credit exposure. Subsequently, they have been used in the management of portfolios, to enhance portfolio yields and in the structuring of synthetic collateralised-debt obligations. We summarise portfolio managers' main uses of credit derivatives below.

Enhancing portfolio returns

Asset managers can derive premium income by trading credit exposures in the form of derivatives issued with synthetic structured notes. The multi-tranching aspect of structured products enables specific credit exposures (credit spreads and outright default), and their expectations, to be sold to specific areas of demand. By using structured notes such as credit-linked notes, tied to the assets in the reference pool of the portfolio manager, the trading of credit exposures is crystallised as added yield on the asset manager's fixed-income portfolio. In this way, the portfolio manager has enabled other market participants to gain an exposure to the credit risk of a pool of assets but not to any other aspects of the portfolio, and without the need to hold the assets themselves.

---

[15] For example, see Satyajit Das, *Credit Derivatives and Credit Linked Notes* (2nd edition) : John Wiley and Sons Ltd, Singapore, 2000, Chapters 2-4.

Reducing credit exposure

Consider a portfolio manager that holds a large portfolio of bonds issued by a particular sector (say, utilities) and believes that spreads in this sector will widen in the short term. Previously, in order to reduce its credit exposure it would have to sell bonds; however, this may crystallise a mark-to-market loss and may conflict with its long-term investment strategy. An alternative approach would be to enter into a credit-default swap, purchasing protection for the short term; if spreads do widen these swaps will increase in value and may be sold at a profit in the secondary market. Alternatively, the portfolio manager may enter into total-return swaps on the desired credits. It pays the counterparty the total return on the reference assets, in return for Libor. This transfers the credit exposure of the bonds to the counterparty for the term of the swap, in return for the credit exposure of the counterparty.

Consider now the case of a portfolio manager wishing to mitigate credit risk from a growing portfolio (say, one that has just been launched). Figure 17.24 shows an example of an unhedged credit exposure to a hypothetical credit-risky portfolio. It illustrates the manager's expectation of credit risk building up to $250 million as the portfolio is ramped up, and then reducing to a more stable level as the credits become more established. A three-year credit-default swap entered into shortly after provides protection on half of the notional exposure, shown as the broken line. The net exposure to credit events has been reduced by a significant margin.

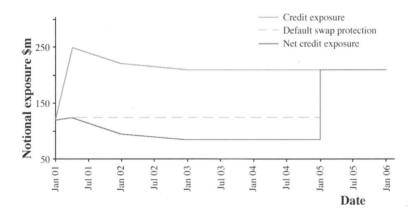

Figure 17.24 Reducing credit exposure

Credit switches and zero-cost credit exposure

Protection buyers utilising credit-default swaps must pay premium in return for laying off their credit-risk exposure. An alternative approach for an asset manager involves the use of credit switches for specific sectors of the portfolio. In a credit switch, the portfolio manager purchases credit protection on one reference asset or pool of assets, and simultaneously sells protection on another asset or pool of assets.[16] So, for example, the portfolio manager would purchase protection for a particular fund and sell protection on another. Typically the entire transaction would be undertaken with one investment bank, which would price the structure so that the net cash flows would be zero. This has the effect of synthetically diversifying the credit exposure of the portfolio manager, enabling it to gain and/or reduce exposure to sectors it desires.

Exposure to market sectors

Investors can use credit derivatives to gain exposure to sectors for which they do not wish a cash-market exposure. This can be achieved with an index swap, which is similar to a TR swap, with one counterparty paying a total return that is linked to an external reference index. The other party pays a Libor-linked coupon or the total return of another index. Indices that are used might include the government-bond index, a high-yield index or a technology-stocks index. Assume that an investor believes that the bank loan market will outperform the mortgage-backed bond sector; to reflect this view the investor enters into an index swap in which he pays the total return of the mortgage index and receives the total return of the bank loan index.

Another possibility is synthetic exposure to foreign currency and money markets. Again we assume that an investor has a particular view on an emerging-market currency. If he wishes, he can purchase a short-term (say, one-year) domestic coupon-bearing note, whose principal redemption is linked to a currency factor. This factor is based on the ratio of the spot value of the foreign currency on issue of the note to the value on maturity. Such currency-linked notes can also structured so that they provide an exposure to sovereign credit risk. The downside of currency-linked notes is that if the exchange rate goes the other way, the note will have a zero return; in effect, a negative return once the investor's funding costs have been taken into account.

---

[16] A pool of assets would be concentrated on one sector, such as utility company bonds.

Credit spreads

Credit derivatives can be used to trade credit spreads. Assume that an investor has negative views on a certain emerging-market government-bond credit spread relative to UK gilts. The simplest way to reflect this view would be to go long a credit-default swap on the sovereign, paying X basis points. Assuming that the investor's view is correct and the sovereign bonds decrease in price as their credit spread widens, the premium payable on the credit swap will increase. The investor's swap can then be sold into the market at this higher premium.

Capital-structure arbitrage

A capital-structure arbitrage describes an arrangement whereby investors exploit mispricing between the yields received on two different loans by the same issuer. Assume that the reference entity has both a commercial bank loan and a subordinated bond issue outstanding, but that the former pays Libor plus 330 basis points while the latter pays Libor plus 230 basis points. An investor enters into a total-return swap in which it effectively is purchasing the bank loan and selling short the bond. The nominal amounts will be at a ratio, for argument's sake let us say 2:1, as the bonds will be more price-sensitive to changes in credit status than the loans.

The trade is illustrated in figure 17.25. The investor receives the "total return" on the bank loan, while simultaneously paying the return on the bond in addition to Libor plus 30 basis points, which is the price of the TR swap. The swap generates a net spread of 175 basis points, given by [(100 bps $\times$ $\frac{1}{2}$) + 250 bps $\times$ $\frac{1}{2}$)].

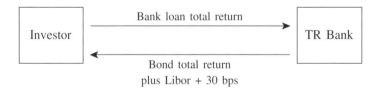

Figure 17.25 Total return swap in capital-structure arbitrage

Synthetic repo

A portfolio manager believes that a particular bond that it does not hold is about to decline in price. To reflect this view the portfolio manager may do one of the following.

- *Sell the bond in the market and cover the resulting short position in repo:* The cash flow out is the coupon on the bond, with capital gain if the bond falls in price. Assume that the repo rate is floating, say Libor plus a spread. The manager must be aware of the funding costs of the trade, so that unless the bond can be covered in repo at general collateral rates[17], the funding will be at a loss. The yield on the bond must also be lower than the Libor plus spread received in the repo.

- *As an alternative, enter into a TR swap:* the portfolio manager pays the total return on the bond and receives Libor plus a spread. If the bond yield exceeds the Libor spread, the funding will be negative. However, the trade will gain if the trader's view is proved correct and the bond falls in price by a sufficient amount. If the breakeven funding cost (which the bond must exceed as it falls in value) is lower in the TR swap, this method will be used rather than the repo approach. This is more likely if the bond is special.

Total-return swaps are increasingly used as synthetic repo instruments, most commonly by investors that wish to purchase the credit exposure of an asset without purchasing the asset itself. This is conceptually similar to what happened when interest-rate swaps were introduced, which enabled banks and other financial institutions to trade interest-rate risk without borrowing or lending cash funds.

Under a TR swap, an asset such as a bond position may be removed from the balance sheet. In order to avoid adverse impact on regular internal and external capital and credit-exposure reporting a bank may use TR swaps to reduce the amount of lower-quality assets on the balance sheet. This can be done by entering into a short-term TR swap with, say, a two-week term that straddles the reporting date. Bonds are removed from the balance sheet if they are part of a sale-plus-TR-swap transaction. This is because legally the bank selling the asset is not required to repurchase bonds from the swap counterparty, nor is the total-return payer obliged to sell the bonds back to the counterparty (or indeed sell the bonds at all on maturity of the TR swap).

---

[17] That is, the bond cannot be *special*. A bond is special when the repo rate payable on it is significantly (say, 20–30 basis points or more) below the *general collateral* repo rate, so that covering a short position in the bond entails paying a substantial funding premium.

Risks in credit-default swaps

Unintended risks

As credit derivatives can be tailored to specific requirements in terms of reference exposure, term to maturity, currency and cash flows, they have enabled market participants to establish exposure to specific entities without the need for them to hold the bond or loan of that entity. This has raised issues of the different risk exposure that this entails compared to the cash equivalent. A recent Moody's special report highlights the unintended risks of holding credit exposures in the form of default swaps and credit-linked notes.[18] Under certain circumstances it is possible for credit-default swaps to create unintended risk exposure for holders, by exposing them to greater frequency and magnitude of losses compared to that suffered by a holder of the underlying reference credit.

In a credit-default swap, the payout to a buyer of protection is determined by the occurrence of credit events. The definition of a credit event sets the level of credit- risk exposure of the protection seller. A wide definition of "credit event" results in a higher level of risk. To reduce the likelihood of disputes, counterparties can adopt the ISDA Credit Derivatives definitions to govern their dealings. The Moody's paper states that the current ISDA definitions do not unequivocally separate and isolate credit risk and, in certain circumstances, credit derivatives can expose holders to additional risks. A reading of the paper would appear to suggest that differences in definitions can lead to unintended risks being taken on by protection sellers. Two examples from the paper are cited below as illustration.

Extending loan maturity

The bank debt of Conseco, a corporate entity, was restructured in August 2000. The restructuring provisions included deferment of the loan maturity by three months, higher coupon, corporate guarantee and additional covenants. Under the Moody's definition, as lenders received compensation in return for an extension of the debt, the restructuring was not considered to be a "diminished financial obligation", although Conseco's credit rating was downgraded one notch. However, under the ISDA definition, the extension of the loan maturity meant that the restructuring was considered

---

[18] Jeffrey Tolk, "Understanding the Risks in Credit Default Swaps", *Moody's Investors Service Special Report*, March 16, 2001.

to be a credit event, and thus triggered payments on default swaps written on Conseco's bank debt. Hence, this was an example of a loss event under ISDA definitions that was not considered by Moody's to be a default.

Risks of synthetic positions and cash positions compared

Consider two investors in XYZ, one of whom owns bonds issued by XYZ while the other holds a credit-linked note (CLN) referenced to XYZ. Following a deterioration in its debt situation, XYZ violates a number of covenants on its bank loans, but its bonds are unaffected. XYZ's bank accelerates the bank loan, but the bonds continue to trade at 85 cents on the dollar, coupons are paid and the bond is redeemed in full at maturity. However, the default swap underlying the CLN cites "obligation acceleration" (of either bond or loan) as a credit event, so the holder of the CLN receives 85% of par in cash settlement and the CLN is terminated. However, the cash investor receives all the coupons and the par value of the bonds on maturity.

These two examples illustrate how, as credit-default swaps are defined to pay out in the event of a very broad range of definitions of a "credit event", portfolio managers may suffer losses as a result of occurrences that are not captured by one or more of the ratings agencies' rating of the reference asset. This results in a potentially greater risk for the portfolio manager compared to the position were it to actually hold the underlying reference asset. Essentially, therefore, it is important for the range of definitions of a "credit event" to be fully understood by counterparties, so that holders of default swaps are not taking on greater risk than is intended.

Conclusions

Credit derivatives are well established instruments in the fixed-income markets, and their flexibility mirrors that of an earlier generation of derivatives such as swaps and options. This chapter has highlighted how they may be used both to hedge credit-risk exposure as well as to enhance portfolio returns. It is clear, though, that users need to be aware of the risks involved in writing credit swaps, such that the legal terms underpinning each contract are clearly defined and communicated.

Appendices

TABLE A17.1 Corporate bond credit ratings

FitchIBCA	Moody's	S&P	Summary Description
Investment Grade			
AAA	Aaa	AAA	Gilt edged, prime, maximum safety, lowest risk, and when sovereign borrower considered "default-free"
AA+	Aa1	AA+	
AA	Aa2	AA	High-grade, high credit quality
AA-	Aa3	AA-	
A+	A1	A+	
A	A2	A	Upper-medium grade
A-	A3	A-	
BBB+	Baa1	BBB+	
BBB	Baa2	BBB	Lower-medium grade
BBB-	Baa3	BBB-	
Speculative Grade			
BB+	Ba1	BB+	
BB	Ba2	BB	Low grade; speculative
BB-	Ba3	BB-	
B+	B1		
B	B	B	Highly speculative
B-	B3		
Predominantly speculative, Substantial Risk or in Default			
CCC+		CCC+	
CCC	Caa	CCC	Substantial risk, in poor standing
CC	Ca	CC	May be in default, very speculative
C	C	C	Extremely speculative
		CI	Income bonds – no interest being paid
DDD			
DD			Default
D		D	

18

Credit Derivatives II: Pricing, Valuation and the Basis[1]

Introduction

In this second chapter on the subject of credit-risk management, we look at the various approaches used in pricing and valuation of credit derivatives. We consider generic techniques and also compare prices obtained using different pricing models. In addition, we highlight the difference in the market between the cash and synthetic spread levels for the same reference name. This is known as the basis and is observed closely in the market.

The pricing of credit derivatives should aim to provide a "fair value" for the credit-derivative instrument. In the sections below, we discuss the pricing models currently proposed by the industry. The effective use of pricing models requires an understanding of the models' assumptions, the key pricing parameters and a clear understanding of the respective limitations of the models. Issues to consider when carrying out credit-derivative pricing include:

- the implementation and selection of appropriate modelling techniques
- the estimation of parameters
- the quality and quantity of data to support parameters and calibration
- the calibration to market instruments for risky debt.

For credit-derivative contracts in which the payout is on credit events other than default, the modelling of the credit evolutionary path is critical. If, however, a credit-derivative contract does not pay out on intermediate stages between the current state and default then the important factor is the probability of default from the current state.

---

[1] This chapter was co-authored with Richard Pereira. All views represented are those of the authors in their private capacity.

We begin by considering the asset-swap pricing method, which was commonly used at the inception of the credit-derivatives market.

Asset-swap pricing

Credit derivatives were originally valued using the asset-swap pricing technique. In addition to its use by dealers, risk-management departments who wished to independently price such swaps also adopted this technique. The asset-swap market remains a reasonably reliable indicator of the returns required for individual credit exposures, and provides a mark-to-market framework for reference assets as well as a hedging mechanism.

A par-asset swap typically combines the sale of an asset such as a fixed-rate corporate bond to a counterparty, at par and with no interest accrued, with an interest-rate swap. The coupon on the bond is paid in return for Libor, plus a spread if necessary. This spread is the asset-swap spread and is the price of the asset swap. In effect, the asset swap allows market participants that pay Libor-based funding to receive the asset-swap spread. This spread is a function of the credit risk of the underlying bond asset, which is why it, in effect, becomes the cornerstone of the price payable on a credit-default swap written on that reference asset.

The generic pricing is given by (18.1),

$$Y_a = Y_b - ir \qquad (18.1)$$

where

Y_a is the asset-swap spread
Y_b is the asset spread over the benchmark
ir is the interest-rate swap spread.

The asset spread over the benchmark is simply the bond (asset) redemption yield over that of the government benchmark. The interest-rate swap spread reflects the cost involved in converting fixed-coupon benchmark bonds into a floating-rate coupon during the life of the asset (or default swap), and is based on the swap rate for that maturity.

Asset-swap pricing: an example

XYZ plc is a Baa2-rated corporate. The seven-year asset swap for this entity is currently trading at 93 basis points; the underlying seven-year bond is hedged by an interest-rate swap with an Aa2-rated bank. The risk-free rate for floating-rate bonds is Libid minus 12.5 basis points (assume the bid-offer spread is six basis points). This suggests that the credit spread for XYZ plc is 111.5 basis points. The credit spread is the return required by an investor for holding the credit of XYZ plc. The protection seller is conceptually long the asset, and so would short the asset as a hedge of its position. This is illustrated in Figure 18.1. The price charged for the default swap is the price of the shorting the asset, which works out as 111.5 basis points each year.

Therefore, we can price a credit default written on XYZ plc as the present value of 111.5 basis points for seven years, discounted at the interest-rate swap rate of 5.875%. This computes to a credit-swap price of 6.25%.

Reference	XYZ plc
Term	Seven years
Interest-rate swap rate	5.875%
Asset swap	Libor plus 93 bps

Default-swap pricing:
Benchmark rate	Libid minus 12.5 bps
Margin	6 bps
Credit-default swap	111.5 bps
Default-swap price	6.252%

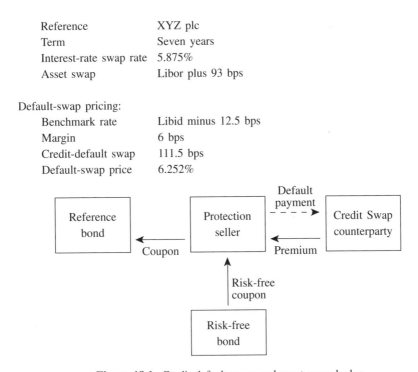

Figure 18.1 Credit-default swap and asset-swap hedge

There are a number of reasons why this approach is no longer applied except perhaps by risk managers or middle-office staff as an independent check.[2] These reflect the respective natures of asset swaps and credit-default swaps as market instruments.

---

[2] See Choudhry, M., "Some Issues in the Asset Swap Pricing of Credit Default Swaps", in Fabozzi, F. (editor), *Professional Perspectives in Fixed Income Portfolio Management*, volume 4, John Wiley, 2003.

We now consider a number of pricing models as used in the credit derivative markets.

Pricing Models

Pricing models for credit derivatives fall into two classes:
- structural models; and
- reduced form models.

We discuss these models below.

Structural models

Structural models are characterised by modelling the firm's value in order to provide the probability of the firm's default. The Black-Scholes-Merton option-pricing framework is the foundation of the structural-model approach. The default event is assumed to occur when the firm's assets fall below the book value of the debt.

Merton applied option-pricing techniques to the valuation of corporate debt. By extension, the pricing of credit derivatives based on corporate debt may in some circumstances be treated as an option on debt (which is therefore analogous to an option on an option model).

Merton models have the following features:
- default events occur predictably when a firm has insufficient assets to pay its debt.
- a firm's assets evolve randomly. The probability of a default is determined using the Black-Scholes-Merton option-pricing theory.

Some practitioners argue that Merton models are more appropriate than reduced-form models when pricing default swaps on high-yield bonds, due to the higher correlation of high-yield bonds with the underlying equity of the issuer firm.

The constraint of structural models is that the behavior of the value of assets and the parameters used to describe the process for the value of the firm's assets are not directly observable and the method does not consider the underlying market information for credit instruments.

Reduced-form models

Reduced-form models are a form of no-arbitrage model. These models can be fitted to the current term structure of risky bonds to generate no-arbitrage prices. In this way, the pricing of credit derivatives using these models will be consistent with the market data on the credit-risky bonds traded in the market. These models allow the default process to be separated from the asset value and are more commonly used to price credit derivatives.

Some key features of reduced-form models include:

- Complete and arbitrage-free credit-market conditions are assumed.
- Recovery rate is an input into the pricing model.
- Credit-spread data is used to estimate the risk-neutral probabilities.
- The use of transition probabilities from credit agencies can be accommodated in some of these models. The formation of the risk-neutral transition matrix from the historical transition matrix is a key step.
- Default can take place randomly over time and the default probability can be determined using the risk-neutral transition matrix.

When implementing reduced-form models it is necessary to consider issues such as the illiquidity of underlying credit-risky assets. Liquidity is often assumed to be present when we develop pricing models. However, in practice, there may be problems when calibrating a model to illiquid positions, and in such cases the resulting pricing framework may be unstable and provide the user with spurious results. Another issue is the relevance of using historical credit-transition data, which is used to project future credit-migration probabilities. In practice, it is worthwhile reviewing the sensitivity of price to the historical credit-transition data when using the model.

Recent models which provide a detailed modelling of default risk include those presented by Jarrow, Lando and Turnbull (1997), Das and Tufano (1996) and Duffie and Singleton (1995).We consider these models in this section.

The Jarrow, Lando and Turnbull (JLT) model

This model focuses on modelling default and credit migration. Its data and assumptions include the use of

- a statistical rating transition matrix which is based on historic data
- risky bond prices from the market used in the calibration process
- an assumption of a constant recovery rate. The recovery amount is assumed to be received at the maturity of the bond.
- a credit-spread assumption for each rating level.

It also assumes no correlation between interest rates and credit-rating migration.

The statistical transition matrix is adjusted by calibrating the expected risky-bond values to the market values for risky bonds. The adjusted matrix is referred to as the "risk-neutral transition matrix". This matrix is key to the pricing of several credit derivatives.

The JLT model allows the pricing of default swaps, as the risk-neutral transition matrix can be used to determine the probability of default. The JLT model is sensitive to the level of the recovery-rate assumption and the statistical rating matrix. It has a number of advantages; as the model is based on credit migration, it allows the pricing of derivatives for which the payout depends on such credit migration. In addition, the default probability can be explicitly determined and may be used in the pricing of credit-default swaps.

The disadvantages of the model include the fact that it depends on the selected historical-transition matrix. The applicability of this matrix to future periods needs to be considered carefully; whether, for example, it adequately describes future credit-migration patterns. In addition, it assumes all securities with the same credit rating have the same spread, which is restrictive. For this reason, the spread levels chosen in the model are a key assumption in the pricing model. Finally, the constant-recovery rate is another practical constraint as, in practice, the level of recovery will vary.

The Das-Tufano model

The Das Tufano (DT) model is an extension of the JLT model. The model aims to produce the risk-neutral transition matrix in a similar way to the JLT model; however, this model uses stochastic recovery rates. The final risk-neutral transition matrix should be computed from the observable term structures. The stochastic recovery rates introduce more variability in the spread volatility. Spreads are a function of factors which may not only be dependent on the rating level of the credit, as in practice credit spreads may change even though credit ratings have not changed. Therefore, to some extent, the DT model introduces this additional variability into the risk-neutral transition matrix.

Various credit derivatives may be priced using this model; for example, credit-default swaps, total-return swaps and credit-spread options. The pricing of these products requires the generation of the appropriate credit-dependent cash flows at each node on a lattice of possible outcomes. The fair value may be determined by discounting the probability-weighted cash flows. The probability of the outcomes would be determined by reference to the risk-neutral transition matrix.

The Duffie-Singleton model

The Duffie Singleton modelling approach considers the three components of risk for a credit-risky product; namely, the risk-free rate, the hazard rate and the recovery rate.

The hazard rate characterises the instantaneous probability of default of the credit-risky underlying exposure. As each of the components above may not be static over time, a pricing model may assume a process for each of these components of risk. The process may be implemented using a lattice approach for each component. The constraint on the lattice formation is that this lattice framework should agree to the market pricing of credit-risky debt.

Here we demonstrate that the credit spread is related to risk of default (as represented by the hazard rate) and the level of recovery of the bond. We assume a zero-coupon risky bond maturing in a small time element Δt where:

λ is the annualised hazard rate
φ is the recovery value
r is the risk-free rate
s is the credit spread

and where its price P is given by

$$P = e^{-\Delta t} ((1 - \lambda\Delta t) + (\lambda\Delta t)\varphi) \ . \tag{18.2}$$

Alternatively, P may be expressed as:

$$P \cong e^{-\Delta t(r+\lambda(1-\varphi))} \tag{18.3}$$

However, as the usual form for a risky zero-coupon bond is

$$P = e^{-\Delta t(r+s)} \tag{18.4}$$

Therefore, we have shown that:

$$s \cong \lambda(1 - \varphi) \tag{18.5}$$

This would imply that the credit spread is closely related to the hazard rate (that is, the likelihood of default) and the recovery rate.

This relationship between the credit spread, the hazard rate and recovery rate is intuitively appealing. The credit spread is perceived to be the extra yield (or return) the investor requires for credit risk assumed. For example:

- as the hazard rate (or instantaneous probability of default) rises, then the credit spread increases; and
- as the recovery rate decreases, the credit spread increases.

A "hazard-rate" function may be determined from the term structure of credit. The hazard-rate function has its foundation in statistics and may be linked to the instantaneous default probability.

The hazard-rate function ($\lambda(s)$) can then be used to derive a probability function for the survival function S(t):

$$S(t) = \exp^{-\int_0^t \lambda(s)ds} \qquad (18.6)$$

The hazard-rate function may be determined by using the prices of risky bonds. The lattice for the evolution of the hazard rate should be consistent with the hazard-rate function implied from market data. An issue when performing this calibration is the volume of relevant data available for the credit.

Recovery rates

The recovery rate usually takes the form of the percentage of the par value of the security recovered by the investor.

The key elements of the recovery rate include:

- The level of the recovery rate
- The uncertainty of the recovery rate based on current conditions specific to the reference credit
- The time interval between default and the recovery value being realised.

Generally, recovery rates are related to the seniority of the debt. Therefore, if the seniority of debt changes, then the recovery value of the debt may change. Also, recovery rates exhibit significant volatility.

Credit-spread modelling

Although spreads may be viewed as a function of default risk and recovery risk, spread models do not attempt to break down the spread into its default-risk and recovery-risk components.

The pricing of credit derivatives which pay out according to the level of the credit spread would require that the credit-spread process is adequately modeled. In order to achieve this, a stochastic process for the distribution of outcomes for the credit spread is an important consideration.

An example of the stochastic process for modelling credit spreads, which may be assumed, includes a mean-reverting process such as:

$$ds = k \ (\mu - s)dt + \sigma \ sdw \qquad (18.7)$$

where

ds is the change in the value of the spread over an element of time (dt)

dt is the element of time over which the change in spread is modeled

s is the credit spread

k is the rate of mean reversion

m   is the mean level of the spread

dw is Wiener increment (sometimes written dW, dZ or dz)

σ is the volatility of the credit spread.

In this model, when s rises above a mean level of the spread, the drift term $(\mu - s)$ will become negative and the spread process will drift towards (revert) to the mean level. The rate of this drift towards the mean is dependent on k the rate of mean reversion.

The pricing of a European spread option requires the distribution of the credit spread at the maturity (T) of the option. The choice of model affects the probability assigned to each outcome. The mean-reversion factor reflects the historic economic features over time of credit spreads to revert to the average spreads after larger-than-expected movements away from the average spread.

Therefore, the European option price may be reflected as:

$$\text{Option price} = E \ [e^{-rT} \ (\text{Payoff}(s,X)] = e^{-rT} \int_0^\infty f(s,X)p(s)ds \qquad (18.8)$$

where :

X is the strike price of the spread option;

$p(s)$ is the probability function of the credit spread

$E[\ ]$ denotes the expected value

$f(s,X)$ is the payoff function at maturity of the credit spread.

More complex models for the credit-spread process may take into account factors such as the term structure of credit and possible correlation between the spread process and the interest process.

The pricing of a spread option is dependent on the underlying process. As an example, we compare the pricing results for a spread-option model including mean reversion to the pricing results from a standard Black Scholes model in Table 18.1.

Expiry in 6 months Risk free rate = 10% Strike = 70bps Credit spread = 60bps Volatility = 20%	Mean-reversion model price	Standard Black Scholes price	% difference between standard Black Scholes and Mean-reversion model price
Mean level = 50bps K=.2			
Put	0.4696	0.5524	17.63%
Call	10.9355	9.7663	11.97%
Mean level = 50 bps K=.3			
Put	0.3510	0.5524	57.79%
Call	11.2031	9.7663	14.12%
Mean level = 80 bps K=.2			
Put	0.8729	0.5524	58.02%
Call	8.4907	9.7663	15.02%
Mean level = 80 bps K=.3			
Put	0.8887	0.5524	60.87%
Call	7.5411	9.7663	29.51%

Table 18.1

Expiry in 12 months Risk free rate = 10% Strike = 70bps Credit spread = 60bps Volatility = 20%	Mean-reversion model price	Standard Black Scholes price	% difference between standard Black Scholes and Mean-reversion model price
Mean level = 50bps K=.2			
Put	0.8501	1.4331	68.58%
Call	11.2952	10.4040	8.56%
Mean level = 50 bps K=.3			
Put	0.7624	1.4331	87.97%
Call	12.0504	10.4040	15.82%
Mean level = 80 bps K=.2			
Put	1.9876	1.4331	38.69%
Call	7.6776	10.4040	35.51%
Mean level = 80 bps K=.3			
Put	2.4198	1.4331	68.85%
Call	6.7290	10.4040	54.61%

Table 18.2

Tables 18.1 and 18.2 show the sensitivity on the pricing of a spread option to changes to the underlying process. Comparing the two tables shows the impact of time to expiry increasing by six months. In a mean-reversion model, the mean level and the rate of mean reversion are important parameters which may significantly affect the probability distribution of outcomes for the credit spread and, hence, the price.

Credit-default swaps

The pricing of a credit-default swap that has a payout on an underlying risky bond (issued by company ABC plc) involves the following key factors when pricing:

- risk-free interest-rate term structure
- risky term structure. Ideally we would determine this by considering the term of the bonds issued by company ABC. However, if a wide term is not available then the bonds of similar credit-risky companies may be used to create a more complete term structure of credit.
- the recovery rate.

For the risk-free interest-rate term structure, the observable money-market and swap curve may be best choice. However, a risk-free interest-rate term structure may also be built from government-bond prices.

The risky term structure and the recovery rate can be used to estimate the risk-neutral probability of default.

$$rs_{Risky} = rs_{Riskfree} *[((1 - p)*1) + (p * R)] \tag{18.9}$$

where:

rs_{Risky} is the risky zero-coupon rate (from the risky term structure)
$rs_{Riskfree}$ is the risk-free zero-coupon rate (from the risk-free term structure)
p is the risk-neutral default probability
R is the recovery rate.

The unknown p can be implied out of the equation (18.9):

$$p = [1/(1 - R)]*[1 - (rs_{risky} / rs_{riskfree})] \tag{18.10}$$

This equation shows that the probability of default is related the risky term structure, risk-free term structure and the recovery rate. In order to determine p, we will make assumptions for a suitable recovery value to be used in the above equation.

The expected value of a single period credit swap may take the form of the expected payout:

$$CDS_1 = rs_{Riskfree} *[(0*(1 - p)) + (p * (1 - R)] \tag{18.11}$$

This reflects the fact that there is no payout on survival of the credit; that is, in the event of no default.

Key issues in the pricing of credit-default swaps include:
- Determining an appropriate assumption for the recovery rate

- Selecting an appropriate risky debt required for calibration and the necessary adjustments to allow for liquidity and embedded options of the risky debt
- Selecting an appropriate risk-free curve
- Allowing for the credit risk of the counterparty and correlation of the underlying credit with the counterparty. We would expect that the cost of credit protection is cheaper if it is purchased from a "high" risk counterparty.

The level of sensitivity of the pricing of credit-default swaps (for example, a one-period credit-default swap pricing analysis) is examined in Table 18.3 below. The table compares the pricing of a default swap based on the inputs in the table. The discussion that follows compares the pricing outputs and attempts to identify sensitivities of the pricing to changes in the inputs.

	A	B	C	D
rs_{Risky}	0.95	0.949	0.95	0.95
$rs_{Riskfree}$	0.97	0.97	0.969	0.97
R	0.5	0.5	0.5	0.3
p	0.041237	0.043299	0.039216	0.029455
Credit-default swap (CDS) price	0.02	0.021	0.019	0.02

Table 18.3

The pricing analysis of the data in Table 18.3 follows.

(i) Credit-default swap price column A / column B = 0.02/0.021 = 0.952381
As a result of changing the risky zero-coupon price by approximately 0.1% (compare column A inputs to column B inputs), we have had a CDS price change of approximately 5%. Clearly, this shows the sensitivity of the CDS price to a change in the risky zero-coupon price. This emphasizes the risk in the estimates of the zero-coupon risky price and the impact of possible adjustments relating to illiquidity and embedded options.

(ii) Credit-default swap price column A / column C = 0.02/0.019 = 1.052632
As a result of changing the risk-free zero-coupon price by approximately 0.1% (compare column A to column C), we have had a CDS price change of approximately 5%. This shows the sensitivity of the CDS price to a

change in the risk-free zero-coupon price. However, given the technology and existing research into yield curves, this is perhaps a smaller risk than (i).

(iii) Credit-default swap price column A / column D = 0.02/0.02=1

The CDS pricing is relatively insensitive to the change in recovery price (column D's recovery is 0.3). However, we note that the risk-neutral default probability (p) is sensitive to the change in the recovery-price assumption. This shows that there is a compensating effect in the pricing of a CDS between the probability of default and the level of recovery. However, care should be taken if the default payoff is fixed (for example, a digital swap) as this compensating effect is removed.

Comparing cash and synthetic markets

The rapid growth of the credit-default swap has resulted in a liquid market in credit-default swaps across the credit curve. Figure 18.2 shows the growth in credit-default swap volumes during 1998–2003.

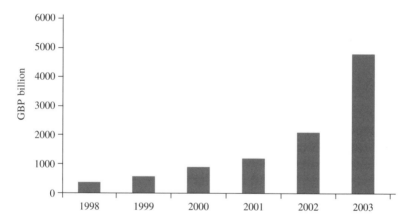

Figure 18.2 Credit-default swap volumes, British Bankers Survey

The liquidity of the credit-derivative market frequently exceeds that available for the same reference market in the cash market. It is this feature that has enabled fund managers to exploit their expertise in credit trading by originating synthetic CDO vehicles that enable them to arbitrage between cash and synthetic markets. These structures are considered in the next chapter. As well as greater liquidity, the synthetic market also offer other potential advantages to investors who would generally consider only the cash markets. These advantages are summarised in Table 18.4.

	Cash bonds	Credit Derivatives
Corporate (issuer) names available	Existing issuers only	Any name required
Liquidity	Variable liquidity	No limit to size of trade
Bid-offer spread	Greater below AAA names	Smaller
Maturity	Fixed dates	Any date required
Principal guaranteed	Rare	Available if reuqired
Coupon	Typcially fixed	Fixed or floating
Yield	Lower	Higher

Table 18.4 Comparing cash and derivatives markets for investors

The difference in pricing between the cash and synthetic markets has already been noted. Because credit derivatives isolate and trade credit as their sole asset, they will be priced at a different level from the asset swap on the same reference asset. This difference is known as the *basis*. The basis is:

$$\text{credit-default spread} - \text{the asset-swap spread}.$$

A positive basis occurs when the credit derivative trades higher than the asset-swap price, and is common. A negative basis describes when the credit derivative trades tighter than the cash-bond asset-swap spread. The factors leading to a positive basis include:

- the delivery option afforded to the protection buyer, when a basket of deliverable obligations is specified in physical settlement, which enables the delivery of the cheapest-to-deliver asset names.
- liquidity resulting in credit-default swaps being the most common means by which a reference name is shorted in the market
- a quoted spread that is always above Libor, despite the fact that AAA and some AA names are funded in the asset-swap market at sub-Libor
- the inability for credit-default swap spreads to be negative.

We illustrate the different trading levels by looking at two issuer names in the Euro-markets, Telefonica and FIAT. Figure 18.3 shows the yield-spread levels for a selection of US-dollar and euro bonds issued by Telefonica, as at November 2002. We note that the credit-default swap price is at levels comparable with the cheapest bond in the group, the 7.35% 2005 bond, issued in US dollars.

A similar picture emerges when looking at a group of FIAT bonds, also from November 2002, as shown at Figure 18.4. Note that the credit curve given by the credit-default swap prices inverts. This is because a year earlier FIAT had issued a very large size "exchangeable" bond that had a July 2004 put date. The basis, previously flat, widened to over 100 basis points due to market-makers hedging this bond with convertible bonds of the same name.

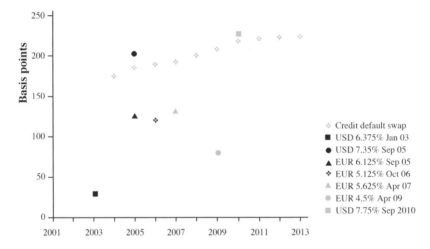

Figure 18.3 Telefonica bond-asset swap and credit-default swap spread levels, November 2002

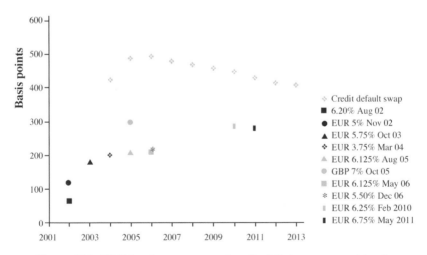

Figure 18.4 FIAT bond asset swap and credit default swap spread levels, November 2002

The basis will fluctuate in line with market sentiment on the particular credit. For instance, for a worsening credit the basis can become positive quite quickly. This is illustrated in Figure 18.5, which shows the widening in spread between the five-year credit-default swap levels with the similar-maturity May 2006 bond of the same name (in this case, British Airways plc). The impact of the deteriorating business outlook in the last quarter of 2001 is prevalent, with the improving situation also illustrated towards the end of the year.

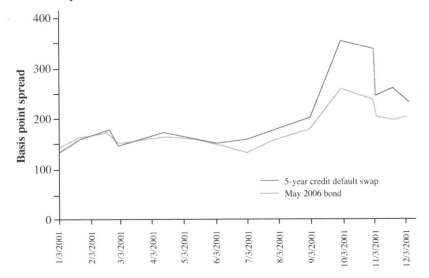

Figure 18.5 British Airways plc, credit-default swap versus bond-spread levels

If plotted graphically, the basis tends to exhibit a smile. This is illustrated in Figure 18.6. The reason for this is that highly rated reference names, such as AA or higher, fund in the asset-swap market at sub-Libor. However, if an entity is buying protection on such a name, it will pay above Libor premiums. The basis therefore tends to increase with better-quality names and results in the smile effect.

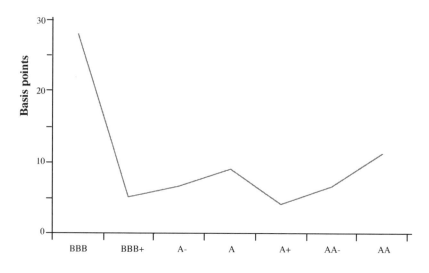

Figure 18.6 Basis smile

Options I

As a risk-management tool, options allow banks and corporates to hedge market exposure but also to gain from upside moves in the market. This makes them unique amongst hedging instruments. Options have special characteristics that make them stand apart from other classes of derivatives. As they confer a right to conduct a certain transaction, but without imposing an obligation to do so, their payoff profile is different from other financial assets, both cash and off-balance-sheet. This makes an option more of an insurance policy than a pure hedging instrument, as the person who has purchased the option for hedging purposes need only exercise it if required. The price of the option is, in effect, the insurance premium that has been paid for peace of mind. Of course, options are also used for purposes other than hedging. As part of speculative and arbitrage trading, and option marke-makers generate returns from managing the risk on their option books profitably. The range of combinations of options that can be dealt today, and the complex-structured products of which they form a part, is constrained only by imagination and customer requirements. Virtually all participants in capital markets will have some requirement that may be met by the use of options.

This chapter is a large one as we first introduce the basics of options and then consider the complex topic of option pricing. A subsequent chapter looks at the main sensitivity measures used in running an option book, and the uses to which options may be put. Key reference articles and publications are listed in the bibliography.

Introduction

An option is a contract in which the buyer has the right, but not the obligation, to buy or sell an underlying asset at a predetermined price during a specified period of time. The seller of the option, known as the writer, grants this right to the buyer in return for receiving the price of the option, known as the premium. An option that grants the right to buy an asset is a call option, while the corresponding right to sell an asset is a put option. The option buyer has a long position in the option and the option seller has a short position in the option.

Before looking at the other terms that define an option contract, we'll discuss the main feature that differentiates an option from all other derivative instruments, and from cash assets. Because options confer on a buyer the right to effect a transaction, but not the obligation (and correspondingly on a seller the obligation, if requested by the buyer, to effect a transaction), their risk/reward characteristics are different from other financial products. The payoff profile from holding an option is unlike that of any other instrument. Let us consider the payoff profiles for a vanilla call option and a gilt futures contract. Suppose that a trader buys one lot of the gilt futures contract at 114.00 and holds it for one month before selling it. On closing the position, the profit made will depend on the contract sale price. If it is above 114.00, the trader will have made a profit, and if below 114.00 she will have made a loss. On one lot, this represents a £1000 gain for each point above 114.00. The same applies to someone who had a short position in the contract and closed it out – if the contract is bought back at any price below 114.00 the trader will realise a profit. The profile is shown in Figure 19.1.

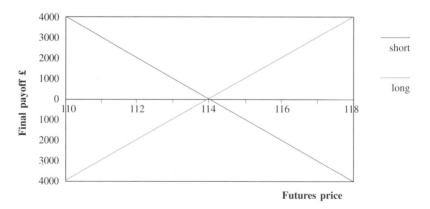

Figure 19.1 Payoff profile for a bond futures contract

This profile is the same for other derivative instruments such as FRAs and swaps, and, of course, for cash instruments such as bonds or equity. The payoff profile therefore has a linear characteristic, and it is linear whether one has bought or sold the contract.

The profile for an option contract differs from the conventional one. Because options confer a right but not an obligation to one party (the buyer), and an obligation but not a right to the seller, the profile will differ according to whether one is the buyer or seller. Supposing now that our trader buys a call option that grants the right to buy a gilt futures contract at a price of 114.00 at some point during the life of the option, her resulting payoff profile will be like that shown in Figure 19.2. If during the life of the option the price of the futures contract rises above 114.00, the trader will exercise her right to buy the future, under the terms of the option contract. This is known as exercising the option. If, on the other hand, the price of the future falls below 114.00, the trader will not exercise the option and, unless there is a reversal in price of the future, it will eventually expire worthless, on its maturity date. In this respect, it exactly like an equity or bond warrant. The seller of this particular option has a very different payout profile. If the price of the future rises above 114.00 and the option is exercised, the seller will bear the loss equal to the profit that the buyer is now benefiting from. The seller's payoff profile is also shown in Figure 19.2, as the dashed line. If the option is not exercised and expires, the trade will have generated premium income for the seller, which is revenue income that contributes to the P/L account.

This illustrates how unlike every other financial instrument this is. The holders of long and short positions in options do not have the same symmetrical payoff profile. The buyer of the call option will benefit if the price of the underlying asset rises, but will not lose if the price falls (except the funds paid for purchasing the rights under the option). The seller of the call option will suffer loss if the price of the underlying asset rises, but will not benefit if it falls (except realising the funds received for writing the option). The buyer has a right but not an obligation, while the seller has an obligation if the option is exercised. The premium charged for the option is the seller's compensation for granting such a right to the buyer.

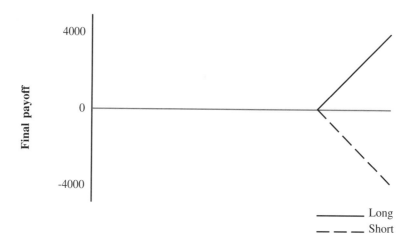

Figure 19.2 Payoff profile for call-option contract

Let us recap on the basic features of the call option. A call option is the right to buy, without any obligation, a specified quantity of the underlying asset at a given price on or before the expiry date of the option. A long position in a call option allows the holder, as shown in Figure 19.2, to benefit from a rise in the market price of the underlying asset. If our trader wanted to benefit from a fall in the market level, but did not want to short the market, she would buy a put option. A put option is the right to sell, again without any obligation, a specified quantity of the underlying asset at a given price on or before the expiry date of the option. Put options have the same payoff profile as call options, but in the opposite direction. Remember also that the payoff profile is different for the buyer and seller of an option. The buyer of a call option will profit if the market price of the underlying asset rises, but will not lose if the price falls (at least, not with regard to the option position). The writer of the option will not profit whatever direction the market moves in, and will lose if the market rises. The compensation for taking on this risk is the premium paid for writing the option, which is why we likened options to insurance policies at the start of the chapter.

Originally, options were written on commodities such as wheat and sugar. Nowadays, these are referred to as options on physicals, while options on financial assets are known as financial options. Today, one can buy or sell an option on a wide range of underlying instruments, including financial products such as foreign exchange, bonds, equities, and commodities, and derivatives such as futures, swaps, equity indices and other options.

Option terminology

Let us now consider the basic terminology used in the options markets.

A call option grants the buyer the right to buy the underlying asset, while a put option grants the buyer the right to sell the underlying asset. There are, therefore, four possible positions that an option trader may put on; long a call or put; and short a call or put. The payoff profiles for each type are shown at Figure 19.3.

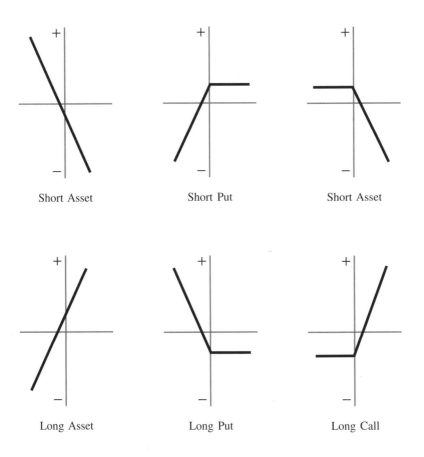

<table>
<tr><td>Short Asset</td><td>Short Put</td><td>Short Asset</td></tr>
<tr><td>Long Asset</td><td>Long Put</td><td>Long Call</td></tr>
</table>

Figure 19.3 Basic option payoff profiles

The strike price describes the price at which an option is exercised. For example, a call option to buy ordinary shares of a listed company might have a strike price of £10.00. This means that if the option is exercised, the buyer will pay £10 per share. Options are generally either American- or European-style, which defines the times during the option's life when it can be exercised. There is no geographic relevance to these terms, as both styles trade can be traded in any market. There is also another type, Bermudan-style options, which can be exercised at pre-set dates.[1] For reasons that we shall discuss later, it very rare for an American option to be exercised ahead of its expiry date, so this distinction has little impact in practice, although of course the pricing model being used to value European options must be modified to handle American options. The holder of a European option cannot exercise it prior to expiry. However, if she wishes to realise its value, she will sell it in the market.

The premium of an option is the price at which the option is sold. Option premium is made up of two constituents, intrinsic value and time value.

The intrinsic value of an option is the value of the option if it is exercised immediately, and it represents the difference between the strike price and the current underlying asset price. If a call option on a bond futures contract has a strike price of 100.00 and the future is currently trading at 105.00, the intrinsic value of the option is 5.00, as this would be the immediate profit gain to the option holder if it were exercised. Since an option will only be exercised if there is benefit to the holder from so doing, its intrinsic value will never be less than zero. So, in our example, if the bond future was trading at 95.00, the intrinsic value of the call option would be zero, not −5.00. For a put option, the intrinsic value is the amount by which the current underlying price is below the strike price. When an option has intrinsic value, it is described as being *in-the-money*. When the strike price for a call option is higher than the underlying price (or for a put option is lower than the underlying price) and has no intrinsic value it is said to be *out-of-the-money*. An option for which the strike price is equal to the current underlying price is said to be *at-the-money*. This term is normally used at the time the option is first traded, in cases where the strike price is set to the current price of the underlying asset.

The time value of an option is the amount by which the option value exceeds the intrinsic value. An option writer will almost always demand a

---

[1] I'm told because Bermuda is mid-way between Europe and America. A colleague also informs me that it's "Asian" for average-rate options because these originated in Japanese commodity markets.

premium that is higher than the option's intrinsic value, because of the risk that the writer is taking on. This reflects the fact that over time the price of the underlying asset may change sufficiently to produce a much higher intrinsic value. During the life of an option, the option writer has nothing more to gain over the initial premium at which the option was sold. However, until expiry there is a chance that the writer will lose if the markets move against her, hence the inclusion of a time-value element. The value of an option that is out-of-the-money is composed entirely of time value.

Table 19.1 summarises the main option terminology that we have just been discussing.

Call	The right to buy the underlying asset
Put	The right to sell the underlying asset
Buyer	The person who has purchased the option and has the right to exercise it if she wishes
Writer	The person who has sold the option and has the obligation to perform if the option is exercised
Strike Price	The price at which the option may be exercised, also known as the *exercise price*
Expiry date	The last date on which the option can be exercised, also known as the maturity date
American	The style of option; an American option can be exercised at any time up to the expiry date
European	An option which may be exercised on the maturity date only, and not before
Premium	The price of the option, paid by the buyer to the seller
Intrinsic value	The value of the option if was exercised today, which is the difference between the strike price and the underlying asset price
Time value	The difference between the current price of the option and its intrinsic value
In-the-money	The term for an option that has intrinsic value
At-the-money	An option for which the strike price is identical to the underlying asset price
Out-of-the-money	An option that has no intrinsic value

Table 19.1 Basic option terminology

Option instruments

Options are traded both on recognized exchanges and in the over-the-counter (OTC) market. The primary difference between the two types is that exchange-traded options are standardised contracts and essentially plain-vanilla instruments, while OTC options can take on virtually any shape or form. Options traded on an exchange are often options on a futures contract; so, for example, gilt option on LIFFE in London is written on the exchange's gilt futures contract. The exercise of a futures options will result in a long position in a futures contract being assigned to the party that is long the option, and a short position in the future to the party that is short the option. Note that exchange-traded options on US Treasuries are quoted in option ticks that are half the bond tick; that is, $1/64^{th}$ rather than $1/32^{nd}$. The same applied to gilt options on LIFFE until gilts themselves switched to decimal pricing at the end of 1998.

Like OTC options, those traded on an exchange can be either American- or European-style. For example, on the Philadelphia Currency Options Exchange both versions are available, although on LIFFE most options are American-style. Exchange-traded options are available on the following:

- ordinary shares: these are traded on major exchanges including the New York Stock Exchange, LIFFE, Eurex, the Chicago Board Options Exchange (CBOE), and SIMEX (in Singapore trade options on corporation ordinary shares).
- options on futures: most exchanges trade an option contract written on the futures that are traded on the exchange, which expires one or two days before the futures contract itself expires. In certain cases such those traded on the Philadelphia exchange, cash settlement is available so that if, for example, the holder of a call exercises, she will be assigned a long position in the future as well as the cash value of the difference between the strike price and the futures price. One of the most heavily traded exchange-traded options contracts is the Treasury bond option, written on the futures contract, traded on the Chicago Board of Trade options exchange.
- stock index options: these are equity-market instruments that are popular for speculating and hedging; for example, the FTSE-100 option on LIFFE and the S&P500 on CBOE. Settlement is in cash and not the shares that constitute the underlying index, much like the settlement of an index futures contract.
- bond options: options on bonds are invariably written on the bond futures contract; for example, the aforementioned Treasury bond

option or LIFFE's gilt option. Options written on the cash bond must be traded in the OTC market.

- interest-rate options: these are also options on futures, as they are written on the exchange's 90-day interest-rate futures contract.
- foreign-currency options: these are rarer among exchange-traded options, and the major exchange is in Philadelphia. Its sterling option contract, for example, is for an underlying amount of £31,250 .

Option trading on an exchange is similar to that for futures, and involves transfer of margin on a daily basis. Individual exchanges have their own procedures; for example, on LIFFE the option premium is effectively paid via the variation margin. The amount of variation margin paid or received on a daily basis for each position reflects the change in the price of the option. So if, for example, an option were to expire on maturity with no intrinsic value, the variation-margin payments made during its life would be equal to the change in value from the day it was traded to zero. The option trader does not pay a separate premium on the day the position is put on. On certain other exchanges, though, it is the other way around, and the option buyer will pay a premium on the day of purchase but then pay no variation margin. Some exchanges allow traders to select either method. Margin is compulsory for a party that writes options on the exchange.

The other option market is the OTC market, where there is a great variety of instruments traded. As with products such as swaps, the significant advantage of OTC options is that they can be tailored to meet the specific requirements of the buyer. Hence, they are ideally suited as risk-management instruments for corporate and financial institutions, because they can be used to structure hedges that match perfectly the risk exposure of the buying party. Some of the more ingenious structures are described in a later chapter on exotic options.

Option pricing: Setting the scene

The price of an option is a function of six different factors, which are:
- the strike price of the option
- the current price of the underlying
- the time to expiry
- the risk-free rate of interest that applies to the life of the option
- the volatility of the underlying asset's price returns
- the value of any dividends or cash flows paid by the underlying asset during the life of the option.

We review the basic parameters next.

Pricing inputs

Let us consider the parameters of option pricing. Possibly the two most important are the current price of the underlying and the strike price of the option. The intrinsic value of a call option is the amount by which the strike price is below the price of the underlying, as this is the payoff if the option is exercised. Therefore, the value of the call option will increase as the price of the underlying increases, and will fall as the underlying price falls. The value of a call will also decrease as the strike price increases. All this is reversed for a put option.

Generally, for bond options a higher time to maturity results in higher option value. All other parameters being equal, a longer-dated option will always be worth at least as much as one that had a shorter life. Intuitively we would expect this because the holder of a longer-dated option has the same benefits as someone holding a shorter-dated option, in addition to a longer time period in which the intrinsic value may increase. This rule is always true for American options, and usually true for European options. However, certain factors, such as the payment of a coupon during the option life, may cause a longer-dated option to have only a slightly higher value than a shorter-dated option.

The risk-free interest-rate is the rate applicable to the period of the option's life. So for our table of gilt options in the previous section, the option value reflected the three-month rate. The most common rate used is the T-bill rate, although for bond options it is more common to see the government-bond repo rate being used. A rise in interest rates will increase the value of a call option, although not always for bond options. A rise in rates lowers the price of a bond, because it decreases the present value of future cash flows. However, in the equity markets it is viewed as a sign that share price growth rates will increase. Generally, however, the relationship is the same for bond options as equity options. The effect of a rise in interest rates for put options is the reverse: they cause the value to drop.

A coupon payment made by the underlying during the life of the option will reduce the price of the underlying asset on the ex-dividend date. This will result in a fall in the price of a call option and a rise in the price of a put option.

Bounds in option pricing

The upper and lower limits on the price of an option are relatively straightforward to set because prices must follow the rule of no-arbitrage pricing. A call option grants the buyer the right to buy a specified quantity of the underlying asset, at the level of the strike price; so, therefore, it is clear that the option could not have a higher value than the underlying asset itself. Therefore, the upper limit or bound to the price of a call option is the price of the underlying asset. Therefore:

$$C \leq S$$

where C is the price of a call option and S is the current price of the underlying asset. A put option grants the buyer the right to sell a specified unit of the underlying at the strike price X. Therefore, the option can never have a value greater than the strike price X. So we may set:

$$P \leq X$$

where P is the price of the put option. This rule will still apply for a European put option on its expiry date. So, therefore, we may further set that the option cannot have a value greater than the present value of the strike price X on expiry. That is,

$$P \leq Xe^{-rT}$$

where r is the risk-free interest for the term of the option life and T is the maturity of the option in years.

The minimum limit or bound for an option is set according to whether the underlying asset is a dividend-paying security or not. For a call option written on a non-dividend paying security, the lower bound is given by:

$$C \geq S - Xe^{-rT}.$$

In fact as we noted early in this chapter, a call option can only ever expire worthless, so its intrinsic value can never be worth less than zero. Therefore $C > 0$ and we then set the following:

$$C \geq \max[S - Xe^{-rT}, 0] .$$

This reflects the law of no-arbitrage pricing. For put options on a non-dividend paying stock, the lower limit is given by:

$$P \geq Xe^{-rT} - S$$

and again the value is never less than zero. So we may set:

$$P \geq \max[Xe^{-rT} - S, 0] \ .$$

As we noted above, payment of a dividend by the underlying asset affects the price of the option. In the case of dividend paying stocks, the upper and lower bounds for options are as follows:

$$C \geq S - D - Xe^{rt}$$

and

$$P \geq D + Xe^{-rt} - S$$

where D is the present value of the dividend payment made by the underlying asset during the life of the option.

We can now look at option pricing and the Black-Scholes model.

Option pricing

Interest-rate products described in this book so far, both cash and derivatives, can be priced using rigid mathematical principles, because on maturity of the instrument there is a defined procedure that takes place such that one is able to calculate a fair value. This does not apply to options because there is uncertainty as to what the outcome will be on expiry; an option seller does not know whether the option will be exercised or not. This factor makes options more difficult to price than other financial-market instruments. In this section we review the parameters used in the pricing of an option, and introduce the Black-Scholes pricing model.

Pricing an option is a function of the probability that it will be exercised. Essentially, the premium paid for an option represents the buyer's expected profit on the option. Therefore, as with an insurance premium, the writer of an option will base his price on the assessment that the payout on the option will be equal to the premium, and this is a function on the probability that the option will be exercised. Option pricing, therefore, bases its calculation on the assessment of the probability of exercise and derives from this an expected outcome and, hence, a fair value for the option premium. The expected payout, as with an insurance company premium, should equal the premium received.

The following factors influence the price of an option.

- **the behaviour of financial prices:** one of the key assumptions made by the Black-Scholes model (B-S) is that asset prices follow a lognormal distribution. Although this is not strictly accurate, it is close enough of an approximation to allow its use in option pricing. In fact, observation shows that while prices themselves are not normally distributed, asset returns are, and we define returns as $\ln(\frac{P_{t+1}}{P_t})$ where P_t is the market price at time t and P_{t+1} is the price one period later. The distribution of prices is called a lognormal distribution because the logarithm of the prices is normally distributed. The asset returns are defined as the logarithm of the price relatives and are assumed to follow the normal distribution. The expected return as a result of assuming this distribution is given by $E\left[\ln\left(\frac{P_t}{P_0}\right)\right] = rt$ where $E[\ ]$ is the expectation operator and r is the annual rate of return. The derivation of this expression is given at Appendix 19.2.

- **the strike price:** the difference between the strike price and the underlying price of the asset at the time the option is struck will influence the size of the premium, as this will have an impact on the probability that the option will be exercised. An option that is deeply in-the-money has a greater probability of being exercised.

- **volatility:** the volatility of the underlying asset will influence the probability that an option is exercised, as a higher volatility indicates a higher probability of exercise. This is considered in detail below.

- **the term to maturity:** a longer-dated option has greater time value and a greater probability of eventually being exercised.

- **the level of interest rates:** the premium paid for an option in theory represents the expected gain to the buyer at the time the option is exercised. It is paid up-front so it is discounted to obtain a present value. The discount rate used, therefore, has an effect on the premium, although it is less influential than the other factors presented here.

The volatility of an asset measures the variability of its price returns. It is defined as the annualised standard deviation of returns, where variability refers to the variability of the returns that generate the asset's prices, rather than the prices directly. The standard deviation of returns is given by (19.1).

$$\sigma = \sqrt{\sum_{i=1}^{N} \frac{(x - \mu)^2}{N - 1}} \qquad (19.1)$$

where x_i is the i'th price relative, μ the arithmetic mean of the observations and N is the total number of observations. The value is converted to an annualised figure by multiplying it by the square root of the number of days in a year, usually taken to be 250 working days. Using this formula from market observations it is possible to calculate the *historic volatility* of an asset. The volatility of an asset is one of the inputs to the B-S model. Of the inputs to the B-S model, the variability of the underlying asset, or its volatility is the most problematic. The distribution of asset prices is assumed to follow a lognormal distribution, because the logarithm of the prices is normally distributed (we assume lognormal rather than normal distribution to allow for the fact that prices cannot – as could be the case in a normal distribution – have negative values). The range of possible prices starts at zero and cannot assume a negative value.

Note that it is the asset price *returns* on which the standard deviation is calculated, and the not the actual prices themselves. This is because using prices would produce inconsistent results, as the actual standard deviation itself would change as price levels increased.

However, calculating volatility using the standard statistical method gives us a figure for historic volatility. What is required is a figure for *future* volatility, since this is relevant for pricing an option expiring in the future. Future volatility cannot be measured directly, by definition. Market-makers get around this by using an option-pricing model "backwards". An option-pricing model calculates the option price from volatility and other parameters. Used in reverse, the model can calculate the volatility implied by the option price. Volatility measured in this way is called implied volatility. Evaluating implied volatility is straightforward using this method and generally more appropriate than using historic volatility, as it provides a clearer measure of an option's fair value. Implied volatilities of deeply in-the-money or out-of-the-money options tend to be relatively high.

The Black-Scholes option model

Most option-pricing models are based on one of two methodologies, although both types employ essentially identical assumptions. The first method is based on the resolution of the partial differentiation equation of the asset-price model, corresponding to the expected payoff of the option security. This is the foundation of the Black-Scholes model. The second type of model uses the martingale method, and was first introduced by Harrison and Kreps (1979) and Harrison and Pliska (1981), where the price of an asset at time 0 is given by its discounted expected future payoffs, under the appropriate probability measure, known as the risk-neutral probability. There is a third type that assumes lognormal distribution of asset returns but follows the two-step binomial process.

In order to employ the pricing models, we accept a state of the market that is known as a *complete market*,[2] one where there is a viable financial market. This is where the rule of no-arbitrage pricing exists, so that there is no opportunity to generate risk-free arbitrage due to the presence of, say, incorrect forward interest rates. The fact that there is no opportunity to generate risk-free arbitrage gains means that a zero-cost investment strategy that is initiated at time t will have a zero maturity value. The martingale property of the behavior of asset prices states that an accurate estimate of the future price of an asset may be obtained from current price information. Therefore, the relevant information used to calculate forward asset prices is the latest price information. This was also a property of the semi-strong and strong-form market-efficiency scenarios described by Fama (1970).

In this section, we describe the Black-Scholes option model in accessible fashion. More technical treatments are given in the relevant references listed in the bibliography.

Assumptions

The Black-Scholes model describes a process to calculate the fair value of a European call option under certain assumptions, and apart from the price of the underlying asset S and the time t, all the variables in the model are assumed to be constant, including – most crucially – the volatility. The following assumptions are made:

- there are no transaction costs, and the market allows short selling
- trading is continuous

---

[2] First proposed by Arrow and Debreu (1953, 1954).

- underlying asset prices follow geometric Brownian motion, with the variance rate proportional to the square root of the asset price
- the asset is a non-dividend-paying security
- the interest rate during the life of the option is known and constant
- the option can only be exercised on expiry.

The B-S model is neat and intuitively straightforward to explain, and one of its many attractions is that it can be readily modified to handle other types of options such as foreign-exchange or interest-rate options. The assumption of the behavior of the underlying asset price over time is described by (19.2), which is a generalised Weiner process, and where a is the expected return on the underlying asset and b is the standard deviation of its price returns.

$$\frac{\mathrm{d}S}{S} = a\mathrm{d}t + b\mathrm{d}W \tag{19.2}$$

The Black–Scholes model and pricing derivative instruments

We assume a financial asset is specified by its terminal payoff value. Therefore, when pricing an option we require the fair value of the option at the initial time when the option is struck, and this value is a function of the expected terminal payoff of the option, discounted to the day when the option is struck. In this section, we present an intuitive explanation of the B-S model, in terms of the normal distribution of asset-price returns.

From the definition of a call option, we can set the expected value of the option at maturity T as:

$$E(C_T) = E[\max(S_T - X, 0)] \tag{19.3}$$

where

S_T is the price of the underlying asset at maturity T
X is the strike price of the option.

From (19.3) we know that there are only two possible outcomes that can arise on maturity; either the option will expire in-the-money and the outcome is $S_T - X$, or the option will be out-of-the-money and the outcome will be 0. If we set the term p as the probability that on expiry $S_T > X$, equation (19.3) can be re-written as (19.4).

$$E(C_T) = p \times (E[S_T \mid S_T > X] - X) \tag{19.4}$$

where $E[S_T \mid S_T > X]$ is the expected value of S_T given that $S_T > X$. Equation (19.4) gives us an expression for the expected value of a call option on maturity. Therefore, to obtain the fair price of the option at the time it is struck, the value given by (19.4) must be discounted back to its present value, and this is shown as (19.5).

$$C = p \times e^{-rt} \times (E[S_T \mid S_T > X] - X) \qquad (19.5)$$

where r is the continuously compounded risk-free rate of interest, and t is the time from today until maturity. Therefore, to price an option we require the probability p that the option expires in-the-money, and we require the expected value of the option given that it does expire in-the-money, which is the last term of (19.5). To calculate p we assume that asset prices follow a stochastic process, which enables us to model the probability function.

The B-S model is based on the resolution of the following partial differential equation,

$$\tfrac{1}{2}\sigma^2 S^2 \left(\frac{\partial^2 C}{\partial S^2}\right) + rS\left(\frac{\partial C}{\partial S}\right) + \left(\frac{\partial C}{\partial t}\right) - rC = 0 \;, \qquad (19.6)$$

under the appropriate parameters. We do not demonstrate the process by which this equation is arrived at. The parameters refer to the payoff conditions corresponding to a European call option, which we considered above. We do not present a solution to the differential equation at (19.6), which is beyond the scope of the book, but we can consider now how the probability and expected-value functions can be solved. For a fuller treatment, readers may wish to refer to the original account by Black and Scholes. Other good accounts are given in Ingersoll (1987), Neftci (1996) and Nielsen (1999), among others.

We wish to find the probability p that the underlying asset price at maturity exceeds X is equal to the probability that the return over the time period the option is held exceeds a certain critical value. Remember that we assume normal distribution of asset-price returns. As asset returns are defined as the logarithm of price relatives, we require p such that:

$$p = prob[S_T > X] = prob\left[return > \ln\!\left(\frac{X}{S_0}\right)\right] \qquad (19.7)$$

where S_0 is the price of the underlying asset at the time the option is struck. Generally, the probability that a normally distributed variable x will exceed a critical value x_c is given by (19.8).

$$p[x > x_c] = 1 - N\!\left(\frac{x_c - \mu}{\sigma}\right) \tag{19.8}$$

where μ and σ are the mean and standard deviation of x respectively and $N(\ )$ is the cumulative normal distribution. We know from our earlier discussion of the behavior of asset prices that an expression for μ is the natural logarithm of the asset-price returns. We already know that the standard deviation of returns is $\sigma\sqrt{t}$. Therefore, with these assumptions, we may combine (19.7) and (19.8) to give us (19.9), that is,

$$p = prob[S_T > X] = prob\!\left[return > \ln\!\left(\frac{X}{S_0}\right)\right] = 1 - N\!\left[\frac{\ln\!\left(\frac{X}{S_0}\right) - \left(\frac{r - \sigma^2}{2}\right)t}{\sigma\sqrt{t}}\right] \tag{19.9}$$

Under the conditions of the normal distribution, the symmetrical shape means that we can obtain the probability of an occurrence based on $1 - N(d)$ being equal to $N(-d)$. Therefore, we are able to set the following relationship, at (19.10).

$$p = prob[S_T > X] = N\!\left[\frac{\ln\!\left(\frac{S_0}{X}\right) + \left(r - \frac{\sigma^2}{2}\right)t}{\sigma\sqrt{t}}\right] \tag{19.10}$$

Now we require a formula to calculate the expected value of the option on expiry, the second part of the expression at (19.5). This involves the integration of the normal distribution curve over the range from X to infinity. This is not shown here, but the result is given at (19.11).

$$E[S_T \mid S_T > X] = S_0 e^{rt}\frac{N(d_1)}{N(d_2)} \tag{19.11}$$

where

$$d_1 = \frac{\ln\!\left(\frac{S_0}{X}\right) + \left(r + \frac{\sigma^2}{2}\right)t}{\sigma\sqrt{t}}$$

and

$$d_2 = \frac{\ln\!\left(\frac{S_0}{X}\right) + \left(r - \frac{\sigma^2}{2}\right)t}{\sigma\sqrt{t}} = d_1 - \sigma\sqrt{t}$$

We now have expressions for the probability that an option expires in-the-money as well as the expected value of the option on expiry, and we incorporate these into the expression at (19.5), which gives us (19.12).

$$C = N(d_2) \times e^{-rt} \times \left[S_0 e^{-rt}\frac{N(d_1)}{N(d_2)} - X\right] \tag{19.12}$$

Equation (19.12) can be re-arranged to give (19.13), which is the famous and well-known Black-Scholes option-pricing model for a European call option.

$$C = S_0 N(d_1) - Xe^{-rt}N(d_2) \qquad (19.13)$$

where
S_0 is the price of the underlying asset at the time the option is struck
X is the strike price
r is the continuously compounded risk-free interest rate
t is the maturity of the option.

and d_1 and d_2 are as before.

What the expression at (19.13) states is that the fair value of a call option is the expected present value of the option on its expiry date, assuming that prices follow a lognormal distribution.

$N(d_1)$ and $N(d_2)$ are the cumulative probabilities from the normal distribution of obtaining the values d_1 and d_2, given above. $N(d_1)$ is the delta of the option. The term $N(d_2)$ represents the probability that the option will be exercised. The term e^{-rt} is the present value of one unit of cash received t periods from the time the option is struck. Where $N(d_1)$ and $N(d_2)$ are equal to 1, which is the equivalent of assuming complete certainty, the model is reduced to:

$$C = S - Xe^{-rt}$$

which is the expression for Merton's lower bound for continuously compounded interest rates, and which we introduced in intuitive fashion in the previous chapter. Therefore, under complete certainty, the B-S model reduces to Merton's bound.

The put-call parity relationship

Up to now we have concentrated on calculating the price of a call option. However, the previous section introduced the boundary condition for a put option, so it should be apparent that this can be solved as well. In fact, the price of a call option and a put option are related via what is known as the put-call parity theorem. This is an important relationship and obviates the need to develop a separate model for put options.

Consider a portfolio Y that consists of a call option with a maturity date T and a zero-coupon bond that pays X on the expiry date of the option. Consider also a second portfolio Z that consists of a put option also with maturity date T and one share. The value of portfolio A on the expiry date is given by (19.14),

$$MV_{Y,T} = \max[S_T - X,0] + X = \max[X,S_T] \qquad (19.14)$$

The value of the second portfolio Z on the expiry date is:

$$MV_{Z,T} = \max[X - S_T,0] + S_T = \max[X,S_T] \qquad (19.15)$$

Both portfolios have the same value at maturity. Therefore, they must also have the same initial value at start time t, otherwise there would be an arbitrage opportunity. Prices must be arbitrage-free; therefore, the following put-call relationship must hold:

$$C_t - P_t = S_t - Xe^{-r(T-t)} \qquad (19.16)$$

If the relationship at (19.15) did not hold, then arbitrage would be possible. So, using this relationship, the value of a European put option is given by the B-S model as shown below, at (19.17).

$$P(S,T) = -SN(-d_1) + Xe^{-rT}N(-d2) \qquad (19.17)$$

EXAMPLE 19.1 The Black–Scholes model

Here, we illustrate a simple applications of the B-S model. Consider an underlying asset, assumed to be a non-dividend-paying equity, with a current price of 25, and volatility of 23%. The short-term risk-free interest rate is 5%. An option is written with strike price 21 and a maturity of three months. Therefore, we have:

$S = 25$
$X = 21$
$r = 5\%$
$T = 0.25$
$\sigma = 23\%$

To calculate the price of the option, we first calculate the discounted value of the strike price, as follows:

$$Xe^{-rT} = 21e^{-0.05(0.25)} = 20.73913.$$

We then calculate the values of d_1 and d_2.

$$d_1 = \frac{\ln(25 / 21) + [0.05 + (0.5)(0.23)^2]0.25}{0.23 \sqrt{0.25}} = \frac{0.193466}{0.115}$$

$$= 1.682313$$

$$d_2 = d_1 - 0.23 \sqrt{0.25} = 1.567313$$

We now insert these values into the main price equation,
$C = 25N(1.682313) - 21e^{-0.05(0.25)}N(1.567313).$

Using the approximation of the cumulative normal distribution at the points 1.68 and 1.56, the price of the call option is:

$$C = 25(0.9535) - 20.73913(0.9406) = 4.3303$$

or 4.3303.

What would be the price of a put option on the same stock?
The values of $N(d_1)$ and $N(d_2)$ are 0.9535 and 0.9406; therefore, the put price is calculated as:

$$P = 20.7391(1 - 0.9406) - 25(1 - 0.9535) = 0.06943$$

If we use the call price and apply the put-call parity theorem, the price of the put option is given by:

$$P = C - S + Xe^{-rT}$$

$$= 4.3303 - 25 + 21e^{-0.05(0.25)}$$

$$= 0.069434$$

This is exactly the same price that was obtained by the application of the put-option formula in the B-S model above.

As we noted early in this chapter, the premium payable for an option will increase if the time to expiry, the volatility or the interest rate is increased (or any combination is increased). Thus, if we keep all the parameters constant but price a call option that has a maturity of six months or $T = 0.5$, we obtain the following values:

$$d_1 = 1.3071, \text{ giving } N(d_1) = 0.9049$$

$$d_2 = 1.1445, \text{ giving } N(d_2) = 0.8740$$

The call price for the longer-dated option is 4.7217.

The Black-Scholes model as an Excel spreadsheet

In Appendix 19.3, we show the spreadsheet formulae required to build the Black-Scholes model into Microsoft® Excel. The user must ensure that the Analysis Tool-Pak add-in is available, otherwise some of the function references may not work. By setting up the cells in the way shown, the fair value of a vanilla call or put option may be calculated. The put-call parity is used to enable calculation of the put price.

Black-Scholes and the valuation of bond options

In this section, we illustrate the application of the B-S model to the pricing of an option on a zero-coupon bond and a plain-vanilla fixed-coupon bond.

For a zero-coupon bond the theoretical price of a call option written on the bond is given by (19.18).

$$C = PN(d_1) - Xe^{-rT}N(d_2) \tag{19.18}$$

where P is the price of the underlying bond and all other parameters remain the same. If the option is written on a coupon-paying bond, it is necessary to subtract the present value of all coupons paid during the life of the option from the bond's price. Coupons sometimes lower the price of a call option because a coupon makes it more attractive to hold a bond rather than an option on the bond. Call options on bonds are often priced at a lower level than similar options on zero-coupon bonds.

EXAMPLE 19.2 B–S model and bond-option pricing

Consider a European call option written on a bond that has the following characteristics:

Price	£98
Coupon	8.00% (semi-annual)
Time to maturity	Five years
Bond price volatility	6.02%
Coupon payments	£4 in three months and nine months
Three-month interest rate	5.60%
Nine-month interest rate	5.75%
One-year interest rate	6.25%

The option is written with a strike price of £100 and has a maturity of one year. The present value of the coupon payments made during the life of the option is £7.78, as shown below.

$$4e^{-0.056 \times 0.25} + 4e^{-0.057 \times 0.25} = 3.9444 + 3.83117 = 7.77557$$

This gives us $P = 98 - 7.78 = £90.22$

Applying the B–S model we obtain:

$$d_1 = [\ln(90.22/100) + 0.0625 + 0.001812] / 0.0602 = -0.6413$$

$$d_2 = d_1 - (0.0602 \times 1) = -0.7015$$

$$C = 90.22N(-0.6413) - 100e^{-0.0625}N(-0.7015)$$
$$= 1.1514$$

Therefore, the call option has a value of £1.15, which will be composed entirely of time value. Note also that a key assumption of the model is constant interest rates, yet it is being applied to a bond price – which is essentially an interest rate – that is considered to follow a stochastic price process.

Interest-rate options and the Black model

In 1976, Fisher Black presented a slightly modified version of the B-S model, using similar assumptions, to be used in pricing forward contracts and interest-rate options. The Black model is used in banks today to price instruments such as swaptions, in addition to bond and interest-rate options like caps and floors.

In this model, the spot price $S(t)$ of an asset or a commodity is the price payable for immediate delivery today (in practice, up to two days forward) at time t. This price is assumed to follow a geometric Brownian motion. The theoretical price for a futures contract on the asset, $F(t,T)$, is defined as the price agreed today for delivery of the asset at time T, with the price agreed today but payable on delivery. When $t = T$, the futures price is equal to the spot price. A futures contract is cash-settled every day via the clearing mechanism, whereas a forward contract is a contract to buy or sell the asset where there is no daily mark-to-market and no daily cash settlement.

Let us set f as the value of a forward contract, u as the value of a futures contract and C as the value of an option contract. Each of these contracts is a function of the futures price $F(t,T)$, as well as additional variables. So we may write at time t the values of all three contracts as $f(F,t)$, $u(F,t)$ and $C(F,t)$. The value of the forward contract is also a function of the price of the underlying asset S at time T and can be written $f(F,t,S,T)$. Note that the value of the forward contract f is not the same as the price of the forward contract. The forward price at any given time is the delivery price that would result in the contract having a zero value. At the time the contract is transacted, the forward value is zero. Over time, both the price and the value will fluctuate. The futures price, on the other hand, is the price at which a forward contract has a zero current value. Therefore, at the time of the trade the forward price is equal to the futures price F, which may be written as:

$$f(F,tF,T) = 0 . \tag{19.19}$$

Equation (19.19) simply states that the value of the forward contract is zero when the contract is taken out and the contract price S is always equal to the current futures price, $F(t,T)$.[3]

The principal difference between a futures contract and a forward contract is that a futures contract may be used to imply the price of forward

---

[3] This assumption is held in the market but does not hold good over long periods, due chiefly to the difference in the way futures and forwards are marked-to-market, and because futures are cash-settled on a daily basis while forwards are not.

contracts. This arises from the fact that futures contracts are repriced each day, with a new contract price that is equal to the new futures price. Hence, when F rises, such that $F>S$, the forward contract has a positive value, and when F falls, the forward contract has a negative value. When the transaction expires and delivery takes place, the futures price is equal to the spot price and the value of the forward contract is equal to the spot price minus the contract price or the spot price.

$$f(F,T,S,T) = F - S \qquad (19.20)$$

On maturity, the value of a bond or commodity option is given by the maximum of zero, and the difference between the spot price and the contract price. Since at that date the futures price is equal to the spot price, we conclude that:

$$C(F,T) = \begin{cases} F - S & \text{if } F \geq S_r \\ 0 & \text{else} \end{cases} \qquad (19.21)$$

The assumptions made in the Black model are that the prices of futures contracts follow a lognormal distribution with a constant variance, and that the Capital Asset Pricing Model applies in the market. There is also an assumption of no transaction costs or taxes. Under these assumptions, we can create a risk-free hedged position that is composed of a long position in the option and a short position in the futures contract. Following the B-S model, the number of options put on against one futures contract is given by $[\partial C(F,t) / \partial F]$, which is the derivative of $C(F, t)$ with respect to F. The change in the hedged position resulting from a change in price of the underlying is given by (19.22) below.

$$\partial C(F,t) - [\partial C(F,t) / \partial F]\partial F \qquad (19.22)$$

Due to the principle of arbitrage-free pricing, the return generated by the hedged portfolio must be equal to the risk-free interest rate, and this together with an expansion of $\partial C(F,t)$ produces the following partial differential equation:

$$\left[\frac{\partial C(F,t)}{\partial t}\right] = rC(F,t) - \tfrac{1}{2}\sigma^2 F^2\left[\frac{\partial^2 C(F,t)}{\partial F^2}\right] \qquad (19.23)$$

which is solved by setting the following:

$$\tfrac{1}{2}\sigma^2 F^2\left[\frac{\partial^2 C(F,t)}{\partial F^2}\right] - rC(F,t) + \left[\frac{\partial C(F,t)}{\partial t}\right] = 0 \ . \qquad (19.24)$$

The solution to the partial differential equation (19.23) is not presented here.

The result, by denoting $T = t$-T and using (19.10) and (19.23), gives the fair value of a commodity option or option on a forward contract as shown at (19.25).

$$C(F,t) = e^{-rT}[FN(d_1) - S_T N(d_2)] \qquad (19.25)$$

where

$$d_1 = \frac{1}{\sigma\sqrt{t}}\left[\ln\left(\frac{F}{S_T}\right) + \tfrac{1}{2}\sigma^2)T\right]$$

$$d_2 = d_1 - \sigma\sqrt{t}$$

There are a number of other models that have been developed for specific contracts; for example, the Garman and Kohlhagen (1983) and Grabbe (1983) models, used for currency options, and the Merton, Barone-Adesi and Whaley or BAW model (1987) used for commodity options. For the valuation of American options, on dividend-paying assets, another model has been developed by Roll, Geske and Whaley. More recently the Black-Derman-Toy model (1990) has been used to price exotic options. A survey of these, though very interesting, is outside the scope of this book.

Comment on the Black–Scholes model

The introduction of the B-S model was one of the great milestones in the development of the global capital markets, and it remains an important pricing model today. Many of the models introduced later for application to specific products are still based essentially on the B-S model. Subsequently, academics have presented some weaknesses in the model that stem from the nature of the main assumptions behind the model itself, which we will summarise here. The main critique of the B-S model appears to center on:

- its assumption of frictionless markets. This is at best only approximately true for large market counterparties.
- the assumption of a constant interest rate. This is possibly the most unrealistic assumption. Interest rates over even the shortest time frame (the overnight rate) fluctuate considerably. In addition to a dynamic short rate, the short-end of the yield curve often moves in

the opposite direction to moves in underlying asset prices, particularly so with bonds and bond options.

• the assumption of lognormal distribution. This is accepted by the market as a reasonable approximation but not completely accurate, and also misses out most extreme moves or market shocks.

• it is a European option only. Although it is rare for American options to be exercised early, there are situations when it is optimal to do so, and the B-S model does not price these situations.

• for stock options, the assumption of a continuous constant dividend yield is clearly not realistic, although the trend in the US markets is for ordinary shares to cease paying dividends altogether.

These points notwithstanding, the Black-Scholes model paved the way for the rapid development of options as liquid tradable products and is widely used today.

Stochastic volatility

The B-S model assumes a constant volatility and for this reason, and because it is based on mathematics, often fails to pick up on market "sentiment" when there is a large downward move or shock. This is not a failing limited to the B-S model, however. For this reason, though, it undervalues out-of-the-money options, and to compensate for this market-makers push up the price of deep in- or out-of-the-money options, giving rise to the volatility smile. This is considered in the next chapter.

The effect of stochastic volatility not being catered for then is to introduce mis-pricing, specifically the undervaluation of out-of-the-money options and the overvaluation of deeply in-the-money options. This is because when the price of the underlying asset rises, its volatility level also increases. The effect of this is that assets priced at relatively high levels do not tend to follow the process described by geometric Brownian motion. The same is true for relatively low asset prices and price volatility, but in the opposite direction. To compensate for this, stochastic volatility models have been developed, such as the Hull-White model (1987).

Implied volatility

The volatility parameter in the B-S model, by definition, cannot be observed directly in the market as it refers to volatility going forward. It is different from historic volatility which can be measured directly, and this value is sometimes used to estimate implied volatility of an asset price. Banks therefore use the value for implied volatility, which is the volatility obtained using the prices of exchange-traded options. Given the price of an option and all the other parameters, it is possible to use the price of the option to determine the volatility of the underlying asset implied by the option price. The B-S model, however, cannot be re-arranged into a form that expresses the volatility measure σ as a function of the other parameters. Generally, therefore, a numerical iteration process is used to arrive at the value for σ given the price of the option; this is usually the Newton-Raphson method.

The market uses implied volatilities to gauge the volatility of individual assets relative to the market. Volatility levels are not constant, and fluctuate with the overall level of the market, as well as for stock-specific factors. When assessing volatilities with reference to exchange-traded options, market-makers will use more than one value, because an asset will have different implied volatilities depending on how in-the-money the option itself is. The price of an at-the-money option will exhibit greater sensitivity to volatility than the price of a deeply in- or out-of-the-money option. Therefore, market-makers will take a combination of volatility values when assessing the volatility of a particular asset.

A final word on option models

We have only discussed the B-S model and the Black model in this chapter. Other pricing models have been developed that follow on from the pioneering work done by Messrs. Black and Scholes. The B-S model is essentially the most straightforward and the easiest to apply, and subsequent research has focused on easing some of the restrictions of the model in order to expand its applicability. Areas that have been focused on include a relaxation of the assumption of constant volatility levels for asset prices, as well as work on allowing for the valuation of American options and options on dividend-paying stocks. However, in practice some of the newer models often require input of parameters that are difficult to observe or measure directly, which limits their application as well. Often there is a difficulty in calibrating a model due to the lack of observable data in the market place. The issue of calibration is an important one in the implementation of a pricing model, and involves inputting actual market data and using this as the parameters for calculation of prices. So, for instance, a model used to calculate the prices of sterling-market options would use data from the UK market, including money-market, futures and swaps rates to build the zero-coupon yield curve, and volatility levels for the underlying asset or interest rate (if it is valuing options on interest-rate products, such as caps and floors). What sort of volatility is used? Some banks use actual historical volatilities but, more usually, it is volatilities implied by exchange-traded option prices that are used. Another crucial piece of data for multi-factor models (following Heath-Jarrow-Morton and other models based on this) is the correlation coefficients between forward rates on the term structure. This is used to calculate volatilities using the model itself.

The issue of calibrating the model is important, because incorrectly calibrated models will produce errors in option valuation. This can have disastrous results, which may be discovered only after significant losses have been suffered. If data is not available to calibrate the model, it may be that a simpler one needs to be used. The lack of data is not an issue for products priced in, say, dollar, sterling or euro, but may be in other currency products if data is not so readily available. This might explain why the B-S model is still widely used today, although markets observe an increasing use of models such as the Black-Derman-Toy (1990) and Brace-Gatarek-Musiela (1994) for more exotic option products.

Many models, because of the way that they describe the price process, are described as Gaussian interest-rate models. The basic process is described by an Itô process:

$$dP_T \, / \, P_T = \mu_T d + \sigma_T dW$$

where P_T is the price of a zero-coupon bond with maturity date T and W is a standard Weiner process. The basic statement made by Gaussian interest-rate models is that:

$$P_T(t) = E_T \exp\left[-\int_t^T r(s)ds\right] .$$

Models that capture the process in this way include Cox-Ingersoll-Ross and Harrison and Pliska. We are only summarising here but, essentially, such models state that the price of an option is equal to the discounted return from a risk-free instrument. This is why the basic B-S model describes a portfolio of a call option on the underlying stock and a cash deposit invested at the risk-free interest rate. This was reviewed earlier. We then discussed how the representation of asset prices as an expectation of a discounted payoff from a risk-free deposit does not capture the real-world scenario presented by many option products. Hence the continuing research into developments of the basic model.

Following on from B-S, under the assumption that the short-term spot rate drives bond and option prices, the basic model can be used to model an interest-rate term structure, as given by Vasicek and Cox-Ingersoll-Ross. The short-term spot rate is assumed to follow a diffusion process

$$dr = \mu dt + \sigma dw$$

which is a standard Weiner process. From this, it is possible to model the complete term structure based on the short-term spot rate and the volatility of the short-term rate. This approach is modified by Heath-Jarrow-Morton (1992), which was reviewed earlier as an interest-rate model.

Appendices

APPENDIX 19.1 Summary of basic statistical concepts

The arithmetic mean μ is the average of a series of numbers. The variance is the sum of the squares of the difference of each observation from the mean, and from the variance we obtain the standard deviation σ, which is the square root of the variance. The probability density of a series of numbers is the term for how likely any of them is to occur. In a normal probability density function, described by the normal distribution, the probability density is given by:

$$\frac{1}{\sqrt{2\pi}e^{\frac{x^2}{2}}}$$

Most option pricing formulae assume a normal probability density function, specifically that movements in the natural logarithm of asset prices follow this function. That is,

$$\ln\left[\frac{\text{today's price}}{\text{yesterday's price}}\right]$$

is assumed to follow a normal probability density function. This relative price change is equal to:

$$\left[1 + r \times \frac{\text{days}}{\text{year}}\right]$$

where r is the rate of return being earned on an investment in the asset. The value

$$\ln(1 + r \times \text{days/years})$$

is equal to $r \times$ days/years where r is the continuously compounded rate of return. Therefore, the value ln(today's price/yesterday's price) is equal to the continuously compounded rate of return on the asset over a specified holding period.

APPENDIX 19.2 Lognormal distribution of returns

In the distribution of asset-price returns, returns are defined as the logarithm of price relatives and are assumed to follow the normal distribution, given by:

$$\ln\left(\frac{P_1}{P_0}\right) \sim N(rt, \sigma\sqrt{t}) \tag{A19.2.1}$$

where

P_t is the price at time t
P_0 is the price at time 0
$N(m,s)$ is a random normal distribution with mean m and standard deviation s
r is the annual rate of return
σ is the annualised standard deviation of returns.

From (A19.2.1) we conclude that the logarithm of the prices is normally distributed, due to (A19.2.2) where P_0 is a constant

$$\ln(P_t) \sim \ln(P_0) + N(rt, \sigma\sqrt{t}) \tag{A19.2.2}$$

We conclude that prices are normally distributed and are described by the relationship,

$$\frac{P_1}{P_0} \sim e^{N(rt, \sigma\sqrt{t})}$$

and from this relationship we may set the expected return as rt.

APPENDIX 19.3 Black–Scholes model in Microsoft® Excel

To value a vanilla option under the following parameters, we can use Microsoft Excel to carry out the calculation as shown in Figure A19.3.1.

Price of underlying	100	
Volatility	0.0691	
Maturity of option	3 months	
Strike price	99.5	
Risk-free rate	5%	

Cell	C	D	
8	**Underlying price**, S	100	
9		Volatility %	0.0691
10	Option maturity years	0.25	
11	**Strike price**, X	99.50	
12	Risk-free interest rate %	0.05	
13			
14			
15			Cell formulae:
16	ln (S/X)	0.005012542	=LN (D8/D11)
17	Adjusted return	0.0000456012500	=((D12-D9)^2/ 2)*D10
18	Time adjusted volatility	0.131434394	=(D9*D10)^0.5
19	d_2	0.038484166	=(D16+D17)/D18
20	$N(d_2)$	0.515349233	=NORMSDIST(D19)
21			
22	d_1	0.16991856	=D19+D18
23	$N(d_1)$	0.56746291	=NORMSDIST(D22)
24	e^{-rt}	0.9875778	=EXP(-D10*D12)
25			
26	**CALL**	6.106018498	=D8*D23-D11*D20*D24
27	**PUT**	4.370009648	* =D26-D8+D11*D24

*By put-call parity, $P = C - S + Xe^{-rt}$

Figure A19.3.1 Microsoft Excel calculation of vanilla option price

Selected Bibliography and References

Black, F. and Scholes, M., "The Pricing of Options and Corporate Liabilities", *Journal of Political Economy* 81, May-June 1973, p.637–659.

Black, F., Derman, E. and Toy, W., "A One-Factor Model of Interest Rates and its Application to Treasury Bond Options", in Hughston, L., (editor), *Vasicek and Beyond*, Risk Publications, 1996.

Bookstaber, R., *Option Pricing and Strategies in Investing*, Addison-Wesley, 1982.

Boyle, P., "Option valuation using a three jump process", *International Options Journal* 3, 1986, p.7–12.

Brace, A., Gatarek, D. and Musiela, M., "The Market Model of Interest Rate Dynamics", in Hughston, L., (editor), *Vasicek and Beyond*, Risk Publications, 1996.

Briys, E, et al, *Options, Futures and Exotic Derivatives*, John Wiley and Sons, 1998.

Choudhry, M., *The Bond and Money Markets: Strategy, Trading, Analysis*, Butterworth-Heinemann, 2001, Chapters 42–49.

Cox, D. and Miller, H., *The Theory of Stochastic Processes*, Chapman & Hall, 1965.

Cox, J. and Ross, S., "The valuation of options for alternative stochastic processes", *Journal of Financial Economics* 3, 1976, p.145–166.

Cox, J., Ross, S. and Rubinstein, M., "Option pricing: A Simplified Approach", *Journal of Financial Economics* 7, October 1979, p.229–264.

Fama, E., "The Behaviour of Stock Prices", *Journal of Business* 38, January 1965, p.34–105.

Debreu, G., "Representation of a preference ordering by a numerical function", in Thrall, R., Coombs, C. and Davis, R., (editors) *Decision Processes*, Wiley, 1954.

Harrison, J. and Kreps, D., "Martingales and arbitrage in multi-period securities markets", *Journal of Economic Theory* 20, 1979, p.381–408.

Harrison, J. and Pliska, S., "Martingales and stochastic integrals in the theory of continuous trading", *Stochastic Processes and Their Applications* 11, 1981, p.216–260.

Haug, E. G., *The Complete Guide to Option Pricing Formulas*, McGraw-Hill, 1998.

Heston, S., "A closed form solution for options with stochastic volatility with application to bond and currency options", *Review of Financial Studies* 6, 1993, p.327–343.

Heston, S., "Invisible parameters in option prices", *Journal of Finance* 48 (3), 1993, p.933–947.

Hull, J. and White, A., "The pricing of options on assets with stochastic volatilities", *Journal of Finance* 42, 1987, p.281–300.

Hull, J. and White, A., "An analysis of the bias caused by a stochastic volatility in option pricing", *Advances in Futures and Options Research* 3, 1988, p.29–61.

Ito, K., "On Stochastic Differential Equations", *American Mathematical Society* 4, 1951, p.1–51.

Joshi, M., *The Concepts and Practice of Mathematical Finance*, Cambridge U.P. 2004.

Klemkosky, R. and Resnick, B., "Put-Call Parity and Market Efficiency", *Journal of Financial Economics* 34, December 1979, p.1141–1155.

Merton, R., "Theory of Rational Option Pricing", *Bell Journal of Economics and Management Science* 4, Spring 1973, p.141–183.

Merton, R., "Option pricing when underlying stock returns are discontinuous", *Journal of Financial Economics* 3, Jan-Mar 1976, p.125–144.

Neftci, S., *An Introduction to the Mathematics of Financial Derivatives*, Academic Press, 1996.

Nielsen, L. T., *Pricing and Hedging of Derivative Securities*, Oxford UP, 1999.

Rendleman, R. and Bartter, B., "Two State Option Pricing", *Journal of Finance* 34, 1979, p.1092–1110.

Rubinstein, M., "Nonparametric tests of alternative option pricing models", *Journal of Financial Economics* 40, 1985, p.455–480.

Scott, L., "Option pricing when the variance changes randomly", *Journal of Financial and Quantitative Analysis* 22, 1987, p.419–438.

Stein, E. and Stein, J., "Stock price distributions with stochastic volatility: an analytic approach", *Review of Financial Studies* 4, 1991, p.113–135.

Whaley, R., "On the Valuation of American Call Options on Stocks with Known Dividends", *Journal of Financial Economics* 9, 1981, p.207–211.

20

Options II

We continue with options in this chapter with a look at how options behave in response to changes in market conditions. To start we consider the main issues that a market-maker in options must consider when writing options. We then review "the Greeks", the measures by which the sensitivity of an option book is calculated. We conclude with a discussion on an important set of interest-rate options in the market, caps and floors.

Behavior of option prices

As we noted in the previous chapter, the value of an option is a function of five factors:

- the price of the underlying asset
- the strike price of the option
- the time to expiry of the option
- the volatility level of the underlying asset-price returns
- the risk-free interest rate applicable to the life of the option.

The Black-Scholes (B-S) model assumes that the level of volatility and interest rates stays constant, so that changes in these will impact on the value of the option. On the expiry date, the price of the option will be a function of the strike price and the price of the underlying asset. However, for pricing purposes an option trader must take into account all the factors above. From Chapter 19 we know that the value of an option is composed of intrinsic value and time value. Intrinsic value is immediately apparent when an option is struck, and a valuation model is essentially pricing the time value of the option. This is considered next.

Assessing time value

The time value of an option reflects the fact that it is highest for at-the-money options and also higher for an in-the-money option than an out-of-the-money option. This can be demonstrated by considering the hedge process followed by a market-maker in options. An out-of-the-money call option, for instance, presents the lowest probability of exercise for the market-maker. Therefore, she may not even hedge such a position. There is a risk, of course, that the price of the underlying will rise sufficiently to make the option in-the-money, in which case the market-maker would have to purchase the asset in the market, thereby suffering a loss. This must be considered by the market-maker, but deeply out-of-the-money options are often not hedged. So the risk to the market-maker is lowest for this type of option, which means that the time value is also lowest for such an option.

An in-the-money call option carries a greater probability that it will be exercised. A market-maker writing such an option will therefore hedge the position, either with the underlying asset, with futures contracts, or via a *risk reversal*. This is a long or short position in a call that is reversed to the same position in a put by selling or buying the position forward (and vice versa). The risk with hedging using the underlying is that its price falls, causing the option not to be exercised and forcing the market-maker to dispose of the underlying at a loss. However, this risk is lowest for deeply in-the-money options, and this is reflected in the time value for such options, which diminishes the more in-the-money the option is.

The highest risk lies in writing an at-the-money option. In fact, the majority of OTC options are struck at-the-money. The risk level reflects the fact that there is greatest uncertainty with this option, because there is an even chance of it being exercised. The decision on whether to hedge is therefore not as straightforward. As an at-the-money option carries the greatest risk for the market-maker in terms of hedging it, the time value for it is the highest.

American options

In the previous chapter, we discussed the B-S and other models in terms of European options, and also briefly referred to a model developed for American options on dividend-paying securities. In theory, an American option will have greater value than an equivalent European option, because of the early-exercise option. This added feature implies a higher value for the American option. In theory, this is correct, but in practice it carries lower weight because American options are rarely exercised ahead of expiry. A holder of an American option must assess if it is ever optimal to exercise it ahead of the expiry date, and usually the answer to this is "no". This is because, by exercising an option, the holder realises only the intrinsic value of the option. However, if the option is traded in the market – that is, sold – then the full value will be realised, including the time value. Therefore, it is rare for an American option to be exercised ahead of the expiry date; rather, it will be sold in the market to realise full value.

As the chief characteristic that differentiates American options from European options is rarely employed, in practical terms they do not have greater value than European options. Therefore, they have similar values to equivalent European options. However, an option-pricing model, calculating the probability that an option will be exercised, will determine under certain circumstances that the American option has a higher probability of being exercised and assign it a higher price.

Under certain circumstances it is optimal to exercise American options early. The most significant is when an option has negative time value. An option can have negative time value when, for instance, a European option is deeply in-the-money and very near to maturity. The time value will be small positive; however, the potential value in deferring cash flows from the underlying asset may outweigh this, leading to a negative time value. The best example of this is for a deeply in-the-money option on a futures contract. By deferring exercise, the opportunity to invest the cash proceeds from the profit on the futures contract (remember, futures are cash-settled daily via the margin process) is lost and this is potential interest income forgone. In such circumstances, it would be optimal to exercise an option ahead of its maturity date, assuming it is an American one. Therefore, when valuing an American option, the probability of it being exercised early is considered and if it is deeply in-the-money this probability will be at its highest.

Measuring option risk: The Greeks

It is apparent from a reading of the previous chapter that the price sensitivity of options is different from other financial-market instruments. This is clear from noting the variables that are required when pricing an option, which we presented by way of recap at the start of this chapter. The value of an option is sensitive to changes in one or any combination of the five variables that are used in the valuation.[1] This makes risk managing an option book more

---

[1] Of course, the strike price for a plain-vanilla option is constant.

complex compared to other instruments. For example, the value of a swap is sensitive to one variable only; the swap rate. The relationship between the change in value of the swap and the change in the swap rate also is a linear one. A bond futures contract is priced as a function of the current spot price of the cheapest-to-deliver bond and the current money-market repo rate. Options, on the other hand, react to moves in any of the variables used in pricing them; more importantly the relationship between the value of the option and the change in a key variable is not a linear one. The market uses a measure for each of the variables and, in some cases, for a derivative of these variables, which are termed the "Greeks" as they are called after letters in the ancient Greek alphabet.[2] In this section, we review these sensitivity measures and how they are used.

Delta

The delta of an option is a measure of how much the value or premium of the option changes with changes in the price of the underlying asset. That is,

$$\delta = \Delta C\ /\ \Delta S.$$

Mathematically the delta of an option is the partial derivative of the option premium with respect to the underlying, given by (20.1).

$$\delta = \partial C\ /\ \partial S$$
$$\text{or} \qquad\qquad (20.1)$$
$$\partial = \partial P\ /\ \partial S$$

In fact, the delta of an option is given by the $N(d_1)$ term in the B-S equation. It is closely related, but not equal, to the probability that an option will be exercised. If an option has a delta of 0.6 or 60%, this means that a $100 increase in the value of the underlying will result in a $60 increase in the value of the option. Delta is probably the most important sensitivity measure for an option, as it measures the sensitivity of the option price to changes in the price of the underlying, and this is very important for option market-makers. It is also the main hedge measure. When an option market-maker wishes to hedge a sold option, she may do this by buying a matching

---

[2] All but one; the term for the volatility sensitivity measure, *vega*, is not a Greek letter. In certain cases, one will come across the use of the term "kappa" to refer to volatility, and this is a Greek letter. However, it is more common for volatility to be referred to by the term "vega".

option, by buying or selling another instrument with the same but opposite value as the sold option, or by buying or selling the underlying. If the hedge is put on with the underlying, the amount is governed by the delta. So, for instance, if the delta of an option written on one ordinary share is 0.6 and a trader writes 1000 call options, the hedge would be a long position in 600 of the underlying shares. This means that of the value of the shares rises by $1, the $600 rise in the value of the shares will offset the $600 loss in the option position. This is known as delta hedging. As we shall see later on, this is not a static situation, and the fact that delta changes, and is also an approximation, means that hedges must be monitored and adjusted, in a processcalled dynamic hedging.

The delta of an option measures the extent to which the option moves with the underlying asset price. At a delta of zero, the option does not move with moves in the underlying, while at a delta of 1 it will behave identically to the underlying.

A positive delta position is equivalent to being long the underlying asset, and can be interpreted as a bullish position. A rise in the asset price results in profit as, in theory, a market-maker could sell the underlying at a higher price or, in fact, sell the option. The opposite is true if the price of the underlying falls. With a positive delta, a market-maker would be over-hedge if running a delta-neutral position. Table 20.1 shows the effect of changes in the underlying price on the delta position in the option book. To maintain a delta-neutral hedge, the market-maker must buy or sell delta units of the underlying asset, although, in practice, futures contracts may be used.

Option	Rise in underlying asset price	Fall in underlying asset price
Long call	Rise in delta: sell underlying	Fall in delta: buy underlying
Long put	Fall in delta: sell underlying	Rise in delta: buy underlying
Short call	Rise in delta: buy underlying	Fall in delta: sell underlying
Short put	Fall in delta: buy underlying	Rise in delta: sell underlying

Table 20.1 Delta-neutral hedging for changes in underlying price

Gamma

Just as the modified-duration measure becomes inaccurate for larger yield changes because of the way it is calculated, there is also an element of inaccuracy with the delta measurement and with delta-hedging an option book. This is because the delta itself is not static, and changes with changes in the price of the underlying. A book that is delta-neutral at one level may not be as the underlying price changes. To monitor this, option market-makers calculate gamma. The gamma of an option is a measure of how much the delta value changes with changes in the underlying price. It is given by:

$$\Gamma = \Delta\delta \: / \: \Delta S$$

Mathematically, gamma is the second partial derivative of the option price with respect to the underlying price; that is:

$$\partial^2 C \: / \: \partial S^2$$

or

$$\partial^2 P \: / \: \partial S^2$$

and is given by (20.2).

$$\Gamma = N(d_1) \: / \: S\sigma\sqrt{T} \qquad (20.2)$$

The delta of an option does not change rapidly when an option is deeply in- or out-of-the-money; so, in these cases, the gamma is not significant. However, when an option is close to or at-the-money, the delta can change very suddenly and at that point the gamma is very large. The value of gamma is positive for long call and put options, and negative for short call and put options. An option with high gamma causes the most problems for market-makers, as the delta hedge must be adjusted constantly, which will lead to high transaction costs. The higher the gamma, the greater is the risk that the option book is exposed to loss from sudden moves in the market. A negative gamma exposure is the highest risk, and this can be hedged only by putting on long positions in other options. A perfectly hedged book is gamma-neutral, which means that the delta of the book does not change.

When gamma is positive, a rise in the price of the underlying asset will result in a higher delta. Adjusting the hedge will require selling the underlying asset or futures contracts. The reverse applies if there is a fall in the price of the underlying. As the hedge adjustment is made in the same direction that the market is moving in, this adjustment is possibly easier to conceptualise for newcomers to a market-making desk. When adjusting a hedge in a rising market, underlying assets or futures are sold, which in itself may generate profit. In a falling market, the delta-hedge is insufficient and must be re-balanced through purchase of the underlying.

However, with a negative gamma, an increase in the price of the underlying will reduce the value of the delta. So to adjust the delta hedge, therefore, the market-maker must buy more of the underlying asset or futures equivalents. However, when the underlying asset-price falls, the delta will rise, necessitating the sale of the underlying asset to rebalance the hedge. In this scenario, irrespective of whether cash or off-balance-sheet instruments are being used, the hedge involves selling assets in a falling market, which will generate losses even as the hedge is being put on. Negative gamma is, therefore, a high-risk exposure in a rising market. Managing an option book that has negative gamma is more risky if the underlying asset-price volatility is high. In a rising market, the market-maker becomes short and must purchase more of the underlying, which may produce losses. The same applies in a falling market. If the desk is pursuing a delta-neutral strategy, running a positive gamma position should enable generation of profit in volatile market conditions. Under the same scenario, a negative gamma position would be risky and would be excessively costly in terms of dynamically hedging the book.

Gamma is the only one of the major Greeks that does not measure the sensitivity of the option premium; rather, it measures the change in delta. The delta of an option is its hedge ratio, and gamma is a measure of how much this hedge ratio changes for changes in the price of the underlying. This is why a gamma value results in problems in hedging an option book, as the hedge ratio is always changing. This ties in with our earlier comment that at-the-money options have the highest value, because they present the greatest uncertainty and hence the highest risk. The relationship is illustrated by the behavior of gamma, which follows that of the delta.

To adjust an option book so that it is gamma-neutral, a market-maker must put on positions in an option on the underlying or on the future. This is because the gamma of the underlying and the future is zero. It is common for market-makers to use exchange-traded options. Therefore, a book that needs to be made gamma-neutral must be re-balanced with options. However, by adding to its option position, the book's delta will alter. Therefore, to maintain the book as delta-neutral, the market-maker will have to re-balance it using more of the underlying asset or futures contracts. The calculation made to adjust gamma is a snapshot in time, and as the gamma value changes dynamically with the market, the gamma hedge must be continually re-balanced, like the delta hedge, if the market-maker wishes to maintain the book as gamma-neutral.

Theta

The theta of an option measures the extent of the change in value of an option with change in the time to maturity. That is, it is

$$\Theta = \Delta C \, / \, \Delta T$$

or

$$-\frac{\partial C}{\partial T} \quad \text{or} \quad -\frac{\partial P}{\partial T}$$

and, from the formula for the B-S model, mathematically it is given for a call option as (20.3) below.

$$\Theta = -\frac{S\sigma}{2\sqrt{2\pi T}} \, e^{\frac{d_1^2}{2}} - Xre^{-rT}N(d_2) \tag{20.3}$$

Theta is a measure of time decay for an option. A holder of a long option position suffers from time decay because as the option approaches maturity, its value is made up increasingly of intrinsic value only, which may be zero as the option approaches expiry. For the writer of an option, the risk exposure is reduced as a result of time decay, so it is favorable for the writer if the theta is high. There is also a relationship between theta and gamma, however. When an option gamma is high, its theta is also high, and this results in the option losing value more rapidly as it approaches maturity. Therefore, a high theta option, while welcome to the writer, has a downside because it is also high gamma. In practice, therefore, there is no gain to be high theta for the writer of an option. The theta value affects certain option strategies. For example, it is possible to write a short-dated option and simultaneously purchase a longer-dated option with the same strike price. This is a play on the option theta: if the trader believes that the time value of the longer-dated option will decay at a slower rate than the short-dated option, the trade will generate a profit.

Vega

The vega of an option measures how much its value changes with changes in the volatility of the underlying asset. It is also known as epsilon (ε), eta (η), or kappa (κ).

We define vega as:

$$v = \Delta C \, / \, \Delta\sigma$$

or

$$v = \frac{\partial C}{\partial \sigma} \quad \text{or} \quad \frac{\partial P}{\partial \sigma}$$

and mathematically from the B-S formula it is defined as (20.4) for a call or put.

$$v = \frac{S\sqrt{\dfrac{T}{2\pi}}}{e^{\frac{d_1^2}{2}}} \tag{20.4}$$

It may also be given by (20.5) below.

$$v = S\sqrt{\Delta T N(d_1)} \tag{20.5}$$

An option exhibits its highest vega when it is at-the-money, and decreases as the underlying and strike prices diverge. Options with only a short time to expiry have a lower vega compared to longer-dated options. An option with positive vega generally has positive gamma. Vega is also positive for a position composed of long call and put options, and an increase in volatility will then increase the value of the options. A vega of 12.75 means that for a 1% increase in volatility, the price of the option will increase by 0.1275. Buying options is the equivalent of buying volatility, while selling options is equivalent to selling volatility. Market-makers generally like volatility and set up their books so that they are positive vega. The basic approach for volatility trades is that the market-maker will calculate the implied volatility inherent in an option price, and then assess whether this is accurate compared to her own estimation of volatility. Just as positive vega is long call and puts, if the trader feels the implied volatility in the options is too high, she will put on a short vega position of short calls and puts, and then reverse the position out when the volatility declines.

Table 20.2 below shows the response to a delta hedge following a change in volatility.

Option position	Rise in volatility	Fall in volatility
Long call		
ATM	No adjustment to delta	No adjustment to delta
ITM	Rise in delta, buy underlying	Rise in delta, sell underlying
OTM	Fall in delta, sell underlying	Fall in delta, buy underlying
Long put		
ATM	No adjustment to delta	No adjustment to delta
ITM	Fall in delta, sell underlying	Rise in delta, buy underlying
OTM	Rise in delta, buy underlying	Fall in delta, sell underlying
Short call		
ATM	No adjustment to delta	No adjustment to delta
ITM	Fall in delta, sell underlying	Rise in delta, buy underlying
OTM	Rise in delta, buy underlying	Fall in delta, sell underlying
Short put		
ATM	No adjustment to delta	No adjustment to delta
ITM	Rise in delta, buy underlying	Rise in delta, sell underlying
OTM	Fall in delta, sell underlying	Fall in delta, buy underlying

Table 20.2 Dynamic hedging as a result of changes in volatility

Managing an option book involves trade-offs between the gamma and the vega, in much the same way as there are trade-offs between gamma and theta. A long in options means long vega and long gamma, which is not conceptually difficult to manage. However, if there is a fall in volatility levels, the market-maker can either maintain positive gamma, depending on her view of whether the fall in volatility can be offset by adjusting the gamma in the direction of the market, or she can sell volatility (that is, write options) and set up a position with negative gamma. In either case, the costs associated with re-balancing the delta must compensate for the reduction in volatility.

Rho

The rho of an option is a measure of how much its value changes with changes in interest rates. Mathematically this is:

$$\partial C \ / \ \partial r$$

or

$$\partial P \ / \ \partial r$$

and the formal definition, based on the B-S model formula, is given at (20.6) for a call option.

$$\rho = Xte^{-rT}N(d_2) \tag{20.6}$$

The level of rho tends to be higher for longer-dated options. It is probably the least used of the sensitivity measures because market interest rates are probably the least variable of all the parameters used in option pricing.

Lambda

The lambda of an option is similar to its delta in that it measures the change in option value for a change in underlying price. However, lambda measure this sensitivity as a percentage change in the price for a percentage change in the price of the underlying. Hence, lambda measures the gearing or leverage of an option. This in turn gives an indication of expected profit or loss for changes in the price of the underlying. From Figure 20.1 we note that in-the-money options have a gearing of a minimum of five, and sometimes the level is considerably higher. This means that if the underlying was to rise in price, the holder of the long call could benefit by a minimum of five times more than if he had invested the same cash amount in the underlying instead of in the option.

This has been a brief review of the sensitivity measures used in managing option books. They are very useful to market-makers and portfolio managers because they enable them to see what the impact of changes in market rates is on an entire book. A market-maker need take only the weighted sum of the delta, gamma, vega and theta of all the options on the book to see the impact of changes on the portfolio. Therefore, the combined effect of changes can be calculated without having to re-price all the options on the book. The Greeks are also important to risk managers and those implementing value-at-risk systems.

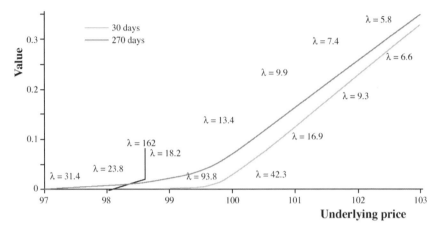

Figure 20.1 Option Lambda

The option smile

Our discussion on the behavior and sensitivity of options prices will conclude with an introduction to the option smile. Market-makers calculate a measure known as the volatility smile, which is a graph that plots the implied volatility of an option as a function of its strike price. The general shape of the smile curve is given at Figure 20.2. What the smile tells us is that out-of-the-money and in-the-money options both tend to have higher implied volatilities than at-the-money options. We define an at-the-money option as one whose strike price is equal to the forward price of the underlying asset.

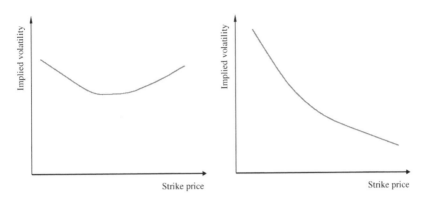

Figure 20.2 The option-volatility smile curve for (i) bond options
and (ii) equity options

Under the B-S model assumptions, the implied volatility should be the same across all strike prices of options on the same underlying asset and with the same expiry date. However, implied volatility is usually observed in the market as a convex function of exercise price, shown in generalised form as Figure 20.2. (In practice, it is not a smooth line or even often a real smile). The observations confirm that market-makers price options with strikes that are less than S, and those with strikes higher than S, with higher volatilities than options with strikes equal to S. The existence of the volatility smile curve indicates that market-makers make more complex assumptions about the behavior of asset prices than can be fully explained by the geometric Brownian-motion model. As a result, market-makers attach different probabilities to terminal values of the underlying asset price than those that are consistent with a lognormal distribution. The extent of the convexity of the smile curve indicates the degree to which the market-price process differs from the lognormal function contained in the B-S model. In particular, the more convex the smile curve, the greater the probability the market attaches to extreme outcomes for the price of the asset on expiry, S_T. This is consistent with the observation that in reality asset-price returns follow a distribution with "fatter tails" than that described by the lognormal distribution. In addition, the direction in which the smile curve slopes reflects the skew of the price-process function; a positively sloped implied volatility smile curve results in a price-returns function that is more positively skewed than the lognormal distribution. The opposite applies for a negatively sloping curve. The existence of the smile suggest asset-price behavior that is more accurately described by non-standard price processes, such as the jump-diffusion model, or a stochastic volatility, as opposed to a constant-volatility model.

Considerable research has gone into investigating the smile. The book references in this and the previous chapter are good starting points on this subject.

Caps and floors

Caps and floors are options on interest rates. They are commonly written on Libor or another interest rate such as euribor, the US Prime rate or a commercial-paper rate. In this section, we review caps, which are essentially calls on an interest rate, while a floor is a put on an interest rate.

A cap is an option contract in which an upper limit is placed on the interest rate payable by the borrower on a cash loan. The limit is known as the cap level. The seller of the cap, who is the market-making bank, agrees to pay to the buyer the difference between the cap rate and the higher rate should interest rates rise above the cap level. The buyer of the cap is long the option and will have paid the cap premium to the seller. Hence, a cap is a call option on interest rates. The cash loan may have been taken out before the cap, or indeed with another counterparty, or the cap may have been set up alongside the loan as a form of interest-rate risk management. If a cap is set up in conjunction with a cash loan, the notional amount of the cap will be equal to the amount of the loan. Caps can be fairly long-dated options; for example, 10-year caps are not uncommon.

In a typical cap, the cap rate is measured alongside the indexed interest rate at the specified fixing dates. So during its life a cap may be fixed semi-annually with the six-month Libor rate. At the fixing date, if the index interest rate is below the cap level, no payment changes hands and if there is a cash loan involved, the borrower will pay the market interest rate on the loan. If the index rate is fixed above the cap level, the cap seller will pay the difference between the index interest rate and the cap level, calculated for the period of the fix (quarterly, semi-annually, etc) on the notional amount of the cap. Individual contracts – that is, each fixing – during the life of the cap are known as caplets. The interest payment on each caplet is given by (20.7).

$$Int = \frac{\max[r - rX, 0] \times (N / B) \times M}{1 + r(N / B)} \qquad (20.7)$$

where

r is the interest-rate fixing for the specified index
rX is the cap level
M is the notional amount of the cap
B is the day-base (360 or 365)
N is the number of days in the interest period (days to the next rate fix).

As with FRAs, any payment made is an upfront payment for the period covered, and so is discounted at the index-rate level.

As it is a call option on a specified interest rate, the premium charged by a cap market-maker will be a function of the probability that the cap is exercised, based on the volatility of the forward interest rate. Caps are frequently priced using the Black 76 model. The strike rate is the cap level, while the forward rate is used as the "price" of the underlying. Using Black's model then, the option premium is given by

$$C = \frac{\emptyset M}{1 + \emptyset rf} \times e^{-rT} \times [rfN(d_1) - rXN(d_2)] \qquad (20.8)$$

where

$$d_1 = \frac{\ln(rf / rX)}{\sigma_f\sqrt{T}} + \frac{\sigma_f}{2}\sqrt{T}$$

$$d_2 = d_1 - \sigma_f\sqrt{T}$$

and
rf is the forward rate for the relevant term (three-month, six-month, etc)
$\emptyset$ is the rate-fixing frequency, such as semi-annually or quarterly
σ_f is the forward rate volatility
T is the time period from the start of the cap to the caplet payment date.

Each caplet can be priced individually and the total premium payable on the cap is the sum of the caplet prices. The Black model assumes constant volatility, and so banks use later models to price products when this assumption is considered to be materially unrealistic.

A vanilla cap-pricing calculator is part of the RATE application software, included in this book.

In the same way as caps and caplets, a floorlet is essentially a put option on an interest rate, with a sequence of floorlets being known as a floor. This might be used, for example, by a lender of funds to limit the loss of income should interest-rate levels fall. If a firm buys a call and sells a floor, this is known as buying a collar because the interest rate payable is bound on the upside at the cap level and on the downside at the floor level. It is possible to purchase a zero-cost collar where the premium of the cap and floor elements are identical. This form of interest-rate risk management is very popular with corporates.

Selected Bibliography and References

Hull, J., *Options, Futures and Other Derivatives* (4th edition), Prentice Hall, 2000.

Kolb, R., *Futures, Options and Swaps* (4th edition), Blackwell, 2003.

Galitz, L., *Financial Engineering* (Revised edition), FT Pitman, 1995.

Marshall, J. and Bansal, V., *Financial Engineering*, New York Institute of Finance, 1992.

Tucker, A., *Financial Futures, Options and Swaps*, West Publishing, 1991.

PART IV

Bond trading and hedging

In the last part of the book we present some insights on trading put together by the author based on his experiences working as a gilt-edged market maker and sterling bond proprietary trader. The topics covered include implied spot yields and market zero-coupon yields, yield curve spread trading and butterfly yields. There are also some observations on the behaviour of the gilt strip market since its introduction in December 1997.

We begin however with an introduction to risk management for a bond or credit trader, and a look at the Value-at-Risk risk measurement tool.

21

Value-at-Risk and Credit VaR

In this chapter, we review the main risk-measurement tool used in banking, known as value-at-risk (VaR). The review looks at the three main methodologies used to calculate VaR, as well as some of the key assumptions used in the calculations, including those on the normal distribution of returns, volatility levels and correlations. We also discuss the use of the VaR methodology with respect to credit risk.

Introducing value-at-risk

Introduction

The introduction of value-at-risk as an accepted methodology for quantifying market risk and its adoption by bank regulators is part of the evolution of risk management. The application of VaR has been extended from its initial use in securities houses to commercial banks and corporates, following its introduction in October 1994 when JP Morgan launched RiskMetrics™ free over the Internet.

VaR is a measure of the worst expected loss that a firm may suffer over a period of time that has been specified by the user, under normal market conditions and a specified level of confidence. This measure may be obtained in a number of ways, using a statistical model or by computer simulation. We can define VaR as follows:

VaR is a measure of market risk. It is the maximum loss which can occur with X% confidence over a holding period of n days.

VaR is the expected loss of a portfolio over a specified time period for a set level of probability. For example, if a daily VaR is stated as £100,000 to a 95% level of confidence, this means that during the day there is a only a 5% chance that the loss the next day will be *greater* than £100,000. VaR measures the potential loss in market value of a portfolio using estimated volatility and correlation. The "correlation" referred to is the correlation that exists between the market prices of different instruments in a bank's portfolio. VaR is calculated within a given confidence interval, typically 95% or 99%; it seeks to measure the possible losses from a position or portfolio under "normal" circumstances. The definition of normality is critical and is essentially a statistical concept that varies by firm and by risk-management system. Put simply, however, the most commonly used VaR models assume that the prices of assets in the financial markets follow a normal distribution. To implement VaR, all of a firm's positions data must be gathered into one centralised database. Once this is complete, the overall risk has to be calculated by aggregating the risks from individual instruments across the entire portfolio. The potential move in each instrument (that is, each risk factor) has to be inferred from past daily price movements over a given observation period. For regulatory purposes, this period is at least one year. Hence, the data on which VaR estimates are based should capture all relevant daily market moves over the previous year.

The main assumption underpinning VaR – and which in turn may be seen as its major weakness – is that the distribution of future price and rate changes will follow past variations. Therefore, the potential portfolio loss calculations for VaR are worked out using distributions from historic price data in the observation period.

VaR is a measure of the volatility of a firm's banking or trading book. A portfolio containing assets that have a high level of volatility has a higher risk than one containing assets with a lower level of volatility. The VaR measure seeks to quantify in a single measure the potential losses that may be suffered by a portfolio.

VaR is therefore a measure of a bank's risk exposure; it is a tool for measuring market risk exposure. There is no one VaR number for a single portfolio, because different methodologies used for calculating VaR produce different results. The VaR number captures only those risks that can be measured in quantitative terms. It does not capture risk exposures such as operational risk, liquidity risk, regulatory risk or sovereign risk. It is important to be aware of what precisely VaR attempts to capture and what it clearly makes no attempt to capture. Also, VaR is not "risk management".

A risk-management department may choose to use a VaR-measurement system in an effort to quantify a bank's risk exposure; however, the application itself is merely a tool. Implementing such a tool in no way compensates for inadequate procedures and rules in the management of a trading book.

Assumption of normality

A distribution is described as normal if there is a high probability that any observation from the population sample will have a value that is close to the mean, and a low probability of having a value that is far from the mean. The normal distribution curve is used by many VaR models, which assume that asset returns follow a normal pattern. A VaR model uses the normal curve to estimate the losses that an institution may suffer over a given time period. Normal distribution tables show the probability of a particular observation moving a certain distance from the mean.

If we look along a normal distribution table we see that at -1.645 standard deviations, the probability is 5%. This means that there is a 5% probability that an observation will be at least 1.645 standard deviations below the mean. This level is used in many VaR models.

Calculation methods

There are three different methods for calculating VaR. They are:
- the variance/covariance (or *correlation* or *parametric* method)
- historical simulation
- Monte Carlo simulation.

Variance-covariance method

This method assumes the returns on risk factors are normally distributed, the correlations between risk factors are constant and the delta (or price sensitivity to changes in a risk factor) of each portfolio constituent is constant. Using the correlation method, the volatility of each risk factor is extracted from the historical observation period. Historical data on investment returns is therefore required. The potential effect of each component of the portfolio on the overall portfolio value is then worked out from the component's delta (with respect to a particular risk factor) and that risk factor's volatility.

There are different methods of calculating the relevant risk factor volatilities and correlations. Two alternatives are:

- simple *historic volatility*: this is the most straightforward method but the effects of a large one-off market move can significantly distort volatilities over the required forecasting period. For example, if using 30-day historic volatility, a market shock will stay in the volatility figure for 30 days until it drops out of the sample range and correspondingly causes a sharp drop in (historic) volatility 30 days *after* the event. This is because each past observation is equally weighted in the volatility calculation.
- to weight past observations unequally: this is done to give more weight to recent observations so that large jumps in volatility are not caused by events that occurred some time ago. One method is to use exponentially weighted moving averages.

Historical simulation method

The historical simulation method for calculating VaR is the simplest and avoids some of the pitfalls of the correlation method. Specifically the three main assumptions behind correlation (normally distributed returns, constant correlations, constant deltas) are not needed in this case. For historical simulation, the model calculates potential losses using actual historical returns in the risk factors and so captures the non-normal distribution of risk-factor returns. This means rare events and crashes can be included in the results. As the risk-factor returns used for revaluing the portfolio are actual past movements, the correlations in the calculation are also actual past correlations. They capture the dynamic nature of correlation as well as scenarios when the usual correlation relationships break down.

Monte Carlo simulation method

The third method, Monte Carlo simulation, is more flexible than the previous two. As with historical simulation, Monte Carlo simulation allows the risk manager to use actual historical distributions for risk-factor returns rather than having to assume normal returns. A large number of randomly generated simulations are run forward in time using volatility and correlation estimates chosen by the risk manager. Each simulation will be different but, in total, the simulations will aggregate to the chosen statistical parameters (that is, historical distributions and volatility and correlation estimates). This method is more realistic than the previous two models and therefore is more likely to estimate VaR more accurately. However, its implementation requires powerful computers and there is also a trade-off in that the time required to perform calculations is longer.

The level of confidence in the VaR estimation process is selected by the number of standard deviations of variance applied to the probability distribution. A standard deviation selection of 1.645 provides a 95% confidence level (in a one-tailed test) that the potential estimated price movement will not be more than a given amount based on the correlation of market factors to the position's price sensitivity.

Explaining value-at-risk

Correlation

Measures of correlation between variables are important to fund managers who are interested in reducing their risk exposure through diversifying their portfolio. Correlation is a measure of the degree to which a value of one variable is related to the value of another. The correlation coefficient is a single number that compares the strengths and directions of the movements in two instruments values. The sign of the coefficient determines the relative directions that the instruments move in, while its value determines the strength of the relative movements. The value of the coefficient ranges from −1 to +1, depending on the nature of the relationship. So if, for exmple, the value of the correlation is 0.5, this means that one instrument moves in the same direction by half of the amount that the other instrument moves. A value of zero means that the instruments are uncorrelated, and their movements are independent of each other.

Correlation is a key element of many VaR models, including parametric models. It is particularly important in the measurement of the variance (hence, volatility) of a portfolio. If we take the simplest example, a portfolio containing just two assets, (21.1) below gives the volatility of the portfolio based on the volatility of each instrument in the portfolio (x and y) and their correlation with one another.

$$V_{port} = x^2 + y^2 + 2xy \cdot r(xy)$$ (21.1)

where

x is the volatility of asset x
y is the volatility of asset y
ρ is the correlation between assets x and y.

The correlation coefficient between two assets uses the covariance between the assets in its calculation. The standard formula for covariance is shown at (21.2):

$$Cov = \frac{\sum_{i=1}^{n} (xi - \bar{x})(yi - \bar{y})}{(n - 1)} \tag{21.2}$$

where the sum of the distance of each value x and y from the mean is divided by the number of observations minus one. The covariance calculation enables us to calculate the correlation coefficient, shown as (21.3):

$$\rho = Cov \frac{(1,2)}{\sigma_1 \times \sigma_2} \tag{21.3}$$

where σ is the standard deviation of each asset.

Equation (21.1) may be modified to cover more than two instruments. In practice, correlations are usually estimated on the basis of past historical observations. This is an important consideration in the construction and analysis of a portfolio, as the associated risks will depend to an extent on the correlation between its constituents.

It should be apparent that from a portfolio perspective a positive correlation increases risk. If the returns on two or more instruments in a portfolio are positively correlated, strong movements in either direction are likely to occur at the same time. The overall distribution of returns will be wider and flatter, as there will be higher joint probabilities associated with extreme values (both gains and losses). A negative correlation indicates that the assets are likely to move in opposite directions, thus reducing risk.

It has been argued that in extreme situations, such as market crashes or large-scale market corrections, correlations cease to have any relevance, because all assets will be moving in the same direction. However, under most market scenarios, using correlations to reduce the risk of a portfolio is considered satisfactory practice, and the VaR number for diversified portfolio will be lower than that for an undiversified portfolio.

Simple VaR calculation

To calculate the VaR for a single asset, we would calculate the standard deviation of its returns, using either its historical volatility or implied volatility. If a 95% confidence level is required, meaning we wish to have 5% of the observations in the left-hand tail of the normal distribution, this means that the observations in that area are 1.645 standard deviations away from the mean. This can be checked from standard normal tables. Consider the following statistical data for a government bond, calculated using one year's historical observations.

Nominal:	£10 million
Price:	£100
Average return:	7.35%
Standard deviation: 1.99%	

The VaR at the 95% confidence level is 1.645 x 0.0199 or 0.032736. The portfolio has a market value of £10 million, so the VaR of the portfolio is 0.032736 x 10,000,000 or £327,360. So this figure is the maximum loss the portfolio may sustain over one year for 95% of the time.

We may extend this analysis to a two-stock portfolio. In a two-asset portfolio, we stated at (21.1) that there is a relationship that enables us to calculate the volatility of a two-asset portfolio; this expression is used to calculate the VaR, and is shown at (21.4):

$$VaR_{port} = \sqrt{w_1^2\sigma_1^2 + w_2^2\sigma_2^2 + 2w_1w_2\sigma_1\sigma_2\rho_{1,2}} \qquad (21.4)$$

where

w_1 is the weighting of the first asset
w_2 is the weighting of the second asset
σ_1 is the standard deviation or volatility of the first asset
σ_2 is the standard deviation or volatility of the second asset
$\rho_{1,2}$ is the correlation coefficient between the two assets.

In a two-asset portfolio, the undiversified VaR is the weighted average of the individual standard deviations; the diversified VaR, which takes into account the correlation between the assets, is the square root of the variance of the portfolio. In practice, banks will calculate both diversified and undiversified VaR. The diversified VaR measure is used to set trading limits, while the larger undiversified VaR measure is used to gauge an idea of the bank's risk exposure in the event of a significant correction or market crash. This is because in a crash situation, liquidity dries up as market participants all attempt to sell off their assets. This means that the correlation relationship between assets ceases to have any impact on a book, as all assets move in the same direction. Under this scenario, then, it is more logical to use an undiversified VaR measure.

Although the description given here is very simple, it nevertheless explains what is the essence of the VaR measure. VaR is essentially the calculation of the standard deviation of a portfolio, which is the used as an indicator of the volatility of that portfolio. A portfolio exhibiting high volatility will have a high VaR number. An observer may then conclude that the portfolio has a ¡igh probability of making losses. Risk managers and traders may use the VaR measure to help them to allocate capital to more efficient sectors of the bank, as return on capital can now be measured in terms of return on risk capital. Regulators may use the VaR number as a guide to the capital-adequacy levels that they feel the bank requires.

Variance-covariance value-at-risk

Calculation of variance-covariance VaR

In the previous section we showed how VaR could be calculated for a two-stock portfolio. Here, we illustrate how this is done using matrices.

Consider the following hypothetical portfolio, invested in two assets, as shown in Table 21.1. The standard deviation of each asset has been calculated on historical observation of asset returns. Note that returns are returns of asset prices, rather than the prices themselves; they are calculated from the actual prices by taking the ratio of closing prices. The returns are then calculated as the logarithm of the price relatives. The mean and standard deviation of the returns are then calculated using standard statistical formulae. This would then give the standard deviation of daily price relatives, which is converted to an annual figure by multiplying it by the square root of the number of days in a year, usually taken to be 250.

Assets	Bond 1	Bond 2
Standard deviation	11.83%	17.65%
Portfolio weighting	60%	40%
Correlation coefficient	0.647	
Portfolio value	£10,000,000	
Variance	0.016506998	
Standard deviation	12.848%	
95% c.i. standard deviations	1.644853	
Value-at-Risk	0.211349136	
Value-at-Risk £	£2,113,491	

Table 21.1 Two-asset portfolio VaR.

The standard equation (shown as (21.4)) is used to calculate the variance of the portfolio, using the standard deviations of the individual assets and the asset weightings. The VaR of the book is the square root of the variance. Multiplying this figure by the current value of the portfolio gives us the portfolio VaR, which is £2,113,491.

The RiskMetric™ VaR methodology uses matrices to obtain the same results that we have shown here. This is because once a portfolio starts to contain many assets, the method we described above becomes unwieldy. Matrices allow us to calculate VaR for a portfolio containing many hundreds of assets, which would require assessment of the volatility of each asset and correlations of each asset to all the others in the portfolio. We can demonstrate how the parametric methodology uses variance and correlation matrices to calculate the variance, and hence standard deviation, of a portfolio. The matrices are shown at Table 21.2. Note that the multiplication of matrices carries with it some unique rules; readers who are unfamiliar with matrices should refer to a standard mathematics textbook.

As shown at Table 21.2, using the same two-asset portfolio described, we can set a 2x2 matrix with the individual standard deviations inside; this is labeled the "variance" matrix. The standard deviations are placed on the horizontal axis of the matrix, and a zero entered in the other cells. The second matrix is the correlation matrix, and the correlation of the two assets is placed in cells corresponding to the other asset. That is why a "1" is placed in the other cells, as an asset is said to have a correlation of 1 with itself. The two matrices are then multiplied to produce another matrix, labeled "VC" in Figure 21.1.[1]

The VC matrix is then multiplied with the V matrix to obtain the variance-covariance matrix or VCV matrix. This shows the variance of each asset; for Bond 1 this is 0.01399, which is expected as that is the square of its standard deviation, which we were given at the start. The matrix also tells us that Bond 1 has a covariance of 0.0135 with Bond 2. We then set up a matrix of the portfolio weighting of the two assets, and this is multiplied by the VCV matrix. This produces a 1x2 matrix, which we need to change to a single number, so this is multiplied by the W matrix, reset as a 2x1 matrix, which produces the portfolio variance. This is 0.016507. The standard deviation is the square root of the variance, and is 0.1284795 or 12.848%, which is what we obtained before. In our illustration it is important to note the order in which the matrices were multiplied, as this will obviously affect

---

[1] Microsoft Excel has a function for multiplying matrices which may be used for any type of matrix. The function is "=MMULT()" typed in all the cells of the product matrix.

the result. The volatility matrix contains the standard deviations along the diagonal, and zeros are entered in all the other cells. So if the portfolio we were calculating has 50 assets in it, we would require a 50x50 matrix and enter the standard deviations for each asset along the diagonal line. All the other cells would have a zero in them. Similarly for the weighting matrix; this is always one row, and all the weights are entered along the row. To take the example just given, the result would be a 1x50 weighting matrix.

	Variance matrix		**Correlation matrix**		**VC matrix**	
			Bond 1	Bond 2		
Bond 1	11.83%	0	1	0.647	0.1183	0.07654
Bond 2	0	17.65%	0.647	1	0.114196	0.1765
	VC matrix		**Variance matrix**		**VCV matrix**	
	0.1183	0.07654	11.83%	0	0.013995	0.013509
	0.1141955	0.1765	0	17.65%	0.013509	0.031152
	Weighting matrix		**VCV matrix**		**WVCV**	
	60%	40%	0.013995	0.013509	0.013801	0.020566
			0.013509	0.031152		
	WVCV		**W**		**WVCVW**	
	0.013801	0.020566	60%		0.016507	
			40%			

Standard deviation 0.1284796

Figure 21.1 Matrix variance-covariance calculation for a two-asset portfolio

The matrix method for calculating the standard deviation is more effective than the first method we described, because it can be used for a portfolio containing a large number of assets. In fact, this is exactly the methodology used by RiskMetrics™ and the computer model used for the calculation will be set up with matrices containing the data for hundreds, if not thousands, of different assets.

The variance-covariance method captures the diversification benefits of a multi-product portfolio because of the correlation coefficient matrix used in the calculation. For instance, if the two bonds in our hypothetical portfolio had a negative correlation, the VaR number produced would be lower. It was also the first methodology introduced, by JP Morgan in 1994. To apply it, a bank would require data on volatility and correlation for the assets in its portfolio. This data is actually available from the RiskMetrics™ website (and other sources), so a bank does not necessarily need its own data. It may wish to use its own datasets, however, should it have them, to tailor the application to its own use. The advantages of the variance-covariance methodology are that:

- it is simple to apply, and fairly straightforward to explain
- datasets for its use are immediately available.

The drawbacks of the variance-covariance are that it assumes stable correlations and measures only linear risk; it also places excessive reliance on the normal distribution, and returns in the market are widely believed to have "fatter tails" than a true-to-normal distribution. This phenomenon is known as leptokurtosis, that is, the non-normal distribution of outcomes. Another disadvantage is that the process requires mapping. To construct a weighting portfolio for the RiskMetrics™ tool, cash flows from financial instruments are mapped into precise maturity points, known as grid points. We will review this later in the chapter. However, in most cases, assets do not fit into neat grid points, and complex instruments cannot be broken down accurately into cash flows. The mapping process makes assumptions that frequently do not hold in practice.

Nevertheless, the variance-covariance method is still popular in the market, and is frequently the first VaR method installed at a bank.

Mapping

The cornerstone of variance-covariance methodologies such as RiskMetrics™ is the requirement for data on volatilities and correlations for assets in the portfolio. The RiskMetrics™ dataset does not contain volatilities for every maturity possible, as that would require a value for very period from 1 day to over 10,950 days (30 years) and longer, and correlations between each of these days. This would result in an excessive amount of calculation. Rather, volatilities are available for set maturity periods, and these are shown in Table 21.2.

RiskMetrics grid points
1 month
3 months
6 month
1 year
2 years
3 years
4 years
5 years
7 years
9 years
10 years
15 years
20 years
30 years

Table 21.2 RiskMetrics™ grid points

If a bond is maturing in six years' time, its redemption cash flow will not match the data in the RiskMetrics™ dataset, so it must be mapped to two periods; in this case, being split to the five-year and seven-year grid point. This is done in proportions so that the original value of the bond is maintained once it has been mapped. More importantly, when a cash flow is mapped, it must split in a manner that preserves the volatility characteristic of the original cash flow. Therefore, when mapping cash flows, if one cash flow is apportioned to two grid points, the share of the two new cash flows must equal the present value of the original cash flows, and the combined volatility of the two new assets must be equal to that of the original asset. A simple demonstration is given at Example 21.1.

EXAMPLE 21.1 Cash–flow mapping

A bond trading book holds £1 million nominal of a gilt strip that is due to mature in precisely six years' time. To correctly capture the volatility of this position in the bank's RiskMetrics™ VaR estimate, the cash flow represented by this bond must be mapped to the grid points for five years and seven years, the closest maturity buckets for which the RiskMetrics™ dataset holds volatility and correlation data. The present value of the strip is calculated using the six-year zero-coupon rate, which RiskMetrics™ obtains by interpolating between the five-year rate and the seven-year rate. The details are shown in Table 21.3.

Gilt strip nominal (£)	1,000,000
Maturity (years)	6
5-year zero-coupon rate	5.35%
7-year zero-coupon rate	5.50%
5-year volatiluty	24.50%
7-year volatility	28.95%
Correlation coefficient	0.979

Table 21.3 Bond position to be mapped to grid points

Note that the correlation between the two interest rates is very close to 1. This is expected because five-year interest rates generally move very closely in line with seven-year rates.

We wish to assign the single cash flow to the five-year and seven-year grid points (also referred to as vertices). The present value of the bond, using the six-year interpolated yield, is £728,347. This is shown in Table 21.5, which also uses an interpolated volatility to calculate the volatility of the six-year cash flow. However, we wish to calculate a portfolio volatility based on the apportionment of the cash flow to the five-year and seven-year grid points. To do this, we need to use a weighting to allocate the cash flow between the two vertices. In the hypothetical situation used here, this presents no problem because six years falls precisely between five years and seven years. Therefore, the weightings are 0.5 for year five and 0.5 for year seven. If the cash flow had fallen in a less obvious maturity point, we would have to calculate the weightings using the formula for portfolio variance. Using these weightings, we calculate the variance for the new "portfolio", containing the two new cash flows, and then the standard deviation for the portfolio. This gives us a VaR for the strip of £265,853.

Interpolated yield	0.05425
Interpolated volatility	0.26725
Present value	728,347.0103
Weighting 5-year grid point	0.5
Weighting 7-year grid point	0.5
Variance of portfolio	0.070677824
Standard deviation	0.265853012
VaR £	265,853

Table 21.4 Cash-flow mapping and portfolio variance

Confidence intervals

Many models estimate VaR at a given confidence interval, under normal market conditions. This assumes that market returns generally follow a random pattern but one that approximates over time to a normal distribution. The level of confidence at which the VaR is calculated will depend on the nature of the trading book's activity and what the VaR number is being used for. The Market Risk amendment to the Basel Capital Accord stipulates a 99% confidence interval and a 10-day holding period if the VaR measure is to be used to calculate the regulatory capital requirement. However, certain banks prefer to use other confidence levels and holding periods; the decision on which level to use is a function of the asset-types in the portfolio, the quality of market data available and the accuracy of the model itself, which will have been tested over time by the bank.

For example, a bank may view a 99% confidence interval as providing no useful information, as it implies that there should only be two or three breaches of the VaR measure over the course of one year. That would leave no opportunity to test the accuracy of the model until a longer period of time had elapsed and, in the meantime, the bank would be unaware if the model was generating inaccurate numbers. A 95% confidence level implies that the VaR level is being exceeded around one day each month, if a year is assumed to contain 250 days.[2] If a VaR calculation is made using 95% confidence, and a 99% confidence level is required for, say, regulatory purposes, we need to adjust the measure to take account of the change in standard deviations required. For example, a 99% confidence interval corresponds to 2.32 standard deviations, while a 95% level is equivalent to 1.645 standard deviations. Thus, to convert from 95% confidence to 99% confidence, the VaR figure is divided by 1.645 and multiplied by 2.32.

In the same way, there may be occasions when a firm will wish to calculate VaR over a different holding period to that recommended by the Basel Committee. The holding period of a portfolio's VaR calculation should represent the period of time required to unwind the portfolio; that is, sell off the assets on the book. A 10-day holding period is recommended but would be unnecessary for a highly liquid portfolio — for example, one holding government bonds.

To adjust the VaR number to fit it to a new holding period we simply scale it upwards or downward by the square root of the time period required. For example, a VaR calculation measured for a 10-day holding period will be $\sqrt{10}$ times larger than the corresponding 1-day measure.

Historical VaR methodology

The historical approach to value-at-risk is a relatively simple calculation, and it is also easy to implement and explain. To implement it, a bank requires a database record of its past profit/loss figures for the total portfolio. The required confidence interval is then applied to this record, to obtain a cut-off of the worst-case scenario. For example, to calculate the VaR at a 95% confidence level, the fifth percentile value for the historical data is taken, and this is the VaR number. For a 99% confidence level measure, the 1% percentile is taken. The advantage of the historical method is that it uses the actual market data that a bank has recorded (unlike RiskMetrics™, for example, for which the volatility and correlations are not actual values, but estimated values calculated from average figures over a period of time, usually the last five years), and so produces a reasonably accurate figure. Its main weakness is that as it is reliant on actual historical data built up over a period of time, generally at least one year's data is required to make the calculation meaningful. Therefore, it is not suitable for portfolios whose asset weightings frequently change, as another set of data would be necessary before a VaR number could be calculated.

To overcome this drawback banks use a method known as historical simulation. This calculates VaR for the current portfolio weighting, using the historical data for the securities in the current portfolio. To calculate historical simulation VaR for our hypothetical portfolio considered earlier,

---

[2] For the 99% confidence level, $250 \times 1\% = 2.5$ days in one year, while 95% confidence is $250 \times 5\%$ or 12.5 days.

comprising 60% of bond 1 and 40% of bond 2, we require the closing prices for both assets over the specified previous period (usually three or five years). We then calculate the value of the portfolio for each day in the period assuming constant weightings.

Simulation methodology

The most complex calculations use computer simulations to estimate value-at-risk. The most common of these is the Monte Carlo method. To calculate VaR using a Monet Carlo approach, a computer simulation is run to generate a number of random scenarios, which are then used to estimate the portfolio VaR. The method is probably the most realistic, if we accept that market returns follow a similar "random walk" pattern. However, Monte Carlo simulation is best suited to trading books containing large option portfolios, whose price behavior is not captured very well with the RiskMetrics™ methodology. The main disadvantage of the simulation methodology is that it is time-consuming and uses a substantial amount of computer resources.

A Monte Carlo simulation generates simulated future prices, and it may be used to value an option as well as for VaR applications. When used for valuation, a range of possible asset prices are generated and these are used to assess what intrinsic value the option will have at those asset prices. The present value of the option is then calculated from these possible intrinsic values. Generating simulated prices, although designed to mimic a "random walk", cannot be completely random because asset prices, although not a pure normal distribution, are not completely random either. The simulation model is usually set to generate very few extreme prices. Strictly speaking, it is asset price *returns* that follow a normal distribution, or rather a lognormal distribution. Monte Carlo simulation may also be used to simulate other scenarios; for example, the effect on option "Greeks" for a given change in volatility, or any other parameters. The scenario concept may be applied to calculating VaR as well. For example, if 50,000 simulations of an option price are generated, the 95th lowest value in the simulation will be the VaR at the 95% confidence level. The correlation between assets is accounted for by altering the random selection program to reflect relationships.

EXAMPLE 21.2 **Portfolio volatilty using variance–covariance and simulation methods**

A simple two-asset portfolio is composed of the following instruments:

	Gilt strip	FTSE100 stock
Number of units	£100 million	£5 million
Market value	£54.39 million	£54 million
Daily volatility	£0.18 million	£0.24 million

The correlation between the two assets is 20%. Using (21.4) we calculate the portfolio VaR as follows:

$$\text{Vol} = \sqrt{s_{bond}^2 + s_{stock}^2 + 2s_{bond}s_{stock}r_{bond,stock}}$$

$$\text{Vol} = \sqrt{0.18^2 + 0.24^2 + (2 \times 0.18 \times 0.24 \times 0.2)}$$

$$= 0.327$$

We have ignored the weighting element for each asset because the market values are roughly equal. The calculation gives a portfolio volatility of £0.327 million. For a 95% confidence level VaR measure, which corresponds to 1.645 standard deviations (in a one-tailed test), we multiply the portfolio volatility by 1.645, which gives us a portfolio value-at-risk of £0.538 million.

In a Monte Carlo simulation, we also calculate the correlation and volatilities of the portfolio. These values are used as parameters in a random-number simulation to throw out changes in the underlying portfolio value. These values are used to re-price the portfolio, and this value will be either a gain or loss on the actual mark-to-market value. This process is repeated for each random number that is generated. In Table 21.5 we show the results for 15 simulations of our two-asset portfolio. From the results we read off the loss level that corresponds to the required confidence interval.

Simulation	Market value: bond	Market value: stock	Portfolio value	Profit/Loss
1	54.35	54.9	109.25	0.86
2	54.64	54.02	108.66	0.27
3	54.4	53.86	108.26	-0.13
4	54.25	54.15	108.4	0.01
5	54.4	54.17	108.57	0.18
6	54.4	54.03	108.43	0.04
7	54.31	53.84	108.15	-0.24
8	54.3	53.96	108.26	-0.13
9	54.46	54.11	108.57	0.18
10	54.32	53.92	108.24	-0.15
11	54.31	53.97	108.28	-0.11
12	54.47	54.08	108.55	0.16
13	54.38	54.03	108.41	0.02
14	54.71	53.89	108.6	0.21
15	54.29	54.05	108.34	-0.05

Table 21.5 Monte Carlo simulation results

As the number of trials is increased, the results from a Monte Carlo simulation approach those of the variance-covariance measure. This is shown in Figure 21.1.

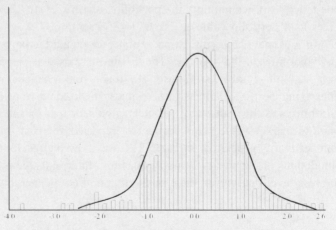

Figure 21.1 The normal approximation of returns
Source: JPMorgan

Value-at-Risk for fixed-income instruments

Perhaps the most straightforward instruments to which VaR can be applied are foreign-exchange and interest-rate instruments such as money-market products, bonds, forward-rate agreements and swaps. In this section, we review the calculation of VaR for a simple portfolio of bonds.

Sample bond portfolio

Table 21.6 details the bonds that are in our portfolio. For simplicity, we assume that all the bonds pay an annual coupon and have full years left to maturity. In order to calculate the value-at-risk, we first need to value the bond portfolio itself. The bonds are valued by breaking them down into their constituent cash flows; the present value of each cash flow is then calculated, using the appropriate zero-coupon interest rate. Note from Figure 21.2 that the term structure is inverted.

Table 21.7 shows the present values for each of the cash flows. The total portfolio value is also shown.

	Bond 1	Bond 2	Bond 3
Nominal value	10,000,000	3,800,000	9,700,000
Coupon	5%	7.25%	6%
Maturity	5	7	2

Table 21.6 Sample three-bond portfolio

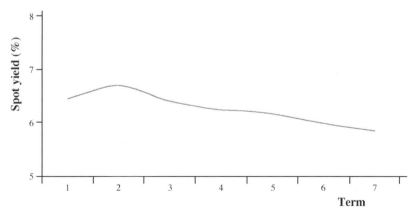

Figure 21.2 Term structure used for valuation

Period	Cash flows: Bond 1	Bond 2	Bond 2	Zero-coupon rates	Discount factor	Present values		
1	500,000	275,500	582,000	6.45	0.939408173	469,704	258,807	546,736
2	500,000	275,500	10,282,000	6.7	0.878357191	439,179	241,987	9,031,269
3	500,000	275,500		6.4	0.830185447	415,093	228,716	
4	500,000	275,500		6.25	0.784664935	392,332	216,175	
5	10,500,000	275,500		6.18	0.740945722	7,779,930	204,131	
6		275,500		5.98	0.705759136	0	194,437	
7		4,075,500		5.87	0.670794678	0	2,733,824	
					Totals	9,496,238	4,078,077	9,578,004
				Portfolio value		23,152,319		

Table 21.7 Bond portfolio valuation

We then use the volatility for each period rate to calculate the VaR. Data on interest-rate volatility for all major currencies is available, for example, from the RiskMetrics™ website. The volatility levels for our hypothetical currency are relatively low in this example. The VaR for each maturity period is then obtained by multiplying the total present value of the cash flows for that period by its volatility level. This is shown in Table 21.8. By adding together all the individual values, we obtain an undiversified VaR for the portfolio. The total VaR is £1.77 million, for a portfolio with a market value of £23.1 million.

Period	Cash flows	Present value	Volatility	Value-at-Risk
1	1,357,500.00	1,275,246.59	0.0687	87,609.44
2	11,057,500.00	9,712,434.64	0.0695	675,014.21
3	775,500.00	643,808.81	0.07128	45,890.69
4	775,500.00	608,507.66	0.0705	42,899.79
5	10,775,500.00	7,984,060.63	0.08501	678,724.99
6	275,500.00	194,436.64	0.08345	16,225.74
7	4,075,500.00	2,733,823.71	0.08129	222,232.53
		Undiversified VaR	1,768,597.39	

Table 21.8 Bond portfolio undiversified VaR

The figure just calculated is the undiversified VaR for the bond portfolio. To obtain the diversified VaR for the book, we require the correlation coefficient of each interest rate with the other interest rates (the correlation will be very close to unity, although the shorter-dated rates will be closer in line with each other than they will be with long-dated rates). We may then use the standard variance-covariance approach, using a matrix of the undiversified VaR values and a matrix with the correlation values. However, the diversification benefit of a portfolio of bonds will be small, mainly because their volatilities will be closely correlated.

Forward-rate agreements

The VaR calculation for a forward-rate agreement (FRA) follows the principles reviewed in the previous section. An FRA is a notional loan or deposit for a period starting at some point in the future; in effect it used to fix a borrowing or lending rate. The derivation of an FRA rate is based on the principle of what it would cost for a bank that traded one to hedge it; this is known as the "breakeven" rate. So a bank that has bought 3v6 FRA (referred to as a "threes-sixes FRA") has effectively borrowed funds for three months and placed the funds on deposit for six months. Therefore, an FRA is best viewed as a combination of an asset and a liability, and that is how one is valued. So a long position in a 3v6 FRA is valued as the present value of a three-month cash-flow asset and the present value of a six-month cash-flow liability, using the three-month and six-month deposit rates. The net present value is taken, of course, because one cash flow is an asset and the other a liability.

Consider a 3v6 FRA that has been dealt at 5.797%, the three-month forward-forward rate. The value of its constituent (notional) cash flows is shown in Table 21.9. The three-month and six-month rates are cash rates in the market, while the interest-rate volatilities have been obtained from RiskMetrics™. The details are summarised in Table 21.9.

Cash flow	Term (days)	Cash rate	Interet rate volatilities	Present value	Undiversified VaR
10,000,000	91	5.38%	0.14%	9,867,765	13,815
−10,144,536	182	5.63%	0.21%	−9,867,765	20,722

Table 21.9 Undiversified VaR for a 3v6 FRA contract

The undiversified VaR is the sum of the individual VaR values, and is £34,537. It has little value in the case of an FRA, however, and would overstate the true VaR, because an FRA is made up of a notional asset and liability, so a fall in the value of one would see a rise in the value of the other. Unless a practitioner was expecting three-month rates to go in an opposite direction to six-month rates, there is an element of diversification benefit. There is a high correlation between the two rates, so the more logical approach is to calculate a diversified VaR measure.

For an instrument such as an FRA, the fact that the two rates used in calculating the FRA rate are closely positively correlated will mean that the diversification effect will be to reduce the VaR estimate, because the FRA is composed notionally of an asset and a liability. From the values in Table 21.12, therefore, the six-month VaR is actually a negative value (if the bank had sold the FRA, the three-month VaR would have the negative value). To calculate the diversified VaR, then, requires the correlation between the two interest rates, which may be obtained from the RiskMetrics™ dataset. This is observed to be 0.87. This value is entered into a 2x2 correlation matrix and used to calculate the diversified VaR in the normal way. The procedure is:

- transpose the weighting VaR matrix, to turn it into a 2x1 matrix
- multiply this by the correlation matrix
- multiply the result by the original 1x2 weighting matrix
- this gives us the variance; the VaR is the square root of this value.

The result is an diversified VaR of £11,051.

Interest-rate swaps

To calculate a variance-covariance VaR for an interest-rate swap, we use the process described earlier for an FRA. There are more cash flows that go to make up the undiversified VaR, because a swap is essentially a strip of FRAs. In a plain vanilla interest-rate swap, one party pays fixed rate basis on an annual or semi-annual basis, and receives floating-rate interest, while the other party pays floating-rate interest payments and receives fixed-rate interest. Interest payments are calculated on a notional sum, which does not change hands, and only interest payments are exchanged. In practice, it is the net difference between the two payments that is transferred.

The fixed rate on an interest-rate swap is the breakeven rate that equates the present value of the fixed-rate payments to the present value of the floating-rate payments. As the floating-rate payments are linked to a reference rate such as LIBOR, we do not know what they will be, but we use the forward rate applicable to each future floating payment date to calculate what it would be if we were to fix it today. The forward rate is calculated from zero-coupon rates today. A "long" position in a swap is to pay fixed and receive floating, and is conceptually the same as being short in a fixed-coupon bond and being long in a floating-rate bond. In effect, the long is "borrowing" money, so a rise in the fixed rate will result in a rise in the value of the swap. A "short" position is receiving fixed and paying floating, so a rise in interest rates results in a fall in the value of the swap. This is conceptually similar to a long position in a fixed-rate bond and a short position in a floating-rate bond.

Describing an interest-rate swap in conceptual terms of fixed- and floating-rate bonds gives some idea as to how it is treated for value-at-risk purposes. The coupon on a floating-rate bond is reset periodically in line with the stated reference rate, usually LIBOR. Therefore, the duration of a floating-rate bond is very low, and conceptually the bond may be viewed as being the equivalent of a bank deposit, which receives interest payable at a variable rate. For market-risk purposes,[3] the risk exposure of a bank deposit is nil, because its present value is not affected by changes in market interest rates. Similarly, the risk exposure of a floating-rate bond is very low and to all intents and purposes its VaR may be regarded as zero. This leaves only the fixed-rate leg of a swap to measure for VaR purposes.

Pay date	Swap rate	Principal (£)	Coupon (£)	Coupon present value (£)	Volatility	Undiversified VaR
7-Jun-00	6.73%	10,000,000	337,421	327,564	0.05%	164
7-Dec-00	6.73%	10,000,000	337,421	315,452	0.05%	158
7-Jun-01	6.73%	10,000,000	335,578	303,251	0.10%	303
7-Dec-01	6.73%	10,000,000	337,421	294,898	0.11%	324
7-Jun-02	6.73%	10,000,000	335,578	283,143	0.20%	566
9-Dec-02	6.73%	10,000,000	341,109	277,783	0.35%	972
9-Jun-03	6.73%	10,000,000	335,578	264,360	0.33%	872
8-Dec-03	6.73%	10,000,000	335,578	256,043	0.45%	1,152
7-Jun-04	6.73%	10,000,000	335,578	248,155	0.57%	1,414
7-Dec-04	6.73%	10,000,000	337,421	242,161	1.90%	4,601
					Total	**10,528**

Table 21.10 Fixed-rate leg of five-year interest-rate swap and undiversified VaR

---

[3] We emphasize for *market*-risk purposes; the credit-risk exposure for a floating-rate bond position is a function of the credit quality of the issuer.

Table 21.10 shows the fixed-rate leg of a five-year interest-rate swap. To calculate the undiversified VaR, we use the volatility rate for each term interest rate; this may be obtained from RiskMetrics™. Note that the RiskMetrics™ dataset supports only liquid currencies; for example, data on volatility and correlation is not available for certain emerging-market economies. Below, we show the VaR for each payment; the sum of all the payments constitutes the undiversified VaR. We then require the correlation matrix for the interest rates, and this is used to calculate the diversified VaR. The weighting matrix contains the individual term VaR values, which must be transposed before being multiplied by the correlation matrix.

Using the volatilities and correlations supplied by RiskMetrics™, the diversified VaR is shown to be £10,325. This is very close to the undiversified VaR of £10,528. This is not unexpected because the different interest rates are very closely correlated.

Using VaR to measure market-risk exposure for interest-rate products enables a risk manager to capture non-parallel shifts in the yield curve, which is an advantage over the traditional duration measure and interest-rate gap measure. Therefore, estimating a book's VaR measure is useful not only for the trader and risk manager, but also for senior management, who by using VaR will have a more accurate idea of the risk-market exposure of the bank. Value-at-risk methodology captures pivotal shifts in the yield curve by using the correlations between different maturity interest rates. This reflects the fact that short-term interest rates and long-term interest rates are not perfectly positively correlated.

Derivative products and Value–at–Risk

The variance-covariance methodology for calculating value-at-risk is considered adequate for trading books that contain mostly products that have a linear payoff profile. This covers money market interest-rate instruments; however the price/yield relationship for bonds exhibits a curved relationship, which gives rise to the convexity property. A trading book with convex instruments will have an added convexity risk exposure, and while most VaR methodologies are able to capture convexity risks adequately, an adjustment to the basic calculation has to be made. Such an adjusted measure is known as the *delta-gamma VaR*. Option products however, have a non-linear payoff profile, and it is more difficult to capture risks associated with option trading books using the variance-covariance approach. In this section we review the delta-gamma approach and its application to bonds and options. The specific risk measures used by option traders are considered in the next section.

Bond convexity

The duration and convexity of fixed income instruments were reviewed in Chapter 2. To recap, the *modified duration* of a bond is an indicator of its sensitivity to interest rates; it measures the change in price of the bond for a 1% change in yield. The higher the level of modified duration in a bond, the more sensitive it is to changes in market interest rates. However the relationship between price and yield in a bond is not a straight-line one; for changes in yield much above 50 basis points, the result given by the modified duration measure becomes increasingly inaccurate. Thus the measure given by a bond's modified duration is only an approximation. The extent of the approximation of modified duration is given by *convexity*, which might be said to be a measure of the error made in using modified duration. Bonds with greater convexity perform differently under the same conditions compared to low convex bonds. For option products, the *delta* of an option is a measure of how much its price moves with respect to changes in the price of the underlying asset. Therefore delta for an option is a similar risk measure to modified duration for bonds. Due to the way it is calculated, the delta figure is also an approximation, and the delta of an option changes as the price of the underlying changes. To measure the change in an option delta with respect o changes in the price of the underlying, traders calculate the *gamma* of the option.

The convex relationship between bond price and yield illustrates that the change in prices for a given change in interest rates is not constant, and nor is it identical, for all but very small amounts, for both upward and downward changes in yield. This feature makes it a difficult property to capture in VaR calculations. Generally the slope of the convex curve flattens out as the yield increases, while it steepens as yields decrease. As this property cannot be captured, and differs among individual bonds, risk managers often overcome the problem with modelling it by simply assuming that the relationship is constant, and using modified duration as the usual risk measure. Under this assumption, we would calculate the VaR for a bond portfolio as described in Example 21.3.

EXAMPLE 21.3 Simplified VaR for a bond portfolio

A portfolio consists of several conventional bonds. The portfolio modified duration is 6.794, and it has a market value of £368 million. Market yields are expected to rise during the year, and the worst-case scenario, to 95% confidence, is a rise in yields of 75 basis points. As the interest-rate scenario is already given to the required degree of confidence, the VaR of the portfolio is given by:

368 million $\times -6.794 \times 0.75\%$

or £18 751 440.

The drawback in assuming constant changes in the price / yield relationship is that it is very inaccurate for large changes in yield. One of the main objectives of risk management is to provide accurate management information on the risk exposure of the bank, particularly under volatile conditions such as a market correction. As these are exactly the type of situation where there are large-scale moves in interest rates, the information contained in a bank's risk reports would be of questionable value.

To overcome this problem, it is necessary to make a convexity adjustment to the duration-based VaR measure. Convexity is the second derivative of duration risk measure, and is derived using a Taylor expansion (this is discussed in greater detail in a separate chapter). The convexity measure is used to provide a more accurate measure of modified duration, and is given by :

$$\tfrac{1}{2} \times CV \times (\Delta r)^2. \tag{21.5}$$

The convexity adjustment is added to the modified duration value. This is demonstrated in Example 21.4.

EXAMPLE 21.4 **Applying the convexity adjustment for a bond**

The analysis is conducted on a hypothetical bond, the 6% 2021, which pays an annual coupon on an actual/actual basis. Its redemption date is 24 January 2021, so the bond has precisely 20 years to maturity. The details are listed in Table 21.11.

Bond	6% 2021
Yield	6.15%
Price	98.30027
Duration	12.08839
Modified duration	11.38803
Convexity	184.21158

Table 21.11 Modified duration and convexity of 6% 2020 bond

The bond has a modified duration of 11.38803, a high value and not unexpected as the bond is very long-dated. The modified duration value is used to estimate the price of the bond resulting from a 1% upward move in yields; we see from Table 21.12 that already, using only modified duration, the new price is over-estimate by approximately one point. The convexity adjustment, using (21.5) is 0.92106%. However the over-estimation is pronounced for a large change, as shown by the 3% upward move in yields. Using the convexity adjustment, which is 8.28952%, the estimated price is considerably closer to the actual price. Note that we are estimating prices for a rise in yields; this means that the bond price will fall, so the modified duration measure is given a negative value. When making the convexity adjustment, we add the value for convexity to the (negative) modified duration value, thus reducing it. For a downward move in yield, modified duration is a positive value, as prices will rise. Adding the convexity adjustment will then increase the value for modified duration.

Yield	7.15%	9.15%	5.00%
Price	87.95764	71.54983	112.46221
MD estimate	86.91224	64.13618	111.39650
MD + *CV* estimate	87.8333	72.42570	113.46889

Table 21.12 Price estimate using convexity adjustment

Convexity is a valuable property in a bond and fund managers frequently look to invest in high convexity bonds; conversely there is usually a convexity premium in a bond, so that it will trade at a lower yield to a bond of similar duration but lower convexity. The attraction of convexity is apparent if the price / yield profile for two bonds is plotted; the bond with higher convexity will outperform the other bond no matter what happens to interest rates. That is, it will rise in price by more for a given fall in yields, and it will drop in price by less for a given rise in yields. Equally therefore, to be short convexity, as a result of running a short position in a bond, can significantly add to a trader's risk. This is because, being short, even a quite small fall in interest rates can substantially increase the risk exposure of the book. This property is even more pronounced with option products.

Option gamma

The gamma measurement for an option is conceptually similar to convexity for a bond. Convexity is a measure of the error made in using modified duration, that is, the curvature of the price / yield relationship. Gamma is the second derivative of an option's delta, so in effect measures the same thing as convexity. As with convexity, it is important for a trader to be aware of the gamma exposure of his book, as at a high gamma level, even very small changes in the price of the underlying asset may lead to substantial mark-to-market losses. A trader who writes options, whether put or call options, is effectively short gamma.

The gamma effect on an option book cannot be captured accurately by most VaR models. This is because the relationship between gamma and the price of the underlying is non-linear. To approximate the VaR measure for an option book, a *delta-gamma* calculation is made, and although it is still not completely accurate, it is a better estimate than the conventional delta-normal approach. However, although intuitively delta-gamma is similar to the convexity adjustment for a bond portfolio, it is not as good an approximation as the convexity measure. This is because behaviour of an option is more unpredictable than that of a bond. A bond instrument may be broken down into a series of zero coupon bonds, so that volatility and other data maybe adjusted for convexity with relative ease. This is not as easy for options, and becomes particularly acute as an option approaches maturity. For example, an at-the-money option will experience extreme movement in its gamma as it approaches maturity, in a way that unpredictable. It is difficult to capture this effect in a VaR model. Nevertheless, the delta-gamma measure is recognised as a close approximation of option book risk, short of using simulation-type VaR models.

The gamma effect has an impact on the distribution of returns from an option book. This transforms the distribution from normal to one with slightly skewed tails, as illustrated by Figure 21.3

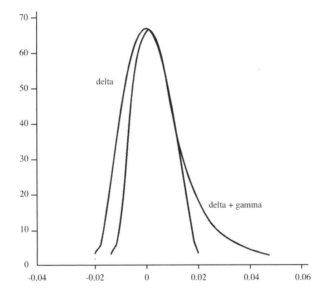

Figure 21.3 Delta + gamma effect

To illustrate the gamma adjustment, consider a position in a bond instrument and a put option on foreign exchange. The details are set out in Table 21.13. The interest-rate and FX volatility and correlation data may be obtained from RiskMetrics. Using these, we calculate the undiversified VaR in the normal manner, multiplying the market value of the instrument by the volatility value to obtain VaR. For the option, we also multiply the value and the volatility by the delta (that is, 1 507 000 × 0.54 × 6.10%). The delta adjustment is required because the price of the option does not "tick-for-tick" with the underlying, but by 0.54 for each unit change in the underlying. The undiversified VaR is 73,753.

Bond nominal	2,000,000
Maturity (years)	2
Market value	1,507,000
Volatility	1.60%
Undiversified VaR	24,112
Nominal value FX option	1,507,000
Delta	0.54
Gamma	3.9
FX volatility	6.10%
Undiversified VaR	49,641
Correlation coefficient	−0.31

Table 21.13 Hypothetical portfolio and undiversified VaR

To calculate the undiversified VaR we require the portfolio variance, which would normally be done in the conventional way using matrices; here there are only two assets so we may use the standard variance equation 36.4. The square root of this is the VaR, which is calculated as:

$$Var_{port} = \sqrt{24,112^2 + 49,641^2 \div (2.-0.31.24,112.49,641)}$$

$$= 41,498.$$

Although the diversified VaR is more realistic a measure, it will not take into account the gamma effect of the option. Previously we allowed for the delta of the option, which was used to modify the volatility level, which changed from 6.10% to 3.294%. The gamma adjustment is made by using equation 36.5, which in this case gives a gamma adjustment of 0.7256%. The delta-gamma approximation for the volatility is therefore 2.568%. Multiplying this by the weighting (the option value) we have a new diversified VaR for the option of 38 700. If we use the same portfolio variance equation we obtain a delta-gamma adjusted diversified VaR of 27 488.

The delta-gamma adjustment is only an approximation of an option book's gamma risk exposure, and it is not as close as a convexity adjustment. This is due mainly to the unpredictable behaviour of gamma as an option approaches maturity, more so if it is a-the-money.

Stress Testing

Risk-measurement models and their associated assumptions are not without limitation. It is important to understand what will happen should some of the model's underlying assumptions break down. Stress testing is a process whereby a series of scenario analyses or simulations are carried out to investigate the effect of extreme market conditions on the VaR estimates calculated by a model. It is also an analysis of the effect of violating any of the basic assumptions behind a risk model. If carried out efficiently, stress testing will provide clearer information on the potential exposures at risk due to significant market corrections, which is why the Basel Committee recommends that it be carried out.

Simulating stress

There is no standard way to undertake stress testing. It is a means of experimenting with the limits of a model. It is also a means to measure the residual risk which is not effectively captured by the formal risk model, thus complementing the VaR framework. If a bank uses a confidence interval of 99% when calculating its VaR, the losses on its trading portfolio due to market movements should not exceed the VaR number on more than one day in 100. For a 95% confidence level the corresponding frequency is one day in 20, or roughly one trading day each month. The question to ask is "What are the expected losses on those days?" Also, what can an institution do to protect itself against these losses? Assuming that returns are normally distributed provides a workable daily approximation for estimating risk but when market moves are more extreme these assumptions no longer add value. The 1% of market moves that are not used for VaR calculations include events such as the October 1987 crash, the bond market collapse of February 1994 and the Mexican peso crisis at the end of 1994. In these cases, market moves were much larger than any VaR model could account for; in fact, the October 1987 crash was a 20 standard deviation move. Under these circumstances, correlations between markets also increase well above levels normally assumed in models.

An approach used by risk managers is to simulate extreme market moves over a range of different scenarios. One method is to use Monte Carlo simulation. This allows dealers to push the risk factors to greater limits. For example, a 99% confidence interval captures events up to 2.33 standard deviations from the mean asset-return level. A risk manager can calculate the effect on the trading portfolio of a 10 standard deviation move. Similarly, risk managers may want to change the correlation assumptions under which they normally work. For instance, if markets all move down together, something that happened in Asian markets from the end of 1997 and emerging markets generally from July 1998 after the Russian bond technical default, losses will be greater than if some markets are offset by other negatively correlated markets.

Only by pushing the bounds of the range of market moves that are covered in the stress-testing process can financial institutions have an improved chance of identifying where losses might occur and, therefore, a better chance of managing their risk effectively.

Stress testing in practice

For effective stress testing, a bank has to consider non-standard situations. The Basel policy group has recommended certain minimum standards in respect of specified market movements. The parameters chosen are considered large moves to overnight marks, and include:

- parallel yield-curve shifts of 100 basis points up and down
- steepening and flattening of the yield curve (two-year to 10-year) by 25 basis points
- increase and decrease in three-month yield volatilities by 20%
- increase and decrease in equity index vales by 10%
- increase and decrease in swap spread by 20 basis point.

These scenarios represent a starting point for a framework for routine stress testing.

Banks agree that stress testing must be used to supplement VaR models. The main problem appears to be difficulty in designing appropriate tests. The main issues are:

- difficulty in "anticipating the unanticipated"
- adopting a systematic approach, with stress testing carried out by looking at past extremes and analysing the effect on the VaR number under these circumstances
- selecting 10 scenarios based on past extreme events and generating portfolio VaRs based on re-runs of these scenarios.

The latest practice is to adapt stress tests to suit the particular operations of a bank itself. On the basis that one of the main purposes of stress testing is to provide senior management with accurate information of the extent of a bank's potential risk exposure, more valuable data will be gained if the stress test is particularly relevant to the bank. For example, an institution such as Standard Chartered Bank, which has a relatively high level of exposure to exotic currencies, may design stress tests that take into account extreme movements in, say, regional Asian currencies. A mortgage book holding option positions only to hedge its cash book — say, one of the former UK building societies that subsequently converted to banks — may have no need for excessive stress testing on, perhaps, the effect of extreme moves in derivatives liquidity levels.

Issues in stress testing

It is to be expected that extreme market moves will not be captured in VaR measurements. The calculations will always assume that the probability of events such as the Mexican peso devaluation are extremely low when analysing historical or expected movements of the currency. Stress tests need to be designed to model for such occurrences. Back-testing a firm's qualitative and quantitative risk-management approach for actual extreme events often reveals the need to adjust reserves, increase the VaR factor, adopt additional limits and controls and expand risk calculations. With back-testing, a firm will take, say, its daily VaR number, which we will assume is computed to 95% degree of confidence. The estimate will be compared to the actual trading losses suffered by the book over a 20-day period and, if there is a significant discrepancy, the firm will need to go back to its model and make adjustments to parameters. Frequent and regular back-testing of the VaR model's output with actual trading losses is an important part of stress testing. To conduct back-testing efficiently, a firm would need to be able to strip out its intra-day profit-and-loss figures, so it could compare the actual change in P/L to what was forecast by the VaR model.

The procedure for stress testing in banks usually involves:
- creating hypothetical extreme scenarios
- computing corresponding hypothetical P/Ls.

One method is to imagine *global* scenarios. If one hypothesis is that the euro appreciates sharply against the dollar, the scenario needs to consider any related areas, such as the effect, if any, on the Swiss franc and Norwegian krone rate, or the effect on the yen and interest rates. Another method is to generate many *local* scenarios and so consider a few risk factors at a time. For example, given an FX option portfolio a bank might compute the hypothetical P/L for each currency pair under a variety of exchange rate and implied volatility scenarios. There is then the issue of amalgamating the results: one way would be to add the worst-case results for each of the sub-portfolios, but this ignores any portfolio effect and cross-hedging. This may result in an over-estimate that is of little use in practice.

Nevertheless, stress testing is one method to account for the effect of extreme events that occur more frequently than would be expected were asset returns to follow a true normal distribution. For example, five-standard-deviation moves in a market in one day have been observed to occur twice every 10 years or so, which is considerably more frequent than given by a normal distribution. Testing for the effects of such a move gives a bank an idea of its exposure under these conditions.

Value-at-risk methodology for credit risk

Credit risk emerged as a significant risk-management issue during the 1990s. In increasingly competitive markets, banks and securities houses began taking on greater credit risk in this period. For instance, consider the following developments:

- Credit spreads tightened during the late 1990s onwards, to the point where blue-chip companies such as BT plc or Shell plc were being offered syndicated loans for as little as 10–12 basis points over Libor. To maintain margin or increased return on capital, banks increased lending to lower-rated corporates.
- The growth in the use of complex financial instruments such as credit derivatives led to the need for more sophisticated analysis and awareness of the risks presented by these instruments.
- Investors were finding fewer opportunities in interest-rate and currency markets, and moved towards yield enhancement through extending and trading credit across lower-rated and emerging-market assets.
- The rapid expansion of high-yield and emerging-market sectors, again lower-rated assets.

The growth in credit exposures and the rise of complex instruments have led to a need for more sophisticated risk-management techniques.

Credit risk

There are two main types of credit risk:
- credit-spread risk
- credit-default risk.

Credit-spread risk

Credit spread is the excess premium, over and above government or risk-free risk, required by the market for taking on a certain assumed credit exposure. Credit-spread risk is the risk of financial loss resulting from changes in the level of credit spreads used in the marking-to-market of a product. It is exhibited by a portfolio for which the credit spread is traded and marked. Changes in observed credit spreads affect the value of the portfolio and can lead to losses for investors.

Credit-default risk

This is the risk that an issuer of debt (obligor) is unable to meet its financial obligations. Where an obligor defaults, a firm generally incurs a loss equal to the amount owed by the obligor less any recovery amount which the firm recovers as a result of foreclosure, liquidation or restructuring of the defaulted obligor. All portfolios of exposures exhibit credit-default risk.

The value-at-risk measurement methodology was first applied for credit risk by JP Morgan, which introduced the CreditMetrics™ tool in 1995. The measurement of credit risk requires a slightly different approach from that used for market risk, because the distribution of credit losses follows a different pattern. In the following sections we describe the approach used to measuring such risk.

Modelling credit risk

Credit-risk VaR methodologies take a portfolio approach to credit-risk analysis. This means that:
- credit risks to each obligor across the portfolio are re-stated on an equivalent basis and aggregated in order to be treated consistently, regardless of the underlying asset class
- correlations of credit-quality moves across obligors are taken into account.

This allows portfolio effects — the benefits of diversification and risks of concentration — to be quantified.

The portfolio risk of an exposure is determined by four factors:
- size of the exposure
- maturity of the exposure
- probability of default of the obligor
- systematic or concentration risk of the obligor.

Credit VaR, like market-risk VaR, considers (credit) risk in a mark-to-market framework. It arises from changes in value due to credit events — that is, changes in obligor credit quality including defaults, upgrades and downgrades.

Nevertheless, credit risk is different in nature from market risk. Typically, market-return distributions are assumed to be relatively symmetrical and approximated by normal distributions. In credit portfolios, value changes will be relatively small upon minor up/downgrades, but can be substantial upon default. This remote probability of large losses produces skewed distributions, with heavy downside tails that differ from the more normally distributed returns assumed for market VaR models. This is shown in Figure 21.4 .

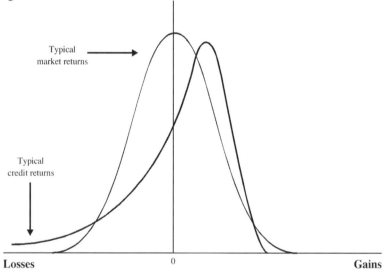

Figure 21.4 Comparison of distribution of market returns and credit returns
Source: JPMorgan 1997

This difference in risk profiles does not prevent us from assessing risk on a comparable basis. Analytical market-VaR models consider a time horizon and estimate value-at-risk across a distribution of estimated market outcomes. Credit VaR models similarly look to a horizon and construct a distribution of value given different estimated credit outcomes.

When modelling credit risk the two main measures of risk are:

- distribution of loss: obtaining distributions of loss that may arise from the current portfolio. This considers the question of what the expected loss is for a given confidence level
- identifying extreme or catastrophic outcomes; this is addressed through the use of scenario analysis and concentration limits.

To simplify modelling, no assumptions are made about the causes of default. Mathematical techniques used in the insurance industry are used to model the event of an obligor default.

Time horizon

The choice of time horizon will not be shorter than the timeframe over which risk-mitigating actions can be taken. CSFB (who introduced the CreditRisk+ model shortly after CreditMetrics™ was introduced) suggest two alternatives:

- a constant time horizon such as one year
- a hold-to-maturity time horizon.

The constant time horizon is similar to the CreditMetrics™ approach and also to that used for market-risk measures. It is more suitable for trading desks. The hold-to-maturity approach is used by institutions such as portfolio managers.

Data inputs

Modelling credit risk requires certain data inputs. For example, CreditRisk+ uses the following:

- credit exposures
- obligor default rates
- obligor default-rate volatilities
- recovery rates.

These data requirements present some difficulties. There is a lack of comprehensive default and correlation data and assumptions need to be made at certain times. The most accessible data is compiled by the credit ratings agencies such as Moody's.

We now consider two methodologies used for measuring credit value-at-risk, the CreditMetrics™ model and the CreditRisk+ model.

CreditMetrics™

CreditMetrics™ is JPMorgan's portfolio model for analysing credit risk, and provides an estimate of value-at-risk due to credit events caused by upgrades, downgrades and default. A software package known as CreditManager is available that allows users to implement the CreditMetrics™ methodology.

Methodology

There are two main frameworks in use for quantifying credit risk. One approach considers only two states: default and no default. This model constructs a binomial tree of default versus no default outcomes until maturity. This approach is shown at Figure 21.5.

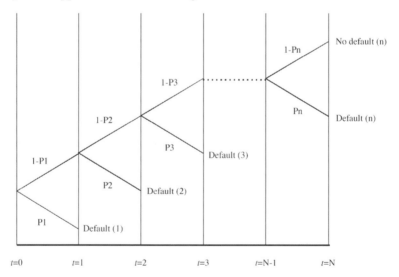

Figure 21.5 A binomial model of credit risk.
Source: JPMorgan

The other approach, sometimes called the RAROC (Risk-Adjusted Return on Capital) approach holds that risk is the observed volatility of corporate-bond values within each credit-rating category, maturity band and industry grouping. The idea is to track a benchmark corporate bond (or index) which has observable pricing. The resulting estimate of volatility of value is then used to proxy the volatility of the exposure (or portfolio) under analysis.

The CreditMetrics™ methodology sits between these two approaches. The model estimates portfolio VaR at the risk horizon due to credit events that include upgrades and downgrades, rather than just defaults. Thus, it adopts a mark-to-market framework. As shown in Figure 21.6, bonds within each credit rating category have volatility of value due to day-to-day credit-spread fluctuations. The figure shows the loss distributions for bonds of varying credit quality. CreditMetrics™ assumes that all credit migrations have been realised, weighting each by a migration likelihood.

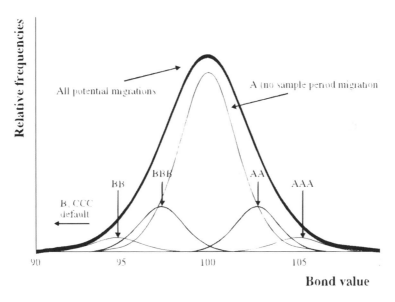

Figure 21.6 Distribution of credit returns by rating
Source: JPMorgan

Time horizon

CreditMetrics™ adopts a one-year risk horizon. The justification given in its technical document[4] is that this is because much academic and credit agency data is stated on an annual basis. This is a convenient convention similar to

---

[4] JPMorgan, *Introduction to CreditMetrics™*, JPMorgan & Co., 1997.

the use of annualised interest rates in the money markets. The risk horizon is adequate as long as it is not shorter than the time required to perform risk-mitigating actions. Users must therefore adopt their risk-management and risk-adjustment procedures with this in mind.

The steps involved in CreditMetrics™ measurement methodology are shown in Figure 21.7, described by JPMorgan as its analytical "roadmap".

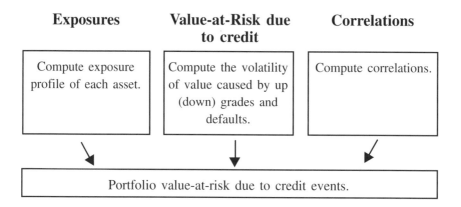

Figure 21.7 Analytics Road Map for CreditMetrics™
Source: JPMorgan 1997

The elements in each step are:
Exposures
- User portfolio
- Market volatilities
- Exposure distributions

VaR due to credit events
- Credit rating
- Credit spreads
- Rating change likelihood
- Recovery rate in default
- Present-value bond revaluation
- Standard deviation of value due to credit-quality changes.

Correlations
- Ratings series
- Models (for example, correlations)
- Joint credit-rating changes

Calculating the credit VaR

CreditMetrics™ methodology assesses individual and portfolio VaR due to credit in three steps:

- Step 1: it establishes the exposure profile of each obligor in a portfolio
- Step 2: it computes the volatility in value of each instrument caused by possible upgrade, downgrade and default
- Step 3: taking into account correlations between each of these events, it combines the volatility of the individual instruments to give an aggregate portfolio risk

Step 1 — Exposure Profiles

CreditMetrics™ incorporates the exposure of instruments such as bonds (fixed- or floating-rate) as well as other loan commitments and market-driven instruments such as swaps. The exposure is stated on an equivalent basis for all products. Products covered include:

- receivables (or trade credit)
- bonds and loans
- loan commitments
- letters of credit
- market-driven instruments.

Step 2 — Volatility of each exposure from up(down)grades and defaults

The levels of likelihood are attributed to each possible credit event of upgrade, downgrade and default. The probability that an obligor will change over a given time horizon to another rating is calculated. Each change (migration) results in an estimated change in value (derived from credit-spread data and — in default — recovery rates). Each value outcome is weighted by its likelihood to create a distribution of value across each credit state, from which each asset's expected value and volatility (standard deviation) of value are calculated.

There are three steps to calculating the volatility of value in a credit exposure:

- the senior unsecured credit rating of the issuer determines the chance of either defaulting or migrating to any other possible credit-quality state in the risk horizon
- revaluation at the risk horizon can be by either (i) the seniority of the exposure, which determines its recovery rate in case of default, or (ii) the forward zero-coupon curve (spot curve) for each credit-rating category which determines the revaluation upon up(down)grade

- the probabilities from the two steps above are combined to calculate volatility of value due to credit-quality changes.

Step 3 — Correlations

Individual value distributions for each exposure are combined to give a portfolio result. To calculate the portfolio value from the volatility of individual asset values requires estimates of correlation in credit-quality changes. CreditMetrics™ itself allows for different approaches to estimating correlations, including a simple constant correlation. This is because of frequent difficulty in obtaining directly observed credit-quality correlations from historical data.

EXAMPLE 21.5

An example of calculating the probability step is illustrated in Figure 21.4. The probabilities of all possible credit events on an instrument's value must be established first. Given this data, the volatility of value due to credit-quality changes for this one position can be calculated. The process is shown in Figure 21.8.

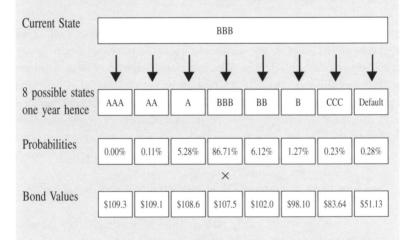

Figure 21.8 Constructing the distribution value for a BBB-rated bond
Source: JP Morgan 1997

CreditManager™

CreditManager™ is the software implementation of CreditMetrics™ as developed by JP Morgan. It is a PC-based application that measures and analyses credit risk in a portfolio context. It measures the VaR exposure due to credit events across a portfolio, and also quantifies concentration risks and the benefits of diversification by incorporating correlations (following the methodology utilised by CreditMetrics™). The CreditManager™ application provides a framework for portfolio credit-risk management that can be implemented "off the shelf" by virtually any institution. It uses the following:

- an obligor credit-quality database: details of obligor credit ratings, transition and default probabilities, industries and countries
- portfolio exposure database, containing exposure details for the following asset types: loans, bonds, letters of credit, total-return swaps, credit-default swaps, interest-rate and currency swaps and other market instruments
- frequently updated market data: including yield curves, spreads, transition and default probabilities
- flexible risk analyses with user-defined parameters supporting VaR analysis, marginal risk, risk concentrations, event risk and correlation analysis
- stress-testing scenarios, applying user-defined movements to correlations, spreads, recovery rates, transition and default probabilities
- customized reports and charts.

CreditManager™ data sources include Dow Jones, Moody's, Reuters and Standard and Poor's. By using the software package, risk managers can analyse and manage credit portfolios based on virtually any variable, from the simplest end of the spectrum — single position or obligor — to more complex groupings containing a range of industry and country obligors and credit ratings.

Generally, this quantitative measure is employed as part of an overall risk-management framework that retains traditional, qualitative methods.

CreditMetrics™ can be a useful tool for risk managers seeking to apply VaR methodology to credit risk. The model enables risk managers to apply portfolio theory and VaR methodology to credit risk. It has several applications, including prioritizing and evaluating investment decisions and, perhaps most important, setting risk-based exposure limits. Ultimately the model's sponsors claim its use can aid in maximizing shareholder value based on risk-based capital allocation. This should then result in increased liquidity in credit markets, the use of a marking-to-market approach to credit positions and closer interweaving of regulatory and economic capital.

CreditRisk+

CreditRisk+ was developed by Credit Suisse First Boston and can, in theory, handle all instruments that give rise to credit exposure including bonds, loans commitments, letters of credit and derivative instruments. We provide a brief description of its methodology here.

Modelling process

CreditRisk+ uses a two-stage modelling process as illustrated in Figure 21.9.

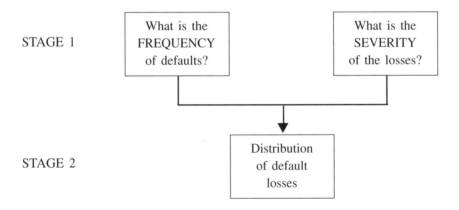

Figure 21.9 CreditRisk+ modelling process

CreditRisk+ considers the distribution of the number of default events in a time period such as one year, within a portfolio of obligors having a range of different annual probabilities of default.

The annual probability of default of each obligor can be determined by its credit rating and then mapping between default rates and credit ratings. A default rate can then be assigned to each obligor (an example of what this would look like is shown in Table 21.15). Default rate volatilities can be observed from historic volatilities.

Credit Rating	One-Year Default Rate (%)
Aaa	0.00
Aa	0.03
A	0.01
Baa	0.12
Ba	1.36
B	7.27

Table 21.15 One-year default rates (%)

Correlation and background factors

Default correlation affects the variability of default losses from a portfolio of credit exposures. CreditRisk+ incorporates the effects of default correlations by using default-rate volatilities and sector analysis.

Unsurprisingly enough, it is not possible to forecast the exact occurrence of any one default or the total number of defaults. Often there are background factors that may cause the incidence of default events to be correlated, even though there is no causal link between them. For example, an economy in recession may give rise to an unusually large number of defaults in one particular month, which would increase the default rates above their average level. CreditRisk+ models the effect of background factors by using default-rate volatilities rather than by using default correlations as a direct input. Both distributions give rise to loss distributions with fat tails.

There are background factors that affect the level of default rates. For this reason, it is useful to capture the effect of concentration in particular countries or sectors. CreditRisk+ uses a sector analysis to allow for concentration. Exposures are broken down into an obligor-specific element independent of other exposures, as well as non-specific elements that are sensitive to particular factors such as countries or sectors.

Distribution of the number of default events

CreditRisk+ models the underlying default rates by specifying a default and a default-rate volatility. This aims to take account of the variation in default rates. The effect of using volatility is illustrated in Figure 21.10, which shows the distribution of default rates generated by the model when rate volatility is varied. The distribution becomes skewed to the right when volatility is increased.

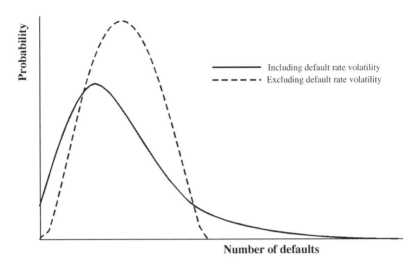

Figure 21.10 CreditRisk+ Distribution of default events
Source: CSFB

This is an important result and demonstrates the increased risk represented by an extreme number of default events. By varying the volatility in this way, CreditRisk+ is attempting to model for real-world shock in much the same way that market-risk VaR models aim to allow for the fact that market returns do not follow exact normal distributions, as shown by the incidence of market crashes.

Application software
CSFB has released software that allows the CreditRisk+ model to be run on Microsoft Excel® as a spreadsheet calculator. The user inputs the portfolio static data into a blank template and the model calculates the credit exposure. Obligor exposure can be analysed on the basis of all exposures being part of the same sector. Up to eight different sectors (government, countries, industry, and so on) can be analysed. The spreadsheet template allows the user to include up to 4,000 obligors in the static data. An example portfolio of 25 obligors and default rates and default-rate volatilities (assigned via a sample of credit ratings) is included with the spreadsheet.

The user's static data for the portfolio will therefore include details of each obligor, the size of the exposure, the sector for that obligor (if not all in a single sector) and default rates. An example of static data is given in Tables 21.16 and 21.17.

Credit Rating	Mean Default Rate	Standard Deviation
A+	1.50%	0.75%
A	1.60%	0.80%
A–	3.00%	1.50%
BBB+	5.00%	2.50%
BBB	7.50%	3.75%
BBB–	10.00%	5.00%
BB	15.00%	7.50%
B	30.00%	15.00%

Table 21.16 Example default-rate data

Name	Exposure (£)	Rating	Mean Default Rate	Default Rate Standard Deviation	Sector Split General economy
Co name	358,475	B	30.00%	15.00%	100%
Co (2)	1,089,819	B	30.00%	15.00%	100%
Co (3)	1,799,710	BBB–	10.00%	5.00%	100%
Co (4)	1,933,116	BB	15.00%	7.50%	100%
Co (5)	2,317,327	BB	15.00%	7.50%	100%
Co (6)	2,410,929	BB	15.00%	7.50%	100%
Co (7)	2,652,184	B	30.00%	15.00%	100%
Co (8)	2,957,685	BB	15.00%	7.50%	100%
Co (9)	3,137,989	BBB+	5.00%	2.50%	100%
Co (10)	3,204,044	BBB+	5.00%	2.50%	100%

Table 21.17 Example obligor data

An example credit-loss distribution calculated by the model is shown below. Figure 21.11 shows the distribution for the basic analysis for a portfolio at the simplest level of assumption; all obligors are assigned to a single sector. The full loss distribution over a one-year time horizon is calculated together with percentiles of the loss distribution (not shown here), which assess the relative risk for different levels of loss. The model can calculate distributions for a portfolio with obligors grouped across different sectors, as well as the distribution for a portfolio analysed over a "hold-to-maturity" time horizon.

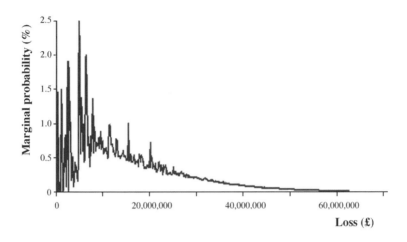

Credit loss distribution

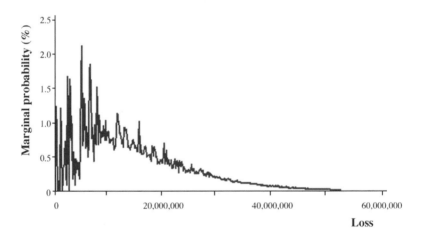

Figure 21.11 Illustration of credit-loss distribution (single-sector obligor portfolio)

Summary of CreditRisk+ model

- **CreditRisk+ captures the main characteristics of credit default events.** Credit default events are rare and occur in a random manner, with observed default rates varying from year to year. The model's approach attempts to reflect this by making no assumptions about the timing or causes of these events and by incorporating a default-rate volatility. It also takes a portfolio approach and uses sector analysis to allow for concentration risk.
- **CreditRisk+ is capable of handling large exposure portfolios.** The low data requirements and minimum assumptions make the model comparatively easy to implement for firms.

However, the model is limited to two states of the world: default or non-default. This means it is not as flexible as CreditMetrics™, for example, and ultimately therefore not modelling the full exposure that a credit portfolio would be subject to.

Applications of Credit VaR

One purpose of a risk-management system is to direct and prioritize actions. When considering risk-mitigating actions, there are various features of risk worth targeting, including obligors having:

- the largest absolute exposure
- the largest percentage level of risk (volatility)
- the largest absolute amount of risk.

A CreditMetrics™-type methodology helps to identify these areas and allow the risk manager to prioritize risk-mitigating action.

Exposure limits

Within bank trading desks, credit-risk limits are often based on intuitive, but arbitrary, exposure amounts. This is not a logical approach because resulting decisions are not risk-driven. Limits should ideally be set with the help of a quantitative analytical framework.

Risk statistics used as the basis of VaR methodology can be applied to limit setting. Ideally, such a quantitative approach should be used as an aid to business judgment and not as a stand-alone limit-setting tool.

A credit committee considering limit setting can use several statistics such as marginal risk and standard deviation or percentile levels. Figure 21.12 illustrates how marginal risk statistics can be used to make credit limits sensitive to the trade-off between risk and return. The lines on Figure 21.12 represent risk/return trade-offs for different credit ratings, all the way from AAA to BBB. The diagram shows how marginal contribution to portfolio risk increases geometrically with exposure size of an individual obligor, noticeably so for weaker credits. To maintain a constant balance between risk and return, proportionately more return is required with each increment of exposure to an individual obligor.

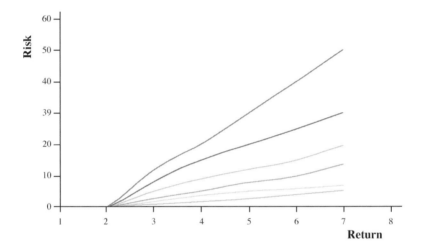

Figure 21.12 Size of total exposure to obligor — risk/return profile

Standard credit-limit setting
In order to equalise a firm's risk appetite between obligors as a means of diversifying its portfolio, a credit-limit system could aim to have a large number of exposures with equal expected losses. The expected loss for each obligor can be calculated as default rate × (exposure amount − expected recovery).

This means that individual credit limits should be set at levels that are inversely proportional to the default rate corresponding to the obligor rating.

Concentration Limits
Concentration limits identified by CreditRisk+-type methodologies have the effect of trying to limit the loss from identified scenarios and are used for managing "tail" risk.

Integrating creditrisk and market-risk functions

It is logical for banks to integrate credit-risk and market-risk management for the following reasons:

- the need for comparability between returns on market and credit risk
- the convergence of risk-measurement methodologies
- the transactional interaction between credit and market risk
- the emergence of hybrid-credit and market-risk product structures.

The objective is for returns on capital to be comparable for businesses involved in credit and market risk, to aid strategic allocation of capital.

EXAMPLE 21.6

Assume that at the time of annual planning a bank's lending manager says his department can make £5 million over the year if they can increase their loan book by £300 million, while the trading manager says they can also make £5 million if the position limits are increased by £20 million.

Assuming that capital restrictions will allow only one option to be chosen, which should it be? The ideal choice is the one giving the higher return on capital, but the bank needs to work out how much capital is required for each alternative. This is a quantitative issue that calls for the application of similar statistical and analytical methods to measure both credit and market risk, if one is compare like with like.

With regard to the loan issue, the expected return is the mean of the distribution of possible returns. Since the revenue side of a loan — that is, the spread — is known with certainty, the area of concern is the expected credit-loss rate. This is the mean of the distribution of possible loss rates, estimated from historical data based on losses experienced with similar quality credits.

In the context of market-price risk, the common-denominator measure of risk is volatility (the statistical standard deviation of the distribution of possible future price movements). To apply this to credit risk, the decision-maker therefore needs to take into account the standard deviation of the distribution of possible future credit-loss rates, thereby comparing like with like.

We have shown that as VaR was being adopted as a market-risk measurement tool, the methodologies behind it were steadily applied to the next step along the risk continuum, that of credit risk. Recent market events, such as bank trading losses in emerging markets and the meltdown of the Long Term Capital Management hedge fund in summer 1998, have illustrated the interplay between credit risk and market risk. The ability to measure market and credit risk in an integrated model would allow for a more complete picture of the underlying risk exposure. (We would add that adequate senior management understanding and awareness of a third type of risk — liquidity risk — would almost complete the risk-measurement picture).

Market-risk VaR measures can adopt one of the different methodologies available; in all of them there is a requirement for the estimation of the distribution of portfolio returns at the end of a holding period. This distribution can be assumed to be normal, which allows for analytical solutions to be developed. The distribution may also be estimated using historical returns. Finally, a Monte Carlo simulation can be used to create a distribution based on the assumption of certain stochastic processes for the underlying variables. The choice of methodology is often dependent on the characteristics of the underlying portfolio, plus other factors. For example, risk managers may wish to consider the degree of leptokurtosis in the underlying asset-returns distribution, the availability of historical data or the need to specify a more sophisticated stochastic process for the underlying assets. The general consensus is that Monte Carlo simulation, while the most IT-intensive methodology, is the most flexible in terms of specifying an integrated market and credit model.

The preceding paragraphs in this section have shown that credit-risk measurement models generally fall into two categories. The first category includes models that specify an underlying process for the default process. In these models, firms are assumed to move from one credit rating to another with specified probabilities. Default is one of the potential states that a firm could move to. The CreditMetrics[TM] model is of this type. The second type of model requires the specification of a stochastic process for firm value. Here, default occurs when the value of the firm reaches an externally specified barrier. In both models, when the firm reaches default, the credit exposure is impacted by the recovery rate. Again market consensus would seem to indicate that the second type of methodology, the firm value model, most easily allows for development of an integrated model that is linked not only through correlation but also the impact of common stochastic variables.

Appendix

APPENDIX 21.1 Assumption of normality

The RiskMetrics™ assumption of conditional multivariate normality is open to criticism that financial series tend to produce "fat tails" (leptokurtosis). That is, in reality there is a greater occurrence of non-normal returns than would be expected for a purely normal distribution. This is shown in Figure A21.1. There is evidence that fat tails are a problem for calculations. The RiskMetrics™ technical document defends its assumptions by pointing out that if volatility changes over time there is a greater likelihood of incorrectly concluding that the data is not normal when in fact it is. In fact, conditional distribution models can generate data that possesses fat tails.

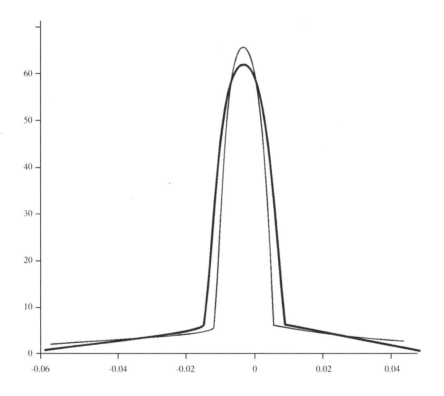

Figure A21.1 Leptokurtosis

Higher moments of the normal distribution

The skewness of a price data series is measured in terms of the third moment about the mean of the distribution. If the distribution is symmetric, the skewness is zero. The measure of skewness is given by

$$\frac{\frac{1}{n} \sum_{i=1}^{n} (x_i - \bar{x})^3}{S^3} \qquad \text{(A21.1)}$$

The kurtosis describes the extent of the peak of a distribution; that is, how peaked it is. It is measured by the fourth moment about the mean. A normal distribution has a kurtosis of three. The kurtosis is given by

$$\frac{\frac{1}{n} \sum_{i=1}^{n} (x_i - \bar{x})^4}{S^4} \qquad \text{(A21.2)}$$

Distributions with a kurtosis higher than three are commonly observed in asset-market prices and are called leptokurtic. A leptokurtic distribution has higher peaks and fatter tails than the normal distribution. A distribution with a kurtosis lower than three is known as platykurtic.

Selected Bibliography and References

Alexander, C., *Risk Management and Analysis*, John Wiley and Sons Ltd, 1996

Beckstrom, R., Campbell, A (eds), *An introduction to VAR*, CATS Software, 1995

Beder, T., "VAR: seductive but dangerous", *Financial Analysts Journal*, 51, 1995, pp. 12-24

Bollerslebv, T., "Generalised Autoregressive Conditional Heteroscedasticity", *Journal of Econometrics*, 31, 1986, pp. 307-327

Chew,L., *Managing Derivatives Risks*, Wiley 1996

Engle, R., "Autoregressive Conditional Heteroscedasticity with Estimates of the Variance of UK Inflation", *Econometrica*, 50, 1982, pp. 987-1008

Jorion, P., *Value-at-Risk*, Irwin, 1997

JP Morgan, *RiskMetrics Technical Manual*, JP Morgan Bank, 1995

JP Morgan & Co., Inc., *CreditMetrics®* - Technical Document, 1997

Schwartz, R., Clifford, W., *Advanced Strategies in Financial Risk Management*, New York Institute of Finance, 1993

22

Government bond analysis, the yield curve and relative-value trading

This chapter examines a number of issues relevant to participants in the fixed-income markets. It is primarily based on unpublished articles written during the time the author was working in the UK gilt market, with certain sections updated for this book. As it is based on government trading experience, the analysis is confined to generic bonds that are default-free. There is no consideration of factors that would apply to corporate bonds, asset- and mortgage-backed bonds, convertibles and other non-vanilla securities, and issues such as credit risk or prepayment risk.

The chapter is broken down as follows: first we consider the redemption yield and duration. This is followed by observations on the implied spot rate and market zero-coupon yields, relative-value trading and butterfly trades.

The determinants of yield

The yield at which a fixed-interest security is traded is determined by the market. This determination is a function if three factors; the term-to-maturity of the bond, the liquidity of the bond and its credit quality. Government securities such as Treasuries are default-free and so this factor drops out of the equation. Under "normal" circumstances, the yield on a bond is higher the greater its maturity, reflecting both the expectations-hypothesis and liquidity-preference theories. Intuitively, we associate higher risk with longer-dated instruments, for which investors must be compensated in the form of higher yield. This higher risk reflects greater uncertainty with longer-dated bonds, both in terms of default and future inflation and interest-rate levels. However, for a number of reasons the yield curve assumes an inverted shape and long-dated yields become lower than short-dated ones.[1] Long-dated yields generally are expected to be less volatile over time than short-dated yields. This is mainly because incremental changes to economic circumstances or other technical considerations generally have an impact for only short periods of time, which affects the shorter end of the yield curve to a greater extent.

The liquidity of a bond also influences its yield level. The liquidity may be measured by the size of the bid-offer spread, the ease with which the stock may be transacted in size, and the impact of large-size bargains on the market. It is also measured by the extent of any specialness in its repo rate. Supply and demand for an individual stock, and the amount of stock available to trade are the main drivers of liquidity.[2] The general rule is that there is a yield premium for transacting business in lower-liquidity bonds.

In the analysis that follows, we assume satisfactory levels of liquidity; that it is straightforward to deal in large sizes without moving the market.

Practical uses of redemption yield and duration

The drawbacks of the traditional gross-redemption yield (henceforth referred to simply as "yield) and duration measures for bond analysis are well documented. That different bonds, even vanilla government securities, can have their yield measured in a number of ways hints, however, at the lack of a satisfactory acceptable measure of return. When assessing the opportunities available in a market, investors will often use the market convention for yield in their analysis. However, the different methods available to calculate yield mean that the comparison of rates of return for different bonds becomes problematic (for example, see Figure 22.1 for the alternative yield measures available for a US Treasury security on the Bloomberg "YA" page). Duration is another measure that can be defined in more than one way, again making comparison between different bonds an issue.

In this section, we look at how the problems inherent in using yield and duration can be mitigated, and how the analysis should proceed when doing this.

---

[1] For a summary of term-structure theories, see Choudhry (2001, Chapter 6).

[2] The amount of stock issued and the amount of stock available to trade are not the same thing. If a large amount of a particular issue has been locked away by institutional investors, this may impede liquidity. However, the existence of a large amount at least means that some of the paper may be made available for lending in the stock loan and repo markets. A small issue size is a good indicator of low liquidity.

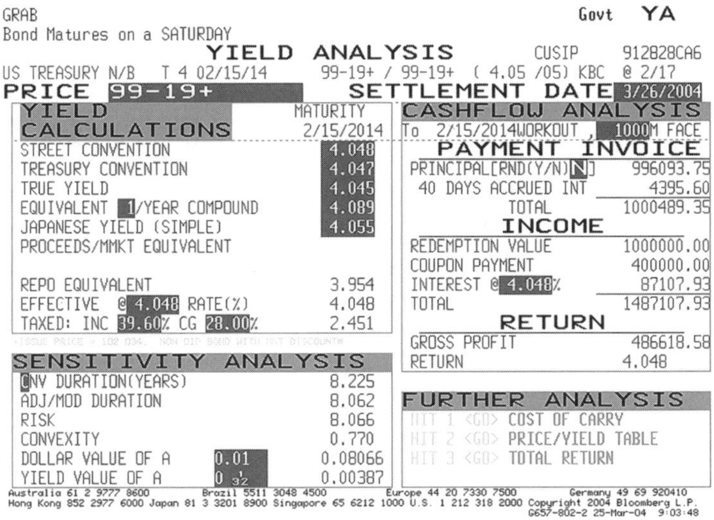

Figure 22.1 Yield calculations for Treasury 4% 2014 on Bloomberg "YA" page.
©Bloomberg LP. Reproduced with permission

The concept of yield

Ideally the yield of an instrument should measure the return achieved from holding it; this would make it a function of the value of the initial investment, the period of the investment and the value of the matured investment. If investment income received during the period is capitalised, this should also be captured by the yield measure, so that we are measuring compounded interest. Under these properties, a yield on a simple instrument such as a T-bill can be defined as shown now.

In the sterling market, the fixed-income interest basis is semi-annual. With this in mind, consider a T-bill with a maturity of m days and a price of P. The true yield rm of the bill is given by

$$P = \frac{100}{(1 + \frac{1}{2}rm)n} \tag{22.1}$$

where n is the number of interest periods from value date until maturity. On an actual/365 basis, one interest period in the gilt market is a half-year or 182.5 days;[3] so, for a 90-day T-bill priced at 98.379 the true yield can be computed by solving

---

[3] The accrued basis in the gilt market is, of course, now actual/actual and not actual/365.

$$98.379 = \frac{100}{(1 + \frac{1}{2}rm)^{90/182.5}}$$

which gives *rm* equal to 0.067389 or 6.739%. That said, the yield quoted on T-bills, when computed using the market price, will often differ from the "true" yield. This is because often yield quotes for bills assume simple interest, rather than compound interest in their calculation. Nevertheless, we are interested in this definition of the true yield because we wish to apply it to longer-dated coupon bonds. Readers are familiar with the definition of bond yield, which involves discounting all the bond's cash flows (its coupons) at a uniform interest rate; yield here is then that interest rate that equates the sum of all the discounted cash flows equal to the observed market price. Let us consider this further.

With a vanilla bond such as a gilt, there are *m* future cash flows of value *C*, which are the bond interest payments calculated as one-half of the bond coupon rate. The *i*th payment is termed C_i, with m_i being the days from value date to maturity. The number of interest periods from today to a cash-flow date or to maturity is simply the days divided by 182.5 and so is denoted $n_i = m_i/182.5$. At a discount interest rate of *r*, the value of the bond's discounted cash flows would be given by (22.2).

$$PV = \frac{C_1}{(1 + \frac{1}{2}r)^{n_1}} + \frac{C_2}{(1 + \frac{1}{2}r)^{n_2}} + \ldots + \frac{C_m}{(1 + \frac{1}{2}r)^{n_m}} \qquad (22.2)$$

This leads easily to the true yield definition for the bond, which is the discount interest rate that equates the current market price of the bond to the discounted value of the cash flows. The market price is the dirty price, which includes accrued interest. We replace *PV* in (22.2) with *P* plus accrued interest, shown at (22.3).

$$P + AI = \frac{C_1}{(1 + \frac{1}{2}rm)^{n_1}} + \frac{C_2}{(1 + \frac{1}{2}rm)^{n_2}} + \ldots + \frac{C_m}{(1 + \frac{1}{2}rm)^{n_m}} \qquad (22.3)$$

We now look at how the true yield for a gilt may differ from the quoted yield.

Yield comparisons from the market

Let's look at a market example. Price quotes are in ticks, or fractions of 32nds. One-half of a tick is denoted by "+". On 10th May 1994, the $10\frac{1}{4}\%$ 1995 gilt, with a maturity date of 21st July 1995, was quoted at a price of

104–28+. To calculate the true yield, and indeed any other yield such as the conventional yield, we use the dirty price of the bond, together with the discounted value of all remaining cash flows.

The bond pays coupon on 21st January and 21st July. For value 11th May 1994 the accrued will be 109 days, which means that the accrued interest is

$$(10.25 \times {}^{1}/_{2}) \times 109 \; / \; 365$$

or 1.53048. The dirty price of the bond is (104–28+ plus 1.53048) or 106.421105.

The remaining bond cash flows are £5.125 on 21st July 1994 and 21st January 1995, and 105.125 on 21st July 1995. However, 21st January 1995 is a Saturday, so the cash flow will not actually be made until Monday, 23rd January. The period from value date to receipt of cash flows is

21st July 1994	71 days
23rd January 1995	230 days
21st July 1995	436 days

The number of interest periods in this term for each cash-flow date is

(71/182.5) or 0.38904
(230/182.5) or 1.26027
(436/182.5) or 2.38904.

Therefore, the true yield is computed as follows

$$106.421105 = \frac{5.125}{(1 + {}^{1}/_{2}rm)^{0.38904}} + \frac{5.125}{(1 + {}^{1}/_{2}rm)^{1.26027}} + \frac{5.125}{(1 + {}^{1}/_{2}rm)^{2.38904}}$$

which solves to give $rm = 0.073241$ or 7.324%.

The conventional yield calculation will almost invariably be different. This is because it ignores delays in the receipt of cash flows when payment dates fall on non-business days, and so the number of interest periods between cash flows are deemed to be in exact one-half year amounts. So the conventional or *consortium* yield for the same bond would be calculated as

$$106.421105 = \frac{5.125}{(1 + {}^{1}/_{2}rm)^{0.38904}} + \frac{5.125}{(1 + {}^{1}/_{2}rm)^{1.24932}} + \frac{5.125}{(1 + {}^{1}/_{2}rm)^{2.38904}}$$

which solves to gives $rm = 0.0732577$ or 7.325%. This shows the true yield to be 0.001% below the consortium yield. This is because under the consortium-yield method the cash flows are received earlier than in the true-yield treatment. Table 22.1 shows this difference in yields for gilts as at 10th May 1994 for value the next day. Note that the difference in the two measures declines to zero from the 6% 1999 gilt onwards. This is because for longer-dated bonds, the discounting of future cash flows is not materially affected by small delays in the treatment of cash-flow receipts, which are only ever a few days if at all, and so there is no difference when computing the true yield.

Gilt	True yield %	Consortium yield	% Difference
10% 15 November 1996	7.171	7.173	0.002
10.5% 21 February 1997	7.379	7.391	0.012
7.25% 30 March 1998	7.780	7.781	0.001
6% 10 August 1999	7.900	7.900	0.000
9% 3 March 2000	8.191	8.191	0.000
7% 6 November 2001	8.220	8.220	0.000
9.75% 27 August 2002	8.484	8.482	-0.002
8% 10 June 2003	8.359	8.359	0.000
6.75% 26 November 2004	8.243	8.243	0.000

Table 22.1 Gilt yields as at 10th May 1994

Measuring true return on a bond

Although we may be satisfied with our true-yield measure, it is not as straightforward as the true-yield measure given for the T-bill earlier. With a single-cash-flow instrument, the actual return generated is straightforward: the maturity value is known, so the return on investment is calculated easily as the increase in value from start to maturity. An investment in a 90-day T-bill at a yield of 5% means that the initial value will increase in value by 5% over 90 days, using semi-annual compounding. We are not able to say this with certainty when confronted with a yield quote for a coupon-bearing bond. A 5% yield on a 90-day T-bill is the return associated with a 90-day maturity, and gives no indications (nor does it attempt to) on the value of the bill after, say, 60 days or the yield available for reinvestment on maturity of the bill. Is there a way to view a bond yield in the same fashion as that for a T-bill? Certainly it would assist investors if there was a way to analyse a bond as if the instrument was a single cash-flow security. This is because investors often buy bonds as assets against liabilities that they are required to discharge on known future dates. If the true return on a bond were known, there would be comfort to the investor that the return achieved would meet requirements. Put very simply, this is the concept of immunisation.

Therefore, if possible we would wish to view bond return in the same way as that for a single cash-flow security: a known initial investment is placed in the market for a set period of time, and the future value of the investment on maturity is calculated. The return on the bond would measure the average rate of capital gain in the investment period. The problem with a bond instrument is that its future value is not known with certainty, and is dependent at the rate at which the investor is able to reinvest interim cash flows; this rate cannot be predicted. There are a number of approaches to get around this problem, which we consider now in simple interest-rate environments.

The first scenario assumes, somewhat unrealistically, a flat yield-curve environment. Further, we expect one movement only in the yield curve, a parallel shift upwards or downwards. A bond instrument is viewed as a package of zero-coupon securities, which would make its theoretical price the sum of the discounted values of each zero-coupon security. This is significant because each cash flow would then be discounted at the interest rate for that specific term, rather than one single "internal rate of return". Under our simple assumptions, we can then measure the return on capital generated from a bond instrument.

The price of the bond, given the redemption yield, is given by (22.3). This is straightforward and conventional. Example 22.1 illustrates the use of this relationship.

EXAMPLE 22.1 **Conventional bond pricing**

We have a hypothetical 5% 2002 semi-annual coupon bond that matures on 8th December 2002. For value on 8th December 2000 the bond has precisely four interest periods to maturity and no accrued interest; its cash flows are 2.50, 2.50, 2.50 and 102.50. If the yield curve on 7th December is flat at 5% (using semi-annual compounding), then the price of the bond is given by

$$PV + AI = \frac{C_1}{(1 + \frac{1}{2}rm)^{n_1}} + \frac{C_2}{(1 + \frac{1}{2}rm)^{n_2}} + \frac{C_3}{(1 + \frac{1}{2}rm)^{n_3}} + \frac{C_4}{(1 + \frac{1}{2}rm)^{n_4}}$$

$$= \frac{2.50}{(1 + 0.025)^1} + \frac{2.50}{(1 + 0.025)^2} + \frac{2.50}{(1 + 0.025)^3} + \frac{2.50}{(1 + 0.025)^4}$$

$$= 2.4390 + 2.3879 + 2.3215 + 92.8600$$

$$= 100.00$$

This is the simplest approach, viewing the bond as a bundle of four zero-coupon securities; however, as the yield curve is flat we can use a uniform discount rate. This is shown and, at a rate of 5% the price of the bond is par.

We now assume a one-off parallel shift in the yield curve to a new level of rm_2, which results in a change in the expected future value of the bond. If there are s interest periods from the value date to a specified "horizon date" this is given by (22.4),

$$P(rm_2, s) = \frac{C_1}{(1 + \frac{1}{2}rm_2)^{n_1-s}} + \frac{C_2}{(1 + \frac{1}{2}rm_2)^{n_2-s}} + \cdots + \frac{C_m}{(1 + \frac{1}{2}rm_2)^{n_m-s}} \quad (22.4)$$

which expresses the fact that the ith cash flow contributes

$$\frac{C_i}{(1 + \frac{1}{2}rm_2)^{n_i-s}}$$

to the future value of the bond. If this cash flow is received ahead of the horizon date then $n_i - s$ will have a negative value, which means we compound C_i to the horizon date at the discount rate rm_2. Otherwise $n_i - s$ will be positive and C_i is discounted backwards to the horizon date at the same rate. So, the same rate rm_2 is used to compound or discount payments received ahead of or after the horizon date.

Remember, we wish to measure the rate of return, or at best approximate it, for a bond. This return is influenced by changes in the yield curve after initial purchase. Let us consider this now. If we have a short-term horizon period and thus small s, a majority of the bond's cash flows will take place after the horizon date. A higher rate rm_2 will produce a lower future value $P(rm_2, s)$. The opposite occurs if s is large; most of the cash flows will then take place before the horizon date, and a higher value rm_2 will actually increase the value of the cash flows as they can be reinvested at a higher rate of interest. If the value of s is sufficiently high, this reinvestment gain may match and exceed the loss suffered due to revaluation of the bond at the higher rate, which would result in a higher future value $P(rm_2, s)$. The reverse effect can occur if $rm_2 < rm$. This is the reinvestment risk borne by the bondholder.

There is a horizon date in between the short-term and long-term dates where the net effect of the change in reinvestment rate on the bond's future value is close to zero. At this horizon date, the bond behaves like a single-cash-flow or zero-coupon security, and so its future value can be predicted with more certainty, irrespective of the change in the yield curve after we have purchased it. Let us call this horizon date s_H. At this date the bond will resemble a zero-coupon security that has s_H interest periods to maturity. We denote P_H as the future value of the bond s_H periods after the purchase date. It can be shown that the rate of return on this bond up to this specific horizon date is the value for rm_H that solves (22.5).

$$P + AI = \frac{P_H}{(1 + \frac{1}{2}rm_H)^{s_H}} \qquad (22.5)$$

In (22.5) the market price is given as clean price plus accrued interest, as before. In fact, it can be shown that the return rm_H is identical to the initial yield value rm. The value that will work for a stable future value is, in fact, the bond's Macaulay duration value. At this point, under the restrictive assumptions we have listed, the effect of a change in yields will not affect the future value of the bond. At this point, the bond's cash flows are said to be immunized and the instrument could be used to match a liability that existed at that date.

The restrictions we imposed limit the usefulness of the analysis. We assume one change only in rates after purchase, and this change is uniform across the term structure. Therefore, in practice an investor must continually adjust his portfolio to maintain its immunization properties. An accessible treatment of the key issues in dynamically managing a portfolio is contained in Fabozzi (1996).

Implied spot rates and market zero-coupon yields[4]

That the duration measure has a number of limitations when used in portfolio management is well known. There are further considerations that limit its use. For instance, the limiting value on duration means that most gilts have duration measures of under 12 years.[5] This makes portfolio immunization difficult when liabilities are very long-dated. The need for

---

[4] This section is based on an unpublished paper originally written in July 1997 when the author was working on the sterling proprietary trading desk in the Treasury division at Hambros Bank Limited. As first written, it pre-dates the introduction of zero-coupon strips in the UK gilt market in December 1997. It was updated as part of a guest lecture delivered at the City University Business School in 2000.

[5] For instance, see Blake (1990), paragraph 5.8.1.

constant rebalancing of the portfolio also adds to the problem. However, investors in zero-coupon bonds do not face these problems, which makes such bonds potentially very attractive securities for investors. Zero-coupon bonds do not suffer from the duration-based drawbacks of coupon bonds, as their duration value is identical to their term to maturity. This makes portfolio matching easier. A five-year zero-coupon bond has a duration of five years when purchased, and after two years its duration will be three years, irrespective of the change in interest rates in that time. A long-dated zero-coupon bond can then be used to match a long-dated investment liability. However, how should the yield on a zero-coupon bond be compared to that on a coupon bond? It is easy to see that we compare a two-year zero-coupon bond with a coupon bond of two years' duration; however, this becomes impractical when dealing with very long-dated zero-coupon bonds, for which no equivalent coupon gilt is usually available. The way around this can be observed in the US Treasury market, where the technique of stripping coupon Treasuries enables us to calculate implied zero-coupon rates with which we can compare actual strip-market yields.

In this section, we attempt to describe the relationship between spot interest rates, the actual market yields that would be observed on zero-coupon bonds and the yields on coupon bonds. We illustrate how an implied spot-rate curve can be derived from the redemption yields and prices observed on coupon bonds, and discuss how this curve may be used to assess relative value in bond yields.

Spot (zero-coupon) yields[6] and coupon bond prices

A gilt is a collection of cash flows, each of which represents an obligation on the part of HM Treasury to service the debt represented by the gilt issue on a semi-annual basis. We can view a gilt as a bundle of individual zero-coupon securities, each maturing on their respective payment date. Viewed in this way, the present value of the gilt becomes the sum of the present values of all the constituent cash flows. Let us consider this first.

Assume that we can observe the spot rates for various maturities and that these rates are r_1, r_2, r_3, ..., r_N. If a bond pays coupon C annually from period 1 to period N its present value using the series of spot rates is given by

---

[6] The term "spot rate" is usually considered to be synonymous with "zero-coupon rate" and it is common to see this written in text books (including this one!). In this chapter, the two terms are not used thus, as we make the distinction between a spot rate derived from coupon bond prices and a zero-coupon rate that is observed on a zero-coupon bond trading in the market.

$$P = \frac{C_1/2}{(1 + \frac{1}{2}r_1)} + \frac{C_2/2}{(1 + \frac{1}{2}r_2)^2} + \frac{C_3/2}{(1 + \frac{1}{2}r_3)^3} + \ldots + \frac{C_{N-1}/2}{(1 + \frac{1}{2}r_{N-1})^{N-1}} + \frac{C_N/2 + 100}{(1 + \frac{1}{2}r_N)^{2N}}$$

$$(22.6)$$

which is, of course, different from the conventional redemption-yield formula with which we are very familiar. Each cash flow is discounted by the specific spot rate that corresponds to the maturity period of the cash flow. It follows that, in order to value a bond in this way, we must know the spot-rate term structure. However, this may not always be readily observable. Gilt prices, on the other hand, are readily observable, and so we may use them to derive spot interest rates. This is examined next.

Deriving the spot-rate term structure from gilts prices

We do not require an active strip market in order to construct a spot interest-rate curve; we can derive a theoretical or *implied* spot-term structure using the yields that are observed on coupon gilts. To illustrate the methodology, we will use a hypothetical set of 10 gilts that are trading in a positive yield-curve environment. The maturity, price and yield for our 10 gilts are shown in Table 22.2. Let us assume that these prices are for settlement on 1ˢᵗ March 1999, and that all the bonds have precisely one, 1.5, two and so on years to maturity; that is, they mature on 1ˢᵗ March or 1ˢᵗ September of their maturity year. The shortest-dated gilt has no intermediate coupon before it is redeemed, and we can therefore treat it as a zero-coupon bond. All the gilts have no accrued interest because the settlement date is a coupon date.

Maturity date	Years to maturity	Coupon (%)	Yield to maturity	Price
1 Sep 99	0.5	5.0	6.00	99.5146
1 Mar 00	1.0	10.0	6.30	103.5322
1 Sep 00	1.5	7.0	6.40	100.8453
1 Mar 01	2.0	6.5	6.70	99.6314
1 Sep 01	2.5	8.0	6.90	102.4868
1 Mar 02	3.0	10.5	7.30	108.4838
1 Sep 02	3.5	9.0	7.60	104.2327
1 Mar 03	4.0	7.3	7.80	98.1408
1 Sep 03	4.5	7.5	7.95	98.3251
1 Mar 04	5.0	8.0	8.00	100.0000

Table 22.2

As we suggested in the previous section, a gilt can be viewed as a bundle of individual zero-coupon securities, so that we may consider its value to be equal to the value of a strip of zero-coupon bonds whose last bond matures at the same time as the coupon bond.

Consider the first bond in Table 22.2. As it matures in precisely six months' time, it is effectively a zero-coupon bond; its yield of 6% is equal to the six-month spot rate. Given this spot rate, we can derive the spot rate for a one-year zero-coupon gilt. The price of a one-year gilt strip must equal the present value of the two cash flows from our 10% one-year coupon gilt. This reflects the principle of no-arbitrage pricing. The cash flows from the one-year coupon gilt are:

1st September 1999	£5
1st March 2000	£5 + £100 = £105

The present value of these cash flows is

$$PV_{Mar00} = \frac{5}{(1 + r_1)} + \frac{105}{(1 + r_2)^2}$$

where

r_1 is one-half of the six-month theoretical spot rate
r_2 is one-half of the one-year theoretical spot rate.

As we illustrated earlier, in a semi-annual coupon environment we take half of the annual discount rate because we are discounting one-half of the annual coupon.

We have assumed that the six-month spot rate is 6%, based on our decision to treat the six-month gilt as a zero-coupon bond; therefore r_1, the yield required to calculate the present value of a semi-annual coupon payment in six months' time, is half of this rate, which is $\frac{1}{2} \times 0.06$, that is 0.03. Therefore, the present value of the one-year coupon gilt is

$$PV_{Mar00} = \frac{5}{(103)} + \frac{105}{(1 + r_2)^2}$$

As the price of the one-year gilt is 103.5322, which we observe in the market, the following relationship must be true :

$$103.5322 = \frac{5}{(103)} + \frac{105}{(1 + r_2)^2}$$

Using this relationship, we are now in a position to calculate the one-year theoretical spot rate as shown below.

$$103.5322 = 4.85437 + \frac{105}{(1 + r_2)^2}$$
$$98.67783 = 105 / (1 + r_2)^2$$
$$(1 + r_2)^2 = 105 / 98.67783$$
$$(1 + r_2)^2 = 1.064069$$
$$(1 + r_2) = \sqrt{1.064069}$$
$$r_2 = 0.03154$$

This is one-half of the one-year spot rate. Doubling this yield gives us the annualised bond-equivalent yield of 0.06308, or 6.308%, which is our theoretical one-year spot rate.

Now that we have obtained our theoretical one-year spot rate, we are in a position to calculate the theoretical $1\frac{1}{2}$-year spot rate. The cash flows for the 7% $1\frac{1}{2}$-year coupon gilt shown in Table 22.2 is shown below.

1st September 1999	£3.50
1st March 2000	£3.50
1st September 2000	£103.50

The present value of this cash-flow stream is :

$$PV_{Sep00} = \frac{3.50}{(1 + r_1)} + \frac{3.50}{(1 + r_2)^2} + \frac{103.50}{(1 + r_3)^3}$$

where r_3 is one-half of the $1\frac{1}{2}$-year theoretical spot rate. We have already established that the six-month and one-year spot rates are 6% and 6.308% respectively, so that r_1 is 0.03 and r_2 is 0.03154. Therefore, the present value of the 7% $1\frac{1}{2}$-year coupon gilt is :

$$PV_{Sep00} = \frac{3.5}{(1.03)} + \frac{3.5}{(1.03154)^2} + \frac{103.5}{(1 + r_3)^3}.$$

We can see from Table 22.2 that the price of the 7% $1\frac{1}{2}$-year gilt is 100.8453; therefore, the following relationship must be true :

$$100.8453 = \frac{3.5}{(103)} + \frac{3.5}{(1.03154)^2} + \frac{103.5}{(1 + r_3)^3}.$$

This equation can then be solved to obtain r_3 which proves to be 0.032035. Again we double this value, which gives us a $1\frac{1}{2}$-year theoretical spot rate of 6.407%.

For the two-year implied spot rate the relationship is

$$99.6314 = \frac{3.25}{(103)} + \frac{3.25}{(1.03154)^2} + \frac{3.25}{(1.032035)^3} + \frac{103.25}{(1 + r_4)^4}$$

which solves to give r_4 equal to 0.0336 and a two-year theoretical spot rate of 6.720%.

This process is repeated, using the two-year spot rate and the 8% September 2001 coupon gilt, so that the relationship used to compute the $2\frac{1}{2}$-year theoretical spot rate is:

$$102.4868 = \frac{4}{(103)} + \frac{4}{(1.03154)^2} + \frac{4}{(1.032035)^3} + \frac{4}{(1.0336)^4} + \frac{104}{(1 + r_5)^5}$$

which solves to give $r_5 = 6.936\%$.

For r_6 the three-year spot rate is 7.394%.

If we carry on the process for the gilts in Table 22.2 we will obtain the results shown in Table 22.3.

Maturity date	Years to maturity	Yield to maturity	Theoretical spot rate (%)
1 Sep 99	0.5	6.00	6.000
1 Mar 00	1.0	6.30	6.308
1 Sep 00	1.5	6.40	6.407
1 Mar 01	2.0	6.70	6.720
1 Sep 01	2.5	6.90	6.936
1 Mar 02	3.0	7.30	7.394
1 Sep 02	3.5	7.60	7.712
1 Mar 03	4.0	7.80	7.908
1 Sep 03	4.5	7.95	8.069
1 Mar 04	5.0	8.00	8.147

Table 22.3

The general relationship used to derive an implied spot rate for the Nth six-month period was given earlier as (22.6), here without the C subscripts.

$$P_n = \frac{C/2}{(1 + \frac{1}{2}r)} + \frac{C/2}{(1 + \frac{1}{2}r_2)^2} + \frac{C/2}{(1 + 1/2r_3)^3} + \ldots + \frac{C/2 + 100}{(1 + 1/2rN)^N} \quad (22.7)$$

We can re-write this expression as (22.8).

$$P_N = \frac{C}{2}\sum_{t=1}^{N-1}\frac{1}{(1 + r_t)^t} + \frac{C/2 + 100}{(1 + r_N)^N}$$ (22.8)

where

r_t for $t=1,2, ...N$-1 is the theoretical spot rates that are already known. This equation can be re-arranged so that we may solve for r_N.

$$r_N = \left[\frac{C/2 + 100}{P_N - \frac{C}{2}\sum_{t=1}^{N-1}\frac{1}{(1 + r_t)^t}}\right]^{\frac{1}{N}} - 1$$ (22.9)

Spot yields and bond yields

Following our description of the process by which spot interest rates can be derived from the prices of bonds observed in the market, in this section we illustrate the relationship between such rates and conventional bond yields.

In Table 22.4 we show the redemption yields for gilts as at 25th June 1997, together with implied spot rates, and the corresponding graph of these yields at Figure 22.2.

Term (years)	Gilt	Conventional Yield %	Spot Yield %	Spread %
0.25	8.75% 1/9/1997	6.508	6.508	0.000
1	7.25% 30/3/1998	6.763	6.770	-0.007
1.5	12% 20/11/1998	6.968	6.978	-0.01
2	6% 10/8/1999	6.956	6.972	-0.016
3	8% 7/12/2000	7.133	7.143	-0.01
4	7% 6/11/2001	7.158	7.179	-0.021
5	7% 7/6/2002	7.118	7.131	-0.013
6	8% 10/6/2003	7.173	7.184	-0.011
7	6.75% 27/11/2004	7.151	7.167	-0.016
8	8.50% 7/12/2005	7.188	7.196	-0.008
9	7.50% 7/12/2006	7.189	7.207	-0.018
10	7.25% 7/12/2007	7.170	7.180	-0.01
11	9% 13/10/2008	7.220	7.239	-0.019
12	8% 25/9/2009	7.235	7.271	-0.036
13	6.25% 25/11/2010	7.255	7.312	-0.057
14	9% 12/7/2011	7.254	7.289	-0.035
15	9% 6/8/2012	7.265	7.307	-0.042
16	8% 27/9/2013	7.254	7.289	-0.035

18	8% 7/12/2015	7.222	7.215	0.007
21	8.75% 25/8/2017	7.267	7.318	-0.051
24	8% 7/6/2021	7.209	7.172	0.037

Table 22.4 Conventional and spot yields, 25 June 1997
Source: Bloomberg; author's notes

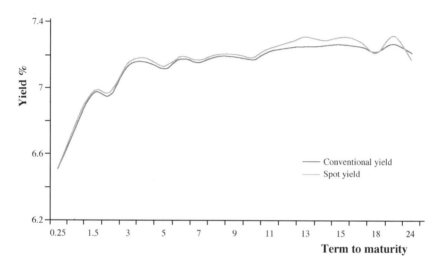

Figure 22.2 Gilt market yields, 25 June 1997
Source: Williams de Broe and Hambros Bank

The redemption-yield curve in Figure 22.2 is a conventional positively sloping curve with a dip at the long end of the term structure at the point of the longest-dated bond. Why is there a spread between the two curves? Remember that the spot yield curve is the theoretical return on a zero-coupon instrument; that is, one that has no coupons paid during its life. However, the redemption-yield curve measures the expected return on instruments that pay a coupon at regular intervals during their life. The rising shape of the curve implies that medium-dated zero-coupon bonds, if they represented actual instruments, would offer a better yield than short-dated zero-coupon bonds. This positively sloping part of the curve influences the relationship between spot yields and bond yields at that part of the curve. For instance, the five-year spot rate is 7.131%, so a five-year zero-coupon bond being priced on 24th June 1997 for settlement the following day in theory should pay 7.131%. The actual five-year coupon bond would pay a series of coupons before the final coupon and principal amount on maturity. This last coupon and principal would indeed be valued at 7.131% on 24th June, as they represent what are in effect zero-coupon payments in five years' time.[7] However, the earlier coupon payments would be valued at lower spot yields, as given by the positively sloping spot-yield curve. We know from earlier in this chapter that the yield on a coupon bond is, in effect, the average of the yields payable on the bundle spot obligations that constitute the bond, so that the final yield on the bond must be below 7.131% when priced for value on 25th June. The yield is, in fact, 7.118%. This is why the spot yields lie above the redemption yields at the short- to medium-end of the curve.

We also note that at the very long-end of the curve the demand for bonds is such that the yields are depressed for the 8% 2015 and 8% 2021 gilts. Again these bonds pay regular coupon but, at the longer-end, their coupons are valued higher by the market, so that these coupons are, in effect, priced at lower yields. This is confirmed by the implied spot-rate curve. The 18- and 24-year spot rates, which would be the theoretical yields on identical-maturity zero-coupon bonds, are 7.215% and 7.172%, respectively. However, the 18- and 24-year bonds themselves are priced at 7.222% and 7.209%.

The implication of this property for potential investors in zero-coupon gilts or strips is clear: in a positively sloping yield-curve environment there is a yield pickup on similar maturity strips, although these will be instruments of higher modified duration.

Consider now gilt yields for 10th November 1996, shown at Table 22.5 and Figure 22.3.

---

[7] We call this is a "five-year" bond as it is the benchmark bond for that period, while accepting that the actual maturity is slightly less than five years. An equivalent zero-coupon bond would also be priced on 24th June 1997 for maturity on 7th June 2002 rather than 25th June 2002, although we would call it a five-year security.

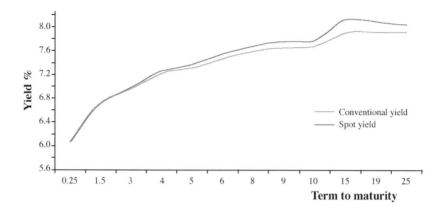

Figure 22.3 Gilt yield curves, 10 November 1996
Source: ABN Amro, Bloomberg; author's notes

Term (years)	Gilt	Conventional Yield %	Spot Yield %	Spread %
0.25	T-Bill	6.06	6.06	0.000
1.5	7.25% 30/3/1998	6.71	6.714	-0.004
3	6% 10/8/1999	6.95	6.979	-0.029
4	8% 7/12/2000	7.22	7.255	-0.035
5	7% 6/11/2001	7.31	7.364	-0.054
6	8% 10/6/2003	7.47	7.542	-0.072
8	6.75% 27/11/2004	7.59	7.690	-0.100
9	8.50% 7/12/2005	7.66	7.762	-0.102
10	7.50% 7/12/2006	7.67	7.780	-0.11
15	9% 12/7/2011	7.90	8.129	-0.229
19	8% 7/12/2015	7.91	8.086	-0.176
25	8% 7/6/2021	7.91	8.046	-0.136

Table 22.5 Conventional and spot yields, 10 November 1996

At this time, the bond yield curve was sloping upwards all the way out the long-bond. The difference in the yields of the 8% 2015 and 8% 2021 is much less pronounced with the curves for June 1997. The effect of this is that although the implied spot rates decrease at the very long end, they do not fall below the bond yield curve. This means that on this earlier date the market was not placing as high a premium on coupon payments made after 19 years as it would be seen to do several months later. This illustration leads nicely on to the next section, when we look at the yields of strips compared to their theoretical yields.

Implied spot yields and zero-coupon bond yields

In an environment in which there is a liquid market in actual zero-coupon securities or strips, we can observe market spot yields from the prices at which the strips are trading. In the previous section, we showed how the prices and redemption yields on coupon bonds can be used to derive an implied spot-yield curve. But how do these implied rates compare to actual strip yields, and how should we expect them to behave vis-à-vis each other? We discuss some of the key issues in this section.

A spot rate could be said to be the rate of return at purchase on a single-cash-flow security held to maturity. It can also, as the previous sections have shown, be viewed as the rate payable on a coupon bond that is viewed as a bundle of individual zero-coupon cash flows, with the bond yield viewed as a complex average of the spot yields on the individual payments. Spot yields as such cannot be actually observed in the market. Zero-coupon securities, on the other hand, are actual market instruments that have been created from stripping individual cash flows from coupon bonds, and trading the resultant cash flows separately.[8] Therefore, the yields observed on zero-coupon bonds will reflect actual market supply and demand for specific securities. This makes zero-coupon yields different from spot yields in practice, notwithstanding the fact that they should be viewed as identical in theory. This reflects how spot yields are derived from other prices and yields, and not observed on market instruments.

How do the two rates differ? If a particular zero-coupon bond is in demand, its price will rise and its yield will fall. The opposite occurs if the bond is not sought after and is being sold by investors and market-makers. The effect of this is that at any time the zero-coupon on yield can and does differ from the equivalent-maturity spot yield, be it higher or lower. If investors value an individual zero-coupon bond lower when it is a stripped security compared to when it is part of a package of zero-coupon cash flows (in a coupon bond), the yield on the zero will be higher than the equivalent-maturity spot rate. The opposite will happen if investors prefer to hold the

---

[8] For more information on this procedure with regard to the gilt strips market, see Choudhry (1999).

zero-coupon security. Despite this reflection of supply and demand, implied spot rates are still important because they allow investors to assess relative value for both zero-coupon bonds and coupon bonds.

Consider Table 22.6 and Figure 22.4; the latter shows the implied spot yields derived from gilt prices on 2nd March 1999, together with the yield for coupon strips and principal strips as at the same date. The yields on principal strips are not joined as a curve, as the comparatively long period between strips would make any conclusions from the resulting curve problematic. These are the yields on the principal or residual cash flow when a bond is stripped. The other cash flows are known as coupon strips.

Two observations are worth making. First, that zero-coupon bonds traded cheap to the spot curve throughout the term structure, indicating that investors were not prepared to hold strips without a premium to the theoretical value. This probably reflected the inverted yield curve, which meant that strips would be trading expensive to coupon bonds of the same maturity. However, strips traded expensive to the spot curve at the 11- to 15-year point of the curve. Second, principal strips trade at lower yields than coupon strips of the same maturity. This reflects the liquidity and demand considerations for principal strips, which investors prefer to hold instead of coupon strips.

Term	Gilt	True yield	Spot yields	Coupon Strip Yield	Principal Strip Yield
0.5	6% 10/8/1999	5.033	5.033	5.068	
1.5*	8% 7/12/2000	5.027	4.977	4.973	5.036
2.5	7% 6/11/2001	4.963	4.927	4.949	
3*	7% 7/6/2002	4.878	4.836	4.91	4.867
4	8% 10/6/2003	4.845	4.789	4.824	
4.5*	6.50% 7/12/2003	4.735	4.687	4.786	4.691
5	6.75% 26/11/2004	4.709	4.658	4.798	
6*	8.50% 7/12/2005	4.78	4.728	4.774	4.74
7*	7.50% 7/12/2006	4.8	4.77	4.781	4.775
8*	7.25% 7/12/2007	4.759	4.721	4.753	4.723
9	9% 13/10/2008	4.72	4.644	4.735	
10*	5.75% 7/12/2009	4.604	4.542	4.723	4.518
11	6.25% 25/11/2010	4.695	4.665	4.711	
12	9% 12/7/2011	4.751	4.721	4.713	
13	9% 6/8/2012	4.787	4.727	4.713	
14	8% 27/9/2013	4.763	4.75	4.71	

16*	8% 7/12/2015	4.711	4.659	4.705	4.670
18	8.75% 25/8/2017	4.729	4.695	4.682	
22*	8% 7/6/2021	4.679	4.609	4.635	4.612
29*	6% 7/12/2028	4.537	4.376	4.402	4.365

* Indicates strippable gilts

Table 22.6 Gilt market gross redemption true yields and implied spot yields on 2 March 1999
Source: Bloomberg

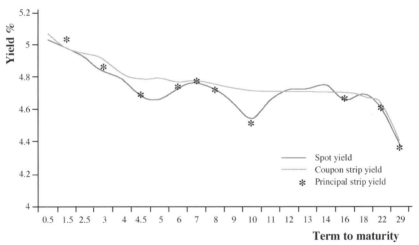

Figure 22.4 Spot and strip yields on 2 March 1999 .
Source: Bloomberg, author's notes

For reference, we graph the curve for the bond yields alongside the spot and zero-coupon yields at Figure 22.5.

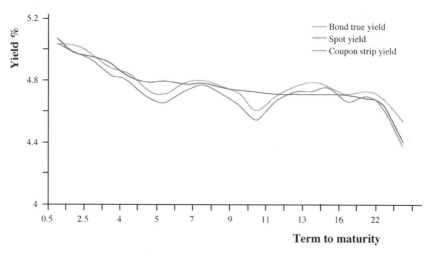

Figure 22.5 Gilt bond, implied spot and coupon strip yields, 2 March 1999
Source: Bloomberg, author's notes

Determining the value of strips

For the investor to identify relative value, it is important to compare curves as we have just described. The three most common ways to calculate the value of a strip are:

- valuation using the bond curve
- the equivalent-duration method
- theoretical zero-coupon curve construction, also known as bootstrapping.

The spread between a strip and a bond with the same maturity is often used as an indicator of strip value. It is essentially a rough-and-ready approach; its main drawback is that two instruments with different risk profiles are being compared against each other. This is particularly true for longer maturities.

When measuring relative value, the equivalent-duration method aligning the strip and coupon bond yields on the basis of modified duration will allow for a better comparison. However, the most common approach of determining the value of a strip is via the derivation of a theoretical zero-coupon curve as just described where we illustrated the relationship between coupon and zero-coupon yield. When the curve is flat, the spot curve will also be flat. When the yield curve is negative, the theoretical zero-coupon curve must lie below the coupon yield curve. This is because the yield on coupon-bearing bonds is affected by the fact that the investor receives part of the cash flow before the maturity of the bond. The discount rates corresponding to these earlier payment dates are higher than the discount rate corresponding to the final payment date on redemption. In addition, the spread between zero-coupon yields and bond yields should increase negatively with maturity, so that zero-coupon bonds always yield less than coupon bonds.

In a positively shaped yield-curve environment the opposite is true. The theoretical zero-coupon curve will lie above the coupon curve. It is interesting, however, to observe the overall steepness of the curves. In general, the steeper the coupon curve is, the steeper the zero-coupon curve will be. It should be remembered that each yearly value of the coupon curve is considered in the derivation of the zero-coupon curve. Hence, a yield curve could, for example, have exactly one-year, 10-year and 30-year yields, while the theoretical zero-coupon 30-year yield could be substantially higher or lower. The derived yield level would depend on whether the points on the term structure in between these maturity bands were connected by a smooth curve or straight line. This argument is sometimes cited as a reason for not using the bootstrapping method, in that the theoretical zero-coupon yields that are obtained are too sensitive for real-world trading. Bond analysts use spline or other curve-smoothing techniques to get around this problem, and produce theoretical values that are more realistic. This issue becomes more important when there are few bonds between large points on the term structure, such that linear interpolation between them produces more inaccurate results. For example, between the 10-year and 30-year maturities there are eight liquid gilts; between 20 and 30 years there are only two gilts.

Strips-market anomalies

From the start of gilt strips trading the market has observed some long-standing anomalies that mirror observations from other strips markets, such as those in the USA and France. These include the following:

Final principal trades expensive

It might be expected that the strip yield curve would behave in a similar fashion to the coupon curve. However, due to supply-and-demand considerations more weight is always given to the final principal strip, and this is indeed so in the gilt strips market.

Longest maturity is the most expensive

A characteristic seen in all well-developed strip markets is that maturities with the longest duration and the greatest convexity trade expensive relative to theoretical values. Conversely, intermediate maturities tend to trade cheap to the curve. This can be observed when looking at the gilt strips and coupon curves.

Principal strips trade at a premium over coupon strips

Principal strips reflect the premium investors are prepared to pay for greater liquidity and, in some markets, for regulatory and tax reasons. This rule is so well established that principal strips will sometimes trade more expensive than coupon strips, even when their outstanding nominal amount is lower than that of coupon strips.

Intermediate-maturity coupons are often relatively cheap

Market-makers in the past have often found themselves with large quantities of intermediate-maturity coupon strips, the residue of client demand for longer maturities. This has occurred with gilt strips where at certain times coupon strips of three to eight years maturity have traded cheap to the curve.

Very short coupon strips trade expensive

In a positively sloped yield-curve environment, short strips are often in demand because they provide an attractive opportunity to match liabilities without reinvestment risk at a higher yield than coupon bonds of the same maturity. We have not observed this in the gilt strips market to date, as the yield curve has been inverted from before the start of trading. However, in France, for example, the short end up to three years is often well bid.

Strips trading strategy

Bond replication through strips

This is the theoretical strategy and the one that first presents itself. The profit potential for a market-maker who strips a gilt lies in arbitrage resulting from a mispricing of the coupon bond. The market mechanism requiring that there be no arbitrage opportunity means the bid price of a gilt must be lower than the offer price of a synthetic gilt (a gilt reconstituted from a bundle of coupon and principal strips). Equally, the offer price of the gilt must be higher than the bid price of a synthetic gilt. Of course, if the above conditions are not satisfied, a risk-free profit can be obtained by trading the opposite way in both instruments simultaneously and simply taking the difference.

The potential profit in stripping a gilt will depend on actual gilt yields prevailing in the market and the theoretical spot-rate yield curve. To illustrate how a GEMM might realise a profit from a coupon-stripping exercise, consider a hypothetical five-year, 8% gilt selling at par (and therefore offering a yield to maturity of 8%) trading in the yield-curve environment we described earlier, and which was shown in Table 22.3. Let us imagine that the market-maker buys the gilt at par and strips it, with the intention of selling the resulting zero-coupon bonds at the yields indicated for the corresponding maturities shown in Table 22.3.

Table 22.7 shows the price that the market-maker would receive for each strip that was created. As we know, the price of the coupon gilt is the discounted total present value of all its cash flows using the required market interest rate. Here, we can equate it to the total present value of all the cash flows from the strips, each discounted at the yield corresponding to its maturity (from Table 22.3). The proceeds received from selling the strips come to a total of £100.4913 per £100 of par value of the gilt originally bought by the GEMM.

Maturity date	Years to maturity	Cash flow	Present value at 8%	Yield to maturity	Present value at yield to maturity
1 Sep 99	0.5	4	3.8462	6.00	6.000
1 Mar 00	1.0	4	3.6982	6.30	6.308
1 Sep 00	1.5	4	3.5560	6.40	6.407
1 Mar 01	2.0	4	3.4192	6.70	6.720
1 Sep 01	2.5	4	3.2877	6.90	6.936
1 Mar 02	3.0	4	3.1613	7.30	7.394
1 Sep 02	3.5	4	3.0397	7.60	7.712
1 Mar 03	4.0	4	2.9228	7.80	7.908
1 Sep 03	4.5	4	2.8103	7.95	8.069
1 Mar 04	5.0	104	70.2587	8.00	8.147
			100.0000		100.4913

Table 22.7

We can show why there is an opportunity to realise this profit. Consider the fourth column in Table 22.7. This shows us how much the market-maker paid for each of the cash flows by buying the entire package of cash flows; that is, by buying the bond at a yield of 8%. For instance, let us examine the

£4 coupon payment due in three years. By buying the five-year gilt priced to yield 8%, the GEMM pays a price based on 8% (4% semi-annual) for that coupon payment, which is £3.1613. However, if we accept the assumptions in this illustration, investors are willing to accept a lower yield, 7.30% (3.65% semi-annual) and purchase a strip with three years to maturity at the price marked.

Thus, investors here are willing to pay £3.2258. On this one coupon payment (now, of course, a strip versus a coupon payment) the GEMM realises a profit equal to the difference between £3.2258 and £3.1613, or £0.0645. From all the strips the total profit is £0.4913 per £100 nominal.

Maturity date	Years to maturity	Cash flow	Present value at 8%	Yield to maturity	Present value at yield to maturity
1 Sep 99	0.5	4	3.8462	6.000	3.8835
1 Mar 00	1.0	4	3.6982	6.308	3.7591
1 Sep 00	1.5	4	3.5560	6.407	3.6390
1 Mar 01	2.0	4	3.4192	6.720	3.5047
1 Sep 01	2.5	4	3.2877	6.936	3.3731
1 Mar 02	3.0	4	3.1613	7.394	3.2171
1 Sep 02	3.5	4	3.0397	7.712	3.0693
1 Mar 03	4.0	4	2.9228	7.908	2.9331
1 Sep 03	4.5	4	2.8103	8.069	2.8020
1 Mar 04	5.0	104	70.2587	8.147	69.7641
			100.0000		~100.0000

Table 22.8

Let us now imagine that instead of the observed yield to maturity from Table 22.7, the yields required by investors are the same as the theoretical spot rates also shown. Table 22.8 shows that in this case the total proceeds from the sale of zero-coupon gilts would be approximately £100 which, being no profit, would render the exercise of stripping uneconomic. This shows that where strips prices deviate from theoretical prices, there may be profit opportunities. We have shown elsewhere that there are differences between observed strip yields and theoretical yields, indicating that there are (often very small) differences between derived prices and actual prices. Do these price differences give rise to arbitrage opportunities? Because of the efficiency and transparency of developed-country bond markets, the answer is usually no. It is the process of coupon stripping that prevents the price of a gilt from trading at a price that is *materially* different from its theoretical price based on the derived spot-yield curve. And where discrepancies arise, any arbitrage activity will cause them to disappear very quickly. As the strips market becomes more liquid, the laws of supply and demand will eliminate obvious arbitrage opportunities, as has already happened in the US Treasury market and is already the norm in the gilts market. However, there will remain occasional opportunities to exploit differences between actual market prices of strips and the theoretical price given by the benchmark (coupon) gilt yield curve.

CASE STUDY Gilt strips yield and cash-flow analysis

The following examples illustrate the yield analysis and cash flows for the 5 $^3/_4$% Treasury 2009, which matures on 7th December 2009, its principal strip and a coupon strip maturing on 7th December 2009. The 5 $^3/_4$% 2009 was the current 10-year benchmark gilt. The market information reflects the position for settlement date 11th February 1999. Interest rate and price data was obtained from Bloomberg and Reuters.

Table 22.9 shows the cash flows paid out to a bondholder of £1 million nominal of the 5 $^3/_4$% 2009. On the trade date (10th February 1999, for settlement on 11th February), this bond traded at 113.15, with a corresponding yield of 4.2224%. The convexity of this bond at this time was 0.820. The relevant spot rates at each of the cash flow dates are shown alongside.

Pay date	Cash flow	Spot	Pay date	Cashflow	Spot
7 Jun 99	28,750.00	5.1474	7 Dec 04	28,750.00	4.2746
7 Dec 99	28,750.00	4.9577	7 Jun 05	28,750.00	4.3168
7 Jun 00	28,750.00	4.8511	7 Dec 05	28,750.00	4.3599
7 Dec 00	28,750.00	4.7376	7 Jun 06	28,750.00	4.3881
7 Jun 01	28,750.00	4.6413	7 Dec 06	28,750.00	4.3603
7 Dec 01	28,750.00	4.5481	7 Jun 07	28,750.00	4.3326
7 Jun 02	28,750.00	4.4614	7 Dec 07	28,750.00	4.3326
7 Dec 02	28,750.00	4.3962	7 Jun 08	28,750.00	4.2942
7 Jun 03	28,750.00	4.3307	7 Dec 08	28,750.00	4.2548

| 7 Dec 03 | 28,750.00 | 4.2654 | 7 Jun 09 | 28,750.00 | 4.2153 |
| 7 Jun 04 | 28,750.00 | 4.2696 | 7 Dec 09 | 1,028,750.00 | 4.1759 |

Nominal	1,000,000	Previous coupon date	7 Dec 98
Duration	8.33	Accrued Interest	10,425.82
Total Cashflow	1,632,500.00	Present Yield	1,141,925.84

Table 22.9 Cash-flow Analysis Treasury $5^3/_4\%$ 2009, yield 4.2224%
Source: Bloomberg

The cash flow for the December 2009 principal strip is shown as Table 22.10. Note that if calling up this security on the Bloomberg system, the ticker is UKTR, comprising the standard UKT (from "United Kingdom Treasury") and the suffix R (from "residual", the Bloomberg term for principal strips). The Bloomberg ticker for coupon strips is UKTS.

The yield on the principal strip at this time was 4.1482%, which corresponds to a price of 64.13409 per £100 nominal. Given that the yield curve is inverted at this time, this is what is expected, a yield lower than the gross redemption yield for the coupon gilt. For a holding of £1 million nominal there is only one cash flow, the redemption payment of £1 million on the redemption date. The convexity for the principal strip was 1.175, which illustrates the higher convexity property of strips versus coupon bonds. Comparing the tables, we can see also that duration for the strip is higher than that for the coupon gilt. Note the analysis for the principal strip gives us a slightly different spot curve.

Pay date	Cash flow	Spot	Pay date	Cashflow	Spot
7 Jun 99	0.00	5.1835	7 Dec 04	0.00	4.2683
7 Dec 99	0.00	4.9577	7 Jun 05	0.00	4.3102
7 Jun 00	0.00	4.8509	7 Dec 05	0.00	4.3529
7 Dec 00	0.00	4.7373	7 Jun 06	0.00	4.3672
7 Jun 01	0.00	4.6411	7 Dec 06	0.00	4.3821
7 Dec 01	0.00	4.5480	7 Jun 07	0.00	4.3571
7 Jun 02	0.00	4.4613	7 Dec 07	0.00	4.3322
7 Dec 02	0.00	4.3952	7 Jun 08	0.00	4.2937

7 Jun 03	0.00	4.3290	7 Dec 08	0.00	4.2543
7 Dec 03	0.00	4.2629	7 Jun 09	0.00	4.2148
7 Jun 04	0.00	4.2651	7 Dec 09	1,000,000.00	4.1753

Nominal	1,000,000	Previous coupon date		7 Dec 98
Duration	10.82	Accrued Interest		0.00
Total Cashflow	1,000,000.00	Present Yield		641,340.87

Table 22.10 Cash-flow Analysis Treasury $5^3/_4\%$ 2009 Principal Strip,
yield 4.1482%
Source: Bloomberg

Finally, we show at Table 22.11 the cash-flow analysis for a coupon strip maturing on 7th December 2009. The yield quote for this coupon strip at this time was 4.4263%, corresponding to a price of 62.26518 per £100 nominal. This illustrates the point on strip prices we referred to earlier; according to a strict interpretation of the law of one price, all strips maturing on the same date should have the same price (the question being asked is, why should an investor have a different yield requirement depending on whether the £100 nominal he receives on maturity was once interest or once principal?). However, as we have already stated, the liquidity differences between principal and coupon strips makes the former easier to trade and also more sought after by investors; hence, the difference in yield between principal and coupon strip. The more liquid instrument trades at the lower yield.

Pay date	Cash flow	Spot	Pay date	Cashflow	Spot
7 Jun 99	0.00	5.2025	7 Dec 04	0.00	4.3217
7 Dec 99	0.00	5.0151	7 Jun 05	0.00	4.3672
7 Jun 00	0.00	4.8927	7 Dec 05	0.00	4.4136
7 Dec 00	0.00	4.7633	7 Jun 06	0.00	4.4353
7 Jun 01	0.00	4.6881	7 Dec 06	0.00	4.4576
7 Dec 01	0.00	4.6108	7 Jun 07	0.00	4.4299
7 Jun 02	0.00	4.5138	7 Dec 07	0.00	4.4023
7 Dec 02	0.00	4.4450	7 Jun 08	0.00	4.3608

7 Jun 03	0.00	4.3761	7 Dec 08	0.00	4.3183
7 Dec 03	0.00	4.3074	7 Jun 09	0.00	4.2758
7 Jun 04	0.00	4.3141	7 Dec 09	1,000,000.00	4.2333

Nominal	1,000,000	Previous coupon date	7 Dec 98
Duration	10.82	Accrued Interest	0.00
Total Cashflow	1,000,000.00	Present Yield	622,651.18

Table 22.11 Cash-flow Analysis, December 2009 Coupon Strip,
yield 4.4263%
Source: Bloomberg

Yield–spread trades[9]

Relative-value trades are common amongst investors who do not wish to put on a naked directional position but rather believe that the yield curve will change shape and flatten or widen between two selected points. Such a trade would involve simultaneous positions in bonds of different maturity. Another relative-value trade may involve high-coupon bonds against low coupon bonds of the same maturity, as a tax-related trade. These trades are concerned with the change in yield spread between two or more bonds rather than a change in absolute interest-rate level. The key factor is that changes in spread are not conditional upon directional change in interest-rate levels; that is, yield spreads may narrow or widen whether interest rates themselves are rising or falling.

Typically, spread trades will be constructed as a long position in one bond against a short position in another bond. If it is set up correctly, the trade will only achieve a profit or incur a loss if there is change in the shape of the yield curve. This is regarded as being first-order risk-neutral, which means that there is no interest-rate risk in the event of change in the general level of market interest rates. In this section, we examine some common yield-spread trades.

Spread–trade risk weighting

A relative-value trade usually involves a long position set up against a short position in a bond of different maturity. The trade must be weighted so that

---

[9] Originally written by the author in June 1997 as an internal paper when at Hambros Bank Limited. The prices quoted are tick prices, that is fractions of a 32nd.

the two positions are first-order neutral, which means the risk exposure of each position nets out when considered as a single trade, but only with respect to a general change in interest-rate levels. If there is a change in yield spread, a profit or loss will be generated.

A common approach to weighting spread trades is to use the basis-point value (BPV) of each bond.[10] Table 22.11 shows price and yield data for a set of benchmark gilts for value date 17th June 1997. The BPV for each bond is also shown, per £100 of stock. For the purposes of this discussion, we quote mid-prices only and assume that the investor is able to trade at these prices.

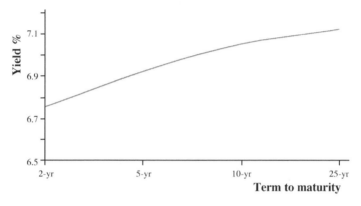

Term	Bond	Price	Accrued	Dirty price	Yield %	Modified duration	BPV	Per £1m nominal
2-yr	6% 10/8/1999	98-17	127	100.62	6.753	1.689	0.016642	166.42
5-yr	7% 7/6/2002	100-10	10	100.50	6.922	3.999	0.040115	401.15
10-yr	7.25% 7/12/2007	101-14	10	101.64	7.052	6.911	0.070103	701.03
25-yr	8% 7/6/2021	110-01	10	110.25	7.120	11.179	0.123004	1230.04

Table 22.12 Gilt prices and yields for value 17th June 1997
Source: Williams de Broe and Hambros Bank Limited; author notes

---

[10] This is also known as "dollar value of a basis point" (DVBP), "present value of a value point" (PVBP) or simply DV01.

An investor believes that the yield curve will flatten between the two-year and 25-year sectors of the curve and that the spread between the 6% 1999 and the 8% 2021 will narrow from its present value of 0.367%. To reflect this view, he buys the 25-year bond and sells short the two-year bond, in amounts that leave the trade first-order risk-neutral. If we assume the investor buys £1 million nominal of the 8% 2021 gilt, this represents an exposure of £1230.04 loss (profit) if there is a 1 basis point increase (decrease) in yields. Therefore, the nominal amount of the short position in the 6% 1999 gilt must equate this risk exposure. The BPV per £1 million nominal of the two-year bond is £166.42, which means that the investor must sell

(1230.04/166.42)

or £7.3912 million of this bond, given by a simple ratio of the two basis-point values. We expect to sell a greater nominal amount of the shorter-dated gilt because its risk exposure is lower. This trade generates cash because the short sale proceeds exceed the long-buy purchase funds, which are respectively

Buy £1m 8% 2021	−£1,102,500
Sell £7.39m 6% 1999	+£7,437,025

What are the possible outcomes of this trade? If there is a parallel shift in the yield curve, the trade neither gains nor loses. If the yield spread narrows by, say, 15 basis points the trade will gain either from a drop in yield on the long side or a gain in yield in the short side, or a combination of both. Conversely, a widening of the spread will result in a loss. Any narrowing spread is positive for the trade, while any widening is harmful.

The trade would be put on the same ratio if the amounts were higher, which is known as scaling the trade. So, for example, if the investor had bought £100 million of the 8% 2021, he would need to sell short £739 million of the two-year bonds. However, the risk exposure is greater by the same amount, so that in this case the trade would generate 100 times the risk. As can be imagined, there is a greater potential reward but at the same time a greater amount of stress in managing the position.

Using BPVs to risk-weight a relative-value trade is common but suffers from any traditional duration-based measure because of the assumptions used in the analysis. Note that when using this method, the ratio of the nominal amount of the bonds must equate the reciprocal of the bonds' BPV ratio. So, in this case the BPV ratio is

(166.42/1230.04)

or 0.1353, which has a reciprocal of 7.3912. This means that the nominal values of the two bonds must always be in the ratio of 7.39:1. This weighting is not static, however; we know from Chapter 2 that duration measures are a snapshot estimation of dynamic properties such as yield and term to maturity. Therefore, for anything but very short-term trades the relative values may need to be adjusted as the BPVs alter over time.

Another method to weigh trades is by duration-weighting, which involves weighting in terms of market values. This compares to the BPV approach which provides a weighting ratio in terms of nominal values. In practice, the duration approach does not produce any more accurate risk weighting.

A key element of any relative-value trade is the financing cost of each position. This is where the repo market in each bond becomes important. In the example just described, the financing requirement is:

- repo out the 8% 2021, for which £1.1 million of cash must be borrowed to finance the purchase; the trader pays the repo rate on this stock
- reverse repo the 6% 1999 bond, which must be borrowed in repo to cover the short sale; the trader earns the repo rate on this stock.

If the repo rate on both stocks is close to the general repo rate in the market, there will be a bid-offer spread to pay but the greater amount of funds lent out against the 6% 1999 bond will result in a net financing gain on the trade whatever happens to the yield spread. If the 8% 2021 gilt is special, because the stock is in excessive demand in the market (for whatever reason), the financing gain will be greater still. If the 6% 1999 is special, the trade will suffer a financing loss.

Figure 22.6(i) and (ii) show the funding considerations for this trade for value 17 June 1997, calculated on the Bloomberg screen RRRA. Both stocks were traded as "general collateral" in the market that day, that is, not special. The financing rate for the 6% 1999 was 6.00%, that for the 8% 2021 stock 6.125%. This reflects the bid-offer spread for GC at that time.

The cash value of the short sale far exceeds that of the long buy, hence over any time horizon the net funding for this trade is positive. From figure 22.6 we see the net funding gain for a one-month trade is £29,698. This is a bonus for the position, as it means there is no "breakeven" level for the spread should the yield curve move in the direction anticipated. In fact the funding gain will cushion against a small move in the wrong direction.

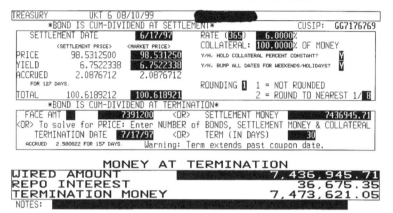

Figure 22.6(i) Bloomberg screen RRRA showing funding calculation for one-month holding in 6% 1999, value 17 June 1997, short sale funding.
© Bloomberg L.P. Used with permission.

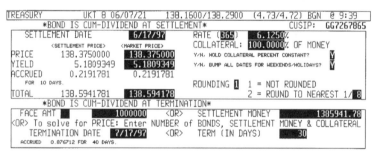

Figure 22.6(i) Bloomberg screen RRRA showing funding calculation for one-month holding in 8% 2021, value 17 June 1997, long position funding.
© Bloomberg L.P. Used with permission.

Identifying yield-spread trades

Yield-spread trades are a type of relative-value position that a trader can construct when the objective is to gain from a change in the spread between two points on the yield curve. The decision on which sectors of the curve to target is an important one and is based on a number of factors. An investor may naturally target, say, the five- and 10-year areas of the yield curve to meet investment objectives and have a view on these maturities. Or a trader may draw conclusions from studying the historical spread between two sectors.

Yield spreads do not move in parallel, however, and there is not a perfect correlation between the changes of short-, medium- and long-term sectors of the curve. The money-market yield curve can sometimes act independently of the bond curve. Table 22.13 shows the change in benchmark yields during 1996/1997. There is no set pattern in the change in both yield levels and spreads. It is apparent that one segment of the curve can flatten while another is steepening, or remain unchanged.

Changes in yield levels

	3-month	1-year	2-year	5-year	10-year	25-year
11/10/96	6.06	6.71	6.83	7.31	7.67	7.91
7/10/97	6.42	6.96	7.057	7.156	7.025	6.921
Change	0.36	0.25	0.227	−0.154	−0.645	−0.989
11/10/97	7.15	7.3	7.09	6.8	6.69	6.47
Change	0.73	0.34	0.033	−0.356	−0.335	−0.451

Changes in yield spread

	3m / 1y	1y / 2y	2y / 5y	5y / 10y	5y / 25y	10y / 25y
11/10/96	−0.65	−0.12	−0.48	−0.36	−0.6	−0.24
7/10/97	−0.54	−0.457	−0.099	0.131	0.235	0.104
Change	0.11	−0.337	0.381	0.491	0.835	0.344
11/10/97	−0.15	0.21	0.29	0.11	0.33	0.22
Change	0.39	0.667	0.389	−0.021	0.095	0.116

Table 22.13 Yield levels and yield spreads during November 1996–November 1997
Source: ABN Amro, Hambros Bank Limited; author notes

Another type of trade is where an investor has a view on one part of the curve relative to two other parts of the curve. This can be reflected in a number of ways, one of which is the butterfly trade, considered in the next section.

Coupon spread

Coupon spreads are becoming less common in the gilt market because of the disappearance of high-coupon or other exotic gilts and the concentration on liquid benchmark issues. However, they are genuine spread trades. The basic principle behind the trade is a spread of two bonds that have similar maturity or similar duration but different coupons.

Table 22.14 shows the yields for a set of high coupon and low(er) coupon gilts for a specified date in May 1993 and the yields for the same gilts six months later. From the yield curves, we see that general yield levels decline by approximately 80–130 basis points. The last column in the table shows that, apart from the earliest pair of gilts (which do not have strictly comparable maturity dates), the performance of the lower-coupon gilt exceeded that of the higher-coupon gilt in every instance. Therefore, buying the spread of the low coupon versus the high coupon should, in theory, generate a trading gain in an environment of falling yields. One explanation for this is that the lower-coupon bonds are often the benchmark, which means the demand for them is higher. In addition, during a bull market, more bonds are considered to be "high" coupon as overall yield levels decrease.

Stock	Term	10-May-93	12-Nov-93
Gilt	1	5.45	5.19
10Q 95	2	6.39	5.39
10 96	3	6.94	5.82
10H 97	4	7.13	5.97
9T 98 and 7Q 98	5	7.31	6.14
10Q 99	6	7.73	6.55
9 00	7	7.67	6.54
10 01	8	8.01	6.82
9T 02	9	8.13	6.95
8 03	10	8.07	6.85
9 08	15	8.45	7.18
9 12	20	8.55	7.23
8T 17	30	8.6	7.22

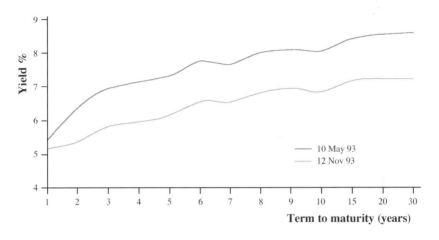

Gilt	Maturity	10/05/1993 Yield %	12/11/1993 Yield %	Yield change %
10Q 95	21-Jul-95	6.393	5.390	-1.003
14 96	10-Jan-96	6.608	5.576	-1.032
15Q 96	3-May-96	6.851	5.796	-1.055
13Q 96	15-May-96	6.847	5.769	-1.078
13Q 97	22-Jan-97	7.142	5.999	-1.143
10H 97	21-Feb-97	7.131	5.974	1.157
7 97	6-Aug-97	7.219	6.037	-1.182
8T 97	1-Sep-97	7.223	6.055	-1.168
15 97	27-Oct-97	7.294	6.113	-1.161
9T 98	19-Jan-98	7.315	6.102	-1.213
7Q 98	30-Mar-98	7.362	6.144	-1.218
6 99	10-Aug-99	7.724	6.536	-1.188
10Q 99	22-Nov-99	7.731	6.552	-1.179
8 03	10-Jun-03	8.075	6.854	-1.221
10 03	8-Sep-03	8.137	6.922	-1.215

Table 22.14 Yield changes on high and low coupon gilts from May 1993 to November 1993

Source: ABN Amro Hoare Govett Sterling Bonds Ltd; Bloomberg; Author's notes

The exception noted in Table 22.14 is the out-performance by the 14% Treasury 1996 over the lower-coupon 10˘% 1995 stock. This is not necessarily conclusive, because the bonds are six months apart in maturity, which is a significant amount for short-dated stock. However, in an environment of low or falling interest rates, shorter-dated investors such as banks and insurance companies often prefer to hold very high-coupon bonds because of the high income levels they generate. This may explain the demand for the 14% 1996 stock,[11] although the evidence at the time was only anecdotal.

Butterfly trades

Butterfly trades are another method by which traders can reflect a view on changing yield levels without resorting to a naked punt on interest rates. They are another form of relative-value trade. Amongst portfolio managers they are viewed as a means of enhancing returns. In essence, a butterfly trade is a short position in one bond against a long position of two bonds, one of shorter maturity and the other of longer maturity than the short-sold bond. Duration-weighting is used so that the net position is first-order risk-neutral, and nominal values are calculated such that the short-sale and long-purchase cash flows net to zero, or very close to zero.

This section reviews key aspects of butterfly trades.

Basic concepts

A butterfly trade is a yield-curve trade par excellence. If the average return on the combined long position is greater than the return on the short position (which is a cost) during the time the trade is maintained, the strategy will generate a profit. It reflects a view that the short-end of the curve will steepen relative to the "middle" of the curve while the long-end will flatten. For this reason, higher-convexity stocks are usually preferred for the long positions, even if this entails a loss in yield. However, the trade is not "risk-free", for the same reasons that a conventional two-bond yield spread is not. Although in theory a butterfly is risk-neutral with respect to parallel changes in the yield curve, changes in the shape of the curve can result in losses. For this reason, the position must be managed dynamically and monitored for changes in risk relative to changes in the shape of the yield curve.

---

[11] This stock also has a special place in the author's heart, although he was No.2 on the desk when the Treasury head put on a very large position in it...!

In a butterfly trade, the trader is long a short-dated and long-dated bond, and short a bond of a maturity that falls in between these two maturities. A portfolio manager with a constraint on running short positions may consider this trade as a switch out of a long position in the medium-dated bond and into duration-weighted amounts of the short-dated and long-dated bond. However, it is not strictly correct to view the combined long position as an exact substitute for the short position; because of liquidity and other reasons the two positions will behave differently for given changes in the yield curve. In addition, one must be careful to compare like with like, as the yield change in the short position must be analysed against yield changes in *two* bonds. This raises the issue of portfolio yield.

Putting on the trade

We begin by considering the calculation of the nominal amounts of the long positions, assuming a user-specified starting amount in the short position. In Table 22.14 we show three gilts as at 25th April 1997. The trade we wish to put on is a short position in the five-year bond, the 7% Treasury 2002, against long positions in the two-year bond, the 6% Treasury 1999, and the 10-year bond, the 7⌣% Treasury 2007. Assuming £10 million nominal of the five-year bond, the nominal values of the long positions can be calculated using duration, modified duration or basis-point values (the last two, unsurprisingly, will generate identical results). The more common approach is to use basis-point values.

	2-year bond	5-year bond	10-year bond
Gilt	6% 1999	7% 2002	7.25% 2007
Maturity date	10 Aug 1999	07 Jun 2002	07 Dec 2007
Price	98-08	99-27	101-06
Accrued interest	2.30137	0.44110	0.45685
Dirty price	100.551	100.285	101.644
GRY %	6.913	7.034	7.085
Duration	1.969	4.243	7.489
Modified duration	1.904	4.099	7.233
Basis Point Value	0.01914	0.0411	0.07352
Convexity	0.047	0.204	0.676

Table 22.15 Bond values for butterfly strategy, June 1997
Source: Author's notes

In a butterfly trade, the net cash flow should be as close to zero as possible, and the trade must be basis-point value-neutral. Using the following notation,

P_1 the dirty price of the short-position
P_2 the dirty price of the long position in the two-year bond
P_3 the dirty price of the long position in the ten-year bond
M_1 the nominal value of short-position bond, with M_2 and M_3 the long position bonds
BPV_1 the basis-point value of the short-position bond

if applying basis-point values, the amounts required for each stock are given by

$$M_1 P_1 = M_2 P_2 + M_3 P_3 \qquad (22.10)$$

while the risk-neutral calculation is given by

$$M_1 BPV_1 = M_2 BPV_2 + M_3 BPV_3 \qquad (22.11)$$

The value of M_1 is not unknown, as we have set it at £10 million. The equations can be rearranged, therefore, to solve for the remaining two bonds, which are

$$M_2 = \frac{P_1 BPV_3 - P_3 BPV_1}{P_2 BPV_3 - P_3 BPV_2} M_1 \qquad (22.12)$$

$$M_3 = \frac{P_2 BPV_1 - P_1 BPV_2}{P_2 BPV_3 - P_3 BPV_2} M_1 \ .$$

Using the dirty prices and BPVs from Table 22.15, we obtain the following values for the long positions. The position required is short £10 million 7% 2002 and long £5.347 million of the 6% 1999 and £4.576 million of the 7⁻% 2007. With these values, the trade results in a zero net cash flow and a first-order risk-neutral interest-rate exposure. Identical results would be obtained using the modified-duration values, and using the duration measures. If using Macaulay duration the nominal values are calculated using

$$D_1 = \frac{MV_2 D_2 + MV_3 D_3}{MV_2 + MV_3} \qquad (22.13)$$

where D and MV represent duration and market value for each respective stock.

Yield gain

We know that the gross-redemption yield for a vanilla bond is that rate r where

$$P_d = \sum_{i=1}^{N} C_i e^{-rn} \qquad (22.14)$$

The right-hand side of (22.14) is simply the present value of the cash-flow payments C to be made by the bond in its remaining lifetime. Expression (22.15) gives the continuously compounded yields to maturity. In practice, users define a yield with compounding interval m, that is

$$r = (e^{rmn} - 1) / m. \qquad (22.15)$$

Treasuries and gilts compound on a semi-annual basis.

In principle, we may compute the yield on a portfolio of bonds exactly as for a single bond, using (22.14), to give the yield for a set of cash flows which are purchased today at their present value. In practice, the market calculates portfolio yield as a weighted average of the individual yields on each of the bonds in the portfolio. This is described, for example, in Fabozzi (1993), and his description points out the weakness of this method. An alternative approach is to weight individual yields using bonds' basis-point values, which we illustrate here in the context of the earlier butterfly trade. In this trade we have

- short £10 million 7% 2002
- long £5.347 million 6% 1999 and £4.576 million 7¼% 2007.

Using the semi-annual adjusted form of (22.14), the true yield of the long position is 7.033%. To calculate the portfolio yield of the long position using market-value weighting, we may use

$$r_{port} = (MV_2 / MV_{port})r_2 + (MV_3 / MV_{port})r_3 \qquad (22.16)$$

which results in a portfolio yield for the long position of 6.993%. If we weight the yield with basis-point values we use

$$r_{port} = \frac{BPV_2 M_2 r_2 + BPV_3 M_3 r_3}{BPV_2 M_2 + BPV_3 M_3} \qquad (22.17)$$

Substituting the values from Table 22.15, we obtain

$$r_{port} = \frac{(1,914)(5.347)(6.913) + (7,352)(4.576)(7.085)}{(1,914)(5.347) + (7,352)(4.576)}$$

or 7.045%.

We see that using basis-point values produces a seemingly more accurate weighted yield, closer to the true yield computed using the expression above. In addition, using this measure, a portfolio manager switching into the long butterfly position from a position in the 7% 2002 would pick up a yield gain of 1.2 basis points, compared to the 4 basis points that an analyst would conclude had been lost using the first yield measure.[12]

The butterfly trade, therefore, produces a yield gain in addition to the capital gain expected if the yield curve changes in the anticipated way.

Convexity gain

In addition to yield pick-up, the butterfly trade provides, in theory, a convexity gain that will outperform the short position irrespective of which direction interest rates moved in, provided we have a parallel shift. This is illustrated in Table 22.16. This shows that the changes in value of the 7% 2002 as interest rates rise and fall, together with the change in value of the combined portfolio.

---

[12] The actual income gained on the spread will depend on the funding costs for all three bonds, a function of the specific repo rates available for each bond. Shortly after the time of writing, the 6% Treasury 1999 went special, so the funding gain on a long position in this stock would have been excessive. However, buying the stock outright would have necessitated paying a yield premium, as demand for it increased as a result of it going special. In the event, the premium was deemed high, an alternative stock was nominated, the $10^1/_4$% Conversion 1999, a bond with near-identical modified-duration value.

Yield change (bps)	7% 2002 value (£)	Portfolio value* (£)	Difference (£)	BPV 7% 2002 (5-year)	BPV 6% 1999 (2-year)	BPV 7.25% 2007 (10-year)
+250	9,062,370	9,057,175	−5,195	0.0363	0.0180	0.0584
+200	9,246,170	9,243,200	−2,970	0.0372	0.0182	0.0611
+150	9,434,560	9,435,200	640	0.0381	0.0184	0.0640
+100	9,627,650	9,629,530	1,880	0.0391	0.0187	0.0670
+50	9,825,600	9,828,540	2,940	0.0401	0.0189	0.0702
0	**10,028,500**	**10,028,500**	**0**	0.0411	0.0191	0.0735
−50	10,236,560	10,251,300	14,740	0.0421	0.0194	0.0770
−100	10,450,000	10,483,800	33,800	0.0432	0.0196	0.0808
−150	10,668,600	10,725,700	57,100	0.0443	0.0199	0.0847
−200	10,893,000	10,977,300	84,300	0.0454	0.0201	0.0888
−250	11,123,000	11,240,435	117,435	0.0466	0.0204	0.0931

* Combined value of long positions in 6% 1999 and 7.25% 2007.
Values rounded. Yield change is parallel shift

Table 22.16 Changes in bond values with changes in yield levels

We observe from Table 22.16 that whatever the change in interest rates, up to a point, the portfolio value will be higher than the value of the short position, although the effect is progressively reduced as yields rise. The butterfly will always gain if yields fall, and protects against downside risk if yields rise to a certain extent. This is the effect of convexity; when interest rates rise, the portfolio value declines by less than the short position value, and when rates fall, the portfolio value increases by more. Essentially, the combined long position exhibits greater convexity than the short position. The effect is greater if yields fall, while there is an element of downside protection as yields rise, up to the +150 basis-point parallel shift.

Portfolio managers may seek greater convexity whether or not there is a yield pick-up available from a switch. However, the convexity effect is only material for large changes in yield; so, if there was not a corresponding yield gain from the switch, the trade may not perform positively. As we noted, this depends partly on the funding position for each stock. The price/yield profile for each stock is shown at Figure 22.7.

Essentially, by putting on a butterfly as opposed to a two-bond spread or a straight directional play, the trader limits the downside risk if interest rates fall, while preserving the upside gain if yields fall.

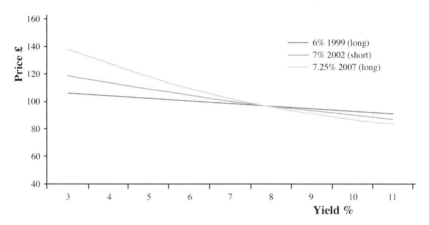

Figure 22.7 Illustration of convexity for each stock in butterfly trade, 27 June 1997

To conclude the discussion of butterfly-trade strategy, we describe the analysis if using the "BBA" screen on Bloomberg. The trade is illustrated at Figure 22.8.

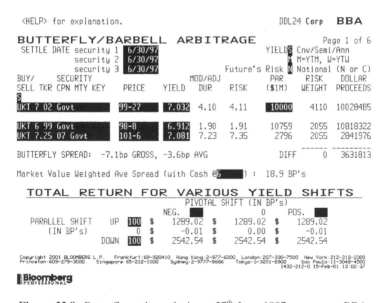

Figure 22.8 Butterfly trade analysis on 27th June 1997, on screen BBA
©Bloomberg L.P. Reproduced with permission

Using this approach, the nominal values of the two long positions are calculated using BPV ratios only. This is shown under the column "Risk Weight", and we note that the difference is zero. However, the nominal value required for the two-year bond is much greater, at £10.76 million, and for the 10-year bond much lower at £2.8 million. This results in a cash outflow of £3.632 million. The profit profile is, in theory, much improved, however; at the bottom of the screen we observe the results of a 100 basis-point parallel shift in either direction, which is a profit. Positive results were also seen for 200 and 300 basis-point parallel shifts in either direction. This screen incorporates the effect of a (uniform) funding rate, input on this occasion as 6.00%.[13] Note that the screen allows the user to see the results of a pivotal shift; however, in this example a 0 basis-point pivotal shift is selected.

This trade, therefore, created a profit whatever direction interest rates moved in.

The spread history for the position up to the day before the trade is shown at Figure 22.9, a reproduction of the graph on Bloomberg screen BBA.

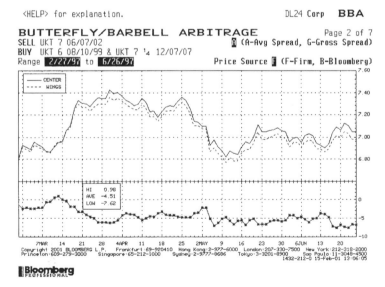

Figure 22.9 Butterfly trade spread history
©Bloomberg L.P. Reproduced with permission.

---

[13] In reality, the repo rate will be slightly different for each stock, and there will be a bid-offer spread to pay. But as long as none of the stocks are special, the calculations should be reasonably close.

CASE STUDY Spread trade

To conclude this chapter we present a further "real-world" analysis conducted when a spread was observed. It concerns two UK gilt benchmark securities, but the principles may be applied to all markets and sectors. The analysis is conducted using standard Bloomberg screens.

On 23 March 2004 we observe that the spread between the two-year and five-year securities is at its lowest since June 2003. The bonds concerned are the 7.75% 2006 and the 5.75% 2009. This is shown at Figure 22.10, the screen SS used to plot spread histories. The widest spread during that time is shown to be 42.3 bps, the narrowest 14.3 bps.

Figure 22.10 Spread summary, 7.75% 2006 versus 5.75% 2009 gilts, 23 March 2004
© Bloomberg L.P. Used with permission

This suggests that a spread widening trade may be worthwhile, with an expectation of widening. Therefore we
- sell the UKT 7.75% 2006 stock
- buy the 5.75% 2009 stock

in duration-weighted ratios.

We conduct a linear regression analysis to determine the relationship between the two securities, that is, the sensitivity of a selected security to a change in the value of another security. As both bonds are UK gilts, we expect a high degree of correlation, and this is shown at Figure 22.11, the screen HRA from Bloomberg. A close relationship between two security price sensitivities is a useful feature in a first-order risk-neutral spread trade, which this is. Figure 22.11 shows that the independent variable has a coefficient of 0.76, a high explanatory value, while the R^2 is 0.974, a very high degree of near-perfect correlation.

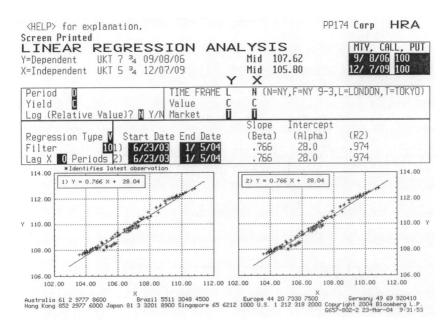

Figure 22.11 Stock linear regression analysis

© Bloomberg L.P. Used with permission

We then conduct the cost of carry analysis. Figure 22.12 shows the repo rates for UK gilts, the HBOS plc prices screen. We enter the respective bid and offer rates into screen CCS, the two-security carry screen. We use a one-month term for this calculation. This is shown at Figure 22.13.

Fixed Income Markets

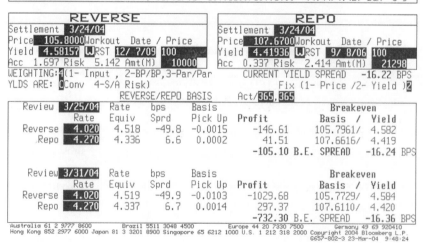

Figure 22.12 HBOS gilt repo rates, 23 March 2004
© Bloomberg L.P. © HBOS plc. Used with permission

Figure 22.13 Two-security carry analysis
© Bloomberg L.P. Used with permission

Finally we calculate the required number of securities. This is shown at Figure 22.14, page PDH2 from Bloomberg. From the respective basis point value, a long position of £10 million of the 2009 stock is balanced with a sale of £21.3 million of the 2006 stock. From Figure 22.14 we see that this produces a zero basis point value to the spread at the time of the trade. For a 30 basis point parallel shift in the yield curve, in either direction, this spread produces a profit (for a down-shift the profit is £55,296 and for a up-shift the gain is £48,611). This is shown at Figure 22.15, page 2 from screen PDH2, while page 3 from the same screen shows the favourable price-yield profile for this spread is shown at Figure 22.16. From this last figure, we note that the price-yield profile remains favourable in either direction, a very desirable position. Of course this is liable to change with pivotal shifts in the yield curve, but at the time of the trade this spread looks very positive and first-order risk-neutral.

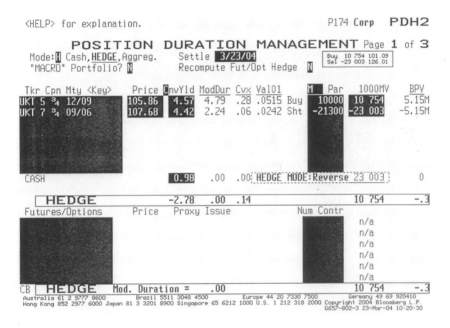

Figure 22.14 Screen PDH2, the calculation of the securities amounts.
© Bloomberg L.P. Used with permission

Fixed Income Markets

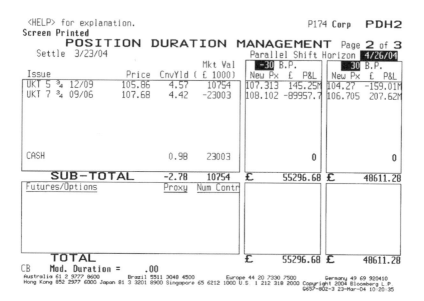

POSITION DURATION MANAGEMENT Page **2** of **3**

Settle 3/23/04   Parallel Shift Horizon 4/26/04

Issue	Price	CnvYld	Mkt Val (£ 1000)	-30 B.P. New Px £ P&L	30 B.P. New Px £ P&L
UKT 5 ¾ 12/09	105.86	4.57	10754	107.313 145.25M	104.27 -159.01M
UKT 7 ¾ 09/06	107.68	4.42	-23003	108.102 -89957.7	106.705 207.62M
CASH		0.98	23003	0	0
SUB-TOTAL		-2.78	10754	£ 55296.68	£ 48611.28
Futures/Options		Proxy	Num Contr		
TOTAL				£ 55296.68	£ 48611.28

CB   Mod. Duration =   .00

Australia 61 2 9277 8600   Brazil 5511 3048 4500   Europe 44 20 7330 7500   Germany 49 69 920410
Hong Kong 852 2977 6000 Japan 81 3 3201 8900 Singapore 65 6212 1000 U.S. 1 212 318 2000 Copyright 2004 Bloomberg L.P.
G657-802-4 23-Mar-04 10:20:35

Figure 22.15 Impact of parallel shift in yield curve.
© Bloomberg L.P. Used with permission

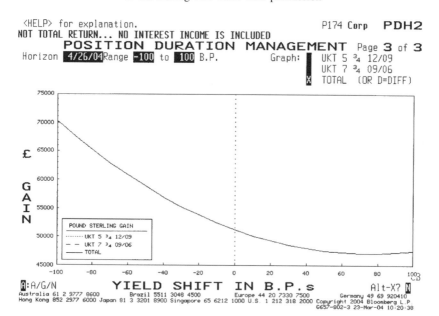

POSITION DURATION MANAGEMENT Page **3** of **3**

Horizon 4/26/04 Range -100 to 100 B.P.   Graph: UKT 5 ¾ 12/09
                                                         UKT 7 ¾ 09/06
                                                       X TOTAL (OR D=DIFF)

YIELD SHIFT IN B.P.s

Australia 61 2 9777 8600   Brazil 5511 3048 4500   Europe 44 20 7330 7500   Germany 49 69 920410
Hong Kong 852 2977 6000 Japan 81 3 3201 8900 Singapore 65 6212 1000 U.S. 1 212 318 2000 Copyright 2004 Bloomberg L.P.
G657-802-3 23-Mar-04 10:20:38

Figure 22.16 Price/yield profile for spread position, showing positive impact
of yield change in either direction, as at 23 March 2004.
© Bloomberg L.P. Used with permission

Selected Bibliography and References

Blake, D., *Financial Market Analysis*, McGraw Hill, 1990.

Choudhry, M., *Introduction to the Gilt Strips Market*, Securities Institute (Services) Limited, 1999.

Choudhry, M., *The Global Repo Markets: Instruments and Applications*, John Wiley, 2004.

Fabozzi, F., *Bond Portfolio Management*, FJF Associates, 1996, Chapters 10-14.

23

Approaches to Trading and Heding

The term "trading" covers a wide range of activity. Market-makers who are quoting two-way prices to market participants may be tasked with providing a customer service, building up retail and institutional volume, or they may be tasked with purely running the book at a profit and trying to maximize return on capital. The nature of the market that is traded will also have an impact on their approach. In a highly transparent and liquid market such as the US Treasury or the UK gilt market the price spreads are fairly narrow, although increased demand has reduced this somewhat in both markets. However, this means that opportunities for profitable trading as a result of mispricing of individual securities, whilst not completely extinct, are rare. It is much more common for traders in such markets to take a view on relative-value trades, such as the yield spreads between individual securities or the expected future shape of the yield curve. This is also called spread trading. A large volume of trading on derivatives exchanges is done for hedging purposes, but speculative trading is also prominent. Very often, bond and interest-rate traders will punt using futures or options contracts, based on their view of market direction. Ironically, market-makers who have a low level of customer business – perhaps because they are newcomers to the market, or for historical reasons or because they do not have the appetite for risk that is required to service the high-quality customers – tend to speculate on the futures exchanges to relieve tedium, often with unfortunate results.

Speculative trading is undertaken on the basis of the views of the trader, desk or head of the department. This view may be an "in-house" view; for example, the collective belief of the economics or research department, or the individual trader's view, which will be formulated as a result of fundamental analysis and technical analysis. The former is an assessment of macroeconomic and microeconomic factors affecting not just the specific bond market itself but the economy as a whole. Those running corporate-debt desks will also concentrate heavily on individual sectors and corporations and their wider environment, because the credit spread – and what drives the credit spread – of corporate bonds is of course key to the performance of the bonds. Technical analysis or charting is a discipline in its own right, and has its adherents. It is based on the belief that over time the patterns displayed by a continuous time series of asset prices will repeat themselves. Therefore, detecting patterns should give a reasonable expectation of how asset prices should behave in the future. Many traders use a combination of fundamental and technical analysis, although chartists often say that for technical analysis to work effectively, it must be the only method adopted by the trader.

A review of technical analysis is presented in Chapter 63 of the author's book *The Bond and Money Markets: Strategy, Trading, Analysis.*

In this chapter, we introduce some common methods and approaches, and some not so common, that might be employed on a fixed-interest desk.

Futures trading

Trading with derivatives is often preferred, for both speculative or hedging purposes, to trading in the cash markets mainly because of the liquidity of the market and the ease and low cost of undertaking transactions. The essential features of futures trading are volatility and leverage. To establish a futures position on an exchange, the level of margin required is very low proportional to the notional value of the contracts traded. For speculative purposes, traders often carry out open – that is, uncovered trading – which is a directional bet on the market. So, therefore, if a trader believed that short-term sterling interest rates were going to fall, he could buy a short sterling contract on LIFFE. This may be held for under a day (in which case, if the price rises the trader will gain), or for a longer period, depending on his view. The tick value of a short sterling contract is £12.50; so, if he bought one lot at 92.75 (that is, 100 − 92.75 or 7.25%) and sold it at the end of the day for 98.85, he made a profit of £125 on his one lot, from which brokerage will be subtracted. The trade can be carried out with any futures contract. The same idea could be carried out with a cash-market product or an FRA, but the liquidity, narrow price spread and the low cost of dealing make such a trade easier on a futures exchange. It is much more interesting, however, to carry out a spread trade on the difference between the rates of two different contracts. Consider Figures 23.1 and 23.2 which relate to the prices for the LIFFE short-sterling futures contract on 22nd March 1999.

```
<HELP> for explanation, <MENU> for similar functions.      P174 Comdty SFR
n <Page> to scroll contracts, n <Go> for history, 98 <Go> to save defaults
  LIF  UK  £  LIBOR  SYNTHETIC  FORWARD  RATES
14:22 Date Days      Last    NRate   6-Mo  1-Yr  18-Mo  2-Yr  3-Yr  4-Yr
 Spot strip 84 Front 95.6805 4.3195  4.461 4.647 4.685 4.751 4.845 4.919
 1)  6/17/04 91 L M4 95.4800 4.5200  4.611 4.763 4.776 4.827 4.900 4.971
 2)  9/16/04 91 L U4 95.3500 4.6500  4.722 4.854 4.843 4.887 4.947 5.016
 3) 12/16/04 91 L Z4 95.2600 4.7400  4.803 4.918 4.898 4.933 4.989 5.041
 4)  3/17/05 91 L H5 95.1900 4.8100  4.866 4.963 4.941 4.969 5.025 5.062
 5)  6/16/05 98 L M5 95.1400 4.8600  4.910 5.007 4.976 4.996 5.058 5.077
 6)  9/22/05 91 L U5 95.1000 4.9000  4.943 5.043 5.005 5.024 5.091
 7) 12/22/05 84 L Z5 95.0700 4.9300  4.982 5.074 5.027 5.057 5.104
 8)  3/16/06 98 L H6 95.0300 4.9700  5.017 5.098 5.049 5.086 5.114
 9)  6/22/06 91 L M6 95.0000 5.0000  5.041 5.112 5.082 5.116
10)  9/21/06 91 L U6 94.9800 5.0200  5.051 5.131 5.111
11) 12/21/06 91 L Z6 94.9800 5.0200  5.056 5.167 5.141      FRA and Bond yld:
12)  3/22/07 90 L H7 94.9700 5.0300  5.082 5.206 5.177      Daytype ACT/365
13)  6/20/07 92 L M7 94.9300b 5.0700 5.148 5.250 5.181      Frequency $
14)  9/20/07 91 L U7 94.8400b 5.1600 5.198 5.292 5.180            m-mkt yield
  Start      End    days years Front  stub  Back    stub  Bond yield ACT/365
 3/25/04   3/25/05  365  1.00  4.32%  84 days 4.78% 8 days   4.594     4.647
 3/25/04   3/25/05  365  1.00  4.32%  84 days 4.78% 8 days   4.594     4.647
 3/25/04   3/25/05  365  1.00  4.32%  84 days 4.78% 8 days   4.594     4.647
 3/25/04   3/25/05  365  1.00  4.32%  84 days 4.78% 8 days   4.594     4.647
 3/25/04   3/25/05  365  1.00  4.32%  84 days 4.78% 8 days   4.594     4.647
Australia 61 2 9777 8600    Brazil 5511 3048 4500    Europe 44 20 7330 7500      Germany 49 69 920410
Hong Kong 852 2977 6000 Japan 81 3 3201 8900 Singapore 65 6212 1000 U.S. 1 212 318 2000 Copyright 2004 Bloomberg L.P.
                                                            G657-802-0 25-Mar-04 14:22:26
```

Figure 23.1 LIFFE short-sterling contract analysis, 25th March 2004
Source: Bloomberg L.P. Used with permission.

Futures exchanges use the letters H, M, U and Z to refer to the contract months for March, June, September and December. So the June 2004 contract is denoted by "M4". From Chapter 3 we know that forward rates can be calculated for any term, starting on any date. In Figure 23.1, we see the future prices on that day, and the interest rate that the prices imply. The "stub" is the term for the interest rate from today to the expiry of the first futures contract, which is called the front month contract (in this case the front month contract is the June 2004 contract) and is 84 days. Figure 23.2 lists the forward rates from the spot date to six months, one year and so on. It is possible to trade a strip of contracts to replicate any term, out to the maximum maturity of the contract. This can be done for hedging or speculative purposes. Note from Figure 23.2 that there is a spread between the cash curve and the futures curve. A trader can take positions on cash against futures, but it is easier to transact only on the futures exchange.

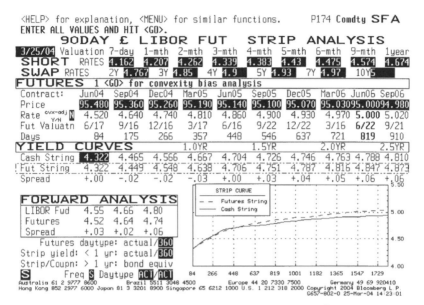

Figure 23.2 LIFFE short-sterling forward rates analysis, 25th March 2004.
Source: Bloomberg L.P. Used with permission.

Short-term money-market interest rates often behave independently of the yield curve as a whole. A money-markets trader may be aware of cash-market trends – for example, an increased frequency of borrowing at a certain point of the curve – as well as other market intelligence that suggests that one point of the curve will rise or fall relative to others. One way to exploit this view is to run a position in a cash instrument such as a CD against a futures contract, which is a *basis spread* trade.

However, the best way to trade on this view is to carry out a spread trade, shorting one contract against a long position in another trade. Consider Figure 23.1; if we feel that three-month interest rates in June 2004 will be lower than where they are implied by the futures price today, but that September 2004 rates will be higher, we will buy the M4 contract and short the U4 contract. This is not a market-directional trade; rather, it's a view on the relative spread between two contracts. The trade must be carried out in equal weights; for example, 100 lots of the June against 100 lots of the September. If the rates do move in the direction that the trader expects, the trade will generate a profit. There are similar possibilities available from an analysis of Figure 23.2, depending on our view of forward interest rates.

Spread trading carries a lower margin requirement than open position trading, because there is no directional risk in the trade. It is also possible to arbitrage between contracts on different exchanges. If the trade is short the near contract and long the far contract (that is, the opposite of our example) this is known as buying the spread and the trader believes the spread will widen. The opposite is shorting the spread and is undertaken when the trader believes the spread will narrow. Note that the difference between the two price levels is not limitless, because the theoretical price of a futures contract provides an upper limit to the size of the spread or the basis. The spread or the basis cannot exceed the cost of carry, that is the net cost of buying the cash security today and then delivering it into the futures market on the contract expiry. The same principle applies to short-dated interest-rate contracts; the net cost is the difference between the interest cost of borrowing funds to buy the "security" and the income accruing on the security while it is held before delivery. The two associated costs for a short-sterling spread trade are the notional borrowing and lending rates from having bought one and sold another contract. If the trader believes that the cost of carry will decrease, she could sell the spread to exercise this view.

The trader may have a longer time horizon and trade the spread between the short-term interest-rate contract and the long bond future. This is usually carried out only by the proprietary trading desk, because it is unlikely that one person would be trading both three-month and 10-year (or 20-year, depending on the contract specification) interest rates. A common example of such a spread trade is a yield-curve trade. If a trader believes that the sterling yield curve will steepen or flatten between the three-month and the 10-year terms, they can buy or sell the spread by using the LIFFE short-sterling contract and the long gilt contract. To be first-order risk-neutral, however, the trade must be duration-weighted, as one short-sterling contract is not equivalent to one gilt contract. The tick value of the gilt contract is £10 however, although the gilt contract represents £100,000 of a notional gilt and the short-sterling contract represents a £500,000 time deposit. We use (23.1) to calculate the hedge ratio, with £1,000 being the value of a 1% change in the value of the gilt contract against £1,250 for the short sterling contract.

$$h = \frac{(100 \times tick) \times P_b \times D}{(100 \times tick) \times P_f} \qquad (23.1)$$

where

tick is the tick value of the contract

D is the duration of the bond represented by the long bond contract

P_b is the price of the bond futures contract

P_f is the price of the short-term deposit contract.

The notional maturity of a long bond contract is always given in terms of a spread; for example, for the long gilt it is $8^3/_4$–13 years. Therefore, in practice, one would use the duration of the cheapest-to-deliver bond.

A butterfly spread is a spread trade that involves three contracts, with the two spreads between all three contracts being traded. This is carried out when the middle contract appears to be mispriced relative to the two contracts either side of it. The trader may believe that one or both of the outer contracts will move in relation to the middle contract. If the belief is that only one of these two will shift relative to the middle contract, then a butterfly will be put on if the trader is not sure which of these will adjust. For example, consider Figure 23.1 again. The prices of the front three contracts are 95.48, 95.35 and 95.26. A trader may feel that the September contract is too low, having a spread of +13 basis points to the June contract, and +9 basis points to the December contract. The trader feels that the September contract will rise, but will that be because June and December prices fall or because the September price will rise? Instead of having to answer this question, all the trader need believe is that the June–September spread will widen and the September–December spread will narrow. To put this view into effect, the trader puts on a butterfly spread, which is equal to the September–December spread minus the June–September spread, which she expects to narrow. Therefore, she buys the June–September spread and sells the September–December spread, which is also known as *selling the butterfly spread*.

Yield curves and relative value

Bond-market participants take a keen interest in both cash and zero-coupon (spot) yield curves. In markets where an active zero-coupon bond market exists, much analysis is undertaken into the relative spreads between derived and actual zero-coupon yields. In this section, we review some of the yield-curve analysis used in the market.

The determinants of government bond yields

Market-makers in government-bond markets will analyse various factors in the market in deciding how to run their book. Customer business apart, decisions to purchase or sell securities will be a function of their views on:

- market direction itself; that is, the direction in which short-term and long-term interest rates are headed
- which maturity point along the entire term structure offers the best value

- which specific issue within a particular maturity point offers the best value.

All three areas are related but will react differently to certain pieces of information. A report on the projected size of the government's budget deficit, for example, will not have much effect on two-year bond yields, whereas if the expectations come as a surprise to the market it could have an adverse on long-bond yields. The starting point for analysis is, of course, the yield curve – both the traditional coupon curve plotted against duration and the zero-coupon curve. Figure 23.3 illustrates the traditional yield curve for gilts on 25 March 2004.

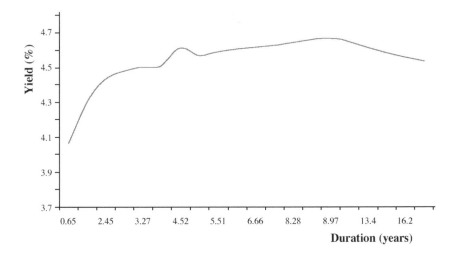

Figure 23.3 Yield and duration of gilts, 25 March 2004

For a first-level analysis, many market practitioners will go no further than Figure 23.3. An investor who has no particular view on the future shape of the yield curve or the level of interest rates may well adopt a neutral outlook and hold bonds that have a duration that matches their investment horizon. If they believed interest rates were likely to remain stable for a time, they might hold bonds with a longer duration in a positive-sloping yield-curve environment, and pick up additional yield but with higher interest-rate risk. Once the decision has been made on which part of the yield curve to invest in or switch in to, the investor must decide on the specific securities to hold, which then brings us on to relative-value analysis. For this, the investor will analyse specific sectors of the curve, looking at individual stocks. This is sometimes called looking at the "local" part of the curve.

An assessment of a local part of the yield curve will include looking at other features of individual stocks in addition to their duration. This recognizes that the yield of a specific bond is not simply a function of its duration, and that two bonds with near-identical duration can have different yields. The other determinants of yield are liquidity of the bond and its coupon. To illustrate the effect of coupon on yield, consider Table 23.1. This shows that, where the duration of a bond is held roughly constant, a change in coupon of a bond can have a significant effect on the bond's yield.

Coupon	Maturity	Duration	Yield
8%	20-Feb-02	1.927	5.75%
12%	5-Feb-02	1.911	5.80%
10%	20-Jun-10	7.134	4.95%
6%	1-Jul-10	7.867	4.77%

Table 23.1 Duration and yield comparisons for bonds in a hypothetical inverted curve environment

In the case of the long bond, under this scenario an investor could both shorten duration and pick up yield, which is not the first thing that an investor might expect. However, an anomaly of the markets is that, liquidity issues aside, the market does not generally like high-coupon bonds, so they usually trade cheap to the curve.

The other factors affecting yield are supply and demand, and liquidity. A shortage of supply of stock at a particular point in the curve will have the effect of depressing yields at that point. A reducing public-sector deficit is the main reason why such a supply shortage might exist. In addition, as interest rates decline – ahead of or during a recession, say – the stock of high-coupon bonds increases, as the newer bonds are issued at lower levels, and these "outdated" issues can end up trading at a higher yield. Demand factors are driven primarily by the investor's views of the country's economic prospects, but also by government legislation; for example, the Minimum Funding Requirement in the UK which compelled pension funds to invest a set minimum amount of their funds in long-dated gilts. This kept yields artificially low until the requirement was removed during 2002.

Liquidity often results in one bond having a higher yield than another, despite both having similar durations. Institutional investors prefer to hold the benchmark bond, which is the current two-year, five-year, 10-year or 30-year bond and this depresses the yield on the benchmark bond. A bond that is liquid also has a higher demand, and thus a lower yield, because it is easier to convert into cash if required. This can be demonstrated by valuing the cash flows on a six-month bond with the rates obtainable in the Treasury-bill market. We could value the six-month cash flows at the six-month bill rate. The lowest obtainable yield in virtually every market[1] is the T-bill yield. Therefore, valuing a six-month bond at the T-bill rate will produce a discrepancy between the observed price of the bond and its theoretical price implied by the T-bill rate as the observed price will be lower. The reason for this is simple: because the T-bill is more readily realisable into cash at any time, it trades at a lower yield than the bond, even though the cash flows fall on the same day.

We have therefore determined that a bond's coupon and liquidity level, as well as its duration, will affect the yield at which it trades. These factors can be used in conjunction with other areas of analysis, which we look at next, when deciding which bonds carry relative value over others.

Characterising the complete term structure

As many readers would have gathered, the yield-versus-duration curve illustrated in Figure 23.3 is an ineffective technique with which to analyse the market.

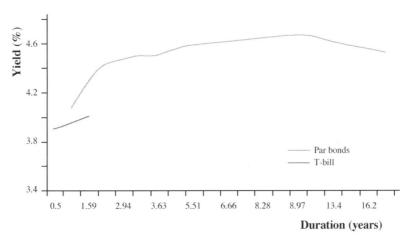

Figure 23.4 T-bill and par-yield curve, March 2004

---

[1] The author is not aware of any market where there is a yield lower than its shortest-maturity T-bill yield, but that does not mean such a market doesn't exist!

This is because it does not highlight any characteristics of the yield curve other than its general shape; this does not assist in the making of trading decisions. To facilitate a more complete picture, we might wish to employ the technique described here. Figure 23.4 shows the bond par-yield curve and T-bill yield curve for gilts in October 1999. Figure 23.5 shows the difference between the yield on a bond with a coupon that is 100 basis points below the par-yield level, and the yield on a par bond. The other curve in Figure 23.5 shows the level for a bond with a coupon that is 100 basis points above the par yield. These two curves show the "low-coupon" and "high-coupon" yield spreads. Using the two figures together, an investor can see the impact of coupons, the shape of the curve and the effect of yield on different maturity points of the curve.

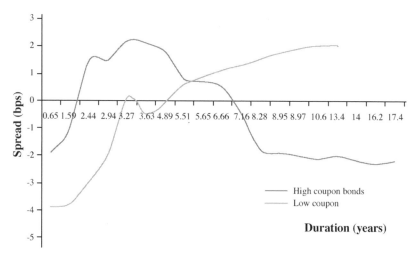

Figure 23.5 Structure of bond yields, March 2004

Identifying relative value in government bonds

Constructing a zero-coupon yield curve provides the framework within which a market participant can analyse individual securities. In a government-bond market, there is no credit-risk consideration (unless it is an emerging-market government market) and, therefore, no credit spreads to consider. There are a number of factors that can be assessed in an attempt to identify relative value.

The objective of much of the analysis that occurs in bond markets is to identify value, and identifying which individual securities should be purchased and which sold. At the overview level, this identification is a function of whether one thinks interest rates are going to rise or fall. At the local level, though, the analysis is more concerned with a specific sector of the yield curve; whether this will flatten or steepen, whether bonds of similar duration are trading at enough of a spread to warrant switching from one into another. The difference in these approaches is one of identifying which stocks have absolute value, and which have relative value. A trade decision based on the expected direction of interest rates is based on assessing absolute value, whether interest rates themselves are too low or too high. Yield-curve analysis is more a matter of assessing relative value. On (very!) rare occasions, this process is fairly straightforward. For example, if the three-year bond is trading at 5.75% when two-year yields are 5.70% and four-year yields are at 6.15%, the three-year would appear to be overpriced. However, this is not really a real-life situation. Instead, a trader might find himself assessing the relative value of the three-year bond compared to much shorter- or longer-dated instruments. That said, there is considerable difference between comparing a short-dated bond to other short-term securities and comparing, say, the two-year bond to the 30-year bond. Although it looks like it on paper, the space along the x-axis should not be taken to imply that the smooth link between one-year and five-year bonds is repeated from the five-year out to the 30-year bonds. It is also common for the very short-dated sector of the yield curve to behave independently of the long end of the curve.

One method used to identify relative value is to quantify the coupon effect on the yields of bonds. The relationship between yield and coupon is given by (23.2):

$$rm = rm_p + c \cdot max(C_{PD} - rm_p, 0) + d \cdot min(C_{PD} - rm_p, 0) \quad (23.2)$$

where

rm is the yield on the bond being analysed
rm_p is the yield on a par bond of specified duration
C_{PD} is the coupon on an arbitrary bond of similar duration to the par bond

and c and d are coefficients.

The coefficient c reflects the effect of a high coupon on the yield of a bond. If we consider a case where the coupon rate exceeds the yield on the similar-duration par bond ($C_{PD} > rm_p$), (23.2) reduces to (23.3):

$$rm = rm_p + c \cdot (C_{PD} - rm_p) \tag{23.3}$$

Equation (23.3) specifies the spread between the yield on a high-coupon bond and the yield on a par bond as a linear function of the spread between the first bond's coupon and the yield and coupon of the par bond. In reality, this relationship may not be purely linear; for instance, the yield spread may widen at a decreasing rate for higher coupon differences. Therefore (23.3) is an approximation of the effect of a high coupon on yield where the approximation is more appropriate for bonds trading close to par. The same analysis can be applied to bonds with coupons lower than the same-duration par bond.

The value of a bond may be measured against comparable securities or against the par or zero-coupon yield curve. In certain instances, the first measure may be more appropriate when, for instance, a low-coupon bond is priced expensive to the curve itself but fair compared to other low-coupon bonds. In that case, the overpricing indicated by the par-yield curve may not represent unusual value but, rather, a valuation phenomenon that was shared by all low-coupon bonds. Having examined the local structure of a yield curve, the analysis can be extended to the comparative valuation of a group of similar bonds. This is an important part of the analysis, because it is particularly informative to know the cheapness or dearness of a single stock compared to the whole yield curve, which might be somewhat abstract. Instead, we would seek to identify two or more bonds, one of which was cheap and the other dear, so that we might carry out an outright switch between the two, or put on a spread trade between them. Using the technique, we can identify excess positive or negative yield spread for all the bonds in the term structure. This has been carried out for five gilts, together with other less-liquid issues as at March 2004 and the results are summarised in Table 23.2.

Bond	Duration (years)	Yield %	Excess yield spread (bps)
6.75% 26-Nov-2004	0.651	4.07	-1.05
8.5% 7-Dec-2005	1.585	4.307	2.08
7.5% 7-Dec-2006	2.453	4.434	-0.08
4.5% 7-Mar-2007	2.782	4.453	0.02
7.25% 7-Dec-2007	3.267	4.502	1.3
5% 7-Mar-2008	3.626	4.51	1.6
5.75% 7-Dec-2009	4.888	4.591	1.7
6.25% 25-Nov-2010	5.506	4.589	3.19
5% 7-Sep-2014	8.28	4.645	-5.6
4.25% 7-Jun-2032	16.172	4.555	-7.7

Table 23.2 Yields and excess yield spreads for selected gilts, 25th March 2004

From the table, as we might expect, the benchmark securities are all expensive to the par curve, and the less-liquid bonds are cheap. Note that the 6.25% 2010 appears cheap to the curve, but the 5.75% 2009 offers a yield pick-up for what is a shorter-duration stock; this is a curious anomaly and one that had disappeared a few days later.[2]

What this section has introduced is the concept of relative value for individual securities, and how the simple duration/yield analysis can be extended to assess other determinants of a bond's yield. Other types of analysis, such as assessing the value of coupon bonds relative to the zero-coupon yield, have been assessed elsewhere in the book. For example, coupon stripping was examined in Chapter 22. We now look at the issues involved in putting on a spread trade.

Yield-spread trades

In the earlier section on futures trading, we introduced the concept of spread trades, which are not market-directional trades but rather the expression of a viewpoint on the shape of a yield curve or, more specifically, the spread between two particular points on the yield curve. Generally, there is no analytical relationship between changes in a specific yield spread and changes in the general level of interest rates. That is to say, the yield curve can flatten when rates are both falling or rising, and equally may steepen

---

[2] In other words, we've missed the opportunity! This analysis used mid-prices, which would not be available in practice.

under either scenario as well. The key element of any spread trade is that it is structured so that a profit (or any loss) is made only as a result of a change in the spread, and not due to any change in overall yield levels. That is, spread trading eliminates market-directional or first-order market risk.

Bond–spread weighting

Table 23.3 shows data for our selection of gilts but with additional information on the basis-point value (BPV) for each point. This is also known as the "dollar value of a basis point" or DV01.

Bond	Duration (yrs)	Yield %	Price	Basis Point Value (BPV)
6.75% 26-Nov-2004	0.651	4.07	101.74	0.00664
8.5% 7-Dec-2005	1.585	4.307	106.79	0.01697
7.5% 7-Dec-2006	2.453	4.434	107.71	0.02639
4.5% 7-Mar-2007	2.782	4.453	100.12	0.02738
7.25% 7-Dec-2007	3.267	4.502	109.26	0.03561
5% 7-Mar-2008	3.626	4.51	101.75	0.03618
5.75% 7-Dec-2009	4.888	4.591	105.88	0.05142
6.25% 25-Nov-2010	5.506	4.589	109.44	0.06004
5% 7-Sep-2014	8.28	4.645	102.91	0.08349
4.25% 7-Jun-2032	16.172	4.555	95.18	0.15252

Table 23.3 Bond basis-point value, 25th March 2004

If a trader believed that the yield curve was going to flatten, but had no particular strong feeling about whether this flattening would occur in an environment of falling or rising interest rates, and thought that the flattening would be most pronounced in the two-year versus 10-year spread, he could put on a spread consisting of a short position in the two-year and a long position in the 10-year. This spread must be duration-weighted to eliminate first-order risk. At this stage we must point out, and it is important to be aware of, the fact that basis-point values, which are used to weight the trade, are based on modified-duration measures. From Chapter 2 we know that this measure is an approximation, and will be inaccurate for large changes in yield. Therefore, the trader must monitor the spread to ensure that the weights are not going out of line, especially in a volatile market environment.

To weight the spread, we use the ratios of the BPVs of each bond to decide on how much to trade. In our example, assume the trader wants to purchase £10 million of the 10-year. In that case, he must sell [(0.08349/0.02639) × 10,000,000] or £31,636,983 of the two-year bond. It is also possible to weight a trade using the bonds' duration values, but this is rare. It is common practice to use the BPV.

The payoff from the trade will depend on what happens to the two-year vis-a-vis the 10-year spread. If the yields on both bonds move by the same amount, there will be no profit generated, although there will be a funding consideration. If the spread does indeed narrow, the trade will generate profit. Note that disciplined trading calls for both an expected target spread as well as a fixed time horizon. Say, for example, that the current spread is 59.7 basis points; the trader may decide to take the profit if the spread narrows to 50 basis points, with a three-week horizon. If at the end of three weeks the spread has not reached the target, the trader should unwind the position anyway, because that was the original target. On the other hand, what if the spread has narrowed to 48 basis points after one week and looks like narrowing further – what should the trader do? Again, disciplined trading suggests the profit should be taken. If, contrary to expectations, the spread starts to widen, if it reaches 64.5 basis points the trade should be unwound, this "stop-loss" being at the half-way point of the original profit target.

The financing of the trade in the repo markets is an important aspect of the trade, and will set the trade's breakeven level. If the bond being shorted (in our example, the two-year bond) is special, this will have an adverse impact on the financing of the trade. The repo considerations are considered in Chapter 6.

Types of bond spreads

A bond spread has two fundamental characteristics. In theory, there should be no P/L effect due to a general change in interest rates, and any P/L should only occur as a result of a change in the specific spread being traded. Note that this assumes that all moves in the yield curve are a parallel shift. Most bond-spread trades are yield-curve trades where a view is taken on whether a particular spread will widen or narrow. Therefore, it is important to be able to identify which sectors of the curve to sell. Assuming that a trader is able to transact business along any part of the yield curve, there are a number of factors to consider. In the first instance, there is the historic spread between the two sectors of the curve. To illustrate in simplistic fashion, if the two–10 year spread has been between 40 and 50 basis points over the last six months but very recently has narrowed to less than 35 basis points, this may indicate imminent widening. Other factors to consider are demand and liquidity for individual stocks relative to others, and any market intelligence that the trader gleans. If there has been considerable customer interest in certain stocks relative to others, because investors themselves are switching out of certain stocks and into others, this may indicate a possible yield-curve play. It is a matter of individual judgment.

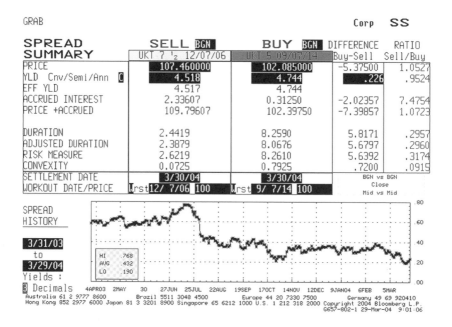

Figure 23.6 Two-year and 10-year spread history, UK gilt market 29 March 2004. *Source*: Bloomberg LP. Used with permission.

An historical analysis requires that the trader identify some part of the yield curve within which he expects to observe a flattening or steepening. It is, of course, entirely possible that one segment of the curve will flatten while another segment is steepening. In fact, this phenomenon is quite common. This reflects the fact that different segments respond to news and other occurrences in different ways.

From Figure 23.6 we see that the two-year versus 10-year spread was at its narrowest in March 2004 during the last 12 months, having reached a high point in July 2003. This might indicate that spread widening was imminent.

A more exotic type of yield curve spread is a *curvature* trade. Consider, for example, a trader who believes that three-year bonds will outperform, on a relative basis, both two-year and five-year bonds. That is, he believes that the two-year/three-year spread will narrow relative to the three-year/five-year spread or, in other words, that the curvature of the yield curve will decrease. This is also known as a butterfly/barbell trade. In our example, the trader will buy the three-year bond, against short sales of both the two-year and the five-year bonds. All positions are duration-weighted. The principle is exactly the same as the butterfly trade we described in the previous section on futures trading.

Hedging bond positions

Hedging is a straightforward concept to understand or describe. However, it is very important that is undertaken as accurately as possible. Therefore, the calculation of a hedge is critical. A hedge is a position in a cash or off-balance-sheet instrument that removes the market-risk exposure of another position. For example, a long position in 10-year bonds can be hedged with a short position in 20-year bonds, or with futures contracts. That is the straightforward part; the calculation of the exact amount of the hedge is where complexities can arise. In this section, we review the basic concepts of hedging, and a case study at the end illustrates some of the factors that must be considered.

Simple hedging approach

The hedge calculation that first presents itself is the duration-weighted approach. From the sample of gilts in Table 23.3, it is possible to calculate the amount of one bond required to hedge an amount of any other bond, using the ratio of the BPVs. This approach is very common in the market; however, it suffers from two basic flaws that hinder its effectiveness. First, the approach assumes implicitly comparable volatility of yields on the two bonds; and, secondly, it also assumes that yield changes on the two bonds are highly correlated. Where one or both of these factors do not apply, the effectiveness of the hedge will be compromised.

The assumption of comparable volatility becomes increasingly unrealistic the more the bonds differ in terms of market risk and market behavior. Consider a long position in two-year bonds hedged with a short-position in five-year bonds. Using the bonds from Table 23.3, if we had a position of £1 million of the two-year, we would short £513,225 of the five-year. Even if we imagine that yields between the two bonds are perfectly correlated, it may well be that the amount of yield change is different because the bonds have different volatilities. For example, if the yield on the five-year bond changes only by half the amount that the two-year does, if there was a five basis-point rise in the two-year, the five-year would have risen only by 2.5 basis points. This would indicate that the yield volatility of the two-year bond was twice that of the five-year bond. This suggests that a hedge calculation that matched nominal amounts, due to BPV, on the basis of an equal change in yield for both bonds would be incorrect. In our illustration, the short position in the five-year bond would be effectively hedging only half of the risk exposure of the two-year position.

The implicit assumption of perfectly correlated yield changes can also lead to inaccuracy. Across the whole term structure, it is not always the case that bond yields are even positively correlated all the time (although most of the time there will be a close positive correlation). Therefore, using our illustration again, imagine that the two-year and the five-year bonds possess identical yield volatilities, but that changes in their yields are uncorrelated. This means that knowing that the yield on the two-year bond rose or fell by one basis point does not tell us anything about the change in the yield on the five-year bond. If yield changes between the two bonds are indeed uncorrelated, this means that the five-year bonds cannot be used to hedge two-year bonds, at least not with accuracy.

Hedge analysis

From the foregoing we note that there are at least three factors that will affect the effectiveness of a bond hedge; these are the basis-point value, the yield volatility of each bond and the correlation between changes in the two yields of a pair of bonds. Considering volatilities and correlations, Table 23.4 shows the standard deviations and correlations of weekly yield changes for a set of gilts during the nine months to March 2004. The standard deviation of weekly yield changes was, in fact, highest for the short-date paper, and actually declined for longer-dated paper. From the table we also note that changes in yield were imperfectly correlated. We expect correlations to be highest for bonds in the same segments of the yield curve, and to decline between bonds that are in different segments. This is not surprising, and indeed two-year bond yields are more positively correlated with five-year bonds and less so with 30-year bonds.

	2-year	3-year	Segment 5-year	10-year	20-year	30-year
Volatility (bp)	20.5	19.5	20.2	20.0	20.1	20.3
Correlation						
2-year	1.000	0.973	0.949	0.919	0.887	0.879
3-year	0.973	1.000	0.961	0.935	0.901	0.889
5-year	0.949	0.961	1.000	0.968	0.951	0.945
10-year	0.919	0.935	0.968	1.000	0.981	0.983
20-year	0.887	0.901	0.951	0.981	1.000	0.987
30-year	0.879	0.889	0.945	0.983	0.987	1.000

Table 23.4 Yield volatility and correlations, selected gilts, March 2004

We can use the standard relationship for correlations and the effect of correlation to adjust a hedge. Consider two bonds with nominal values M_1 and M_2; if the yields on these two bonds change by Δr_1 and Δr_2. the net value of the change in position is given by:

$$\Delta PV = M_1 BPV_1 \Delta r_1 + M_2 BPV_2 \Delta r_2 \qquad (23.4)$$

The uncertainty of the change in the net value of a two-bond position is dependent on the nominal values, the volatility of each bond and the correlation between these yield changes. Therefore, for a two-bond position we set the standard deviation of the change in the position as (23.5):

$$\sigma_{pos} = \sqrt{M_1^2 BPV_1^2 \sigma_1^2 + M_2^2 BPV_2^2 \sigma_2^2 + 2M_1 M_2 BPV_1 BPV_2 \sigma_1 \sigma_2 \rho} \qquad (23.5)$$

where ρ is the correlation between the yield volatilities of bonds 1 and 2. We can rearrange (23.5) to set the optimum hedge value for any bond using (23.6):

$$M_2 = - \frac{\rho BPV_1 \sigma_1}{BPV_2 \sigma_2} M_1 \qquad (23.6)$$

so that M_2 is the nominal value of any bond used as a hedge given any nominal value M_1 of the first bond, and using each bond's volatility and the correlation. The derivation of (23.6) is given in the appendix. A lower correlation leads to a smaller hedge position, because where yield changes are not closely related, this implies greater independence between yield changes of the two bonds. In a scenario where the standard deviation of two bonds is identical, and the correlation between yield changes is 1, (23.6) reduces to:

$$M_2 = \frac{BPV_1}{BPV_2} M_1 \tag{23.7}$$

which is the traditional hedge calculation based solely on basis point values.

CASE STUDY HEDGING A PORTFOLIO OF EUROBONDS WITH US TREASURIES

Consider a portfolio of value $10,000,000 composed of the following US$ Eurobonds:
  7% 2000
  7.75% 2002
  9% 2004
  9% 2006

A trader is concerned that yields will rise over the next 48 hours, and decides to construct a short position of $ 100 million of U.S. Treasuries that will hedge the portfolio of US$ Eurobonds against the expected rise in yields. To determine the accuracy of hedge the trader will compare the change in value of the US$ Eurobond portfolio to that of the short position of the US Treasury hedge. All the possible hedge bonds under consideration are given below.

Bond	Dirty price	Duration	Convexity
T7% 1999	100.375512	1.852	4.165
T7% 2000	99.994565	2.623	7.987
T7% 2000	100.71875	3.089	10.917
T7% 2002	99.668545	4.176	19.823
T7% 2004	100.262295	5.284	32.634
T8% 2007	99.315217	6.905	57.913
T9$^3/_4$% 2012	110.011395	8.168	90.636
T7$^1/_2$% 2022	90.654891	10.895	178.898
T8$^3/_4$% 2026	106.116885	10.794	186.779
T8% 2027	97.769361	11.251	199.657

The Eurobond portfolio has the following initial values:

Value	Duration	Convexity
$10,000,000	4.550	27.218

The duration and market value can be matched analytically with any two bonds provided the duration of one of the bonds is less than that of the portfolio and the duration of the other bond is greater than that of the portfolio.

The trader might elect to do the following:

- he can attempt to match both duration and convexity by constructing two portfolios with a duration of 4.550, one with a convexity greater than 27.218 and the other with a convexity less than 27.218. Assume these portfolios are called "A" and "B"respectively. Inspection of the table given above suggests the following bonds would be suitable components of these two portfolios:

    A: T7% 2000 and T8% 2007
    B: T7% 2002 and T7% 2004

Having identified two bonds with duration below and above 4.550 the trader then calculates the nominal value required for each bond using the simultaneous equation method giving an overall portfolio duration of 4.550.

Portfolio A:

Bond	Nominal required	Duration	Combined Duration	Convexity
T7% 2002	6,644,185	4.176	4.550	24.151
T7% 2004	3,369,000	5.284		

Portfolio B:

As above, but with following bonds:

Bond	Nominal Value required	Combined Duration	Duration	Convexity
T7% 2000	6,127,300	3.089	4.550	28.911
T8% 2007	3,855,059	6.905		

There are now two portfolios with the same duration. Therefore, however the portfolios are combined, the duration will remain at 4.550. We now need to determine what amounts of each portfolio are required, such that the combined portfolio convexity is 27.218, matching the convexity of the Eurobond portfolio. The trader can use simple proportions to determine the amount of each portfolio which would be necessary to form a new portfolio of convexity 27.218. The exact amounts are:

A: 0.356   B: 0.644

Thus the composition of the hedging portfolio, which has a value of $10 million is:

T7% 2000	3,945,464 nominal
T7% 2002	2,365,484 nominal
T7% 2004	1,199,442 nominal
T8% 2007	2,482,828 nominal

Assume that the yield curve scenario two days later is a curvature twist around the 5 year maturity. The market value of the Eurobond portfolio improves by $75,984 to $10,075,984. The suggested combination of US Treasuries would mirror this gain as a loss – the suggested possible solution does result in a loss of $76,512 – a difference of -$528.

Introduction to bond analysis using spot rates and forward rates in continuous time[3]

This section analyses further the relationship between spot and forward rates and discusses briefly how this can be applied in bond analysis.

The relationship between spot and forward rates

In the discussion to date, we have assumed discrete time intervals and interest rates in discrete time. Here, we consider the relationship between spot and forward rates in continuous time. For this, we assume the mathematical convenience of a continuously compounded interest rate.

The rate r is compounded using e^r and an initial investment M earning $r(t,T)$ over the period $T - t$, initial investment at time t and for maturity at T, where $T > t$, would have a value of $Me^{r(t,T)(T-t)}$ on maturity.[4] If we denote the initial value M_t and the maturity value M_T then we can state $M_t e^{r(t,T)(T-t)} = M_T$ and therefore the continuously compounded yield, defined as the continuously compounded interest rate $r(t,T)$ can be shown to be

$$r(t,T) = \frac{log(M_T/M_t)}{T - t} .$$

(23.8)

We can then formulate a relationship between the continuously compounded interest rate and yield. It can be shown that

$$M_T = M_t e^{\int_t^T r(s)ds}$$

(23.9)

where $r(s)$ is the instantaneous spot interest rate and is a function of time. It can further be shown that the continuously compounded yield is actually the equivalent of the average value of the continuously compounded interest rate. In addition, it can be shown that

$$r(t,T) = \frac{\int_t^T r(s)ds}{T - t} .$$

(23.10)

In a continuous time environment, we do not assume discrete time intervals over which interest rates are applicable but, rather, a period of time in which a borrowing of funds would be repaid instantaneously. So we

---

[3] This section is a revised and updated version of the section in Chapter 50 of Choudhry (2001).

[4] e is the mathematical constant 2.7182818… and it can be shown that an investment of £1 at time t will have grown to e on maturity at time T (during the period $T - t$) if it is earning an interest rate of $1/(T - t)$ continuously compounded.

define the forward rate $f(t,s)$ as the interest rate applicable for borrowing funds where the deal is struck at time t; the actual loan is made at s (with $s > t$) and repayable almost instantly. In mathematics, the period $s - t$ is described as infinitesimally small. The spot interest rate is defined as the continuously compounded yield or interest rate $r(t,T)$. In an environment of no arbitrage, the return generated by investing at the forward rate $f(t,s)$ over the period $s - t$ must be equal to that generated by investing initially at the spot rate $r(t, T)$. So we may set

$$e^{\int_t^T f(t,s)ds} = e^{r(t)dt} \tag{23.11}$$

which enables us to derive an expression for the spot rate itself, which is

$$r(t,T) = \frac{\int_t^T f(t,s)ds}{T - t} . \tag{23.12}$$

The relationship described by (23.12) states that the spot rate is given by the *arithmetic* average of the forward rates $f(t,s)$, where $t < s < T$. How does this differ from the relationship in a discrete time environment? From Chapter 3 we know that the spot rate in such a framework is the *geometric* average of the forward rates,[5] and this is the key difference in introducing the continuous time structure. Equation (23.12) can be rearranged to

$$r(t,T)(T - t) = \int_t^T f(t,s)ds \tag{23.13}$$

and this is used to show (by differentiation) the relationship between spot and forward rates, given below:

$$f(t,s) = r(t,T) + (T - t)\frac{dr(t,T)}{dT} \tag{23.14}$$

If we assume we are dealing today (at time 0) for maturity at time T, then the expression for the spot rate becomes

$$r(0,T) = \frac{\int_0^T f(0,s)ds}{T} \tag{23.15}$$

so we can write

$$r(0,T) \cdot T = \int_0^T f(0,s)ds . \tag{23.16}$$

---

[5] To be precise, if we assume annual compounding, the relationship is one plus the spot rate is equal to the geometric average of one plus the forward rates.

This is illustrated in Figure 23.7 which is a diagrammatic representation showing that the spot rate $r(0,T)$ is the average of the forward rates from 0 to T, using the hypothetical value of 5% for $r(0,T)$. Figure 23.7 also shows the area represented by (23.16), to the period 0.7T.

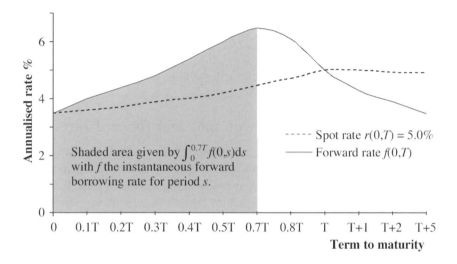

Figure 23.7 Diagrammatic representation of the relationship between spot and forward rate.
The spot rate $r(t, T)$ is the average of the forward rates between t and T.

What (23.14) implies is that if the spot rate increases then, by definition, the forward rate (or "marginal" rate as has been suggested that it may be called[6]) will be greater. From (23.14) we deduce that the forward rate will be equal to the spot rate plus a value that is the product of the *rate* of increase of the spot rate and the time period $(T - t)$. In fact, the conclusions simply confirm what we already discovered in the discrete time analysis in Chapter 3, that the forward rate for any period will lie above the spot rate if the spot rate term structure is increasing, and will lie below the spot rate if it is decreasing. In a constant spot-rate environment, the forward rate will be equal to the spot rate.

---

[6] For example, see Section 10.1 of Campbell, Lo and Mackinlay (1997), Chapter 10 of which is an excellent and accessible study of the term structure, and provides proofs of some of the results discussed here. This book is written in very readable style and is worth purchasing for Chapter 10 alone.

However, it is not as simple as that. An increasing spot-rate term structure only implies that the forward rate lies above the spot rate, but not that the forward rate structure is itself also *increasing*. In fact, one can observe the forward-rate term structure to be increasing or decreasing while spot rates are increasing. As the spot rate is the average of the forward rates, it can be shown that in order to accommodate this, forward rates must in fact be *decreasing* before the point at which the spot rate reaches its highest point. This confirms market observation. An illustration of this property is given in Appendix 23.2. As Campbell *et al.* (1997) state, this is a property of average and marginal cost curves in economics. An introduction to the integration function is given at Appendix B.

Bond prices as a function of spot and forward rates[7]

In this section, we describe the relationship between the price of a zero-coupon bond and spot and forward rates. We assume a risk-free zero-coupon bond of nominal value £1, priced at time t and maturing at time T. We also assume a money-market bank account of initial value $P(t,T)$ invested at time t. The money-market account is denoted M. The price of the bond at time t is denoted $P(t,T)$ and if today is time 0 (so that $t > 0$) then the bond price today is unknown and a random factor (similar to a future interest rate). The bond price can be related to the spot rate or forward rate that is in force at time t.

Consider the scenario below, used to derive the risk-free zero-coupon bond price[8].

The continuously compounded *constant* spot rate is r as before. An investor has a choice of purchasing the zero-coupon bond at price $P?t,T?$, which will return the sum of £1 at time T or of investing this same amount of cash in the money-market account, and this sum would have grown to £1 at time T. We know that the value of the money-market account is given by $Me^{r(t,T)(T-t)}$. If M must have a value of £1 at time T, then the function $e^{-r(t,T)(T-t)}$ must give the present value of £1 at time t and, therefore, the value of the zero-coupon bond is given by

$$P(t,T) = e^{-r(t,T)(T-t)} \quad . \tag{23.17}$$

---

[7] For more details, see Neftci (2000), Chapter 18, Section 3. This is an excellent, readable text.
[8] This approach is also used in Campbell et al. (q.v.).

If the same amount of cash that could be used to buy the bond at t, invested in the money-market account, does *not* return £1 then arbitrage opportunities will result. If the price of the bond exceeded the discount function $e^{-r(t,T)(T-t)}$ then the investor could short the bond and invest the proceeds in the money-market account. At time T, the bond position would result in a cash outflow of £1, while the money-market account would be worth £1. However, the investor would gain because in the first place $P(t,T) - e^{-r(t,T)(T-t)} > 0$. Equally, if the price of the bond was below $e^{-r(t,T)(T-t)}$, then the investor would borrow $e^{-r(t,T)(T-t)}$ in cash and buy the bond at price $P(t,T)$. On maturity, the bond would return £1, which proceeds would be used to repay the loan. However, the investor would gain because $e^{-r(t,T)(T-t)} - P(t,T) > 0$. To avoid arbitrage opportunities we must therefore have

$$P(t,T) = e^{-r(t,T)(T-t)} \ . \tag{23.18}$$

Following the relationship between spot and forward rates, it is also possible to describe the bond price in terms of forward rates.[9] We show the result only here. First we know that

$$P(t,T)e^{\int_t^T f(t,s)ds} = 1 \tag{23.19}$$

because the maturity value of the bond is £1, and we can rearrange (23.19) to give

$$P(t,T) = e^{-\int_t^T f(t,s)ds} \ . \tag{23.20}$$

Expression (23.20) states that the bond price is a function of the range of forward rates that apply for all $f(t,s)$; that is, the forward rates for all time periods s from t to T (where $t < s < T$, and where s is infinitesimally small). The forward rate $f(t,s)$ that results for each s arises as a result of a random or stochastic process that is assumed to start today at time 0. Therefore, the bond price $P(t,T)$ also results from a random process; in this case, all the random processes for all the forward rates $f(t,s)$.

The zero-coupon bond price may also be given in terms of the spot rate $r(t,T)$, as shown at (23.18). From our earlier analysis we know that

$$P(t,T)e^{r(t,T)(T-t)} = 1 \tag{23.21}$$

---

[9] For instance, see *ibid*, Section 4.2.

which is rearranged to give the zero-coupon bond price equation

$$P(t,T) = e^{-r(t,T)(T-t)} \qquad (23.22)$$

as before.

Equation (23.22) describes the bond price as a function of the spot rate only, as opposed to the multiple processes that apply for all the forward rates from t to T. As the bond has a nominal value of £1, the value given by (23.22) is the discount factor for that term; the range of zero-coupon bond prices would give us the discount function.

What is the importance of this result for our understanding of the term structure of interest rates? First, we see (again, but this time in continuous time) that spot rates, forward rates and the discount function are all closely related, and given one we can calculate the remaining two. More significantly, we may model the term structure either as a function of the spot rate only, described as a stochastic process, or as a function of all of the forward rates $f(t,s)$ for each period s in the period $(T - t)$, described by multiple random processes. The first yield-curve models adopted the first approach, while a later development described the second approach.

Appendices

APPENDIX 23.1 Summary of derivation of optimum hedge equation

From equation (23.5) we know that the variance of a net change in the value of a two-bond portfolio is given by

$$\sigma_{pos}^2 = M_1^2 BPV_1^2 \sigma_1^2 + M_2^2 BPV_2^2 \sigma_2^2 + 2M_1 M_2 BPV_1 BPV_2 \sigma_1 \sigma_2 \rho \ . \quad (A23.1.1)$$

Using the partial derivative of the variance σ^2 with respect to the nominal value of the second bond, we obtain

$$\frac{\partial \sigma^2}{\partial^2 M^2} = 2M_2 BPV_2^2 \sigma_2^2 + 2M_1 BPV_1 BPV_2 \sigma_1 \sigma_2 \rho \ . \qquad (A23.1.2)$$

If (A23.1.1) is set to zero and solved for M_2 we obtain (A23.1.3) which is the hedge quantity for the second bond.

$$M_2 = -\frac{\rho BPV_1 \sigma_1}{BPV_2 \sigma_2} M_1 \qquad (A23.1.3)$$

APPENDIX 23.2

Illustration of forward-rate structure when spot-rate structure is increasing
We assume the spot rate $r(0,T)$ is a function of time and is increasing to a
high point at $\overline{T}$. It is given by

$$r(0,T) = \frac{\int_0^T f(0,s)ds}{T} \quad . \tag{A23.2.1}$$

At its high point, the function is neither increasing nor decreasing, so we
may write

$$\frac{dr(0,\overline{T})}{dT} = 0 \tag{A23.2.2}$$

and therefore the second derivative with respect to T will be

$$\frac{d^2r(0,\overline{T})}{dT^2} < 0 \tag{A23.2.3}$$

From (23.14) and (A23.2.2) we may state

$$f(0,\overline{T}) = r(0,\overline{T}) \tag{A23.2.4}$$

and from (A23.2.3) and (A23.2.4) the second derivative of the spot rate is

$$\frac{d^2r(0,\overline{T})}{dT^2} = \left[\frac{df(0,\overline{T})}{dT} - \frac{dr(0,\overline{T})}{dT}\right]\frac{1}{T} < 0 \tag{A23.2.5}$$

From (A23.2.2) we know the spot rate function is zero at $_T$, so the
derivative of the forward rate with respect to T would therefore be

$$\frac{df(0,\overline{T})}{dT} < 0 \tag{A23.2.6}$$

So, in this case, the forward rate is decreasing at the point T when the
spot rate is at its maximum value. This is illustrated hypothetically at Figure
23.7 and it is common to observe the forward-rate curve decreasing as the
spot rate is increasing.

Selected Bibliography

Brennan, M. and Schwartz, E., "A continuous time approach to the pricing of bonds", *Journal of Banking and Finance* 3, 1979, p.134ff.

Brennan, M. and Schwartz, E., "Conditional predictions of bond prices and returns", *Journal of Finance* 35, 1980, p.405ff.

Choudhry, M., *Bond Market Securities*, FT Prentice Hall, 2001.

Campbell, J., Lo, A. and MacKinley, A., *The Econometrics of Financial Markets*, Princeton, 1997.

Fisher, L. and Leibowitz, M., "Effects of alternative anticipations of yield curve behaviour on the composition of immunized portfolios and on their target returns", in Kaufmann, G., et al. (editors.), *Innovations in Bond Portfolio Management*, Jai Press, 1983.

"Out of Debt", *The Economist*, 12 February 2000.

Neftci, S., *An Introduction to the Mathematics of Financial Derivatives* (2nd edition), Academic Press, 2000.

Statistical Concepts

Mean and standard deviation

In finance, two fundamental concepts are the mean and standard deviation of a series of numbers. Imagine that there are five dot-com companies that are suffering cash-flow problems. The year-end operating losses for these companies are £1,000, £2,000, £3,000, £5,000 and £9,000. The mean or average loss suffered by the companies is

$$(1,000 + 2,000 + 3,000 + 5,000 + 9,000)/5 \text{ or } £4,000.$$

An analyst of this particular dot-com sector may wish to know how much variation (or perhaps "dispersion") away from the mean value has occurred. Therefore, we require a measure of the variance of the raw data. This is a measure of the dispersion for each item away from the mean (here denoted as $\overline{X}$). Individual measures may be either positive or negative, and so to remove the effects of the sign we take the square of each deviation before adding them together. This is shown below.

X	$(X - \overline{X})$	$(X - \overline{X})^2$
1000	−3000	9,000,000
2000	−2000	4,000,000
3000	−1000	1,000,000
5000	1000	1,000,000
9000	5000	25,000,000
		40,000,000

If we are calculating variance for a sample of the population, rather than the entire population itself, then the total of the squared sums is divided by $(n-1)$ where n is the number of observations (so here $n = 5$). The reason for this can be found in any text book on statistics. So, in our example, the variance is [40,000,000/4] or 10,000,000. In fact, this value measures £-squared, which in our particular example does not in itself tell us very much. We, therefore, use a measure known as *standard deviation*. The standard deviation is the square root of the variance, but as it measures (here) actual £ units, it is more illustrative. The standard deviation is given by the square root of the variance. Here, the standard deviation is $\sqrt{10,000,000}$ or £3,162.28. This means that the average (or mean) loss is £4,000, and the standard deviation is £3,162. This indicates the extent of the dispersion around the mean of the underlying data, which in this case is quite high. Statistically, the mean and variance of a set of data are given at (AA.1) and (AA.2).

$$x = \frac{\sum_{i=1}^{n} x_i}{n} \qquad\qquad (AA.1)$$

$$\sigma^2 = \frac{\sum_{i=1}^{n} (x_i - \bar{x})}{n - 1} \qquad\qquad (AA.2)$$

If we are calculating variance for the population rather than a sample of the population, the denominator of (AA2) is simply n.

The statistics used in Value-at-Risk calculations are based on well-established concepts. There are standard formulae for calculating the mean and standard deviation of a set of values. If we assume that X is a random variable with particular values x, we can apply the basic formula to calculate mean and standard deviation. Remember that the mean is the average of the set of values or observations, while the standard deviation is a measure of the dispersion away from the mean of the range of values. In fact, the standard deviation is the square root of the variance, but the variance, being the sum of squared deviations of each value from the mean, divided by the number of observations, has little use for us.

We say that the random variable is X, so the mean is E(X). In a time series of observations of historical data, the probability values are the frequencies of the observed values. The mean is

$$E(X) = \left[\sum_{i} x_i\right] / n$$

where the assigned probability to a single value among n is $1/n$ and where n is the number of observations.

The standard deviation of the set of values is

$$\sigma(X) = (1 \, / \, n)\sqrt{\sum_i [x_i - E(X)]^2} \ .$$

The probability assigned to a set of values is given by the type of distribution and, in fact, from a distribution we can determine mean and standard deviation depending on the probabilities p_i assigned to each value x_i of the random variable X. The sum of all probabilities must be 100%. From probability values, then, the mean is given by

$$E(X)\left[\sum_i p_i x_i\right] / \, n \ .$$

The variance is the weighted average by the probabilities of the squared deviations from the mean; so, of course, the standard deviation – which we now call volatility – is the square root of this value. The volatility is given by:

$$\sigma(X) = \sqrt{\sum_i p_i [x_i - E(X)]^2} \ .$$

In the example below at Table AA1, we show the calculation of mean, variance and standard deviation as calculated from an Excel spreadsheet. The expectation is the mean of all the observations, while the variance is, as we noted earlier, the sum of squared deviations from the mean. The standard deviation is the square root of the variance.

Dates	Observations	Deviations from mean	Squared deviation
1	22	4.83	23.36
2	15	−2.17	4.69
3	13	−4.17	17.36
4	14	−3.17	10.03
5	16	−1.17	1.36
6	17	−0.17	0.03
7	16	−1.17	1.36
8	19	1.83	3.36
9	21	3.83	14.69
10	20	2.83	8.03
11	17	−0.17	0.03
12	16	−1.17	1.36
Sum	206	Sum	85.67
Mean	17.17	Variance	7.788
		Standard deviation	2.791

Table AA1

What happens when we have observations that can assume any value within a range, rather than the discrete values we have seen in our example? When there is a probability that a variable can have a value of any measure between a range of specified values, we have a continuous distribution.

Probability distributions

A probability distribution is a model for an actual or empirical distribution. If we are engaged in an experiment in which a coin is tossed a number of times, the number of heads recorded will be a discrete value of 0, 1, 2, 3, 4, or so on, depending on the number of times we toss the coin. The result is called a discrete random variable. Of course, we know that the probability of throwing a head is 50%, because there are only two outcomes in a coin-toss experiment, heads or tails. We may throw the coin three times and get three heads (it is unlikely but by no means exceptional); however, performing the experiment a great number of times should produce something approaching our 50% result. So an experiment with a large number of trials would produce an empirical distribution which would be close to the theoretical distribution as the number of tosses increases.

This example illustrates a discrete set of outcomes (0, 1, 2, 3); in other words, a discrete probability distribution. It is equally possible to have a continuous probability distribution: for example, the probability that the return on a portfolio lies between 3% and 7% is associated with a continuous probability distribution because the final return value can assume any value between those two parameters.

The normal distribution

A very commonly used theoretical distribution is the normal distribution, which is plotted as a bell-shaped curve and is familiar to most practitioners in business. The theoretical distribution actually looks like many observed distributions such as the height of people, shoe sizes, and so on. The distribution is completely described by the mean and standard deviation. The normal distribution $N(\mu,\sigma)$ has mean μ and standard deviation σ. The probability function is given by

$$P(X = x) = (1 \: / \: \sigma\sqrt{2\pi}) \exp \: [-(x - \mu)^2 \: / \: 2\sigma^2].$$

The distribution is standardised as N(0, 1) with mean of 0 and standard deviation of 1. It is possible to obtain probability values for any part of the distribution by using the standardised normal distribution curve and converting variables to this standardised distribution; thus the variable $Z = (X - \mu) \: / \: \sigma$ follows the standardised normal distribution N(0, 1) with probability :

$$P(Z = Z) = (1 \: / \: \sqrt{2\pi}) \exp \: [-Z^2 \: / \: 2] \: .$$

The Central Limit Theorem (known also as the law of large numbers) is the basis for the importance of the normal distribution in statistical theory and, in real life, a large number of distributions tend towards the normal, provided that there is a sufficient number of observations. This explains the importance of the normal distribution in statistics. If we have large numbers of observations – for example, the change in stock prices, or closing prices in government bonds – it makes calculations straightforward if we assume that they are normally distributed.

Often, as we have seen in the discussions on value–at–risk, it is convenient to assume that the returns from holding an asset are normally distributed. It is often convenient to define the return in logarithmic form as:

$$\ln \left(\frac{P_t}{P_{t-1}} \right)$$

where

P_t is the price today
P_{t-1} is the previous price

If this is assumed to be normally distributed then the underlying price will have a lognormal distribution. The lognormal distribution never goes to a negative value, unlike the normal distribution, and hence is intuitively more suitable for asset prices. The lognormal distribution is illustrated as Figure AA1.

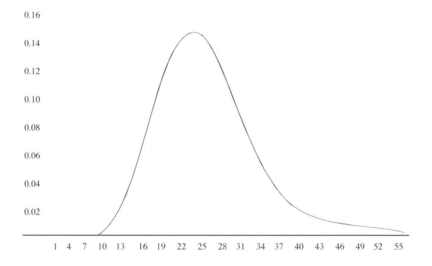

Figure AA1 The lognormal distribution

The normal distribution is assumed to apply to the returns associated with stock prices and, indeed, all financial time series observations. However, it is not strictly accurate, as it implies extreme negative values that are not observed in practice. For this reason the lognormal distribution is used instead, in which case the logarithm of the returns is used instead of the return values themselves; this also removes the probability of negative stock prices. In the lognormal distribution, the logarithm of the random variable follows a normal distribution. The lognormal distribution is asymmetric, unlike the normal curve, because it does not have negatives at the extreme values.

Confidence intervals

Assume an estimate x of the average of a given statistical population where the true mean of the population is μ. Suppose that we believe that on average $\bar{x}$ is an unbiased estimator of μ. Although this means that on average $\bar{x}$ is accurate, the specific sample that we observe will almost certainly be above or below the true level. Accordingly, if we want to be reasonably confident that our inference is correct, we cannot claim that μ. is precisely equal to the observed $\bar{x}$.

Instead, we must construct an interval estimate or confidence interval of the following form:

$$μ = \bar{x} +/- \text{sampling error}$$

The crucial question is: how wide must this confidence interval level be? The answer of course will depend on how much $\bar{x}$ fluctuates. We first set our requirements for level of confidence; that is, how certain we wish to be statistically. If we wish to be incorrect only 1 day in 20 – that is we wish to be right 19 days each month (a month assumed to have 20 working days) – that would equate to a 95% confidence interval that our estimate is accurate. We also assume that are observations are normally distributed. In that case we would expect that the population would be distributed along the lines portrayed in Figure AA2.

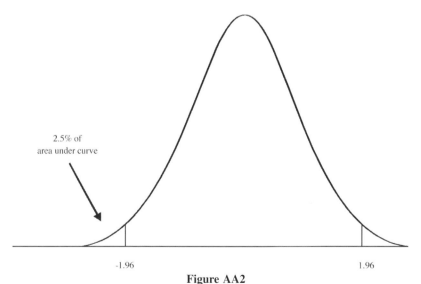

2.5% of
area under curve

-1.96　　　　1.96

Figure AA2

In the normal distribution, 2.5% of the outcomes are expected to fall more than 1.96 standard deviations from the mean. So that means 95% of the outcomes would be expected to fall within +/– 1.96 standard deviations. That is, there is a 95% chance that the random variable $\bar{x}$ will fall between $\mu-1.96$ standard deviations and $\mu+1.96$ standard deviations. This would be referred to as a "two-sided" (or "two-tailed") confidence interval. It gives the probability of a move upwards or downwards by the random variable outside the limits we are expecting.

In the financial markets, we do not, however, expect negative prices, so that values below zero are not really our concern. In this scenario, it makes sense to consider a one-sided test if we are concerned with the risk of loss: a move upward into profit is of less concern (certainly to a risk manager anyway!). From the statistical tables associated with the normal distribution we know that 5% of the outcomes are expected to fall more than 1.645 (rounded to 1.65) standard deviations from the mean. This would be referred to as a one-sided confidence interval.

B

Basic Tools

In this appendix we provide a very brief summary overview of some the main statistical tools that are mentioned in the text. There are no derivations or proofs, and interested readers can access any number of text books on statistics and econometrics.

Summation and product operators

Summation is indicated by the use of the Greek capital letter Σ, pronounced sigma. Thus, we have

$$\sum_{i=1}^{N} x_i = x_1 + x_2 + x_3 + \ldots\ldots + x_N .$$

The double summation operator is also used; thus

$$\sum_{i=1}^{n}\sum_{j=1}^{m} x_{ij} = \sum_{i=1}^{n}(x_{i1} + x_{i2} + \ldots\ldots + x_{im}) .$$

The product operator is given by

$$\prod_{i=1}^{n} x_i = x_1 \cdot x_2 \cdot x_3 \cdot\ldots\ldots\cdot x_N .$$

Standard Brownian motion and the dynamics of the asset-price process

A normal random variable, also termed a Gaussian random variable, with mean 0 and variance 1 is defined by a probability density function of the form

$$f(x) = \frac{1}{\sqrt{2\pi}} \exp\left[-\frac{x^2}{2}\right] \qquad (AB1)$$

where

$$\int_{-\infty}^{+\infty} f(x)\mathrm{d}x = 1$$

A normally distributed variable x with mean 0 and variance 1 is denoted by $x \rightarrow N(0,1)$. Given two real numbers a and b, then $a + bx$ would be normally distributed with a mean of a and standard deviation of b. This is expressed as

$$a + bx \rightarrow N(a,b^2) . \qquad (AB2)$$

Standard Brownian motion (Z, $t \geq 0$), sometimes written as W_t, is a continuous time stochastic process. For a given state of the world ω, the sample path $t \mapsto Z(t,\omega)$ is a function of time. Standard Brownian motion exhibits the following properties:

- $Z_0 = 0$
- for all $t \geq 0$ and $h \geq 0$, the value of $Z_{t+h} - Z_t$ is independent of all previous values of the process
- for all $t \geq 0$ and $h \geq 0$, $Z_{t+h} - Z_t \rightarrow N(0,h)$;
- the distribution of Z_h is identical to the distribution of $Z_{t+h} - Z_t$; that is, it is a Gaussian variable with mean 0 and variance h.

A *random walk* is defined thus: if Z_t, $t \geq 0$ is a standard Brownian motion and $T > 0$, then the value of Z_T is regarded as an infinite sum of infinitely small independent Gaussian increments. Assume that $A > 0$ and the infinitesimally small time increment $\Delta t = T / A$ and that the time interval $[0, T]$ is divided into A sub-intervals each of duration Δt. We have the following

$$Z_T \sim \sum_{i=1}^{A} \chi_i \sqrt{\Delta t} \qquad (AB3)$$

where

$$\chi_i \rightarrow N(0,1)$$

and where χ_i is independent. We then have

$$E(Z_T) = \sum_{i=1}^{A} E(\chi_i)\sqrt{\Delta t} = 0 \tag{AB4}$$

and

$$\text{var}(Z_T) = \sum_{i=1}^{A} \text{var}(\chi_i\sqrt{\Delta t}) + 2\sum_{i<j} \text{cov}(\chi_i\sqrt{\Delta t}, \chi_j\sqrt{\Delta t}) \tag{AB5}$$

$$= \sum_{i=1}^{A} \Delta t + 0 = A\Delta t = T .$$

Therefore, we have

$$Z_t \rightarrow N(0,1).$$

As each sub-interval decreases in duration to 0, at the limit of $A \rightarrow \infty$ we obtain Brownian motion Z, which is also known as a Weiner process.

To define a generalisation of standard Brownian motion Z_t, assume a process X given by

$$\forall t \geq 0, X_t = X_0 + bt + \sigma Z_t . \tag{AB6}$$

We then have

$$X_t \rightarrow N(x_0 + bt, \sigma^2 t) . \tag{AB7}$$

The value of X now, or at time $t = 0$ is given by X_0. In (AB7) the drift term of the process is b and its volatility is σ^2. Informally, we may then write

$$dX_t = bdt + \sigma dZ_t \tag{AB8}$$

where X is a generalised Brownian motion.

In continuous-time pricing models, the dynamics of an asset price P at time t is described by

$$\frac{dP_t}{P_t} = \mu dt + \sigma dZ_t \tag{AB9}$$

where Z is the standard Brownian motion or Weiner process. Expression (AB9) is also written as

$$dP_t = \mu P_t d_t + \sigma P_t dZ_t \tag{AB10}$$

and it can be shown that

$$\frac{\Delta P_t}{P_t} \to N(\mu \Delta t, \sigma^2 \Delta t) \qquad \text{(AB11)}$$

where $\Delta P_t / P_t$ is the ratio of the change in price of the asset between time t and $t + \Delta t$; in other words, the return on the asset during this time. A diagram of the generalised price process is at Figure AB1.

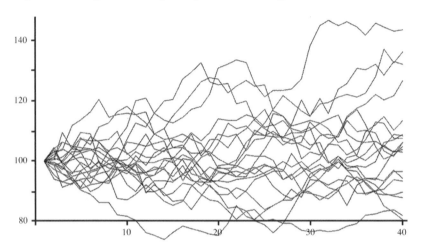

Figure AB1 The generalised price processs.

The integral calculus

The process of differentiation is demonstrated by

$$y = 6x^3 + 2x^2 + 3x$$

where

$$\frac{\mathrm{d}y}{\mathrm{d}x} = 18x^2 + 4x + 3 \ .$$

The reverse of this process is integration, indicated by

$$\int 18x^2 + 4x + 3\mathrm{d}x$$

where $\mathrm{d}x$ is used to indicate the original differentiation with respect to x.

If we know that

$$\int g(x)\mathrm{d}x = f(x)$$

then

$\int_a^b g(x)\mathrm{d}x$ is defined as $f(a) - f(b)$ and is the definite integral between a and b of the function $g(x)$.

Figure AB2 shows part of the function $y = f(x)$ between the points a and b on the x-axis. Imagine that we wish to find the area A between the curve, the x-axis and the lines $x = a$ and $x = b$. We divide the area A into strips of width δx and height y. These strips are approximately rectangles.

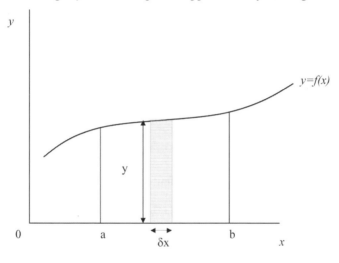

Figure AB2

Again approximating, we can say that the area of each strip $\delta A = y \delta x$, so that

$$\frac{\delta A}{\mathrm{d}x} \approx y \ . \tag{AB12}$$

As the value of δx becomes progressively smaller and approaches (but does not reach) zero, any strips become closer to a rectangle and the approximation given by (AB12) approaches an equality, so that we then get

$$\frac{\mathrm{d}A}{\mathrm{d}x} \approx y \ . \tag{AB13}$$

However, $y = f(x)$, which means we can state

$$\frac{dA}{dx} \approx f(x) . \qquad \text{(AB14)}$$

Therefore, we can state

$$A = \int f(x)dx.$$

We let the integral be

$$A = g(x).$$

At the point a on the x-axis $A = 0$, which also means that $g(a) = 0$, and at the point b on the x-axis we would have A equal to the whole area, which would allow us to set

$$A = g(b).$$

But as $g(a) = 0$ at this point, we can set

$$A = g(b) - g(a). \qquad \text{(AB15)}$$

The expression at (AB15) is actually

$$\int_a^b f(x)dx$$

which is usually written

$$\int_a^b ydx .$$

Hence, using the definite integral allows us to calculate the area under the graph.

Stochastic integrals

If X is a generalised Brownian motion described by

$$X_t = X_0 + bt + \sigma Z_t \qquad \text{(AB16)}$$

at time t, for the time interval $t_0 = 0 < t_1 < t_2 < \ldots\ldots < t_{A-1} < t_A = t$ we have

$$X_t = X_0 + \sum_{i=1}^{A}\left[b(t_i - t_{i-1}) + \sigma(Z_{ti} - Z_{ti}-1)\right] \qquad \text{(AB17)}$$

At the limit where A goes to infinity, we obtain

$$X_t = X_0 + \int_0^T\left[bdt + \sigma dZ_t\right] . \qquad \text{(AB18)}$$

If the variables b and Σ are functions of t and X_t and are not constant, then the process X can be shown to be defined as

$$X_t = X_0 + \int_0^T\left[b(t,X_t)dt + \sigma(t,X_t)dZ_t\right] . \qquad \text{(AB19)}$$

which describes the limit position as A approaches infinity. At this point, we have

$$dX_t = b(t,X_t)dt + \sigma(t,X_t)dZ_t \qquad \text{(AB20)}$$

and X is described as a *diffusion* process. This process has the following properties
- the value of the process at time $t = 0$ is X_0
- the instantaneous *drift* of the process at time t is given by $b(t, X_t)$
- the instantaneous standard deviation or *volatility* of the process at time t is given by $\sigma(t,X_t)$.

The integral $\int_0^T \sigma(t,X_t)dZ_t$ is called a stochastic integral.

C

Introduction to the Mathematics of Fixed Income Pricing[1]

Appendix B introduced the techniques for handling the dynamics and calculus of stochastic variables such as interest rates. In this section we introduce the fundamentals of mathematical finance with respect to fixed income pricing. An extended and through discussion of the content of this section can be found in Choudhry (2004).

To begin we need to state the following sets of assumptions, generally adopted from Merton's[2] pricing method:

- There are no transaction cost or taxes
- There exists an exchange market for borrowing and lending at the same rate of interest (no bid-offer spread)
- The term structure is "flat" and known with certainty
- There is a rational and competitive market
- Market participants prefer to increase wealth
- There are no arbitrage opportunities.

The main prerequisite of mathematical finance that is imperative in understanding fixed income are risk neutral valuation and arbitrage pricing theory. In this introduction we will establish the probabilistic setting in which these concepts are formulated.

As stated in Musiela and Rutkowski (1998), an economy is a family of filtered space $\{(\Omega,I,\mu):\mu\in P\}$[3], where the filtration satisfies the usual

---

[1]   This section was co-written with Mohamoud Dualeh.
[2]   Robert C. Merton, "Continuous-Time Finance", 1998
[3]   To forecast a random variable, one utilises some information denoted by the symbol I_t. See more of this in Neftci (2000) pp. 97

conditions[4], and P is a collection of mutually equivalent probability measures on the measurable space.[5] We model the subjective market uncertainty of each investor by associating to each investor a probability measure from P. Investors with more risky tolerance will be represented by probability measures that weight unfavourable events relatively lower, whereas conservatives investors are characterised by probability measures that weight unfavourable relatively higher. Moreover, it is assumed that investment information is revealed to each investor simultaneously as events in the filtration.

Since the measures in P are mutually equivalent, the investors agree on the events that have and have not occurred. We refer the reader to Neftci (2000) for an excellent example of this. It is convenient to further assume that investors initially have no other information, that is, the filtration is trivial with respect to each probability measure in P. This assumption asserts that the initial information available to investors is objective.

The foundation of a working knowledge of fixed income finance rests on an understanding of the inherent relationship between the various interest rates and bonds. Consider the economy $\{(\Omega, I, \mu) : \mu \in P\}$ on the interval $[0,T]$ and a Markov process[6] X_t with $I \equiv \sigma(X_{:0 \leq s \leq t})$. Implicit in this statement is the assumption that the state variable7 probability $P \equiv P^x$ associated with X_t belongs to P for some fixed elements X of the state space X_t.

Setting the scene further, a zero coupon or discount bond of maturity T is a security that pays the holder one unit of currency at time T. The prices of government and corporate discount bonds at time $t \leq T$ are denoted $B(t,T)$ and $\tilde{B}(t,T)$ respectively. The local expectation hypothesis (L-EH) relates the discount bond to the instantaneous interest rate, or the spot rate for borrowing of the loan over the time interval $[t, t+dt]$.

Denote the riskless spot rate by $r_t = r(X_t)$ and assume that it is a non-negative, adapted process with almost all sample paths integrable on the $[0,T]$ with respect to the Lebesgue measure.

The L-EH asserts that

$$B(t,T) = E_P(\exp(-\int_t^T r(Xs)ds \mid I_t)$$

---

[4] See Karatzas and Shreve (1991) section 2.7 and Korn and Korn (2000) pp. 18.
[5] For a definition of measurable space and how to construct this see Jeffrey S. Rosenthal (2000) section 2.
[6] See Choudhry (2004) pp. 185 for a lucid definition of Markov process.
[7] See Choudhry (2004), pp. 144.

As defined in Musiela and Rutkowski (1998), the economic interpretation of this hypothesis is that "... the current bond price equals the expected value ... of the bond price in the next (infinitesimal) period, discounted at the current short-term rate".[8]

This statement is better understood in a discrete time setting. In fact using a left sum approximation to the integral with partition $\{t_i\}_{t=0}^{n}$ of $[0,T]$ yields

$$B(0,T) = E_P(\exp(-\sum_{i=L}^{n} r(X_{t_{i-1}})\Delta t_i))$$

$$= E_P(\exp(-r(X_{t_0})\Delta t_L)\exp(-\sum_{i-2}^{n} r(X_{t_{i-1}})\Delta t))$$

$$= (\exp(-r(X)t_L)E_P(E_P(\exp(-\sum_{i-2}^{n} r(X_{t_{i-1}})\Delta t_i \mid I_{t_i}))$$

$$= (\exp(-r(X_{t_0})t_L)E_P^X(B(t,T))$$

Under the assumption of no arbitrage, it can be shown that above equation holds under the risk neutral measure.[9] Naturally as similar relationship holds between the risky bond and the risky spot rate.

Bond pricing

The process B_t is referred to as an accumulation factor or savings account.[10] B_t represents the price of a riskless security that continuously compounds at the spot rate. More precisely it is the amount of cash at time t that accumulates by investing \$1 initially, and continually rolling over a bond with an infinitesimal time to maturity. See Musiela and Rutkowski (1998) page 268 for more detail on this.

Therefore an adapted process B_t of finite variation with continuous sample path is given by

$$B_t = \exp(\int_0^t r(X_s)ds) .$$

---

[8] See ibid, pp. 283.
[9] We refer to the interested reader to Ingersoll (1987).
[10] See Pliska (1997) chapter 1.

When security S_t is divided by the saving account the resultant process is the price process of the security discounted at the riskless rate.[11]

We consider next a coupon-bearing bond, with fixed coupon payments $c_1,\ldots,c_n$ at predetermined times $T_1,\ldots,T_n$ with $T_n = T$.

The price of the coupon bond is simply the present value of the sum of these cash flows. Denoting the price of a riskless coupon bond at time by $cB(t,T)$, we have

$$B_c(t,T) = \sum_{i=1}^{n} c_i B(t,T)$$

A similar relationship holds for the risky coupon bond.

However the coupons are typically structured by setting $c_i = c$ for $i = 1,\ldots n-1$ and $c_n = N+c$, where N is the principal or face value, and c is a fixed amount that is generally quoted as a percentage of N called the coupon rate. A problem that arises in comparing coupon bonds is that uncertainty about the rate at which the coupons will be reinvested causes uncertainty in the total return of the coupon bond. Hence, coupon bonds of different coupon rates and payment dates are not directly comparable. The standard way to overcome this problem is to extend the notion of a yield to maturity to coupon bearing bonds.

Yield to Maturity (YTM)

In Musiela and Rutkowski (1998) the continuously compounded riskless yield to maturity $Y_c(t) = Y_c(t;c_1,\ldots,c_n.T1,\ldots T_n)$ is derived as the unique exposition to the equation

$$B_c(t) = \sum_{T_i>t} c_i e^{-Y_c(t)(T_i-t)}$$

and stands for the total return on the coupon bond under the assumption that each of the coupon payments occurring after t is reinvested at the rate $Y_c(t)$. The risky yield to maturity is defined in a similar fashion.

Expectation Hypothesis

There are number of excellent textbooks that the reader is encouraged to read which provides the necessary background, in particular Ingersoll (1987) and Choudhry (2004).

---

[11] In other words, the bank account is the Numeraire.

The yield to maturity expectation hypothesis (YTM-EH) relates the riskless YTM and the riskless spot rate. Musiela and Rutkowski (1998) state that this hypothesis as the assertion that

"... the [continuously compounded] yield from holding any [discount] bond is equal to the [continuously compounded yield expected from rolling over a series of single period [discount] bonds".

To gain a better understanding of this statement, we first observe that the YTM of a discrete time setting with the partition $\{t_i\}_{i=0}^{n}$ of $[t,T]$, we have that the yield of a discount bond $B(t_{i-1},t_i)$ is given by

$$Y(t_{i-1},t_i) = r(X_{t_{i-1}})$$

from which we deduce that the bond price is given by

$$B(t_{i-1},t_i) = \exp(-r(X_{t_{i-1}})\Delta t_i) \ .$$

Since the YTM-EH asserts that the yield of $B(t,T)$ is equal to the yield expected from rolling over a series of discount bonds $B(t_{i-1},t_i)$, it follows that

$$Y(t,T) = \frac{1}{T-t}\ln(B(t,T)) = -\frac{1}{T-t}E_p\left[\ln\left(\sum_{i-L}^{n}B(t_{i-L},t_i)\right)\middle| I_t\right]$$

$$= -\frac{1}{T-t}E_p\left[\sum_{i-L}^{n}r(X_{t_{i-1}})\Delta t_i\middle| I_t\right] \ .$$

Taking the limit, as the mesh of the partition tends to zero; we obtain the continuously time discount bond price and YTM under the YTM-EH:

$$B(t,T) = \exp\left[-E_p\left(\int_t^T r(X_s)ds\right)\middle| I_t\right]$$

$$Y(t,T) = \frac{1}{T-t}\left[E_p\left(\int_t^T r(X_s)ds\right)\middle| I_t\right] \ .$$

The last interest rate that we will consider is the instantaneous forward interest rate, or forward rate for borrowing or lending over the time interval $[s,s+ds]$ as seen from time $[t \leq s]$. This will be denoted by $f(t,s)$ in the riskless case and $\tilde{f}(t,s)$ in the risky case.

If the dynamics of the process $\{f(t,s)\}_{t \leq s \leq T}$ are specified, then the price of the discount bond is defined by

$$B(t,T) = \exp\left(-\int_t^T f(s,t)ds\right)$$

Alternatively, if the dynamics of the discount bond are known, then we have

$$f(t,T) = \frac{\partial}{\partial T} \ln B(t,T) \ ,$$

provided that this derivation exists!

Therefore the YTM-EH asserts that the forward rate is an unbiased estimate of the spot rate under the state variable probability measure P. See Choudhry (2004) chapter 2, equation (2.18). For the relationship between the spot and forward rate we refer the reader to read further in chapter 3 of Choudhry (2004).

References

Bjork, T., *Arbitrage Theory in Continuous Time*. Oxford 1997

Choudhry, M., *Analysing & Interpreting the Yield Curve*, John Wiley 2004

Ingersoll, J., *Theory of Financial Decision Making*, Rosman and Littlefield 1987

Karatzas, I and Shreve, S., *Brownian Motion and Stochastic Calculus*, Spinger 1991

Korn, R., and Korn, E., *Option Pricing and Portfolio Optimisation*, AMS 2000

Musiela, M., and Rutkowski, M., *Martingale Methods in Financial Modelling*, Spinger 1997

Neftci, S., *An Introduction to the Mathematics of Financial Derivatives*, Academic Press 2000

Pliska, S., *Introduction to Mathematical Finance: Discrete Time Models*, Blackwell 1997

Rosenthal, J., *A First Look at Rigorous Probability Theory*, World Scientific 2000

Glossary

A

Accreting: An accreting principal is one which increases during the life of the deal. See **amortising**, **bullet**.

Accreting swap: Swap whose notional amount increases during the life of the swap (opposite of **amortising** swap).

Accrued interest: The proportion of interest or coupon earned on an investment from the previous coupon-payment date until the value date.

Accrued benefit obligation: Present value of pension benefits that have been earned by an employee to date, whether vested in the employee or not. It can be an important measure when managing the asset/liability ration of pension funds.

Accumulated value: The same as **future value**.

ACT/360: A day/year count convention taking the number of calendar days in a period and a "year" of 360 days.

ACT/365: A day/year convention taking the number of calendar days in a period and a "year" of 365 days. Under the ISDA definitions used for interest-rate swap documentation, ACT/365 means the same as **ACT/ACT**.

ACT/ACT: A day/year count convention taking the number of calendar days in a period and a "year" equal to the number of days in the current coupon period multiplied by the coupon frequency. For an interest-rate sway, that part of the interest period falling in a leap year is divided by 366 and the remainder is divided by 365.

Add-on factor: Simplified estimate of the potential future increase in the replacement cost, or market value, of a derivative transaction.

All-in price: See **dirty price**.

All or nothing: Digital option. This option's **put** (call) pays out a predetermined amount ("the all") if the index is below (/above) the strike price at the option's expiration. The amount by which the **index** is below (/above) the **strike** is irrelevant; the payout will be all or nothing.

American option: An option which may be exercised at any time during its life.

Amortising: An amortising principal is one which decreases during the life of a deal, or is repaid in stages during a loan. Amortising an amount over a period of time also means accruing for it pro rata over the period. See **accreting, bullet**.

Annuity: An investment providing a series of (generally equal) future cash flows.

Appreciation: An increase in the market value of a currency in terms of other currencies. See **depreciation, revaluation**.

Arbitrage: The process of buying securities in one country, currency or market, and selling identical securities in another to take advantage of price differences. When this is carried out simultaneously, it is, in theory, a risk-free transaction. There are many forms of arbitrage transactions. For instance, in the cash market a bank might issue a money-market instrument in one money center and invest the same amount in another center at a higher rate, such as an issue of three-month US-dollar CDs in the United States at 5.5% and a purchase of three-month Eurodollar CDs at 5.6%. In the futures market, arbitrage might involve buying three-month contracts and selling forward six-month contracts.

Arbitrageur: Someone who undertakes arbitrage trading.

ARCH: (autoregressive conditional heteroscedasticity) A discrete-time model for a random variable. It assumes that variance is stochastic and is a function of the variance of previous time steps and the level of the underlying.

Arithmetic mean: The average.

Asian option: An Asian option depends on the average value of the underlying over the option's life.

Ask: See **offer**.

Asset: Probable future economic benefit obtained or controlled as a result of past events or transactions. Generally classified as either current or long-term.

Asset & Liability Management (ALM): The practice of matching the term structure and cash flows of an organisation's asset and liability portfolios to maximize returns and minimize risk.

Asset allocation: Distribution of investment funds within an asset class or across a range of asset classes for the purpose of diversifying risk or adding value to a portfolio.

Asset securitisation: The process whereby loans, receivables and other illiquid assets in the balance sheet are packaged into interest-bearing securities that offer attractive investment opportunities.

Asset-backed security: A security which is collaterised by specific assets — such as mortgages — rather than by the intangible creditworthiness of the issuer.

Asset swap: An interest-rate swap or currency swap used in conjunction with an underlying asset such as a bond investment. See **liability swap**.

Asset-risk benchmark: Benchmark against which the riskiness of a corporation's assets may be measured. In sophisticated corporate risk-management strategies the dollar risk of the liability portfolio may be managed against an asset-risk benchmark.

Asset-sensitivity estimates: Estimates of the effect of risk factors on the value of assets.

At-the-money (ATM): An option is at-the-money if the current value of the underlying is the same as the strike price. See **in-the-money, out-of-the-money**.

Auction: A method of issue where institutions submit bids to the issuer on a price or yield basis. Auction rules vary considerably across markets.

Average cap: Also known as an average rate cap, a cap on an average interest rate over a given period rather than on the rate prevailing at the end of the period. See also **average price (rate) option**.

Average price (rate) option: Option on a currency's average exchange rate or a commodity's average spot price in which four variables have to be agreed between buyer and seller: the premium, the **strike** price, the source of the exchange rate or commodity price data and the sampling interval (each day, for example). At the end of the life of the option, the **average spot exchange rate** is calculated and compared with the strike price. A cash payment is then made to the buyer of the option that is equal to the face amount of the option times the difference between the two rates (assuming the option is **in-the-money**; otherwise it expires worthless).

Average worst-case exposure: The expression of an exposure in terms of the average of the worst-case exposure over a given period.

B

Back-testing: The validation of a model by feeding it historical data and comparing the results with historical reality.

Backwardation: The situation when a forward of futures price for something is lower than the spot price (the same as forward discount in foreign exchange). See **contango**.

Balance sheet: Statement of the financial position of an enterprise at a specific point in time, giving assets, liabilities and stockholders' equity.

Band: The Exchange Rate Mechanism (ERM II) of the European Union links the currencies of Denmark and Greece in a system which limits the degree of fluctuation of each currency against the Euro within a band (of 15% for the drachma and $2^1/_4\%$ for the krone) either side of an agreed par value.

Banker's acceptance: See **Bill of Exchange**.

Banking book: As described under Bank rules and the EU capital adequacy directives (CAD), a bank's outstanding transactions that relate to customer lending or long-term investments.

Barrier option: A barrier option is one which ceases to exist, or starts to exist, if the underlying reaches a certain barrier level. See **knock in/ out**.

Base currency: Exchange rates are quoted in terms of the number of units of one currency (the variable or counter currency) which corresponds to one unit of the other currency (the base currency).

Basis: The underlying cash-market price minus the futures price. In the case of a bond futures contract, the futures price must be multiplied by the conversion factor for the cash bond in question.

Basis points: In interest-rate quotations, 0.01%.

Basis risk: A form of market risk that arises whenever one kind of risk exposure is hedged with an instrument that behaves in a similar, but not necessarily identical, way. For instance, a bank trading desk may use three-month interest-rate futures to hedge its commercial-paper or euronote program. Although eurocurrency rates, to which futures prices respond, are well correlated with commercial-paper rates they do not always move in lock-step. If, therefore, commercial-paper rates move by 10 basis points but futures prices dropped by only seven basis points, the three bp gap would be the basis risk.

Basis swap: An interest-rate swap where both legs are based on floating-rate payments.

Basis trade: Buying the basis means selling a futures contract and buying the commodity or instrument underlying the futures contract. Selling the basis is the opposite.

Basket option: Option based on an underlying basket of bonds, currencies, equities or commodities.

Bearer bond: A bond for which physical possession of the certificate is proof of ownership. The issuer does not know the identity of the bondholder. Traditionally the bond carries detachable coupons, one for each interest-payment date, which are posted to the issuer when payment is due. At maturity, the bond is redeemed by sending in the certificate for repayment. These days, bearer bonds are usually settled electronically, and while no register of ownership is kept by the issuer, coupon payments may be made electronically.

Bear spread: A spread position taken with the expectation of a fall in value in the underlying.

Benchmark: A bond whose terms set a standard for the market. The benchmark usually has the greatest liquidity, the highest turnover and is usually the most frequently quoted. It also usually trades expensive to the yield curve, due to higher demand for it among institutional investors.

Beta: The sensitivity of a stock relative to swings in the overall market. The market has a beta of one, so a stock or portfolio with a beta greater than one will rise or fall more than the overall market, whereas a beta of less than one means that the stock is less volatile.

Bid: The price at which a market-maker will buy bonds. A tight bid-offer spread is indicative of a liquid and competitive market. The bid rate in a **repo** is the interest rate at which the dealer will borrow the **collateral** and lend the cash. See **offer**.

Bid figure: In a foreign-exchange quotation, the exchange rate omitting the last two decimal places. For example, when EUR/USD is 1.1910/20, the big figure is 1.19. See **points**.

Bid-offer: The two-way price at which a market will buy and sell stock.

Bilateral netting: The ability to offset amounts owed to a counterparty under one contract against amounts owed to the same counterparty under another contract – for example, where both transactions are governed by one master agreement. Also known as **cherry-picking**.

Bill: A **bill of exchange** is a payment order written by one person (the drawer) to another, directing the latter (drawee) to pay a certain amount of money at a future date to a third party. A bill of exchange is a bank draft when drawn on a bank. By accepting the draft, a bank agrees to pay the face value of the obligation if the drawer fails to pay, hence the term "bankers acceptance". A **Treasury bill** is short-term government paper of up to one year's maturity, sold at a discount to principal value and redeemed at par.

Bill of exchange: A short-term, **zero-coupon** debt issued by a company to finance commercial trading. If it is guaranteed by a bank, it becomes a banker's acceptance.

Binomial pricing model: A tool for valuing an option based on building a **binomial tree** of all the possible paths both up and down that the underlying asset price might take, from start until expiry. It assumes each up or down move is by a given amount.

Binomial tree: A mathematical model to value options, based on the assumption that the value of the underlying can move either up or down a given extent over a given short time. This process is repeated many times to give a large number of possible paths (the "tree") which the value could follow during the option's life.

BIS: Bank for International Settlements.

Black-Scholes: A widely used option-pricing formula devised by Fischer Black and Myron Scholes and published in 1973.

Blended interest-rate swap: Result of adding forward swap to an existing swap and blending the rates over the total life of the transaction.

Bloomberg: The trading, analytics and news service produced by Bloomberg LP; also used to refer to the terminal itself.

Bond basis: An interest rate is quoted on a bond basis if it is on an **ACT/365**, **ACT/ACT** or **30/360** basis. In the short term (for accrued interest, for example), these three are different. Over a whole (non-leap) year, however, they all equate to 1. In general, the expression "bond basis" does not distinguish between them and is calculated as ACT/365. See **money-market basis**.

Bond futures: Contracts traded on a recognised futures exchange that are standardised agreements to buy or sell a fixed nominal amount of a government bond. The contract is based on a "notional" bond, and a specified basket of actual bonds may be delivered against the contract.

Bond-equivalent yield: The yield which would be quoted on a US treasury bond which is trading at par and which has the same economic return and maturity as a given treasury bill.

Bootstrapping: Building up successive zero-coupon yields from a combination of coupon-bearing yields.

BPV: Basis-point value. The price movement due to a one basis-point change in yield.

Bräss/Fangmeyer: A method for calculating the yield of a bond similar to the **Moosmüller** method, but in the case of bonds which pay coupons more frequently than annually, using a mixture of annual and less-than-annual **compounding**.

Break forward: A product equivalent to a straightforward option, but structured as a forward deal at an off-market rate which can be reversed at a penalty rate.

Broken date: A maturity date other than the standard ones (such as one week, one, two, three, six and 12 months) normally quoted. Also known as a "cock-date" by FRA traders.

Broker-dealers: Members of the London Stock Exchange who may intermediate between customers and market-makers; may also act as principals, transacting business with customers from their own holdings of stock.

Bulldog: Sterling domestic bonds issued by non-UK domiciled borrowers. These bonds trade under a similar arrangement to gilts and are settled via the Central Gilts Office (now CREST).

Bull spread: A spread position taken with the expectation of a rise in value in the **underlying**.

Bullet: A loan/deposit has a bullet maturity if the principal is all repaid at maturity. See **amortising**.

Business intelligence tools: Term used to describe the latest generation of access tools, which are expected to support both data extraction and subsequent analysis.

Butterfly: Either an option spread that comprises the purchase of a call (or put) combined with the purchase of another call (or put) at a different strike, plus the sale of two calls at a mid-way strike, **OR**, a bond spread of one short position and a long position in two other bonds.

Buy/sell-back: Opposite of **sell/buy-back**.

C

Cable: The exchange rate for sterling against the US dollar.

CAD: The European Union's Capital Adequacy Directive.

Calendar spread: The simultaneous purchase/sale of a futures contract for one date and the sale/purchase of a similar futures contract for a different date. See **spread**.

Callable bond: A bond which provides the borrower with an option to redeem the issue before the original maturity date. In most cases, certain terms are set before the issue, such as the date after which the bond is callable and the price at which the issuer may redeem the bond.

Call option: An option to purchase the commodity or instrument underlying the option. See **put**.

Call price: The price at which the issuer can call in a bond or preferred bond.

Cancelable swap: Swap in which the payer of the fixed rate has the option, usually exercisable on a specified date, to cancel the deal (see also **swaption**).

Cap: A series of borrower's **IRG**s, designed to protect a borrower against rising interest rates on each of a series of dates.

Capital adequacy ratio: A ratio calculated to meet banking regulators' requirements, and made up of the size of a bank's own funds (available capital and reserves) as a proportion of its risky assets (the funds it has lent to credit risky borrowers).

Capital market: Long-term market (generally longer than one year) for financial instruments. See **money market**.

Capped option: Option where the holder's ability to profit from a change in value of the underlying is subject to a specified limit.

Caption: Option on a **cap**.

Cash: See **cash market**.

Cash market: The market for trading an actual financial instrument for its true value. The cash market is the underlying market for derivatives contracts.

Cash-and-carry: An arbitrage trade in which a trader sells a bond futures contract and simultaneously buys the CTD bond, to lock in perceived mis-pricing in the implied future price of the bond. A reverse cash-and-carry is a purchase of futures against a sale of cash bonds. The key measure to analyse is the repo rate for the CTD, and whether the CTD is expected to be unchanged on futures expiry.

CBOT: The Chicago Board of Trade, one of the two futures exchanges in Chicago, USA, and one of the largest in the world.

CD: See **certificate of deposit**

Cedel: Centrale de Livraison de Valeurs Mobilieres; a clearing system for Euro-currency and international bonds. Cedel is located in Luxembourg and is jointly owned by a number of European banks.

Ceiling: The same as **cap**.

Central bank repo: A central bank repo is when the central bank lends funds (provide liquidity) to the market; as such it is a reverse repo in market terms.

Central Gilts Office: The office of the Bank of England which runs the computer-based settlement system for gilt-edged securities and certain other securities (mostly **Bulldogs**) for which the Bank acts as Registrar.

Central line theorem: The assertion that as sample size, n, increases, the distribution of the mean of a random sample taken from almost any population approaches a normal distribution.

Certificate of deposit (CD): A money-market instrument of up to one year's maturity (although CDs of up to five years have been issued) that pays a bullet interest payment on maturity. After issue, CDs can trade freely in the secondary market, the ease of which is a function of the credit quality of the issuer.

CGBR: Central Government Borrowing Requirement.

CGBCR: Central Government Net Cash Requirement.

CGO reference prices: Daily prices of gilt-edged and other securities held in CGO which are used by CGO in various processes, including revaluing stock-loan transactions, calculating total consideration in a repo transaction, and DBV assembly.

Cheapest to deliver: (Or CTD). In a bond futures contract, the one underlying bond among all those that are deliverable, which is the most price-efficient for the seller to deliver.

Cherry-picking: See **bilateral netting**

Classic repo: Repo is short for "sale and repurchase agreement" – a simultaneous spot sale and forward purchase of a security, equivalent to borrowing money against a loan of collateral. A reverse repo is the opposite. The terminology is usually applied from the perspective of the repo dealer. For example, when a central bank does repos, it is lending cash (the repo dealer is borrowing cash from the central bank).

Clean deposit: The same as **time deposit**.

Clean price: The price of a bond excluding accrued coupon. The price quoted in the market for a bond is generally a clean price rather than a **dirty price**.

Close-out netting: The ability to net a portfolio of contracts with a given counterparty in the event of default. See also **bilateral netting**.

CMO: Central Money-markets Office which settles transactions in Treasury bills and other money-market instruments, and provides a depository.

CMTM: Current **mark-to-market** value. See **current exposure** and **replacement cost**.

Collar: The simultaneous sale of a **put (or call) option** and purchase of a call (or put) at different strikes – typically both **out-of-the-money**.

Collateral: An asset of value, often of good credit quality, such as a government bond, given temporarily to a counterparty to enhance a party's creditworthiness. In a **repo**, the collateral is sold temporarily by one party to the other and bought back on maturity.

Commercial paper: A short-term security issued by a company or bank, generally with a zero coupon.

Competitive bid: A bid for the stock at a price stated by a bidder in an auction. **Non-competitive bid** is a bid where no price is specified; such bids are allotted at the weighted-average price of successful competitive bid prices.

Compound interest: When some interest on an investment is paid before maturity and the investor can reinvest it to earn interest on interest, the interest is said to be compounded. Compounding generally assumes that the reinvestment rate is the same as the original rate. See **simple interest.**

Compound option: Option on an option, the first giving the buyer the right, but not the obligation, to buy the second on a specific date at a predetermined price. There are two kinds. One, on currencies, is useful for companies tendering for overseas contracts in a foreign currency. The interest-rate version comprises **captions** and **floortions**.

Consideration: The total price paid in a transaction, including taxes, commissions and (for bonds) accrued interest.

Contango: The situation when a forward or futures price for something is higher than the spot price (the same as forward premium in foreign exchange). See **backwardation**.

Contingent option: Option where the premium is higher than usual but is only payable if the value of the underlying reaches a specified level. Also known as a contingent premium option.

Continuous compounding: A mathematical, rather than practical, concept of compound interest where the period of compounding is infinitesimally small.

Contract date: The date on which a transaction is negotiated. See **value date**.

Contract for differences: A deal such as an **FRA** and some futures contracts, where the instrument or commodity effectively bought or sold cannot be delivered; instead, a cash gain or loss is taken by comparing the price dealt with the market price, or an index, at maturity.

Conventional gilts (included double-dated): Gilts on which interest payments and principal repayments are fixed.

Conversion factor: In a bond futures contract, a factor to make each deliverable bond comparable with the contract's notional bond specification. Defined as the price of one unit of the deliverable bond required to make its yield equal the notional coupon. The price paid for a bond on delivery is the futures settlement price times the conversion factor.

Convertible currency: A currency that may be freely exchanged for other currencies.

Convexity: A measure of the curvature of a bond's price/yield curve (mathematically, $\dfrac{d^2P}{dr^2}$ / dirty price).

Correlation matrices: Statistical constructs used in the **value-at-risk** methodology to measure the degree of relatedness of various market forces.

Corridor: The same as **collar**.

Cost of carry: The net running cost of holding a position (which may be negative) – for example, the cost of borrowing cash to buy a bond, less the coupon earned on the bond while holding it.

Cost volatility: Volatility relating to operational errors or the fines and losses a business unit may incur. Reflected in excess costs and penalty charges posted to the profit and losses. See also **revenue volatility**.

Counterparty risk: The risk that the other side to a transaction will default on payments owed by it during the transaction and/or on maturity.

Counterparty risk weighting: See **risk weighting**.

Country risk: The risks, when business is conducted in a particular country, of adverse economic or political conditions arising in that country. More specifically, the credit risk of a financial transaction or instrument arising from such conditions.

Coupon: The interest payment(s) made by the issuer of security to the holders, based on the coupon rate and the face value.

Coupon swap: An interest-rate swap in which one leg is fixed-rate and the other floating-rate. See **basis rate**.

Cover: To cover an exposure is to deal in such a way as to remove the risk – either reversing the position, or hedging it by dealing in an instrument with a similar but opposite risk profile. Also the amount by how much a bond auction is subscribed.

Covered call/put: The sale of a covered call option is when the option writer also owns the underlying. If the underlying rises in value so that the option is exercised, the writer is protected by his position in the underlying. Covered puts are defined analogously. See **naked**.

Covered-interest arbitrage: Creating a loan/deposit in one currency by combining a loan/deposit in another with a forward foreign-exchange swap.

CP: See **commercial paper**.

Credit (or default) risk: The risk that a loss will be incurred if a counterparty to a derivatives transaction does not fulfill its financial obligations in a timely manner.

Credit derivatives: Financial contracts that involve a potential exchange of payments in which at least one of the cash flows is linked to the performance of a specified underlying credit-sensitive asset or liability.

Credit-equivalent amount: As part of the calculation of the risk-weighted amount of capital the Bank for International Settlements (BIS) advises each bank to set aside against derivative credit risk, banks must compute a credit-equivalent amount for each derivative transaction. The amount is calculated by summing the **current replacement cost**, or market value, of the instrument and an **add-on factor**.

Credit-risk (or default-risk) exposure: The value of the contract exposed to default. If all transactions are marked-to-market each day, such positive market value is the amount of previously recorded profit that might have to be reversed and recorded as a loss in the event of counterparty default.

Credit spread: The interest-rate spread between two debt issues of similar duration and maturity, reflecting the relative creditworthiness of the issuers.

Credit swaps: Agreement between two counterparties to exchange disparate cash flows, at least one of which must be tied to the performance of a credit-sensitive asset or to a portfolio or index of such assets. The other cash flow is usually tied to a **floating-rate index** (such as **Libor**) or a fixed rate or is linked to another credit-sensitive asset.

Credit value-at-risk (CVAR): See **value-at-risk (VAR)**.

CREST: The paperless share-settlement system through which trades conducted on the London Stock Exchange can be settled. The system is operated by CRESTCo and was introduced in 1996.

CRND: Commissioners for the Reduction of the National Debt, formally responsible for investment of funds held within the public sector – for example, the National Insurance Fund.

Cross: See **cross-rate**.

Cross-currency repo: A repo in which cash and stock are denominated in different currencies.

Cross-rate: Generally an exchange rate between two currencies, neither of which is the US dollar. In the American market, spot cross is the exchange rate for US dollars against Canadian dollars in its direct form.

CTD: See **cheapest to deliver**.

cum-dividend: literally "with dividend", stock that is traded with interest or dividend accrued included in the price.

Cumulative default rate: See **probability of default**.

Currency option: The option to buy or sell a specified amount of a given currency at a specified rate at or during a specified time in the future.

Currency swap: An agreement to exchange a series of cash flows determined in one currency, possibly with reference to a particular fixed or floating interest-payment schedule, for a series of cash flows based in a different currency. See **interest-rate swap**.

Current assets: Assets which are expected to be used or converted to cash within one year or one operating cycle.

Current liabilities: Obligations which the firm is expected to settle within one year or one operating cycle.

Current yield: Bond coupon as a proportion of clean price per 100; does not take principal gain/loss or time-value of money into account. See **yield to maturity**, **simple yield to maturity**.

Curve fitting: Plotting or estimating the yield curve from market-observed yield data.

Cylinder: The same as **collar**.

D

DAC-RAP: Delivery against collateral-receipt against payment. Same as **DVP**.

Daily range: The difference between the high and low points of a single trading day.

Day-count: The convention used to calculate accrued interest on bonds and interest on cash. For UK gilts, the convention changed to actual/actual from actual/365 on 1st November 1998. For cash, the convention in sterling markets is actual/365.

DBV (delivery by value): A mechanism whereby a CGO member may borrow from or lend money to another CGO member against overnight gilt collateral. The CGO system automatically selects and delivers securities to a specified aggregate value on the basis of the previous night's CGO reference prices; equivalent securities are returned the following day. The DBV functionality allows the giver and taker of collateral to specify the classes of security to be included within the DBV. The options are: all classes of security held within CGO, including strips and bulldogs; coupon-bearing gilts and bulldogs; coupon-bearing gilts and strips; only coupon-bearing gilts.

DEaR: Daily earnings at risk.

Debenture: In the US market, an unsecured domestic bond, backed by the general credit quality of the issuer. Debentures are issued under a trust deed or indenture. In the UK market, a bond that is secured against the general assets of the issuer.

Debt Management Office (DMO): An executive arm of the UK Treasury, responsible for cash management of the government's borrowing requirement. This includes responsibility for issuing government bonds (gilts), a function previously carried out by the Bank of England. The DMO began operations in April 1998.

Default correlation: The degree of covariance between the probabilities of default of a given set of counterparties. For example, in a set of counterparties with positive default correlation, a default by one counterparty suggests an increased probability of a default by another counterparty.

Default probability: See **probability of default**.

Default risk: See **credit risk**.

Default-risk exposure: See **credit-risk exposure**.

Default start options: Options purchased before their "lives" actually commence. A corporation might, for example, decide to pay for a deferred-start option to lock into what it perceives as current advantageous pricing for an option that it knows it will need in the future.

Deferred-strike option: Option where the strike price is established at future date on the basis of the spot foreign-exchange price prevailing at that future date.

Delegation costs: Incentive costs incurred by banks in delegating monitoring activities.

Deliverable bond: One of the bonds which is eligible to be delivered by the seller of a bond futures contract at the contract's maturity, according to the specifications of that particular contract.

Delivery: Transfer of gilts (in settlements) from seller to buyer.

Delivery versus payment (DVP): The simultaneous exchange of securities and cash. The assured payment mechanism of the CGO achieves the same protection.

Delta (δ): The change in an option's value relative to a change in the underlying's value.

Delta neutral: An option portfolio contracted to have zero delta.

Depreciation: A decrease in the market value of a currency in terms of other currencies. See **appreciation, devaluation**.

Derivative: Strictly, any financial instrument whose value is derived from another, such as a forward foreign-exchange rate, a futures contract, an option, an interest-rate swap, etc. Forward deals to be settled in full are not always called derivatives, however.

Devaluation: An official one-off decrease in the value of a currency in terms of other currencies. See **revaluation, depreciation**.

Diffusion effect: The potential for increase over time of the credit exposure generated by a derivative: as time progresses, there is more likelihood of larger changes in the underlying market variables. Depending on the type and structure of the instrument, this effect may be moderated by **amortisation effect**.

Digital option: Unlike simple European and American options, a digital option has fixed payouts and, rather like binary digital circuits, which are either on or off, pays out either this amount or nothing. Digital options can be added together to create assets that exactly mirror index price movements anticipated by investors. See **one-touch all-or-nothing**.

Direct: An exchange-rate quotation against the US dollar in which the dollar is the **variable currency** and the other currency is the **base currency**.

Dirty price: The price of a bond including accrued interest. Also known as the "all-in" price.

Discount: The amount by which a currency is cheaper, in terms of another currency, for future delivery than for spot, is the forward discount (in general, a reflection of interest-rate differentials between two currencies). If an exchange rate is "at a discount" (without specifying to which of the two currencies this refers), this generally means that the **variable currency** is at a discount. See **premium.**

Discount factor: A factor by which one multiplies a future known cashflow, to obtain its present value.

Discount house: In the UK money market, originally securities houses that dealt directly with the Bank of England in T-bills and bank bills, or discount instruments; hence the name. Most discount houses were taken over by banking groups and the term is not generally used, as the BoE now also deals directly with clearing banks and securities houses.

Discount rate: The method of market quotation for certain securities (US and UK treasury bills, for example), expressing the return on the security as a proportion of the face value of the security received at maturity – as opposed to a **yield**, which expresses the yield as a proportion of the original investment.

Discount swap: Swap in which the fixed-rate payments are less than the internal rate of return on the swap, the difference being made up at maturity by a balloon payment.

Diversified: A portfolio that has been invested across a range of assets such that its credit risk is minimised. This is achieved by having a mixture of assets whose individual credit risks are uncorrelated with each other.

Dividend discount model: Theoretical estimate of market value that computes the economic or the net present value of future cash flows due to an equity investor.

DMO: The UK Debt Management Office.

Down-and-in option: Barrier option where the holder's ability to exercise is activated if the value of the underlying drops below a specified level. See also **up-and-in option**.

Down-and-out-option: Barrier option where the holder's ability to exercise expires if the value of the underlying drops below a specified level.

Dual-currency option: Option allowing the holder to buy either of two currencies.

Dual-currency swap: Currency swap where both the interest rates are fixed rates.

Dual-strike option: Interest-rate option, usually a **cap** or a **floor**, with one floor or ceiling rate for part of the option's life and another for the rest.

Duration: A measure of the weighted-average life of a bond or other series of cash flows, using the present values of the cash flows as the weights. See **modified duration**.

Duration gap: Measurement of the interest-rate exposure of an institution.

Duration weighting: The process of using the modified-duration value for bonds to calculate the exact nominal holdings in a spread position. This is necessary because £1 million nominal of a two-year bond is not equivalent to £1 million of, say, a five-year bond. The modified-duration value of the five-year bond will be higher, indicating that its "basis-point value" (bpv) will be greater and that, therefore, £1 million worth of this bond represents greater sensitivity to a move in interest rates (risk). As another example, consider a fund manager holding £10 million of five-year bonds. The fund manager wishes to switch into a holding of two-year bonds with the same overall risk position. The basis-point values of the bonds are 0.041583 and 0.022898, respectively. The ratio of the bpvs are 0.041583/0.022898 = 1.816. The fund manager, therefore, needs to switch into £10m × 1.816 = £18.160 million of the two-year bond.

DV01: An acronym for "dollar value of an 01", meaning price value of a basis point. The change in value of a bond or derivative for a 1 basis point change in its yield. Also known as "Dollar value of a basis point" or DVBP.

DVP: Delivery versus payment, in which the settlement mechanics of a sale or loan of securities against cash is such that the securities and cash are exchanged against each other simultaneously through the same clearing mechanism and neither can be transferred unless the other is.

E

Early exercise: The exercise or assignment of an option prior to expiration.

ECU: The European Currency Unit, a basket composed of European Union currencies, now defunct following introduction of the euro currency.

Effective rate: An effective interest rate is the rate which, earned as simple interest over one year, gives the same return as interest paid more frequently than once per year and then compounded. See **nominal rate**.

Efficient-frontier method: Technique used by fund managers to allocate assets.

Embedded option: Interest-rate-sensitive option in debt instrument that affects its redemption. Such instruments include **mortgage-backed securities** and **callable bonds.**

End-end: A money-market deal commencing on the last working day of a month and lasting for a whole number of months, maturing on the last working day of the correlation.

Epsilon (ε): The same as **vega**.

Equity: The residual interest in the net assets of an entity that remains after deducting the liabilities.

Equity options: Options on shares of an individual common stock.

Equity warrant: Warranty, usually attached to a bond, entitling the holder purchase share(s).

Equity-linked swap: Swap where one of the cash flows is based on an equity instrument or index, when it is known as an equity-index swap.

Equivalent life: The weighted-average life of the principal of a bond where there are partial **redemptions**, using the **present values** of the partial redemptions as the weights.

Equivalent rate: The interest rate that returns the same amount as another quoted interest rate but at a different compounding basis.

ERA: See **exchange-rate agreement**.

Eta (η): The same as **vega**.

Euribor: The reference rate for the euro currency, set in Frankfurt.

Euro: The name for the domestic currency of the European Monetary Union. Not to be confused with **Eurocurrency**.

Euroclear: An international clearing system for international securities. Euroclear is based in Brussels and managed by Morgan Guaranty Trust Company.

Eurocurrency: A Eurocurrency is a currency owned by a non-resident of the country in which the currency is legal tender. Not to be confused with **Euro.**

Euro-issuance: The issue of gilts (or other securities) denominated in Euro.

Euromarket: The international market in which **Eurocurrencies are** traded.

European: A European **option** is one that may be exercised only at **expiry**. See **American**.

Exchange controls: Regulations restricting the free convertibility of a currency into other currencies.

Exchange-rate agreement: A **contract for differences** based on the movement in a **forward-forward** foreign-exchange swap price. Does not take account of the effect of **spot** rate changes as an **FXA** does. See **SAFE**.

Exchange-traded: Futures contracts are traded on a futures exchange, as opposed to **forward** deals which are **OTC. Option** contracts are similarly exchange traded rather than **OTC**.

Ex-dividend (xd) date: A bond's record date for the payment of coupons. The coupon payment will be made to the person who is the registered holder of the stock on the xd date. For UK gilts, this is seven working days before the coupon date.

Exercise: To exercise an **option** (by the **holder**) is to require the other party (the **writer**) to fulfill the underlying transaction. Exercise price is the same as **strike** price.

Exotic option: An option that is not plain vanilla, any complex option.

Expected (credit) loss: Estimate of the amount a derivatives counterparty is likely to lose as a result of default from a derivatives contract, with a given level of probability. The expected loss of any derivative position can be derived by combining the distributions of credit exposures, rate of recovery and probabilities of default.

Expected default rate: Estimate of the most likely rate of default of a counterparty expressed as a level of probability.

Expected rate of recovery: See **rate of recovery**.

Expiry: An option's expiry is the time after which it can no longer be **exercised**.

Exposure: Risk to market movements.

Exposure profile: The path of worst-case or expected exposures over time. Different instruments reveal quite differently shaped exposure profiles arising from the interaction of the diffusion and amortisation effects.

Extinguishable option: Option in which the holder's right to exercise disappears if the value of the underlying passes a specified level. See also **barrier option**.

Extrapolation: The process of estimating a price or rate for a particular value date, from other known prices, when the value date required lies outside the period covered by the known prices. See **interpolation**.

F

Face value: The principal amount of a security generally repaid ("redeemed") all at maturity, but sometimes repaid in stages, on which the **coupon** amounts are calculated.

Fence: The same as **collar**.

Fixing: See **Libor fixing**.

Floating rate: An interest rate set with reference to an external index. Also, an instrument paying a floating rate is one where the rate of interest is re-fixed in line with market conditions at regular intervals, such as every three or six months. In the current market, an exchange rate determined by market forces with no government intervention.

Floating-rate CD: CD on which the rate of interest payable is re-fixed in line with market conditions at regular intervals (usually six months).

Floating-rate gilt: Gilt issued with an interest rate adjusted periodically in line with market interbank rates.

Floating-rate note: Capital-market instrument on which the rate of interest payable is re-fixed in line with market conditions at regular intervals (usually six months).

Floor: A series of lender's **IRG**s, designed to protect an investor against falling interest rates on each of a series of dates.

Floortion: Option on a **floor**.

Forward: In general, a deal for value later than the normal value date for that particular commodity or instrument. In the foreign-exchange market, a forward price is the price quoted for the purchase or sale of one currency against another where the value date is at least one month after the **spot** date. See **short date**.

Forward band: Zero-cost collar; that is, one in which the premium payable as a result of buying the **cap** is offset exactly by that obtained from selling the **floor**.

Forward break: See **break forward**.

Forward-exchange agreement: A **contract for differences** designed to create exactly the same economic result as a foreign-exchange cash **forward-forward** deal. See **ERA, SAFE**.

Forward/forward: Short-term exchange of currency deposits. (See also **forward/forward deposit**).

Forward-forward yield curve: A yield curve of zero-coupon rates for periods starting at a future point, say 1 month or 1 year from today.

Forward-rate agreement (FRA): Short-term interest-rate **hedge**. Specifically, a contract between buyer and seller for an agreed interest rate on a notional deposit of a specified maturity on a predetermined future date. No principal is exchanged. At maturity, the seller pays the buyer the difference if rates have risen above the agreed level, and vice versa.

Forward swap: Swap arranged at the current rate but entered into at some time in the future.

FRA: See **forward-rate agreement**.

FRCD: See **floating-rate CD**.

FRN: See **floating-rate note**.

Framework document: Sets out the DMO's responsibilities, objectives and targets, its relationship with the rest of the Treasury and its accountability as an Executive Agency.

Fraption: Option on a forward-rate agreement. Also known as an interest-rate guarantee.

FSA: The Financial Services Authority, the body responsible for the regulation of investment business, and the supervision of banks and money-market institutions in the UK. The FSA took over these duties from nine "self-regulatory organisations" that had previously carried out this function, including the Securities and Futures Authority (SFA), which had been responsible for regulation of professional investment business in the City of London. The FSA commenced its duties in 1998.

FTSE-100: Index comprising 100 major UK shares listed on The International Stock Exchange in London. Futures and options on the index are traded at the London International Financial Futures and Options Exchange (**LIFFE**).

Funding reserve: A specified (say, 10bp) multiple of the aggregate value of the funding gap, across the maturity structure.

Funds: The **USD/CAD** exchange rate for value on the next business day (standard practice for **USD/CAD** in preference to **spot**).

Fungible: A financial instrument that is equivalent in value to another, and easily exchanged or substituted. The best example is cash money, as a £10 note has the same value and is directly exchangeable with another £10 note. A bearer bond also has this quality.

Future: A futures contract is a contract to buy or sell securities or other goods at a future date at a predetermined price. Futures contracts are usually standardised and traded on an exchange.

Future exposure: See **potential exposure**.

Future value: The amount of money achieved in the future, including interest, by investing a given amount of money now. See **time-value of money**, **present value**.

Futures contract: A deal to buy or sell some financial instrument or commodity for value on a future date. Unlike a **forward** deal, futures contracts are traded only on an exchange (rather than **OTC**), have standardised contract sizes and value dates, and are often only **contract for differences** rather than deliverable.

FXA: See **forward-exchange agreement**.

G

G7: The "Group of Seven" countries: the USA, Canada, the UK, Germany, France, Italy and Japan.

Gamma (Γ): The change in an option's delta relative to a change in the underlying's value.

Gap: The difference in the maturity profile of assets versus liabilities by time bucket.

Gap ratio: Ratio of interest-rate-sensitive assets to interest-rate-sensitive liabilities; used to determine changes in the risk profile of an institution with changes in interest-rate levels.

Gapping: Feature of commodity markets whereby there are large and very rapid price movements to new levels followed by relatively stable prices.

GDP: Gross domestic product, the value of total output produced within a country's borders.

GEMM: A gilt-edged market-maker, a bank or securities house registered with the Bank of England as a market-maker in gilts. A GEMM is required to meet certain obligations as part of its function as a registered market-maker, including making two-way price quotes at all times in all gilts and taking part in gilt auctions. The Debt Management Office now makes a distinction between conventional gilt GEMMs and index-linked GEMMs, known as IG GEMMs.

General collateral (GC): Securities, which are not "special", used as collateral against cash borrowing. A repo buyer will accept GC at any time that a specific stock is not quoted as required in the transaction. In the gilts market, GC includes DBVs.

GIC: Guaranteed investment contract.

Gilt: A UK Government sterling-denominated, listed security issued by HM Treasury with initial maturity of over 365 days when issued. The term "gilt" (or gilt-edged) is a reference to the primary characteristic of gilts as an investment: their security.

Gilt-edged market-maker: See **GEMM.**

GMRA: Global Master Repurchase Agreement, the industry-standard legal agreement describing repo transactions. Issued under the auspices of the Bond Market Association in the US and the International Securities Market Association (ISMA).

GNP: Gross national product, the total monetary value of a country's output, as produced by citizens of that country.

Gold warrant: Naked or attached warrant exercisable into gold at a predetermined price.

Gross-redemption yield: The same as **yield to maturity**; "gross" because it does not take tax effects into account.

GRY: See **gross-redemption yield.**

H

Haircut: The value of collateral required over and above the loan value in a repo, required by the lender of cash. Also called **margin**.

Hedge ratio: The ratio of the size of the position it is necessary to take in a particular instrument as a hedge against another, to the size of the position being hedged.

Hedging: Protecting against the risks arising from potential market movements in exchange rates, interest rates or other variables. See **cover**, **arbitrage**, **speculation**.

Herstatt risk: See **settlement risk**.

High-coupon swap: Off-market coupon swap where the coupon is higher than the market rate. The floating-rate payer pays a front-end fee as compensation. Opposite of low-coupon swap.

Historical simulation methodology: Method of calculating **value-at-risk (VAR)** using historical data to assess the likely effect of market moves on a portfolio.

Historic rate rollover: A **forward-rate swap** in FX where the settlement exchange rate for the near date is based on a historic **off-market** rate rather than the current market rate. This is prohibited by many central banks.

Historic volatility: The actual **volatility** of an instrument or asset, recorded in market prices over a particular period in the past.

Holder: The holder of an **option** is the party that has purchased it.

I

IDB: Inter-dealer broker; in this context a broker that provide facilities for dealing in bonds between market-makers.

IG: Index-linked gilt whose coupons and final redemption payment are related to the movements in the Retail Price Index (RPI).

Immunisation: This is the process by which a bond portfolio is created that has an assured return for a specific time horizon irrespective of changes in interest rates. The mechanism underlying immunization is a portfolio structure that balances the change in the value of a portfolio at the end of the investment horizon (time period) with the return gained from the reinvestment of cash flows from the portfolio. As such, immunization requires the portfolio manager to offset interest-rate risk and reinvestment risk.

Implied repo rate: The breakeven interest rate at which it is possible to sell a bond **futures contract**, buy a **deliverable bond**, and **repo** the bond out. See **cash and carry**.

Implied volatility: The **volatility** used by a dealer to calculate an **option** price; conversely, the volatility implied by the price actually quoted.

Index option: An **option** whose **underlying** security is an index. Index options enable a trader to bet on the direction of the index.

Indexed notes: Contract whereby the issuer usually assumes the risk of unfavorable price movements in the instrument, commodity or index to which the contract is linked, in exchange for which the issuer can reduce the cost of borrowing (compared with traditional instruments without the risk exposure).

Index swap: Sometimes the same as a **basis swap**. Otherwise, a swap like an **interest-rate swap** where payments on one or both of the legs are based on the value of an index – such as an equity index, for example.

Indirect: An exchange-rate quotation against the US dollar in which the dollar is the **base currency** and the other currency is the **variable currency**.

Initial margin: The excess either of cash over the value of securities, or of the value of securities over cash in a repo transaction at the time it is executed and, subsequently, after margin calls.

Interbank: The market in unsecured lending and trading between banks of roughly similar credit quality.

Interest-rate cap: See **cap**.

Interest-rate floor: See **floor**.

Interest-rate guarantee: An **option** on an **FRA[needs to be added]**.

Interest-rate option: Option to pay or receive a specified rate of interest on or from a predetermined future date.

Interest-rate swap: An agreement to exchange a series of cash flows determined in one currency, based on fixed- or **floating**-interest payments on an agreed **notional** principal, for a series of cash flows based in the same currency but on a different interest rate. May be combined with a **currency swap**.

Intermarket spread: A spread involving futures contracts in one market spread against futures contracts in another market.

Internal rate of return: The yield necessary to discount a series of cash flows to an **NPV** of zero.

Interpolation: The process of estimating a price or rate for value on a particular date by comparing the prices actually quoted for value dates either side. See **extrapolation**.

Intervention: Purchases or sales of currencies in the market by central banks in an attempt to reduce exchange-rate fluctuations or to maintain the value of a currency within a particular band, or at a particular level. Similarly, central bank operations in the money markets to maintain interest rates at a certain level.

In-the-money: A **call (put) option** is in-the-money if the underlying is currently more (less) valuable than the **strike** price. See **at-the-money**, **out-of-the-money**.

Intrinsic value: The amount by which an option is in-the-money.

IRG: See **interest-rate guarantee**.

IRR: See **internal rate of return**.

IRS: See **interest-rate swap**.

ISMA: The International Securities Market Association. This association compiled, with the PSA (now renamed the Bond Market Association), the PSA/ISMA Global Master Repurchase Agreement.

Issuer risk: Risk to an institution when it holds debt securities issued by another institution. (See also **credit risk**).

Iteration: The mathematical process of estimating the answer to a problem by seeing how well an estimate fits the data, adjusting the estimate appropriately and trying again, until the answer is close to the actual. Used, for example, in calculating a bond's **yield** from its price.

J

Junk bonds: The common term for high-yield bonds; higher-risk, low-rated debt.

K

Kappa (κ): An alternative term to refer to volatility; see **vega**.

Kick-in note: An index-linked hybrid bond whose enhanced return is triggered if the index reaches a certain level above or below where it is when the note is issued.

Knock out/in: A knock out (in) **option** ceases to exist (starts to exist) if the underlying reaches a certain trigger level. See **barrier option**.

L

Lambda (λ): The same as **vega**.

Large exposure: A risk exposure to a bank caused by having a large part of lending made to one counterparty. Under EU CAD, an extra risk number must be allocated for this risk.

Lender option: Floor on a single-period forward-rate agreement.

Leptokurtosis: The non-normal distribution of asset-price returns. Refers to a probability distribution that has a fatter tail and a sharper hump than a normal distribution.

Level payment swap: Evens out those fixed-rate payments that would otherwise vary; for example, because of the amortisation of the principal.

Leverage: The ability to control large amounts of an underlying variable for a small initial investment.

Liability: Probable future sacrifice of economic benefit due to present obligations to transfer assets or provide services to other entities as a result of past events or transactions. Generally classed as either current or long-term.

Liability swap: An interest-rate swap or currency swap used in conjunction with an underlying liability such as a borrowing. See **asset swap**.

LIBID: The London Interbank Bid Rate, the rate at which banks will pay for funds in the interbank market.

LIBOR: The London Interbank Offered Rate, the lending rate for all major currencies up to one-year maturity set at 1100 hours each day by the British Bankers' Association.

Libor fixing: The Libor rate "fixed" by the British Bankers' Association (BBA) at 1100 hours each day, for maturities up to one year.

LIBID: See **Libor**.

LIFFE: The London International Financial Futures and Options Exchange, the largest futures exchange in Europe.

LIMEAN: The arithmetic average of Libor and Libid rates.

Limit up/down: Futures prices are generally not allowed to change by more than a specified total amount in a specified time, in order to control risk in very volatile conditions. The maximum movements permitted are referred to as limit up and limit down.

Liquidation: Any transaction that closes out or offsets a futures or options position.

Liquidity: A word describing the ease with which one can undertake transactions in a particular market or instrument. A market where there are always ready buyers and sellers willing to transact at competitive prices is regarded as liquid. In banking, the term is also used to describe the requirement that a portion of a banks assets be held in short-term risk-free instruments, such as government bonds, T-Bills and high-quality Certificates of Deposit.

Loan-equivalent amount: Description of derivative exposure which is used to compare the credit risk of derivatives with that of traditional bonds or bank loans.

Lognormal: A variable's **probability distribution** is lognormal if the logarithm of the variable has a normal distribution.

Lognormal distribution: The assumption that the log of today's interest rate, for example, minus the log of yesterday's rate is normally distributed.

Long: A long position is a surplus of purchases over sales of a given currency or asset, or a situation which naturally gives rise to an organisation benefiting from a strengthening of that currency or asset. To a money-market dealer, however, a long position is a surplus of borrowings taken in over money lent out, (which gives rise to a benefit if that currency weakens rather than strengthens). See **short**.

Long-dated forward: Forward foreign-exchange contract with a maturity of greater than one year. Some long-dated forwards have maturities as great as 10 years.

Long-term assets: Assets which are expected to provide benefits and services over a period longer than one year.

Long-term liabilities: Obligations to be repaid by the firm more than one year later.

Lookback option: Option that allows the purchaser, at the end of a given period of time, to choose as the rate for exercise any rate that has existed during the option's life.

Low-coupon swap: Tax-driven swap, in which the fixed-rate payments are significantly lower than current market interest rates. The floating-rate payer is compensated by a front-end fee.

LSE: London Stock Exchange.

LTV: Loan-to-value, the ratio of the loan amount over the value of the asset. A lending risk ratio calculated by dividing the total amount of the mortgage or loan by the appraised value of the asset.

M

Macaulay duration: See **duration**.

Manufactured dividend: A payment from the repo buyer to the repo seller during the term of the trade, representing the coupon or dividend received by the temporary owner (repo buyer) of the security being repo'd. Also applies in a stock loan transaction.

Mapping: The process whereby a treasury's derivative positions are related to a set of risk "buckets".

Margin: Initial margin is **collateral**, placed by one party with a counterparty at the time of the deal, against the possibility that the market price will move against the first party, thereby leaving the counterparty with a credit risk. Variation margin is a payment or extra collateral transferred subsequently from one party to the other because the market price has moved. Variation margin payment is either, in effect, a settlement of profit/loss (for example, in the case of a **futures** contract) or the reduction of credit exposure (for example, in the case of a **repo**). In gilt **repos**, variation margin refers to the fluctuation band or threshold within which the existing collateral's value may vary before further cash or **collateral** needs to be transferred. In a loan, margin is the extra interest above a **benchmark** (for example a margin of 0.5% over **Libor**) required by a lender to compensate for the credit risk of that particular borrower.

Margin call: A request following marking-to-market of a repo transaction for the initial margin to be reinstated or, where no initial margin has been taken, to restore the cash/securities ratio to parity.

Margin default rate: See **probability of default**.

Margin transfer: The payment of a **margin call**.

Market comparables: Technique for estimating the fair value of an instrument for which no price is quoted by comparing it with the quoted prices of similar instruments.

Market-maker: Market participant who is committed, explicitly or otherwise, to quoting two-way bid-and-offer prices at all times in a particular market.

Market risk: Risks related to changes in prices of tradable macroeconomic variables, such as exchange-rate risks.

Mark-to-market: The act of revaluing securities to current market values. Such revaluations should include both coupon accrued on the securities outstanding and interest accrued on the cash.

Matched book: This refers to the matching by a repo trader of securities repoed in and out. It carries no implications that the trader's position is "matched" in terms of exposure, for example, to short-term interest rates.

Maturity date: Date on which stock is redeemed.

Mean: Average.

Minmax option: One of the strategies for reducing the cost of options by forgoing some of the potential for gain. The buyer of a currency option, for example, simultaneously sells an option on the same amount of currency but at a different strike price.

MLV: Maximum likely potential increase in value.

Modified duration: A measure of the proportional change in the price of a bond or other series of cash flows, relative to a change in yield. (Mathematically $- \dfrac{dP}{di}$ / dirty price.) See **duration**.

Modified following: The convention that if a value date in the future falls on a non-business day, the value date will be moved to the next following business day, unless this moves the value date to the next month; in which case, the value date is moved back to the last previous business day.

Momentum: The strength behind an upward or downward movement in price.

Money market: Short-term market (generally up to one year) for financial instruments. See **capital market**.

Money-market basis: An interest rate quoted on an ACT/360 basis is said to be on a money-market basis. See **bond basis**.

Monte Carlo simulation: Technique used to determine the likely value of a derivative or other contract by simulating the evolution of the underlying variables many times. The discounted **average** outcome of the simulation gives and approximation of the derivative's value. Monte Carlo simulation can be used to estimate the **value-at-risk**

(VAR) of a portfolio. Here, it generates a simulation of many correlated market movements for the markets to which the portfolio is exposed, and the positions in the portfolio are revalued repeatedly in accordance with the simulated scenarios. This gives a probability distribution of portfolio gains and losses from which the **VAR** can be determined.

Moosmüller: A method for calculating the yield of a bond.

Mortgage-backed security (MBS): Security guaranteed by pool of mortgages. MBS markets include the US, UK, Japan and Denmark.

Moving average convergence/divergence (MACD): The crossing of two exponentially smoothed moving averages that oscillate above and below an equilibrium line.

Multi-index option: Option which gives the holder the right to buy the asset that performs best out of a number of assets (usually two). The investor would typically buy a call allowing him to buy the **equity**.

N

Naked: A naked **option** position is one not protected by an off-setting position in the **underlying**. See **covered call/put**.

Negative divergence: When at least two indicators, indexes or averages show conflicting or contradictory trends.

Negotiable: A security which can be bought and sold in a **secondary market** is negotiable.

Net present value: The net present value of a series of cash flows is the sum of the present values of each cash flow (some or all of which may be negative).

NLF: National Loans Fund, the account which brings together all UK Government lending and borrowing.

Noise: Fluctuations in the market which can confuse or impede interpretation of market direction.

Nominal amount: Same as **face value** of a security.

Nominal rate: The quoted interest rate, rather than the **effective rate** to which it is equivalent.

Non-deliverable forward: A forward FX contract that does not result in exchange of actual cash currency amounts on maturity, but instead has a single net payment representing the change between the traded forward rate and the spot rate on maturity.

Normal: A normal **probability distribution** is a particular distribution assumed to prevail in a wide variety of circumstances, including the financial markets. Mathematically, it corresponds to the probability density function:

Notional: In a bond futures contract, the bond bought or sold is a standardised non-existent notional bond, as opposed to the actual bonds which are **deliverable** at maturity. **Contracts for differences** also require a notional principal amount on which settlement can be calculated.

Novation: Replacement of a contract or, more usually, a series of contracts with one new contract.

NPV: See **net present value**.

O

O/N: See **overnight**.

Odd date: See **broken date**.

Off-balance sheet: A transaction whose nominal value is not entered on the balance sheet, because the principal amount is not traded. The standard accounting treatment for "contracts for differences".

Offer: The price at which a market-maker will sell bonds. Also called "ask".

Off-market: A rate which is not the current market rate.

Off-market coupon swap: Tax-driven swap strategy, in which the fixed-rate payments differ significantly from current market rates. There are high- and low-coupon swaps.

One-touch all-or-nothing: Digital option. The option's put pays out a predetermined amount (the "all") if the index goes below (above) the strike price at any time during the option's life. How far below (above) the strike price the strike price the index moves is irrelevant; the payout will be the 'all" or nothing. **Opening leg:** The first half of a repo transaction (see **closing leg**).

Open interest: The quantity of **futures** contracts (of a particular specification) which have not yet been closed out by reversing. Either all **long** positions or all **short** positions are counted but not both.

Operational Market Notice: Sets out the DMO's (previously the Bank's) operations and procedures in the gilt market.

Operational risk: Risk of loss occurring due to inadequate systems and control, human error, or management failure.

Opportunity cost: Value of an action that could have been taken if the current action had not been chosen.

Option: The right (but not the obligation) to buy or sell securities at a fixed price within a specified period.

Option forward: See **time option**.

Ornstein-Uhlenbeck equation: A standard equation that describes mean reversion. It can be used to characterise and measure commodity price behavior.

OTC: Over the counter. Strictly speaking, any transaction not conducted on a registered stock exchange. Trades conducted via the telephone between banks, and contracts such as FRAs and (non-exchange traded) options are said to be "over-the-counter" instruments. OTC also refers to non-standard instruments or contracts traded between two parties; for example, a client with a requirement for a specific risk to be hedged with a tailor-made instrument may enter into an OTC structured-option trade with a bank that makes markets in such products.

Out-of-the-money: A **call (put) option** is out-of-the-money if the **underlying** is currently less (more) valuable than the strike price. See **at-the-money**, **in-the-money**.

Outright: An outright (or **forward** outright) is the sale or purchase of one foreign currency against another value on any date other than spot. See **spot**, **swap**, **forward**, **short date**.

Over the counter: An OTC transaction is one dealt privately between any two parties, with all details agreed between them, as opposed to one dealt on an exchange – for example, a **forward** deal as opposed to a **futures contract**.

Overborrowed: A position in which a dealer's liabilities (borrowings taken in) are of longer maturity than the assets (loans out).

Overlent: A position in which a dealer's assets (loans out) are of longer maturity than the liabilities (borrowings taken in).

Overnight: A deal from today until the next working day ("tomorrow").

P

Paper: Another term for a bond or debt issue.

Par: The face value, or 100%. In foreign exchange, when the **outright** and **spot** exchange rates are equal, the **forward swap** is zero or par. When the price of a security is equal to the face value, usually expressed as 100, it is said to be trading at par. A par-swap rate is the current market rate for a fixed **interest-rate swap** against **Libor**.

Par yield curve: A curve plotting maturity against **yield** for bonds priced at par.

Parity: The official rate of exchange for one currency in terms of another which a government is obliged to maintain by means of intervention.

Participation forward: A product equivalent to a straightforward **option** plus a **forward** deal, but structured as a forward deal at an **off-market** rate plus the opportunity to benefit partially if the market rate improves.

Path-dependent: A path-dependent **option** is one which depends on what happens to the **underlying** throughout the option's life (such as the **American** or **barrier** option) rather than only at expiry (a **European** option).

Peak exposure: If the worst-case or the expected credit-risk exposures of an instrument are calculated over time, the resulting graph reveals a credit-risk exposure profile. The highest exposure marked out by the profile is the peak exposure generated by the instrument.

Periodic-resetting swap: Swap where the floating-rate payment is an average of floating rates that have prevailed since the last payment, rather than the interest rate prevailing at the end of the period. For example, the average of six one-month **Libor** rates rather than one six-month Libor rate.

Pips: See **points**.

Plain vanilla: See **vanilla**.

Points: The last two decimal places in an exchange rate. For example, when EUR/USD is 1.1910/1.1920, the points are 10/20. See **bid figure**.

Portfolio variance: The square of the **standard deviation** of a portfolio's return from the mean.

Positive cash-flow collar: Collar other than a zero-cost collar.

Potential exposure: Estimate of the future replacement cost, or positive market value, of a derivative transaction. Potential exposure should be calculated using probability analysis based on broad confidence intervals (for example, two standard deviations) over the remaining term of the transaction.

Preference shares: These are a form of corporate financing. They are normally fixed-interest shares whose holders have the right to receive dividends ahead of ordinary shareholders. If a company were to go into liquidation, preference shareholders would rank above ordinary shareholders for the repayment of their investment in the company. Preference shares ("prefs") are normally traded within the fixed-interest division of a bank or securities house.

Premium: For a bond, the amount by which the price is over par. In the FX market, the amount by which a currency is more expensive, in terms of another currency, for future delivery than for spot, is the forward premium (in general, a reflection of interest-rate differentials between two currencies). If an exchange rate is "at a premium" (without specifying to which of the two currencies this refers), this generally means that the **variable currency** is at a premium. See **discount**.

Present value: The amount of money which needs to be invested now to achieve a given amount in the future when interest is added. See **time-value of money, future value**.

Pre-settlement risk: As distinct from credit risk arising from intra-day settlement risk, this term describes the risk of loss that might be suffered during the life of the contract if a counterparty to a trade defaulted and if, at the time of default, the instrument had a positive economic value.

Price-earnings ratio: A ratio giving the price of a stock relative to the earnings per share.

Price factor: See **conversion factor**.

Primary market: The market for new debt, into which new bonds are issued. The primary market is made up of borrowers, investors and the investment banks which place new debt into the market, usually with their clients. Bonds that trade after they have been issued are said to be part of the secondary market.

Probability distribution: The mathematical description of how probable it is that the value of something is less than or equal to a particular level.

Probit procedures: Methods for analysing qualitative dependent methods where the dependent variable is binary, taking the values zero or one.

Put: A put option is an option to sell the commodity or instrument **underlying** the option. See **call**.

Put-call parity: The theory that demonstrates the relationship between the call price and put price of an option with otherwise identical terms.

PVB: Price value of a basis point, the change in value of a bond or derivative contract resulting from a 1 basis point change in its yield, or in the level of interest rates.

Q

Quanto: An option that has its final payoff linked to two or more underlying assets or reference rates.

Quanto swap: A **swap** where the payments in one or both legs are based on a measurement (such as the interest rate) in one currency but payable in another currency.

Quasi-coupon date: The regular date for which a **coupon** payment would be scheduled if there was a coupon payable. Used for price/yield calculations for **zero-coupon** bonds.

R

Range forward: A **zero-cost collar** where the customer is obliged to deal with the same bank at spot if neither limit of the collar is breached at **expiry**.

Rate of recovery: Estimate of the percentage of the amount exposed to default – that is, the credit-risk exposure – that is likely to be recovered by an institution if a counterparty defaults. The recovery value of a deposited asset is dependent on its rate of recovery.

Record date: A **coupon** or other payment due on a security is paid by the issuer to whoever is registered on the record date as being the owner. See **ex-dividend, cum-dividend**.

Redeem: A security is said to be redeemed when the principal is repaid.

Redemption yield: The rate of interest at which all future payments (coupons and redemption) on a bond are discounted so that their total equals the current price of the bond (inversely related to price).

Re-denomination: A change in the currency unit in which the nominal value of a security is expressed (in context, from sterling to euro).

Reduced-cost option: Generic term for options for which there is a reduced premium, either because the buyer undertakes to forgo a percentage of any gain, or because he offsets the cost by writing other options (for example, minmax, range forward). See also **zero-cost option**.

Refer: The practice whereby a trader instructs a broker to put "under reference" any prices or rates he has quoted to him, meaning that they are no longer "firm" and the broker must refer to the trader before he can trade on the price initially quoted.

Register: Record of ownership of securities. For gilts, excluding bearer bonds, entry in an official register confers title.

Registered bond: A bond for which the issuer keeps a record (register) of its owners. Transfer of ownership must be notified and recorded in the register. Interest payments are posted (more usually electronically transferred) to the bondholder.

Registrar's Department: Department of the Bank of England which maintains the register of holdings of gilts.

Reinvestment rate: The rate at which interest paid during the life of an investment is reinvested to earn interest-on-interest which, in practice, will generally not be the same as the original yield quoted on the investment.

Relative-performance option: Option whose value varies in line with the relative value of two assets.

Replacement cost: The present value of the expected future net cash flows of a derivative instrument. Aside from various conventions dealing with the **bid/ask** spread, synonymous with the "market value" or "current exposure" of an instrument.

Repo: Usually refers in particular to **classic repo**. Also used as a term to include classic repos, **buy/sell-backs** and **securities lending.**

Repo rate: The return earned on a repo transaction expressed as an interest rate on the cash side of the transaction.

Repurchase agreement: See **repo**.

Return on assets: The net earnings of a company divided by its assets.

Return on equity: The net earning of a company divided by its equity.

Return on value-at-risk (ROVAR): An analysis conducted to determine the relative rates of return on different risks, allowing corporations to compare different risk-capital allocations and capital-structure decisions effectively.

Revaluation: An official one-off increase in the value of a currency in terms of other currencies. See **devaluation**.

Reverse: See **reverse repo**.

Reverse repo: The opposite of a **repo**.

Rho (ρ)**:** The change in an option's value relative to a change in interest rates.

Risk-free rate: The interest rate payable on an investment that carries zero credit risk. Usually associated with the 90-day Treasury bill rate.

Risk reversal: Changing a long (or short) position in a call option to the same position in a put option by selling (or buying) forward, and vice versa.

Risk-weighted asset: Assets that carry an element of credit risk and so must be weighted in accordance with relative risk, for capital adequacy purposes under Basel regulations.

Rollover: See **tom/next**. Also refers to a renewal of a loan.

Running yield: Same as **current yield**.

Rump: A gilt issue so designated because it is illiquid, generally because there is a very small nominal amount left in existence.

S

S/N: See **spot/next**.

S/W: See **spot-a-week**.

SAFE: See **synthetic agreement for forward exchange**.

Sale and repurchase agreement: The full name for repo.

Secondary market: The market in instruments after they have been issued. Bonds are bought and sold after their initial issue by the borrower, and the marketplace for this buying and selling is referred to as the secondary market. The new-issues market is the primary market.

Securities and Exchange Commission: The central regulatory authority in the United States, responsible for policing the financial markets, including the bond markets.

Securities lending: When a specific security is lent against some form of collateral. Also know as stock lending.

Security: A financial asset sold initially for cash by a borrowing organisation (the "issuer"). The security is often negotiable and usually has a maturity date when it is redeemed.

Sell/buy-back: Simultaneous spot sale and forward purchase of a security, with the forward price calculated to achieve an effect equivalent to a classic repo.

Settlement: The process of transferring stock from seller to buyer and arranging the corresponding movement of funds between the two parties.

Settlement bank: Bank which agrees to receive and make assured payments for gilts bought and sold by a CGO member.

Settlement date: Date on which transfer of gilts and payment occur, usually the next working date after the trade is conducted.

Settlement risk: The risk that occurs when there is a non-simultaneous exchange of value. Also known as "delivery risk" and "Herstatt risk".

Sharpe ratio: A measure of the attractiveness of the return on an asset by comparing how much risk premium the investor can expect it to receive in return for the incremental risk (volatility) the investment carries. It is the ratio of the risk premium to the volatility of the asset.

Short: A short position is a surplus of sales over purchases of a given currency or asset, or a situation which naturally gives rise to an organisation benefiting from a weakening of that currency or asset. To a money-market dealer, however, a short position is a surplus of money lent out over borrowings taken in (which give rise to a benefit if that currency strengthens rather than weakens). See **long**.

Short date: A deal for value on a date other than spot but less than one month after spot.

Simple interest: When interest on an investment is paid all at maturity or not reinvested to earn interest on interest, the interest is said to be simple. See **compound interest**.

Simple yield to maturity: Bond coupon plus principal gain/loss amortised over the time to maturity, as a proportion of the clean price per 100. Does not take time-value of money into account. See **yield to maturity, current yield**.

SLA: Service Level Agreement, in this context between the DMO and service suppliers in the Bank and HM Treasury.

Special: A security which for any reason is sought after in the repo market, thereby enabling any holder of the security to earn incremental income (in excess of the **General Collateral** rate) through lending them via a repo transaction. The repo rate for a special will be below the GC rate, as this is the rate the borrower of the cash is paying in returning for supplying the special bond as collateral. An individual security can be in high demand for a variety of reasons; for instance, if there is sudden heavy investor demand for it, or (if it is a benchmark issue) it is required as a hedge against a new issue of similar-maturity paper.

Speculation: A deal undertaken because the dealer expects prices to move in his favor, as opposed to **hedging** or **arbitrage**.

Spot: A deal to be settled on the customary value date for that particular market. In the foreign-exchange market, this is for value in two working days' time.

Spot yield curve: The current zero-coupon yield curve.

Spot/next: A transaction from **spot** until the next working day.

Spread: The difference between the bid and offer prices in a quotation. Also a strategy involving the purchase of an instrument and the simultaneous sale of a similar related instrument, such as the purchase of a **call option** at one **strike** and the sale of a call option at a different strike.

Square: A position in which sales exactly match purchases, or in which assets exactly match liabilities. See **long**, **short**.

Standard deviation (σ): A measure of how much the values of something fluctuate around its mean value. Defined as the square root of the **variance**.

Step-down swap: Swap in which the fixed-rate payment decreases over the life of the swap.

Step-up swap: Swap in which the fixed-rate payment increases over the life of the swap.

Stock lending: See **securities lending**.

Stock-index future: Future on a stock index, allowing a hedge against, or bet on, a broad equity-market movement.

Stock-index option: Option on a stock-index future.

Stock option: Option on an individual stock.

Straddle: A position combining the purchase of both a call and put at the same strike for the same date. See **strangle**.

Strangle: A position combining the purchase of both a call and a put at different strikes for the same date. See **straddle**.

Street: The "street" is a term for the market, deriving originally from "Wall Street". A US term for market convention; so, in the US market is the convention for quoting the price or yield for a particular instrument.

Stress testing: Analysis that gives the value of a portfolio under a range of **worst-case** scenarios.

Strike: The strike price or strike rate of an option is the price or rate at which the holder can insist on the underlying transaction being fulfilled.

Strip: A zero-coupon bond which is produced by separating a standard coupon-bearing bond into its constituent principal and interest components. To strip a bond is to separate its principal amount and its coupons and trade each individual cash flow as a separate instrument ("*s*eparately *t*raded and *r*egistered for *i*nterest and *p*rincipal"). Also, a strip of **futures** is a series of short-term futures contracts with consecutive delivery dates, which together create the effect of a longer-term instrument (for example, four consecutive three-month futures contracts as a **hedge** against a one-year swap). A strip of **FRA**s is similar.

Swap: A foreign-exchange swap is the purchase of one currency against another for delivery on one date, with a simultaneous sale to reverse the transaction on another value date. See also **interest-rate swap, currency swap**.

Swaption: An **option** on an **interest-rate swap, currency swap**.

Switch: Exchanges of one gilt holding for another, sometimes entered into between the DMO and a GEMM as part of the DMO's secondary-market operations.

Synthetic: A package of transactions which is economically equivalent to a different transaction (for example, the purchase of a **call option** and simultaneous sale of a **put** option at the same **strike** is a synthetic **forward** purchase.)

Synthetic agreement for forward exchange: A generic term for **ERA**s and **FXA**s.

T

T/N: See **tom/next**.

Tail: The difference in maturity between assets and liabilities (also known as "gap" or interest rate tail). In FX markets, the exposure to interest rates over a forward-forward period arising from a mismatched position (such as a two-month borrowing against a three-month loan). A forward foreign-exchange dealer's exposure to **spot** movements.

Tap: The issue of a gilt for exceptional market-management reasons and not on a pre-announced schedule.

TED spread: A term referring to the spread in a trade involving a long/short futures position against a short/long government bond position. Also the futures strip hedge page on Bloomberg. Originally referred to as "Treasury-Eurodollar spread".

Term: The time between the beginning and end of a deal or investment.

Theta (θ): The change in an option's value relative to a change in the time left to expiry.

Tick: The minimum change allowed in a futures price.

Tick value: The change in value of a futures contract for a one tick movement in price.

Time bucket: The maturity group into which a loan or other exposure is placed. For instance, time buckets of o/n, o/n – 1week, 1week – 3month, 3month – 6month and 6month – 12month may be calculated, and assets and liabilities placed in buckets according to their maturity.

Time deposit: A non-**negotiable** deposit for a specific term.

Time option: A forward currency deal in which the value date is set to be within a period rather than on a particular day. The customer sets the exact date two working days before settlement.

Time-value for money: The concept that a future cash flow can be valued as the amount of money which it is necessary to invest now in order to achieve that cash flow in the future. See **present value, future value**.

Today/tomorrow: See **overnight**.

Tom/next: A transaction from the next working day ("tomorrow") until the day after ("next day" – that is, **spot** in the foreign-exchange market).

Total-return swap: Swap agreement in which the total return of bank loans or credit-sensitive securities is exchanged for some other cash flow usually tied to **Libor**, or other loans, or credit-sensitive securities. It allows participants to effectively go **long** or **short** the credit risk of the **underlying** asset.

Traded option: Option that is listed on and cleared by an exchange, with standard terms and delivery months.

Trading book: A bank's investment, trading and short-term activity, grouped into the trading book for regulatory capital purposes.

Tranche: One of a series of two or more issues with the same coupon rate and maturity date. The tranches become fungible at a future date, usually just after the first coupon date.

Transaction risk: Extent to which the value of transactions that have already been agreed is affected by market risk.

Transparent: A term used to refer to how clear asset prices are in a market. A transparent market is one in which a majority of market participants are aware of what level a particular bond or instrument is trading.

Trigger option: See **barrier option**

Treasury bill: A short-term security issued by a government, generally with a zero **coupon**.

True yield: The yield on a bond that is equivalent to the quoted discount or zero-coupon rate.

Tunnel: The same as **collar**.

Tunnel options: Set of collars, typically zero-cost, covering a series of maturities from the current date. They might, for example, be for dates six, 12 or 24 months ahead. The special feature of a tunnel is that strike price on both sets of options, not just on the options bought, is constant.

U

Uncovered option: When the writer of the option does not own the underlying security. Also known as a **naked option**.

Undated gilts: Gilts for which there is no final date by which the gilt must be redeemed.

Underlying: The underlying of a futures or option contract is the commodity of financial instrument on which the contract depends. Thus, underlying for a bond option is the bond; the underlying for a short-term interest-rate futures contract is typically a three-month deposit.

Underwriting: An arrangement by which a company is guaranteed that an issue of debt (bonds) will raise a given amount of cash. Underwriting is carried out by investment banks, who undertake to purchase any part of the debt issue not taken up by the public. A commission is charged for this service.

Unexpected-default rate: The distribution of future default rates is often characterised in terms of an expected-default rate (for example, 0.05%) and a worst-case default rate (for example, 1.05%). The difference between the worst-case default rate and the expected-default rate is often termed the "unexpected default" (that is, 1%=1.05 − 0.05%).

Unexpected loss: The distribution of credit losses associated with a derivative instrument is often characterised in terms of an **expected loss** or a **worst-case loss**. The unexpected loss associated with an instrument is the difference between these two measures.

Up-and-away option: See **up-and-out option**.

Up-and-in option: Type of barrier option which is activated if the value of the underlying goes above a predetermined level. See also **down-and-in option**.

Up-and-out option: Type of barrier option that is extinguished if the value of the underlying goes above a predetermined level. See also **down-and-out option**.

V

Value-at-risk (VAR): Formally, the probabilistic bound of market losses over a given period of time (known as the holding period) expressed in terms of a specified degree of certainty (known as the confidence interval). Put more simply, the VAR is the worst-case loss that would be expected over the holding period within the probability set out by the confidence interval. Larger losses are possible but with a low probability. For instance, a portfolio whose VAR is $20 million over a one-day holding period, with a 95% confidence interval, would have only a 5% chance of suffering an overnight loss greater than $20 million.

Value date: The date on which a deal is to be consummated. In some bond markets, the value date for coupon accruals can sometimes differ from the settlement date.

Vanilla: A vanilla transaction is a straightforward one.

VAR: See **value-at-risk**

Variable currency: Exchange rates are quoted in terms of the number of units of one currency (the variable or counter currency) which corresponds to one unit of the other currency (the **base currency**).

Variance (σ^2): A measure of how much the values of something fluctuate around its mean value. Defined as the average of (value − mean)^2. See **standard deviation**.

Variance-covariance methodology: Methodology for calculating the **value-at-risk** of a portfolio as a function of the **volatility** of each asset or liability position in the portfolio and the correlation between the positions.

Variation margin: The band agreed between the parties to a repo transaction at the outset within which the value of the collateral may fluctuate before triggering a right to call for cash or securities to reinstate the initial margin on the repo transaction.

Vega: The change in an option's value relative to a change in the **underlying's volatility**.

Volatility: The **standard deviation** of the continuously compounded return on the **underlying**. Volatility is generally annualised. It measures the price fluctuation of an asset or derivative. See **historic volatility**, **implied volatility**.

W

Warrant: A security giving the holder a right to subscribe to a share or bond at a given price and from a certain date. If this right is not exercised before the maturity date, the warrant will expire worthless.

Warrant-driven swap: Swap with a warrant attached allowing the issuer of the fixed-rate bond to go on paying a floating rate in the event that she exercises another warrant allowing her to prolong the life of the bond.

When-issued trading: Trading a bond before the issue date; no interest is accrued during this period. Also known as the "grey market".

Worst-case (credit-risk) exposure: Estimate of the highest positive market value a derivative contract or portfolio is likely to attain at a given moment or period in the future, with a given level of confidence.

Worst-case (credit-risk) loss: Estimate of the largest amount a derivative counterparty is likely to lose, with a given level of probability, as a result of default from a derivatives contract or portfolio.

Worst-case default rate: The highest rates of default that are likely to occur at a given moment or period in the future, with a given level of confidence.

Write: To sell an option is to write it. The person selling an option is known as the **writer**.

Writer: The same as "seller" of an **option**.

X

X: Used to denote the strike price of an option; sometimes this is denoted using the term K.

Y

Yield: The interest rate which can be earned on an investment, currently quoted by the market or implied by the current market price for the investment – as opposed to the **coupon** paid by an issuer on a security, which is based on the coupon rate and the face value. For a bond, generally the same as yield to maturity unless otherwise specified.

Yield curve: Graphical representation of the maturity structure of interest rates, plotting yields of bonds that are all of the same class or credit quality against the maturity of the bonds.

Yield-curve option: Option that allows purchasers to take a view on a yield curve without having to take a view about a market's direction.

Yield-curve swap: Swap in which the index rates of the two interest streams are at different points on the yield curve. Both payments are re-fixed with the same frequency whatever the index rate.

Yield to equivalent life: The same as **yield to maturity** for a bond with partial redemptions.

Yield to maturity: The **internal rate of return** of a bond – the yield necessary to discount all the bond's cash flows to an **NPV** equal to its current price. See **simple yield to maturity**, **current yield**.

YTM: See **yield to maturity**.

Z

Zero-premium option: Generic term for options for which there is no premium, either because the buyer undertakes to forgo a percentage of any gain or because he offsets the cost by **writing** other options.

Zero-cost collar: A **collar** where the premiums paid and received are equal, giving a net zero cost.

Zero-coupon: A zero-coupon security is one that does not pay a **coupon**. Its price is correspondingly less to compensate for this. A zero-coupon **yield** is the yield which a zero-coupon investment for that term would have if it were consistent with the **par yield curve**.

Zero-coupon bond: Bond on which no coupon is paid. It is either issued at a discount or redeemed at a premium to face value.

Zero-coupon rate: The interest rate on a zero-coupon bond, sometimes called the spot rate. The two terms are not strictly synonymous however.

Zero-coupon swap: Swap converting the payment pattern of a zero-coupon bond, either to that of a normal, coupon-paying **fixed-rate** bond or to a **floating rate**.

Zero-coupon yield: The yield returned on a zero-coupon bond.

Index